MANAGEMENT INFORMATION SYSTEMS

MANAGEMENT INFORMATION SYSTEMS

Third Edition

RAYMOND McLEOD, Jr.

Texas A&M University

SCIENCE RESEARCH ASSOCIATES, INC.
Chicago, Henley-on-Thames, Sydney, Toronto

An IBM Company

Dedication

The dedication of a computer book to Thomas J. Watson, Jr., president of IBM during its early computer years, would be justified based on that fact alone. I have another, more personal, reason. I was an IBM sales trainee in the San Antonio office when Mr. Watson paid a visit and addressed the employees. He was asked about the progress of a contest to sell punched card machines, and he replied that he "didn't know" about the contest, explaining his concern at the top level with problems of a longer-term nature. At first, I was surprised that this man I so admired didn't know everything. I later came to appreciate the courage that it took to admit a lack of knowledge when it would have been so easy to say "Oh, it's going quite well." That has been one of the important lessons of my life— that when you don't have the answer it is a sign of intelligence, not ignorance, to say "I don't know." I owe that lesson to Mr. Watson.

Acquisition Editor	Michael Carrigg
Project Editor	Byron Riggan
Copy Editors	Elizabeth Derman/Don Weggeman
Compositor	Graphic Typesetting Service
Illustrators	Jim McDermott/Patrick Long
Cover and Text Designer	Carol Harris
Cover Photographer	Peter Menzel/Stock, Boston

Library of Congress Cataloging-in-Publication Data

McLeod, Raymond.
  Management information systems.

  Includes index.
  1. Management information systems. I. Title.
T58.6.M424 1986   658.4′038   85-19585
ISBN 0-574-21995-1

10 9 8 7 6

Preface

Although the subject of management information systems (MIS) is usually offered in schools of business, it is difficult to conceive of a career path that will not eventually involve use of the computer as a management tool. All people who have managerial responsibilities—including those in organizations such as churches, military branches, museums, and hospitals as well as business firms—need more than a computer literacy. They need an MIS literacy. These people are the users of the MIS.

In addition to managers, there are information specialists—systems analysts, programmers, data base administrators, network managers, and EDP auditors—who support the managers. These specialists help managers to recognize problems that can be solved with the aid of the MIS, formulate computer-based solutions, and implement workable information systems. Information specialists also need to understand the importance of information to the managerial role.

Future managers and future information specialists travel different paths during their collegiate programs. But at some point the two bodies of material—the managerial and the technical—must merge. The MIS course provides such a point. Both groups of students study the same material in the same setting of managerial problem solving. Because the two groups eventually will work together in designing and implementing information systems, it is important that a spirit of cooperation and understanding develop as soon as possible. The MIS course provides the perfect setting, and this textbook has been written especially to facilitate such a joint study.

Total Classroom Support

Since there is little course standardization from campus to campus, every effort has been made to provide instructional flexibility. The logical grouping of material into textbook parts, chapters, and topics within chapters enables the instructor to select the material that is relevant to his or her own situation. Further flexibility is provided by an updated Case Book and a Software Package. These items permit the student to become personally involved in solving MIS-related problems and using the computer as a decision support system (DSS).

In addition, an Instructor's Guide includes a range of items designed to facilitate the coverage of the course material in the classroom. The Instructor's Guide also includes six appendices dealing with the tools of systems analysis and design—flowcharting, data flow diagrams, the data dictionary, structured English, HIPO (Hierarchy plus Input, Processing, Output), and Warnier-Orr diagrams. To understand the data flow diagrams in Chapter 9 and to solve several problems at the end of Chapter 17 require an understanding of certain material in the appendices. The instructor can duplicate and distribute this material on an "as required" basis.

Like the previous two editions, this book has a management orientation. Emphasis is on the problem to be solved and the information needed. It is both possible and preferable for the manager to obtain information without getting wrapped up in the technical details of the computer, so those details are omitted here. The intent is to provide a solid foundation of the MIS material on which instructors in this and following courses can build in explaining the subject and describing its specific application to particular career areas.

The Basis for the New Edition

Although the second edition was the top-selling MIS text, it needed substantial updating to reflect the rapidly changing computer field. Two surveys provided the basis for the revisions. First, I surveyed the major U.S. colleges and universities to determine how the MIS course is being taught as well as to project future trends. The results of that survey were published in the Fall 1985 issue of the *Journal of Management Information Systems*. Second, SRA surveyed the users of the second edition for their appraisal of things they liked and did not like and for their suggestions for improvement. The Third Edition has been designed to provide the coverage that the participants in the two surveys indicate they need. A sound empirical base therefore exists for the content.

Organization

This edition continues the same time-tested organization. Part One consists of a single-chapter overview that describes what an MIS is and why you should be studying it.

Part Two is devoted to theory and its application to problem solving. A process that can be followed in solving problems is explained, using the computer as a decision support system. A mastery of this process, called the systems approach, is a valuable skill for every person entering an organization.

Part Three deals with the computer. Chapter 5 describes the capabilities of the computer as an information processor in the MIS. Chapter 6 addresses the class of computers that is currently receiving the most attention—microcomputers—and Chapters 7 and 8 address two popular topics that apply to all classes of computers—the data base and data communications.

Part Four is new, viewing the MIS as a composite of three major subsystems—data processing, office automation, and decision support. Chapter 9 presents an integration of data processing subsystems that might be found in a distribution organization such as a retailer, wholesaler, or manufacturer. Chapter 10 describes ten office automation applications such as word processing and electronic mail and explains how they can be used in an MIS. Chapter 11 elaborates on the various views of decision support and explains how DSS differs from MIS.

Part Five presents a subdivision of the MIS based on the users. Chapter 12 describes an executive information system used by the managers on the top level, and Chapters 13, 14, and 15 tailor the MIS to managers in the marketing, manufacturing, and finance areas.

Part Six tells how the MIS evolves through a life cycle, including planning (Chapter 16), analysis, design, and implementation (Chapter 17), and operation (Chapter 18). Chapter 19 extends the cycle into the future by addressing directions that the MIS might take. One of the future directions encompasses artificial intelligence and its subset expert systems.

New Features

The most obvious new material consists of the three new chapters on data processing, office automation, and executive information systems. However, all the other chapters have been rewritten to incorporate new material or to make them easier to understand. New topics have been integrated throughout—information resource management (Chapter 1), the role of intuition in decision making (Chapter 4), data base management systems for micros (Chapter 7), local area networks (Chapter 8), prewritten application software (Chapter 9), noncomputer sources of information (Chapter 12), EDP auditing (Chapter

15), prototyping (Chapter 17), and the corporate information officer (Chapter 19), to name a few.

The basic diagrams used in the Second Edition have been retained to provide the underlying structure, but there are many more supporting explanations from MIS literature than previously. The Third Edition therefore not only continues to be an easily comprehensible description of MIS, but also ties that description to the contributions by many sources from both academia and industry. A selected bibliography is included at the end of each chapter to direct students to the best sources of additional information.

Another evident change is the addition of more end-of-chapter problems as well as a second case problem for selected chapters. Students have the option of solving some of the problems with prewritten software such as electronic spreadsheets and word processors. The cases provide an excellent means of applying the chapter concepts to a real-life situation. The names of the firms and persons in the cases are fictitious, although many of the situations are those that I have experienced while working with organizations of all kinds.

The intent of the extensive revision of the previous edition is to provide the most up to date description of MIS possible—a description that will assist you in harnessing the power of the electronic computer in your career.

Acknowledgments

Throughout the book I use the terms *we* and *our*. Sometimes I am referring to the persons who produced the book, including SRA vice president and publisher Michael G. Crisp, acquisition editor Michael Carrigg, project editor Byron Riggan; as well as Elliott Derman and Cathy Rundell of Graphic Typesetting Service; the reviewers, Marilyn G. Kletke of Oklahoma State University, George P. Schell of the University of Tulsa, and Guy L. Langsford of California State University at Northridge; all of the current users who participated in the survey; as well as my secretary at Texas A&M, Sherry Erickson, and my typist in Boulder, Colorado, Chris Davis of Words-to-the-Wise. Each of these persons played a key role.

At other times, when I say *we* and *our,* I am including you, the reader. The book is truly a team effort, and both students and faculty have played an important part. I receive much useful feedback from my own students and also from users around the world. Since the First Edition was published in 1979, there have been only two major changes to the schematic models of the information systems in the text, and one came from one of my undergraduate students, Debra Dusek. She suggested the addition of an internal auditing subsystem for the financial information system, and that change is reflected in this edition.

I have received the assistance of many persons both in academia and industry. My colleagues at Texas A&M University were very helpful. Management professors Robert Albanese and Carl Zeithaml, marketing professors Charles Futrell and Valarie Zeithaml, professor of production management Norman Gaither, professors of business computing science Marietta Tretter, Joobin Choobineh, Lewis Myers, Jr., James Sena, and Wayne Headrick and his wife Barbara contributed materials, ideas, and suggestions. Assistance was also provided by Texas A&M graduate students Bill Owens and Heon Kook, who prepared many of the computer printouts. My colleague at Texas Christian University, professor Jack W. Jones, made a major contribution through his participation in the study of executive information systems, as did professor John C. Rogers of Montana State University, through his participation in the study of marketing information systems. Professor John R. Hauser of the Massachusetts Institute of Technology contributed material relating to marketing intelligence systems.

Respondents to the user questionnaire included William H. Anderson of Montgomery College, George Bannon of Moravian College, Stephen L. Barclay of Our Lady of the Lake University, John F. Barlow, College of Commerce, Dublin, Ireland, Mehdi Beheshtian of the University of Missouri at St. Louis, Charles P. Bilbrey of James Madison University, Roger Bloomquist of the University of North Dakota, Thomas A. Browdy of Washington University, Ronald E. Burke of Grayson College, Carl Clavadetscner of California State University at Stanislaus, Thomas A. Dahlstrom of Eastern College, Barbara B. Denison of Wright State University, Brian L. Dos Santos of the University of Wisconsin at Madison, John Eatman of the University of North Carolina at Greensboro, James M. Haine of the University of Wisconsin at Stevens Point, James A. Hall of Lehigh University, Donald L. Haney of St. Mary's University, T. L. Honeycutt of North Carolina State University, Archibald How of York College of Pennsylvania, Stephanie Howe of Iowa State University, Carl K. Howell of Florida Institute of Technology, Armond D. Inselberg of Synapse Computer Corporation, Lawrence A. Jadico of Spring Garden College, J. A. Justice of the University of Wisconsin at River Falls, Prasad V. Kilari of the University of Wisconsin at Superior, Frederick G. Kohun of Robert Morris College, John F. Lelane, San Jose State University, Charles M. Lutz of Utah State University, T. E. Manore of Old Dominion University, Jugoslav Milutinovich of Temple University, Josephine F. Morecroft of Virginia Commonwealth University, Joanna D. Mulholland of Philadelphia College of Textiles and Science, Margaret Nagle of Dominian College of Blauvelt, Ata Nahouraii of Indiana University of Pennsylvania, Virginia Z. Ogozalek of Worchester State College, W. James Petru of Aurora College, Cleve Pillifant of the U.S. Naval Academy, Sam H. Roy of Moorhead State University, Marian Sackson of Pace University, George Schneller of Baruch College— City University of New York, John F. Schrage of Southern Illinois University at Edwardsville, Janet Shalhoop of the University of Central Florida, Do Yeong Shin of Shaw University, Bonnie Simmons of North Central College, Peggy C. Smith of the University of Tulsa, William E. Spaulding of San Diego State University, Eugene F. Stafford of Iona College, Matilde K. Stephenson of St. Mary's University, Robert Lewis Stokes of the University of North Carolina at Charlotte, Andrew Varanelli, Jr. of Pace University, Jerry Wegenast of North Dakota State University, Glen J. Wiebe of Bethel College, and Richard M. Zugarek of Elizabethtown College.

Contributors from industry included Peter J. Hennessey III, and Donald Bender of Government Personnel Mutual Life Insurance Company, Joseph M. (Jody) Grant of Texas American Bank/Fort Worth, Martha Scott of United Services Automobile Association, Bill Guthrie of Elder Oil Tools, MIS consultant Gary P. Bennington, Bob Camp formerly of Pier 1 Imports, Steve Gaskin of Information Resources, Inc., and Joe Foster, James L. Daily, Jr., John Easton, John Adams, David Biles, James M. Baird, and Virginia Malinowski of Tenneco. I am also indebted to the following computer stores in College Station, Texas— YES Computers, Radio Shack Computer Center, and ComputerLand.

Finally, I would like to recognize my wife, Martha, who has inspired me to achieve goals that I never would have thought possible, and our children, Sharlotte and Glenn, who know all too well how much time it takes to write a book. And, I will always remember the sacrifices made on earlier projects by my older children—Mickey, Gregg, Chris, Suzanne, and Melinda, my best proofreader ever at age 12.

Even though I have received much help along the way, I alone am responsible for the contents of this work. In some cases I was advised to do one thing, and I elected to do otherwise. Any errors or shortcomings are my own doing.

Those of us who have produced the book believe it to be the most comprehensive, manager-oriented description of MIS to appear on the market. We sincerely hope that your experiences prove us right. Please address any suggestions for further improvement to the publisher or to me.

Raymond McLeod, Jr.
Department of Business Analysis and Research
College of Business
Texas A&M University
College Station, Texas 77843

Contents

PART THREE   THE INFORMATION PROCESSOR   151

PART SIX   MANAGING THE MIS   677

Part One

INFORMATION MANAGEMENT

Managers have always used information to perform their tasks, so the subject of management information is nothing new. What *is* new is the current availability of better information. The innovation that makes this possible is the electronic computer.

The computer is a relatively new tool, since it became popular only about thirty years ago. It was first applied to business tasks mainly as an accounting tool. More recently, the value of the computer as a producer of management information has been recognized. The term *management information system (MIS)* was coined to describe this new area of computer application. The term MIS was quickly adopted by the business world, although there has been considerable controversy about what it actually means. Originally the term was restricted to systems producing information for managers. Today, the term is generally used to describe the firm's overall computer system. A new term, *decision support system (DSS)*, refers to any computer application that helps the manager make decisions.

More and more firms are using computers to produce information. Computers, even small, inexpensive ones, are capable of generating large volumes of information. These information-producing systems are designed by computer professionals working closely with the persons who are to use the information—the users. In some cases, the users are designing the systems themselves.

The control that the MIS designers have over the firm's information system is called *information management*. This term implies that information is a resource, and it can be managed. The objective of Part One is to introduce the topic of information management.

Chapter 1

Introduction to Information Management

Learning Objectives

After studying this chapter, you should:

- Understand why there is so much interest in the use of computers for management support
- Know what is meant by a physical system, supersystem, and subsystem, and how they relate to a business organization
- Appreciate the importance of a conceptual information system as it relates to the physical system
- Know the difference between data and information, and the basic processes for transforming data into information
- Understand one definition of MIS, and know the necessary components and how they are integrated
- Be familiar with how the MIS concept has evolved and how MIS relates to the DSS concept
- Be aware of efforts to link office automation and artificial intelligence to the MIS and DSS
- Appreciate the difficulty of justifying the MIS economically
- Understand how the MIS evolves through a series of phases, and recognize the primary roles played by the manager and the information specialist
- Understand the necessity for a firm to adopt a formal policy of information resource management

Introduction

This book regards information as one of the basic resources available to the manager—just as valuable as human, material, or financial resources. Information is especially valuable because it *represents* the other, tangible, resources. This representation becomes more important as the scale of operation increases.

The manager of a small newsstand in the lobby of a hotel can manage by observing the tangible ingredients—himself or herself, the merchandise, the cash register, the room, and the customer flow. As the scale increases to a firm with several hundred or several thousand employees, with operations scattered over a wide area, the manager relies less on observation of the physical operation and more on information representing that operation. He or she uses many reports or information displays to reflect the firm's condition. It is easy to imagine the almost complete reliance that the chairman of the board of General Motors or Texaco or Sears must place on information. These executives probably regard information as their most valuable resource.

If information is recognized as a resource, then it follows that information, like other resources, can be managed. The other resources (personnel, money, material, and machines) are acquired and assembled to be available for use when needed. Very often the assembly process entails converting an essentially raw material into a refined form, such as training an employee or constructing a piece of special machinery. Once these resources are assembled, the manager is responsible for using them in the most efficient way. The manager attempts to minimize the amount of time during which resources are idle and to keep them functioning at their highest efficiency. Finally, the manager must replace these resources at a critical time—before inefficiency or obsolescence affects the entire organization.

The management of information as a resource follows the same pattern. The manager is responsible for gathering raw data and processing it into usable information. He or she must assure that appropriate individuals within the organization receive the information in the proper form at the proper time so that it can assist in the management process. And finally, the manager must discard out-of-date, incomplete, or erroneous information and replace it with information that is usable. This activity is called *information management*.

Importance of Information Management

Interest in information management has increased during recent years—not only in the world of business but in all areas where resources must be managed. Two main reasons account for this: the increasing complexity of the management task and improved decision-making tools.

Increasing complexity of the management task

Management has always been a difficult task, but it is more so today than ever before. One reason is the sheer *size of organizations*. In addition to an increase in the number of organizations (especially the very small ones), the large ones have grown larger. For example, sales of *Fortune 500* firms increased from $1,219 billion in 1978 to $1,759 billion in 1984, while assets increased from $899 billion to $1,409 billion. These increases were accomplished with a reduction in the number of employees from 15.8 million to 14.2 million. Similar reductions in the labor force were felt throughout U.S. industry during the early eighties as firms turned increasingly to automation and felt the effects of recession and inflation. *Economic influences* contribute to the complexity of management.

Another factor is the *increasing complexity of technology* employed within the organization. The effort to keep pace with technology must be continuous. It is possible today to buy a pocket calculator more powerful than one of the first room-sized computers—and at a fraction of the cost. Fifteen years ago, only large firms could afford to purchase or lease computers. Today computer technology is more readily available. The lack of a computer with sufficient power and capacity is no longer a deterrent to solving a problem. More likely, the deterrent will be the difficulty of formulating a solution in terms of instructions that the computer can follow. Today, managers throughout many companies can access a central computer through typewriterlike terminals in their offices. In some companies, managers have small computers by their desks, as in Figure 1-1. Very often, these

Figure 1-1 Many managers have computing equipment in their offices.

small computers are linked to a central computer to form an integrated problem-solving network. The computer is not the only example of increasing technological complexity. Increasing mechanization is occurring in almost every part of the firm; examples include factory robots and automated merchandise storage and movement.

In addition to this increase in the scale and complexity of operations, the manager's *time frame* for action is shrinking. Managers must act quickly in response to pressures from customers, competition, and stockholders. The entire span of business operations is moving more rapidly today than ever before; sales representatives cover their territories by jet, sales orders arrive at headquarters by satellite transmission, and filled orders are shipped the same day.

This desire to operate in the most efficient manner has been strengthened by the increasing competition for the consumer's dollar. *Competitive pressure* is applied not only by firms headquartered within the firm's own country, but in other countries as well. This effect of international competition is most clearly seen in the U.S. steel industry where a 6.2 cent loss was recorded in 1982 for each sales dollar. This compares to a 5 cent profit in 1975 before imports from other countries, notably Japan, began to take their toll.

Not all environmental pressures favor production; some, ironically, favor *non*production. This is true in the case of products and services that society, or some part of it, finds undesirable. Thus, *social pressure* adds another dimension to the task of business decision making. Decisions must be based on economic factors, but social costs and payoffs must be considered as well. Plant expansion, new products, new sales outlets, and similar actions affecting the local and national community must all be weighed in terms of their short- and long-term impacts.

All of these factors—organization size, economic influences, technology complexity, shrinking time frames, and competitive and social pressure—influence the management task.

Availability of decision-making tools

Even as the manager's task has become more complex, there has been a movement under way to improve the effectiveness of decision making. Central to this movement are quantitative techniques and electronic devices such as computers. During the 1950s, efforts to solve business problems with advanced mathematics were called *operations research (OR)*. These efforts were usually designed to solve manufacturing problems. During the 1960s, the term *management science* became popular, as quantitative methods were applied on a broader scale—in finance and marketing, for example. The increasing popularity of the computer in the late sixties and seventies led to attempts to harness the power of this electronic giant for mathematical computations. Terms such as *management information system (MIS)* and *decision support system (DSS)* represent currently popular means of assisting the manager with computer-produced information. MIS refers to the overall application of the computer in a firm, with the emphasis on supporting management's information needs. DSS refers to efforts applied in a more focused way—on a particular problem faced by a particular manager.

The Modern Manager

A manager is anyone who is responsible for directing the use of any types of resources. The resources can be personnel, equipment, money, or even information. Such a broad definition involves many people that are not ordinarily regarded as managers—pastors, band directors, senators, football coaches, and so on.

Where managers are found

Managers can be found practically everywhere, but it is important to recognize that they exist on various levels within an organization. Managers at the top, such as the president and vice presidents, are often called *executives*. The top level has been referred to as the *strategic planning level*, recognizing the impact that decisions have on the entire organization for years to come. Middle-level managers include regional managers, product directors, and division heads. Their level has been called the *management control level*, recognizing the responsibility to put plans into action and to ensure that goals are met. Lower-level managers include department heads, supervisors, and group leaders, and are responsible for accomplishing the plans and tactics specified by managers on upper levels. The lower level has been called the *operational control level* in recognition of the fact that it is where the operations of the organization occur.

In addition to these organizational levels, managers can be found in various *functional areas* such as marketing, manufacturing, finance, and personnel. Some of the names of the functional areas are unique to particular industries, whereas some names are universally applied. For example, you would find an underwriting division only in an insurance company, but you could find a personnel department in any organization. Figure 1-2 illustrates how managers can be grouped by level and functional area in a manufacturing firm.

What managers do

It is important to recognize both differences and similarities that exist between the various levels of management and functional areas. Some managers perform well on one level, but not on others. The same can be said for the functional areas. A good accounting department head might fail miserably as a sales department head. Even in light of the obvious differences, it is generally agreed that all managers perform the same functions or play the same roles. It has long been recognized that *management functions* include planning, organizing, staffing, directing, and controlling. All managers perform these functions to some degree, although perhaps with varying emphasis. More recently the idea of *managerial roles* has become popular—viewing the manager's duties in major categories such as interpersonal, informational, and decisional.

Even though managers have been performing their functions and playing their roles for many years, there is more and better support today than ever before. Modern managers utilize the available tools and procedures to increase their

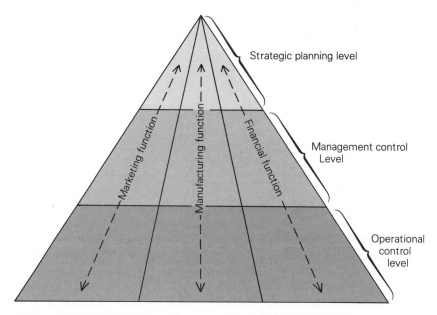

Figure 1-2 Managers can be found on all levels and in all functional areas of the organization.

effectiveness and likelihood of success. The tools and procedures combine with basic management skills to achieve levels of performance that were impossible only a few years ago. For example, a modern manager can use the computer as a tool to transmit messages electronically throughout the organization; such a procedure was not feasible for the manager of the sixties or even seventies.

Management Skills

It would be possible to list many skills that a successful manager should possess, but two stand out as being basic— decision making and communications. Managers on all levels and in all functional areas must decide on strategies, tactics, and operations, and they must communicate with persons reporting to them, to other managers, and to persons outside the organization.

If the idea of computer-based decision support can be criticized as having a fundamental weakness, it is perhaps the overemphasis on decision making. Managers do things in addition to making decisions. If records were kept of how managers spend their time, the time spent actually making decisions would be quite small, whereas the time spent in gathering information from many types of communications would be quite large.

Communications

Managers receive and transmit information orally and in writing. *Oral communications* include conversations that occur during meetings, while touring facilities, when someone unexpectedly walks into the manager's office, and on the telephone. The scene for oral communications can also involve business lunches, social events, and conventions. *Written communications* include reports prepared by computer and by other means, memos, letters, and periodicals. Figure 1-3 shows the manager receiving information by means of these media and using the

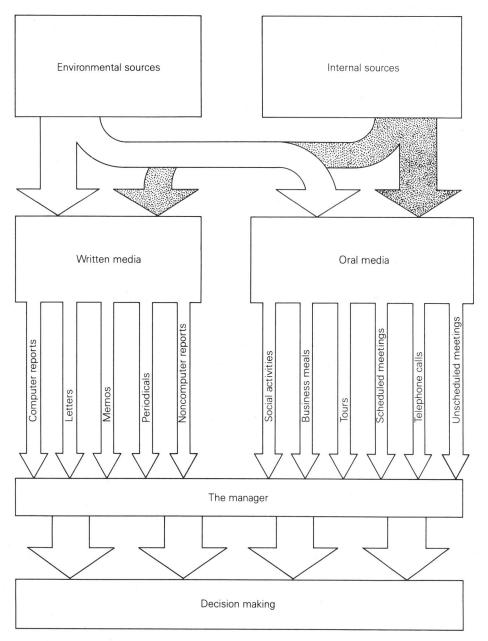

Figure 1-3 The manager receives oral and written information from sources outside and inside the firm for use in decision making.

information in decision making. All of the media are available to every manager, and all are used to some extent. Individual managers, however, have their own preferences. One manager may favor telephone conversations over computer printouts, and another manager may feel just the opposite. A manager will assemble a mix of communications media to fit his or her management style.

Decision making

Managers make decisions during the process of solving problems. Usually, it is necessary to make multiple decisions to solve a single problem. The term *problem solving* implies that something detrimental has happened, or will happen, to the organization. The manager acts to minimize the adverse effects or ensure that the same problem doesn't recur. The term should also include managerial behavior aimed at capitalizing on opportunities. Managers don't limit their attention to things that are going wrong. They also seek to maximize the benefits from things that are going right. It is necessary to engage in *decision making* in both instances.

Computer literacy

The computer is a tool that can support both communications and decision making. The manager can get the best results from computer use when that tool is understood. The term *computer literacy* has been coined to represent the knowledge of the computer that is necessary to function effectively in today's world. Public school systems have responded to this need for computer knowledge by designing curricula that begin with kindergarten students, and include computer terminology, computer history, using prewritten programs, coding programs, and surveying careers in computing.

Today, most college graduates who enter management training programs have had computer courses. These management trainees know the basics and can communicate with the firm's computer staff. Thus, managers and specialists can jointly develop computer-based systems to help solve business problems.

Many of the senior managers in today's organizations, however, studied neither quantitative solutions to business problems nor computers in college. Some never went to college, and those who did took courses that were generally nonquantitative. Senior managers who have seen the need to augment their education have enrolled in programs conducted by business societies such as the American Management Association, or pursued Master of Business Administration (MBA) degrees through special evening or weekend programs. Computer manufacturers also offer executive courses in particular techniques and systems.

During the early years of the computer, few people in any organization understood the new technology, and their level of understanding was often low. This problem is gradually disappearing as more and more computer-trained managers enter organizations and work their way to the top. Not all companies have management staffs who are generally knowledgeable about computers, but many do. Surprisingly, company size is not the key factor. Some small firms with progressive leadership are making very effective use of computers.

MIS literacy

In addition to understanding the computer as a tool in a general sense, the modern manager should understand how the computer is used in management. This knowledge can be termed *MIS literacy* and builds on computer literacy. MIS literacy includes an understanding of the strengths and weaknesses of the computer when applied to business problems, and also an ability to use the computer as a decision support system. Computer use can be achieved alone, or with help from computer experts.

A person can achieve computer literacy in an introductory computer course. This fundamental literacy can be expanded with additional courses or experience. The objective of this textbook is to facilitate the achievement of MIS literacy.

The Manager and Systems

A *systems orientation* is often associated with modern management. This view implies that the manager must know what a system is and how the concept relates to her or his area of responsibility. A manager who thinks of a firm as an integration of functional areas working toward a common goal is actually regarding the firm as a system. The areas are integrated by flows of resources, such as material and information, and each area depends on the others for survival. The firm is then a physical system just as a machine (such as an automobile or a computer) is a system.

To complete this systems orientation, the manager must recognize the importance of the firm's environment. The firm depends not only on its environment for life-giving resources, but also makes a contribution to that environment. Regarding business operations as systems embedded within larger systems is an abstract way of thinking. But this abstraction prevents the manager from getting lost in the details of the job and emphasizes the importance of ensuring that the major parts work together.

What is a system?

When the word *system* is used in relation to business operations, it identifies a group of elements or parts that are integrated through the common purpose of achieving some objective. Let us take the key terms in the definition and expand on them.

1. *A group of elements*: A system must have more than one elemental part. A rock, for example, is not a system. But it can be part of a system, such as a wall.

2. *Integrated elements*: All parts of a system must have some logical relationship. Mechanical systems satisfy this requirement. For example, watches, cars, bicycles, and video cassette recorders have been designed to do specific jobs, and all of the parts contribute to performing those jobs.

Many people assume that the elemental parts of a system must work together in a synchronized manner. Although this is desirable, it is not necessary. A wristwatch that does not keep accurate time is still a system; it is just a poor system.

3. *Common purpose to achieve an objective*: A system is designed to achieve one or more objectives. All elements work toward the achievement of the system goal rather than toward separate goals for each element.

Mechanical systems are designed to achieve a coordinated operation. Systems comprised of humans, such as workers in an office, lack this built-in coordination, and it is difficult to attain. The manager of such human systems must motivate participants to coordinate so that system objectives can be reached.

Elements of a system

The elements of a system are integrated, as illustrated in Figure 1-4. In this view, the system transforms input into output. A control mechanism monitors the system and regulates its operation so that the transformation process is executed properly.

When this diagram, or model, is used to explain a building's heating system, the input represents the fuel—electricity, natural gas, coal, and so on. The heating process transforms this fuel into heat—the output. The control mechanism is the thermostat, which can be set at a desired level of performance.

When the model illustrates a business firm, the input consists of basic resources—machinery, materials, money, personnel, and information. The transformation process converts these resources into the output of the firm—products or services. The control is performed by the management. As in the example of the heater, the performance of the firm can be established to achieve a certain level. It is the manager's job to assure this level of performance.

What is a subsystem?

Systems often consist of smaller systems, or subsystems. A *subsystem* is simply a system contained within a larger one. Therefore a subsystem is also a system. This

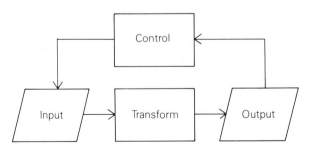

Figure 1-4 Component parts of a system.

means that systems exist on several levels, and sometimes small ones are part of larger ones.

An automobile can be regarded as a system. But it is made up of several subsidiary, or lower-level, systems—the engine system, the body system, and the frame system. Each in turn may be composed of lower-level systems; for example, the engine system is a combination of a carburetor system, a generator system, a fuel system, and so on. And these systems may be subdivided further into subsystems or elemental parts. The parts of a system therefore may be either systems (groups of parts) or individual parts. Figure 1-5 illustrates this relationship.

In a business firm, the basic functional units—such as marketing, finance, and manufacturing—are the subsystems. Each of these, in turn, consists of subsystems. The marketing department, for example, is made up of advertising, sales, and marketing research subsystems.

When a system is a part of a larger system, that larger system is often called a *supersystem* or *suprasystem*. For example, the Internal Revenue Service is itself a system, and it is also part of a larger system—the federal government. Here the federal government is a supersystem, or suprasystem.

The business system

What the manager manages is the system of the firm or the organization. The organization may have *profit* objectives; or it may be *nonprofit*. Also, it may be *private*, as in the case of a corporation or proprietorship, or it may be *governmental*. In the discussion that follows, the term *firm* is not restricted to profit-seeking business organizations. The term applies to any type of organization. The fundamentals of information management described in this book apply to any type of organization.

The manager's major responsibility is to assure that the firm meets the established goals or objectives. Effort is required to make the various parts of the firm work together as they should. The manager is the control element in the system, keeping it on course as it moves forward to achieve its goals.

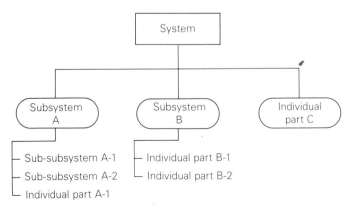

Figure 1-5 System composition.

Of course, the system of the firm fits into one or more larger systems or suprasystems. If the firm is a bank, for example, it is part of the financial community. Also, it is part of both the local community and the business community. See Figure 1-6.

The system of the firm also comprises smaller systems, or subsystems. The subsystems of the bank may be the departments for savings accounts, demand deposits (checking accounts), installment loans, and so on. Although each of these subsystems has its own objectives and goals, these subsidiary objectives support and contribute to the overall objectives of the firm (the bank).

Physical systems and conceptual systems

The business firm is a *physical system*. The system is tangible; it can be seen, touched, or kicked. The buildings, trucks, employees, machines, and materials are all physical entities. The manager is concerned with managing this physical system.

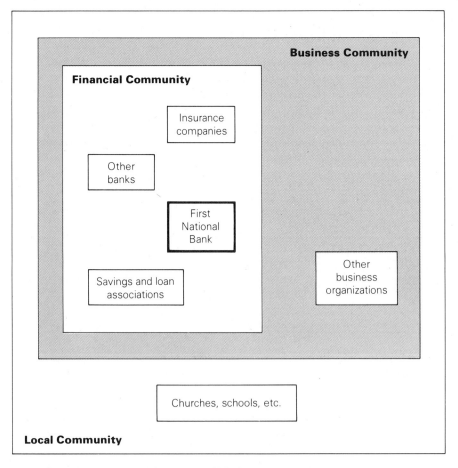

Figure 1-6 The firm as a subsystem within larger systems.

What, then, is a conceptual system? A *conceptual system* is a system that *represents* a physical one. The conceptual system commonly exists as an idea in someone's mind, as figures or lines on a sheet of paper, or as magnetized areas of a computer storage medium. How and where the information is stored is unimportant. What matters is what the information represents. The physical system is important for what it is; the conceptual system is important for its representation of the physical system. For example, the data in a computer storage unit is a conceptual system representing the physical system of the firm.

A good example of the importance of the conceptual system is provided by Lee Iacocca, describing the situation at Chrysler when he became chairman in 1978:

> A couple of months after I arrived, something hit me like a ton of bricks. We were running out of cash! Gradually, I was finding out that Chrysler had no overall system of financial controls—nobody in the whole place seemed to fully understand what was going on when it came to financial planning and projecting. I couldn't find out *anything*. This was probably the greatest jolt I've ever had in my business career. I already knew about the lousy cars, the bad morale and the deteriorating factories. But I simply had no idea that I wouldn't even be able to get hold of the right numbers so that we could begin to attack some basic problems.[1]

Iacocca could handle the poor state of Chrysler's physical system, but he was unprepared for the poor state of the conceptual system.

Data Versus Information

Many people use the terms *data* and *information* interchangeably. This is acceptable in informal conversation, but to computer people there is a difference. *Data* is something used as a basis for discussion, decision making, calculating, or measuring. For example, data might be the number of hours worked for each employee in the company. When this data is processed, it can be converted into information. For example, when the hours worked by each employee are multiplied by his or her hourly rate, the product is the gross earnings. And, when the figures for gross earnings are added, the sum is the total payroll amount for the entire firm. This payroll amount would be information to the owner of the firm. *Information* is processed data, or meaningful data. Information tells someone something that he or she did not previously know.

You might have heard the expression "One person's junk is another person's treasure." In discussing data and information, we could say, "One person's data is another person's information." Let's get back to our example of the gross earnings figures for a firm's employees. These separate figures are information to each employee—each figure tells an employee how much money he or she earned last week. But to the company's owner, these figures are data. The owner wants

[1] "Iacocca: An Autobiography," *Newsweek* 104 (October 8, 1984): 62.

to know the total payroll for the firm, and the individual figures (the data) must be processed to produce this amount.

Data processing

The system that processes the data is called a *data processing system*. Figure 1-7 shows that input data is transformed into output information.

Data processing can be performed manually, with the help of a keydriven device such as a pocket calculator or typewriter, or with a computer. The processing consists of one or more of the following operations:

1. *Recording* transaction data to create a file of transaction records
2. *Sorting*, sequencing, or arranging the records of a single file
3. *Merging* the ordered contents of two or more files
4. *Calculating* amounts by performing one or more mathematical operations
5. *Accumulating* amounts to develop summary totals
6. *Storing* data or information for future use
7. *Retrieving* stored data or information when it is needed
8. *Reproducing* or duplicating data or information for multiple uses
9. *Displaying* or printing the output of the processing (the information) for the intended users

During the early years of computer use, the emphasis was on the processing of data. The computer was used mainly for traditional accounting functions, and little output was generated for the firm's managers. Today information output is receiving most of the attention as firms design management information systems and decision support systems.

Data storage

There is usually a lag between the time that data is gathered and the time that it is transformed into information. For example, payroll data is retained until the end of the pay period when payroll reports are prepared. There also may be a lag

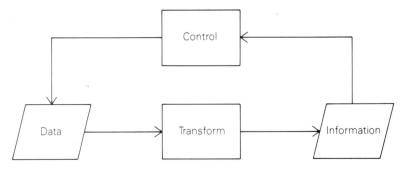

Figure 1-7   A data processing system transforms data into information.

between the time that data is processed and when the output of that processing is presented to the user. As an example, precomputed totals may be retained so as to minimize the response time when they are requested by the user. The reservoir of data and information, retained for whatever purpose, is the firm's data base, data bank, or data store. We will use the term *data base*.[2] The data base is an important ingredient in an MIS

The Management Information System (MIS)

Although the term *MIS* has been around since the mid-sixties, there is still no universal agreement as to its meaning. In this book, we are going to use MIS to include *all* data processing within an organization. This comprehensive definition means that the MIS does more than just produce information for managers

Definition of MIS

An MIS can be defined as

> The formal and informal systems that provide past, present, and projection information in a written and oral form relating to the firm's internal operations and its environment. It supports the managers and employees and key environmental elements by furnishing information in the proper time frame to assist in decision making.[3]

Several key words capture the essence of what the MIS is and how it is used:

1. *Formal and informal*: A formal system is one defined by a procedure. Examples are computer programs and scheduled meetings. An informal system is enacted in response to an unanticipated or nonrepetitive event. Unscheduled meetings and unexpected telephone calls are examples. The MIS includes all systems that provide information—formal and informal.

2. *Past, present, and projection information*: Information is provided to the manager to make it possible to know where the firm has been, where it is now, and where it is going. Before computers were available, most systems used by managers were designed to provide only past information. Those systems, using punched card machines, keydriven machines, or manual processes, generated historical reports for the manager. The manager used those reports as a basis for deciding what should be done in the future. The systems were so slow that the manager seldom had a good

---

[2]In this introductory chapter, we use the term *data base* in a very broad sense—to include all of the data available to the MIS. Some people use the term in a very narrow sense—to include only computer-stored files that are interconnected in special ways. In later chapters we will discuss the options for maintaining the firm's data resource.

[3]This definition paraphrases one coined by Walter J. Kennevan in 1970. See his article "MIS Universe," in the September 1970 issue of *Data Management*, p. 63.

idea of what was happening presently. By the time present performance was reported, it was past history

   An important characteristic, then, of the modern MIS is the ability to report information about the present and to project into the future—an ability that was generally unavailable before the computer era.

3. *Written and oral*: Most of the information that managers receive from the computer is in a written form—primarily displays of numeric and alphabetic material. It is also possible to obtain graphical information from the computer. Practically all of the oral information received by the manager comes from noncomputer sources, although it is possible to obtain computer output in the form of an audio response. It is important to recognize the importance of both computer and noncomputer information to the manager's MIS.

4. *Internal and environmental information*: Information is provided about what is happening both inside and outside the firm. Compared to previous systems that provided mainly internal information, the MIS places great value on environmental information. This environmental information is especially important to top-level managers. The president of a Fort Worth bank, for example, receives more information on the local community and the national economy than on internal matters left to competent lower-level managers.

5. *Managers and employees*: Many firms would cease to operate if they lost the use of their computers for any length of time. Airlines, newspapers, and banks are examples. Since operational-level employees such as reservation clerks, typesetters, and tellers rely on computers in their work, it is necessary to include them along with their managers as users of the MIS.

6. *Key environmental elements*: The firm has an obligation to report certain financial data to the government, to keep stockholders apprised of the status of their investments, to inform customers of amounts owed the firm, and so forth.

7. *Proper time frame*: The information from the MIS must be available when it is needed. This requirement of responsiveness is especially critical for information describing the current operation. Often the conceptual information system must respond immediately to the needs of the physical system—perhaps within seconds. The term *realtime* describes systems with a response ability fast enough to adapt a physical system immediately to changing environmental conditions. As the size of the firm increases, the need for responsiveness demands a computer—and often a larger and more expensive computer as the need for a fast response intensifies.

8. *Assist in decision making*: The MIS is designed to help the manager make decisions. The intent is not to make decisions for the manager, but to provide information support. The information earmarked for employees and environmental elements can also be considered as useful in decision

making. The government decides whether the firm has satisfied its tax liabilities, stockholders decide whether to sell or buy, and customers decide how much to pay and when.

MIS components

While it is not absolutely necessary that the MIS include a computer, a noncomputer-based system is the exception. *We will assume from this point on that our MIS is computer-based. And, we will concentrate our interest on the manager as the primary user of the MIS output.*

The computing equipment is known as the *hardware*, and it is the easiest of the MIS components to acquire. The story is told of one manager who simply telephoned a local computer store and had a small computer delivered in a taxicab.

In addition to the hardware, it is necessary to provide instructions describing the processes that the hardware is to perform. These instructions are the *software*. There are basically two types of software. The first is *application software*, which processes the firm's data. Payroll programs, inventory programs, and forecasting programs are good examples. The second type of software is *system software*, which causes the computer to perform certain operations such as compiling programs (converting them from a programming language such as BASIC or Pascal to a machine language that the computer can understand), sorting data, or retrieving data from storage. Application software can be prepared by the firm's programming staff or acquired from a software vendor. System software is almost always acquired from a hardware vendor.

If a firm elects to use a computer to process its data, then it must have a staff of *information specialists*. If it prepares its own application software, it must have programmers and systems analysts. Even if it purchases prewritten application software, it must have data entry operators and other operational-area personnel, and managers. These human resources are organized into an *information services staff*. In a small organization using a microcomputer, the information services staff may consist of only a single employee.

If the hardware and software are to convert data into information, a firm must first acquire a *data base*. The data base includes data describing all of the important transactions and details of the firm's operations.

With all of the resources identified so far—the hardware, the software, the information services staff, and the data base— a firm can now use a computer to produce information. To close the loop, the firm needs an *information-oriented management staff* to identify what information they need, to use that information, and to work to refine and improve both the information and the MIS over time. These managers are the users of the information product, and they are perhaps the most difficult to acquire. The ideal management staff is one that is MIS literate.

Most importantly, the firm must possess *progressive executive leadership* in the form of a president, board of directors, or executive committee to serve as a motivating force. Even when all of the other resources are present, if top management isn't enthusiastic about the MIS and doesn't provide the necessary support, then developing a good information system will be difficult or even impossible.

An MIS model

The resources of a good information system are illustrated in Figure 1-8. At the bottom is the *physical system of the firm*—the workers and all of the facilities and equipment used to produce the firm's products and services. *Internal data* is gathered throughout the physical system and directed to the *information process- ing resources*. These resources include the computer and the information services staff. The *software library* (or collection of programs) and the *data base* are used to convert *data* into *information* that is directed to the *executive leadership and*

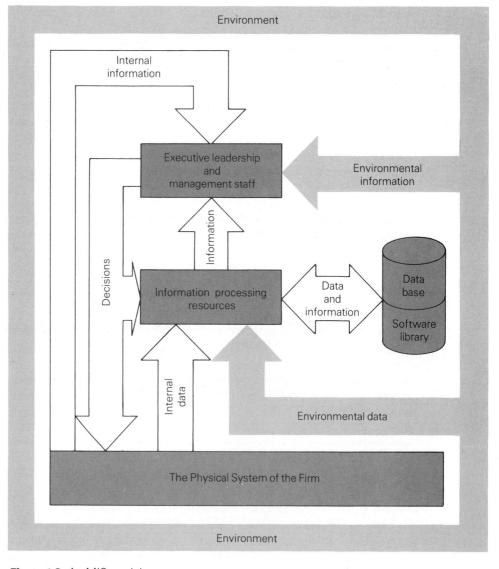

Figure 1-8 An MIS model.

management staff—the users. These users make *decisions* directed at the physical system of the firm and at the information processing resources. These decisions produce changes designed to improve operations.

The model illustrates a loop—data is gathered from the firm, transformed into information, and used to make decisions that are transmitted back to the data origin. The ongoing looping process allows the firm to monitor its effectiveness in achieving its information goals.

The *environment* is important to the firm and to the MIS. As the model shows, *environmental data* is also used to produce information. And some *environmental information* is transmitted directly to the users from the environment without passing through the computer system. Managers acquire a great deal of environmental information by reading business publications such as *The Wall Street Journal,* by developing good relationships with customers and suppliers, and by engaging in community and industry activities.

You will also notice another arrow labeled *internal information* that bypasses the computer. This is information passed along by word of mouth, observation, conversation, interoffice memos, and the like, describing activities within the firm. Internal information ranges from formal reporting activities to informal communications among employees around the water cooler.

In sum, the model illustrates not only the resources of the MIS, but also the important looping activity, the interrelationships between the firm and its environment, and the noncomputerized information flows. The MIS is a network of data and information flows similar to the nervous system of the body, reporting on both internal and external conditions and facilitating appropriate responses to those conditions. Computers speed this information flow and make it possible to process certain types of data that would otherwise be impractical or impossible to convert into information.

An MIS example

A medium-sized life insurance company recently implemented an information system to be used mainly by its marketing division. The system consists of a notebook of computer printouts prepared on a monthly basis. Some of the printouts are intended to help marketing managers plan future personnel hiring programs. One of the reports is illustrated in Figure 1-9. The report is a projection for the next 48 months (the horizontal rows) of the sales and corresponding personnel needs. Reading from left to right, the report identifies the month, the sales goal for that month, the portion of the sales to be made by sales agents currently employed by the company, and the portion to be made by new agents. New agents will be needed to help the firm increase its sales over time and to replace current agents who leave the firm. The number of agents needed to meet the sales goals are identified in the center columns of the report. The "To hire" column identifies the number of agents to be hired that month. This projection of needed agents is important and, by itself, would justify preparation of the report. The information specialists and marketing managers, working together to design this report, went one step further. They identified, in the right-hand columns, the number of full-time recruiters needed to hire the new agents. The

9/25/85

SUMMARY REPORT 1.0
PROJECTIONS REPORT
ASSUMED GROWTH RATE .120

MO	DATE	PRODUCTION POINTS GOAL	CURRENT AGENTS	NEW AGENTS	ON BOARD AGENTS ALL AGENTS	CURRENT AGENTS	NEW AGENTS	TO HIRE	RECRUITERS ALL CURRENT	CURRENT	NEW	TO HIRE
1	9 / 85	159070	159070	0	212	212	0	14	14	14	0	0
2	10 / 85	173411	160410	13001	233	214	19	14	14	13	1	1
3	11 / 85	178790	157320	21470	241	210	31	14	14	13	1	0
4	12 / 85	184169	151500	32669	249	202	47	14	14	12	2	1
5	1 / 86	163000	145680	17320	219	194	25	14	14	12	2	0
6	2 / 86	165000	138320	26680	222	184	38	13	13	11	2	0
7	3 / 86	166000	133970	32030	224	178	46	13	13	11	2	0
8	4 / 86	168000	126550	41450	227	168	59	12	12	10	2	0
9	5 / 86	169000	120750	48250	229	160	69	11	11	10	1	0
10	6 / 86	171000	114840	56160	232	152	80	10	10	9	1	0
11	7 / 86	173000	110490	62510	235	146	89	10	10	9	1	0
12	8 / 86	174000	106120	67880	237	140	97	10	10	9	1	0
13	9 / 86	176000	101770	74230	240	134	106	10	10	8	2	1
14	10 / 86	178000	98850	79150	243	130	113	11	11	8	3	1
15	11 / 86	180000	95950	84050	246	126	120	12	12	8	4	1
16	12 / 86	182000	93030	88970	249	122	127	13	13	8	5	1
17	1 / 87	184000	90130	93870	252	118	134	13	13	8	5	1
18	2 / 87	185000	87210	97790	254	114	140	13	13	7	6	1
19	3 / 87	187000	85760	101240	257	112	145	14	14	7	7	1
20	4 / 87	189000	82840	106160	260	108	152	15	14	7	7	1
21	5 / 87	191000	81240	109760	263	106	157	15	15	7	8	1
22	6 / 87	194000	78170	115830	267	102	165	14	14	6	8	1
23	7 / 87	196000	73710	122290	271	96	175	15	15	6	9	1
24	8 / 87	198000	72260	125740	274	94	180	15	15	6	9	1
25	9 / 87	200000	70810	129190	277	92	185	16	16	6	10	1
26	10 / 87	202000	69360	132640	279	90	189	16	16	6	10	1
27	11 / 87	204000	67890	136110	282	88	194	16	17	6	11	1
28	12 / 87	207000	66440	140560	287	86	201	17	17	6	11	1
29	1 / 88	209000	66440	142560	290	86	204	17	17	6	11	1
30	2 / 88	211000	64990	146010	293	84	209	17	17	5	12	1
31	3 / 88	213000	63540	149460	296	82	214	17	17	5	12	1
32	4 / 88	216000	63540	152460	300	82	218	17	18	5	12	1
33	5 / 88	218000	63540	154460	303	82	221	18	18	5	13	1
34	6 / 88	221000	62090	158910	307	80	227	18	18	5	13	1
35	7 / 88	223000	60620	162380	310	78	232	18	19	5	14	1
36	8 / 88	226000	57630	168370	315	74	241	19	19	5	14	1
37	9 / 88	228000	59250	168750	317	76	241	19	19	5	14	1
38	10 / 88	231000	57800	173200	321	74	247	19	19	5	14	1
39	11 / 88	233000	57800	175200	324	74	250	19	19	5	14	1
40	12 / 88	236000	57800	178200	329	74	255	20	20	5	15	1
41	1 / 89	239000	57800	181200	333	74	259	20	20	5	15	1
42	2 / 89	242000	54880	187120	337	70	267	20	20	5	15	1
43	3 / 89	244000	54880	189120	340	70	270	20	20	5	15	1
44	4 / 89	247000	54880	192120	344	70	274	20	20	5	15	1
45	5 / 89	250000	56330	193670	349	72	277	20	20	5	15	1
46	6 / 89	253000	56330	196670	353	72	281	20	20	4	16	1
47	7 / 89	256000	56330	199670	357	72	285	20	20	4	16	1
48	8 / 89	258000	56330	201670	360	72	288	20	20	4	16	1
TOTAL								751				38

POINTS PER PRODUCTIVE AGT (YRS 1-5+) 1450 1470 1540 1620 1600
ON-BOARD/PRODUCTIVE RATIO = 2/1
NEW ON-BOARD PER MONTH PER RECRUITER = 1
ESTIMATE OF COST FROM REPORT 1.9 IS $4258000
RT:BASERT...FN:SUMREPORT

Figure 1-9 A report of personnel projections prepared by a life insurance company.

report represents a type of chain reaction. The company's top management projected sales goals for the next four years. These goals were converted into the number of agents needed to meet the goals and the number of recruiters needed to hire the new agents. The same information in a graphical form is illustrated in Figure 1-10.

The computer programs preparing these printouts can be regarded as a decision support system. The DSS assists marketing management in solving the problem of building a sales force to accomplish the firm's goals.

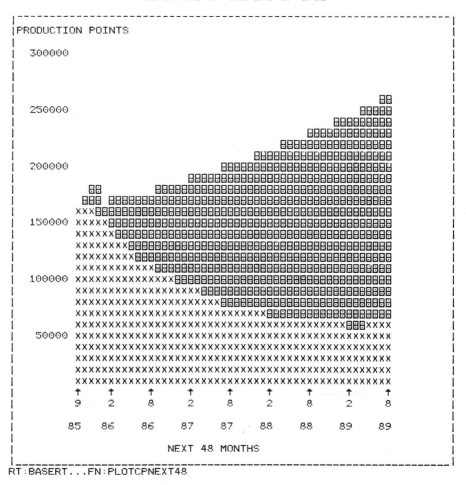

Figure 1-10 A graphical display of personnel projections using a standard computer printer.

The Evolution of the MIS Concept

Managers have always used information for decision making, and the systems providing that information could have been called management information systems. However, it took the computer revolution to call management's attention to the importance of its information systems.

The initial focus on data

During the precomputer era, firms generally ignored the possibility of generating information for managers. It was not until the mid-fifties that computers were marketed on a widespread basis. Acceptance of computers was gradual, with application limited to the same areas handled by the keydriven and punched card machines (i.e., accounting applications).

Before long, however, users and vendors recognized the inherent power of the computer—its ability to do jobs never before possible. Managers in the manufacturing area realized that the computer could be used for superior production scheduling and more sophisticated inventory control. Engineers saw the potential for design work. News of the power of computers spread throughout the firm.

During this period, which lasted until the mid-sixties, the use of computers was called *electronic data processing*, or *EDP*. The term is hardly used at all anymore. When it is used, the term has a somewhat negative connotation—the limited use of computers for processing accounting data rather than producing management information.

The refined focus on information

A few farsighted individuals recognized that the computer could do more than process data. Among them were H. P. Luhn and Stephen E. Furth of IBM, who developed a use of computers known as *information retrieval*. This development occurred during the late fifties and early sixties. Information retrieval is the most likely predecessor of the MIS. It involves the storage of particular data files for the subsequent purpose of retrieving selected portions. An example is the storage of abstracts of scientific journals so that scientists can selectively retrieve those that relate to their projects.

Although information retrieval and MIS are similar, there are two major distinctions. First, information retrieval seeks only to store specialized data, such as titles and abstracts of printed publications or the contents of court records. Second, information retrieval does not calculate or accumulate; it is primarily concerned with storing, retrieving, and displaying.

In 1964 a new generation of computer hardware was introduced that exerted a strong influence on the manner in which computers were employed. Hardware improvements are classified by generation. In the first generation, computers were constructed of vacuum tubes; in the second, they were constructed of transistors. The third generation, introduced in 1964, consisted of the first use of semiconductor chip circuitry. This generation offered much greater processing speed and data storage capacity per user's dollar. A firm could use a computer with large-capacity storage units and data communications equipment for a relatively small increase in overall cost. The concept of using the computer as a *management information system*, or *MIS*, was promoted by computer vendors to justify this additional equipment. The concept was accepted readily by many computer users, since a real need existed for better management information. The time was ripe for the development of a new use for the computer.

The road traveled by these pioneering firms was not easy. As with many new ideas, actual accomplishments seldom matched those initially envisioned. There are several reasons why many of the first MIS efforts failed—a general lack of computer literacy among users, an ignorance of the management role among information specialists, expensive and limited hardware and software, and so on. But one error in particular characterized the early systems—they were too ambitious. Firms believed that they could build a giant information system to support all managers. System designs snowballed, and the task became overwhelming. Some firms stuck it out, invested more resources, and eventually developed workable systems, although more modest in size than originally projected. Other firms decided to scrap the entire MIS idea and retreated to EDP.

The current focus on decision making and communication

While many watched from the sidelines as firms grappled with their giant system designs, some information scientists at the Massachusetts Institute of Technology (MIT) formulated a different approach to information for managers. These scientists were Michael S. Scott Morton, G. Anthony Gorry, and Peter G. W. Keen, and their approach was named *decision support systems*, or *DSS*. A DSS is an information-producing system aimed at a particular decision a manager must make. The problems that the DSS can best attack are semistructured ones—those with some aspects that can be described quantitatively and others that must be handled subjectively. Instead of attempting to install one giant MIS, DSS proponents recommend focusing on separate problems and designing a decision support system for each.

Some people feel that DSS replaced MIS, and they regard the MIS concept as being obsolete. One often-heard criticism is that the MIS overloaded the manager with too much information that was not needed. This happened frequently in early efforts, but it was not because the MIS concept was faulty. The failures occurred because the concept was poorly implemented.

Other people regard the DSS, MIS, and data processing as existing in a hierarchy, with DSS at the top. The DSS provides the most decision support by actively involving the manager and making available special analytical software in addition to the data base. The MIS, on the other hand, plays a more passive role by simply providing information that the manager must then interpret and apply.

A third view holds that DSS is a new part of the MIS concept, in which MIS is the overall structure, encompassing both DSS and data processing. This view provides the underlying organization of our text and will be developed in the following chapters.

Since about 1980 interest has been aimed at another area of computer application—*office automation (OA)*. Office automation seeks to facilitate communication and increase productivity among managers and office workers through the use of electronic and electro-mechanical devices. Office automation got its start in 1964 when IBM announced its Magnetic Tape/Selectric Typewriter (MT/ST)—a typewriter that could type automatically from words recorded on magnetic tape. This automatic typing operation was soon transferred to small systems containing some of the circuitry found in small computers—the microprocessor. These small systems were called word processors. IBM has been joined in this booming business by over 30 other firms including Wang, Lanier, NBI, and Philips.

The early word processors were designed specifically for that type of use. During this same time period, users of large computer systems realized that word processing could be accomplished from a keyboard terminal linked to the computer. Special programs such as the University of Waterloo's SCRIPT enabled the central computer to perform word processing functions such as document storage, rearrangement of paragraphs, and replacement of words. The next step was to perform word processing on a microcomputer, or *micro*, and that approach is currently receiving the most interest. A micro such as a Macintosh, an IBM PC, or a TI Professional can use a word processing program such as WordStar to perform word processing, and use other programs to perform data processing.

In addition to word processing, office automation also includes electronic mail, teleconferencing, voice mail, electronic mail, electronic calendaring, document transmission, image storage and retrieval, and other means of increasing the productivity of the office worker. There is a real need for improvement here. During the 1970s, factory productivity increased by 85-90%, whereas office productivity increased by only 4%. Where the movement toward office automation will lead is anybody's guess; in any case, it will be widespread. Office automation could possibly become the umbrella under which all business applications of the computer are integrated—data processing, MIS, and DSS.

The view taken in this book is that MIS serves as this umbrella, and that data processing, DSS, and office automation are parts of MIS. This view is illustrated in Figure 1-11.

The emerging focus on consultation

There is a movement presently under way to link *artificial intelligence (AI)* to the MIS. The basic idea of AI is that the computer can be programmed to perform some of the same logical reasoning as a human. The accomplishments to date in applying AI to business have been modest, but this will no doubt change. A special subclass of AI, expert systems, is receiving the most attention in business. An *expert system* is one that functions as an expert in an area. For example, an expert system could provide some of the same type of assistance to a manager as would come from a management consultant. During the next few years, we can expect DSS to embrace expert systems. The DSS will then not simply assist the manager in making a decision in the same way as the DSS has been programmed, but will be able to suggest better ways to make the decision.

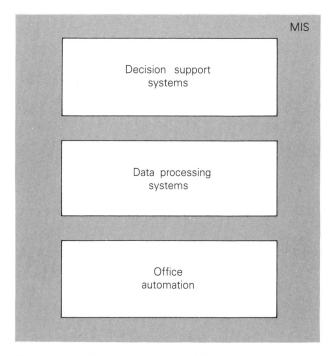

Figure 1-11 MIS provides the overall structure for decision support systems, data processing, and office automation.

Figure 1-12 shows how the various concepts relative to business information have evolved. The chronological pattern of some of the concepts is well documented—the solid arrows. Some of the relationships are still not fully understood—the dashed arrows.

Justifying the MIS

MIS resources should be justified in the same manner as any other sizable expenditure. During the EDP era, firms justified the cost of a computer and its associated expenses by comparing the costs with those of the displaced manual, keydriven, or punched card systems. Even though the computer costs exceeded the costs of the keydriven and punched card equipment, fewer people were required for the computer system. The computer was justified on the basis of displaced clerical costs. Few of these clerical workers actually lost their jobs, however, since management decided to transfer them elsewhere in the company where their skills could be better utilized.

Another way of justifying EDP was the added efficiency or reduced investment it made possible. This approach was common in the manufacturing and marketing areas. One of the first computer applications was inventory control,

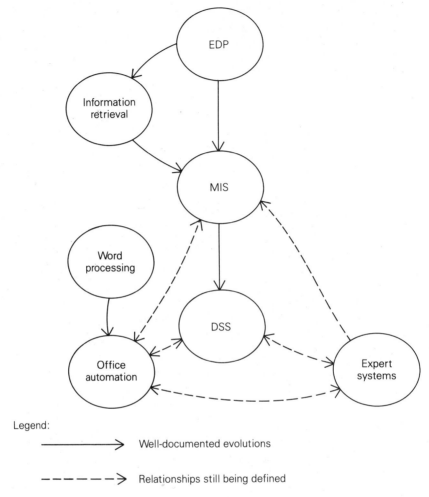

Legend:

——————————> Well-documented evolutions

— — — — — —> Relationships still being defined

Figure 1-12 The evolution of the MIS concept.

and firms often reduced their inventory investment with EDP. If EDP could reduce a $10 million inventory by 3%, then $300,000 was available to invest elsewhere.

With the advent of MIS, computer justification became more difficult. An MIS can produce a valuable report, such as the projection of personnel needs for the insurance company, but how valuable is the report? Under normal circumstances a report's monetary value is difficult to assess. A firm could implement the report and then, using the report, compare total profit for the period with the profit during a prior period. For this comparison to be valid, the report would have to be the only change in the firm's operations—hardly a feasible possibility in a dynamic business setting. There are usually many actions or combinations of actions that could contribute to increased profit, and singling out one is almost impossible.

So the modern manager faces a problem. How does he or she justify something when its worth can't be exactly measured? Quite simply, the manager has to have faith that the MIS contributes more to revenues than to costs. This is not an unusual approach. Millions of dollars are spent on advertising each year, even though the revenue value of advertising is impossible to measure.

Because of the difficulty of justifying an MIS, firms approach the decision very seriously. Much manager and staff time is spent evaluating the impact that the MIS will have on the organization. Although the process is largely subjective, justifying the MIS is a key step in the achievement of this valuable resource.

Achieving the MIS

A computer-based MIS is achieved by assembling the MIS resources identified earlier. Some firms are farther along in this assembly process than others, and probably no firm feels that it has assembled all of the resources that it needs. The process of developing an MIS is never ending, as firms strive to take advantage of new technology and methodology. Although much has been accomplished in MIS design in recent years, much more remains to be accomplished. Firms will be involved in MIS implementation projects for years to come.

The evolutionary process followed in achieving an MIS is called the *MIS life cycle.* In some respects, the MIS is like a living organism—it is born, it grows and matures, it functions, and sooner or later it dies. A given MIS will eventually be replaced by a newer or better one as the firm's needs change.

As the MIS develops, it passes through several phases. In Part Six of this book, the MIS life cycle phases are identified as:

- Planning
- Analysis and design
- Implementation
- Operation and control

Figure 1-13 illustrates how these phases fit into a circular pattern. When an MIS becomes obsolete and must be replaced, the firm begins a new life cycle by initiating the planning phase.

Management responsibility for the MIS

The manager is ultimately responsible for the MIS. She or he is responsible both for developing it and for using it. The information specialists serve as valuable technical assistants. As the MIS evolves, the manager must plan the life cycle and then control the specialists as they set out to achieve the new system. After the MIS has been implemented, the manager must control the resources to keep system performance within tolerances. The manager's overall responsibility and the phase-by-phase support by the information specialists are illustrated in Figure 1-14.

The information specialists play a vital role in the development of an MIS. They often trigger the manager's interest in a new system by informing the manager of a new technology or method. The specialist is trained to solve systems

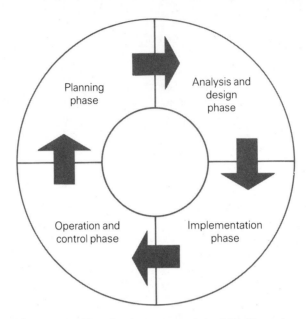

Figure 1-13 The circular pattern of the MIS life cycle.

problems and knows the correct procedure to follow to convert an ill-defined problem into a specific description of the solution process. Both the manager and the specialist follow this procedure to identify, evaluate, and select alternate solutions and to identify appropriate hardware and software. The specialist recommends a particular system design, but it is the manager's responsibility to approve implementation. Once the manager makes the decision, it is the information specialist's task to implement the system.

Managing the MIS

The first computer systems in business were located in the accounting area—the same place where the punched card machines had been located. As the computer's popularity increased, it was relocated as a separate support function for the entire firm. Very often the manager of the firm's computer resource has vice-presidential status. Under this arrangement, the firm's computer resources are managed by the information specialists. When a user, such as a manager, wants to obtain computer output, he or she communicates the output specifications to a systems analyst. It is the systems analyst's responsibility to decide how the computer can best be applied and to describe the approach using diagrams and other graphical tools. This documentation is then passed along to a programmer. The programmer prepares the code that enables the computer to produce the needed output. This communication chain is pictured in Figure 1-15a.

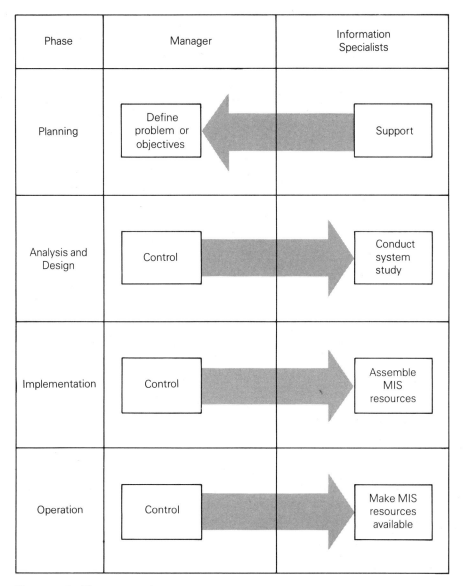

Figure 1-14 The cooperative MIS development process.

End-user computing

As users became more computer and MIS literate, they became dissatisfied with the communication chain. Very often it took months to get output from the computer because of the tedious nature of the information specialists' work. The world wide shortage of information specialists only added to the delay. Some firms accumulated backlogs of jobs awaiting computer processing that required from two to three years to clear.

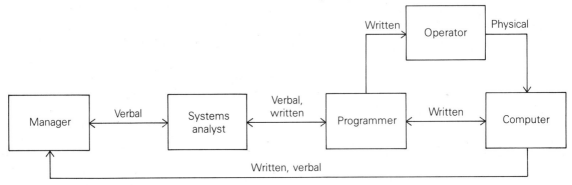

(a) The communication chain.

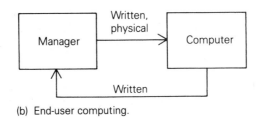

(b) End-user computing.

Figure 1·15 End-user computing shortens the communication chain.

At the same time, new software was easier for the user to use. The software was said to be *user friendly*. This new software was not as tedious as the traditional computer languages. The new software was regarded as a *fourth-generation language*, recognizing its extension beyond languages of earlier generations such as COBOL, FORTRAN, and PL/I.

The combination of the backlog and the new, user-friendly software stimulated many users to do their own computing using terminals connected to their firm's central computers. This concept became known as *end-user computing*, and it is illustrated in Figure 1-15b. The key to end-user computing is a high degree of computer literacy on the part of the user.

The immediate reaction to this concept is that there will no longer be a need for systems analysts, programmers, and even operators. This is an unfounded fear. Some jobs, such as the firm's payroll calculations and records, are best performed in the central computing facility. Information specialists will still be needed to design and maintain these systems. Users will do their own computing for those jobs that do not have to be performed in a central location. In many cases, information specialists will be needed to help users set up their own systems.

The information center

As the concept of end-user computing spread, users wanted to expand the scope of their computer-related abilities. In 1970 Security Pacific Bank in Los Angeles established an *information center* to encourage their employees to do their own computing rather than contract it out to computer service bureaus. In 1976 IBM

Canada began promoting the information center as a facility dedicated to support end-user computing. The idea spread quickly during the early eighties and now many large firms have information centers.

The information center is a location where hardware and user-friendly software are available for use by the firm's employees. Initially the hardware included terminals, printers, and graphics plotters. Several information specialists are also available for "hand holding" help as users become self-sufficient. The specialists frequently conduct training seminars to teach new software and hardware. Most information centers are operated by the information services departments.

The microcomputer boom

The information center idea was conceived before the small computer (microcomputer) boom began in the late seventies. This boom was timed perfectly—users were becoming more computer literate, the information center concept had only begun to whittle away at the job backlog, and the new micros were both inexpensive and easy to operate. Users began to obtain their own micros at an unexpected rate.

Although this increased user interest in computing is healthy, it also has its drawbacks. The wide selection of microcomputer hardware and software makes it possible for a firm to acquire a hodgepodge of incompatible systems. Many firms have felt that it is better to standardize micros and software and permit only certain brands to be purchased. This standardization facilitates exchange of hardware and software among users, interconnection of hardware, and user training. Also, microcomputers are now included among the hardware offered by information centers. Users can use the micros in the information center or check them out and take them to their offices.

Information resource management

The increased computer literacy of users and the ease with which users can acquire their own computing facilities have made many firms realize that a new corporate attitude toward computing is needed. Information centers are only a step toward support of end-user computing; activities are still carried on in a disjointed fashion, often leading to inefficiencies. For example, two users in different areas may simultaneously be developing systems to prepare the same report. It is necessary for the firm's top management to devise a long-range plan specifying the firm's information requirements and identifying how existing technology will be applied. This corporate attitude toward the concept of information management has been named *information resource management*, or *IRM*.

Several ingredients should be present if a firm is to implement IRM:

1. The top computer executive should report directly to the president.
2. The firm should have a data administrator who establishes and enforces policies and procedures concerning company data.
3. The information services group (the computer department) should have a documented understanding of data flow throughout the firm.

4. A long-range plan should identify how information needs are to be satisfied through personal computing (microcomputers), remote computer
   use from terminals, and centralized computing.
5. The top computer manager should establish company-wide MIS policies
   where necessary.[4]

The IRM concept is just getting started. In 1985 a survey of 41 MIS managers
revealed that only six firms had fully implemented IRM. Twenty-seven firms had
begun implementation, but eight firms had no plans. IRM is a formal corporate
policy toward management of the information resource and should bring about
order to the dynamic and often undisciplined condition of computer use in business firms.

Summary

Information is a resource to be managed. The value of information increases as
the management task becomes more complex. Managers are found on all levels
and in all functional areas of the organization. The managers augment their basic
decision-making and communications skills with computer usage to increase their
productivity and performance levels. An understanding of how to use a computer
to help solve business problems is termed MIS literacy.

A system is an integration of parts, all contributing to the achievement of
an overall goal. This structural system consists of a transformation process that
converts input resources to output and is controlled in some manner. The manager
can regard his or her firm as a system. With a systems orientation, managers can
appreciate fully the importance of the environment to the system, and they can
conceptualize the subdivision of the system into subsystems.

The manager must manage this physical system. But this task becomes more
difficult as the size of the firm increases. The manager of a large firm must monitor
the physical system by using another system, a conceptual system that represents
the physical one. This conceptual system is an information system—a management information system (MIS).

The MIS provides information for decision making. The information comes
from both formal and informal systems and can be in a written or an oral form.
The information describes both the internal operation of the firm and its environment. Also, the information describes what has happened in the past, what is
happening now, and what is likely to happen in the future. The information is
used for decision making by managers, employees, and persons in the firm's
environment.

There is a difference between information and data. Data includes items and
elements of fact that are transformed into information—processed or meaningful
data. This transformation is called data processing.

---

[4]This list was adapted from Tor Guimaraes, "IRM Revisited," *Datamation* 31 (March 1, 1985):
134.

The computer-based MIS is composed of resources—hardware, software, an information services staff, a data base, an information-oriented management staff, and progressive executive leadership. Before the MIS, computers were used for electronic data processing (EDP) and for information retrieval. Recently, the emphasis has shifted to decision support systems (DSS), office automation (OA), and expert systems.

It is rather easy to identify the costs of an MIS. More difficult, however, is a measurement of the value of the information produced. Yet decisions to implement an MIS are usually made in a sound, businesslike manner. Managers are confident that the value of the MIS exceeds its cost, even though the value cannot be measured exactly.

It is the manager's responsibility to see that an information system is designed and implemented. This responsibility cannot be delegated. Information specialists and managers must work together, but the manager must both initiate and control the effort.

For years, information specialists worked to encourage computer use. Now the combination of increasing computer literacy and low-cost, user-friendly hardware and software is causing much computer use to become decentralized. Information centers are an effort to serve users' information needs in an organized way—but more is needed. A company-wide policy toward computer use, called information resource management, must originate at the top management level. Many firms are currently embarking on a policy of IRM.

In this first chapter we have only presented the big picture of MIS. In the remaining chapters we will expand on each of these topics.

Key Terms

information management	physical system, conceptual system
operations research (OR)	data, information
management science	data processing system
strategic planning level	data base
management control level	management information system (MIS)
operational control level	
functional area of the firm	hardware
management function	software
managerial role	application software
problem solving	system software
decision making	information specialist
computer literacy	electronic data processing (EDP)
MIS literacy	information retrieval
systems orientation	decision support system (DSS)
system, subsystem, supersystem, suprasystem	office automation (OA)
	artificial intelligence (AI)

expert system   information center
MIS life cycle   information resource management
end-user computing   (IRM)

Key Concepts

Information as a resource to be managed

The increasing complexity of management

The similarity in basic tasks performed by all managers

MIS literacy as a step beyond computer literacy; addressing how to use the computer in business

Why the manager should think in systems terms

The firm as a physical system

The MIS as a conceptual system

The difference between data and information

The inclusion of oral and written information from both formal and informal systems in the MIS design

The inclusion of employees and persons in the environment, along with managers, as users of MIS output

The inclusion of software, data, information specialists, and users along with the computer in a computer-based MIS

The direct flow of some information to the manager, bypassing the data processing step

The progression in computer use beginning with EDP, leading to information retrieval, MIS, and DSS

The current efforts aimed at integrating OA and AI into the MIS

The difficulty of justifying the MIS on a dollars and cents basis

The evolutionary character of the MIS life cycle, controlled by the manager

The impact of computer literacy, microcomputers, and a heavy backlog of jobs on the firm's computing resources

Information resource management

Questions

1. How can information be managed? Explain.

2. In what ways is management becoming more complex?

3. Name two ways to classify all managers.

4. Is information more valuable to the manager of a large firm than of a small one? Explain.

5. Is a manager of a large firm more likely to have a computer-based MIS than a manager of a small firm? Explain your answer, and describe how the situation has changed over the past ten years.

6. How does a manager become computer literate? MIS literate?

7. Why should a manager think of the organization as a system? Is it a physical system or a conceptual system?

8. A recent ad for a razor with a replaceable double blade referred to it as a "shaving system." Is the razor really a system? What are its elements? What is the objective?

9. What is the control mechanism in a firm?

10. Can a subsystem also be a system? Explain.

11. Each day, a large metropolitan telephone company will print thousands of bills. Are the bills data or information? Explain.

12. List the components of an MIS.

13. Must a firm have a computer to have a data base?

14. Give an example of (1) environmental information, (2) environmental data, (3) internal information, and (4) internal data. Which of these would you probably find in *The Wall Street Journal*?

15. In order to print the report of personnel projections, the insurance company has to know how much insurance, on the average, an agent can sell in a month. What other things does the company need to know? Where does it get the information?

16. Distinguish between EDP, information retrieval, MIS, and DSS.

17. What type of hardware is used to perform word processing? Is software also needed?

18. Describe how artificial intelligence can be incorporated into an MIS.

19. What factors result in users doing their own computing? What is good about end-user computing? Is there anything bad? Explain.

20. If a firm establishes an information center, has it implemented IRM? If not, what else must be done?

Problems

1. Go to the library and obtain a book on introductory management. Learn what skills a manager should possess. List them. Identify your source.

2. While in the library, look up a definition of computer literacy. Copy it and identify the source.

3. After reading the chapter, make up your own definition of MIS. Do not refer back to the one in the book.

4. Draw a diagram of an MIS showing: internal and environmental sources, oral and written information, formal and informal systems, and the three classes of users. You do not have to include anything else.

5. A new insurance company wants to plan its sales expenses for its first 12 months of operation. They want to sell $100,000 of insurance in the first

month and increase that by $20,000 each month. One agent can sell $10,000 per month. An agent's salary is $2,000 per month, and each month an agent incurs the following expenses: $50 telephone, $100 travel, $10 entertainment. Sketch out the Expense Report, showing the various expenses across the top, and the 12 months down the side. Fill in the numbers. If you are familiar with an electronic spreadsheet such as VisiCalc or Lotus 1-2-3, you can use it.

CASE PROBLEM: Freeway Ford

You are a sales representative for Automobile Software, Inc., a national firm that markets a software package for car dealers. One day while you are talking with James Kahler, the sales manager for Freeway Ford, you learn that his firm has a problem with its inventory. The manual records they maintain do not accurately reflect the inventory status—the numbers and types of automobiles and trucks on the lot. Whenever a new shipment arrives from Detroit, it takes several days to update the inventory cards. A salesperson might have a buyer who wants a particular car, and the car may be on the lot, but the salesperson will never know it. A sale is lost because of poor information. Another problem arises when two salespersons sell the same car to two buyers. This happens because the inventory records are not updated immediately after a sale.

You know that your software package, called SMART (Sales Management for Automobile Retail Trade), will solve the problem. Once a dealer gets SMART, the computer records are updated from a typewriterlike terminal as soon as a new-car shipment arrives or a sale is made. The computer records always reflect exactly what is on the lot. Versions of SMART are available for most popular small computers. The cost of both the software and hardware is well within the reach of most metropolitan new-car dealerships.

Your next step is to approach the new president of Freeway Ford, Phil Rains, and give your sales pitch. As you begin to tell Rains of your product's merits, he stops you and says: "Listen, I'm new on the job. I'm a recent graduate of a top Pacific Coast school, with a degree in systems theory. If you could just explain how your product will help us, in systems terms, I think I can understand. Now, go ahead."

Assignment

Describe, in systems terms, how SMART can benefit Freeway Ford.

Selected Bibliography

Introduction to Information Management

Ackoff, Russell L., "Management Misinformation Systems," *Management Science* 14 (December 1967): B147–B156.

Benson, David H., "A Field Study of End User Computing: Findings and Issues," *MIS Quarterly* 7 (December 1983): 35–45.

Cowan, William M., "The 'I Center'—An Office Resource Comes of Age," *Office Administration and Automation* 45 (February 1984): 30ff.

Dearden, John, "MIS is a Mirage," *Harvard Business Review* 50 (January-February 1972): 90–99.

Guimaraes, Tor, "The Evolution of the Information Center," *Datamation* 30 (July 15, 1984): 127ff.

Guimaraes, Tor, "IRM Revisited," *Datamation* 31 (March 1, 1985): 130ff.

Head, Robert V., "Information Resource Center: A New Force in End User Computing," *Journal of Systems Management* 36 (February 1985): 24–29.

McKenney, James L., and F. Warren McFarlan, "The Information Archipelago—Maps and Bridges," *Harvard Business Review* 60 (September-October 1982): 109–119.

Meyer, Ken, and Mike Harper, "User Friendliness," *MIS Quarterly* 8 (March 1984): 1–3.

Michaelsen, Robert, and Donald Michie, "Expert Systems in Business," *Datamation* 29 (November 1983): 240ff.

Ryan, Hugh, "End-User Game Plan," *Datamation* 29 (December 1983): 241ff.

Sprague, Ralph H., Jr. "Guest Editor's Introduction," *Data Base* 12 (Fall 1980): 2–7.

Part Two

FUNDAMENTAL PRINCIPLES

Management information systems are very real. They consist of managers, information specialists, data, information, communication channels, and often computers for storage and processing. The business student can expect to become a part of such a system, either as a provider of information or as a user.

There is a great deal to learn about management information systems. The subject is primarily a composite of two complete fields—management and computer science. Additional principles are drawn from physical sciences such as biology and botany, and from social sciences such as sociology and psychology. Much of the MIS material has developed during the past few years as firms created their computer-based systems. Other material, however, has evolved over the past century as the subject of business management has become more refined.

The purpose of Part Two is to provide a theoretical foundation—a basic structure—upon which to build an understanding of information systems. This is a general framework, applying to a wide variety of situations. The framework should prove useful in preparing for both business and nonbusiness careers.

This part of the book addresses three basic topics. The first is *theory*. Theories of management, organizations, and systems are presented. The second topic is a *general model* of a firm as a physical system with a conceptual information system. The third is an approach to business problem solving, the *systems approach*.

Each topic relates to the idea of a system. This relatively new way to view business is used in this book to help you understand an important part of a business organization—its management information system.

## Chapter 2

Theory of Management and Organizations

Learning Objectives

After studying this chapter, you should:

- Understand and appreciate how theory facilitates both the study and the practice of business
- Recognize that management theory concerns all managerial activity, and that organization theory is a subset concerning the allocation of all resources—not just personnel
- Be able to identify several different schools of management and organization theory, and understand their differences
- Understand Henry Mintzberg's concept of managerial roles
- Recognize some of the major strengths and weaknesses of the Japanese school of management and organization theory
- Appreciate the contributions of the different schools to MIS design and use
- Appreciate what is meant by general systems theory, why it was developed, and how it applies to multiple disciplines—including business
- Be able to relate systems theory to business organizations

Introduction

This chapter lays the theoretical foundation for the material to follow. It describes theories of both management and organizations, the two large and important bodies of theory in the study of management information systems. Also included is a description of systems theory and how it relates to both the manager and the organization. We will not attempt a full description of management and organization theories. The sole purpose of discussing theory in this text is to lay the groundwork for studying information management. Consequently, we will be selective in our coverage of theory, keeping this objective in sight.

Theory

Many people don't get excited about theory. In fact, some dislike it. To these people, theory is unrealistic. They say, "That's just a theory," when they feel something is not true.

Actually, these people are not altogether wrong. Theory does not mean truth; nor does it mean untruth. When something always holds true, it is no longer a theory, but a *law*. Probably the most widely understood law is the law of gravity, which relates to the behavior of physical objects. It has been proven and everyone accepts it. A number of such laws provide the basis for the physical sciences, such as physics and chemistry.

What is theory?

Nearly everyone has heard the term *theory* and has a conception of its meaning. Because the term has several different meanings, theory probably means one thing to one person and another to somebody else. Any dictionary will show six or eight different definitions.

The definition, or meaning, of theory that is of interest to the study of information management deals with a set of propositions. *Theory is a coherent group* of *general propositions* that are used as *principles* to *explain* some class of *phenomena.*

Coherent Group   Just as an efficient system comprises multiple parts that work together, a theory comprises a coherent group of parts that fit together in a logical way. A theory, then, is a type of system. The system consists of propositions designed to explain certain phenomena. The interest here, however, is not in theory *as a system* but in a theory *of* systems.

The general propositions   A proposition is something offered for acceptance. A general proposition is one used to apply to a variety of situations.

Principles   Principles are generally accepted rules of behavior or action. These are the component parts of a theory. A theory, then, contains multiple principles that fit together in a logical, coherent manner.

Explanation   The purpose of theories in business is to explain the various business phenomena.

Class of phenomena   A class of phenomena relates to some particular area of activity. The phenomena of interest here are those generally accepted rules used to explain management and organizations.

Theory in business

Business is not a physical science. In fact, some doubt that it is a science of any kind. If business is a science, then it is a social science—one dealing with people.

In general, it is much harder to predict what people will do than what a nonliving object will do. For this reason, the social sciences have fewer laws than the physical sciences. In business there are more theories than laws. These theories represent what people believe to be true but have not proven true in all cases. The manager applies judgment to the use of theories. The manager realizes that the theory does not tell the entire story, but that it does provide an idea of what to expect under general conditions. The manager must then determine whether the theory applies to the situation at hand.

Since business is so complex and covers so many areas, there is no single theory *of* business. There are, however, theories *in* business. One area of business that has inspired many theories is the study of consumer behavior. Efforts have mainly focused on applying theories developed in psychology and sociology to business situations.

Why study theory?

A theory in isolation is worth very little. The real value of theory is in its application to a real situation in order to accurately explain that situation. Theories of business do not seek to answer the question *What exists?* Usually *what exists* is very apparent to the observer, in this case the manager. The manager knows what is happening if an adequate information system is available. What the manager usually does not know, however, is *why it exists*. Theories seek to provide the needed explanation.

As an example, assume a manager knows that certain employees are motivated better by nonmonetary than by monetary rewards. If the manager knows why nonmonetary rewards work better for certain employees, then that type of reward can be intelligently applied in appropriate situations. Thus the manager can make better decisions because he or she understands why a certain behavior occurs.

Jay W. Forrester, an MIT professor, recognized the need for theory in business almost 30 years ago:

> To develop the status of a profession, management must discover the underlying principles which unify its separate aspects. It must develop a basic theory of behavior. It must learn how to convert experiences and particular case examples into a contribution to this general theory. And, finally, it must be able to employ the basic principles of the theory as a useful practical guide for explaining and solving new problems as they arise. By accomplishing these aims, management will become a true profession during the next generation.[1]

Theory provides the manager with a better understanding of the complex system of business. This understanding helps the manager do a better job.

---

[1] Jay W. Forrester, "Industrial Dynamics: A Major Breakthrough for Decision Makers," *Harvard Business Review* 36 (July–August 1958): 37.

Information and theory

Many managers use theories learned in school. Others develop their own from experience. Most theories begin as approximations, then undergo refinement as more is learned about the phenomena involved (Figure 2-1). In effect, the manager's information system helps the manager develop theories.

The theory tells the manager what to expect. The information system tells what is happening. If real activity differs from what was expected, the theory is refined. Over a period of time, the manager can develop theories that accurately predict the behavior of the business system.

Management Theory

We will direct most of our attention in this chapter to the development of theories of management. We can paraphrase our earlier definition of theory to define *management theory* as a coherent group of general propositions used as principles to explain the practice of management. This general body of knowledge describes the roles that managers play, the functions that they perform, and the skills that they need to do both jobs well.

These theories have been developed, for the most part, by managers who have learned through trial and error and who have gradually identified propositions that serve as useful guidelines. The managers and other people who study

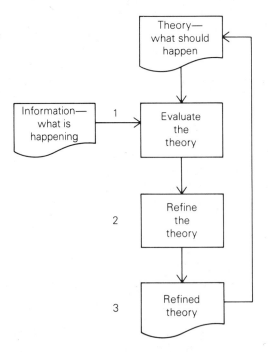

Figure 2-1 Information is used to refine theories.

the art of management have assembled these propositions into the theories that now form an integral part of the literature of business.

Management theory includes everything relating to the managerial task—including organization. Organization theory is so important to the MIS that we will treat it separately later in the chapter.

There have been many theories of business management. Those that share a number of basic principles are grouped into *schools.* The first school was the *classical* school, followed by the *behavioral,* the *decision theory,* and, most recently, the *contingency* schools. As we discuss each of these schools, we will highlight their relevance to the MIS.

The classical theory of management[2]

Frederick W. Taylor (1856–1915) is known as the *father of scientific management.* Taylor was the first industrial engineer (IE), or systems analyst. He studied the activities of American steelworkers. Using time-and-motion studies, Taylor sought to identify the best way to perform menial tasks such as shoveling coal. By experimenting with shovels of different sizes for different materials, he was able to increase worker productivity from 16 to 59 tons per day. Taylor believed that maximizing productivity was the key to maximizing the profits of the firm and the earnings of the employees. Management was quick to embrace scientific management, but organized labor resisted it, claiming that it was dehumanizing.

Performance standards Taylor's attention was aimed at the worker level in the organization; he didn't contribute much to improve upper-level management. His main contribution, in terms of a systems theory of management, was his attention to *performance standards.* Taylor believed that standards should be established to regulate the methods used and time taken for each task. Taylor's idea of standards is equally applicable to management.

If the workers and the managers meet their standards, then the firm will accomplish its objectives. The objectives represent an accomplishment to be achieved. Standards are similar to a thermostat setting that establishes an acceptable temperature range for a heater or an air conditioner. For the heater or air conditioner, the objective is human comfort.

The difference between standards and objectives is very important, for we will be using both terms throughout the remainder of the book. *Objectives* are what the organization attempts to accomplish. *Standards* are measures of performance that, when met, should accomplish the stated objectives. Objectives are usually defined for the firm and for its important units. They tend to be broad, general statements. Standards can apply to the firm, its units, and even individual employees. They should be stated in specific, quantifiable terms so that the degree of accomplishment can be measured. Table 2-1 presents a list of several objectives that a firm might adopt, along with some standards of performance.

----

[2] Based on Andrew D. Szilagyi, Jr., *Management and Performance* (Santa Monica: Goodyear Publishing Co., 1981), pp. 57–84.

Table 2-1   Examples of objectives and corresponding standards of performance

Objectives	Standards of Performance
Satisfy customer needs	Achieve an annual sales volume of at least $25 million
	Maintain a 20% share of the market
	Maintain an annual growth rate of 15%
Produce a return on investment for the owners	Pay dividends to stockholders each quarter
	Maintain the price of the firm's common stock above $85 per share
Operate efficiently	Realize an after-tax profit of 15% of sales
	Maintain a record of accident-free days
	Keep employee turnover below 10%
Invest in the future	Invest a minimum of 15% of sales in research and development
Develop sources of supply	Achieve stockouts on no more than 2% of the items in inventory during the year
	Keep the number of backorders to less than 5% of all orders processed
	Have no plant shutdowns due to unavailable raw materials
Operate ethically	Successfully defend the firm against legal actions filed by customers, suppliers, and the government
Take advantage of modern methods	Invest no less than 10% of sales revenue in automation, computerization, and mechanization

Each manager is the control mechanism of her or his system. The manager keeps the system performance on target with respect to its objectives by comparing the performance to standards.

Management by exception   We can also credit Taylor with another contribution to management theory—the *exception principle*. This idea, that one should only pay attention to exceptions from the standard, is known today as *management by exception*. The manager only becomes involved in cases of exceptional (very good or very bad) performance. Management by exception conserves the manager's time by directing attention to problems and opportunities, and this focused effort is facilitated by the MIS.

Management functions A second important contributor to classical theory was a Frenchman, Henri Fayol (1841–1925), who was the first to develop a theory of administrative management. Fayol recognized a difference between operating and managerial activities, and sought to improve management, whereas Taylor concentrated on operations. Fayol is most famous for his definition of *management functions*—the activities that managers perform.

According to Fayol, all managers plan, organize, staff, direct, and control. Listed in a logical order, the first task is to *plan* what is to be done. Then the proper *organization* structure must be established to permit implementation of the plan. The manager then must *staff* for the planned activity by acquiring the necessary resources. While the term staff suggests personnel resources, all types of resources should be included. Once these resources have been assembled, the next task is to *direct* their use in the performance of the planned activities. Finally, the manager must *control* the activities in order to meet the designated objectives.

Management levels Fayol believed that all managers perform these functions, regardless of their level in the organization. This theory has been called the *universality of management functions*—it applies universally to all managers on all levels.

We introduced the topic of management levels in Chapter 1 and used the names strategic planning (top), management control (middle), and operational control (lower). These names were coined by Robert N. Anthony in his 1965 book on planning and control, and, as we shall see in a later chapter, form a theoretical basis for the DSS concept.

All levels *plan,* but managers on the top levels plan farther into the future than those on the bottom. Top-level managers project the firm's activities five or more years into the future. Middle-level managers are involved with what the firm will be doing from one to five years into the future. Lower-level managers are mainly concerned with meeting objectives for the current year. A manager's *planning horizon,* therefore, is a way to identify her or his management level.

Although all levels *organize,* they organize different parts of the firm. Top-level managers determine the overall, general organization of the firm. The details of how each part is organized are left to lower-level managers.

The *staff* function also is performed on all levels, but in a different manner. Top-level managers are concerned with the acquisition of those resources used on their level. For example, the president will personally select the vice presidents, but leave the selection of lower-level employees to lower-level managers.

All managers *direct* resources to attain objectives. But the top level is most interested in accomplishing long-range, general objectives. Lower levels are more interested in immediate, specific objectives.

As the managers direct their resources, they exercise *control* over them. Top levels aim for long-range control, whereas lower levels have more short-term concerns.

Figure 2-2 shows that managers on different levels divide their time differently among the various functions. The diagrams, as are many in this book, are *conceptual representations* in that there is little empirical evidence to support

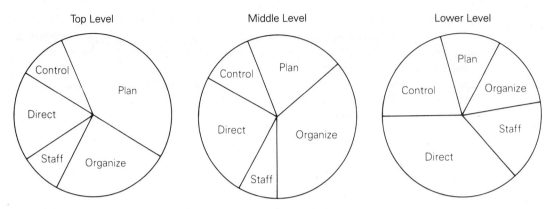

Figure 2-2   Influence of management level on management function.

them. The diagrams are intended to convey *general conditions,* and you should keep in mind that each manager has his or her own unique style.

As a general rule, the higher you are in the organization, the more time you spend planning. The lower you are, the more time you spend staffing, directing, and controlling. Managers on the middle level spend much time organizing.

The management levels have a significant effect on two basic aspects of MIS design. First, they influence the source of data or information; and second, they influence how the information is presented. These design aspects are shown in Figure 2-3.

The different levels demand information from different sources. Top-level managers have a greater need for environmental information than do managers on lower levels. According to the figure, a president may receive as much as half of his or her information from the environment. A lower-level manager, such as a department head, receives practically all of his or her information from internal sources. It is important to note that even though top-level managers are the ones most interested in the environment, they still have a definite internal focus.

The management level also influences how the information should be presented to the manager. Lower-level managers need detailed descriptions: exactly how many overtime hours were worked last week, the average hourly cost of operating a forklift truck, how many units were produced on machine A, and so on. Top-level managers are exposed to so much information that it must be summarized into only the most important facts. Middle-level managers work with both detailed and summary information.

These are general rules about the information needs of the three management levels. Individual preference is also a factor. Some top-level managers like detailed information. One executive, commenting on his newly found ability to use the computer, said, "I've always felt that the answers were in the detail. Now, at last, I can pore through some of that detail. That's my style."[3]

---

[3] John F. Rockart and Michael E. Treacy, "The CEO Goes On-line," *Harvard Business Review* 60 (January–February 1982): 86.

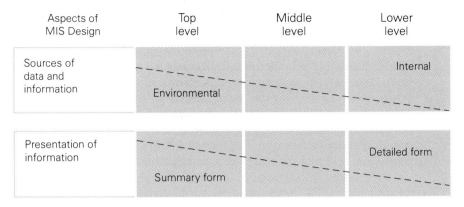

Figure 2-3 Influence of management level on MIS design.

Early MIS efforts were criticized for helping only lower-level managers. There were two reasons for this low-level approach. First, the information specialists were able to grasp the information needs of lower-level managers more quickly. The work of the upper-level managers was less routine and repetitive, and thus more difficult to analyze. Second, the first information systems were used mainly for control. The computer reports compared actual performance with standards, pointing out areas needing attention. As Figure 2-2 shows, most of this control occurs on the lower level.

More recently, the MIS has been applied to planning. Statistical techniques such as forecasting methods, and also mathematical models facilitating "what-if" simulations, enable managers to look into the future. Since planning is primarily an upper-level function, recent MIS efforts have mainly supported top- and middle-level managers.

These examples of different uses of the MIS, based on management level, are easy to observe. Fayol's theory of management functions helps us understand why these differences exist. This understanding is very important to the people designing the MIS—both managers and information specialists.

The behavioral theory of management

In a well-known case now called "the Hawthorne experiment," a team of Harvard researchers, headed by Elton Mayo and Fritz J. Roethlisberger, studied the effects of illumination on productivity at the Western Electric Hawthorne plant at Cicero, Illinois, between 1927 and 1932. The more they studied the relationship, the more confusing it became. Productivity seemed to increase regardless of whether the lighting was increased, reduced, or kept the same. As it turned out, the experimental groups of employees were not responding to the lighting, but to the attention that was being shown them. This response to attention was named the *Hawthorne effect,* and the Hawthorne experiments heralded the beginning of the behavioral school.

The behavioral school has been characterized by two groups, both placing more emphasis on the *people* in the jobs than on the jobs themselves. The Hawthorne researchers, as part of the *human relations movement,* were among the first to gain a better understanding of people at work in organizations. These researchers were later joined by highly trained behavioral scientists. These scientists became known as the *social systems* group. More sophisticated research techniques were applied by this group, whose efforts produced the body of material describing *organizational behavior.* The social systems group has greatly influenced the study of management in modern business schools, as evidenced by the many textbooks and courses titled *Organizational Behavior.*

It is more difficult to relate the MIS to the behavioral school than to the classical school. The classical school, with its emphasis on efficiency and productivity, is highly compatible with the design of many computerized management information systems. This is unfortunate. The designers of early systems paid little attention to the people involved. The systems often looked good on paper but were unacceptable to the employees who were expected to provide the input data, and to the managers who were expected to use the output information.

Had the designers of early information systems paid more attention to behavioral theory, both the number and the severity of MIS failures would probably have been reduced. Employees felt threatened by the computer; they feared that they would lose their jobs. Management made little effort to communicate the objectives of the computer project to the employees. When the computer was installed, employees in effect sabotaged it by doing their computer-related jobs poorly or not at all. The performance of the managers was frequently no better. Although intended primarily to help the managers, systems were often designed without the managers' participation. Many managers rejected the MIS, feeling that it was forced on them without their consent or involvement.

The research that came out of the human relations group can be applied to increase the chances of a successful MIS. These findings recognized that employees have various needs, and that there are ways that these needs can be satisfied. The chain reaction linking the employees' needs to the firm's objectives is pictured in Figure 2-4. The first step is to recognize the employees' needs. In step 2, the manager develops motivators to inspire the employees to work toward the objectives of the firm. The work is performed in step 3, and the firm meets its objectives in step 4. The key to the chain reaction comes in step 2 when the motivators are seen by the employees as ways to satisfy their needs.

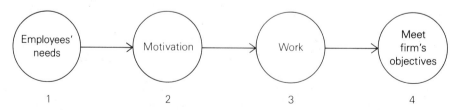

Figure 2-4 Objectives of the firm are met by satisfying needs of the employees.

The social systems group worked along the same lines as this model. They also recognized the importance of the individual if the group, or firm, is to meet its objectives. They believed that the objectives of both the individual and the group must be compatible. Therefore, when the manager sets a goal for a system, it must be one the employees will regard as compatible with their personal goals.

The designers of today's information systems are paying more attention to behavioral considerations. Most of the attention is being directed at the use of video display terminals by clerical workers. The terms *ergonomics, human engineering,* and *human factors considerations* have been used to describe this attention to primarily physical considerations of employees while integrating machines into work activity. We will return to this topic in Chapter 10 when we address office automation.

Less attention is being given to the impact of the MIS on management. Perhaps the reasoning is that the MIS is the manager's own doing, and she or he should be able to cope with it. There are indications, however, that some managers have difficulty in handling the abstraction and formality of the MIS. We have introduced the idea of using a conceptual system to manage the physical system. Some managers have difficulty with this. Because they cannot tear themselves away from the physical system, they maintain their personal contacts, for example, by touring the facilities. As the manager increases computer use, the need to obtain information through social interaction is lessened. Many managers prefer their informal social contacts over the formal, often regimented computer-based systems.

The behavioral school has made some solid contributions to the design of information systems. The school concentrates on the importance of objectives and how they can be achieved. It would be foolish for a manager of a business system to ignore these suggestions. The business system is not simply a mechanical structure. Its performance level is determined by the people working in it. The behavioral school suggests how these people can be motivated to work together as a system.

The decision theory school of management

New quantitative techniques were developed during World War II for military purposes in order to use limited resources more efficiently and to improve decision making. After the war, the techniques were applied in business situations to accomplish the same results. At the same time, the electronic computer arrived on the scene, and together the two innovations—quantitative techniques and the computer—formed an exciting problem-solving tool.

The name given to these quantitative techniques is *operations research,* or *OR.* The term *management science* is also used. Larger organizations and the government formed operations research staffs composed of persons with the necessary quantitative expertise.

The body of theory that stresses the use of quantitative techniques in decision making is known as the decision theory school. Herbert A. Simon is generally regarded as the father of this school. Much of his attention has been focused on the types of decisions made by managers. He distinguished between programmed and nonprogrammed decisions. *Programmed decisions* are those that are repetitive and routine and can be described in a procedure. Simon was not referring to computer programming. *Nonprogrammed decisions* are those that are novel and unstructured and there is no cut-and-dried method for handling them.

Simon and the other early founders of the decision theory school, James G. March and Richard M. Cyert of Carnegie-Mellon University, believed upper-management level decisions to be less programmed than those at the bottom. They also saw the manager's job as one of "programming," or routinizing, the procedures made by subordinates.

Decision theory concentrates on decision making and provides tools for improving this aspect of managerial work. Central to the quantitative approach is the *mathematical model*—an equation, or set of equations, that represents a business situation. Actually, any mathematical formula can be considered a model. A widely used business model is the EOQ (economic order quantity) model:

$$EOQ = \sqrt{\frac{2AS}{R}}$$

where A is the cost of acquiring or purchasing inventory items, S is the annual sales, and R is the retention or carrying cost. The EOQ is the order quantity that strikes the best (lowest) balance between purchasing and carrying costs. Some mathematical models used in business include hundreds or thousands of such formulas.

The decision theory school has greatly influenced MIS design and use. Quantitative techniques demand the use of a computer, and the problems attacked are some of the most difficult that a manager can face. There are managers, however, who have not embraced the decision theory school. These managers believe that human skills are the key to solving problems of organization, motivation, staffing, and leadership. Additionally, there are several concerns with the quantitative approach.

1. *Development time*: The time to create and test the model may be excessive for a problem that demands a quick decision.

2. *Lack of good input data*: The models require good input data, which is not always available. The model can be no better than its input.

3. *Requirement for quantitative skills*: Many managers do not have the necessary quantitative skills and cannot communicate effectively with people who do. Managers often hesitate to turn over decision-making authority to an OR specialist.

4. *Difficulty of modeling business problems*: Some business situations are so complex that it is difficult to see all of the variables and their effects. Attempts to solve these problems with overly simple models lead to poor decisions.

As we go about the task of describing the modern MIS, you will recognize the influence of the decision theory school. Always remember that its techniques are not ends in themselves, but only contributions to improved management, supplementing the contributions of other schools of management theory.

The contingency theory of management

Efforts to apply the principles of the classical, behavioral, and decision theory schools have not always been successful. None of the principles work in all situations. One group of theorists believe that success is contingent on the situation. This group is known as the contingency, or situational, school. The school has a large following because it encourages flexibility in the solution of complex problems that the other schools, with their specialized focus, cannot offer.

According to this school, the situation affecting management practice is the environment of the manager. This environment consists of the *external environment* (the economic, political, and social influences on the firm) and the *internal environment* (the constraints imposed by a firm's resources). The internal constraints consist of the technology used in the production process, the tasks performed by the employees, and the people themselves. To cite an example, the internal environment of a supervisor of a welding shop, where a majority of the workers have little or no college education, is different from that of a project leader of a group of research and development engineers.

The manager must be constantly aware of changes in both environments and capable of obtaining the information necessary to understand the current situation and where it might lead. In this view of management, the MIS can play an important role by providing good information and facilitating good decisions.

Mintzberg's Managerial Roles

Henri Fayol's management functions have formed one of the fundamentals of management theory since they were published in 1916. However, they have not been immune to criticism. The most widely publicized criticism has come from Henry Mintzberg, who believes that much of what managers do cannot be conveniently pigeon-holed in the five functions. He asks, for example, what function a manager is performing when emergency arrangements are being made to continue production after a factory has burned down, or when presenting a gold watch to a retiring employee.[4]

As a doctoral student at MIT gathering data for his thesis, Mintzberg observed five top-level executives. Out of this research evolved his concept of *managerial roles*. We give Mintzberg special attention for two reasons. First, his contemporary views of management have not attracted a great deal of criticism and are generally regarded as good descriptions of what managers do. Second, although Mintzberg does not speak highly of computer-based MIS, his role concept provides an excel-

---

[4] Henry Mintzberg, "The Manager's Job: Folklore and Fact," *Harvard Business Review* 53 (July–August 1975): 49.

lent framework for designing better management information and decision support systems.

According to Mintzberg, the manager's title provides her or him with a formal authority over an organizational unit. This authority produces a status that enables the manager to play three categories of roles—interpersonal, informational, and decisional. This view is illustrated in Figure 2-5. The 10 roles that managers play are listed in the rectangles, which represent the three basic role categories.

The interpersonal category includes figurehead, leader, and liaison. *Figurehead* includes ceremonial duties such as giving visiting dignitaries tours of the

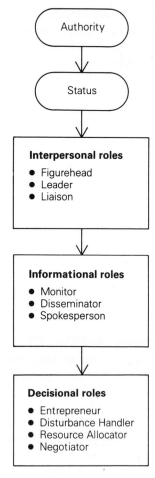

Figure 2-5 Mintzberg's managerial roles.

Source: Reprinted by special permission of the MIS Quarterly, Volume 6, Number 4, December 1982. Copyright 1982 by the Society for Information Management and the Management Information Systems Research Center.

facilities. As *leader,* the manager maintains the unit by hiring and training the staff and providing motivation and encouragement. In the *liaison* role, contacts are made with persons outside the manager's own unit—with peers and others in the unit's environment.

The informational category is the basis for the appeal of Mintzberg's theory to information specialists. This category recognizes information as an important ingredient in management work. As a *monitor,* the manager is constantly on the lookout for information bearing on the performance of the unit. The manager's sensory perceptors scan both the internal activity of the unit and the environment. When the manager receives valuable information to be passed along to others in the unit, he or she serves as a *disseminator.* Finally, the manager must serve as a *spokesperson* by passing information along to those outside the unit—superiors and persons in the environment.

The third role category recognizes the manager as a decision maker. The manager must serve as an *entrepreneur,* making rather permanent improvements to the unit such as changing the organizational structure. As a *disturbance handler,* the manager reacts to unanticipated events such as the devaluation of the dollar in a foreign country where the firm has operations. As a *resource allocator,* the manager controls the purse strings of the unit, determining which subsidiary units get what resources. The last role sees the manager serving as a *negotiator,* resolving disputes both within the unit and between the unit and its environment.

Mintzberg believed that all managers play all roles, although certain roles are more important to certain managers. In a 1983 mail survey of 180 managers, Cynthia M. Pavett and Alan W. Lau found that management level had a significant influence on how the managers valued eight of the roles.[5] Top-level managers placed higher values on their roles of figurehead, liaison, monitor, disseminator, spokesperson, resource allocator, and negotiator than did low-level managers. The only role valued more highly by the low-level managers was that of leader. Other studies have found no influence by management level on the leadership role—managers on all levels regard it as having the same value. The Pavett and Lau study also revealed some effect of functional area on perceived value of the roles. Mintzberg had hypothesized that sales managers spend relatively more time in interpersonal roles, for example.

Mintzberg's managers were not big users of computer output. He says, ". . . it has become increasingly evident that these giant MIS systems are not working—that managers are simply not using them." He adds, "Every bit of evidence suggests that the manager identifies decision situations and builds models not with the aggregated abstractions an MIS provides, but with specific tidbits of data."[6]

We must keep in mind that his study was completed in 1968, and computer-based MIS and DSS designs have come a long way since that time. Some current studies, however, have revealed a continued reluctance at the top-management level to embrace computer support.

---

[5] Cynthia M. Pavett and Alan W. Lau, "Managerial Work: The Influence of Hierarchical Level and Functional Specialty," *Academy of Management Journal* 26 (Number 1, 1983): 170–177.

[6] Mintzberg, p. 52.

Mintzberg offered three suggestions for information specialists as they develop management information systems:

1. Do not attempt to learn what information a manager needs only by asking questions. Learn by studying the manager, observing how time is spent, with whom, and where. Armed with this insight, design improved monitoring systems.
2. Try to get as much of the manager's knowledge into the computer storage as possible. This will minimize the information loss caused by turnover, and will facilitate dissemination to others.
3. Attempt to develop formal systems that include more of the informal information that managers prefer.

We will return to Mintzberg's role theory in later chapters as we describe office automation and executive information systems.

Importance of Management Theory to Information Management

The firm's information system is intended to help the manager manage. In order to do so, the people designing the MIS must understand management. This is why *the manager must be directly involved in the design of the MIS.* He or she is more likely to have this understanding than is an information specialist.

The manager should understand theories of management. The MIS can then be designed to help the manager apply these theories to the management of available resources. The understanding of management must come first. It is a prerequisite for a good MIS.

The manager's recognition of the psychological impact of an MIS on a firm and its employees is another reason why management theory is important. Since much of management theory is concerned with the psychology of management, this understanding can help win acceptance of the MIS.

As we conclude our discussion of management theory, we should recognize that an MIS is not a cure for poor management. The basic management skill must be present for an effective MIS to be realized.

Organization Theory[7]

Organization theory concerns the arrangement or assembly of a firm's resources. It deals with structure. Usually, the structure is thought of as relating only to people, as with an organization chart. But this arrangement of people also entails an arrangement of other resources—money, machines, and material. For exam-

---

[7] Based on Szilagyi, pp. 291–317; and Robert Albanese, *Managing: Toward Accountability for Performance,* 3rd ed. (Homewood, Ill.: Richard D. Irwin, 1981), pp. 492–501, 579–602.

ple, the people in the marketing department are given operating funds, machines (such as company cars), and material (such as sales manuals and free samples). When people are classified by organizational unit, these other resources go along with them.

Like management theory, organization theory has evolved through a series of schools: first the *classical* school, followed by the *behavioral* school, and then the *contingency* school. The past few years have seen a great deal of interest in the *Japanese* approach to management. Much of this theory relates to the organization, and we will recognize those features that relate to information management and decision making.

The classical theory of organization

Frederick Taylor and his scientific management group viewed employees in a strictly economic sense—more or less as appendages of their machines, working to achieve higher productivity. These theorists ignored the firm's environment, and their emphasis was strictly on making internal operations as efficient, rational, and predictable as possible. High productivity was considered a direct result of the best work methods. The scientific management group believed that the best organizational structure for implementing these methods was one with clear lines of authority and responsibility, management control, and economic (monetary) rewards for good work. The organization chart is an example of how classical theory has influenced the modern-day organization.

Henri Fayol had a wider view of management than did Taylor and his colleagues, and he contributed more toward the organization of workers into groups. Fayol identified a set of *organization principles*. We have singled out and explained in systems terms some of Fayol's principles that apply to the firm as a system.

- *Division of labor*: Resources are grouped into specialized units, or subsystems. Such specialization can improve efficiency and productivity.
- *Unity of command*: There is one control point in the system.
- *Unity of direction*: Subsystems should work together toward the system's goals.
- *Subordination of individual interest to the common goal*: All subsystems should contribute to the achievement of the system's goals.

Although these principles were almost fifty years old when the systems concept became popular, they serve as guidelines for good system performance.

Another principle important to MIS designers is that of *functional organization*. Fayol used the term *departmentation,* meaning that the firm's resources should be segregated in departments based on purposes, processes, customers, geographic area, and so on. Today the functional form of organization is the most prevalent, with resources distributed among the functional areas of manufacturing, marketing, and finance. Sometimes these functional areas do not work together as they should, and this makes it difficult to implement an MIS. Although the MIS can contribute to coordination among functional areas, the MIS should not be viewed as a way to achieve coordination after all else has failed.

In summary, classical organization theory is very formal and rigid. The resources must be arranged along functional lines in an exact manner. The structure should be reflected in an organization chart, and all members of the organization should have specific, well defined duties.

The behavioral theory of organization

Behavioral scientists saw that classical organization theory did not tell the whole story. It was too inflexible. Managers and workers alike grew tired of the formal, rigid structure and established their own "unofficial" arrangement. This informal structure exists in all organizations. It does not appear on an organization chart, but it is there.

The communication portion of this informal structure is known as *the grapevine.* The grapevine enables one employee to communicate with another without following the lines of the organization chart. Horizontal and diagonal communications exist, as illustrated in Figure 2-6. The figure also shows a vertical

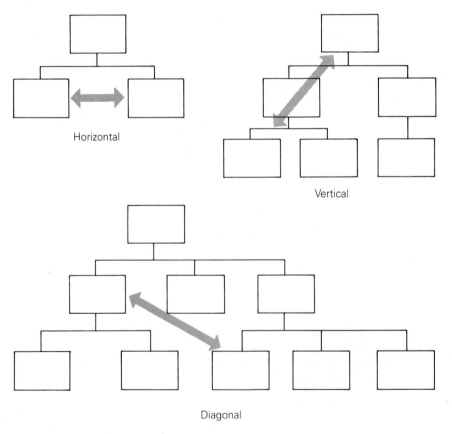

Figure 2-6 Informal communication flows.

link, bypassing an intermediate level. This vertical link is common as managers acquire information from their subordinates, often making contacts three or four levels down.

The informal information flow is of special interest because the MIS is responsible for an important part of the communication within a firm—the information and decision flow. Up until now, however, the MIS has been unsuccessful in capturing the information of the informal network. Although Mintzberg is not associated with the behavioral, or any other, school, he states that "most work just cannot get done without some informal communication."[8] His five managers spent 65–80% of their time communicating verbally, and about 45% of their time communicating outside of their formal organizational structure.

In addition to informal communication flows, there are informal flows of *influence* or *power* that fail to show up on the charts. Some people accumulate power over and above that of their formal positions. As the MIS designer becomes involved in an MIS project, he or she should attempt to identify all the individuals who will have an effect on the success of the project. All of the people influencing the success of the MIS should be involved in its design—regardless of their formal position in the organization.

The contingency theory of organization

In practice, none of the theories of organization discussed up to now is effective in all situations. Functional organization is the most widespread, but it becomes cumbersome as the firm grows larger. Firms that outgrow the functional structure often superimpose another structure on top of it.

This two-dimensional approach to organization can be visualized as a matrix. In fact, when an organization is structured as in Figure 2-7, it is called a *matrix organization.* The rows of the matrix represent one organizational subdivision, and the columns represent another. In the figure, the rows represent the firm's products, and the columns represent the functional areas. The matrix structure is popular in firms with large government contracts, such as aerospace. Someone is designated *project manager,* and he or she assembles a staff that cuts horizontally across functional lines.

A contingency theory of organization is based on the notion that there is no single best way to organize. Different approaches are possible, and the appropriate one should be used in each situation. Matrix organization, for example, might be right for aerospace but wrong for a bank. The contingency theory recognizes the influence of the environment on organization, and sees different structures as ways of coping with environmental demands and changes. Finally, this theory recognizes that several different structures usually exist within a firm at the same time.

---

[8] Mintzberg, *The Structuring of Organizations* (Englewood Cliffs, N.J.: Prentice-Hall, 1979), p. 49.

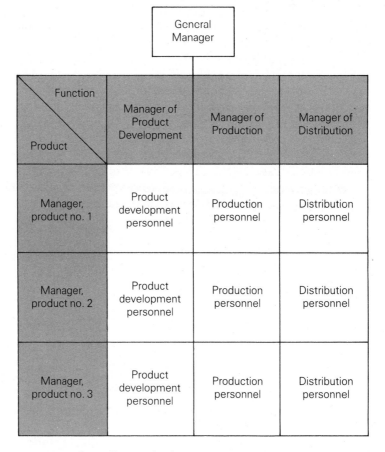

Figure 2-7 A matrix organization structure.

The Japanese theory of organization

The best evidence of the effectiveness of the Japanese approach to business is the manner in which their products have captured key consumer markets such as electronics, cameras, automobiles, and motorcycles. Perhaps the key to success has been the extent to which Japanese workers have become involved with their firms. Writer William G. Ouchi calls this involvement *Theory Z* and offers it as the way that U.S. business can compete.[9]

Charles Y. Yang, an American executive in a Japanese firm, identifies three characteristics of the Japanese culture that stimulate the high degree of worker involvement:[10]

---

[9] William G. Ouchi, *Theory Z: How American Business Can Meet the Japanese Challenge* (Reading, Mass.: Addison-Wesley, 1981).

[10] Charles Y. Yang, "Demystifying Japanese Management Practices," *Harvard Business Review* 62 (November–December 1984): 172 ff.

- *Organic harmony* The performance of the group receives more attention than individual performance. Emphasis is on togetherness, achieved by paternalistic personnel policies and the concept of consensus (group) decision making.

- *Vertical relationships* The employee is more loyal to his company than to his profession. For example, a Sony electronics engineer takes more pride in being employed by Sony than in being an engineer. Firms breed this loyalty by guaranteeing lifetime employment and looking after their employees' welfare.

- *Dualistic perceptions* The concepts of *tatemae* (formality) and *honne* (essence) are at the core of Japanese organizational theory. The top executive follows a practice of tatemae in assuring nonproductive subordinates of a series of promotions, and also a limited participation in decision making. This subordinate group is called the *madoqiwa-zoku*. In a formal sense, these subordinates play key roles. The top executive, however, singles out certain select subordinates, the *jitsuryoku-sha*, on whom he or she relies heavily for decision support.

Yang points out that many Japanese managers worry about the adverse effects of these practices and that some firms are adopting American practices. For one thing, the bottom-up style of *consensus decision making* is very slow. A *ringi* document is circulated among all of the managers who have the opportunity to make known their agreement by affixing their seal. The method is good for morale and permits a sharing of risks, but it takes a long time to reach a decision.

Ouchi offers Theory Z as a way to compete. He spells out strategies dealing with productivity, trust, subtlety, and intimacy. Firms taking a cooperative, long-term view can give employees incentives to be more *productive*. Firms can earn their employees' *trust* by being open and honest. *Subtlety* involves a more personal relationship between supervisor and employees than is normally found in U.S. industry. It also involves the idea of letting employees manage much of their own work. *Intimacy* is achieved by making the firm a place where solid relations can be stimulated. Ouchi points out that a number of U.S. firms such as Hewlett-Packard, Rockwell, Eli Lilly, and Intel have already implemented Theory Z.

If one reviews the history of IBM, he or she can see evidence of Theory Z. During the early years, each IBM office had an annual IBM family dinner, and T. J. Watson, Sr., the founder, traveled around the country attending the dinners. Employees were encouraged to think of themselves as members of the IBM family. While IBM has been criticized for its paternalistic policies, they most likely contributed much to its success.

Importance of Organization Theory to Information Management

The MIS provides an opportunity for improved communication and decision flow in organizations of all forms. In designing the MIS, attention must be given to the levels of management and the organizational groupings (by functional area, product, and so on) and to the effect that these structures have on information needs.

Attention must also be directed to the informal organization structure. Management should try to identify information needs that are not being fulfilled by the formal system and to incorporate as many of these flows into the formal MIS as possible. Certainly those informal power centers of the organization that can influence the success of the MIS should be identified and included in the design effort.

Finally, the MIS can keep management informed of environmental needs and changes that influence the organizational structure. The structure can then be adapted to the environment.

In addition to the influence of the MIS on the organization, the organization influences the MIS. A good MIS cannot be expected in a firm where the parts—the divisions and departments—do not work together.

The organizational implications of the MIS go beyond setting up a new MIS department. An understanding of the basics of organizational theory is a must for MIS designers.

Systems Theory

We paid considerable attention to the subject of systems in Chapter 1. We recognized that managers use a management information system to manage the physical system of the firm. A systems orientation is often identified as a characteristic of the modern manager. When a manager has a systems orientation, he or she views the firm as a system with all elements, or subsystems, working toward the overall goals. The firm transforms input resources into output, a process monitored and controlled by management. The manager is the feedback loop. The manager uses the firm's objectives to keep the system on course.

General systems theory

The idea of viewing something as a system is not unique to business. In fact, a movement has been under way for quite some time to use the system as a means of better understanding all phenomena. The idea was initially presented in 1937 by Ludwig von Bertalanffy, a German biologist. He gave the name *general systems theory* to a new discipline dedicated to formulating principles that apply to systems in general, whatever the nature of their component elements or the relations or forces between them.

Von Bertalanffy addressed a number of system fundamentals, including open versus closed systems, steady state, and feedback. An *open system* communicates with its environment, relying on that environment for life-giving inputs, and contributing something to the environment in return. A *closed system* does not have this environmental relationship. An open system reaches a *steady state* by maintaining a continuous, balanced flow of inputs and outputs. Through a *feedback* process, the system monitors its output so that its input might be adjusted to maintain the steady state. It is easy to visualize a gas heater, an animal, a human being, and a business firm as open systems using feedback to maintain a steady state. This universal application of systems principles is what von Bertalanffy had in mind when he presented the idea of a general systems theory. He did not imply that there is *one* theory that explains *everything*. Rather, all entities comprising multiple parts can be viewed as systems.

A number of years passed until, in 1956, economist Kenneth Boulding presented general systems theory in another manner. He described the theory as

> the skeleton of science in the sense that it aims to provide a framework or structure of systems on which to hang the flesh and blood of particular disciplines and particular subject matters in an orderly and coherent corpus of knowledge.[11]

Boulding took two approaches. First, he recognized that certain phenomena can be found in several disciplines. He listed as common phenomena: populations, individuals in environments, growth, and information and communication. For example, animals are examples of individual organisms existing in environments, exhibiting growth over time, perhaps living in packs or populations, and employing some types of communication. The same phenomena can be seen in a business firm.

Second, Boulding provided a hierarchical ranking of system types. This hierarchy, with the most simple system type on the bottom and the most complex on the top, is illustrated in Figure 2-8.

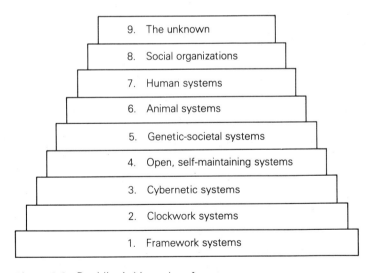

Figure 2-8 Boulding's hierarchy of systems.

---

[11] Kenneth E. Boulding, "General Systems Theory: The Skeleton of Science," *Management Science* 2 (April 1956): pp. 197–208.

The simplest type is the *framework* that integrates several nonmoving parts, such as a straight chair or a hammer. Next is the *clockwork* system that includes parts with predetermined motions, such as a hair dryer or an electric drill. *Cybernetic* systems are more complex in that they are self-controlled, such as heaters with thermostats. These are all nonliving systems. The next level of complexity is represented by the simplest type of living system—the cell. This system type is called an *open, self-maintaining* system. The cells can be integrated to form the next higher system—*genetic-societal* systems, such as a plant. *Animal* systems are followed by *human* systems, and then groups of humans forming *social organizations*. Boulding believes that the most complex type of system is the one not yet discovered—the *unknown* system.

With the groundwork laid by von Bertalanffy and Boulding, other theorists provided more specific descriptions of how systems theory applies to the business firm.

A systems view of the firm

In their 1966 book, Daniel Katz and Robert L. Kahn identified two problems in understanding organizations.[12] The first was defining what was included in the organization and what was not. The second was identifying the organization's goals. Very often analysts, such as information specialists, will define an organization's boundaries based on its name. For example, if they are studying the marketing department, they include only those resources within that department. This ignores the influence of outside resources such as customers and the manufacturing department. Also, the analysts will simply accept the organization's written goal statement or a description provided by the chief executive officer as representing what the organization seeks to accomplish.

Katz and Kahn offered the concept of an open system, promulgated by von Bertalanffy, as the means of overcoming both of these problems. They viewed the organization as an *energetic input-output system*. The organization accepts energy from its environment and transforms this energy into output that reactivates the system. This is an example of Boulding's level four—open, self-maintaining system. Applying this interpretation to a firm, the energy inputs are raw materials and labor. These are transformed into products that are sold to customers. The money received from customers is used to buy more raw materials and labor. Such a system does not run down. Conversely, it can acquire more energy than it needs, store the surplus, and actually increase its transformation rate or scale of operation. The name given to the running down of a closed system is *entropy*. Open systems exhibit *negative entropy* by stockpiling excess energy.

By using the concept of an open system, it is possible to identify those resources and elements contained within the organization. They are the ones contributing to production of output energy; the goals of the firm are those outcomes that provide for the energetic source to produce the same type of output.

---

[12] Daniel Katz and Robert L. Kahn, *The Social Psychology of Organizations* (New York: John Wiley & Sons, 1966), pp. 14–29.

Networks of resource flows

The view taken by Katz and Kahn, that the organization is a flow of energy through the physical system of the firm, is very abstract. It is not easy to see all firms in such a simplified manner.

Other theorists from the business area have used the concept of flows in a less abstract way. Jay W. Forrester used five flows—information, materials, money, manpower, and capital equipment—to show the need for all of the functional units to work together.[13] He coined the term *industrial dynamics* to represent the fluctuations in business activity caused by sudden changes in certain of the flows.

Mintzberg used four flows—authority, material, information, and decision processes.[14] He succeeded in capturing the complexity of these flows as pictured in Figure 2-9. Mintzberg's diagram pictures the flows vertically between the levels

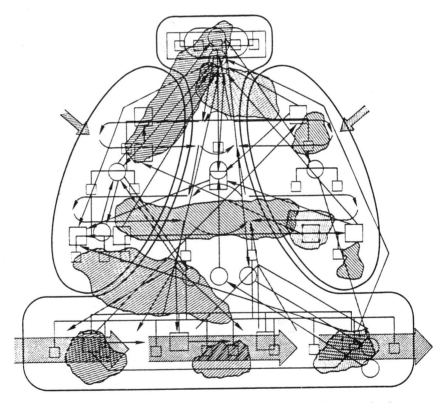

Figure 2-9 Mintzberg's flows through the different parts of an organization.
Source: Henry Mintzberg, The Structuring of Organizations: A Synthesis of the Research, *© 1979, p. 64. Reprinted by permission of Prentice Hall, Englewood Cliffs, New Jersey.*

---

[13] Jay W. Forrester, "Industrial Dynamics: A Major Breakthrough for Decision Makers," *Harvard Business Review* 36 (July–August 1958): pp. 37–66.

[14] Mintzberg, pp. 35–64.

of the *line organization* (the part directly responsible for producing the firm's output) and the *staff organization* (those groups supporting the line groups).

Richard J. Hopeman, an author of a series of books on manufacturing management, used five flows—materials, money, manpower, information, and machines—to describe the operation of a factory.[15] We will use Hopeman's flows to present a systems theory of management and organization. This theory can be applied to any type of firm.

A Systems Theory of Management and Organization

The resources that the manager controls do not remain within the firm but flow through it. The firm can be regarded as a system of flow networks representing physical resources and information, as shown in Figure 2-10. These networks originate outside the firm, flow through the firm, and finally return to the environment.

Four of the flow networks carry physical resources—personnel, material, machines, and money. The fifth flow is that of information—the conceptual representation of the physical system. Managers use information to manage the physical resources when direct contact with those resources becomes difficult. While information is valuable to all managers, it is an absolute necessity for managers in large firms and for managers on upper levels.

Most of the flow of physical resources occurs at the lower, or operational, level. The flows of machines and material are at this level as they move through the manufacturing process. Money also flows at the operational level—between the firm and its customers, vendors, and financial institutions. Management is very interested in these flows but does not participate in them directly. Instead, managers monitor the physical flows by using the information flow. The only major physical flow at upper levels is personnel; management is actively involved in personnel through organizing, staffing, directing, and motivating other employees on those same levels.

Even though the firm may be considered in flow network terms, it is seldom organized along those lines. Instead, firms are normally organized by functional group. Some firms have approached the flow network structure while maintaining an essentially functional organization. This is usually done by separating the material flow and assigning it to a new function—*logistics*. This new functional area is responsible for all material flows from the environment, through the firm, and back to the environment. Other firms have separated out particular parts of the material flow and assigned them to *product managers* or *brand managers*.

If firms have been organized or subdivided other than by flow network, then what is the value of thinking in flow network terms? The main advantage is that

[15] Richard J. Hopeman, *Systems Analysis and Operations Management* (Columbus, Ohio: Charles E. Merrill, 1969), pp. 125–150.

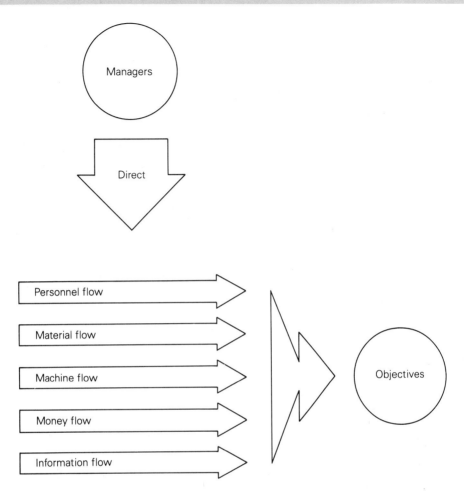

Figure 2-10 The firm viewed as a system of resource flows.

it recognizes the firm as a single system, not a conglomeration of several systems. It is possible to trace a single flow from the environment, through the firm, and back to the environment without being confused by the functional complexities that vary from one type of organization to another. Even when a firm is organized functionally, the manager and the information specialist can think in flow network terms to isolate and understand problems. Flow network organization is an abstraction that enables managers to focus on important elements without getting tangled up in details.

Because functionalism is so widely accepted, and because it can be followed along with the systems approach, it has been included in this book. A structure for an information system is presented along functional lines in Part Five. This structure reflects the direction that functionally organized firms have followed in the design of management information systems.

Summary

Our purpose in this chapter has been to lay a foundation for study of the MIS. Although the MIS is relatively new, theoretical work that went on long ago is still applicable. A knowledge of management, organization, and systems theory is important in the design of an MIS. The theory enables the manager and the information specialist to understand *why* certain behavior occurs. With this understanding, the MIS and its development project can be designed to meet user needs, thereby assuring their cooperation.

Management theory is the overall body of knowledge related to every aspect of the management process. The classical theorists, including Frederick W. Taylor and Henri Fayol, were concerned with increasing productivity. Taylor's work with standards of performance and management by exception contribute significantly to modern MIS design and use. Fayol's management functions provide the information specialist with an understanding of the activities needing information support.

The behavioral theorists were more concerned with the people performing the work than with the work itself. The human relations group grew out of the Hawthorne studies and was later joined by behavioral scientists, forming a social systems group. The importance of behavioral theory is easily overlooked—which is exactly what happened in early MIS designs. Early system failures were due in part to the insufficient attention given to the human aspects. Present-day system designers are more aware of the importance of behavioral theory than were designers of early systems.

Decision theory has assumed a key role in the MIS. Information systems use mathematical models to support the manager's decision making. But you must be careful not to lose sight of the fact that decision modeling presents several problems and that it does not address all of the areas of managerial responsibility.

The unique limitations of each of the schools of management theory led to the establishment of a new school that recognizes the relative effectiveness of different techniques in different situations. This is the contingency school, which uses the manager's environment (external and internal) as the starting point. The environment influences how problems are solved.

We paid special attention to Henry Mintzberg's theory of managerial roles because it shows the link between information and decision making. His recognition of the importance of oral information and informal information systems helps explain the difficulties of implementing computer-based designs, especially at the executive level.

Organization theory is the subset of management theory that concerns the arrangement of the firm's resources. The classical school, led by Fayol, stressed formal, functional relationships. The behavioral school emphasized informal communications and power centers in the organization. These behavioral considerations are important to the MIS designer, who must capture more of the informal information flows and achieve broad-based cooperation during the MIS implementation project. The contingency school recognizes the influence of the situation on organization. Matrix structure is an example of how a functional organization can adapt to special needs such as those faced in aerospace. Finally, we recognized the unique characteristics of the Japanese school, identified some weaknesses, and included some suggestions for U.S. firms to follow so that they can compete better.

We concluded our discussion of theory by illustrating how the firm can be viewed in systems terms. General systems theory offers the structure and behavior of both open and closed systems as a means of improving our knowledge of the physical and social sciences. This general systems theory has been applied to the business firm, stressing flows of energy and other resources. Such a view permits the manager to see her or his role as the controller of the system and the importance of information to the feedback process. This systems theory will be expanded in the next two chapters.

Key Terms

law	organization theory
theory	organization principles
proposition	functional organization
principle	the grapevine
management theory	matrix organization
objective, standard	project manager
management by exception	Theory Z
management functions	consensus decision making
universality of management functions	general systems theory
	open, closed system
planning horizon	steady state
Hawthorne effect	feedback
ergonomics, human engineering, human factors considerations	energetic input-output system
programmed, nonprogrammed decisions	entropy, negative entropy
	industrial dynamics
mathematical model	line, staff organization
external, internal environment	logistics
managerial roles	product manager, brand manager

Key Concepts

The role of theory in explaining and understanding phenomena

How information is used to develop theory

The grouping of theorists into schools

The contributions of the schools to MIS design and use

Management by exception

The universality of management functions

Levels of management

The importance of human behavior to a successful MIS

The specialized nature and limited scope of the decision theory school

The importance of the environment to the contingency school

Roles that managers play

Functional organization structure

Informal organizational relationships

Importance of employee involvement to Japanese success

The universal applicability of systems theory to entities and phenomena existing in various disciplines

Business firms as networks of resource flows

Questions

1. Does a theory have to be true all the time? If not, what is its value?
2. What is theory?
3. What is the question that theory enables the user to answer?
4. How is information used to develop theories?
5. What concepts or ideas did Taylor contribute that are useful in designing an MIS?
6. Is a standard the same as an objective? Explain.
7. Are management functions the same as functional areas? Explain.
8. Why were early MIS efforts most successful at the lower-management level?
9. How can a manager achieve improved employee performance by using the Hawthorne effect?
10. Which management theory did designers of early information systems overlook?
11. What is the primary tool of the decision theory school of management theory? What are some problems with its use?
12. What are the three main categories of managerial roles developed by Mintzberg? Are the categories "played" in a sequential order? Explain.
13. Is it a good idea for a manager to establish lines of communication outside of those shown on the organization chart? Explain.
14. How do Japanese firms get all of the employees to work together as a system? Would the same approach work in another country like the U.S., Canada, or England where the culture is so different?
15. Are there any disadvantages to the Japanese approach? Explain.
16. What situations should exist before a firm attempts to implement an MIS?
17. Which of Boulding's systems levels represents the firm, a computer, an organization chart, a central-heating system?

18. What are the two problems that Katz and Kahn sought to solve by viewing the firm as an open system?

19. Which flow did Katz and Kahn include in their system model? Did Forrester, Mintzberg, and Hopeman include the same flow? Explain.

20. Use the concept of resources flowing through a firm to explain why the MIS is so important to upper-level managers.

Problems

1. Obtain a copy of Boulding's article on general systems theory. Your instructor will tell you how to go about obtaining it. Read it and write a short paper titled "How Boulding's Concepts Relate to Business." Your instructor will tell you how long the paper should be and whether it should be typed.

2. Repeat problem 1, only using the Duncan article listed in the bibliography. The title should be "How Duncan's Concepts Relate to Business."

CASE PROBLEM: Pacific Metals

You have been unhappy with your job as assistant director of MIS at a San Diego trucking firm for quite some time. You believe that you have some good ideas about implementing decision support systems, but your boss won't listen to you. You respond to several classified ads and get an invitation from one of the companies to have an interview with the owner, a Mr. Ferrell. The company is Pacific Metals, a fabricator of sheet metal products such as vent-a-hoods and air conditioning ducts. After checking around, you learn that they have recently installed a medium-sized computer and are using it mostly for data processing. This may be your chance to show your stuff.

You arrive several minutes early and the receptionist shows you to Mr. Ferrell's office. After the normal pleasantries about the weather, Mr. Ferrell begins to tell you what he has in mind. Although Pacific has been using computers for many years, the managers are not benefiting very much. Mr. Ferrell tells you that he wants to implement decision support applications throughout the company.

You ask why this hasn't been tried before, and Mr. Ferrell turns the conversation to his management staff:

"None of our managers, including myself, know much about the computer.

I think we're probably afraid of it. Our previous data processing manager tried to get something started but didn't have any luck. He wanted to form some type of MIS steering committee made up of our vice presidents of manufacturing, engineering, personnel, marketing, and finance. He even wanted me to be on it. We could never get everybody together at the time—seems like we always had something more important to do. But, that's not unusual; we have never been much for meetings."

You ask Mr. Ferrell if he wants managers on all levels and in all functional areas to receive computer support, and he replies, "Definitely." You ask where the managers are presently getting their information, and Mr. Ferrell replies "Everywhere but the computer. Most managers have their own little systems—reports typed by their secretaries, logs they keep themselves, personal contacts with their subordinates, and so on."

You ask Mr. Ferrell to tell you more about the separate systems that each manager has. You ask if the managers get along well together and develop joint systems. Mr. Ferrell immediately responds by saying, "Not well at all. That's a problem I've always had. Some of them fight like cats and dogs. They're more interested in their departments looking good than in Pacific showing a profit."

You ask if the managers have had a good preparation for their jobs—business degrees, industry education programs, and so on, and Mr. Ferrell replies "No, most have been around for years and worked their way up from the bottom." He laughs as he says that most graduated from the "school of hard knocks," and have learned through trial and error.

You feel like you have the picture and ask Mr. Ferrell what he is looking for in a new computer manager. He says, "I want you to make decision support your number one priority. I want a working system within 12 months that we can all be proud of. Money is no object. Hardware, software, staff, you name it. You can have anything you want. If you're successful, you'll be one of the highest-paid computer people in San Diego. But if you fail, you're out. Now tell me, are you interested?"

You think for a few minutes, swallow hard, and say, "I guess not. It doesn't sound like what I had in mind."

Mr. Ferrell looks at you like he can't believe his ears. "What's the matter?" he says. "Did I say something wrong?"

Questions

1. Why did you turn down the job?

2. Make a list of the things that Pacific should do, in the proper sequence, before you would be interested.

3. Do you think that the managers have theories of management? Of organization? What school, or schools, do you think they support?

4. If you were to view Pacific as a system, which part would be the weakest? Refer to Figure 1-4. Which resource flow? Refer to Figure 2-10.

CASE PROBLEM: Judson's Department Store

Alice Long is head buyer for the largest department store in Little Rock—Judson's. She has six buyers reporting to her, and she specializes in buying ladies' clothes. She travels to market in Dallas four times a year to buy clothing for the coming season. She gets several computer reports at the end of each month showing dollar sales by item, profit by item, and sales by item for clearance sales at the end of the season to dispose of unsold stock. Additional orders for items that are selling well are usually placed after the season begins. Sometimes, however, these replenishment items arrive too late and are still in stock when the season is over. Alice becomes alarmed at the quantity of items that must be marked down and sold at a loss. She decides that perhaps she can get some better information from the computer that will help her and her buyers purchase the right items in the right quantities that will be sold before the end of the season.

Alice asks Prentice Delaney, the MIS manager, for help; he assigns one of his systems analysts, Sue Scott, to help Alice solve her problems. Prentice tells Alice that Sue doesn't have any assignments right now, and Alice can use her for as long as she likes.

During the first meeting, Sue takes a note pad from her purse and asks Alice, "What information do you need?" Alice hasn't thought about it that much and says, "I really can't say. Buying fashion merchandise is more of an art than a science. We can use last season's sales as some kind of a guide, but a lot depends on how new styles will be received. I'm afraid that I can't be very specific. I just thought that the computer might be of some help."

Sue puts her blank note pad back in her purse and says, "Well, I'm afraid that if you don't know what information you need, we can't be of much help. Why don't you think about it for a while and give me a call when you can be more specific. Sorry."

Questions

1. Whose responsibility is it to define Alice's information needs?
2. Does Alice need information about the past? The present? The future? Give examples.
3. Should Alice's information come from formal systems, such as the computer? From informal systems such as personal contacts? Explain your answer.
4. Does Alice need environmental information? Internal information? Explain.
5. Explain in systems theory terms what is wrong with Judson's buying system.
6. How could Sue be more helpful to Alice? What would you suggest that Sue do?

Selected Bibliography

Theory of Management and Organizations

Anthony, Robert N., *Planning and Control Systems: A Framework for Analysis*
(Cambridge: Harvard University Graduate School of Business
Administration, 1965).

Boulding, Kenneth E., "General Systems Theory—the Skeleton of Science,"
Management Science 2 (April 1956): 197–208.

Duncan, Otis Dudley, "Social Organization and the Ecosystem," in Robert E.
L. Faris, ed., *Handbook of Modern Sociology* (Chicago: Rand McNally,
1964); pp. 36–45.

Forrester, Jay W., "Industrial Dynamics: A Major Breakthrough for Decision
Makers," *Harvard Business Review* 36 (July-August 1958): 37–66.

Hopeman, Richard J., *Systems Analysis and Operations Management*
(Columbus, Ohio: Charles E. Merrill, 1969).

Katz, Daniel, and Robert L. Kahn, *The Sociology of Organizations* (New York:
John Wiley & Sons, 1966), pp. 14–29.

Mintzberg, Henry, *The Nature of Managerial Work* (New York: Harper &
Row, 1973), pp. 132–152.

Mintzberg, Henry, "The Manager's Job: Folklore and Fact," *Harvard Business
Review* 53 (July-August 1975): 49–61.

Mintzberg, Henry, *The Structuring of Organizations* (Englewood Cliffs, N.J.:
Prentice-Hall, 1979), pp. 35–64.

Ouchi, William G., *Theory Z: How American Business Can Meet the Japanese
Challenge* (Reading, Mass.: Addison-Wesley, 1981).

Pavett, Cynthia M., and Alan W. Lau, "Managerial Work: The Influence of
Hierarchical Level and Functional Specialty," *Academy of Management
Journal* 26 (Number 1, 1983): 170–177.

Schoderbek, Peter P., Charles G. Schoderbek, and Asterios G. Kefalas,
Management Systems: Conceptual Considerations, 3rd ed. (Plano, Texas:
Business Publications, 1985).

Simon, Herbert A., *The New Science of Management Decision,* revised ed.
(Englewood Cliffs, N.J.: Prentice-Hall, 1977).

Szilagyi, Andrew D., Jr., *Management and Performance* (Santa Monica: Goodyear, 1981), pp. 57–84, 291–317.

von Bertalanffy, Ludwig, "General System Theory: A Critical Review," *General Systems* 7 (1962): 1–20.

Weinberg, Gerald M., *An Introduction to General Systems Thinking* (New York: John Wiley & Sons, 1975).

Yang, Charles Y., "Demystifying Japanese Management Practices," *Harvard Business Review* 62 (November-December 1984): 172ff.

Zuboff, Shoshana, "New Worlds of Computer-Mediated Work," *Harvard Business Review* 60 (September-October 1982): 142–152.

Chapter 3

The General Systems Model of the Firm

Learning Objectives

After studying this chapter, you should:

- Know what a model is, what types exist, and how they are used
- Appreciate the special capability of the mathematical model when used in decision support
- Appreciate the value of a general model
- Know the elemental parts of the general systems model, their relationships, and their roles
- Understand the concept of management by exception
- Be able to visualize how the general systems model can be used as the basis for evaluating any type of organization
- Be able to use the general systems model in a real business setting, with practice

Introduction

We have seen that a systems theory of organization views the firm as an open system. The system receives resources from the environment, transforms those resources in some manner, and makes the transformed resources available to the environment. In this chapter, we describe in detail how a manufacturing organization can be regarded as a system. We develop a diagram of the system processes that can be applied to any type of organization. We call the diagram "the general systems model of the firm."

Models

The model has become a popular device in business. It is used to facilitate understanding and to aid in decision making. An analysis of business literature during the past fifteen years shows an almost geometric increase in the discussion of models in textbooks and periodicals. If the scope of the analysis were pushed back thirty or forty years, it would appear that modeling is a recent innovation that, like the computer and management science techniques, came into its own only recently. This conclusion is not completely true. Modeling has always been an important decision-making tool, but only recently has it attracted the attention of business writers.

What is a model?

A *model* is an abstraction of something; it is something that represents something else.

The word *model* usually brings to mind the people pictured in fashion ads. This type of model is an abstraction of something, as the person viewing the ad puts himself or herself in the model's place. Fashion models—female and male alike—are employed by advertisers to show viewers how they could look wearing a particular dress or suit. The model represents the hundreds or thousands of potential purchasers who view the ad.

The idea of a conceptual system was presented in Chapter 1. A conceptual system also has the function of representing something—in this case, a physical system. Therefore, both a model and a conceptual system are used to represent something else. In fact, the two terms can be used interchangeably.

Types of models

Since models of all kinds have become popular in recent years, a number of efforts have been made to classify the various kinds. The classification scheme discussed below consists of four types:

1. Physical models
2. Narrative models
3. Graphical models
4. Mathematical models

The fashion model is a *physical model,* as are childhood toys such as dolls and toy airplanes. Most physical models are three-dimensional representations, and in many cases the models are smaller than the object represented. For example, a scale model of a new shopping mall can sit on top of a table in the architect's office. But reduced size is not a requirement, and some models are the same size as their counterparts. The styling models used by automakers are examples.

Regardless of size, these physical models represent something else—consumers, babies, and automobiles. For one reason or another, the model serves a purpose that cannot be fulfilled by the real thing; real babies cannot stand the physical wear suffered by dolls, and automakers can hardly stand the financial wear of using real automobiles as styling prototypes.

The physical model pictured in Figure 3-1 is a Hybrid II anthropomorphic dummy developed by General Motors for use in automobile crash testing. The model serves its purpose by providing some characteristic not evident in the object being modeled. In some cases this characteristic is *economy;* in others it is *availability*—the model is more readily available than the real object. Availability is the reason for the GM crash dummy. There wasn't a long line of human volunteers for the work.

Of the four types, the physical model probably has the least value for the business manager. Managers usually do not need to see something in three-dimensional form in order to understand it or to make decisions.

One type of model managers use daily is seldom recognized as a model; this

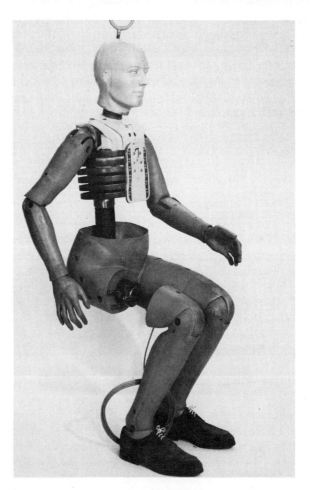

Figure 3-1 An automobile crash-testing dummy—a physical model.

is the *narrative model*. Since the narrative can be either written or spoken, the narrative model is used by everyone who speaks or writes, which makes it the most popular type.

The narrative represents a subject or topic, and the representation is accomplished with words. The listener or reader can understand the subject from the narrative. At least, that is the intent. All written and oral communications in business are narrative models. Therefore, both the written information of the computer and the verbal information of the informal communication system are examples of narrative models.

Another type of model in constant use is the *graphical model*. This is an abstraction of lines, symbols, or shapes, often with a narrative explanation. Graphical models include pie charts, bar charts, layered charts, and scatter diagrams. Graphical models are used to communicate the financial status of the firm to its stockholders. Many annual reports contain colorful graphs of financial indicators such as sales and profit. Graphics are also used to communicate information to managers. The graphical model in Figure 3-2 is called a break-even chart. It depicts the point at which revenues and costs are equal. Beyond that point, the firm begins to show a profit. The availability of special graphics software for microcomputers has focused more attention on the use of graphics in decision support than ever before.

Graphical models are also used in the design of information systems. Many of the tools used by the systems analyst and programmer are graphical in nature. The most popular of these models is the flowchart. The flowchart symbols represent processes to be performed and also input and output files. The systems analyst and the programmer use the flowchart both to help understand the system

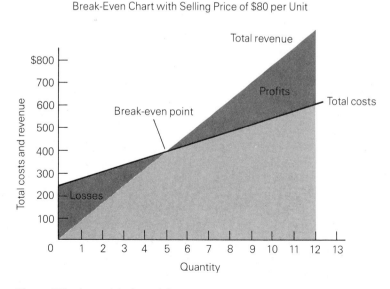

Figure 3-2 A graphical model.

and to communicate with each other and with users. Refer to the appendices for examples of graphical design and documentation tools.

The fourth type of model, the *mathematical model,* is responsible for most of the recent interest in models for decision making. This interest has been stimulated by improvements in both computer hardware and modeling software.

Any mathematical formula or equation is a model, and most of us have had years of experience with mathematics dating back to elementary school. The mathematical model, then, is no stranger.

Many of the mathematical models that business managers use are similar to those used in mathematics courses. For example, the break-even formula used to calculate the break-even point in Figure 3-2 is simply

$$\text{BEP} = \frac{\text{TFC}}{\text{P} - \text{C}}$$

where: BEP = break-even point in units sold
TFC = total fixed costs
P = sales price per unit
C = unit variable cost

Figure 3-3 shows a computer program, written in the BASIC language, to compute the break-even point. A manager can use this model to simulate the effect of different prices on the break-even point. The BASIC program is a mathematical model, representing the calculations in a program language. Assuming total fixed costs of $250 and unit variable costs of $30, a price of $80 produces

```
10 PRINT "ENTER TOTAL FIXED COSTS";
20 INPUT F
30 PRINT "ENTER UNIT VARIABLE COST";
40 INPUT C
50 PRINT "ENTER SALES PRICE";
60 INPUT P
70 LET B = F/(P-C)
80 PRINT
90 PRINT "BREAKEVEN POINT IS";B
100 PRINT
110 PRINT "DO YOU WANT TO TRY ANOTHER PRICE? ENTER Y-YES/N-NO";
120 INPUT R$
130 IF R$ = "Y" THEN 60
140 IF R$ = "N" THEN 999
150 PRINT "YOU SHOULD ENTER Y OR N, TRY AGAIN"
160 GOTO 120
999 END
```

Figure 3-3 A BASIC program to compute the break-even point.

a break-even point of 5 units, and a price of $100 produces a break-even point of 3.6 units. The manager can sit at a terminal or microcomputer and play the "what-if" game, trying out different prices until a preferred one is identified. Figure 3-4 shows the output—the dialog between the manager and the computer.

The break-even model uses only one equation. Many of the more complex mathematical models used in business use numerous equations—often hundreds of them. A financial planning model developed by the Sun Oil Company during the early years of MIS used approximately 2000 equations.[1] But large models tend to be cumbersome and difficult to use. The trend today is toward smaller models serving as decision support systems.

Because the language of mathematics is universal, mathematical models know no cultural, political, or geographic boundaries. Anyone who understands the language and knows the meaning of the symbols can understand the model regardless of its origin; this is one of the main advantages of a mathematical model.

Another advantage is precision in describing the interrelationships among the parts of an object. Mathematics can handle relationships expressed in more than the two dimensions of the graphical model or the three of the physical model. To the mathematician, and to the business manager who recognizes the complexity of business systems, the multidimensional ability of the mathematical model is of great value.

Use of models

We noted earlier that the value of the model lies in its ability to depict some characteristic not evident in the object being modeled. Economy and availability are important reasons to use a model rather than the real thing. Another reason is simplicity. It is common to use a model more simple in construction than the real object. While this leads to benefits in economy—a desirable goal—the primary reason for using simplified models is *understanding*. When the system being modeled is complex, it is easier to understand its interrelationships and workings

```
ENTER TOTAL FIXED COSTS? 2000
ENTER UNIT VARIABLE COST? 75
ENTER SALES PRICE? 125
BREAKEVEN POINT IS 40
DO YOU WANT TO TRY ANOTHER PRICE? ENTER Y-YES/N-NO? N
```

Figure 3-4 Output from the break-even-point model.

[1] George W. Gershefski, "Building a Corporate Financial Model," *Harvard Business Review* 47 (July–August 1969): 39.

if these are presented in a simplified way. For example, a map only shows the cities, towns, highways, lakes, and so forth. If more detail were included, the map would be too cluttered to be useful.

Each type of model discussed above can vary in detail. But as a rule, less detail is included when the objective of the model is to facilitate understanding. A physical model can represent only features of interest; a narrative can be boiled down to a summary; a diagram can show only the main relationships; and a mathematical equation can contain only primary ingredients. In each, an effort is made to present the model in a simplified form, frequently the first step to understanding. Once these simple models are understood, they can be made more complex, but they still only represent the system being modeled and *never* match it exactly.

A model is an abstraction of reality, and models exist in various degrees of abstraction. Mathematical models are perhaps the most abstract; in fact, it is difficult for many to understand how a physical system, such as a business firm, can be represented by a series of mathematical equations. If you can accept that the equations represent different parts of the system in an extremely precise way, you can appreciate the value of the mathematical model to the manager.

The recent interest in modeling has been due less to the value of models as aids to understanding, however, than to a second important feature—their ability *to predict*. Because the manager is concerned with the impact of decisions on the firm, the ability to look into the future before deciding is of great value. Only the mathematical model offers this predictive power. If the manager is able to predict with the other types of models, it is because of the greater understanding that the models provide. The manager must use this understanding to project what might happen in the future. The mathematical model, on the other hand, does the projecting for the manager. For example, the break-even model provides the manager with a projection of when total revenue will equal total cost.

You should not get the idea that mathematical models enable the manager to predict the future perfectly. *No* model is ever that good. Because the model is only a simplification or approximation of the real system, the result is a device that can be expected to behave similarly but not identically to the real system. Despite this lack of perfect accuracy, the model is such an improvement over anything previously available that the model-oriented manager accepts its shortcomings and takes advantage of its strong points. As long as the manager is aware of the shortcomings, and considers their possible influence on the behavior of the model, this situation is acceptable.

The mathematical model adds a dimension to decision support that was not present twenty years ago. There are many types of mathematical models—each designed to address a particular type of business problem. The models permit the analysis of multiple influences, which interact in various ways to affect some aspect of the firm's operations. The models provide the manager with a look into the future and enable the manager to see the possible outcomes of a particular decision strategy. Using models therefore helps managers better understand the complexity of the systems that they manage. We will return to the subject of mathematical modeling in Chapter 11 when we address decision support systems.

General versus specific models

Because all models only approximate the system being modeled, they are all somewhat general in nature. However, as Table 3-1 illustrates, some models are more general than others. Models can fit on a continuum ranging from the very general to the very specific. All types of models can exist at any point on the continuum.

The examples of very general models in Table 3-1 have the primary advantage of wide applicability. The baby doll can represent any baby, and the break-even formula can be used by any type of firm. This wide applicability is also a limitation. While describing many objects in a rough way, the general model fails to describe any object specifically.

You must use a specific model rather than a general model if you want to describe a relationship or condition unique to a particular situation. Using organizational relationships as an example, an organization chart can show the exact relationships within the particular firm. The advantage is accuracy, gained at the expense of another advantage—general applicability. One firm's chart probably cannot describe the organizational structure of another firm.

Each type of model has its purpose, and the type selected depends on the needs to be fulfilled. If a manager wants to understand a particular situation, the specific model is helpful. If the purpose is to understand a wide variety of situations, the general model is more applicable.

The value of a general model

Business education at the college level is general in approach. You take courses that will help you in the wide variety of employment situations that you may later encounter. Few business courses are aimed at a particular type of organization or profession.

This book is also general in approach. The principles and fundamentals found here can be applied to any type of information system in any type of organization. This chapter will present a *general systems model* of a business firm.

Table 3-1 Degrees of Generality in Models

Model	Very general	Very specific
Physical	A department store mannequin	A likeness of John F. Kennedy in a wax museum
Narrative	An article on "Ethics in Business"	The Continental Oil Company policy manual
Graphical	The break-even chart (Figure 3-2)	The graph of personnel projections for the insurance company (Figure 1-10)
Mathematical	The break-even formula	The Sun Oil Company financial planning model

The model is intended for use in a wide variety of situations. It should provide an effective way to view any type of firm and its information system. The model is primarily narrative, supported by a graphical diagram that portrays its parts and relationships.

The simplicity of the general systems model of the firm facilitates a basic understanding of the firm. This basic understanding will be augmented by additional material later in the book and in later business courses. When you begin your business career with a particular company, you need only add the unique characteristics of your company to the model.

The transition from the classroom to the firm is often an awkward period in a person's career. The first few days on a new job can be confusing. The environment is new and different—new faces, facilities, and terminology. When something familiar appears, it can serve as a reference point and provide a feeling of stability. The general systems model of the firm can serve as such a reference point. You can learn the basic activities performed in any organization and their fundamental interrelationships. You will therefore be prepared to encounter these activities and to use the model as a useful framework.

Besides providing a framework for orientation, the general systems model can be a yardstick for evaluating the new firm. You expect certain elements and relationships. Using the model as a checklist of what should be encountered can help you identify the parts of the firm that offer opportunities for improvement. You need not always accept the new firm as it is; you will eventually be asked to suggest improvements. The general systems model can indicate the need for improvement and pinpoint where this improvement should occur.

The General Systems Model

The systems theory of management and organization recognizes the firm as a physical system. In addition, management uses a conceptual system, the MIS, to manage the physical system. In this chapter, both of these systems are integrated to form a general systems model of the firm. First, we will describe the physical elements, and then we will add the conceptual elements.

The physical system

The system model presented in the first chapter provides the basis for studying the physical system of the firm. As seen in Figure 3-5, input resources are transformed into output resources. Input resources come from the environment, and output resources are returned to the same environment. The physical system of the firm is therefore an open system, interacting with its environment by means of physical resource flows. You recall from Chapter 2 that von Bertalanffy is credited with recognizing the ability to view many things as open systems. Other persons, such as Katz and Kahn, Forrester, Hopeman, and Mintzberg, have applied the concept of resources flowing through an open system of a business firm.

Figure 3-5 can represent a manufacturing operation where raw materials are transformed into finished goods. This is essentially a flow of materials without

Figure 3-5 The physical system of the firm.

reference to any of the other flows of physical resources, such as personnel, machines, and money, that enter into the transformation process. There is no doubt that these other flows are involved—personnel and machines transform the raw materials into finished goods, and money pays for the material, personnel, and machines. These latter resources also flow through the firm much like the material flow. Each of the physical flows is described below.

Material flow Input materials are received from vendors or suppliers of raw materials, parts, and assembled components. These materials are held in a storage area (raw-materials inventory) until required for the transformation process; then they are released to the manufacturing activity (work-in-process inventory). At the conclusion of the transformation, the materials, now in some finished form, are placed in a storage area (finished-goods inventory) until they are shipped to customers.

It is important to note, at this early stage in our discussion, the contrast between the resource flows and functional organization structure. Taking the material flow as an example, three or more functional areas are involved. The input of the raw materials is the responsibility of the purchasing department, the transformation is accomplished by manufacturing, and the output is accomplished by marketing. If the material is to flow smoothly, it is necessary for the functional units to work together.

Personnel flow Personnel input originates from several points in the environment. Some workers are provided by organized labor unions, some are not. Some are recruited by the firm and some by private employment agencies. Some are found in the local community and some result from a nationwide search. Some come from college campuses and others do not. A firm obtains personnel from many sources to meet a wide range of requirements.

This personnel input is usually processed by the personnel department of the firm and assigned to separate work areas. While in those areas, the employees are used in the transformation process, either directly or indirectly. They might be available to the firm briefly or for a long period. Some may leave the firm shortly after joining it. Others remain for fifty years or more to receive their gold watches. Whether the duration is short or long, the personnel resource flows through the firm, and at some point each employee exits. The personnel department processes the termination, and the resource is returned to its environment— the local community, a competitor, organized labor, or some other environmental element. In some firms the personnel department is a part of manufacturing, where most of the employees are located. More often, however, the personnel department reports directly to an administrative vice president who may have other areas of responsibility as well.

Machine flow   Machines are obtained from specialized vendors and suppliers who manufacture and distribute them. Unlike the other physical resources, machines invariably remain in the firm for a long period. Rarely is a machine acquired one day and released the next. Ultimately, however, all machines return to the environment. In many cases, machines wear out or become obsolete and are scrapped. Some machines can be traded in on newer models or sold to other organizations that have a use for them.

While in the firm, machines are seldom stored. Rather, they are almost continually available, either as delivery trucks in the marketing department, desktop calculators in the accounting department, or machine tools in the manufacturing department. Because of special supply sources, the lack of in-firm storage, and special disposal outlets, the machine flow is the simplest flow of physical resources. However, control of the machine flow is diffused among all functional areas using the machines.

Money flow   Money is obtained primarily from the owners who provide investment capital, and the firm's customers who provide sales revenue. Other sources include loans from financial institutions, government loans and grants, and interest income from investments.

While many sources provide money, the responsibility for controlling the money flow lies with the accounting department. The accounting department is part of the finance functional area. The accounts receivable section of the accounting department collects money owed the firm by its customers, and the accounts payable section pays debts owed by the firm.

The flow of money through the firm is unusual in one respect. Physical money seldom flows through the firm. Rather, there is a flow of something representing money—checks, credit card slips, and so forth. Only on the retail level does cash change hands, and even here cash is giving way to credit transactions and electronic funds transfers.

The money flow, therefore, connects the firm to its financial institutions, customers, vendors, stockholders, and employees. In some cases the firm holds specific funds for a long time, such as certificates of deposit representing an interest-bearing investment. In other cases, there is a quick turnover of money, as when sales revenue is quickly converted into checks payable to vendors and employees.

The diffusion of resource control

We have seen how the resources flow from one functional area of the firm to another. That flow is illustrated in Figure 3-6. This is a simplified diagram showing only those departments identified in our discussion, and not showing some of the flows between departments. For example, personnel and machines are often transferred from one department to another.

The purpose of the diagram is to show that a basic incompatibility exists

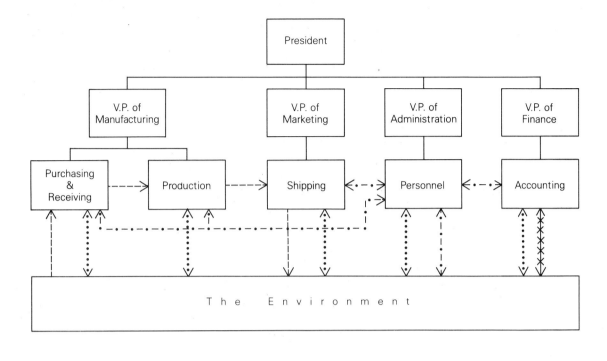

Legend:

Material flow -------->   Machine flow ···········>

Personnel flow • — • — • •>   Money flow ×××××××>

Figure 3-6 Flow of physical resources through a functionally organized firm.

between functional organization and resource flows. Functional organization does nothing to simplify the flow. The fact that the functional organization works at all under these circumstances is somewhat of a miracle. Managers prefer the functional organization over any other type, and it is a constraint that must be accepted by designers of both physical and conceptual business systems.

The finance function is the only one corresponding to a resource flow—money. The finance function may be regarded as a pipeline for money flowing through the firm.

There have been efforts to isolate the material flow in functionally organized firms. Portions of the manufacturing and marketing functions that handle material flow are set up as a separate unit. In the early 1960s, Stanley H. Brewer and James Rosenzweig coined the term *rhochrematics* to represent the material flow from the source of supply, through the firm, and to the customer.[2] The term was derived from the Greek "rhoe" meaning a flow such as a river, and "chrema" meaning materials.

---

[2] Stanley H. Brewer and James Rosenzweig, "Rhochrematics and Organizational Adjustments," *California Management Review* 3 (Spring 1961): pp. 52–71.

Although Brewer and Rosenzweig were on the right track, their term didn't stick. Instead, the new organization became known as *logistics*. Many firms formed logistics units in the 1960s and '70s and realized dramatic economies and efficiencies. Many of these systems are already growing obsolete and are being updated with the latest technology.

The conceptual system

As illustrated in Figure 3-5, the physical system is an open system in terms of its environmental links. It has no feedback loop or control mechanism. Such a system is called an *open-loop system*. There is no feedback from system output to effect changes in system input. A system that incorporates feedback is known as a *closed-loop system*. The concept of open- and closed-loop systems applies equally to closed systems.

Examples of open-loop systems are not hard to find. A good example is a small electric space heater. When the heater is turned on, it gives off heat. It may give off too much or too little. It has no self-regulating mechanism to maintain a certain temperature.

There are probably a few business firms of the open-loop type. They set off on a particular course and never change direction. If they get out of control, nothing is done to restore equilibrium. The result is system destruction, or bankruptcy.

The feedback loop   Most business firms have a closed feedback loop. The control mechanism built into this loop is management. A business firm, therefore, can be regarded as a closed-loop system.

Figure 3-5 could have included feedback and control elements. Those additions are reflected in Figure 3-7.

The reason that management and the feedback loop were not included in the discussion of the physical system is that they are both integral parts of the conceptual information system. It is true that both managers and devices contributing to the flow of information (such as computers, telephone networks, and the like) are physical resources; but they are also elements of the conceptual information system. Because we are primarily interested in studying how resources work together

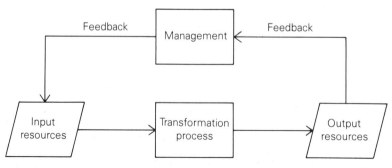

Figure 3-7 The physical system of the firm as a controlled system.

to form a conceptual system, we have included the physical feedback elements in our discussion of the conceptual, rather than the physical, system.

With the addition of the feedback loop to the physical system, management can control the system by becoming an integral part of the loop. The control process involves receiving information about the system, evaluating it, and transmitting information back to the system when some type of change must be made. The feedback loop, therefore, provides a communication channel for the fifth basic resource—information.

Management control As shown in Figure 3-7, management receives information about the system's output. Many management reports fall into this category— sales analyses by customer, distribution costs, inventory statistics, and so on. Since the main purpose of the firm as a system is to produce some type of output, a measure of the output is an integral part of system control.

Figure 3-8 is an example of a report of system output—a sales report of fast-moving products. The detailed sales data during the month is retained on a computer storage medium such as a magnetic disk or diskette, which is used to print the report at the end of the month. A computer program arranges all of the detailed data by product number, accumulates the sales amounts for each product, sorts these amounts into descending order, selects the products at the top of the list (such as the top 10%), and prints the report. The report calls the manager's attention to the products that are selling best. The manager then tries to determine

ITEM NUMBER	ITEM DESCRIPTION	YEAR-TO-DATE SALES VOLUME	PERCENT OF TOTAL YEAR-TO-DATE SALES*
400293	BRAKE PIPE	$ 1,702.93	.068
319421	DOOR HANDLE GASKET	1,624.00	.065
786402	CLUTCH DRIVEN PLATE	1,403.97	.056
190796	CARPET SNAP	1,102.00	.044
001007	SPARK PLUG	1,010.79	.040
739792	HOSE CLIP	949.20	.038
722210	RUBBER PLUG	946.73	.038
410615	UPPER DOOR HINGE	938.40	.038
963214	REAR TUBE SHOCK	922.19	.037
000123	NEEDLE VALVE	919.26	.037
	TOTALS	$11,519.47	.461

*BASED ON YEAR-TO-DATE SALES OF $24,988.00

Figure 3-8 A sales report of fast-moving products.

why these products sell well, and possibly uses the findings to increase the sales of other products.

Feedback on system output is valuable to the manager. However, certain additions and refinements can be made to describe the conceptual system better. First, the manager gathers information other than that relating to the firm's output. The manager also must know the status of the firm in terms of internal processes and inputs. For example, the manager wants information describing the production efficiency of the manufacturing operation, and how well vendors are meeting the firm's needs for input material. Figure 3-9 reflects the addition of information-gathering activities to the input and processing parts of the physical system.

In Figure 3-10 we can see a report describing one aspect of the system's input. This vendor analysis compares all of the vendors used to procure a certain raw material in the past. The comparison includes price, delivery time, and product quality. A buyer in the purchasing department could request such a report before deciding on the supplier of the next order of the raw material.

Figure 3-11 illustrates an aspect of internal processing that can be reported to management. In this example, a production manager wants to know the status of a certain job. The job number is keyed into a terminal, and the terminal displays the information, as shown in the figure. The manager knows that the job has reached step 4 in department 410, that the step was begun at 10:15 A.M. on October 8, and that the job should be completed by 9:30 A.M. on October 14.

Getting back to our discussion of the general model, we should realize that information does not always travel directly from the physical system to the manager. The manager is usually removed from the physical system and must get information through some type of communication network. Sometimes the information is not immediately made available to the manager but is held in storage until needed.

The information processor Figure 3-12 includes the addition of an element called the *information processor*. In this discussion we assume that the information processor is a computer. You may recall from Chapter 1 that there are other ways

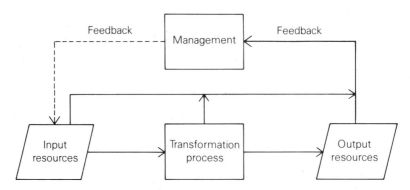

Figure 3-9 Multiple information sources monitor the physical system.

```
-----------------------------------------------------------------------------------
ITEM NUMBER              410615
ITEM DESCRIPTION         UPPER DOOR HINGE

VENDOR                       -LAST TRANSACTION-        UNIT     DAYS TO   PERCENT
NUMBER     VENDOR NAME      DATE PURCH ORD NO QTY      PRICE    RECEIPT   REJECTS
-----------------------------------------------------------------------------------
 3062    CARTER AND SONS    7/12   1048-10    360     $8.75      12        .00
 4189    PACIFIC MACHINING  4/13    962-10    350      9.10       8        .02
 0140    A.B.MERRIL & CO.   1/04    550-10    350      8.12       3        .00
 2111    BAY AREA METALS    8/19   1196-10    360     11.60      19        .04
-----------------------------------------------------------------------------------
```

Figure 3-10 A vendor analysis report.

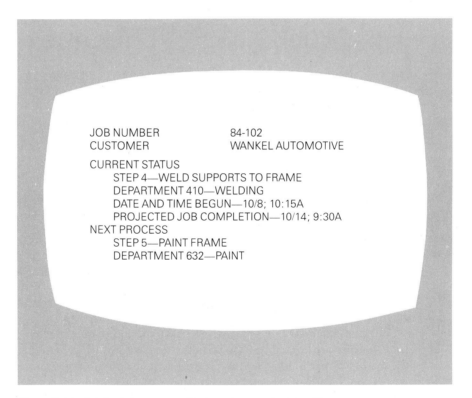

Figure 3-11 A job status report displayed on a television-like screen.

to process data—manually and with keydriven machines. The general systems model is just as applicable to those noncomputer systems.

Figure 3-13 identifies the important parts of a computer-based information processor. The concept of a *data base* was introduced in Chapter 1. If the information system is computerized, the data is housed in some type of computer storage. The computer uses programs in the software library to perform the

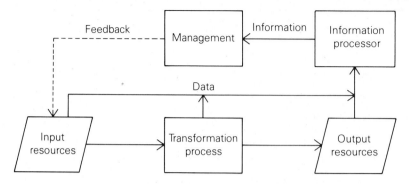

Figure 3-12 Adding the information processor to the conceptual information system.

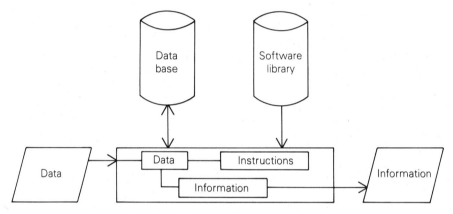

Figure 3-13 An information processor.

processing. The *software library* is the collection of all application and system programs that enable the computer to process the firm's data in the desired manner. One of the system programs is the data base management system (DBMS), which is used to manage the data in the data base.

When a certain process is to be performed, the appropriate program is selected from the software library and copied in the primary storage area of the computer (the large rectangle in the center of Figure 3-13). The program is executed, causing the necessary data to be selected from the data base and copied into primary storage. The data is transformed into output information.

As the manager identifies information needs, he or she should consider the following important characteristics of information.

1. *Quality*: How accurate must the information be? Very often, as in monetary accounting, the information must be very accurate—to the penny. In other situations, such as sales forecasting, the information need only approximate what actually exists or can be expected to happen.
2. *Quantity*: How much information is needed? The computer can produce

information faster than the manager can digest it. The manager should receive only the amount of detail necessary to understand the situation and make a decision. The MIS can be designed to produce information initially in summary form, and to produce increasing levels of detail on demand.

3. *Timing*: How quickly must an action in the physical system be reported to the manager? All managers would like an instantaneous signal, but that may not be necessary. Perhaps the manager cannot take immediate action even if the information is made available without delay.

4. *Cost versus return*: As the manager considers requirements in terms of quality, quantity, and timing, the cost also must be recognized. Most firms simply cannot afford a perfect system and must settle for something less. The cost of information should never exceed its value.

5. *Presentation mode*: How will the information be presented—in the form of numbers, narrative, or graphics? Will the information be printed or displayed on a television-type screen, or will it be presented in an audible form?

The manager is the best person to identify the information that he or she needs. The systems analyst, however, can work with the manager, and provide the stimulus and the logical, systematic format for considering information needs. Together, manager and analyst identify and understand a problem, delineate the decisions necessary to solve the problem, and identify the information that the manager needs to make the appropriate decisions. The analyst uses these information specifications to identify the processes (or programs) required to produce the information. At the same time, the analyst identifies the input data needed by the programs. This type of chain reaction, illustrated in Figure 3-14, originates with a problem, identifies decisions and their information needs, and produces program and data requirements. This is how the contents of the software library and the data base are determined.

Standards Another element in the evolving model of the conceptual information system addresses the manager's need for standards to measure the firm's actual performance. You recall from Chapter 2 that Frederick W. Taylor saw the need to set standards for production workers. Here we are talking about one or more standards for the firm and for each of its subsystems.

If the manager receives a report indicating that yesterday's sales were $25,000, is that good or bad? Without some standard of performance, it would be impossible to tell. If the firm never before had reached that sales level, the performance would be good; if sales normally averaged $30,000, the performance would be bad. The need for performance standards can also be seen in a thermostatically controlled heating system. If the thermostat is to maintain a certain temperature, it must first be set to the appropriate level. Similarly, if a business firm is to perform at a certain level or rate, some standard of performance must be established. In many cases, the managers set the performance level; but in others the level is

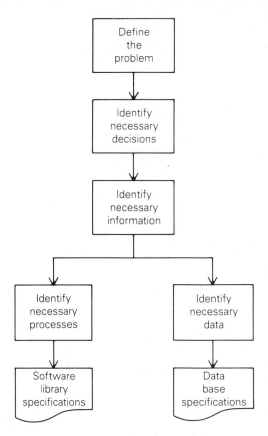

Figure 3-14 Software library and data base specifications begin with definitions of problems.

established by an element in the environment such as the government or the local community.

The manager controls the system by comparing (1) actual performance, as reflected by information provided by the information processor, to (2) the standards of performance. Figure 3-15 illustrates the addition of standards. It is important to note that the standards are made available to the information processor as well as the manager. This approach enables the information processor to relieve the manager of much of the monitoring activity. The information processor can tell the manager when actual performance varies too much from the standards—management by exception.

Before we conclude the discussion of standards, we should return to our earlier discussion (in Chapter 2) of the distinction between standards and objectives. Here we are describing a firm as a system, and a system is designed to meet certain objectives. Our firm has objectives, but they do not appear in the model. The model includes the levels of performance (the standards) necessary for the firm to meet its objectives.

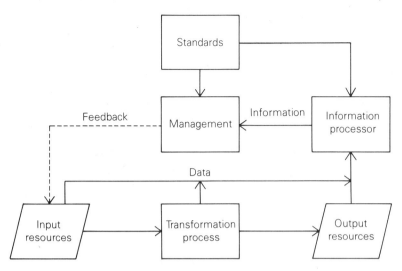

Figure 3-15 Adding performance standards to the conceptual information system.

Management by exception Most managers have so many responsibilities that they find it practically impossible to give each the attention it deserves. Managers learn to direct their attention to either extremely bad or extremely good performance. Students of management often fail to appreciate why exceptionally good performance should be called to the attention of the manager. If something good happens, the manager should know why so that she or he can get the same thing to happen more often.

Management by exception requires that both high and low standards of performance be established. For example, if daily shoe sales should range from 125 to 200 pairs, the manager is signaled only when the sales fall below 125 or rise above 200.

Management by exception offers three basic *advantages*:

1. The manager is relieved from monitoring activity that is progressing in a normal manner and requires no attention.
2. Since fewer decisions are made, each can receive more thorough attention.
3. It is a positive approach since opportunities as well as problems are identified.

There are some *constraints*, however, that must be recognized:

1. It is not always easy to quantitatively measure certain types of business performance. An example is customer attitudes toward the firm's products.
2. An effective information system that accurately monitors various types of performance is essential.
3. Attention must continually be directed to the standards. Are they at the correct level? Have they become obsolete?

4. The manager must not grow passive and simply wait for performance boundaries to be exceeded. Most likely, performance standards have not been established for all parts of the firm's operations. Also, the information system may not report actual performance in the manner desired.

Management by exception is an integral part of the MIS concept. The manager's time is effectively used as the MIS assumes some of the responsibilities for monitoring the physical system.

Decision flow   Another addition to the general model is necessary to reflect how management decisions can change the physical system. Just as the manager must gather data from all three elements in the physical system—input, processing, and output—it is important that the manager also be able to effect changes in the performance of all three elements. In the model drawn in Figure 3-15, the manager can only communicate feedback instructions or decisions to the input element. This limitation would prohibit the manager from responding quickly to changes throughout the entire system. If information from the data base indicates that activity in either the transformation processing or the output area requires adjustment, the manager must be able to effect such change directly, without having to work through the input area. This modification is made in Figure 3-16; the feedback from the manager to the physical system is relabeled "decisions" to reflect the manner in which the manager changes the system's performance.

The basic feedback loop as drawn initially in Figure 3-7 still represents signals from the physical system used for control; but the signals are in three different forms—data, information, and decisions. The data is transformed into information by the information processor, and the information is transformed into decisions by the manager. The information processor and the manager are the

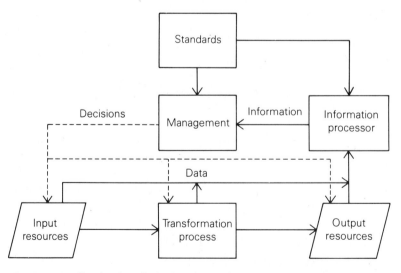

Figure 3-16   Changes made in the physical system through the decision flow.

two key elements in the feedback loop—they work together to transform data into needed decisions. This is the decision support system (DSS) concept.

The environment

In Chapter 2, the discussion of the contingency school of management theory used the terms *external environment* and *internal environment.* These are the environments of the *manager,* and they include elements both outside and inside the firm. Also, when we discussed Mintzberg's managerial roles, we saw that some involve interaction with persons outside the manager's *unit.* The persons could well be in other departments in the firm. Here, and for the remainder of the text, we are concerned with the environment of the *firm.* We will use the term *environment* to describe all of the influences outside the firm.

As the discussion in the next chapter will indicate, the influence of the environment on the firm can be very complex. An attempt to show this effect in the general model would complicate it unnecessarily. Therefore, the final form of the general model recognizes only that resources flow into the firm from the environment and from the firm back to the environment. That addition is made in Figure 3-17.

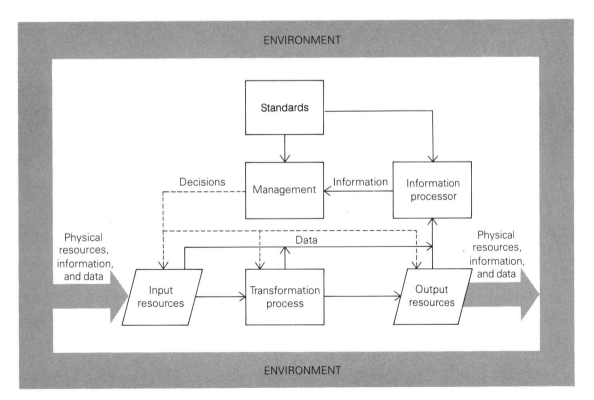

Figure 3-17 The general systems model of the firm.

All five types of resources—personnel, machines, material, money, *and information*—enter the firm from the environment. The physical resources flow through the physical system at the bottom of the model. The conceptual resource—information—first enters the input area of the physical system and then enters the information processor, where it is stored or made available to the manager. *Data* gathered from the environment follows the same path.

Use of the General Model

It is rather easy to relate our general model to a manufacturing firm. The flow of materials through the physical system and the control exercised by the manager in assuring that production goals are met by the firm are both very apparent. It is not quite so easy to relate the model to other types of organizations, especially those providing services rather than products, and those of a nonprofit nature. In the sections below, three types of organizations are explained in terms of the model. Our objective is to show that the model is general in the true sense and can provide a basic structure for the analysis of any type of organization.

A football team

The management control of a football team is exercised by the coaching staff. The coaches must use their resources in the most efficient way. Most teams have standards that they wish to meet during a season (such as winning at least eight games) or during a single game (such as limiting the opposition to no more than 10 first downs). The team's standards are mostly quantitative, and there is little question of whether they have been reached. Fans and sportswriters can make this determination very easily.

The most important resource available to the coaches is personnel. Some material is involved (such as uniforms, footballs, adhesive tape, and the like), but it is not as important to the success of the team as are the players. Very little machinery is involved. Movie projectors, whirlpool baths, and weight machines are about the extent of it. Money may or may not be an important resource, depending on the type of team; certainly, no professional team could exist without it. For a team that is more modest in its performance level, money plays a lesser role.

Clearly the management of the organization—the coaching staff—has a mixture of resources with which to work, and these resources have different relative values. Much of the success of a football team is due to the skill of the coaching staff, but much is determined by the resources available. The coach must do the best he can with what he has.

These resources flow through the organization. In a college team, the players are available for only four years, much equipment is used for only a single season, and supplies often last only days. The team begins the season with a budgeted amount of funds, which are probably spent by the time the last game rolls around. During the time that the resources are available, the coaches must integrate them into a smoothly functioning team.

All coaches have a conceptual information system of some sort. Coaches on the sandlot level rely entirely on observation from the sidelines. This basic approach can be augmented at higher levels by assistant coaches in the pressbox, by game films, and even by computer systems. Many professional teams use computers to decipher the strategy of opponents. As a general rule, data does not reside in the data base for a long period of time. During a game, the coaching staff can usually determine by half-time the causes of their team's problems. As this information becomes available to the coaches, they make decisions that alter the team's performance. The purpose of such changes is to help the team meet its objectives.

The football team is a service organization. It produces entertainment for its followers and perhaps some profit for its owners. It uses resources gathered from its environment and returns an output to the environment in the form of entertainment. Although the organization is quite different in many respects from a business firm, there are many similarities to the general systems model. The model provides a framework useful for evaluating the team. A new head coach will take stock of his resources, evaluate the nature of the goals, and pass judgment on the information system in preparing for the upcoming season. The model serves as a normative, or ideal, picture of how the organization should be structured.

A law firm

There are several obvious differences between a law firm and a football team. The law firm usually comprises a small number of people who perform their tasks through mental, rather than physical, activity. The overriding objective of the law firm is profit rather than entertainment.

Even with these basic differences, a law firm can be described by the same general model used for the football team. Each law firm is subjected to management control. In a large firm this control is exercised by the partners; in a small firm of only a single lawyer, this control is performed on a part-time basis by that person.

The main responsibility of the person or persons managing the law firm is to assure that it meets its objectives. It is doubtful that the goals of the law firm are as specific as those of the football team. A law firm probably does not strive to win a certain percentage of court cases or to handle some minimum number of divorce settlements. We can assume a profit objective, however, since management realizes that profit is the key to continued operation and service.

The transformation process in the law firm is one of converting the raw materials (clients with legal problems) into finished products (clients whose legal problems have been solved). This transformation is accomplished by the lawyers, who represent the most important resource available to the firm. One could argue that information is the most important resource. That ingredient is absolutely necessary in legal practice. Everyone has seen pictures of attorneys' offices with bookshelves filled with law books. Any lawyer will tell you, however, that you have to know where to look in the books.

Some law firms use computers to provide information in a fraction of the time required to obtain it through library research. A special information retrieval system called WESTLAW is offered by the West Publishing Company on a subscription basis. A legal data base is maintained in St. Paul, Minnesota, containing results of federal court cases dating back to 1925, and of state court cases dating back as far as 1945 for some states. A lawyer enters a request for case information into a terminal or a microcomputer with a data communications ability. The request is transmitted to St. Paul, where the data is retrieved and transmitted back to the law office. Output can be displayed on a screen or printed.

The performance of a law firm lends itself to the general model. Management of the firm monitors the process by which legal problems are transformed into solutions. Information facilitating this control is provided from the physical system and derived from a data base. When standards are not being met, decisions are made to alter the physical system. If too few legal problems are being converted into solutions (the firm is losing too many cases), the partners can hire additional lawyers, replace existing lawyers, reassign lawyers to different types of cases, hire legal secretaries, and so forth.

The general model provides a structure for the basic elements of a legal firm. A new partner can expect to find these elements regardless of whether he or she has ever before served in that particular firm or has any previous knowledge of its structure. The new partner expects to find standards (for the firm and perhaps for individual lawyers), an information system, and a personnel resource capable of performing the transformation process in a manner acceptable to the managing partners.

A newspaper publisher

A newspaper publisher is usually a profit-seeking organization. A management team is formed to assemble the resources necessary to achieve and maintain profitable operations. These resources include personnel such as reporters, press operators, and carriers, who play roles in creating and delivering the printed product. Machines such as typesetting equipment and printing presses are necessary to the production process. The primary materials are newsprint and ink, and all of these resources are acquired with money.

The transformation of the raw material into the finished product is very rapid. You can go to bed before a Monday night football game is over and read the final score in your morning paper, printed a hundred miles away. It is management's responsibility to achieve this responsive system. The management uses an MIS to monitor both the environment and the physical system of the firm. The cry "Stop the presses!" captures the urgency of newspaper management. This expression was famous long before the computer. Today it could easily be "Stop the computer!" since most big-city papers and many smaller ones have computerized typesetting operations. Television-like terminals have replaced typewriters for many reporters and data entry personnel.

For a modern newspaper publisher, the computer plays two roles. As a piece of production equipment, it is part of the physical system of the firm, transforming the input copy into a printed newspaper. It is also part of the conceptual system, keeping management informed of the status of the overall physical system.

The newspaper organization needs standards specifying market coverage, readership rates, level of advertising revenues, daily deadlines, profit margins, and so on. The MIS helps management channel resources toward the achievement of specified objectives.

Managers of the newspaper organization can use the general model to pinpoint the source and nature of problems in the physical system. If the newspaper doesn't get out on time, or if it contains too many errors, management knows that the cause of the problem is a resource flow not measuring up to the standards. Perhaps there are not enough resources, such as reporters or carriers, or perhaps the resources are not being used efficiently. But the real cause of the poor physical system might be the conceptual system. Perhaps the physical system is poorly managed. The general model shows two elements integrated into the feedback control loop—management and the information processor. If either of these elements is not performing in the desired way, the physical system will not be in control.

A new employee of a newspaper can use the general systems model to evaluate how well the newspaper measures up to the normative model. The new employee can study the quantity and quality of the resources, and the efficiency with which they are used. She or he can check to determine how data and information are gathered from the physical system and from the environment. The information processor and its data base and software library can be studied, as well as the information flow to management. The employee can verify that standards exist, and that they are being used by management for decision making. When the newspaper—or any other firm—is given this type of scrutiny, the areas needing improvement are easily identified. The general systems model of the firm is an effective systems analysis tool.

Summary

A general systems model of the firm can be used to understand the structure of both the physical system of the firm and the conceptual information system and how they interrelate.

A model is an abstraction of something, and there are four types— physical, narrative, graphical, and mathematical. All types provide some feature not evident in the object being modeled. These features, economy and availability, permit the user to better understand the object being modeled and often (for mathematical models) to predict the future with a limited degree of accuracy.

All four types of models can range from general to specific. A general model has wide applicability, but does not address any particular situation in an exact way. The general systems model of the firm can be used to analyze any type of organization, but not as exactly as one designed for that particular purpose.

We introduced the general systems model element by element, with attention to both the resource flow through the physical system and the feedback flow through the conceptual system. The feedback flow originates as data, is transformed into information by the information processor, and is then used by the manager to make decisions.

The general model depicts the firm as an open system (it interacts with its environment) and as a closed-loop system (it has a feedback loop). No firm can be a completely closed system, shut off from its environment. But a poorly managed firm can resemble an open-loop system—one with no feedback mechanism.

Management follows a practice of management by exception by using the information processor to monitor the physical system. By including standards in the data base, the information processor can determine whether system performance is within established upper and lower limits.

This chapter serves only to introduce the general systems model. Each part of the model will be analyzed in more detail in the following chapters. As you will see, the beauty of the general systems model is its simplicity: it is useful to anybody in any situation. It is also a basic tool of the systems approach to business analysis, which is the subject of the next chapter.

Key Terms

model

physical, narrative, graphical, mathematical model

general systems model of the firm

logistics

open-loop system, closed-loop system

information processor

software library

management by exception

Key Concepts

A model as an abstraction of some phenomenon

Different types of models

The two basic uses of models

Comparative advantages of general and specific models

The value of a general systems model as a systems analysis tool

The manner in which the physical resources flow through the various functional areas

The use of media representing money, rather than money itself, to transfer funds both within the

firm and between the firm and its environment

Difficulty of assigning resource flow responsibility in a functionally organized firm

Open-loop versus closed-loop systems

Characteristics of information

How the MIS facilitates management by exception

The three different forms of the feedback loop—data, information, and decisions

Questions

1. Why is the term *model* used to describe someone who poses for clothing ads?
2. Name the four basic types of models. Which is used the least in management decision making? Which has a predictive ability?
3. What are the two main reasons for using a model?
4. Only one of the physical resource flows is restricted to a single functional area. Name the resource and the functional area.
5. Which material flow does logistics handle? Name the two functions from which the logistics operation was derived.
6. What is the difference between an open-loop and a closed-loop system? Which of these types describes a business firm?
7. The physical system of the firm is composed of four resource flows. What are they? Should the manager try to speed up or slow down these flows? Explain.
8. Are managers and the information processor a part of the physical or the conceptual system? Explain.
9. Is the sales report of fast-moving products pictured in Figure 3-8 an example of a management-by-exception report? What about the vendor analysis report in Figure 3-10, and the production status report in Figure 3-11? Explain your reasoning.
10. What part of the information processor contains stored data? Stored programs?
11. Name five characteristics of information that the manager should consider.
12. Comment on the following statements:
    a. Information produced by the MIS should contain no errors.
    b An MIS should provide the manager with as much information as possible.
    c. A good MIS must produce information no later than five seconds after it is requested.
13. Arrange the following items in sequence, based on the order in which they are specified by the systems analyst: data, information, problem, processes, decisions.
14. How does the work of Frederick W. Taylor relate to the general systems model?
15. Since a system is intended to meet objectives, shouldn't objectives be a part of the general systems model?
16. Why would a manager want to be bothered with a signal that things are going better than planned?
17. In what form(s) does the feedback loop exist in a firm?
18. By what route through the model does information gathered from the environment travel to the manager?
19. What machines might flow through a law firm? What materials? What information?

20. Is the computer in a newspaper a part of the physical system? The conceptual system? Explain.

Problems

1. Write a short paper describing the operation of a supermarket in terms of the general systems model. Your instructor will tell you how long the paper should be and whether it need be typed.

2. Repeat problem 1, using a hospital.

3. Assume that you are a purchasing agent (buyer) analyzing the vendor analysis report in Figure 3-10. Which vendor would you select for your next purchase? Why?

CASE PROBLEM: Conway Container Corp.

Conway Container Corp. is a manufacturer of metal and plastic containers, such as motor oil cans, milk cartons, and frozen-juice cans. Ralph McCann, Jr., assumed the presidency of Conway upon graduation from college. One of McCann's first actions was to install a Macintosh computer—one of the hottest-selling small systems. The Macintosh is used to compute payroll, maintain inventory records, prepare purchase orders, and handle the firm's accounts payable.

In the inventory system, the Macintosh maintains a master record for each inventory item, describing its balance on hand, reorder point, order quantity, and so on. Each time an inventory transaction is processed, the new balance is compared to the reorder point. When the balance drops below the reorder point, the computer prints a purchase order. The purchase orders are sent to McCann so that he can check them for accuracy, verify the need to make the purchase, and initial them. After Ralph's approval (which might take as long as two days, because of his busy schedule), the multiple-part purchase order forms are separated. The original copy is sent to the supplier, the second copy is placed in an unfilled-purchase-order file, and the third copy is sent to the receiving department.

Quite often the ordered materials do not arrive soon enough, and production must be delayed. This results in missed deliveries and lost business. McCann is dismayed over the poor performance of the inventory system, especially after having made it one of his top-priority computer applications. If the situation doesn't improve, McCann is going to revert back to a manual system and take the Macintosh home to his children so that they can play some electronic games.

Questions

1. Is McCann using his Macintosh to produce management information?

2. Is the Macintosh properly positioned in the feedback loop of Conway's inventory system?

3. Is McCann properly positioned in the feedback loop of the inventory system?

4. What is the problem?

5. How can the problem be solved? Briefly outline a strategy that you would recommend to McCann.

CASE PROBLEM: Oil Field Equipment Co.

"Oil Field" sells equipment and supplies to offshore drilling rigs in the Gulf of Mexico. The warehouse is located in Bossier City, Louisiana, and deliveries are made by helicopter. The competition is keen, and customers switch suppliers quickly when delivery becomes slow or stock is unavailable.

Although Oil Field has a fast delivery capability, its order filling procedure is relatively primitive. The company does not use a computer but performs most tasks manually.

Orders are taken over the phone by four order clerks who type the data on "picking tickets." Only in very rare instances are all four operators busy at the same time. When this happens and another call comes in, the customer is put on hold.

The picking ticket is typed in duplicate—one copy is placed in an "open order suspense file," and the other is placed in the "warehouse basket." The suspense file is a manila folder that contains picking ticket copies for all orders received but not yet filled. As orders are filled and materials delivered, the copies are removed from the file by the warehouse clerk. Twice a day Mr. Hall, the order department manager, looks through the open order file. If an order has not been filled in four hours (the picking ticket contains the time of day that the order was received), he telephones Mr. Williams, the warehouse supervisor, to find out the reason for the delay. Usually, the order has been filled and the material is on its way, but the warehouse clerk (who reports to Mr. Williams) has failed to remove the suspense copies. This happens quite often. The warehouse clerk is supposed to come into the order department once each hour to remove suspense file copies for filled orders, and pick up picking tickets for new orders. The warehouse clerk places the removed suspense copies in a "filled order file" for use the next day by typists in the billing department in preparing invoices to be sent to the customers requesting payment.

After the warehouse clerk picks up the picking tickets for new orders from the warehouse basket, he takes them to the warehouse where he gives them to Mr. Williams. Mr. Williams, in turn, gives them to any of the five stock clerks who might be available at the time. The stock clerks walk through the warehouse and pull the merchandise from the shelves. The merchandise is taken to the packing area where it is packed for delivery. The picking and packing operation usually goes smoothly with little delay.

Since Oil Field has no computer, it has had to devise a manual system for recognizing when it is time to order replenishment stock from its suppliers. Oil

Field uses a method called the "two-bin plan." Most of their items such as pipe fittings, washers, bolts, and so forth are kept loose in large containers (called bins) on the shelves. Actually there are two bins for each item—one in the front and one at the back of the shelf. Each set of bins may contain hundreds of small items.

Once each year Mr. Williams reviews the monthly sales reports of the items and decides which reorder points will be appropriate. The reorder point is the quantity that triggers a purchase order for replenishment stock. When the balance on hand drops below the reorder point, a purchase order is prepared by the purchasing department. Mr. Williams is familiar with which suppliers supply most of the items, and about how long it usually takes to get delivery. For example, if monthly sales of a 5½" flange average 200 and the supplier delivery time is two weeks, a reorder point of 100 is set. A quantity of 100 is available for sale while awaiting replenishment by the supplier. Mr. Williams has been doing this job for six years, but it takes more time each year. The number of items stocked by Oil Field has grown to over 10,000.

Once Mr. Williams sets a reorder point, that quantity is placed in the rear bin. Any additional items are placed in the front bin. As the stock clerks fill orders, they are instructed to take items from the front bin. When the front bin becomes empty, they know that the reorder point has been reached and it is time to reorder. In that case, they mark an asterisk next to the item number on the picking ticket. At the end of the day the warehouse clerk takes all of the processed picking tickets to the purchasing department. The two buyers go through the tickets, noting those items with asterisks. Purchase orders are then typed.

The two-bin plan works well most of the time, but turnover among the stock clerks is high, and they often forget to mark the asterisks. The next clerk to pull that item sees the empty front bin but assumes that a replenishment order has been placed. Before long the quantity in the rear bin has been removed and Oil Field is out of stock on that item.

Questions

1. Make a list of the problems that Oil Field is having with the conceptual system.
2. Make a list of the problems that Oil Field is having with the physical system.
3. Assume that Oil Field must continue to use a manual system. Make a list of the things that they should do to improve the overall system. Assume that any additional personnel can be hired.

Selected Bibliography

General Systems Model of the Firm

Brewer, Stanley H., and James Rosenzweig, "Rhochrematics and Organizational Adjustments," *California Management Review* 3 (Spring 1961): 72–81.

Gershefski, George W., "Building a Corporate Financial Model," *Harvard Business Review* 47 (July-August 1969): 61–72.

Hopeman, Richard J., *Systems Analysis and Operations Management*, (Columbus, Ohio: Charles E. Merrill, 1969), pp. 125–150.

Meador, Charles Lawrence, and David N. Ness, "Decision Support Systems: An Application to Corporate Planning," *Sloan Management Review* 15 (Winter 1974): 51–68.

Shapiro, Roy D., "Get Leverage From Logistics," *Harvard Business Review* 62 (May-June 1984): 119–126.

Sharman, Graham, "The Rediscovery of Logistics," *Harvard Business Review* 62 (September-October 1984): 71–79.

Shim, Jae K., and Randy McGlade, "Current Trends in the Use of Corporate Planning Models," *Journal of Systems Management* 35 (September 1984): 24–31.

Chapter 4

The Systems Approach

Learning Objectives

After studying this chapter, you should:

- Understand how the MIS is involved in the problem-solving process
- Know the difference between structured and unstructured problems, and how they relate to the DSS concept
- Recognize that a firm of any size can have some influence over its environment
- Be familiar with the elements of the systems approach and how they fit together to form a powerful problem-solving tool
- Be able to use the systems approach, with practice, to solve business problems
- Appreciate individual differences in problem-solving styles and how they affect MIS design
- Realize that managers do not always solve problems in a systematic manner, but rely to varying degrees on intuition

Introduction

In the two previous chapters we devoted considerable attention to the subject of systems. In Chapter 2 we concluded with a brief description of a systems theory of management and organization. That theory was explained in more detail in Chapter 3 as we described the general systems model of the firm.

In this chapter we continue our attention to the firm as a system by describing how the manager can solve problems or capitalize on opportunities. We present an orderly, systematic method that the manager can follow.

The computer can play a key role in this method, called the *systems approach*. However, we should not lose sight of the fact that information from noncomputer sources is frequently used. Also, we will recognize in this chapter that managers do not always solve problems in an orderly, systematic fashion. More and more attention is being given to the use of intuition in problem solving. We recognize the noncomputer sources and the unsystematic methods, but our attention is focused on a systematic use of a computer-based MIS.

Problem Solving

The term *problem solving* brings to mind the correction of things that are going *wrong*. Managers make decisions to prevent these wrong things from happening or to minimize their effect once they occur.

Managers usually respond quickly to harmful influences, but they also respond to things that are going *right*. When managers spot performance that is going exceptionally well, they act to make it even better or to achieve the same good performance in other areas. We define a *problem* as a potentially harmful condition that management is required to prevent or minimize, or a potentially beneficial condition that management should exploit.

The importance of problem solving

The purpose of the information system is to help the manager solve problems. Certainly managers do other things. In fact, problem solving might account for only a small portion of a manager's time. However, the importance of problem solving is not based on the amount of time spent doing it, but rather on the consequences. A set of decisions to solve a problem might require only a few hours, but could affect the firm's profits to the tune of thousands or even millions of dollars.

Decision making and problem solving

Some people use the terms decision making and problem solving interchangeably. This is acceptable in casual conversation, but there is a difference.

Managers make decisions to solve problems. A *decision* is a selection of a strategy or action. *Decision making* is the act of selecting the strategy or action that the decision maker believes to offer the best solution. Usually there is a choice of strategies or actions that the decision maker can consider. One of the keys to problem solving is the identification of decision alternatives.

Several decisions are ordinarily required in order to solve a single problem. Consider, for example, the decisions that must be made by U.S. automakers to address the problem of competition from other countries. Decisions must be made relative to design, production, advertising, distribution, maintenance, and so forth.

Elements of a problem-solving process

Several elements are critical if a manager is to begin a successful problem-solving process. Naturally, there must be a *problem* and a *problem solver* (the manager).

The other elements are less obvious; but if any are absent, the end results are likely to be poor. All of these elements are pictured in Figure 4-1.

The solution to the problem must best enable the system to meet its objectives, as reflected in the performance standards. Therefore, the *standards* must be specified clearly. These standards describe the *desired state* that the system should achieve. In addition, the manager must have available *information* that describes the *current state* of the system. If the current state and the desired state are the same, there is no problem and the manager takes no action. If the two states are different, some problem is the cause and must be solved. In some cases, there is more than one problem to solve.

The figure indicates that the problem-solving elements—managers, standards, and information—are also the elements of the conceptual information system from the general systems model. In fact, these are the elements that achieve the solution. The information system is therefore a system to be used in problem solving.

The difference between the current state of the system and the desired state represents the *solution criterion,* or what it will take to bring the current state to the desired state. For example, if the standard is to sell a minimum of 125 pairs of ski boots a day, and sales are averaging 75 pairs, the solution to the problem must be one that can increase sales by at least 50 pairs. This is the solution criterion.

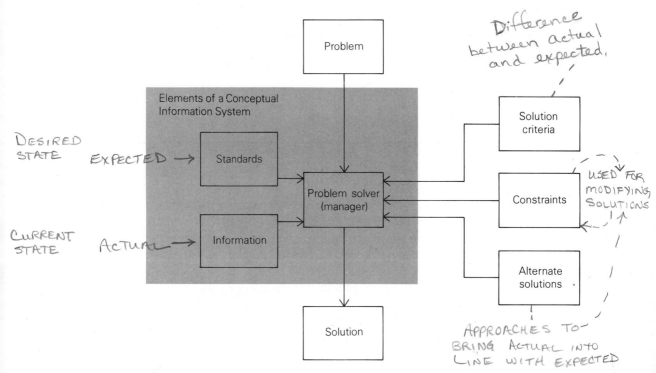

Figure 4-1 Elements of a problem-solving process.

Of course, if the current state happens to represent a *higher* level of performance than the desired state, the task is *not* to bring the current state in line. Rather, the task is to keep the current state at the higher level. If continued high-level performance can be anticipated, then the desired state should be revised upward.

We have recognized that an important part of problem solving is the consideration of *alternate solutions*. It is the manager's responsibility to identify these alternatives and to evaluate each one. As computers have been applied to support the manager in this problem-solving process, they have been little help in identifying alternatives. That task is left largely to the manager. Once the alternatives have been identified, the information system can be used to evaluate them individually.

As the alternate solutions are considered, the manager must be aware of any possible *constraints*. These can be internal or environmental. *Internal constraints* are in the form of limited resources—personnel, money, material, machines, or information. Some alternate solutions can be eliminated because they demand unavailable resources.

Environmental constraints can be just as real. Government laws may prohibit certain solutions. A whole host of laws, mostly on the federal level, establish constraints on practically every facet of business operation. Also, constraints applied by the other elements of the external environment, such as competition, vendors, and so on, can prohibit certain alternatives.

Once all of these elements exist and the manager understands them, a *solution* to the problem is possible. All problems have solutions. Some solutions may be difficult to recognize, some may not be easy to achieve, and some may not be optimal, but they do exist.

Problems versus symptoms

It is important to recognize the distinction between problems and symptoms. The *symptoms* are the conditions produced by the problem. Very often the manager sees symptoms rather than the problems themselves. The symptoms are like the tip of the iceberg; the manager must look beneath the symptoms to locate the real cause of the difficulty.

This process of sorting through symptoms to find problems is the task facing a medical doctor when a patient complains of some ailment, such as constant headaches. Something is causing the headaches, and the doctor must determine whether it is nervous tension, poor vision, poor diet, or something else. The manager faces the same task when he or she is confronted with a symptom such as low profits. Something is causing the low profits. The problem is the *cause* of the low profits.

Decision and problem structure

The various decisions made in the day-to-day operation of a firm can be classified into broad types. The most popular classification scheme in the MIS area was by G. Anthony Gorry and Michael S. Scott Morton in their original description of the decision support system (DSS) concept. Gorry and Scott Morton showed that decisions fall on a continuum, with one end representing structured decisions and the other end representing unstructured decisions. *Structured decisions* are those of a routine nature for which a prescribed solution procedure exists. *Unstructured decisions* are novel, nonrepetitive challenges that must be met with creativity, initiative, and originality. An example of a structured decision is the economic order quantity (EOQ) decision. The key variables have been identified and assembled in the EOQ formula. The break-even formula is another example. These formulas can be used by nonmanagers and even by computers to solve structured problems. Gorry and Scott Morton based their classification of decision structure on Herbert Simon's concept of programmed decisions. Managers make programmed decisions to solve structured problems.

An example of a truly unstructured problem is hard to find. Almost all problems have some structure. Nevertheless, we could argue that some problems are so unique and complex that they deserve to be called unstructured. The problem of how to determine the social value of a corporation is a good example. The solution would involve some measure of the firm's contribution to the good of society, which would differ from the traditional economic value measured by profit. No suitable measure has yet been found to solve this difficult problem. Managers make nonprogrammed decisions to solve unstructured problems.

Computers can solve structured problems without the manager's involvement, once appropriate procedures have been established. But the manager has to do most of the work to solve unstructured problems. In between the two extremes lies a vast area of *semi-structured problems* that can be solved by the manager with help from the computer. The manager and the computer make *semi-structured decisions* to solve semi-structured problems. This is the area of the decision-support system (DSS).

The Systems Approach

Central to the DSS concept is the identification and isolation of a problem or set of related problems, followed by a systematic solution process. The idea is to subdivide the complexity of business into manageable units—separate problems—which you handle one at a time.

A search for the origin of the systems approach leads to John Dewey, a philosophy professor at Columbia University around the turn of the century. In a 1910 book, he identified three series of judgments involved in adequately resolving a controversy.[1]

1. Recognize the controversy
2. Weigh alternative claims
3. Form a judgment

---

[1] John Dewey, *How We Think* (New York: D. C. Heath & Company, 1910), pp. 101–107.

Dewey didn't use the term systems approach, but he recognized the sequential nature of problem solving—beginning with a problem, considering alternate solutions, and selecting the best one.

Dewey did use the term *scientific method,* an approach to problem solving that has been used in physical sciences (such as chemistry and physics) and in behavioral sciences (such as psychology and sociology). The steps of the scientific method are:

1. Observing
2. Formulating a hypothesis
3. Predicting what will happen in the future
4. Testing the hypothesis

For example, assume that psychologists have *observed* that rats physically handled by researchers learn faster than those left alone. Their *hypothesis* states "Physical handling facilitates learning." The psychologists *predict* that rats handled physically will learn faster than those not handled. The hypothesis is *tested* by designing an experiment in which some rats are handled and others are not. The results are then evaluated.

The application of the scientific method to business problem solving has been named the *systems approach.* The steps are:

1. Define the problem
2. Gather data describing the problem
3. Identify alternate solutions
4. Evaluate the alternatives
5. Select the best alternative
6. Implement the solution
7. Follow up to assure that the solution is effective

The systems approach could be considered simply as an application of common sense to human problem solving. It is characterized by first understanding the problem and then considering the alternate ways of solving it.

The systems approach and decision making

Earlier, we recognized how multiple decisions are required to solve a single problem. The steps of the systems approach provide a good way to categorize the decisions that must be made. Each step of the systems approach requires at least one decision. This relationship is illustrated in Table 4-1.

The systems approach and the MIS

The MIS should be used as a support system for the decisions made while applying the systems approach. A DSS can be designed to support each decision, as illustrated in Figure 4-2. The systems approach serves as a bridge between the problem and the DSS, providing a framework for the various decisions.

Table 4-1 The systems approach requires decision making at each step

Step	Decisions
1. Define the problem.	Where is the problem? What is causing the problem? Is this the true cause?
2. Gather data describing the problem.	What kind of data should be gathered? Who will use the data? Does new data need to be gathered, or does data already exist? Who will gather data? How will the data be gathered?
3. Identify alternate solutions.	How many alternatives should be identified? Are there other alternatives? Are these alternatives feasible?
4. Evaluate the alternatives.	Which criteria should be used? How does each alternative measure up to each criterion? Do all criteria have equal weight?
5. Select the best alternative.	Is there enough information to make a selection? Which alternative measures up best to the criteria? Has the selection process been fair and unbiased?
6. Implement the solution.	When should this solution be implemented? How should this solution be implemented?
7. Follow up to assure that the solution is effective.	Who should perform the evaluation? How well is the solution meeting the objectives?

The figure depicts one DSS used to solve a single problem. Some might prefer to think of one DSS for each decision. The size of the problem is the determining factor. If the problem is too large and complex for a single DSS, then you must use multiple support systems.

A series of steps

We have seen that the systems approach is a series of steps. We are going to expand on the number of steps as we apply the systems approach to a business firm. We are going to package the steps in three phases—preparation effort, definition effort, and solution effort. Figure 4-3 shows the phases and the subsidiary steps. Each is discussed below.

Preparation Effort

You do not have to await the arrival of a problem before using the systems approach. First, you should gain a systems orientation, and we refer to that process as *preparation effort*—getting ready.

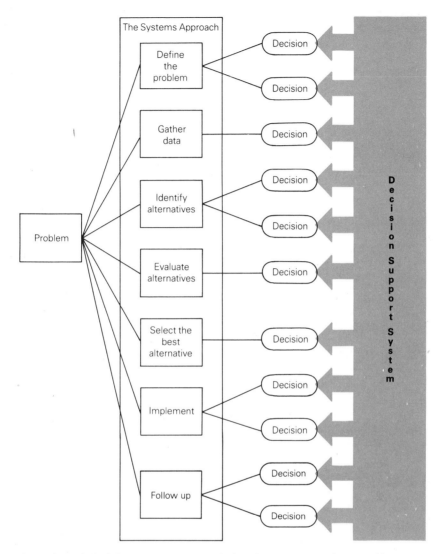

Figure 4-2 A decision support system helps the manager solve a problem.

1. Regard the firm as a system

The manager must be able to see his or her firm as a system. This requirement must be met even if the firm is organized functionally or some other way. The manager must be able to integrate mentally all of the resources so that they form a single system. This is how the general systems model of the firm illustrated in Figure 4-4 fits in. The manager must be able to see how the model fits the firm.

2. Recognize the environmental system

The firm's relationship to its environment is also important. The environment represents a larger system, of which the firm is a subsystem. The environment

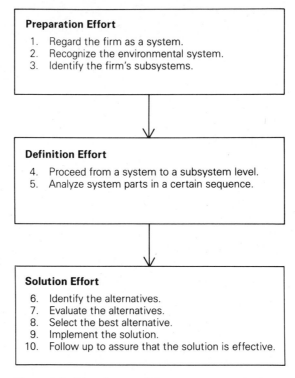

Preparation Effort

1. Regard the firm as a system.
2. Recognize the environmental system.
3. Identify the firm's subsystems.

Definition Effort

4. Proceed from a system to a subsystem level.
5. Analyze system parts in a certain sequence.

Solution Effort

6. Identify the alternatives.
7. Evaluate the alternatives.
8. Select the best alternative.
9. Implement the solution.
10. Follow up to assure that the solution is effective.

Figure 4-3   The phases of the systems approach.

requires certain products and services, and this provides a reason for the firm's existence. The firm's objectives are geared to meeting some of these needs.

The environment also furnishes the firm with all of the resources used to produce the products and services. The firm, therefore, is created from the environment. The management of the firm, playing an entrepreneurial role, recognizes environmental needs, acquires the resources to meet those needs, and then manages the resources.

There are many ways to look at the *environmental system.* One is to identify eight separate members or elements, as shown in Figure 4-5.[2] Each element is actually a subsystem within a larger system called *society.*

The *vendors* supply the materials used by the firm to produce goods and services for the *customers. Labor* provides the personnel resources, and the *financial community* provides the money resources, as do the *stockholders or owners. Competition* places a constraint on what the firm does, and often motivates the firm to satsify the needs of the environment in a better way. The *government,* on the federal, state, and local levels, also provides constraints; in addition, it can assist the firm by buying products and services, providing information, and pro-

---

[2] Based on Richard J. Hopemen, *Systems Analysis and Operations Management* (Columbus, Ohio: Charles E. Merrill, 1969), pp. 79–103.

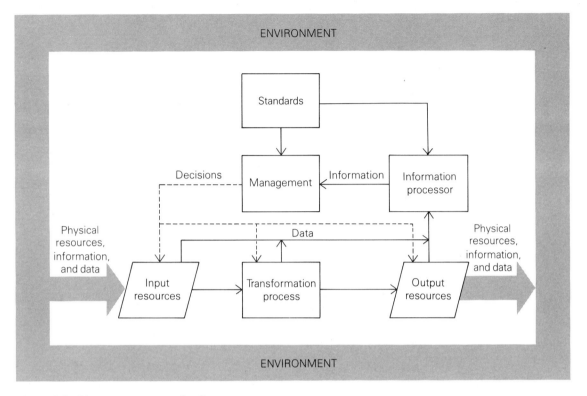

Figure 4-4 The manager sees the firm as a system.

viding research and development funds. In recent years, the *local community* has assumed a larger role in this environmental system. The firm demonstrates its responsibility to this community by using antipollution and safety measures and by supporting charitable and civic programs.

Resource flows connect the firm with these environmental elements. All types of resources flow back and forth, but some flows are more frequent than others. Material flow to customers, money flow to stockholders, machine flow from vendors, and personnel flow from labor are all primary. Other flows such as money flow from the government (for research, for example), material flow to vendors (for returned merchandise), and personnel flow to the competition (for employees "pirated" by other firms) exist on a secondary level.

Not *all* resources flow between the firm and *all* environmental elements. For example, machines normally do not flow from the firm to the stockholders, money should not flow to competitors, and material should not flow to labor. The only resource that connects the firm with all of the elements is information. In most cases the manager strives to expedite the information flow by building an inter-firm information network exclusive of the competition. The manager strives to suppress the flow of information *from* the firm *to* its competitors.

Resource flows are further complicated by the influence that one environmental element can have on another. An element can have an *indirect influence*

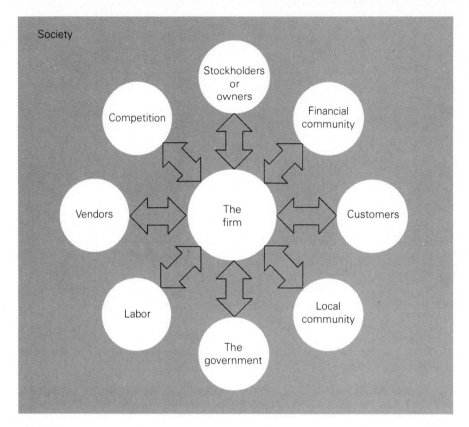

Figure 4-5   Elements in the environment of the firm.

on the firm, often as effective as one of a direct nature. An example is a strike by organized labor against a vendor, resulting in a lack of needed materials. The vendor might have to shut down its manufacturing process. Similar indirect influences involve the competition, the government, the financial community, and the local community.

The idea of the firm as an open system gives special importance to the environment, providing the resources that flow into the firm and accepting the resources that flow from the firm. It is easy to understand, and has long been the attitude, that the firm is at the mercy of its environment. This attitude has been especially easy to adopt as government has grown larger and more powerful, competition has grown keener, and supplies such as energy have grown more scarce. This attitude is *reactive*—the firm must live within the environmental constraints and simply react to them.

Recently, however, more attention has been directed at the firm adopting a *proactive* environmental attitude. This attitude recognizes the ability of a firm to influence its environment. Jay Galbraith calls this new, aggressive approach *envi-*

ronmental management—changing the context in which the firm operates.[3] According to Galbraith, a firm can adopt three basic strategies in influencing its environment. *Independent strategies* are those that the firm can carry out using its own resources so that it can function better in its environment. *Cooperative strategies* involve cooperation with other elements in the environment for the same purpose. *Strategic maneuvering* enables the firm to actually alter its environment.

Carl and Valarie Zeithaml, business professors at Texas A&M, have taken Galbraith's idea of environmental management and shown how the marketing function can play a key role.[4] They list a number of separate strategies under each of Galbraith's three categories, and provide examples. Table 4-2 reproduces a portion of their framework.

It is not difficult to see how an industry giant such as Phillip Morris, General Electric, and 3M can influence its environment. It is more difficult to see how a small, local business can implement the same strategy, but it is possible. The concept of competitive aggression provided by the Zeithamls could be implemented by a firm of any size, for example.

A proactive posture such as environmental management recognizes the importance of the environment to the firm, but encourages the firm to influence its environment positively. This is a new attitude to incorporate into a manager's systems orientation.

3. Identify the firm's subsystems

Once the firm is seen as a system in a larger environmental system, it is next necessary to identify the major system parts of the firm. These parts are the subsystems of the firm, and they can take several forms. The easiest for the manager to see are the *functional areas* of finance, manufacturing, and marketing. Each can be regarded as a separate subsystem. Each subsystem exists on the same level within the firm; one is not superior to the others. This arrangement is shown in Figure 4-6. Each functional subsystem in the figure is illustrated with an input, transformation, and output box, recognizing that each subsystem is in fact a system.

The president of the firm must integrate these subsystems into a single system. To do so the president must think in systems terms. So should the vice presidents in charge of the functional areas.

How are these subsystems integrated or connected? They are connected by the resources that flow through the firm. This is where a systems theory of organization is useful. When the manager can see how resources flow from one functional area to another, he or she can appreciate the need for an integrated system.

---

[3] Jay R. Galbraith, *Organization Design* (Reading, Mass.: Addison-Wesley, 1977), pp. 204–221.

[4] Carl P. and Valarie A. Zeithaml, "Environmental Management: Revising the Marketing Perspective," *Journal of Marketing* 48 (Spring 1984): 46–53.

Table 4-2   Environmental management strategies

Environmental Management Strategy	Definition	Examples
Independent Strategies		
Competitive aggression	Focal organization exploits a distinctive competence or improves internal efficiency of resources for competitive advantage.	Product differentiation. Aggressive pricing. Comparative advertising.
Voluntary action	Voluntary management of and commitment to various interest groups, causes, and social problems.	McGraw-Hill's efforts to prevent sexist stereotypes. 3M's energy conservation program.
Legal action	Company engages in private legal battle with competitor on antitrust, deceptive advertising, or other grounds.	Private antitrust suits brought against competitors.
Political action	Efforts to influence elected representatives to create a more favorable business environment or limit competition.	Corporate constituency programs. Issue advertising. Direct lobbying.
Cooperative Strategies		
Implicit cooperation	Patterned, predictable, and coordinated behaviors.	Price leadership.
Co-optation	Process of absorbing new elements into the leadership or policymaking structure of an organization as a means of averting threats to its stability or existence.	Consumer representatives, women, and bankers on boards of directors.
Coalition	Two or more groups coalesce and act jointly with respect to some set of issues for some period of time.	Industry association. Political initiatives of the Business Roundtable and the U.S. Chamber of Commerce.
Strategic Maneuvering		
Domain selection	Entering industries or markets with limited competition or regulation coupled with ample suppliers and customers; entering high growth markets.	IBM's entry into the personal computer market. Miller Brewing Company's entry into the light beer market.

Table 4-2 Environmental management strategies *(continued)*

Environmental Management Strategy	Definition	Examples
	Strategic Maneuvering	
Diversification	Investing in different types of businesses, manufacturing different types of products, vertical integration, or geographic expansion to reduce dependence on single product, service, market, or technology.	Marriott's investment in different forms of restaurants. General Electric's wide product mix.
Merger & acquisition	Combining two or more firms into a single enterprise; gaining possession of an ongoing enterprise.	Merger between Pan American and National Airlines. Phillip Morris's acquisition of Miller Beer.

Source: Carl. P. Zeithaml and Valarie A. Zeithaml, "Environmental Management: Revising the Marketing Perspective," Journal of Marketing 48 (Spring 1984): 50–51. Reprinted with permission.

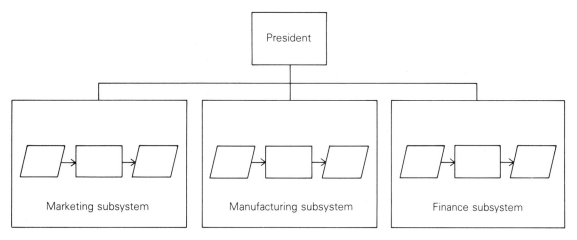

Figure 4-6 Functional subsystems in the firm.

Figure 4-7 shows some of the more important resource flows that connect the subsystems. The numbered paths in the figure are explained as follows:

1. The marketing subsystem gets information from the environment describing needs for products and services.
2. This information is transmitted to the other functional subsystems so that they can determine what the firm must produce if the needs are to be met.
3. The finance subsystem obtains money from the environment and makes

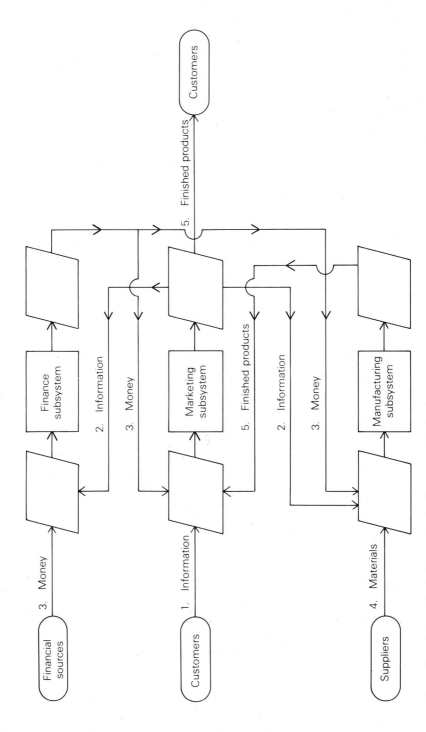

Figure 4-7 Interaction of functional subsystems in the firm.

it available to the manufacturing and marketing subsystems so that they can perform their functions.

4. The manufacturing subsystem transforms raw material resources into finished products.

5. These products are distributed to customers by the marketing subsystem.

The manager also can regard the *levels of management* as subsystems. This concept is pictured in Figure 4-8. Here the subsystems have a superior-subordinate

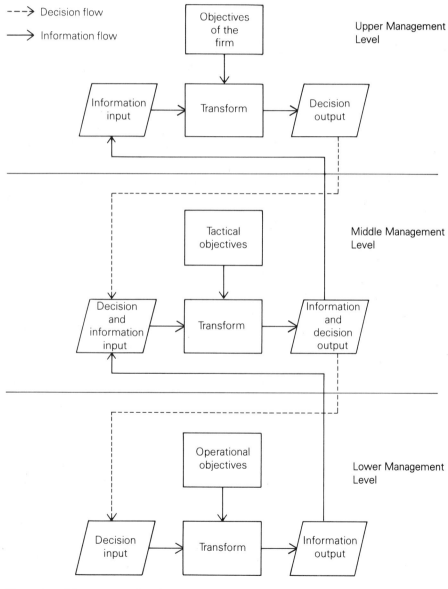

Figure 4-8 Management levels as subsystems.

relationship and are connected by information flows. Top management makes decisions that filter down through the organization. These decisions enable the organization to meet its objectives. Information flows up through the organization from the lower level, where the firm creates the products and services for the environment. When the manager sees the firm arranged in this manner, the importance of information flows is clear. Without these flows, upper-level management is cut off from the physical system of the firm.

Figure 4-8, in its simplified form, fails to illustrate two key points about information flow. First, it is not necessary that the information flow up through the middle level to get to the top level. The top level can get information directly from the lower level. Second, only internal information is shown. Managers on all three levels make use of environmental information as well. The environmental information can enter the firm on any level.

The manager can also use *resource flows* as a basis for dividing the firm into subsystems. These are the resources that we identified in the previous chapter—personnel, materials, machines, money, and information. This approach would require a very strong systems orientation since the firm usually is not organized this way. The manager would have to look beyond the functional structure and isolate the flows. This approach is much easier when the firm has incorporated certain of the flows into the organization structure, such as the establishment of a logistics function.

When a manager can see the firm as a system of subsystems existing within an environment, he or she has a systems orientation. The manager has completed the preparation effort and is ready to use the systems approach in problem solving.

Definition Effort

Most descriptions of the systems approach begin with a step named "define the problem." The logic is sound—you can't solve a problem unless you understand it. *Problem definition* includes two subsidiary actions—problem identification and problem understanding. First, the manager must learn that a problem exists, or may exist in the future. This is *problem identification*. Once the problem is identified, it must be defined in terms of its location and nature. This is *problem understanding,* and it is accomplished by gathering information in some manner—personal interviews, observation, surveys, and data search. In this phase, we describe two procedures that may be followed in defining the problem to be solved.

Before we discuss these procedures, we should recognize that something *triggers* the problem solving. The manager may search for a problem to solve, or the problem may be called to the attention of the manager. The information processor will often call problems to the attention of the manager.

The manager or someone in the manager's unit usually identifies the problem or a symptom. These persons are on the scene, and understand the system. Consequently, they are in a better position to detect difficulties or opportunities than is an information specialist. Once the problem is identified, the manager can call upon the information specialist to assist in problem understanding. The information specialist—the systems analyst—is skilled in converting an ill-defined problem into the specifications of a new or revised system. The systems analyst uses a combination of the information-gathering methods listed above, plus the analysis tools described in the appendices.

4. Proceed from a system to a subsystem level

As the manager attempts to understand how the firm is performing, the analysis should begin with the top system, or supersystem, and proceed level by level to the lower ones. The analysis proceeds from the supersystem to the system and then to the subsystem. This is not a new idea. In his 1910 book, Dewey explained:

> The analytic method is supposed to begin with the physical whole, the solar system or globe, and to work down through its constituent portions till the immediate environment is reached. The underlying conceptions are of physical wholes and physical parts.[5]

The first level to occupy the manager's attention is the *environment*. The manager must know what elements exist within the environment and how they relate to the firm. Emphasis must be placed on what resources are provided and what constraints are imposed by the environment.

Next, the manager studies the position of the *firm* in the environment. Is the system in equilibrium with its environment? Are resources flowing between the firm and its environment in the desired manner? Is the firm meeting its objectives of providing products and services to the environment?

Finally, the manager analyzes the firm in terms of its *subsystems*. Are the subsystems integrated into a smoothly functioning unit? Are all subsystems working toward system goals?

As an example of this approach, assume that you are a top-management consultant, and you have been called in by one of the large U.S. automakers to solve its major problem of low sales. After you shake hands with the chairman of the board to seal the pact, you immediately turn your attention to your client firm's environment. You fully recognize the problem of foreign imports—especially those from Japan. You decide to study an indirect environmental impact— the Japanese automakers' success with U.S. customers.

After you understand the environmental problem, you study your client company, learning about the product line, designs for the future, strengths and weaknesses, and so on. In studying the firm's resources, you look for reasons why sales are low and for strengths that can be expanded. This analysis of the firm leads to a study of the subsystems. You visit car dealers' showrooms and service departments to see firsthand how the firm interacts with its market.

Once you have completed this top-to-bottom study, you assemble your facts and report back to the top with your recommendations. You describe the problem and specify the levels in the system where the problem exists. To complete your

---

[5] Dewey, pp. 114–115.

report, you recommend changes in different subsystems that you believe will correct the problem. The same approach can be followed for any size firm, and for any system level such as a division or a department. The approach can also be followed by managers and systems analysts as well as consultants.

In the past, the manager has relied heavily on systems analysts and consultants to help understand problems. Their help will continue to be used, but it is becoming increasingly important for this work to be done by the manager. The concept of end-user computing is based on the assumption that the user is self-sufficient. This self-sufficiency does not involve simply interacting with a computer. Rather, self-sufficiency implies an ability to do one's own work from the time a problem is identified until it is solved. End user computing or problem solving begins with an analysis of the performance of the highest-level system and progresses to lower-level systems.

5. Analyze system parts in a certain sequence

While on a system level, the manager studies each element of the system in sequence. This analysis begins at the level of the firm as a system. Is the firm meeting its responsibilities to the environment? If not, what part is defective? The analysis proceeds in the sequence shown in Figure 4-9. The steps below correspond to the numbered blocks in the figure.

1. *Evaluate standards*: The performance standards for a firm are usually stated in the form of annual plans, budgets, and quotas. The annual performance is subdivided into the desired performance level by month. As the firm meets these standards, it moves toward the short- and long-term objectives that have been established.

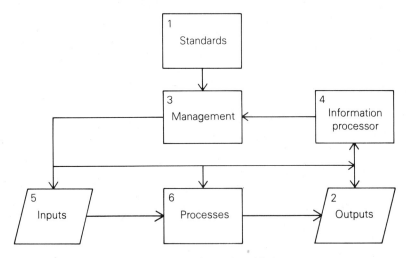

Figure 4-9 Each part of the system is analyzed in sequence.

The standards must have certain characteristics. They must be *valid*. That is, they must be a good measure of system performance. For example, a certain high sales volume may not be a valid standard if the goal of the firm is to achieve a certain level of profitability. Perhaps high profits can be achieved at low sales volumes. The standards also must be *realistic*. A 20% increase in sales is not very realistic if it has never before been achieved and there is nothing to warrant such optimism. Standards must be *understandable* to those who are expected to meet them, and they should be *measurable*. If the standard is "maximum profits," the manager never knows whether the standard has been achieved. "Realize a profit of 10% of sales" is the type of standard that leaves no doubt about its degree of attainment.

2. *Compare output with standards*: Once the manager is satisfied with the standards, he or she next evaluates the performance of the firm. The output of the firm is compared with the standards.

   If the firm is meeting its standards, there is no need to continue with the systems approach to problem solving. There is no problem to solve. The manager can reevaluate the standards in the light of good current performance. Perhaps the performance level can be increased in the future.

   If the firm is not meeting its standards—in all or in part— the manager must identify the cause or causes. A problem exists that must be solved. The remaining system elements are possible locations of the problem or problems.

3. *Evaluate management*: A critical appraisal is made of the firm's management. Are there adequate numbers of managers in the different areas and on the different levels? The signals that indicate this to be a problem are (1) managers working excessively long hours and (2) projects that never get completed.

   The quality of the management team also must pass inspection. Do the managers have the skills and experience needed to perform their duties? Errors in judgment, excessive costs, and high employee turnover are signals that management quality might not be satisfactory. A good knowledge of management theory is valuable in this part of the analysis.

4. *Evaluate the information processor*: It is possible that a good management team is present, but the team is simply not getting the information that it needs. If this is the case, the needs must be identified and an adequate information system must be designed and implemented.

   The question could be asked "Doesn't a poor information processor indicate poor management?" It is possible that the managers simply have not had time to devote to their information processor. Perhaps things have been going so well that the information processor has been continually shoved to the background. This is a much healthier situation than one of poor management. The information processor problem is much easier to solve than the poor management problem.

   There is one point that you should not overlook as we proceed with this element-by-element analysis. With the exception of the system's output, the analysis begins with the *conceptual* elements of the system—standards, management, and information processor. These are yardsticks to use in determining whether the *physical* elements are performing as they should. Information management strives to achieve a high performance level of the conceptual elements, whereas management of the physical resources aims at the input, transformation, and output elements.

5. *Evaluate the firm's input resources*: When this level of the system analysis is reached, the adequacy of the management and information processor resources are no longer a question. But what about the rest of the resources? Does the firm have the right number of workers, and do they have the right skills? And what about the machine and material resources? Are they adequate? What about money? Is there enough available for the firm to obtain the physical resources that it needs to meet its objectives?

   Some compromise may be necessary here. Some resources may not exist in the quantities and qualities desired. Even if this is true, the limitations may be overcome through good management of available resources. If good management cannot solve the resource problem, then the manager should start over with step 1 and reevaluate the standards. Some realistic standards must be adopted.

   At this point, the organizational structure of the firm can also be assessed. Has management assembled the resources effectively? Are the resources functioning as an efficient physical system? A good knowledge or organization theory facilitates this portion of the analysis.

6. *Evaluate the transformation process*: It is possible that the problem lies within the physical system—how the resources are used. Inefficient procedures and practices might be the cause. Automation, robotics, and computer-aided design and computer-aided manufacturing (CAD/CAM) are all examples of efforts to make the transformation process more efficient, effective, and economical.

If the analysis of the firm as a system indicates problems, they will probably be solved on the subsystem level. It is then necessary to analyze selected subsystems in the same manner that the firm was studied.

Take, for example, a firm that is having problems with a new product. The information system reports that too many products are being returned by customers because of defective parts. An evaluation of the transformation process indicates sloppy production work. The manager then shifts attention to the manufacturing subsystem of the firm. Each of the elements of the manufacturing subsystem is examined in the same sequence as the overall firm. The sequence in Figure 4-9 is followed on successively lower levels until the cause of the problem is found.

Let's pause and review our progress. After adopting a systems way of thinking, something triggered a problem-solving process. We examined the firm in its environment by starting at the top system level and working down. This is a *vertical analysis*. On each level, we studied the elements of that system in a certain sequence. This is a *horizontal analysis*.

Figure 4-10 shows this vertical and horizontal process. The analysis starts with the top system level—that of the firm—and proceeds from one system element to another. As soon as the problem element is identified, the analysis drops to the next lower system level. That level is analyzed, element by element, and the problem element on that level is identified. If necessary, the analysis drops to still lower system levels.

As Figure 4-11 shows, it is unnecessary to analyze all six elements on each level. As soon as the problem element is identified, attention is focused on that element by studying it on a lower system level. For example, assume that a firm's top management is alerted to the fact that the firm is not meeting its annual sales standards. The firm is below quota each month. Hence the output of the firm is not up to standard. The next system element, management, is studied and determined to be deficient. There is no need at this point to continue with the analysis on the firm level, as the subsequent elements are of a lower priority. We follow the priority sequence on each level, studying the most important elements first.

The problem element (in this case, management) must be understood once it is identified. The nature of the management deficiency must be explored. Perhaps you learn that a high turnover of managers in the marketing division has kept the firm from meeting its standards. The analysis turns to the marketing division to learn more about the problem.

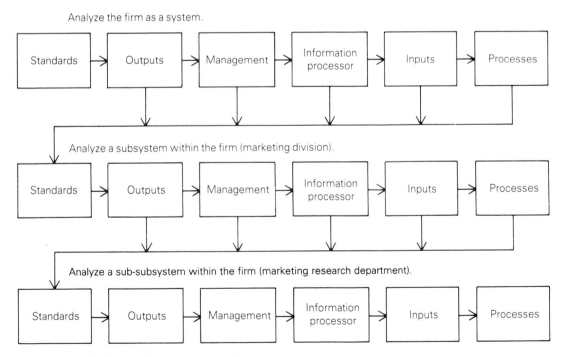

Figure 4-10 Vertical and horizontal analysis process.

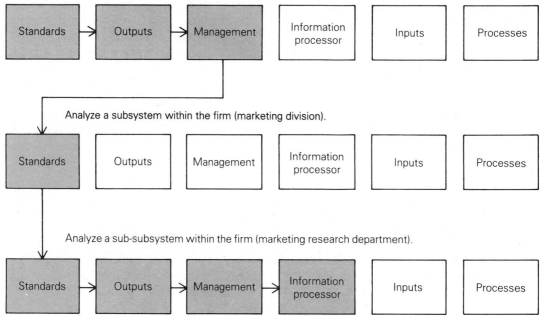

Figure 4-11   The systems approach provides the path to problem identification.

In analyzing the marketing system, you learn that managers have been leaving the firm because they felt that the annual sales quotas were unreasonable. The problem lies within the standards established for marketing management. Continued study of the problem on the marketing level discovers that the primary reason for the unrealistic quotas is a poorly functioning marketing research department. The department is not doing a good job of measuring the market potential that the managers should be expected to achieve.

Analysis next drops to the lower system level—the marketing research department—and its elements are analyzed. You learn that the problem in the marketing research department is an inadequate information processor. The firm has a computer, but the marketing research routines need improving. You can now direct your attention toward solving the problem.

The signals received at the higher system levels—low sales, deficient management, high management turnover, and poor quotas—were only symptoms of the problem: a poor marketing research information processor. Usually the symptoms appear first, and the manager must trace the symptoms to the problem. The systems approach provides the path for the manager to follow.

The procedure that we followed in this example is one of problem identification and understanding. Management became aware of a problem (problem identification) by comparing performance to quota for the firm as a system. When a problem was signaled, management learned more about it (problem understanding) by analyzing system elements in sequence on successively lower levels.

One of the most important tasks facing the manager is problem definition. Mintzberg calls this step *diagnosis* and says that it "seems to be the crucial step in strategic decision making, for it is in that routine that the whole course of decision making is set."[6] Once the manager understands the problem, it can be solved.

Solution Effort

Solution effort involves a consideration of the feasible alternatives, a selection of the best, and its implementation.

6. Identify the alternatives

The manager seeks to identify *different* ways to solve the *same* problem. As a general rule, this is easier for the experienced manager; the manager recalls solutions that have worked (or have not worked) in the past. Experience is not the only key, however, as creativity and intuition identify completely new solutions.

As an example of how alternate solutions are identified, assume that the problem is a computer that cannot handle the increasing volume of transactions. Three alternatives might exist: (1) add more devices to the existing computer to increase its capacity and speed, (2) replace the existing computer with a larger computer, (3) replace the existing computer with a network of smaller computers that work together as a unit.

7. Evaluate the alternatives

Once the alternatives have been identified, they must be compared in terms of how well they enable the firm to meet its objectives.

It is necessary to consider both the *advantages* and *disadvantages* of each alternative. It is rare when an alternative has no disadvantages. Table 4-3 shows how the three computer alternatives are compared. It is common to identify several *evaluation criteria,* and to consider how well each alternative meets these criteria. The criteria in the example relate to cost of operation, user training, responsiveness, data security, and ability to adapt to changing user needs. The manner in which each alternative measures up to the criteria provides the advantages and disadvantages of implementing that alternative as a problem solution.

You should understand two points relative to the example in Table 4-3. First, the evaluation criteria will vary from one situation to the next. The five criteria used here are for illustration only. Second, it is best to evaluate the alternatives quantitatively when possible. For example, it would be better to state for alternative 1: "The operating costs will be $53,800 per month" than to state "small increase." The quantitative measure makes the evaluation easier. Of course, you

---

[6] Henry Mintzberg, "Planning on the Left Side and Managing on the Right," *Harvard Business Review* 54 (July–August 1976): 55.

Table 4-3 Comparison of advantages and disadvantages of the alternatives

	Alternative 1: *Upgrade existing system*	*Alternative 2:* *Install larger system*	*Alternative 3:* *Install microcomputer network*
Advantages	1. Small increase in cost of operation 2. No user training required 3. Provides maximum data security	1. Very responsive to information requests 2. Good data security 3. Easily adaptable to changing user needs	1. Slight decrease in cost of operation 2. Slightly adaptable to changing user needs
Disadvantages	1. Moderately responsive to information requests 2. Not easily adaptable to changing user needs	1. Large increase in cost of operation 2. Much user training required	1. Some user training required 2. Only moderately responsive to information requests 3. Presents data security problems

must have good supporting data for the quantitative evaluations, and the data is not always available.

8. Select the best alternative

Mintzberg identified three ways that managers go about selecting the best alternative:

1. analysis—systematic evaluation of options, considering their consequences on the organization's goals.
2. judgment—mental process of a single manager.
3. bargaining—negotiations between several managers.[7]

As we study the systems approach, we emphasize the analysis. We should not lose sight of judgment and bargaining also being used.

9. Implement the solution

The problem is not solved when the best solution is selected. It is necessary to implement the solution. In our example, it would be necessary to install the required computing equipment.

10. Follow up to assure that the solution is effective

Simply making the implementation is not sufficient. The manager should follow up to make certain that the solution achieves the planned performance. Perhaps

---

[7] Ibid., p. 55.

the solution was supposed to show a decreased cost of operations but the decrease has never materialized. It then becomes necessary to look into the situation to identify the cause of variance from the anticipated results. The manager therefore sticks with the solution until she or he is certain that the problem has been solved.

Review of the Systems Approach

We have identified several elements, or characteristics, of the systems approach. Although it is not difficult to understand each one separately, effectively fitting them together requires some effort. Managers develop this integrative skill through experience.

A good starting point is the *preparation effort* that the manager should expend before problem solving begins. The manager should see the firm as a system residing within a larger environmental system and consisting of several subsystems. This orientation represents the outer ring in Figure 4-12. Now the manager is ready to look for a problem, or to respond to one if it presents itself.

The manager defines problems by proceeding from system to subsystem, and by analyzing system parts in a certain sequence. Together these activities constitute *definition effort* in the upper circle in Figure 4-12.

Once the problem has been defined, it can be solved by following the remaining five steps of the systems approach, as illustrated in the lower circle of the figure—the *solution effort*.

The Computer and the Systems Approach

The computer should serve as a decision support system—supporting the manager at each step of the systems approach. The support is in the form of computations and information necessary to the solution process.

It is easier for the computer to support some steps than others. The steps involving programmed decisions can be performed well, but the steps involving nonprogrammed decisions do not receive as much support. The steps that the computer supports the best are those of the definition effort where the computer provides problem signals, and provides information useful to pinning down the problem to a particular system level or part.

The computer support is less for the solution effort. The manager usually has to identify the alternatives, but, once identified, the computer can produce information to be used in the evaluation. The manager has to select the best solution and implement it. Once implemented, the computer can inform the manager whether the solution is performing as intended.

The computer is a tool that can support the manager in problem solving. The MIS-literate manager can make use of the tool but will have to supplement it with knowledge, creativity, and logic in taking several of the steps.

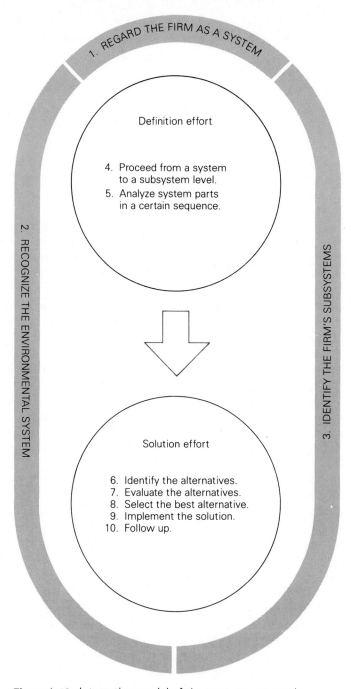

Figure 4-12 Integrative model of the systems approach.

Examples of the Systems Approach

Let's look again at the three types of organizations described in the previous chapter—a football team, a law firm, and a newspaper publisher. We will describe how each organization's management can use the systems approach to understand and solve a problem that is having a negative effect on the firm.

A football team

Assume that a four-year college has just hired a new head football coach. He must decide if he has any problems. If he thinks in systems terms, he views his squad as a system, composed of subsystems, existing in a larger environment. The subsystems are offensive players, defensive players, and specialty players (kickers, returners, and so on). The environment consists of the team's athletic conference.

The coach remembers the last words of the chancellor as he signed his one-year contract: "Win the championship next year, or else." He knows what his *standards* are. He must somehow raise the quality of the output to championship caliber in one year. He starts with the team's *output* and reviews the past won-lost record. Last year it was 2–9. The year before that it was 0–11. Now he's beginning to understand why the school changed coaches. The previous teams were not meeting their standards.

The team's *management* is the next focus. The new coach was able to select his own staff of assistants, and he got the people that he wanted. He is confident that he has the right leadership. He is also satisfied with the quality of his *information processor*. His assistant coaches have proven abilities for preparing team scouting reports, and serving as observers in the pressbox.

What about *input resources*? Looking at the files on the team members, he notices very few highly recruited high-school players. His team is composed mainly of players that nobody else wanted. Here is a problem. The team has inadequate input resources. The coach drops down to the subsystem level to learn more about this personnel shortage. He reviews last season's game films and sees that most of the losses were caused primarily by a poor kicking game. The team needs a better kicker. This completes the problem definition phase. Now, the coach must start solving the problem.

The coach *identifies the alternatives*. He can develop the kicking ability of a player already on the squad. He can recruit a graduating high-school kicker. Or he can recruit a graduating junior-college kicker. He *evaluates the alternatives*, looking at the advantages and disadvantages of each. He remembers what the chancellor said about next year, and decides to *select the alternative* of recruiting the junior-college kicker since that alternative offers the best chance for a quick solution. He *implements the solution* by signing an All-American junior-college kicker. He has to wait a while to *follow up on the solution*—until the end of the coming season. If his team meets its standards, he will know that he made the right decisions. If he must look for another job, he will be a lot more experienced the next time a kicking problem arises.

A law firm

Our firm consists of three partners, two secretaries, a part-time bookkeeper, and a part-time researcher (a law school student). The founder of the firm (one of the partners) has become increasingly concerned about the firm's financial condition. The loss of a highly publicized case last year seems to have affected the firm's image, and several clients have switched to other firms.

The founder reviews the past year's trial record and sees too many lost cases. This *output* is unacceptable, even though no specific *standards* exist for the percentage of cases that should be won. The founder is satisfied, however, with the firm's standards. He and the other partners have agreed on the importance of an image of being winners.

Since the partners also serve as lawyers, they represent the *management* and an important *input resource*. The founder believes that the partners are good managers, but as lawyers they often have difficulty with certain types of cases. For example, one lawyer took on a trademark infringement case even though he had little background in business law. He lost the case, and the client company was critical of the counsel that they had received.

The problem does not seem to involve an inadequate *information processor*. The part-time researcher and one of the secretaries have performed good research. There is no evidence that better information would have made a difference in the firm's past performance.

The legal staff appears to be inadequate to their task. The firm is spread too thin—cases are taken on without reference to the lawyers' abilities. The standards are too ambitious for the resources. The problem of unreasonable standards is reflected in the symptoms: a poor financial condition, a tarnished image, a low client load, lost clients, lost cases, and difficulty with certain kinds of cases.

The partners discuss the founder's conclusions and agree that the firm should have a more central focus. They decide that the firm should select some type of law and specialize in it. There are not enough resources to be all things to all clients. While the *standards* at first appeared satisfactory, a comparison with the resources indicates the need to rethink what the firm is attempting to accomplish.

The firm selects criminal law as its specialty, and the standards are revised to focus on the new area.

In this example the firm is so small that the analysis can be performed without studying subsystems. The systems approach is applied to fit the unique characteristics of the system under study.

A newspaper publisher

The *Rapid City Herald* has been gradually losing its market leadership to its crosstown rival, the *Rapid City Bugle*. After reviewing the *Herald*'s annual financial report, the board of directors hired a marketing research firm to survey area readers and find out how each of the two papers is perceived.

The survey of the *environment* revealed a conservative and mature, yet old-fashioned and boring, image of the *Herald*. The *Herald* appeals to an older market, whereas the *Bugle* is seen as youthful, fresh, and exciting. *Herald* readers most enjoyed the column on needlepoint and the series on Medicare.

The problem is that management has been out of touch with market needs. The image of the *Herald* must change, but more importantly, steps must be taken to ensure that management doesn't again lose contact. The MIS can help keep the managers informed.

When the board meets to decide on the solution, one member recommends a column on vacation spots for swingers, but it is voted down as being too piecemeal. The chairman of the board, just back from an American Management Association conference on decision making, suggests that they follow the systems approach. The other members agree to try.

The board forms a project team, consisting of the president and the four vice presidents, to apply the approach. The team examines each element in the system of the firm in sequence. The *standards* are restated by dividing the market into submarkets based on age, income, and ethnic origin. Specific standards are established for each group. The *management* team is evaluated as strong and competent. The *information system,* however, is almost nonexistent. The computer has been used almost solely for typesetting, and generates no worthwhile management reports. The team decides to reorganize the data processing organization—moving it from a department within the controller's division to separate divisional status. The director of data processing is told that if she can develop an effective MIS during the next two years, she will be promoted to vice president.

The MIS is to be used to provide management with environmental information. Annual readership surveys will be conducted, and economic and demographic (age, income, education, and so on) statistics will be maintained in the data base. Management intends to use the MIS to do a better job of keeping in touch with its market. A new set of standards, a revised organizational structure, and new plans for using the computer as part of an MIS are expected to solve the problem.

In this example, the analysis began at the appropriate level—the environment. The marketing researchers gathered data for a better understanding of environmental relationships. The management could identify the problem on the environmental level without studying the firm as a system. They directed their attention to the problem's solution and evaluated the elements of the firm as a system. For each element they asked, "How can this element contribute to a better understanding of environmental needs?"

The application of the systems approach to each of the three examples above has been quite different. The systems approach is simply an organized problem-solving format. It does not guarantee success. *How* it is used is the key. The manager must use the technique with skill and imagination.

Personal Factors Influencing Problem Solving

Throughout this book, we paint a picture of a manager who aggressively seeks out problems to solve. That seems to be the way things should work. In actual practice, however, all managers do not adopt such an aggressive posture. It may not be their nature, and they may not have time.

Each manager has a unique decision-making or cognitive style. Three dimensions appear to provide an opportunity for individual differences among managers. These dimensions are their problem-sensing styles, their information-gathering styles, and their information-using styles.[8]

Managers fall into three basic categories in terms of their *problem-sensing styles*:

- *Problem avoider*—The manager who takes a positive attitude and assumes that everything is fine. An effort is made to block out the possibility of problems by ignoring information or avoiding thorough planning.
- *Problem solver*—The manager who neither looks for problems nor blocks them out. If a problem arises, it gets solved.
- *Problem seeker*—Here is our aggressive manager.

In addition to the differences in how managers sense problems, there are differences in how they develop and evaluate alternatives. Managers can exhibit one of two *information-gathering styles*—their attitude toward the total volume of information available to them:

- *Preceptive style*—The manager adheres to management by exception and screens out everything not meeting certain criteria, such as relevance to his or her area of responsibility.
- *Receptive style*—The manager wants to look at everything and then determine its meaning. This style is illustrated by the chief executive officer (CEO) who said, "Your staff really can't help you think. The problem with giving a question to the staff is that they provide you with the answer. You learn the nature of the real question you should have asked when you muck around in the data."[9]

Managers also tend to favor one of two different *information-using styles*—the way that they use information to solve a problem:

- *Systematic style*—The manager pays particular attention to following a prescribed method of problem solving, such as the systems approach.
- *Intuitive style*—The manager does not favor any certain method, but rather uses the approach that seems suited to the situation.

It is important to recognize these individual differences. All too often the MIS is described with statements that supposedly apply to all managers. State-

---

[8] The information-gathering and information-using styles were first presented by James L. McKenney and Peter G. W. Keen, "How Managers' Minds Work," *Harvard Business Review* 52 (May–June 1974): 79–90. Andrew D. Szilagyi, Jr. added the problem-sensing style in *Management and Performance* (Santa Monica: Goodyear Publishing Co., 1981), pp. 220–225.

[9] John F. Rockart and Michael E. Treacy, "The CEO Goes On-Line," *Harvard Business Review* 60 (January–February 1982): 86.

ments such as "Upper-level managers use summarized information" probably hold true *most* of the time but not all of the time. The most important element in the MIS is the manager, and he or she is only human. No two are exactly alike, and they use the MIS in different ways.

The Role of Intuition

In this chapter we have emphasized the systematic approach to problem solving. There is increasing support for a less formal view—one including intuition. We have attempted to incorporate this new thinking into our description by recognizing the limitations of the computer and the nonprogrammed nature of many of the decisions.

What is intuition?

Intuition is a way of venturing into an unknown area and sensing the problems and opportunities that may not be readily apparent. It is a subset of logical thinking where the steps of the process are hidden in the subconscious.[10]

Brain style in management

Much of the attention aimed at management intuition has recognized differences in how the left and right sides of the brain function. In addition to controlling parts of the body (the left side of the brain controls the right side of the body, and vice versa), the sides of the brain control certain thought processes.

The left side of most people's brains is where logical thought processes are found. Data is processed sequentially, such as the decoding of spoken language. The right side is where thought processes are intuitive. Data is processed in parallel—multiple pieces at a time. A good example is the way we perceive visual images, such as graphs.

The systems approach that we have described is an example of "left-brain thinking." Weston H. Agor, a professor at the University of Texas at El Paso, has tested over 2,000 managers, and has found top-level managers, female managers, and managers with Asian backgrounds to be most adept at using intuition.

Agor suggests the following strategy for a manager to follow in developing intuitive skills:

1. Believe in it.
2. Practice it.
3. Create a supportive personal and organizational environment in which intuitive skills are valued and applied in day-to-day life to make decisions.

---

[10] Taken from definitions offered by Weston H. Agor, "Using Intuition to Manage Organizations in the Future," *Business Horizons* 27 (July–August 1984): 51.

Henry Mintzberg has concluded that brain processes might be the explanation for the behavior exhibited by the five executives that he studied. He believes that managers use both sides of the brain, but right-side, intuitive processes are most important at the top level. Mintzberg recommends that managers use left-brain processes (systematic analysis) while planning, and use right-brain processes (intuition) while carrying out the plan.

DSS Integrates Analysis and Intuition

Agor cites the failure of many left-side strategies as the reason for current interest in intuition. Perhaps he is referring to early MIS efforts more than recent DSS designs. The DSS concept assumes an interaction between the manager and the decision support systems—usually a computer. The computer handles the structured part of the problem, and the manager handles the unstructured part. The DSS therefore supports the manager's analytic processes while the manager fills in the gaps with intuition. The DSS concept is compatible with the idea that intuition is a key ingredient in problem solving.

Summary

The conceptual information system is a problem-solving system consisting of the manager, information, and standards. Other elements enter into the problem-solving process—solution criteria, constraints, and alternate solutions.

A popular way to classify problems is to place them on a continuum ranging from structured to unstructured. The computer can solve structured problems, the manager must solve the unstructured problems, and the manager and computer working together can solve the semistructured problems. The semistructured area is the target of the DSS concept.

Modeled after the scientific method, the systems approach is used in business to solve problems. Most definitions of the systems approach include a series of seven steps from problem definition to implementation and follow-up.

The systems approach requires decision making at each step. The MIS can support the manager by providing information for each decision. The steps of the systems approach provide a bridge between a single problem and the multiple decisions needed to solve it. A single DSS can support the manager in solving a manageable problem; larger problems require more than one DSS.

In addition to the steps, the systems approach requires that the manager regard the firm as a system, recognize the environmental system, and identify subsystems in the firm. These are all orientations that the manager should adopt before a problem arises. While looking for the source of a problem and understanding it, the manager proceeds from system to subsystem level and analyzes the parts in a certain sequence. Once the problem has been defined, the manager evaluates the various alternatives before selecting and implementing the best.

The systems approach is a general method, applicable to any type of organization. We used the systems approach to identify a problem of inadequate input resources for a football team, unreasonable standards for a law firm, and a non-existent information processor for a newspaper publisher. The systems approach is not an inflexible procedure, but rather a guideline adaptable to specific decision-making situations.

Descriptions of decision making and decision makers frequently overlook exceptions to the rule. Personal factors create three basic problem-sensing styles—problem avoiders, solvers, and seekers. Managers also differ in how they gather information (preceptive and receptive), and how they use the information to solve problems (systematic and intuitive).

The way that managers use the sides of their brains may help explain management behavior. Managers, especially those on the top level, have demonstrated a preference for information coming from informal systems in contrast to the structured information provided by the computer. Designers of information systems should be aware of personal differences and the need for informal systems and subjective processes.

We have now completed the theory part of our study of the MIS. This theory will provide a solid foundation as we proceed to study the computing equipment that can be used in an MIS, the various types of MIS software, information subsystems, and the MIS life cycle. The remaining chapters will reveal *what* is happening in MIS. The theory will help us understand *why*.

Key Terms

---

problem solving

problem

decision

decision making

desired state, current state

solution criterion

internal constraint, environmental constraint

symptom

structured problem, unstructured problem, semistructured problem

scientific method

systems approach

preparation effort

environmental system

indirect environmental influence

reactive, proactive environmental attitude

environmental management

definition effort

problem definition, problem identification, problem understanding

problem trigger

vertical analysis, horizontal analysis

solution effort

evaluation criteria

cognitive style

problem-sensing style

problem avoider, problem solver, problem seeker

information-gathering style

preceptive style, receptive style

information-using style

systematic style, intuitive style

intuition

Key Concepts

The elements that must be present to solve a problem

Problems versus symptoms

The varying degrees of problem structure and how they relate to the DSS concept

The logical nature of the systems approach as a problem-solving tool

The multiple decisions needed to solve a single problem

The relationship between the problem, the systems approach, and the DSS

How to gain a systems orientation

How a firm can influence its environment

How the elements of the environment form a supersystem

The flow of resources between environmental elements, and between subsystems of the firm

The separation of the problem-solving process into definition effort and solution effort

The systematic way that system levels and elements can be analyzed

Individual differences in problem-solving styles

The importance of intuition in problem solving, and how the DSS concept incorporates both intuition and analysis

Questions

1. What are the elements of the problem-solving process? Which of these elements also appear in the general systems model of the firm?

2. What type of problem, if any, is the DSS intended to solve?

3. List the seven traditional steps of the systems approach.

4. What are the three phases of effort in applying the systems approach?

5. What steps are included in the first phase?

6. What is the difference between a reactive and a proactive attitude toward the environment? Which attitude is reflected in environmental management?

7. What steps are included in the second phase of the systems approach?

8. List the elements of a system in the order in which they are analyzed.

9. List four desired characteristics of standards.

10. Distinguish between horizontal and vertical analysis.

11. What steps are included in the third phase of the systems approach?

12. What are the three ways of selecting the best alternative, according to Mintzberg?

13. Which steps of the systems approach (definition and solution effort) receive strong support from the computer? Which steps do not receive strong support?

14. Could a good MIS conceivably change a problem solver into a problem seeker? Explain your reasoning.

15. In what ways could an MIS support a manager who has a receptive style of information gathering?

16. Can you see any relationship between information-using style (systematic versus intuitive) and degree of managerial experience? Explain.

17. What types of thought processes does the left side of the brain control? The right side?

18. Which side of the brain does Mintzberg recommend that the manager use in planning? In executing the plan?

19. What three strategies does Agor suggest for developing intuitive skills?

20. How does the DSS concept incorporate both analysis and intuition?

Problems

1. Assume that you are going to use the systems approach in buying a car. Make a list of the evaluation criteria that you would use.

2. Make a list of questions that you would ask a manager in order to categorize her or him as a problem avoider/solver/seeker, preceptive/receptive gatherer, and systematic/intuitive user.

CASE PROBLEM: Far East Imports

Far East Imports is a 140-store retail chain with annual sales of $250 million. Headquartered in Oakland, California, the chain specializes in low-cost, imported goods such as rugs, chairs, glassware, and clothing.

Bob Crump, the president, likes to review computer reports before visiting the stores. He spends much of his time on these tours, talking with the store personnel. The tours build company morale by demonstrating that the president really cares about the employees, and the tours also allow Bob to keep in touch with what is going on.

Far East has one large computer at its corporate headquarters, plus medium-sized computers at its warehouses in San Francisco, Denver, and Trenton, New Jersey. Also, there are many microcomputers scattered throughout the company.

Bob receives about 15 periodic reports from the computer—some weekly and some monthly. He has a file cabinet behind his desk, and his secretary files the most current version of each report in the cabinet so that Bob can have easy access.

Bob has been trying to get a new report prepared but has not been able to get any help from the MIS department. The MIS department has been very busy implementing a new inventory system and has not taken on any new jobs during the past 8 months. As a result, there is a backlog of jobs, such as Bob's, to be put on the computer. Bob knows that he could apply pressure and get his report, but he wants the inventory system to be implemented on schedule. He has decided to be patient.

He calls the new report his "dogs" report. It would list those items that are not selling well. Armed with such information before going on a tour, Bob could ask the store personnel why specific items are not selling. "If anybody knows why items don't sell, it's the store personnel," Bob reasons.

Perhaps the most difficult part of the Far East operation is the source of supply. Most of the items are imported from the Orient, and it often takes months to receive an order. This long lead time requires Far East to place an order well in advance of the needed delivery date. This situation makes the ordering decision very critical. If the buyers don't order enough, the firm loses sales. If the buyers order too much or order the wrong items, Far East is stuck with the dogs.

Bob is very pleased with his firm's operations. Sales are going according to the long-range plan, and his in-house management training program is showing good results. Each executive must spend three days in a store each year to maintain the same closeness with the operation that Bob receives from his tours.

One day Bob's wife drops by his office for lunch. She is the buyer for a line of ethnic clothing that was recently added. Over lunch, the conversation turns to her job. She tells Bob that it is time to place orders for next year's shipments, and she is very nervous. She is not certain what styles and what quantities to order. "If I only had some good information . . ." she explains. "With so little experience on this job, I don't know what is selling well and what is not." Bob tries to console her by telling her that he is in the same situation, but that things will get better.

Questions

1. Are there any problems at Far East relating to their objectives or standards? Explain.
2. What about the output? Explain.
3. What about management? Explain.
4. What about the information processor? Explain.
5. What is the basic problem? What are symptoms of the problem?
6. Name three possible solutions.
7. Which solution do you recommend? Briefly explain why.

CASE PROBLEM: Micro-Scan Corp.

By age 35, Herb Thomas had amassed a fortune through shrewd deals in the stock market. A finance major in college, he developed a "system" for knowing when to buy and sell. His college roommate, Bill Simpson, an engineering major, wrote a program to perform the logical analysis that Herb had devised. Herb used the program to speed up his investment decisions.

Everything went so well for Herb after college that life was no longer a challenge. One Saturday morning, while having a cup of coffee at the country club, who should walk in but Bill Simpson. It had been years since they last saw each other, and each brought the other up to date on his career. Bill explained that he had developed an electronic device that could read data into a computer from microfilm. The more Bill described his invention, the more interested Herb became. Before they left the club, they agreed to form a company to manufacture the reader. Herb would put up the money, and Bill would provide the product.

The first three years of operations exceeded the owners' highest expectations, although they had set no specific goals. A key order came in from a large oil company, and the dominoes began to fall. By the end of the fifth year, virtually every major oil company was a user. The reader seemed perfectly tailored to the credit card processing most oil companies performed.

At this point, Bill suggested that the firm get its own computer. He sought to convince Herb that Micro-Scan had outgrown its manual system. With 500 employees and sales hovering at the $25 million mark, Bill saw the need to computerize. Herb, however, was a firm believer in the service bureau approach— letting someone else do the processing for a monthly fee. "That way, they have all of the problems," he said. Herb convinced Bill that the service bureau route was the way to go, and they decided to start with some basic accounting applications—inventory, payroll, billing, and accounts receivable.

Shortly after the service bureau arrangement had begun, company sales began to slip. The oil company market had been saturated, and nobody else was buying. Herb and Bill attempted to make inroads into the banking industry, but bankers had no interest in microfilm reading. Similar attempts to enter the retailing, insurance, and government markets also ended in failure. Within a year, a third of the work force was laid off, and Herb and Bill were forced to sell much of their stock in order to avoid bankruptcy. The stock was bought by Pacific Investors, which became the majority stockholder.

The first thing Pacific did was to replace Herb as president with one of their own executives, Lisa Tanaka. Herb was named executive vice president, and Bill kept his title of chief scientist.

On Lisa's first day, she called Herb and Bill into her office and explained that she wanted to make a complete reappraisal of the firm, its products, its market, and its future. A new start was needed, and Pacific was looking to her to get Micro-Scan moving again. After listening intently, Bill asked "And just how do you plan to solve our problems?" To which Lisa replied, "With the systems approach, of course."

Questions

1. What will Lisa study first as she applies the systems approach? Is there a problem there?

2. Which part of the Micro-Scan system is defective? Explain why.

3. What symptoms could Herb and Bill have used to lead them to the problem?

4. How do you think Lisa will solve the problem?

Selected Bibliography

The Systems Approach

Agor, Weston H., "Using Intuition to Manage Organizations in the Future," *Business Horizons* 27 (July-August 1984): 49–54.

Dewey, John, *How We Think* (New York: D. C. Heath & Company, 1910), pp. 101–115.

Doyle, James R., and Jack D. Becker, "Computer Assisted Planning (CAP) at Dinero International Bancorporation," *MIS Quarterly* 7 (September 1983): 33–46.

Galbraith, Jay R., *Organization Design* (Reading, Mass.: Addison-Wesley, 1977), pp. 204–221.

Huber, George P., "Cognitive Style as a Basis for MIS and DSS Designs: Much Ado About Nothing?," *Management Science* 29 (May 1983): 567–597.

Johnson, Richard A., Fremont E. Kast, and James E. Rosenzweig, *The Theory and Management of Systems*, 2nd ed. (New York: McGraw-Hill, 1967), pp. 280–282.

McGinnis, Michael A., "The Key to Strategic Planning: Integrating Analysis and Intuition," *Sloan Management Review* 26 (Fall 1984): 45–52.

McKenney, James L., and Peter G. W. Keen, "How Managers' Minds Work," *Harvard Business Review* 52 (May-June 1974): 79–90.

Martin, Merle P., "Problem Identification," *Journal of Systems Management* 28 (December 1977): 10–15.

Martin, Merle P., "Problem Identification Indicators," *Journal of Systems Management* 29 (September 1978): 36–39.

Mintzberg, Henry, "Planning on the Left Side and Managing on the Right," *Harvard Business Review* 54 (July-August 1976): 49–58.

Mosard, Gil, "Problem Definition: Tasks and Techniques," *Journal of Systems Management*, 34 (June 1983): 16–21.

Robey, Daniel, and William Taggart, "Human Information Processing in Information and Decision Support Systems," *MIS Quarterly* 6 (June 1982): 61–73.

Schoderbek, Peter P., Charles G. Schoderbek, and Asterios G. Kefalas, *Management Systems: Conceptual Considerations*, 3rd ed. (Plano, Texas: Business Publications, 1985), pp. 259–283.

Simon, Herbert A., *The New Science of Management Decision* (New York: Harper & Brothers, 1960), pp. 54ff.

Zeithaml, Carl P., and Valarie A. Zeithaml, "Environmental Management: Revising the Marketing Perspective," *Journal of Marketing* 48 (Spring 1984): 46–53.

Part Three

THE INFORMATION PROCESSOR

We recognized earlier that a firm need not have a computer to have an information system. Most of the material presented in the first four chapters applies to any kind of information system, whether it be manual, keydriven machine, or computer. This book deals mainly with computer-based management information systems, and the computer plays an important role in the remainder of the chapters. However, we must not lose sight of the fact that *the computer does not play the most important role. That role must be played by the manager.* The manager not only uses the information output but also participates in the design and implementation of the system.

The primary objective of this part of the book is to provide the future manager with a working knowledge of computer hardware and software fundamentals. Another objective is to present these topics in the context of an MIS to benefit future information specialists who will work with the managers in implementing the MIS. Part Three provides a common language, making possible improved communications between information specialists and users.

Chapter 5 presents the concepts that apply to computers of all sizes—how data is processed, input and output units, storage, system software, and the roles played by information specialists. Chapter 6 applies these concepts to the class of computers that is generating the most current interest—microcomputers. Chapter 7 explains data base concepts and data base management systems, while Chapter 8 addresses the subject of data communications.

Chapter 5

Computer Concepts

Learning Objectives

After studying this chapter, you should:

- Recognize the computer as one type of information processor
- View the computer as both a physical and conceptual system
- Identify the groupings of computers based on their size
- Understand the difference between batch and online processing, and between timesharing and distributed processing
- Gain an understanding of the possible input and output options
- Recognize the difference between primary and secondary storage, and between two types of secondary storage—sequential and direct
- Understand how data is stored and retrieved using magnetic tape, and direct access storage devices such as magnetic disk
- Understand what is meant by application and system software
- Know how the information services staff might be organized

Introduction

In Chapter 1 we noted that MIS literacy builds upon computer literacy. In this chapter, we cover the concepts that contribute to computer literacy. We do not include everything to make you computer literate. In order to be computer literate, you should know how to use the computer by coding your own programs and using prewritten software. Those skills are best learned in a separate course or book.

Perhaps you have already been introduced to some or all of these concepts. If that is the case, and you are using this book as a part of a course, your instructor will tell you which portions of the chapter to study. If you are using the book as a part of a self-study program, you can review the chapter topics and decide which ones are of interest. Even if you have prior computer experience, it might be worthwhile to use the chapter to put things into perspective before more advanced computer and application topics are addressed.

All of these topics have relevance to a computer-based MIS. This chapter will recognize such relevance and use it for a foundation for later chapters.

The Information Processor in the General Systems Model

Chapter 3 presented the general systems model of the firm as a basic structure showing the important resource flows in any type of organization. The conceptual system gathers data from the physical system and transforms that data into information for the manager. This chapter introduces some basic concepts relating to the use of a computer as an information processor. These concepts apply to computers of any size, but we will respond to the microcomputer boom by specifically relating the concepts to those small systems in the next chapter.

Figure 5-1 illustrates the parts of the general systems model discussed in this chapter. Most of the discussion will center on the information processor itself, but attention will also be directed to data gathering, data communications, storage, and software.

Types of information processors

Today there are three basic types of information processors—manual, keydriven, and computer. *Manual systems* do not employ any mechanical or electronic devices;

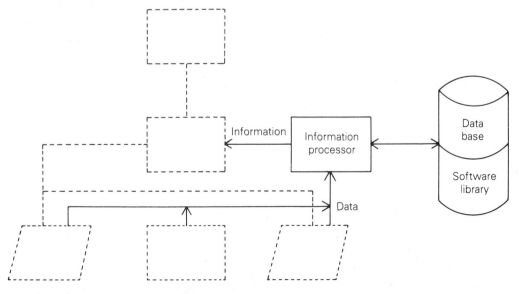

Figure 5-1 Information processor components.

the work is done essentially with pencil and paper. Much data is processed manually, but in small volumes. It would be difficult to find a firm using only a manual system. Most manual systems are used in conjunction with keydriven and/or computer systems. The largest computer users employ numerous manual systems where small volumes and nonrepetitive procedures do not justify more elaborate designs.

Keydriven systems use devices operated by pressing keys—typewriters, pocket calculators, cash registers, and so on. These devices are not connected to a computer. Many small firms that have not yet adopted computer processing use a combination of keydriven and manual systems. Keydriven devices permit the processing of larger volumes than do manual systems, but are not cost efficient when the volumes get too large. Since each machine must have a human operator, the cost accelerates quickly as the scale of operation increases. Keydriven systems offer greater accuracy than manual systems.

Computer systems came onto the scene with the installation of the first Remington Rand UNIVAC in 1951 at the U.S. Census Bureau. Their popularity increased in a rather slow, deliberate way until the mid-1970s when a new breed of small computers was introduced. The early 1980s saw sales boom for these small computers. Since the prices start at around $1,000, these small systems are within the budget of practically all firms.

Computers are able to handle much larger volumes than keydriven or manual systems. They also offer greater accuracy and responsiveness. Computers enable a transformation of data into information that is often impossible or impractical with other approaches. Had the electronic computer not been invented, we most likely would not have concepts such as MIS and DSS.

But the computer has its disadvantages. A firm usually has to make a sizeable investment in hardware, software, and personnel before a return is realized. Also, computers present challenges in terms of security and control. Firms must be prepared to pay the cost of computer processing. Properly used, the computer becomes an essential resource to the firm. Most managers of computer-using firms say "We couldn't get along without it."

The computer as a physical system

We made a distinction in Chapter 1 between physical and conceptual systems. The computer is a physical system; it is a group of integrated elements with the common purpose of achieving some objective. The elements are the various electronic units connected with wires and cables. The objective is the successful processing of data and generating of information as specified by the user.

The technology of computers has changed dramatically in the past thirty-odd years, but the basic architecture has not. Figure 5-2 shows this architecture, and it is called the *computer schematic*. All computers to date, large and small, have conformed to this architecture.

The computer has one or more input devices for entering data into the transformation and control part of the system—called the *central processing unit*, or *CPU*. The CPU contains a *storage unit* where data and programs are stored. Any calculations or logical decisions are made in the *arithmetic and logic unit*, and

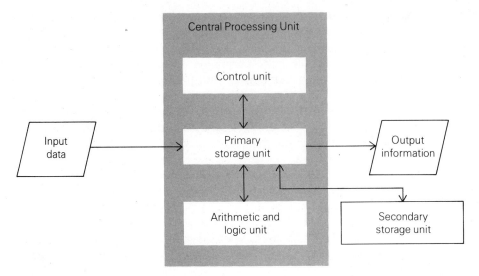

Figure 5-2 The computer schematic.

the entire computer system is controlled by the *control unit*. Processed data and information are transmitted from the storage unit to one or more output devices.

In addition to the primary storage unit, constructed of integrated circuits and containing thousands of locations where characters are stored, there is a secondary storage unit. The secondary storage unit maintains data on a medium such as magnetic disk or magnetic tape and contains millions or billions of locations.

In a small computer, several devices and units can be packaged in a single cabinet. As a general rule, however, a separate cabinet is used for each unit. In a large system, twenty or thirty or more separate cabinets can be interconnected with cables. Even though computer systems can be quite different in appearance and performance, they can all be represented by the computer schematic shown in Figure 5-2.

Computer contents as a conceptual system

You recall from Chapter 3 that the information processor, standards, and management comprise the conceptual information system. The computer, when used as the information processor, plays an important role in this conceptual system.

The data stored in the secondary storage is called the *data base*. The data represents the physical condition of the firm. An inventory record magnetically stored on a disk says that 60 pairs of jogging shoes are on hand. An inspection of the warehouse storage area should reveal an identical number of pairs. The magnetic codes on the disk represent the physical entities in the warehouse.

The programs that cause the computer to carry out the procedures that process the data are also kept in secondary storage. These program files represent the *software library*. The software can cause changes in the data base to reflect changes in the physical system. For example, someone buys a pair of jogging shoes, and software updates the data base accordingly.

Both the data base and software library are pictured in Figure 5-1 as parts of the information processor. These parts enable the computer to represent the physical condition of the firm.

Computer Sizes

As we have noted, computers come in different sizes. The smallest are the *micro-computers*, followed by the slightly larger *minicomputers*. These are the small-scale systems. On a higher level are the *medium-scale* and *large-scale* systems. At the top of the ranking are the *supercomputers*.

Microcomputers

Microcomputers, often called *personal computers (PCs)* or *micros*, cost about $1,000 to $4,000. The most popular computer in this category for business applications is the IBM PC, followed by the Apple II and Macintosh, and the Tandy TRS-80. Products from firms such as Digital Equipment Corporation (DEC), Hewlett-Packard, and Commodore are also popular.

These small systems can serve as information processors for small firms or as intelligent terminals in a larger computer network. An *intelligent terminal* can perform some limited processing, such as editing data, in addition to serving as an input/output device. Primary storage for most micros is in the 64–256KB range. *KB* stands for *kilobyte*, or one thousand bytes. A *byte* is a unit of storage that represents one character. Actually, a kilobyte is 1,024 bytes, so a 64KB computer can store 65,536 characters.

A microcomputer system consists of a drawer-size CPU, a keyboard terminal (usually with a television-like display), a diskette unit that can hold one or two diskettes, and possibly a printer. The television-like display is called a *CRT*, for *cathode ray tube*. The most popular programming language used in micros is BASIC, and a wide variety of packaged, prewritten application software is also available. This software (both custom prepared and prewritten) performs the firm's processing, such as maintaining accounting records.

Minicomputers

Minicomputers cost about $4,000 to $150,000. The most popular minicomputers, or *minis*, are the Data General Nova, DEC PDP-11, various models from Hewlett-Packard, and the IBM Series/1. These systems can serve as information processors in small- to medium-sized firms or as processors in computer networks for large firms. Primary storage capacity starts at about 32KB and can go as high as a million bytes—a *megabyte (MB)*. A system typically consists of a CPU, several disk drives, a high-speed printer, perhaps a few magnetic tape units, and a number of terminals. Programming languages include BASIC, Pascal, and FORTRAN. Much prewritten application software is also available.

Medium- and large-scale systems

Medium- and large-scale systems, often called *mainframes*, are the direct descendants of the hardware and software developed during the early computer generations. Prices start at about $80,000 and can go as high as $10 million. Any type of hardware configuration can be assembled, using a wide variety of input/output and secondary storage devices. The full range of programming languages is offered, with FORTRAN, COBOL, PL/1, and APL the most popular. Although much packaged application software is available, users tend to develop their own. These systems serve as information processors or as central systems in computing networks for larger business organizations.

IBM holds a lion's share of this market with its 43XX medium-scale line and its large-scale line of 370, 303X, and 308X computers. (The X means that there are several models in the category, such as 3031, 3032, and so on.) In 1985 IBM announced a new 309X line called the "Sierra." Other firms competing for this medium- and large-scale computer market are Honeywell, Burroughs, NCR, CDC, Amdahl, and Sperry.

Supercomputers

This category is unusual in that IBM has elected not to compete. These are the largest and fastest computers available but are typically not used for commercial data processing. Instead they are used in specialized areas such as aircraft design and computer-generated movies. The first supercomputer was the ILLIAC IV, made by Burroughs. The market was quickly dominated by Cray with its Cray-1 and CDC with its CYBER 205. As of mid-1984, Cray had delivered about 70 machines, and CDC about 15. Japanese firms such as Fujitsu and NEC are expected to compete for this business. The total market is expected to reach 200 systems by 1987.

Realistically, these systems are not designed to handle business data processing, even for the largest firms. The value of the supercomputers to the MIS is their influence on future, lower-priced, smaller-scale computer design.

Basic Approaches to Computer Processing

There are two basic ways that a computer can process business data. It can do it now, or it can do it later. If a transaction is to be processed *now*, the data must be entered into the computer while the transaction occurs or immediately afterward. The computer then performs all of the necessary processes and produces the needed outputs. Then the computer can handle another transaction. This approach is called *transaction processing* or *online processing*. We will use the term online. *Online* means that a device, such as a terminal, is connected to a computer. A device that is not connected to a computer (such as a keypunch machine) is said to be *offline*.

If a transaction is to be processed *later*, it can be held until a number of such transactions can be processed as a group. This assembly-line approach to data processing offers the advantage of low cost and is the most popular way to handle large data volumes. This approach is called *batch processing*. The main disadvantage to batch processing is the outdated nature of the files as the transactions are collected into a group. The files are only current immediately after they are updated, which might be only once a day. For example, if a firm batches its sales transactions and processes them against the inventory file in the evening, the file only reflects the real inventory situation until the beginning of the next work day. As the next day's sales transactions build up, the file gradually becomes less valuable as a conceptual representation of the physical system.

Batch processing

Figure 5-3 illustrates how batched transaction data passes through a series of sort and update steps to update three master files. This diagram is a *system flowchart* showing the work flow through an entire system of several programs. If you are unfamiliar with flowcharting, refer to Appendix A. The flowchart symbol for the files in the figure indicates that they are recorded on magnetic tape. Before a master file can be updated in a batch fashion, the transactions must be sorted into the sequence of the master file.

The data files can be stored on either magnetic tape or disk. Regardless of the medium, a completely new file is created with each update—changes are not made directly to the old file. In this way, the old files can be retained for backup.

Online processing

Figure 5-4 is a system flowchart showing the same file-updating process, this time with each transaction entered online. The symbol at the top represents keyed input, such as from a terminal. The symbol at the right represents magnetic disk storage containing the three files. Changes are made directly to the files—new ones are not created.[1]

Assume that the transaction is a sale by salesperson 23 to customer 4002 for a dozen of product 12Y at a price of $10 each. The single transaction record is entered into primary storage and the inventory record for product 12Y is obtained from the disk file. The CPU can direct a reading mechanism to the area in secondary storage where the inventory record is located. This procedure is accomplished in a fraction of a second, without searching through the file.

The inventory record is updated to reduce the balance on hand by a dozen. In a like manner, the record for customer 4002 is updated to show an increase of $120 in accounts receivable. Finally, the record for salesperson 23 is updated with the $120 sale. This transaction is completed before the next is entered.

With online processing, the data files are current as of the last transaction handled. If a manager wants to know an inventory balance, or the amount of a

---

[1]The type of processing (batch or online) determines whether a new file is created. The technology (tape or disk) is not a consideration. Magnetic disk storage can be used in either a batch or online manner, but magnetic tape cannot. Magnetic tape can be used only in batch processing.

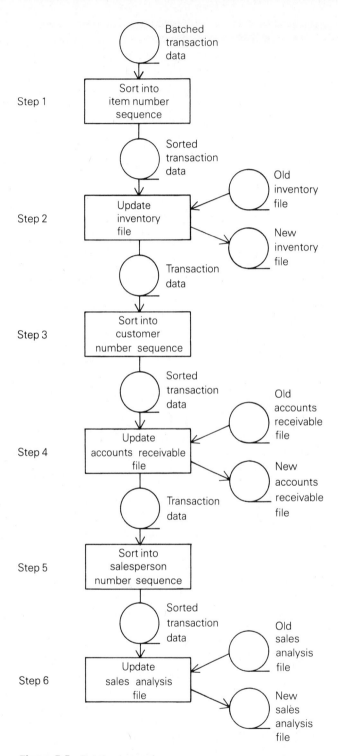

Figure 5-3 Batch processing.

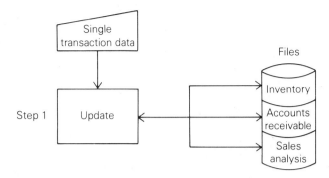

Figure 5-4 Online processing.

customer's receivables, or the sales volume of a salesperson, that information is available in a current form.

Online processing requires some type of online input/output ability, such as that provided by a terminal, plus a secondary storage technology that can respond quickly to the online requests for processing. The secondary storage must be able to directly access the data, without a sequential search. Such a storage is said to have a *direct access* capability, and is called a *DASD—direct access storage device*. Magnetic disk is the most popular form of DASD.

An online system provides a much more current representation of the physical system of the firm than that provided by a batch system. For this reason, online systems are increasingly popular.

Computer networks

In addition to batch and online processing, you have probably heard the terms *timesharing* and *distributed processing*. They are special adaptations of the batch and online approaches whereby the computing equipment is linked using data communications channels or circuits.

Timesharing Modern computers operate at such fast speeds that users must work hard to keep up with them. It takes a lot of jobs to keep the computer busy. Indeed, the more users, the more cost efficient. One approach developed to permit this multiple use is known as *timesharing*. All that is needed is a central computer large enough to handle several users at the same time, data communications circuits and terminals, and the software required to control the hardware.

Many terminals can be attached to a central computer by means of the circuits. The terminal users can thus *share* the *time* of the computer. Data can be entered through a keyboard and transmitted to the central computer. The processing required by each terminal user is performed, perhaps using central data files, and the output is transmitted back to the appropriate terminal, where it is printed or displayed. The computer is usually so responsive that each user begins to think of his or her terminal as the computer itself.

An individual or firm can purchase timesharing services from a commercial computer service center. The user furnishes the data, programs, and terminal, and pays for the communication and computer time used. This can be an attractive alternative for a new computer user, especially a small firm. More computing power can often be obtained for less money than if the firm acquired its own system. The WESTLAW legal retrieval system discussed in Chapter 3 is an example of a purchased timesharing service.

Distributed processing During the mid-seventies firms began to spread their computing power throughout the organization. They distributed computers, often minis, to regional, area, and branch offices and plants. This approach is called *distributed processing*, or *distributed data processing (DDP)*. Distributed processing requires multiple computers interconnected in some manner. Two basic network arrangements are in current use. One, called the *star network*, illustrated in Figure 5-5, includes a *host* computer (usually larger than the others) and any number of satellite systems. The satellite systems are called *distributed processing systems (DPS)*. The star network concept is the most popular of the two approaches. In the other arrangement, called a *ring network*, there is no host. All systems are comparable in importance. Figure 5-6 illustrates this approach.

The availability of the necessary hardware and software makes distributed processing an attractive alternative for large, geographically dispersed operations.

There are various options that a firm can consider when it takes a DDP approach. The processing at each DPS site can be accomplished in either a batch or online manner. Also, the firm can centralize its data base at the host site (in a star network) or distribute the data base among the DPSs.

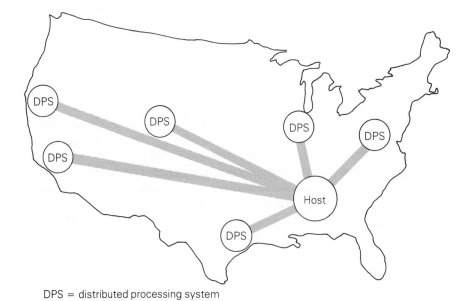

DPS = distributed processing system

Figure 5-5 A star network.

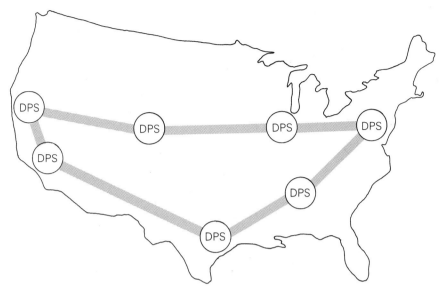

DPS = distributed processing system

Figure 5-6 A ring network.

The main advantage of DDP is that the firm's computing resource is moved closer to the user. Users of a DPS have their own information processor and possibly their own data base and do not have to rely on headquarters for their computing support. But DDP is not without its problems. More sophisticated software is required to link the processors, especially in a ring network. New problems of data and program security are also introduced when users have access to other DPSs and the host. The advantages outweigh the disadvantages, however, for the larger firm with operations spread over a large geographic area.

Input Options

We will now discuss the basic computer units in more detail. The discussion will emphasize how the units are used in an MIS. First, we will discuss how to enter data into the computer.

Figure 5-7 shows the available options. The input hardware devices are shaded. The devices enter data from three sources: (1) data gathered from the physical system of the firm, (2) data gathered from the environment, and (3) data provided by the manager. Very often the manager must enter data such as specifications of information to be retrieved from the data base or specifications to guide a mathematical model. Most of the input data, however, is gathered from the firm's internal operations as recorded by the accounting system.

Some of the gathered data is first recorded on some type of medium, such as punched cards, magnetic tape, or magnetic disk. *Offline keydriven devices*, operated by data entry operators, convert source data to a computer-readable medium.

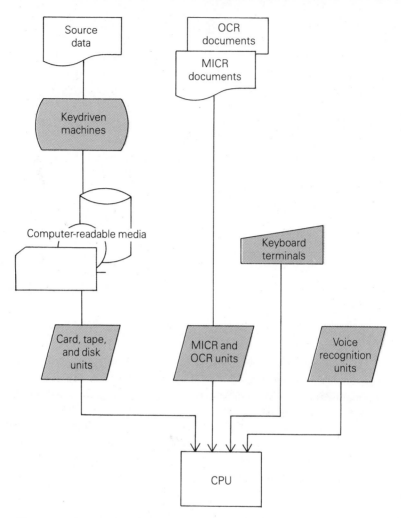

Figure 5-7 Input options.

Then another group of machines—*input devices* (card, disk, and tape units attached to the computer system)—enter the media-recorded data into the CPU.

Other data is originally recorded in a form that is acceptable to the computer. Little or no keying is required. This approach is called *source data automation*— the source medium is designed in such a manner that its data can enter the computer directly, a process also called *direct entry*. The optical character recognition (OCR) units in supermarkets that read the bar codes on packaged items are a good example, as are the magnetic ink character recognition (MICR) units in banks that read data from checks. In the latter case, the only data that must be keyed onto the check is the amount.

A third basic way to enter data into the computer is to key it into an *online keydriven device*, such as a keyboard terminal. With this option, no computer-readable medium is required.

A fourth option permits data input in audible form, using a *voice recognition unit.* These relatively new units recognize specific vocabularies spoken by designated users.

The trend is away from the offline keydriven devices. As recently as ten years ago, the most popular medium was the punched card, but it became obsolete around 1980. We will concentrate on the approaches that are currently popular (keyboard terminals and MICR/OCR) or are expected to be popular in the future (voice recognition).

Keyboard terminals

There are two basic types of keyboard terminal. One displays output on a CRT. The other prints output on a continuous paper form. Both types use typewriterlike keyboards for data entry. Unlike offline keydriven devices, online terminals provide convenient and effective means of *output* as well as input.

A CRT terminal, also called an *alphanumeric display terminal* and a *video display terminal,* is all-electronic, noiseless, and economical. CRTs can display information very rapidly, filling the screen with characters much faster than the characters can be printed on paper. This speed makes the CRT ideal for displaying information in response to a manager's inquiries (or queries). For example, a complete stock status report for an inventory item can be displayed within a few seconds after the query is made. CRT terminals offer a variety of special features:

- *Graphics*: Information can be displayed in graphical form such as pie charts, bar charts, and maps.
- *Color*: Multiple colors can be displayed on certain models.
- *Reverse video*: Characters can be green, amber, or white on a black background, or black on a green, amber, or white background.
- *Cursor*: A special character such as an underline mark can move about on the screen to identify, for example, the position where the next character should be entered. Cursors can be controlled by the computer (for some terminals) or by the operator.
- *Scrolling*: Lines move up or down by one line as a new line is added.
- *Paging*: Some terminals have enough storage capacity to store two or more "pages" of data and can display a page upon request.
- *Protected format*: Some characters on the screen can be protected from inadvertent erasure. In this procedure a "form" is displayed on the screen for the user to complete.

A terminal with paper output is called a *hardcopy terminal,* since the term *hardcopy* describes anything in printed form. Another name is *teleprinter terminal.* The hardcopy terminal uses a mechanical printing device. Therefore it is noisier, somewhat slower, and more subject to failure than a CRT. In addition, the hardcopy terminal is usually more expensive. These disadvantages are overcome by a strong need to obtain a printed copy of terminal input and/or output. A lawyer using the WESTLAW system, for example, would likely want a printed copy of the retrieved court cases.

Hardcopy terminals use the same printing technology as printers attached to small computers. We will discuss that technology later in this chapter.

Both types of terminals (CRT and hardcopy) are good input and output devices in an MIS. The units can be located in the manager's office, and information can be produced in a report or a graphic format. The CRT is especially good for graphs, which can be displayed in two or more colors.

We will describe only keyboard terminals in this chapter. Several other types of terminals will be covered in Chapter 8, where the topic is data communications.

Voice recognition

There has been an infatuation with being able to "talk to the computer" since the first computers were built. Keyboard input is extremely slow, and not everyone knows how to type. A big breakthrough in input technology came in 1970 when Threshold Technology began to manufacture a voice recognition system. In 1978 Interstate Electronics Corporation introduced the first voice-operated intelligent terminal. The user tailors the system to recognize her or his voice by repeating a word several times. The words comprise a *vocabulary* recognizable by the terminal or computer. This is an example of a *speaker-dependent system*. See Figure 5-8.

Texas Instruments offers a "speech command system" for its TI Professional micro. It is speaker dependent and can be conditioned to recognize a maximum of 50 words for each of 9 vocabularies. A manager can condition the TI Professional to recognize certain requests for information such as "Graph the year-to-date sales." The micro decodes the request, assembles the instructions necessary to accomplish the tasks, and produces the requested output.

An improvement over these technologies would be a *speaker-independent system* that could recognize anybody's voice. Several firms are currently working on such a device.

MICR and OCR

The American banking industry was among the first to establish a standard approach to computer use. In the mid-fifties, the American Banking Association devised a standard *type font* (or style) to be used in processing checks. After you write a check, the amount is encoded in a magnetic ink by the first bank to process it. The amount is entered by a keydriven machine called an *encoder*. After the amount is encoded, the check can be processed on a *reader sorter*. The reader sorter performs two main functions. First, it reads the encoded data and records it on a storage medium such as tape or disk. This process of reading the magnetic-encoded characters is called *magnetic ink character recognition (MICR)*. Next, the reader sorter sorts all of the checks for each bank into separate stacks. Checks on other banks are forwarded to the clearinghouse, and checks written by the bank's own customers are then sorted into customer batches. At the end of the month, the computer prints a statement for each customer using tape or disk data created by the reader sorter. The statement and the checks are mailed to the customer.

Figure 5-8 A voice recognition unit.

Had it not been for MICR, the banking system could not have handled the large volume of checks during the past twenty-five years. But MICR is not a permanent cure. Bankers fear that the future volume of checks will be too great, even for MICR. One alternative being implemented on a gradual basis to reduce the number of checks is called *electronic funds transfer (EFT)*.

In electronic funds transfer, money is transferred from one account to another electronically. Employers deposit employees' earnings directly into the employees' checking accounts. Withdrawals from the accounts are authorized by customers as purchases are made at retail stores, for example. The paper documents (the checks) are eliminated; all transfers are electronic. The *automated teller machines (ATMs)* currently in use by many banks are also part of the EFT system.

In addition to checks, there are other types of paper documents that create processing problems because of their large volumes. Examples are credit card invoices, airline tickets, insurance claims, vehicle registrations, and court records. *Optical character recognition (OCR)* equipment has been designed to read the data from these and other forms at high speeds. The data is printed in ordinary ink, but the forms usually must be specially designed to facilitate the reading process. The input device that reads the data into the CPU is called a *scanner*.

A standard OCR type font, called OCR-A, has been adopted for use in the U.S. In Europe, the standard font is OCR-B. Manufacturers of OCR equipment produce machines to read these or other fonts. Examples appear in Figure 5-9. A machine designed to read only one font is called a *single-font reader*. A machine designed to read several specific fonts is called a *multiple-font reader*. A machine that can read nearly all fonts intermixed, without being restricted to a predetermined set, is called a *multifont reader*.

In addition to reading *machine-printed* characters, OCR units can read *marks* made with any type of writing instrument, not just a soft-lead pencil. As long as the mark is dark, it can be read. Several manufacturers produce equipment that can read *hand-printed numbers*. The numbers must be printed in boxes, and must match a predefined pattern or style, such as:

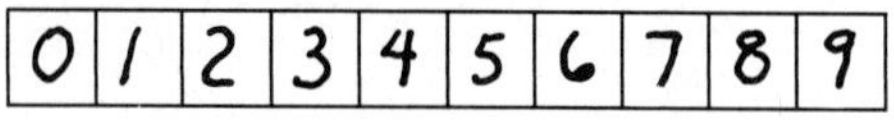

$$0 \quad / \quad 2 \quad 3 \quad 4 \quad 5 \quad 6 \quad 7 \quad 8 \quad 9$$

In addition to numeric data, some of these readers can read selected alphabetic letters (three or four) and special characters. At present, no unit on the market can read *hand-printed alphanumeric* data, which would include all letters, all numbers, and a set of special characters. There has been even less success in reading *handwritten* data.

We are presently in the midst of an OCR boom in retailing. Many department stores use *point-of-sale (POS)* terminals with *OCR wands*. In Figure 5-10, a retail clerk optically reads product identification data from a price tag. Data is then transmitted to the store's central computer, where the appropriate records are

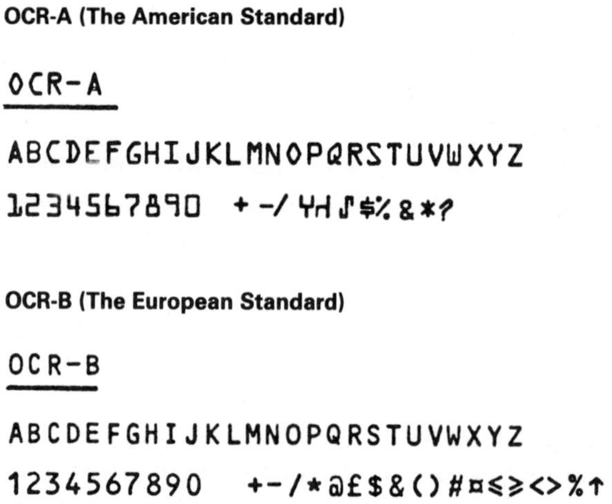

OCR-A (The American Standard)

OCR-A

ABCDEFGHIJKLMNOPQRSTUVWXYZ

1234567890   + -/ ¥H ∫ $% & *?

OCR-B (The European Standard)

OCR-B

ABCDEFGHIJKLMNOPQRSTUVWXYZ

1234567890   +-/*∂£$&()#¤≤≥<>%↑

Figure 5-9 The American and European standard OCR type fonts.

Figure 5-10 A retail terminal with an OCR wand.

updated immediately. For example, inventory records can be updated to reflect the sale. This is an example of online processing.

Another retail application of OCR is in the supermarket industry. The bar code printed on food labels is called the *universal product code (UPC)*. Part of the bar code identifies the manufacturer, and part identifies the specific item. Each checkout register contains an OCR unit that reads the bar code. If an item has no code printed on it, the clerk must enter the code on a keyboard. As each item is handled, the store computer retrieves the price from storage. When all item data has been entered, the computer calculates the tax, and totals the bill. The store computer can record transaction data on cassette tape or floppy disk, or it can communicate with a large central computer. The store manager can use a terminal to obtain information describing the store's performance.

Although developed for the food industry, the OCR bar code has been adopted in other areas as well. A good example of a manufacturing application is provided by the Electric Boat Division of General Electric. Bar-code hardware costing $20,000 and software costing $80,000 were purchased to track the flow of tools and supplies. This has been a good investment since, in 1984 alone, $320,000 was saved through reduced manufacturing costs. Workers use the new system to check out tools from the tool crib. Each worker wears a badge containing a bar code, and the tools are also bar coded. A wand is used to record which tool is checked out (or returned) by which worker.

Bar codes can also facilitate the tracking of products flowing through the plant and through the firm's distribution network. Bar codes on work-in-process products and on cartons of finished products can be scanned by stationary scanners or hand-held wands to provide immediate data input to the computer.

Output Options

There are several options for producing computer output, as illustrated in Figure 5-11. Information or data can be recorded on a permanent medium, such as paper, microfilm, or punched cards, or the information can be displayed on a CRT or presented audibly. In addition, data or information recorded on microfilm can be converted to printed form or displayed on a viewer.

Printers

Beginning with the first computer, the most common way to obtain human-readable output has been the printer. Currently there are three types of printers in use. The first printers were called *line printers* since they print a line at a time. Next came slower-speed, less expensive *serial printers* that print one character at a time like a typewriter. Most recently there have been successful efforts to produce very high speed printers, called *page printers*. Both line and serial printers are online devices. Some page printers can be operated offline.

These printers use two basic technologies—impact and nonimpact. An *impact printer* causes a print "hammer" to strike the paper to form the character (as in a typewriter). A *nonimpact printer* causes characters to be printed by means of some chemical or heat process, or by spraying the characters onto the paper from an ink jet.

Line printers   Line printers are impact printers that can print multiple characters on a line simultaneously. The first line printers used a mechanism of 120 *print wheels*—one wheel per printing position. Each wheel had the characters embossed around the perimeter. Next came the *print drum*, a metal cylinder with embossed characters around the surface. Drums, still in use, have a set of characters for each printing position. Most line printers today print a 132-character line. Another popular technology is the *print chain*, which looks like a bicycle chain with two embossed characters on each link. There are five sets of characters on the chain. The chain rotates in a horizontal plane, and hammers fire at the appropriate time to cause the characters to print. The most recent development is the *print band*, a steel ribbon with embossed characters that moves in the same horizontal plane as the chain.

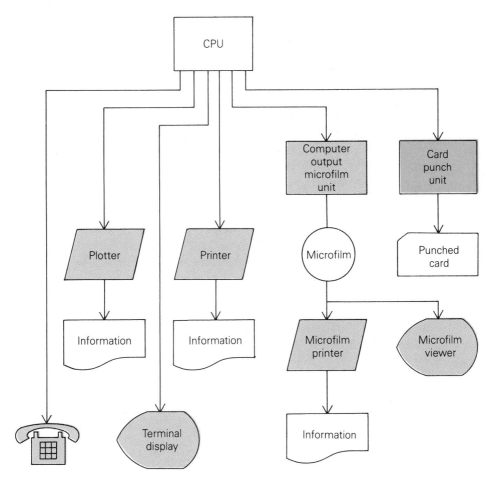

Figure 5-11 Output options.

About three-fourths of all line printers on the market today operate in the 200–650 lpm (lines per minute) range. Most of the remainder operate at higher speeds—up to 3,600 lpm.

Throughout the computer era, line printers have been the workhorse output device, capable of high volumes. They are found on most medium- and large-scale systems. Some systems include multiple printers.

Serial printers Serial printers are often called *character printers* because they print one character at a time, using the same technology as hardcopy terminals. Serial printers provide the printed output for practically all micros and for a large number of minis.

Some serial printers use an impact mechanism such as dot matrix and daisywheel. One model of the *dot matrix* printer moves a column of seven pins across the paper and selectively actuates the pins at five successive intervals to form the character. This mechanism is called a "5 by 7" dot matrix—the characters are formed by a matrix of five columns across and seven rows down. Most dot matrix printers operate in the 80–160 cps (characters per second) range, but some are so fast that they are cutting into the lower end of the line printer market. Speeds of 300 lpm are common, and 600 and 900 lpm have been achieved.

The other type of impact serial printer is the *daisy wheel*, which uses a flat plastic disk with petallike projections, each containing an embossed character, as on a typewriter print bar. A daisy wheel printer is slower than a dot matrix printer, but the quality is better—often referred to as *letter quality*.

Other serial printers are of the nonimpact variety, using thermal, Xerographic, and ink-jet processes. A *thermal* printer uses a heat process. *Ink-jet* printers spray droplets of ink onto the paper. Xerox uses the *Xerographic* principle (naturally). Because of their high cost and inability to print more than a single copy, nonimpact serial printers are still quite rare.

Some serial printers have a *graphics capability*. Dot matrix printers can prepare excellent graphics. Since these printers are used on microcomputers, a graphics capability is affordable by most firms.

Page printers Page printers are used by organizations with very large volumes of printed output, such as the federal government, insurance companies, and banks. The printers produce mostly data documents, such as claim checks and bank statements, rather than management reports. Speeds range from 6 to 150 ppm (pages per minute), with the low-speed units eating into the line printer market.

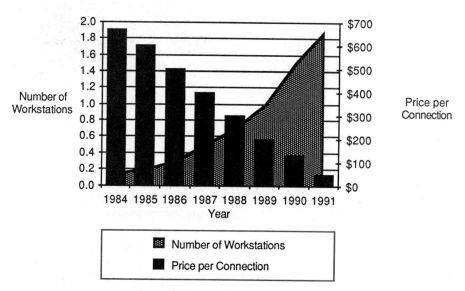

Figure 5-12 Graphical output produced by a serial printer.

The first page printer was the Xerox 1200, introduced in 1973. IBM followed with their 20,000 lpm model 3800 in 1975. Xerox and IBM have been joined by Honeywell, Canon, Fujitsu, and several others. A large number of nonimpact technologies are used, several of which are called *laser printers* because they incorporate a pinpoint beam of light that causes a toner to be attracted to a photosensitive drum. The process is similar to that of a Xerox copier. Advances in laser technology are reducing the cost to a point where the printers will be competitive with daisywheel serial printers. Figure 5-12 was prepared on a laser printer attached to a microcomputer.

Today printed output represents an important way for the manager to receive information from the computer. But interest in online devices and graphics is increasing. This interest, combined with the high cost of printed output, indicates that the printer will probably become less significant in future MIS designs.

Plotters

Special output devices called *plotters* are used to display information graphically on paper. There are two types—the pen plotter and the electrostatic plotter.

The *pen plotter* uses from one to ten pens with different colored ink to draw lines. The pens can be pressurized ball point, liquid ink, nylon tip, or liquid ball. The pen plotter moves the pen quite rapidly, at speeds approximating 30 inches per second. But since only one pen can be used at a time, a rather complex graph can require several minutes to complete.

Pen plotters come in three styles. In the *flatbed plotter*, the paper remains stationary on a large table. The pens move in two directions across the width and length of the paper, tracing the path of both the X and Y axes. In the *drum plotter*, the paper is wrapped around two rollers, with the pen mechanism in between. The rollers move the paper back and forth, and this action, combined with the movement of the pens, draws lines at the proper angles on the paper. *Hybrid plotters* combine the two technologies.

Electrostatic plotters use a Xerographic-type process and can produce graphs much more quickly than a pen plotter. They are not as popular, however, as pen plotters.

If a user wants hardcopy graphical output, there are two options—plotter or serial printer. Graphs prepared by a plotter can be larger (up to 36 inches wide and no limit on length) than those prepared on a serial printer. Previously, plotters offered an exclusive advantage of color, but now several serial printers can produce color output.

We also recognize that a graphics option is available for keyboard terminals. The vivid graphics that are possible with video games provide a good idea of what is possible with a CRT—color, three dimensions, and even motion.

Graphics have long been considered a preferred type of output for the manager. One of the founders of the DSS concept, Michael S. Scott Morton, recognized graphics as a way of reducing a large volume of data to a manageable size. But research to date does not build a strong case for graphics. Gerardine DeSanctis, a professor at the University of Minnesota, reviewed the findings of 29 research projects, and found that 7 projects concluded that graphs were better than tables, 12 concluded that tables were better than graphs, and 10 concluded that there was no difference.[2] More research is needed to better understand the value of graphical output. Computer-prepared graphics are now within the price range of most managers. The question is, "Are they worth the price?"

Audio response

Audio output, or *audio response,* has not been difficult for computer equipment manufacturers to achieve. Words are recorded on a magnetic drum in much the same manner as sound is recorded by a tape recorder. The stored computer program can select words from the drum to form a sentence, which is usually transmitted over a communication line or circuit.

Audio response units can store a vocabulary of from 30 to as many as 1500 words. With an audio response unit as part of the computer system, any pushbutton telephone becomes a terminal. For example, assume that a manager wants to know the stock status of a particular inventory item. The manager dials the computer number and keys in a code identifying a "request for a stock status" along with the item number. The keying is done on the telephone's pushbuttons. The computer retrieves the inventory record from the data base and selects vocabulary words to form a response. The computer might respond, for example, "ITEM ONE-FOUR-THREE-SIX BALANCE ON HAND FOUR HUNDRED AND SIXTY-TWO QUANTITY ON ORDER EIGHT HUNDRED AND FORTY-SIX."

We saw in Chapter 2 that some managers prefer verbal information. Audio response enables computers to satisfy this preference in a limited, formal way.

Other output

Some firms still produce *punched card output.* GTE encloses a punched card with the telephone bill. The card serves as a *turnaround document*—you return it with your payment. Most firms use OCR turnaround documents. The documents eliminate the need to key the payment data into the computer.

As we pointed out earlier, it is possible to produce microfilm images with a computer. This is called *computer output microfilm (COM).* COM is being incorporated into office automation systems for image storage and retrieval. We will wait until Chapter 10 to discuss this use of microfilm.

Putting the Input and Output (I/O) Devices in Perspective

We have identified many of the available I/O devices. Not all firms need all of the devices, and not all of the devices have the same level of importance to an MIS

The manager works with some of the devices or with their output. These devices make a *direct* contribution to the MIS. This group includes hardcopy and CRT terminals that a manager can use to interact with the computer, printers of

---

[2]Gerardine DeSanctis, "Computer Graphics as Decision Aids: Directions for Research," *Decision Sciences* 15 (Fall 1984): 463–487.

microimage terminals that provide images of documents, and both audio response and voice recognition units that permit audible interaction with the computer.

Other devices make an *indirect* contribution to the MIS. These devices convert large volumes of data to computer-readable form for entry into the data base. Although these devices do not produce information, they do provide the data resource from which information is produced. These data input devices include both offline and online keydriven devices, keyed media input units, MICR, OCR, and voice recognition units.

Figure 5-13 illustrates the role of these units in (1) providing a path for the data flow from the physical system of the firm to the data base, (2) providing a two-way communication path between the manager and the computer, and (3) providing a communication path from the manager to the physical system.

Of these three paths, the third is the least developed. If the manager is to communicate to the physical system through the MIS, the link will primarily involve office automation developments such as electronic mail, voice mail, word processing, and teleconferencing.

The figure illustrates vividly how the I/O devices, as part of the formal MIS, provide a link between the manager and the physical system. In conjunction with the other MIS resources, these devices provide a "window" through which the manager can view the operation of the firm.

Storage

There are two basic types of computer storage. *Primary storage* is built into the CPU, whereas *secondary storage* is usually housed in a separate unit, or units. Primary storage is very fast—its contents can be accessed in millionths or billionths of a second. But primary storage has a limited capacity. Although the cost per byte has continued to decrease, there is not enough capacity to store all of a firm's files. Secondary storage supplements the capacity of primary storage. Secondary storage has an almost infinite capacity, measured in millions and billions of bytes. Some secondary storage media (such as magnetic disks) offer direct access, but magnetic tape does not. The access speed of secondary storage is slower than that of primary storage.

Primary storage

In early computers, primary storage was constructed of small doughnut-shaped magnetic cores with wires running through them. Magnetic core storage gave way to *metal-oxide semiconductor (MOS)* chip storage in the 1970s. The capacity of MOS storage has increased dramatically since its introduction. The first chips could store only 1KB. By 1980 the capacity had increased to 64KB. Capacity today is 256KB, and is expected to reach 1MB before 1990.

Primary storage has five different uses. These may be described as the *five conceptual areas* of storage. The areas are not physical, in that the storage is not

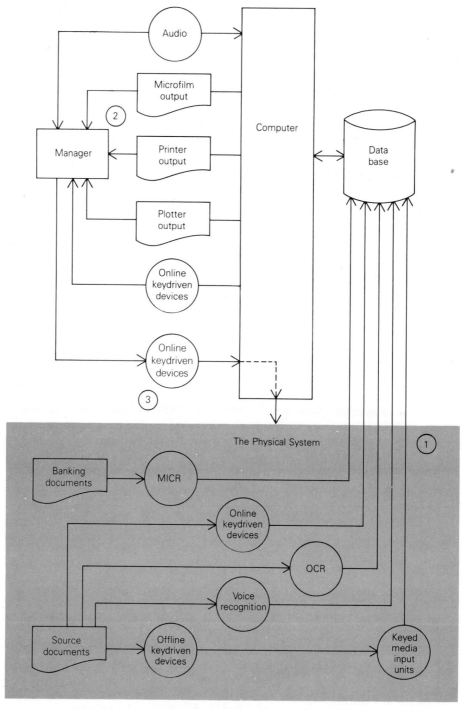

Figure 5-13   Input/output devices in the MIS.

permanently partitioned in this manner. In fact, nothing physically distinguishes the five areas; the distinction is only in how the areas are used. The conceptual areas are illustrated in Figure 5-14.

As data enters the storage from an input device, it is placed in the *input area*. The program in the *application program area* is the list of instructions that guides the computer to the solution of a problem or the completion of a task. The application program performs the necessary calculations, logical decisions, movements, and so on, and places data and information in the *output area*. The data and information are transmitted from this output area to an output device. Most programs require a separate storage area to contain intermediate totals, constants, descriptive characters, and the like. This separate area is the *working area*. The execution of the application program is controlled by system programs in the *system program area*. We will discuss system programs later in the chapter.

The hierarchy of data

In order to appreciate how secondary storage is used, we must first understand how business data is organized. Business data exists in a hierarchy, with names identifying each level. At the lowest level is the *data element*, such as an employee number. All of the data elements that describe an object or subject are assembled to form a *record*. For example, all of the payroll data about an employee form a payroll record. All of the records of a type are accumulated in a *file*. A firm has one or more payroll files—perhaps a salaried payroll file, an hourly payroll file, and so forth. All of the files available for computer processing are called a *data base*.

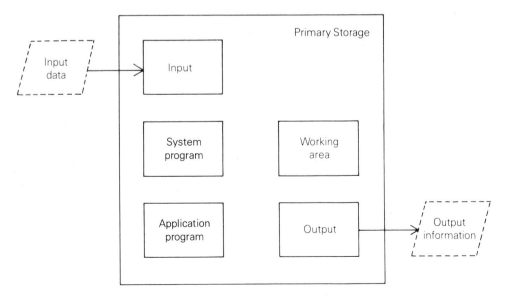

Figure 5-14 The five conceptual areas of primary storage.

Secondary storage

There are two basic types of secondary storage—sequential and direct. In *sequential storage* the data records are arranged in sequence based on a code called the key. The *key* is simply a data element that identifies a particular record. For example, the key for a payroll file would most likely be the employee's number. If the payroll file is arranged sequentially, the records are ordered using the key with the lowest numbered record first and the highest numbered record last. This is an ascending sequence; it is also possible to arrange records in a descending sequence.

The most common medium for sequential storage is magnetic tape. Sequential storage offers both economy and efficiency. Very little storage space and time are wasted in creating and updating the files. However, the main restriction is that records must be processed sequentially. In *sequential processing*, the first record on the tape must be processed first, the second must be processed second, and so on.

Direct storage was invented to overcome the sequential processing requirement of sequential storage. With direct storage an access mechanism can move a read/write head directly to the desired record—DASD.

Magnetic disk storage is the most common type of DASD. There are two basic types of disks—the metal *hard disks* of the larger systems, and the plastic *diskettes*, or *floppies* of the mini/micro systems.

In addition to disks, other types of DASD are magnetic tape cartridges and metal-oxide-semiconductor (MOS) chips. The cartridges provide exceptionally large capacities at modest speeds. The MOS devices provide the opposite support—modest capacities at high speeds. Disks represent an attractive compromise for the vast area between the two.

Direct storage is designed for direct access, facilitating online processing. But it is also possible to use a DASD as a sequential medium and to process the data in batches. When we discussed batch and online processing earlier in the chapter, we drew the distinction between "now" and "later." If you handle a transaction now (online processing), you need DASD. If you handle a transaction later (batch processing), you can use magnetic tape or DASD.

Magnetic Tape

Magnetic tape has consistently provided an attractive storage alternative. It is fast—data can be read or written at speeds from 20KB to 1250KB per second. It is compact—a 2400-foot reel of half-inch-wide tape can contain more than 140 million bytes of data. It is economical—a reel of tape costs about $30.

Computer tape is used in basically the same manner as sound recording tape. But instead of recording sound magnetically in frequencies, computer tape records data magnetically in combinations of bits. *Bit* is a contraction of *binary digit*— it is an area of storage that can be magnetized either "on" or "off." A byte is comprised of eight bits. The bits of a byte are written across the width of the tape, making it possible to record a large number of bytes on an inch of tape. The standard *recording densities* are 200, 556, 800, 1600, and 6250 bytes per inch (bpi).

To record data, you place a reel of tape on a *magnetic tape unit*, often called a *tape drive*. The leading portion of the tape is automatically threaded through a read/write mechanism and wrapped around the hub of a takeup reel. The process is analogous to loading film in a movie projector. As data is written onto the tape or read from it by the read/write mechanism, the tape winds onto the takeup reel. When all the data has been read from the file or written onto it, the reels rewind and you remove the source reel.

How data is recorded on tape

Figure 5-15 shows how the parts of a tape are used for different purposes. Part of the tape is used to attach the tape to the two reels. These parts are called *leaders*.

In many systems the first and last records on the tape are used for control purposes. These records are known as *labels*. The one at the beginning of the tape is the *header label*. The one at the end is the *trailer label*. The header identifies the reel to assure that the operator mounts the reel required by the program. The

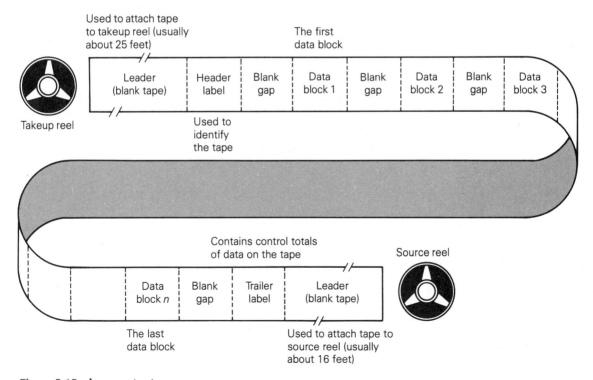

Figure 5-15   A computer tape.

trailer label includes totals accumulated from records on the reel; the totals are used for control purposes.

Most of the tape is used for recording data. This data is written as *blocks* in the area between the labels. The tape unit writes the blocks one at a time and later reads them one at a time. A block can contain a single record, as in Figure 5-16, or multiple records.

Uses of magnetic tape

One use of magnetic tape is as an *input* medium. For example, payroll data showing employee number and hours worked can be keyed onto a tape using a key-to-tape device. The tape data can then be read into primary storage for a computation of payroll amounts, as in Figure 5-17. A second use is as a *master file* medium. In the payroll example, the payroll master file is maintained on tape. A master file contains important data that is kept up to date. Both the input payroll data file and the payroll master file are in sequence by employee number.

An input payroll data record is read into primary storage along with the payroll master record. With both employee records in primary storage, the computer can multiply hourly rate (from the master record) by hours worked (from the payroll data record) to obtain gross pay. Then deductions are made, using data from the master record, to calculate net pay. While all of this data is in primary storage, a payroll check is printed on the printer. Before the next employee's records are read, an updated payroll master record is written. This updated record contains data such as gross pay to date, income tax to date, social security tax to date, and so on. These amounts reflect the results of the calculations just completed.

The updated file is never written back onto the input reel because it is difficult to do so without inadvertently erasing data in adjacent areas. It is always written onto another reel. This is the third use of magnetic tape—as an *output* medium. The new file will provide the master data the next time that payroll computations are made; it now contains the current data.

Magnetic tape also can be used as a *historical storage* medium. Since a reel

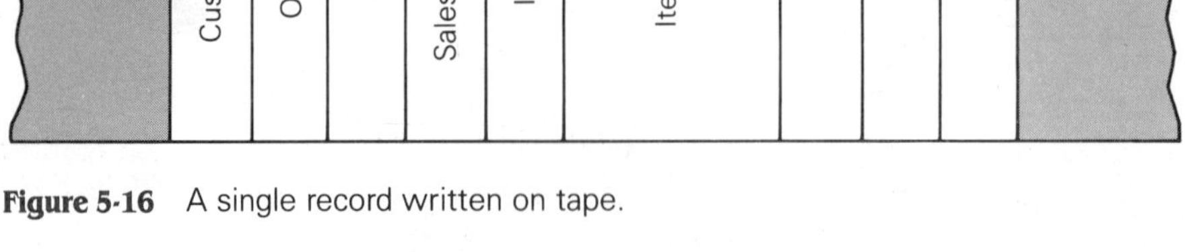

Figure 5-16   A single record written on tape.

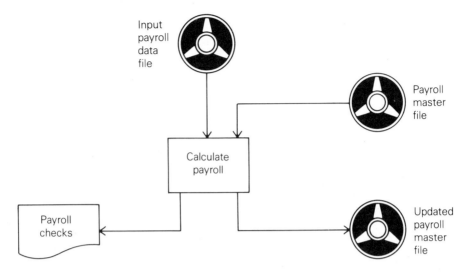

Figure 5-17 Updating the payroll master file using magnetic tape.

of tape is so inexpensive and contains so much data in a small area, tape is ideal for historical storage. Accounting procedures require that historical data be retained for a period of time, but the frequency of use is too low to keep the data in a more expensive form.

A final use of magnetic tape is for *intermediate storage* of data awaiting further processing. For example, a reel can provide the communication between one computer program and another, such as between the payroll computation described above and a program that prints a payroll report for management. In addition, tape reels can be mailed or delivered to other computer sites.

Direct Access Storage Devices

The first DASDs were magnetic disks, similar to phonograph records. The disks were mounted in a stack on a vertical, rotating shaft in much the same manner as records in a jukebox. All disks rotated at the same time, and a single access mechanism moved up and down and in and out to read and write data. Disks are still the most popular DASD medium, but today's units are greatly improved over the initial designs.

The first major improvement was to provide an *access mechanism* for each disk. The mechanism need only move in and out of the disk stack, eliminating the up-and-down movement. Figure 5-18 shows a disk stack containing eleven disks. This is only an example; other disk stacks have different specifications— more or fewer disks, two access mechanisms, and so on. The access mechanism includes an *access arm* that moves between two disk surfaces. At the end of the arm is a pair of *read/write heads*—one for the surface above and one for the surface below.

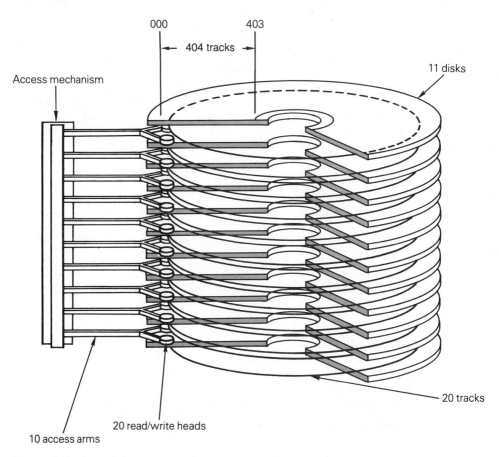

Figure 5-18 A comblike access mechanism.

Data is not recorded on the top surface of the top disk or on the bottom surface of the bottom disk. Data is recorded only on the inner surfaces. Of the twenty disk surfaces used for recording, only nineteen contain data. The other is used by one of the read/write heads to synchronize the movement of the access arm.

The disk stack in Figure 5-18 provides 404 tracks per surface. Each track has a capacity of 13,030 bytes. When the access mechanism is positioned to read one of the 404 tracks of a disk, there are actually nineteen tracks arranged in a vertical stack, or *cylinder*.

The cylinder of data is created by all read/write heads moving in unison. If one head is positioned on, say, track 103, then all of the heads must be positioned on their tracks 103. The cylinder concept is important because it recognizes how data should be stored in a disk stack to minimize access time. The *access time* is the interval from the time the CPU transmits a command (such as read, or write) to a DASD, until the read/write head begins to read data from or write data to the record location.

The cylinder concept encourages the storage in one cylinder of all the data needed to process a transaction. The access mechanism is moved to that cylinder, and then multiple reads and writes can be performed without the need to reposition the access mechanism.

In addition to the comblike access mechanism, other improvements over early units include greater capacity and reduced access times.

How data is recorded on a disk

As on magnetic tape, the characters are recorded on a disk in the form of magnetized bits using the same coding structure of eight data bits per byte. But on disks the bytes are recorded *serially* (one bit after the other) along the track, rather than in the *parallel* form of the tape (across the width). Each record is preceded by its address, separated from the record by a gap. These addresses enable the computer to identify a particular record on the track.

How DASD records are addressed

When it becomes necessary to move the access mechanism to a particular location in a DASD, the CPU must provide an address of that location. The address must specify the cylinder, the read/write head, and the sequence of the record on the track. Figure 5-19 provides an example of the address of the fifteenth record on cylinder 104 served by head 12. The size of the address (number of digits) will vary from one DASD to another. This particular address format (cylinder, head, and record), however, is used in most systems.

When the CPU issues the address for a read operation, the access mechanism is moved to the proper location and the data is read into primary storage for processing. On a write operation, data is written from primary storage to the area specified by the address. When the data is written, it erases the record that was previously recorded. If a master file record is being updated, the old record is lost. This is a basic difference between DASD and magnetic tape.

How records are arranged in a DASD file

As seen earlier, magnetic tape records are arranged sequentially. Records can be recorded on a DASD in the same way, as shown in Figure 5-20. This *sequential* organization permits the DASD to be used like a magnetic tape. This is especially useful for applications such as payroll where the economies of batch processing can be realized and direct access is not required.

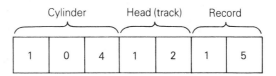

Figure 5-19 A DASD address identifying cylinder, head, and record locations.

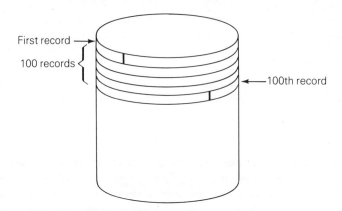

Figure 5-20 Sequential organization of a DASD file.

Another type of file organization is *indexed sequential,* shown in Figure 5-21. As the name implies, the records are arranged sequentially, as in sequential storage. But there is something extra—an index. The *index* serves as a directory of the records in the file. Although Figure 5-21 shows the index separate from the file, it is usually recorded on the first few tracks.

The index contains a key for each record in the file. The keys are listed in the index sequentially, and with each key is the DASD address of the record. The index is used in much the same manner as a telephone directory, with the key identifying the needed record and the address identifying where that record can be found. The key is provided by the computer program that requires data from the record. The index is read into primary storage from the DASD, and the key is compared with each entry in the index until a match is found. The corresponding address is then used to send the access mechanism to the location where the record is stored. The advantage of this approach is direct access. The disadvantage is the time-consuming routine that must be followed in order to access the record.

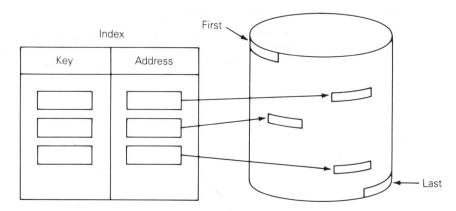

Figure 5-21 Indexed sequential organization of a DASD file.

First, the index must be accessed and read into primary storage. Then, the data record must be accessed. Two movements of the access mechanism are required (unless the data record is located in the same cylinder as the index). This disadvantage can be overcome by using the direct type of file organization, as illustrated in Figure 5-22.

With *direct* organization, the data address can be generated by the program requiring the record. The address is used to send the access mechanism to the correct location. The easiest approach is to use the key as the address. For example, part number 34125 could identify cylinder 34, read/write head 12, and the fifth record on the track. Unfortunately, few coding schemes exactly match the addressing scheme of the DASD. For example, part numbers contain too many positions, include letters as well as numbers, and do not run in continuous sequences.

Some type of arithmetic can be used to convert the key into an acceptable address. This use of arithmetic is called a *hashing scheme*. In Figure 5-22, part number 149107432 is divided by 1,000,000, and the remainder, 107432, is used as the address. A number of such hashing schemes have been devised.

A potential advantage of direct addressing is that it may require only a single movement of the access mechanism to access a particular record. Since access movements are time-consuming, faster computer use is possible with direct organization than with the other file organizations. A potential disadvantage is that records may become distributed unequally in the DASD. It is possible for the hashing scheme to produce the same address for more than one key. These duplicates are called *synonyms*. In this case, all but the first record assigned to a given location must be placed in an *overflow area*. The access mechanism is sent to the first location, finds that the record is elsewhere, and looks in the overflow area. One or more additional movements of the access mechanism might be required. This time-consuming activity should not occur very often. If it does, a new hashing scheme should be devised—one producing fewer synonyms. A rule of thumb is a maximum of 20% synonyms. When more than one out of five calculated storage addresses produces a synonym, it is time to find a new hashing scheme.

Part number 149107432

Hashing scheme: divide by 1,000,000 and use remainder for the address

$$\frac{149107432}{1,000,000} = 149.107432 = 107432$$

Location 107432

Figure 5-22   Direct organization of a DASD file.

The above file organizations (sequential, indexed sequential, and direct) are used for data records in the data base. Another organization, *partitioned*, is used for programs in the program library. Figure 5-23 shows how the software library is partitioned into areas for each program. The access mechanism can be directed to the location of the first instruction in a partition by means of a *directory*. The directory contains the name and beginning address of each *member* (program) in the file. The entire program or subprogram can then be called into primary storage sequentially, one instruction at a time.

Uses of DASD

DASD makes its greatest contribution to the MIS as a *file* medium. DASD units are used for both data and programs that are active enough to warrant the expense. It costs more to maintain data on DASD than on magnetic tape. A file should not be kept on DASD unless the cost is justified.

In online processing, it is impossible to anticipate which program, file, or record will be required next. For this reason, all must be kept in a "ready" state. This procedure is shown in Figure 5-24. Programs are called from the DASD to perform certain computations. Also, data from the DASD is made available to the programs.

DASD permits a manager to *query* the data base and receive information within seconds. A manager can use a terminal to obtain information, such as year-to-date sales statistics for each region. Perhaps this information prompts the need to obtain additional information, such as sales statistics for a certain branch. The manager can enter a second query, and a third, and so on. In this manner, the manager can use the MIS as a decision support system—identifying problems, their nature, and their causes.

DASD can also serve as an *input medium* produced by a key-to-disk system. It is unlikely to serve as an *output medium*, however, because records of files organized indexed sequential or direct are updated *in place*, not replaced by new records as in magnetic tape processing. Also, since all records of a transaction

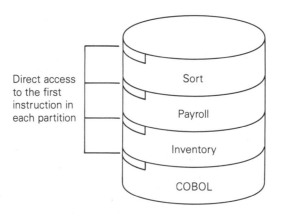

Figure 5-23 Partitioned organization of a DASD file.

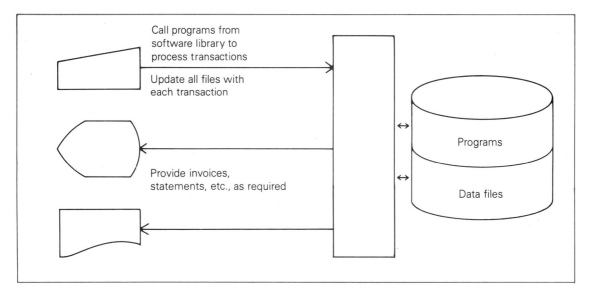

Figure 5-24 DASD makes data and programs immediately available.

are updated before another transaction is handled, it is usually not necessary to create *intermediate* files. However, when such files are necessary, DASD is excellent. And finally, the cost of the DASD storage space, while continuing to decrease, is too great to consider for use as a *historical storage medium.*

A Comparison of Magnetic Tape and DASD

Table 5-1 compares magnetic tape and DASD for the five major uses. Both types of secondary storage are best suited for file media. Tape is good when there is no

Table 5-1 Magnetic tape and DASD as secondary storage media

Use	*Magnetic Tape*	*DASD*
Input	Both secondary storage media play minor roles as input media—the trend is toward online data entry and source data automation.	
File	Good	Excellent
Output	Good in batch processing	Not a large volume of activity with online processing
Historical Storage	Excellent	Poor
Communication	Good for both site-to-site and program-to-program communication	Poor for site-to-site communication. Excellent for program-to-program communication when necessary

need to query the file for status information between batch updating cycles. DASD offers excellent file capabilities—facilitating online processing and immediate response to a manager's queries. Because of its lower cost, magnetic tape is the most commonly used historical storage medium.

Magnetic tape was effective during early computer generations, when the emphasis was on the batch processing of accounting data. The evolution to online processing and decision support systems, coupled with continued refinements in disk technology, have made DASD the preferred secondary storage medium.

Software

We have recognized that software is maintained in the software library and includes application software—the programs that process the firm's data. Another type of program, system software, is also stored in the software library. In this section, we address the important features of these software types.

Application software

Application software is produced inhouse, by the firm's programmers, or purchased off-the-shelf from outside organizations—software or hardware vendors. Programmers use a *procedural language* that specifies the steps that the computer is to follow. The most popular procedural languages in business are Assembler, COBOL, PL/I, RPG and BASIC. Also frequently used are FORTRAN, APL, Pascal, and C.

System software

While an application program may be of value only to a particular industry or firm, system software can be utilized by all users of a particular computer. System software enables the user to perform basic operations such as translating programs from the language used by the programmer (such as BASIC) to the language used by the computer (called *machine language*). This translation is performed by programs called *assemblers, compilers,* and *interpreters.* These programs are controlled by a master program called an *operating system.* The operating system manages the resources comprising the computer system and directs the overall operation.

It is impossible to use most computers without the operating system. There are exceptions. For example, many micros have a programming language built into their primary storage. The IBM PC contains a limited version of BASIC that is activated when you turn on the system. But if you want to use any other software, you must use the operating system. For example, assume that you want to code a program in regular BASIC (not the limited version). You insert a diskette containing the operating system and turn on the computer. The operating system asks for the date and time, and then you must specify the language that you want to use by typing "BASIC." The operating system retrieves the BASIC translator from the diskette, and now you can code the program. The operating systems for larger computers may require you to enter more data—such as an account number and a password.

The ability to call up the appropriate language translator is only one of the operating system's duties. It also calls up *utility programs* that perform such basic tasks as sorting and merging data files, printing data from disks, and so on. The operating system also handles the *scheduling* of the computer units so that multiple users can be accommodated at one time—*multiprogramming*. Most small computers do not have this multiprogramming capability, but larger ones do. An operating system that permits multiprogramming is a prerequisite to timesharing.

The operating system also interfaces with two other important system software packages—the data base management system (DBMS) and the teleprocessing monitor. The DBMS controls the data base, and we will devote Chapter 7 (The Data Base) to it. The teleprocessing monitor controls the use of data communications facilities connected to the computer, and we will explain this operation in Chapter 8 (Data Communications).

Portions of the operating system, called the *control program*, reside in primary storage at all times while the system is in use. This is the conceptual storage area labeled "system program" in Figure 5-14. Figure 5-25 positions the operating system in relation to other system and application programs.

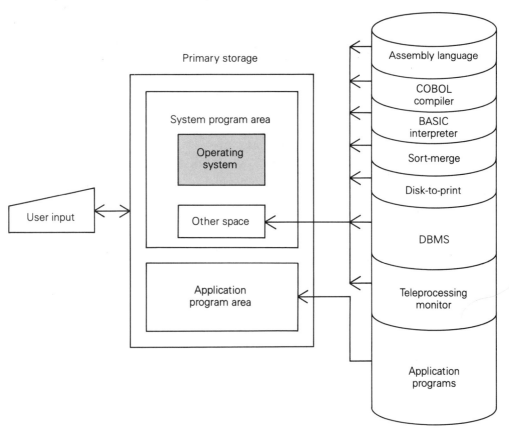

Figure 5-25 Central role of the operating system.

When the user wants to create a program, the proper translator is read into the system program area. The translated program can be written in the application program area and executed at that time, or it can be written onto secondary storage for later retrieval and execution. The operating system can call a translated application program from secondary storage and execute the program without the need to translate it each time. The operating system can also call the other system programs when they are needed.

The Information Services Staff

We have used the name *information specialist* to refer to any computer professional or expert. Historically, there have been three categories of information specialists—the systems analysts who interface with the user, the programmers who create the computer code, and the operators who operate the equipment. We viewed these information specialists as a communication chain in Figure 1-15a. These specialists are organized into a department or division and are managed by someone with responsibility for the firm's computer resources. Various names have been given to the department—data processing, MIS, information systems, and information services. We will use the name information services, recognizing its service function to the firm. Various titles have also been assigned to the manager of information services. This person may be a vice president or a lower-level manager.

During recent years, it has become necessary to add two additional types of specialists in the information services organization—a data base administrator and a network manager. The *data base administrator (DBA)* is responsible for the firm's computerized data base, and the *network manager* is responsible for the data communications network. Figure 5-26 illustrates an information services organization structure that would be found in a firm with a large-scale computing operation. Other structures are also popular.

We will provide additional descriptions of the information services organization and personnel throughout the remainder of the book.

Summary

Information processing can be performed manually, with keydriven machines, or with computers. Computers are most effective when data volumes are large, processing is complex, and/or fast retrieval of stored data is required. The computer is a physical system, but its contents (data and programs) are an important part of the conceptual system of the firm.

Computers come in all sizes. The smallest are called microcomputers or personal computers. Next come minicomputers, followed by medium-scale and large-scale computers, and supercomputers. Supercomputers are not often used to process business data; microcomputers are presently receiving the most attention.

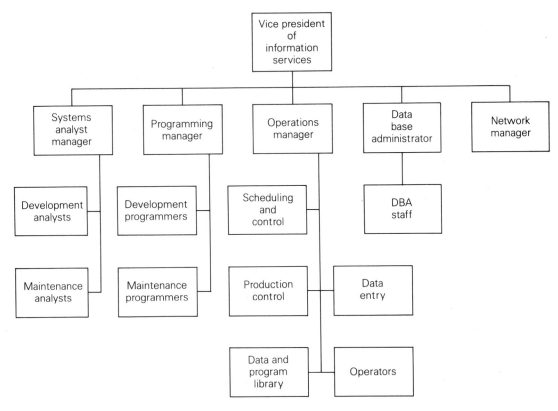

Figure 5-26 The information services organization.

Data can be processed in batches or online. Timesharing involves multiple users sharing a single computer. Distributed processing involves multiple computers. Timesharing and distributed systems can process data in batches or online.

The most popular way to enter data into a computer is with a keyboard terminal. MICR and OCR handle large-volume inputs in banking and retailing. OCR is being adopted in areas such as manufacturing and distribution, but MICR is being replaced by electronic funds transfer. Voice recognition is expected to increase in popularity, especially as an input option for micros.

The line printer has been the output workhorse in the past, but more and more information is being printed by serial printers and displayed on CRT terminals. Plotters offer a graphics capability, as do some serial printers and terminals. Other output forms such as audio response, COM, and punched cards are used in special situations.

The manager interacts directly with only a few of the input-output devices, but other devices enter data into the data base. They all, therefore, play a role in the MIS.

Primary storage is housed in the CPU. It is fast but restricted in capacity. Primary storage can be viewed as having conceptual subdivisions for input, output, working area, application programs, and system programs. Secondary storage augments primary storage but is relatively slow. Magnetic tape is a form of secondary storage but must be used sequentially. Magnetic disk is a type of direct access storage device (DASD) that enables transactions to be processed as they occur—in a random order. Magnetic tape is used primarily on larger systems for master files processed in batches, and for historical storage. DASD files are used on systems of all sizes and provide the fast access to the software library and the data base important to all computer-based MIS and DSS designs.

A combination of application and system software is necessary in order to use the hardware. The operating system is the most important system software, directing the performance of translators, utility programs, DBMS, and data communications packages.

Information specialists are organized in a separate unit that we will call information services. This department includes systems analysts, programmers, operations personnel, data base administrators and a network manager. This department is often managed by a vice president.

We will expand on this foundation of computer concepts in the next three chapters as microcomputers, the data base, and data communications are addressed in greater detail.

Key Terms

manual, keydriven, computer systems

computer schematic

central processing unit (CPU)

arithmetic and logic unit

control unit

microcomputer (micro), personal computer (PC)

intelligent terminal

byte, kilobyte (KB)

cathode ray tube (CRT)

minicomputer (mini)

megabyte (MB)

medium-scale, large-scale computer (mainframe)

supercomputer

online, online processing

transaction processing

offline

batch processing

direct access storage device (DASD)

timesharing

distributed processing, distributed data processing (DDP)

star, ring network

host computer

distributed processing system (DPS)

offline keydriven device

source data automation, direct entry

online keydriven device

voice recognition unit

alphanumeric display, video display terminal

cursor

scrolling

hardcopy

teleprinter, hardcopy terminal

speaker-dependent, speaker-independent system

type font

encoder

reader sorter

magnetic ink character recognition
(MICR)

electronic funds transfer (EFT)

automated teller machine (ATM)

optical character recognition (OCR)

scanner

point of sale (POS)

wand

universal product code (UPC)

line, serial, page printer

impact, nonimpact printer

dot matrix printer

daisywheel printer

letter-quality printer

laser printer

pen plotter, electrostatic plotter

audio response

turnaround document

computer output microfilm (COM)

I/O (input/output) device

primary, secondary storage

metal-oxide semiconductor (MOS)

sequential, direct storage

sequential processing

key

hard disk

diskette, floppy

bit

recording density

magnetic tape unit

header, trailer label

master file

access mechanism

access arm

read/write head

cylinder

access time

sequential, indexed sequential,
direct, partitioned organization

hashing scheme

synonym

procedural language

operating system

multiprogramming

control program

information specialist

data base administrator (DBA)

network manager

Key Concepts

The relative advantages and disadvantages of the three types of information processor—manual, keydriven, and computer

The computer as both a physical system and a part of the conceptual system

How data can be processed in batches or online

The difference between timesharing and distributed processing

How the selection of input, output, and storage units enables a firm to tailor a computer to its own needs

How the five uses of primary storage can be viewed as conceptual areas

The hierarchy of data—from data elements (at the bottom) to records, files, and the data base (at the top)

The process of updating a master file using magnetic tape and magnetic disk

Cylinders of data in a DASD

How data and programs are organized in a DASD

The role of the operating system in the MIS

How the various information specialists form a service unit for the entire firm

---

Questions

1. What are the advantages of using a computer as an information processor? The disadvantages?

2. Is the computer a physical system? A conceptual system? Explain?

3. What are the different computer sizes? Which size is called a mainframe?

4. What is the capacity (in characters) of a computer with 128 KB of primary storage?

5. What are the two basic approaches to computer processing? Which approach requires magnetic tape? DASD?

6. Explain the difference between timesharing and distributed processing.

7. What features have contributed to the popularity of keyboard terminals?

8. What is the main difference between MICR and OCR? Which is losing popularity? Why?

9. Which type of printer uses only impact technology? Nonimpact technology? Which type of printer mechanism produces "letter quality"?

10. What different output devices can be used to prepare graphs?

11. Explain how a manager can use voice recognition in an MIS. Do the same for audio response.

12. What are the two basic types of computer storage? Of secondary storage? In answering the second part, do not use names of storage media.

13. Arrange the following terms in order based on their position in the data hierarchy (starting at the top): record, data base, file, data element.

14. If a magnetic tape unit records data at a density of 800 bpi, how many characters can be recorded in a 10-inch strip?

15. What hardware devices comprise a DASD access mechanism?

16. Explain the cylinder concept.

17. Using the DASD address format in Figure 5-19, what does the address 0110603 specify?

18. Which DASD organization(s) is (are) used for data files? For programs?

19. What conditions would cause you to select magnetic tape over DASD as your secondary storage medium?

20. Name five classifications of employees that you would find in an information services department. (Hint: two of these have become necessary in recent years.)

Problems

1. Draw a schematic of a computer system containing: (1) a CPU, (2) 4 keyboard terminals, (3) 2 DASD units, (4) 4 magnetic tape units, (5) a plotter, (6) a line printer. Use the flowchart symbols from Appendix A.

2. Draw a system flowchart showing how a master file on magnetic tape is updated from a transaction file also on magnetic tape. Do the same for a master file on DASD updated from data entering the system using a keyboard terminal.

3. Draw an organization chart similar to the one in Figure 5-26, but with the following changes: (1) the DBA reports to the systems analyst manager, (2) three systems team managers also report to the systems analyst manager— one each for marketing, manufacturing, and finance, (3) a group of analysts report to each team manager; the analysts are not subdivided into development and maintenance groups.

CASE PROBLEM: O'Meara Brothers Grocery Wholesalers

O'Meara Brothers is a wholesale grocery firm located in Bozeman, Montana. It buys supermarket items from producers, stores them in its warehouse, and delivers them in its fleet of trucks to supermarkets in the Pacific Northwest. They use a Hewlett-Packard 3000 minicomputer primarily for inventory control. Data describing inventory receipts from producers is entered into the HP-3000 using online keyboard terminals. The inventory file, consisting of 25,000 separate items, is stored on magnetic disk.

You are a recent college graduate with a degree in business computer systems. You have just been hired by Big Sky Computer Sales, a firm that sells hardware and software of all types produced by other firms. Big Sky serves as a broker, securing sales orders and then directing the shipment of merchandise to the customers by the suppliers.

Your sales territory includes Montana, Idaho, and part of Wyoming. One day while driving through Bozeman, you notice the large O'Meara building and decide to make a sales call. You are lucky that Fran Wilding, the general manager, is able to see you.

Wilding describes the operation, and you ask if they have any problems. Wilding explains that it sometimes takes a long time to get data into the computer for inventory receipts. When the suppliers' trucks arrive, they are backed up to the receiving dock where O'Meara warehouse clerks move the merchandise to its location using fork-lift trucks. There are 18 clerks, supervised by Michael O'Meara, the warehouse manager. O'Meara has an office and a secretary who maintains files, types correspondence, and takes care of miscellaneous clerical duties. At the time the merchandise is delivered to the warehouse area, the clerks fill out receiving reports (identifying the item, producer, and quantity), and the reports are held in O'Meara's office until the next pickup of company mail. The reports are then delivered to the MIS department where the data is keyed into the HP-3000. Sometimes the data is not entered until the day after the merchandise is received in the warehouse.

You ask Wilding if the merchandise cartons received from the producers have UPC bar codes on them, and she replies "Some do, and most don't." You ask if all of the cartons have markings identifying the supplier, the merchandise type, and the quantity, and Wilding says that all suppliers are required to attach a label to each carton including a 5-digit supplier code assigned by O'Meara, an 8-digit item number, and the quantity. If a carton contains more than a single item type, all are identified on the carton label. The data entry operators in the MIS department key this data from the receiving reports into the HP-3000.

Questions

1. Why isn't the HP-3000 doing a better job of serving as a conceptual system of the physical inventory?

2. What type(s) of computing equipment could solve the problems? Briefly describe how it would be used.

3. Could Michael O'Meara use the same equipment to obtain management information from the computer? Explain.

CASE PROBLEM: Wellborn's Department Stores

Wellborn's is a Midwest chain of seventeen department stores, with headquarters in Chicago. The VAX 11 at headquarters is used for inventory, sales analysis, and charge account collections. The VAX is a medium-scale computer with sufficient speed and capacity to handle the Wellborn's volume with room to spare. Any type of storage unit or input/output device can be attached to the VAX.

Sales clerks in each of the seventeen stores enter sales data on paper sales forms. The data includes customer name and address, items purchased, quantities, and prices. Charge account sales are identified with a special code. The forms are mailed daily to headquarters, where the data is keyed onto magnetic tape using key-to-tape units. The tape is then read by the VAX. Once in the computer, the data is used to update inventory and sales files on magnetic tape. Charge account data is recorded on a collection file (also on magnetic tape) that is used monthly to prepare printed statements. In addition to the statement, a punched card turn-around document is enclosed. When the customer pays the bill, the card data is read by a card reader, and the receivable amount is removed from the collection file. Printed management reports are also prepared on the line printer on a monthly basis. The reports include a list of inventory items showing monthly sales and quantities on hand, and a list of all past-due collections (those over thirty days old).

The store managers have been complaining because they don't have enough information on inventory status and collections. They claim that their information is outdated when they receive it because of the delays caused by mailing and keyboard entry. As a rule, it takes four days after the end of the month to enter all of the month's sales data in the computer. It takes three or four more days for the reports to reach managers by mail. And the managers get the reports only once a month. The reports are practically useless, the managers complain, because they do not represent the actual status of the stores' inventories and collections.

Questions

1. What is the problem?
2. In which part of the general systems model of the firm is the problem located?
3. Which type of processing does Wellborn's use—batch or online? Do they use timesharing or distributed processing?
4. What input devices, if any, do they need? Explain how they would be used.
5. What storage devices, if any, do they need? Explain their use.
6. What output devices, if any, do they need? Explain their use.

Selected Bibliography

Computer Concepts

Allen, F. E., "The History of Language Processor Technology in IBM," *IBM Journal of Research and Development* 25 (September 1981): 535–548.

Auslander, M. A., D. C. Larkin, and A. L. Scherr, "The Evolution of the MVS Operating System," *IBM Journal of Research and Development* 25 (September 1981): 471–482.

Austin, Sandy, "Field Guide to Daisies," *Business Computer Systems* 3 (February 1984): 131ff.

Austin, Sandy, "Feature Attractions," *Business Computer Systems* 4 (February 1985): 79ff.

Bashe, C. J., and Others, "The Architecture of IBM's Early Computers," *IBM Journal of Research and Development* 25 (September 1981): 363–375.

Bernstein, Amy, "Bar Codes Earn Their Stripes," *Business Computer Systems* 4 (February 1985): 68ff.

Bohl, Marilyn, *Introduction to IBM Direct Access Storage Devices* (Chicago: Science Research Associates, 1981).

Borrell, Jerry, "Graphics Users Gain From Vendors' Rivalry," *Mini-Micro Systems* 18 (April 19, 1985): 83ff.

Buchanan, Jack R., and Richard G. Linowes, "Understanding Distributed Data Processing," *Harvard Business Review* 58 (July-August 1980): 143–153.

Buchanan, Jack R., and Richard G. Linowes, "Making Distributed Data Processing Work," *Harvard Business Review* 58 (September-October 1980): 143–161.

Dalrymple, Rick, "Leaner Page Printers Bid for Office Space," *Mini-Micro Systems* 18 (April 19, 1985): 55ff.

DeSanctis, Gerardine, "Computer Graphics as Decision Aids: Directions for Research," *Decision Sciences* 15 (Fall 1984): 463-487.

Friedman, Roy R., "Minicomputer Companies Move Toward Industry-Standard Software," *Mini-Micro Systems* 17 (April 1984): 137ff.

Harris, J. P., and Others, "Innovations in the Design of Magnetic Tape

Subsystems," *IBM Journal of Research and Development* 25 (September 1981): 691–699.

Levine, Ronald D., "Supercomputers," *Scientific American* 246 (January 1982): 118ff.

Li, Lindsay, "Drawing Conclusions," *Business Computer Systems* 3 (April 1984): 115ff.

Mace, Scott, "Affordable Color," *Infoworld* 6 (October 1, 1984): 42–43.

Mendez, Raul, and Steve Orszag, "The Japanese Supercomputer Challenge," *Datamation* 30 (May 15, 1984): 112ff.

Rushinek, Avi, and Sara Rushinek, "Distributed Processing: Implications and Applications for Business," *Journal of Systems Management* 35 (July 1984): 21–27.

Sammet, Jean E., "History of IBM's Technical Contributions to High Level Programming Languages," *IBM Journal of Research and Development* 25 (September 1981): 520–534.

Simpson, David, "Line Printer Leaders Lower Prices, Improve Reliability," *Mini-Micro Systems* 17 (September 1984): 175ff.

Strassmann, Paul A., and Charles F. Willard, "The Evolution of the Page Printer," *Datamation* 24 (May 1978): 167–170.

Verity, John W., "Upstarts Outshine the Stars," *Datamation* 30 (November 15, 1984): 34ff.

Verity, John W., "Up, Up, and Away," *Datamation* 31 (May 15, 1985): 32ff.

Watson, Collin J., and Russell W. Driver, "The Influence of Computer Graphics on the Recall of Information," *MIS Quarterly* 7 (March 1983): 45–53.

Weizer, Norman, "Sierra: Where Will It Lead?," *Datamation* 31 (May 15, 1985): 84ff.

Whieldon, David, "Small But Powerful Printers," *Computer Decisions* 17 (March 26, 1985): 114ff.

Woods, Tom, "The Laser Factor," *Business Computer Systems* 3 (July 1984): 96ff.

Chapter 6

Microcomputer Systems

Learning Objectives

After studying this chapter, you should:

- Know how the micro boom got started
- Appreciate the impact that microcomputers are having on the MIS
- Understand the basic features of microcomputer hardware
- Know the distinguishing features of the three most popular operating systems for micros
- Know what procedural languages are being used to create custom programs for micros
- Have a good understanding of types of prewritten micro software for particular business applications
- Be familiar with the features of electronic spreadsheets, and how they have evolved into integrated decision support packages
- Be familiar with some of the more popular brands of micros
- Appreciate some of the control problems that micros are causing, and some of the solutions that are being pursued
- Have an idea of how to go about selecting a micro to use in an MIS

Introduction

We are in the midst of the second computer revolution. The first one involved the use of large computers—mainframes—by larger organizations. That revolution has had time to run its course. Most of the larger firms now have computers, and there are fewer breakthroughs in mainframe hardware and software. The second revolution is that of small computers—minicomputers and microcomputers. These smaller computers enable smaller organizations to enjoy the benefits of computer processing. But the small computers are having major effects on larger organizations as well.

In this chapter, we examine the effect that the small computer boom is having on the MIS. We make specific reference to microcomputers as they are receiving the most current attention. Much of the material also relates to minicomputers.

The Small-Computer Boom

The first computers to feature small size were called *minicomputers*. The mini-computer era got its start in 1963, when Digital Equipment Corporation (DEC) announced its PDP-5, selling for $27,000. The PDP-5 was followed in 1965 by the more powerful PDP-8, selling for only $18,000. These first two minicomputers set the trend toward smaller size, more powerful performance, and lower cost.

At first, minicomputers (or *minis*) were not applied to business data processing tasks, but to scientific and production problems. In manufacturing, minis were used to monitor and control production machines, to test products, and to control heating, power, and water systems. Perhaps one reason why business applications were not attempted on the early minis is that the established computer manufacturers, such as IBM, Burroughs, and National Cash Register (NCR), did not offer minicomputer systems. They did not want to replace their larger, more expensive units with minis. Another deterrent was the fact that early minis, offered by firms with little commercial experience (such as DEC, Data General, Hewlett-Packard, and Wang) did not have the system or application software that the commercial users required.

But the momentum of the minicomputer was unstoppable. In 1970 IBM shipped its first mini, the System/3. Other old-line manufacturers, such as Burroughs, Honeywell, UNIVAC, and NCR, followed suit with their small systems. These systems, marketed for business applications, are often called *small business computers*.

The early minis were easily distinguished from their larger counterparts. These small systems were limited in terms of internal operations, software support, and input/output equipment. Purchase prices ranged from $3,000 to $50,000, and primary storage seldom exceeded 32KB.

The distinctive features of the minis soon blurred. Minis often had more storage, processed data faster, and generally outperformed larger systems. The name "mini" no longer seemed appropriate.

In the late 1970s another boom emerged—the even smaller *microcomputer* (or *micro*). The beginnings of the microcomputer era can be traced back to 1971 when Ted Hoff, an Intel Corporation engineer, designed the first *microprocessor*—or "computer on a chip." This microprocessor, the Intel 4004, consisted of 2250 transistors on an MOS chip measuring 0.117 by 0.159 inch. Within four years of the 4004 introduction, approximately twenty different microprocessors were placed on the market by firms such as Rockwell International and National Semiconductor. A modern microprocessor is pictured in Figure 6-1.

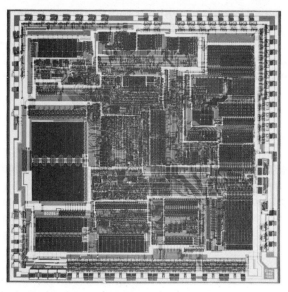

Figure 6-1 A microprocessor.
Source: Intel Corporation.

A microprocessor is not a computer. It only provides part of the CPU circuitry. In order for the microprocessor to have a special value in business information processing, it must be integrated with storage and input/output units. This integration produces the microcomputer.

The first microcomputer was the Altair 8800, offered in kit form in 1975 for about $400 and featuring the Intel 8080 microprocessor. The next year, Steve Jobs and Stephen Wozniak started work on the Apple computer in their garage. Their efforts were initially just for fun, but in 1977 they formed a partnership, got an order from a local store, and started producing and selling Apples in volume. Improvements in the initial design led to the Apple II, which became the heart of the micro boom.

Also in 1977 two other successful micro efforts were launched. Commodore International, a Canadian firm, announced their PET, and Radio Shack announced their TRS-80. Both the PET and TRS-80 enjoyed immediate success as individuals purchased them primarily for home use. The term *personal computer* captured the notion that an individual can have her or his own computer. Computers had stepped out of large organizations and into the home.

It took a move by IBM to lend legitimacy to the micro as a business computing tool. In 1980 a group of IBM engineers, led by Don Estridge, began working on the computer that was to become known simply as the PC.[1] The IBM PC was announced in August of 1981, and it quickly began competing successfully with the industry leaders—the Apple, Commodore, and Radio Shack units.

---

[1]Don Estridge and his wife Mary Anne died in the crash of Delta Flight 191 at DFW airport on August 2, 1985.

Within two years, IBM had shipped almost 750,000 systems and was second only to Apple in annual sales.[2]

The immediate success of the IBM PC was due to several factors, not the least of which was IBM's reputation for quality and service in supporting business users. But the PC did not follow the pattern set by previous IBM products. For one thing, most of the PC units were produced by other firms. The diskette drives were initially produced by Tandon Corporation, the CRT display was from Taiwan, and the printer was produced by Epson. IBM used highly automated production techniques to assemble the CPU and the keyboard in large quantities and at low cost.

In addition to the innovative (for IBM) hardware strategy, the software approach was also unique in that IBM elected not to produce it themselves. Rather, they encouraged software firms to provide both system and application programs. This open invitation produced the largest number of software packages available for any computer—some 1,500 separate programs.[3]

A third innovative strategy involved marketing. IBM decided not only to sell the PC through its own sales network, but also to license retailers such as ComputerLand. The potential purchaser, therefore, had a choice of sources.

The PC popularity has added momentum to the microcomputer boom initiated by Apple, Radio Shack, and Commodore. Those firms have continued to develop newer, better products such as the Apple Lisa, the Macintosh, and Tandy TRS-80 Model 2000. Dozens of other firms have also joined in the competition. Some of the firms have jumped on the IBM PC bandwagon and developed PC clones called *PC compatibles*. By 1984 the compatibles had acquired about 10 percent of the micro market, compared to the 28 percent represented by the IBM PC.[4]

The microcomputer boom shows no signs of slowing down. The 1984 entry of AT&T Information Systems with its PC6300 micro will cause IBM and the others to work even harder to produce improved products. In 1985 it was estimated that one-third of all American companies were using micros in some way, and by 1990 three-fourths of all computing resources will be controlled by end users.[5] Many of these end users will be using personal computers either as standalone information processors or as part of larger computer networks.

The Role of Micros in the MIS

It is easy to think of micros serving as information processors in small firms. Many are, and that is one reason why the micro boom has such significance to

---

[2]"Personal Computers: And the Winner is IBM," *Business Week* (October 3, 1983): 76.

[3]*PC World 1985 Annual Software Review.*

[4]Dennis Kneale and Alan Freeman, "Commodore Unit Signs License Accord Over IBM-Compatible Computer Gear," *The Wall Street Journal* (March 1, 1984): 10.

[5]Louis E. Raho and James A. Belohlav, "Integrating Personal Computers into Organizations: Problems, Benefits, and Training Issues," *Journal of Systems Management* 36 (March 1985): 16–17.

MIS. Were it not for the micros, many small firms could not afford a computer-based information processor.

But micros are used in large firms as well. Some managers have their own micros and are using them as *personal information processors*. These managers prepare or purchase their own software and build their own data bases. In some firms, the micros are linked with other computers to form a network. In these configurations, the micros can serve as intelligent keyboard terminals connected to other computers, or as stand-alone processors.

As information processors or as intelligent terminals in a network, the micros provide the manager with information. This is the most popular role of micros in an MIS. But more and more attention is being given to the use of micros as a means of communicating decisions to the physical system of the firm. This use is one that office automation contributes to the MIS. Managers can use micros to generate electronic mail or voice mail messages to others in the firm, resulting in altered performance of the physical system. Word processing is also used to prepare paper documents to communicate decisions within the firm.

These uses of micros are illustrated in Figure 6-2. We will provide more information on networked micros in Chapter 8 (Data Communications) and on decision communication in Chapter 10 (Office Automation).

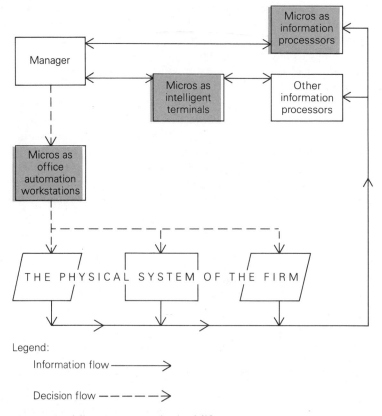

Figure 6-2   Microcomputers in the MIS.

Microcomputer Hardware

Micros fit the computer schematic presented in Chapter 5. The schematic is redrawn in Figure 6-3 to provide a guide for our examination of hardware components. All computers consist of the components in the figure, but the packaging varies depending on system size.

The IBM PC pictured in Figure 6-4 includes all of the components of the schematic. The keyboard is the input device, the large unit just behind the key-

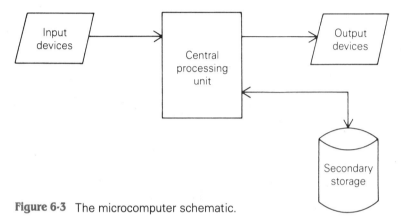

Figure 6-3 The microcomputer schematic.

Figure 6-4 The IBM Personal Computer.

Source: Reprinted from page 1-4, Guide to Operations
(Copyright 1983 International Business Machines Corporation).

board houses the CPU (called the *system unit*) and secondary storage, and the CRT screen sitting on top is the output device. Secondary storage is provided by one or two diskette drives mounted on the right front of the system unit.

It is very common to attach a serial printer as a second output device. Such a printer is pictured in Figure 6-5. A wide variety of serial printers are available.

The CPU

The CPU often consists of a large printed circuit board with many electronic devices such as MOS chips mounted on it. In the IBM PC, this board, called the *motherboard*, measures 8½ by 12 inches. Figure 6-6 is a layout showing where the more important items are located.

Two microprocessors are located in the upper right-hand corner. IBM selected the Intel 8088 to perform the control functions of the CPU and the optional Intel 8087 to supplement the arithmetic and logic unit. Many other microcomputers use these same components.

The primary storage is subdivided into *read-only memory (ROM)* and *random-access memory (RAM)*. These terms are a product of the microcomputer era. ROM stores prewritten routines loaded into the computer by the manufacturer. You can read these routines and execute them, but you cannot alter them. ROM is software in a hardware form. The IBM PC has 40KB of ROM. A limited version of the BASIC language occupies 32KB, and something called RIOS (pronounced rye-ose) occupies the remaining 8KB. RIOS stands for ROM Basic Input/ Output System, and it controls the transfer of data between the CPU and other units.

RAM provides storage for application and system programs as well as input, output, and working areas. These are the conceptual areas identified in Chapter 5. You can write data on RAM as well as read data from it. The IBM PC comes with 256KB of RAM, expandable to 640KB. Earlier micros offered smaller capac-

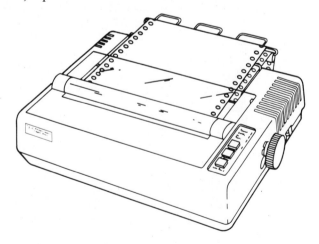

Figure 6-5 A serial printer used with IBM PC.

Source: Reprinted from page 1-4, Guide to Operations *(Copyright 1983 International Business Machines Corporation).*

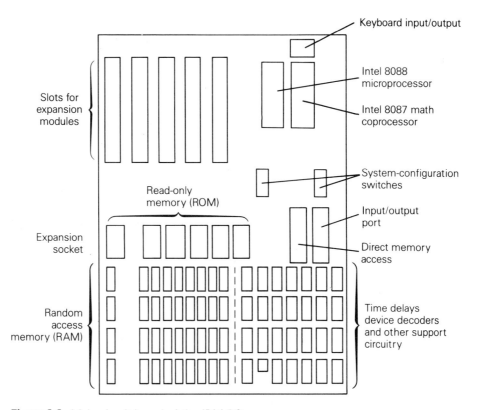

Keyboard input/output

Intel 8088 microprocessor

Intel 8087 math coprocessor

Slots for expansion modules

System-configuration switches

Input/output port

Read-only memory (ROM)

Expansion socket

Direct memory access

Random access memory (RAM)

Time delays device decoders and other support circuitry

Figure 6-6 Main circuit board of the IBM PC.

ities, usually 32KB, but much of today's sophisticated software requires at least 64KB.

In the upper left-hand corner of the motherboard are located slots for adding extra electronic components. The IBM PC offers five such slots. The extra circuitry is packaged on *expansion boards* (pictured in Figure 6-7) that are plugged into available slots. The capacity and performance of your system is upgraded by buying the additional components and plugging them in. For example, you can add extra RAM by plugging in a memory expansion board or add a graphics capability by plugging in a graphics board.

Most micros are constructed in this same manner but offer greater or lesser capacity and flexibility. As an example, the Macintosh has no expansion slots, whereas the TRS-80 Model 2000 has four. Many of the PC compatibles come with 512KB RAM standard, whereas the Compaq portable includes only 128KB.

Input

Micros use fewer types of input devices than do larger computers. You don't normally find OCR and MICR readers attached to a micro, for example. The common practice is to key data directly into a micro using the keyboard.

The IBM PC keyboard is pictured in Figure 6-8. The area in the center is arranged the same as a typewriter—number keys across the top, space bar at the bottom, and upper and lower shift. In addition, there are some keys unique to

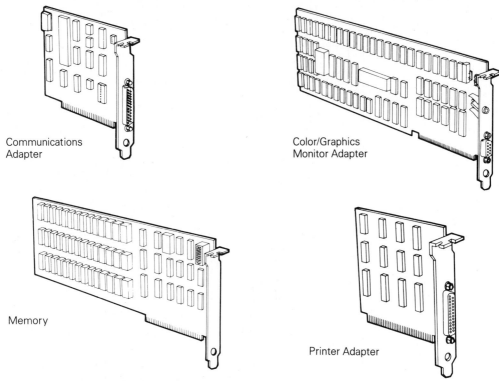

Figure 6-7 Expansion boards.

Source: Reprinted from pages 1-6 and 1-7. Guide to Operations *(Copyright 1983 International Business Machines Corporation).*

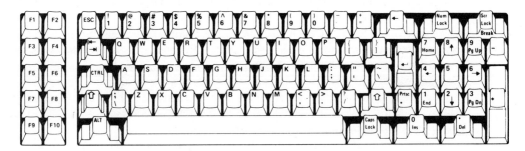

Figure 6-8 The IBM PC keyboard.

computer operation such as "Ctrl," "PrtSc," and "Del." The Ctrl (Control) key is used in conjunction with other keys to perform special functions. As an example, when using WordStar (a word processing package), pressing the Y key while holding down the Ctrl key causes a line to be deleted. The PrtSc (Print Screen) key causes the screen display to be printed on the printer, and the Del (Delete) key is used to correct errors.

There is a block of ten keys at the right of the keyboard marked with numbers and arrows. This area is referred to as a *numeric keypad*. The numbers are arranged like a pocket calculator. If you are adept at using a calculator, you can use these keys to enter numbers, rather than use the keys across the top. The arrows are used to control the cursor on the screen—up, down, left, and right.

There are other keys with arrows. The large key to the left of the numeric keypad marked with a crooked arrow (⏎) is called the Enter key. You use it to enter data that you have just keyed into the keyboard and displayed on the screen.

The 10 keys at the left are called *function keys*. They are labeled F1 to F10, and each one performs a special function depending on the software being used. For example, if you are using the WordStar word processing package and press the F10 key, the cursor moves to the end of the file that you have created.

Not all micro keyboards are arranged identically to the IBM PC. The PC keyboard has been criticized for being hard to use because of its large size and the location of some of the keys. Some keyboards have the cursor keys arranged in a different pattern, and some do not include function keys.

Some older micros (such as the TRS-80 Model 1 and the Apple II) have the keyboard built into the CPU cabinet. On the IBM PC, the keyboard is separate, attached to the system unit by a coiled cord such as that used on a telephone. This arrangement allows you to move the keyboard around on the table without moving the system unit.

There is another input device that you usually don't find on an IBM PC, and it is a *mouse*. This is a small box, about the size of a pack of cigarettes, that is attached to the CPU with a cable. The Macintosh, pictured in Figure 6-9, features the mouse as an easy-to-use input device. You move the mouse around on the table, and the cursor (in this case a pointer arrow) moves around on the screen in the same pattern. You can "point" the cursor to certain areas, press the button on the mouse, and cause things to happen. For example, if you are using the Jazz software package, you can use the mouse to cause a bar graph to change from a vertical to a horizontal arrangement.

Output

We discussed serial printers in Chapter 5 and will not repeat that material here. There are a wide variety from which to choose, ranging in price from about $200 to $3,000. A big factor is whether you want letter quality printing. If so, that requirement usually (but not always) means higher cost.

The other primary output device is the CRT screen. This unit is called a *monitor* or a *display* and comes in two basic types—just like televisions. One model uses only one color in addition to black. The color can be white, green, or amber. This is your black and white TV. On the IBM PC, the two-color monitor is called a *monochrome display*. The other basic type uses multiple colors, like a color TV. On the IBM PC, this unit is called a *color monitor*.

A screen has a predetermined capacity for the number of lines, and the number of characters on each line. The IBM PC displays 25 lines of 80 characters. Most monitors are in this ballpark. The early Apple II displayed only 40 characters on a line, and this feature restricted its use for some business applications.

If your micro has a graphics capability (such as a graphics board in the IBM PC system unit), you can display graphs on the monitor and print them on a graphics printer or a plotter. It is possible to attach an ink-pen plotter to a micro, and such configurations do an excellent job of printing graphs. If a company has

Figure 6-9 The Macintosh features "mouse" input.
Source: Courtesy of Apple Computer, Inc.

an information center, they probably have a micro with a plotter for use as a graphics system. Of course, in order to output graphics to a plotter, printer, or screen, you need the graphics software. The Lotus 1-2-3 package did much to promote graphical output, and many DSS packages now feature that option.

Secondary storage media

The secondary storage for most micros is provided by diskettes or "floppies." The first diskettes were 8″ in diameter and were used in key-to-disk data entry devices. IBM shipped the first such unit, the 3740, in 1973. In 1976 Schugart Associates brought out the first 5¼″ diskette, which has been adopted for most micros. Sony developed a 3½″ size in 1981 for its first micro, but that size has been slow to catch on. The small diskette is used in the Macintosh, however, as well as in very small portables that we will discuss later. It seems logical that such small diskettes will increase in popularity as the recording densities become greater. The Macintosh diskette has a capacity of 400KB, almost twice that of the first 8″ diskette.

Figure 6-10 shows a diskette in its sealed, protective cover. The entire package is inserted into the diskette drive, label up, with the oval read/write opening facing the computer. A rotating spindle is inserted through the large hole in the diskette, and the plastic diskette is rotated inside its cover. Data is read and written through the oval opening. Some diskette drives can only read and write data on one side of the diskette; they are called *single-sided drives*. Others, called *double-sided drives*, can handle both sides. The early IBM PC drives were single-sided, but a double-sided option was added in 1982.

Another pair of terms that you hear are single density and double density. A *double-density drive* records the data bits twice as close together as a *single-density drive*. IBM achieved this ability in 1977, and the PC drives have always been double density.

There are a couple of other diskette features that we should recognize. The *timing hole* is used to locate the beginning of a recording area. Most diskettes have only a single hole in the plastic that can be detected through the hole in the cover. These diskettes are called *soft-sectored* since the micro software determines the layout of the diskette. A *hard-sectored* diskette has multiple (10, 16, or 32) holes in the plastic, and the micro hardware determines the diskette layout.

The *write-protect notch* is a safety feature. When it is covered by a small piece of tape, the micro cannot write data on the diskette. You can protect valuable data and programs by covering the notch. This practice, plus that of making

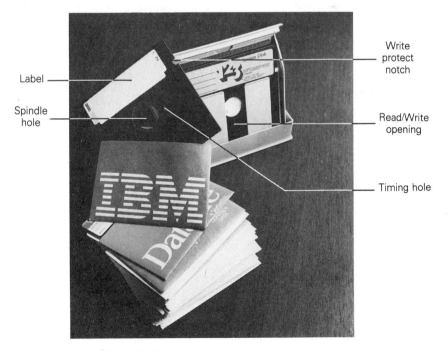

Figure 6-10 A diskette.

backup copies, is a good habit. It greatly reduces the possibility that your data and programs will be inadvertently "clobbered" (erased or altered).

When you go to a computer store to buy a diskette, you have to understand these terms. The clerk will ask you "single-sided or double? Single-density or double? Soft-sectored or hard?" A single-sided, single-density diskette doesn't mean that it won't work on a double-sided, double-density drive. It simply means that the manufacturer has verified that only one side is free from flaws and can record data at the lower density. Many micro users save money by using the less expensive single-sided, single-density diskettes on double-sided, double-density drives.

Diskette layout

The layout of a diskette used on the IBM PC is shown in Figure 6-11. The data bits are recorded serially in circular tracks. On the IBM PC, there are 40 tracks per side. These tracks are numbered 00–39 on one side and 40–79 on the other. Each diskette surface is divided into *sectors*, like slices of a pie. IBM PC diskettes created using earlier operating systems had 8 sectors per diskette side. Current operating systems use 9 sectors numbered 0–8. Each length of track within a sector contains 512 bytes. The bits are recorded more densely on inner tracks, but the capacity is the same.

Some micros have two diskette drives, some have only one, and some have none. A two-drive system enables you to keep your write-protected program diskette in one drive and your data diskette in the other, for example.

We saw in Chapter 5 that each record in a DASD must have an address. The diskette is a DASD; therefore, an addressing scheme is required. If the PC is to

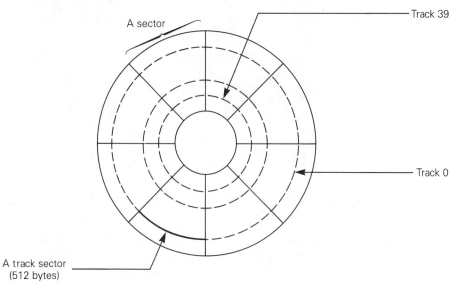

Figure 6-11 The layout of a diskette.

read or write diskette data, the address must specify the drive, the track, and the sector. The format of a diskette address might appear as:

Drive   Track   Sector

| 1 | | 2 | 9 | | 5 |

This address sends the read/write mechanism on diskette drive 1 to track 29, and data is either read from sector 5 or written onto it. All 512 bytes are read or written in one operation.

We should note that an address such as the above is used by the computer, not the user. The user need only supply the name of the file, such as PAYROLL. In some cases, the diskette drive must also be specified, such as B:PAYROLL. On the IBM PC, the left-hand drive is called the "A: drive," and the one on the right is the "B: drive."

Hard disks

A diskette handled by a single-sided IBM PC drive has a capacity of 184,320 bytes (40 × 9 × 512). The capacity is 368,640 for a double-sided drive. This seems like a lot, but some applications require more. The need for larger capacity has caused some users to add a *hard-disk drive* to their micros. This is a metal disk with greater capacity and speed than a floppy. The name *Winchester disk* is often used to describe the hard disk. "Winchester" was the code name that IBM used for the first such unit, introduced in 1973 for its mainframe computers. Actually, "Winchester" describes a special type of metal disk—one with the disk and its access mechanism encased in a contamination-free covering.

Early hard disks had a 10MB capacity, but these soon became obsolete when IBM announced the PC AT with a 20MB hard disk. Now, the 20MB capacity is the industry standard. During the next few years, the capacity should increase to 40MB. Most of the current hard disk drives fit into the same area required for a 5¼" diskette. One hard disk with 10MB capacity fits into an expansion board slot of the CPU.

It is a good idea to always keep duplicate copies of your secondary storage. This practice applies to both diskettes and hard disks. You make backup copies of diskettes by using the operating system's disk copy command. You keep the two copies in separate locations. You make a backup copy of your hard disk by "dumping" its contents onto diskettes or magnetic tape. When using diskettes, this copying process can be time consuming. Almost 30 diskettes are needed to contain the contents of a 10MB hard disk. But the user who ignores the practice is leaving himself or herself open to trouble.

Putting the hardware in perspective

A micro has fewer hardware devices than a mainframe, such as high-speed MICR and OCR input, line and page printers, and so on. But you can get hardware devices such as online keyboard input and DASD that were characteristic of the more expensive mainframes just a few years ago. The micro puts a very powerful decision-support tool in the hands of the manager.

Since the hardware is so inexpensive, practically any organization can afford a micro. This has its benefits for smaller organizations that otherwise could not own a computer. But the low cost also has its drawbacks—it's easy to buy a computer that is not for you. The hardware may be fine, but it may not come with the needed programs. The software is the key to using a micro in an MIS.

Microcomputer Software

In Chapter 5 we distinguished between system software and application software. In this chapter, we will discuss two major categories of system software for micros—operating systems and procedural languages. We will delay our discussion of data base management systems until Chapter 7 (Data Base). In this chapter, we will also discuss three categories of application software—prewritten application packages, electronic spreadsheets, and integrated packages.

Operating systems

It is the general practice to write operating systems for particular microprocessors. The first popular micro operating system was *CP/M (Control Program for Microprocessors)* by Digital Research. CP/M was designed for microprocessors such as the Intel 8080 and 8085 and also the Zilog Z80. These early microprocessors handled 8 bits at a time. All of the pathways inside the microprocessor were like 8-lane highways, allowing all 8 bits of a byte to be transmitted at one time. These early computers were called *8-bit word machines*—each group of bits transferred in parallel is called a *word*. The number of bits handled at a time is *one* of the factors influencing processing speed. The more bits handled at once the faster.

Then, along came the IBM PC. IBM chose the Intel 8088, with an ability to process 16 bits at a time. This circuitry gave the PC an advantage over its competitors—the 8-bit Apple II and TRS-80. IBM contracted with Microsoft Corporation to provide the operating system for the 8088-based PC. The operating system is called *PC-DOS*, the DOS (pronounced "dahss") standing for disk operating system. It serves a disk-oriented computer. IBM allowed Microsoft to market their own version, called *MS-DOS*. This was part of IBM's strategy to encourage software firms to develop programs for the PC. The software firms could design their programs to work in conjunction with MS-DOS.

All during this time, another operating system was slowly gaining support, most of which was outside the business community. In 1969 Bell Telephone Laboratories designed an operating system called *UNIX*. UNIX is special in that it permits multiple users to share the computer at one time—multiprogramming. Historically, micros have generally been used by only one person at a time. To accommodate multiple users, the micro configuration requires multiple input/

output devices, an operating system that can allocate the hardware to the users, and a microprocessor such as the Intel 80286 that permits multiple users. The IBM PC AT has such a multiuser ability.

Since it was not written with business users in mind, UNIX has been slow in gaining acceptance outside the scientific community. But there are UNIX supporters in business who believe it to be the best bet for the future.

IBM ignored UNIX for a long time—but in early 1985 was working on five versions. Altogether there are approximately 40 UNIX versions on the market, including names like PC/IX, VENIX, and XENIX. Whether any of these versions will gain widespread support from business users is anyone's guess. Some basic improvements will be necessary to adapt UNIX to a business environment. Much depends on the degree to which IBM lends support.

There is no question, however, about which operating system is currently dominant. It is MS-DOS. It is not fancy, but it gets the job done. It is very user friendly, and that feature has contributed to the popularity of MS-DOS micros as decision support systems.

Procedural languages

There has always been general agreement that BASIC is the most popular programming language for micros. Invented by Dartmouth professors John G. Kemeny and Thomas E. Kurtz in 1962, BASIC was quickly accepted because of the ease with which it could be learned. It was originally intended for use on mainframe terminals, but William Gates and Paul Allen, the cofounders of Microsoft, developed the first micro version in 1975.

The main problem with BASIC is that there are no standards such as with FORTRAN and COBOL. Many BASIC versions have evolved over the years and some major differences exist. A BASIC program written for an Apple IIe might not run on a Radio Shack TRS-80, for example.

The number of different versions of a language provides a measure of the popularity of the language. The language developers are attracted to languages that can be sold. Figure 6-12 shows the number of versions of the more popular languages available for the IBM PC. BASIC is the clear leader, followed in order by FORTRAN, C, and Pascal. Then come LISP, FORTH, and COBOL. In addition, there are languages such as PL/I, Assembler, and Ada with only one or two versions.

All of the languages in Figure 6-12 are not used in business. C and FORTH feature very succinct code that is difficult to modify and update. Pascal has difficulty in handling DASD files. LISP is used in artificial intelligence—just emerging in business. The popular business languages are BASIC, FORTRAN, and COBOL.

BASIC is likely to remain the primary language for years to come. It can handle both data processing and decision support applications equally well. This feature makes it a good language for small firms that may have only one programmer. And, since it is not intimidating, computer-literate managers can use it to obtain information not available from prewritten software.

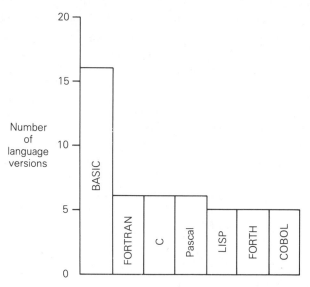

Figure 6-12 Language versions available for the IBM PC.
Source: PC World 1985 Annual Software Review.

Prewritten application software

Most of the prewritten application software performs *accounting functions* such as payroll, inventory, and general ledger. We will investigate these packages in Chapter 9 (Data Processing Systems).

Since about 1982, a large number of micro software packages have been produced that the manager can use in decision making. Some of these packages focus on management problems in general, whereas others aim at particular problems. An example of a *general DSS package* is Executive Package, from Alpha Software Corp. It addresses 40 key business problems including those found in planning, budgeting, and scheduling. Another example is Decision-Analyst from Executive Software, Inc. It assists the manager in selecting the best solution by quantitatively evaluating the various alternatives.

A good example of a DSS package aimed at a *particular type of problem* is Forwork from Percs Software. Forwork is used to manage projects, such as the construction of a new building or design of a new product. It can control up to 4,096 projects at one time and produce reports for as many as 255 managers on 16 levels.

A large number of *statistical packages* have been prepared for micros. Some of these packages include only a single statistical routine such as regression analysis. Most, however, offer a variety of routines. Table 6-1 lists 21 of these packages and shows some of the routines offered.[6]

---

[6]Most of the packages listed are analyzed in more detail in James Carpenter, Dennis Deloria, and David Morganstein, "Statistical Software for Microcomputers," *Byte* 9 (April 1984): 234ff.

Table 6-1   Some statistical packages for micros

Package	Discriminant analysis	Factor analysis	Multiple regression	Paired T tests	ANOVA N-way
ABSAT			*	*	2
AIDA			*	*	1
A-Stat		*	*	*	2
Dynacomp Multilin			*		
Dynacomp ANOVA					5
HSD Stats Plus				*	2
HSD Regress II			*		
HSD ANOVA II					5
Introstat				*	2
Microstat			*	*	2
Micro-TSP			*		
Number Cruncher		*	*	*	4
NWA Statpak			*	*	3
SAM	*	*	*	*	10
SpeedSTAT, Vol. II			*		
SPS		*	*		1
STATGRAPHICS	*	*	*	*	12
STAN			*		
Statpro	*	*	*	*	3
SYSTAT	*	*	*	*	30
TWG ELF	*	*	*	*	2

The availability of both plotters and graphics printers for micros has stimulated a great deal of activity in producing *graphics packages*. Some of the packages include Chartstar, Chartmaster, Graphwriter, and PFS Graph. These packages take output from other programs and produce a variety of graphs—such as bar, line, and pie chart. The graphs can be in black and white or multiple colors. The EXEC*U*STAT package from Statistical Graphics Corporation integrates statistics and graphics. An example of the graphic output from a statistical analysis is shown in Figure 6-13.

Electronic spreadsheets

Daniel S. Bricklin and Robert M. Frankston, of Personal Software, triggered the interest in DSS software with their VisiCalc electronic spreadsheet package. Released in 1979, it became the largest-selling package in computer history by reaching the 200,000 mark in 1982. These sales stimulated numerous other companies to bring out their own spreadsheets—Multiplan, CalcStar, SuperCalc, EasyCalc, and so on. By the end of 1984, it was estimated that some 2.5 million spreadsheet packages had been sold.

VisiCalc is a success because it is very logical in its design and can be learned quickly by someone with limited computer skills. It was the first DSS package to be truly user friendly.

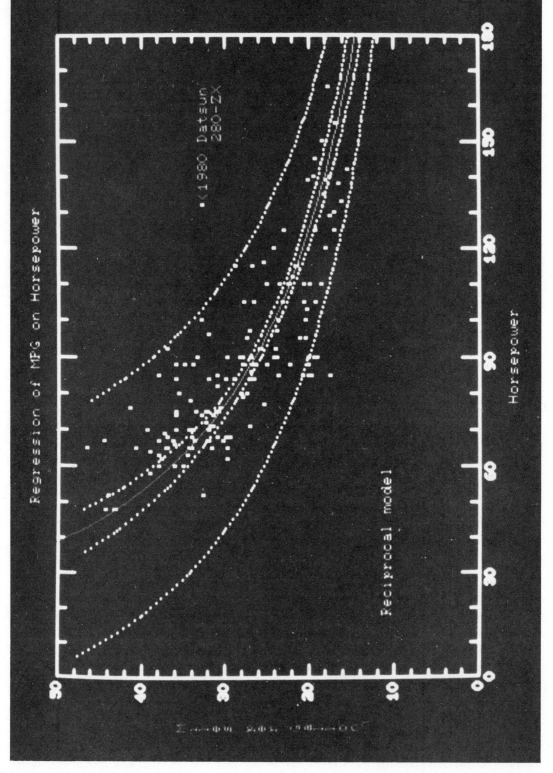

Figure 6-13 Graphical output from a statistical package.

An *electronic spreadsheet* displays data in a grid of columns and rows. This is the way that many people are taught to view data in accounting courses. The electronic spreadsheet is just a modern version of the ledger sheets that accountants and financial analysts have used for years. The VisiCalc spreadsheet consists of 254 rows and 63 columns. More modern packages provide greater size. Lotus 1-2-3 has 256 columns, and Symphony has 1,024.

The intersection of each row and column is a *cell*, which can contain a number, a label such as "Net Profit," or a formula. You can design the spreadsheet so that it functions as a dynamic what-if model by using the columns as time periods. Figure 6-14 is a model that simulates the effect of a price change over the next three years. When you make a change to the contents of one cell, the software updates all other cells that use the changed value. In the pricing model, a change in price produces changes in other income and expense cells. This ease of reflecting changes throughout the spreadsheet enhances its value to the user.

Integrated software

VisiCalc triggered interest in electronic spreadsheets. WordStar triggered a similar interest in word processing, and dBASE II popularized data base management systems. We have also seen that there are graphics packages. All of these packages are designed to be used separately, but users frequently want to take data from one package and use that data in another package. For example, take data from a data base, use it in a spreadsheet, and prepare a graph.

There have been four basic approaches to solving this problem of package integration. The first, the *product family*, was conceived by VisiCorp (the new name adopted by Personal Software). VisiCorp developed other packages that can transfer data to and from VisiCalc. VisiFile is a DBMS that can provide data

```
DECISIONS:

    PRICE                   15.00
    QUANTITY SOLD           25000              26500              28090

RESULTS:                                       YEAR
                            1                  2                  3


SALES REVENUE            375000.00          397500.00          421350.00

EXPENSES
    MANUFACTURING       112500.00          119250.00          126405.00
    MARKETING            75000.00           79500.00           84270.00
    ADMINISTRATION       66250.00           69625.00           73202.50

    TOTAL               253750.00          268375.00          283877.50

GROSS PROFIT            121250.00          129125.00          137472.50
```

Figure 6-14 Using the spreadsheet as a dynamic, what-if model.

to VisiCalc, and VisiTrend/Plot can use the VisiCalc output to prepare graphs. The packages are designed to be used together.

The second approach includes *file conversion utilities* such as Software Art's DIF and Microsoft's SYLK. With DIF (data interchange format), you use a special file name extension when producing a data file on one package to be used on another. For example, PFS:Graph accepts the DIF format; you can create a spreadsheet using another package and transfer it to PFS:Graph for printing.

The third approach is called *all-in-one applications package*. This is the method used by Lotus 1-2-3, Context MBA, and Framework that incorporates multiple packages into one. 1-2-3 integrates a spreadsheet, a data base system, and a graphics package. MBA includes these same packages, plus data communications and word processing. When you buy one of these integrated packages, you can perform the various functions, but you cannot select packages for each function. You take the package as is.

The most flexible approach is the *operating environment* composed of a program that integrates packages of your choice. Examples are VisiCorp's VisiOn, Quarterdeck Software's DESQ, and Microsoft's Windows. These packages enable you to continue using your favorite packages such as WordStar and dBASE II but tie them together so that output from one can provide input for another.

Integrated packages are currently receiving the most attention of all micro software. The next few years will see additional improvements in this area, to capitalize on the high level of interest triggered by 1-2-3.

Putting the software in perspective

As we have seen, there is much system and application software for micros. Much of the software, such as accounting packages, is intended for firms with no computer literacy. The firms are expected to use the software as is, without understanding what is going on inside the computer. Other software is quite sophisticated, and provides a powerful tool to managers with MIS literacy.

Micro software tailors the hardware to the specific needs of a firm or manager. The software enables the hardware to be used in solving problems in both large and small firms.

Some Popular Micros

We have highlighted the IBM PC in our hardware discussion. We selected the PC because of its wide acceptance.

The IBM PC has undergone minor refinements since its announcement, and it has stimulated the addition of other members to the "IBM PC family." A lower-priced PCjr. was added and then withdrawn because of slow sales—proving that even IBM can make a mistake. Higher-priced, higher-performance members appear to be doing well—the PC XT, PC AT, PC XT/370, and 3270 Personal Computer. There is also a PC Portable. The XT offers a 10MB hard disk as a standard feature, and a second can be added. The AT offers high-capacity diskettes (1.2MB) and a 20MB hard disk. The XT/370 and 3270 can be used as terminals connected to mainframes or as stand-alone processors. The PC line accounts for approximately 6 percent of IBM's revenue and no doubt will be expanded as users' needs change and new technologies are discovered.

The Tandy 2000

The Tandy TRS-80 Model 2000, pictured in Figure 6-15, uses the MS-DOS operating system, and is an "IBM PC compatible." The keyboard includes a numeric keypad and function keys. The microprocessor is the Intel 80186, which is about 40 percent faster than the 8088 used in the IBM PC. The standard RAM capacity is 128KB, expandable to 768KB. The two diskette drives record data on 80 tracks

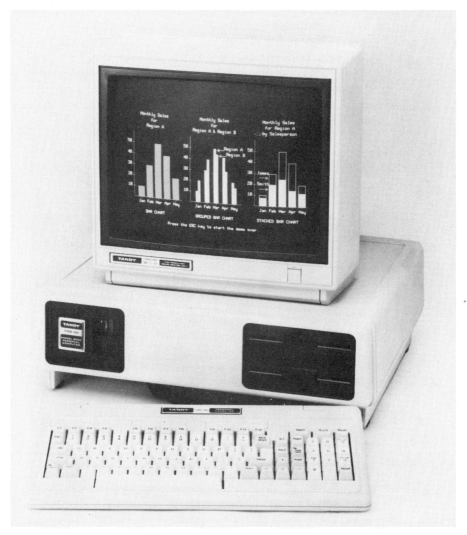

Figure 6-15 The Tandy TRS-80 Model 2000.
Source: Courtesy Tandy Corporation.

per side—giving the 5¼″ diskettes a capacity of 720KB each. The standard monochrome display is green and black on a 12-inch screen. An optional 14-inch color monitor is also available.

Software includes BASIC, COBOL, FORTRAN, and Pascal languages, the PFS:Write and Multimate word processors, the dBASE II DBMS, a graphics package, a report writer, and Lotus 1-2-3.

AT&T Personal Computer 6300 Plus

The AT&T 6300 Plus is aimed at the high end of the microcomputer market, and competes head-on with the high performance IBM PC AT. The 6300 Plus is based on an Intel 80286 microprocessor and comes with 512KB RAM standard. RAM can be expanded to 7MB by adding chips and cards to the motherboard.

A unique feature of the 6300 Plus, pictured in Figure 6-16, is its ability to run both MS-DOS and UNIX operating systems. This feature makes the 6300 Plus appealing to both scientific and business users.

The 6300 Plus contains features that indicate it was designed with the user in mind. The keyboard is easy to use, the screen includes a non-glare front and has a swivel base for easy positioning. The screen offers a graphics capability exceeding that of the IBM PC.

AT&T's first entry into the microcomputer market was the 6300—introduced about a year earlier. It was strictly an IBM compatible aimed at the PC XT. The 6300 Plus indicates a revised AT&T strategy of developing systems reflecting their own architectures rather than those of IBM.

Figure 6-16   AT&T Personal Computer 6300 Plus.
Source: AT&T.

Apple Macintosh

The Macintosh was announced in 1984 as the ultimate in user friendliness. The mouse, pictured in Figure 6-9, relieves the user of many keyboard operations. The advertising emphasizes that if you can point, you can use the Macintosh.

The keyboard closely resembles that of a typewriter—no numeric keypad (a separate unit is optional), no cursor keys, and no function keys. The mouse is used to move the cursor and initiate functions.

The standard configuration includes 128KB of RAM (expandable to 512KB), one 3½″ diskette drive holding 400KB, and a 9-inch black-and-white screen. Optional hardware includes a second diskette drive, a dot matrix printer, and circuitry to attach the Macintosh to a data communications network. The Macintosh uses its own proprietary operating system, accompanied by the MacWrite word processing package and the MacPaint graphics package. The Jazz spreadsheet package was developed especially for the Macintosh. All of the software makes liberal use of the mouse.

The "lap tops"

The first portable micros were about the size of attache cases and weighed in the neighborhood of 30 pounds. The COMPAQ, Columbia VP, and Eagle Spirit XL are examples. Then, the size got even smaller—about the size of a notebook. This new group is known as the *lap tops*. It includes the Hewlett-Packard 110 (pictured in Figure 6-17), the TRS-80 Model 100, the Data General One, and others. The Hewlett-Packard unit is unique in that Lotus 1-2-3 is built into ROM.

One can picture the busy executive carrying a lap top along on business trips. Their battery power (in addition to AC) facilitates this use. Some of the lap tops (such as the 110) do not include diskette drives, whereas others (such as the Data

Figure 6-17 The Hewlett-Packard 100 lap-top.
Source: Courtesy Hewlett-Packard Company.

General One) use a 3½″ size. Output is usually provided by a liquid crystal diode (LCD) technology similar to that of a digital watch. The LCD can display from 8 lines of 40 characters each (for the TRS 100) to 25 lines of 80 characters each (for the Data General One).

It doesn't matter whether a manager wants to use a micro in the office, at home, or on the road—there is a model available to meet each need.

The Impact of the Micro on Decision Making

Some managers have elected to use the micro, and some have not. Robert Hightower, a business unit manager for Wavetek, uses 1-2-3 and the Volkswriter word processing package to prepare analyses of his product line. Previously, using BASIC, it took 8 to 12 hours to conduct an analysis. With 1-2-3 and Volkswriter, it now takes about half an hour with the help of his secretary, who enters the data into the spreadsheet. Mr. Hightower states, "More important than the time involved is the immediacy and better quality of the results."[7]

Thomas Haberkorn, director of financial accounting, American Medical Association, also recognizes the improved quality provided by his Apple Lisa. The spreadsheets, graphics, and word processing provided by the Lisa show big improvements over the previous manual system in terms of both time and quality. Haberkorn also recognizes that "There's more creativity on everyone's part. We keep coming up with new uses and better ways of doing routine accounting jobs."[8]

But not all manager experiences with micros have been so successful. One of the nation's largest energy companies gave each of its corporate executives a Lisa to take home for use as a personal computer. Within weeks, the executives started bringing them back—the executives were not interested. Perhaps the executives didn't receive the proper training. In the same firm, a vice president in the financial area taught himself how to use the Multiplan spreadsheet on his office Corona micro. Within a year he turned to his micro for analytical support each time a special project came up. Micros received a mixed response from executives in this company.

We have previously recognized that all managers are different, and this difference is reflected in how they use computers. John Dearden, a Harvard professor who has recognized weaknesses in computer-based decision support for 15 years, says this about the use of personal computers by top managers and by managers in small firms:

> I believe that the job of the top manager has not been affected significantly by the computer. Most important management jobs have not been solved by automation. If interested, a top manager should get a personal computer—provided it is not used to harass operating managers, the computer will do no harm and it may be effective for

---

[7] Patrick Flanagan, "What I Use My PC For," *Office Administration and Automation* 45 (February 1984): 27.

[8] Ibid., p. 55.

certain things. However, I do not believe that it will have an important impact on the way the manager manages. If a manager does not wish to use a personal computer, his or her performance will not be adversely affected.

In my opinion, the greatest impact of the personal computer will be on managers of small businesses. Small businesses tend to be limited in both the quality and quantity of their staff because of financial constraints. Managers of these small businesses may be able to use the computer for analysis as well as retrieval of information.[9]

Two comments about this quote are in order. First, Mr. Dearden was especially pessimistic concerning micro use at the top management level. As we shall see in Chapter 12 (Executive Information Systems), these managers have special needs. Managers on lower levels may have different reasons for using the computer. Second, the quote was made in 1983, and, as we have seen in this chapter, significant improvements have been made in micro-based DSS software since that date. Still, the reality should be recognized: the micro will not appeal to all managers.

You should not be influenced too much by stories of successes or failures. Just because they happened to someone else doesn't mean that they will happen to you. Be aware of what the computer can do—its strengths and limitations—and use it where it can make a contribution.

Integrating Micros Into the MIS

For years, information specialists encouraged others in the firm to use the corporate computer. The specialists were so successful that the demand for computer support often exceeded the resources, and backlogs of work built up. When the micro came along, many disgruntled users decided to take matters into their own hands. They began to procure their own micros and do their own work. While it is easy to see why many users chose to follow this route, it is also easy to see the potential problems. For one thing, if everyone had their own information processor, there would be no central data base for everyone to share. It would be difficult to implement an MIS under those conditions.

It is important that firms include micros in their long-range plan of information resource management. In deciding on a corporate policy concerning micros, top management can consider three basic strategies: (1) give users complete freedom in obtaining micros, (2) proclaim that no user micros will be purchased and that all computing will be done on the central computer, or (3) settle on a more moderate view of permitting user micros as long as they meet certain specifications. The first strategy (complete freedom) could result in inefficient computing, with everyone running in a different direction—each "reinventing the wheel." The second strategy (no micros) ignores the potential role that a micro can play in the MIS. Most firms who consider the consequences adopt the third alternative of setting guidelines for users to follow.

---

[9]John Dearden, "Will the Computer Change the Job of Top Management?" *Sloan Management Review* 25 (Fall 1983): 59–60.

It is important that top management be involved in setting the guidelines by first making a *policy statement*. The policy statement should clarify responsibilities and establish incentives for all parties. Next, middle-level management can put the policy into effect by establishing committees and acquiring resources.

Metropolitan Life is a good example of how micro guidelines can be set. The electronic steering committee, comprised of senior officers of all departments, issued a policy statement establishing an "info center." The info center evaluated various micros and selected one as the standard. Departments can obtain their own micros, but they must be the standard brand. The requisitions are processed by the info center. The info center also provides service, such as training classes, to departments that have obtained their own micros.

Mitre Corp. took a different approach. They decided to establish a personal computer support center (PCSC) as a means of channeling user micro needs in one direction. They did not want a proliferation of incompatible micros at the 5,000-employee firm. The PCSC provides a variety of Apple and IBM micros for employee use when needed. The PCSC has been a success in that it is heavily used—24 hours a day, 7 days a week. An average of 1,000 telephone calls inquiring about service are received each month. But the PCSC did not eliminate micro purchases by departments. If anything, the PCSC stimulated such purchase by assuring the users that their first micro experiences were positive ones. Two years after the PCSC opened its door, there were over 400 micros in Mitre offices. But all have been purchased within the guidelines.

At both Metropolitan and Mitre, management saw a need to coordinate micro purchases. Both the info center and the PCSC were established as a part of the firm's computer organization. Both firms recognized the importance of the information specialists working with the users so that all parts of the firm's computing resource fit together.

Choosing a Micro

Many individuals and firms have followed the worst possible approach in getting a micro. They buy the micro first and then decide what to do with it. The software is so important to what the micro can do that many of these "impulse purchases" have left the buyers with hardware that cannot do the job because needed software did not exist.

Choosing a micro, or any computer, is a classic example of the use of the systems approach. First you identify your needs; then you evaluate the alternate systems (hardware and software); you select and implement the best; and you follow up to ensure that your needs are being satisfied.

In the section below, we list the steps to be taken in selecting a micro and implementing it as a decision support tool.

1. *Learn about computers.* Read newspapers, magazine articles, and books. Visit computer stores and observe demonstrations, talk with salespersons and anyone else who appears knowledgeable. Ask questions. Enroll

in courses. Consider evening classes at the local college, as well as short seminars offered by computer stores. There are many two- or three-day seminars offered by various organizations that are geared especially for managers. Some are general and some specific; some are introductory and some are advanced. The American Management Association offers a number of such courses.

2. *Define the computer applications in general terms.* Assuming that you are a business manager, just what job will the computer do? Will it solve some problems that have been bothering you, or will you use it to improve an already good organization, or both? The basic decision is the application area—will it be data processing, DSS, or office automation? Don't bite off too much at first. Take a key application first. Perhaps it is inventory. Doing that job well could save you money and give you the stimulus to tackle other, perhaps more difficult, applications. Don't waste valuable time on applications just because they are easy; meet your challenges head-on.

3. *Set objectives.* What must the computer do to satisfy you? If it is inventory, for example, how much must the investment be reduced, or how much must the service level be increased?

4. *Establish constraints.* How much can you spend? What resources, such as personnel time, can you dedicate to the computer project? This will define the hardware and software market for you to consider.

5. *Define the computer applications in specific terms.* Talk with other people in your organization. Sound them out on your plan. Ask for input. Think about how the computer will be used. Be as specific as you can in an effort to understand fully the job to be done. If you haven't enlisted the help of an expert by now, this might be a good time. A computer consultant or a computer specialist in your accounting firm can do a lot in just a short time. They may appear to be expensive, but not as expensive as a misdirected, ill-defined computer project that ultimately leads to failure.

6. *Survey the software market.* What packages meet your needs? Which are close? Ask the people at the computer store for advice. Look at the books and magazines on their shelves, and buy the ones that appear helpful. Go to the library and look through back issues of the computer magazines such as *Byte, Mini-Micro Systems, PC World,* and *PC Magazine.* Contact business people outside your firm who are using micros, and see what software they recommend. Define your needs and then measure how well the packages satisfy them. If this activity gets to be too much for you, call in an expert who can help you focus on the essentials.

7. *Verify the software performance.* See a demonstration of the software. Use the actual package, not a demo diskette, with your own sample data. Think about your job in detail and try to think of problems that you might encounter and how they can be solved. Find out whether the software can be modified, and, if so, the cost.

8. *Identify and evaluate the hardware.* More likely than not, the software will run on more than one piece of equipment. Consider not only price, but the support that the manufacturer and the retailer can provide. Will they be there when you need them? Can you purchase a maintenance contract? If so, what is the cost, and who will do the work?

9. *Identify other resources needed.* Are you going to rely entirely on off-the-shelf software, or will you be doing some programming yourself? Should you hire one or more computer professionals—systems analysts, programmers, operations personnel? Look at your plan in a long-range sense. What people will you need? Where will they come from? Can you get them? What will they cost? In addition to personnel, think about facilities, space, supplies, user education, and all areas where the computer will likely impact the firm. What should you do to get the system on the air?

10. *Select the hardware and software, and prepare for implementation.* Assuming that your analysis hasn't discouraged you, make the decision of what computer and software to buy. Then, get your data in a form that will be acceptable to the computer. This might be a big task. Prepare the physical facilities and educate the users. Set a date for conversion and stick with it. Give thought to backup should the system fail.

11. *Implement the system.* Cut over one application at a time until the entire system is functioning.

12. *Evaluate the performance.* Set a date for a post-implementation review, such as 90 days after conversion is complete. Give the system time to settle down. Is it meeting the objectives set in step 3? This is a good time to call in an unbiased third party, a person who has not previously been involved in the implementation project. Even your consultant, who has helped you over the rough spots, might be inclined to assure you that "everything is rosy" when it is not. You should expect an accurate appraisal from someone who does not have a vested interest in the system.

Summary

Minicomputers started the evolution to smaller and less expensive computers with little, or no, loss in processing capability. Minicomputers with software and input/output devices required by business are called small business computers. The microcomputer revolution got its start with the development of the microprocessor—a computer on a chip. Actually, the microprocessor includes only the control circuitry of the CPU and possibly the arithmetic and logical circuitry. Primary storage is added in the form of ROM and RAM. ROM enables you to read routines recorded by the computer manufacturer, but you cannot write in that area. RAM enables you to store data and programs and later retrieve them.

A microcomputer can serve as the information processor of a small firm or of an individual manager. A micro can also be used as an intelligent terminal to communicate with other computers in a network, and as a means to transmit decisions to the physical system of the firm.

Input to the micro is usually provided by the keyboard. The keyboard includes regular typewriter keys plus keys unique to a computer such as function keys. Another input device is the mouse, found on the Macintosh and other computers seeking to achieve a degree of user friendliness greater than that provided by the keyboard.

Output is produced on serial printers and the CRT display—a monochrome display or color monitor. Information can be displayed in a graphic form using graphics circuitry in the CPU and graphics software. The graphs can be displayed on the screen, or printed by a graphics printer or a plotter.

Secondary storage is most often provided by 5¼″ diskettes, but some micros (the Macintosh and some lap tops for example) use a smaller 3½″ size. Data can be recorded on one or both sides, and in double or single density. Records are stored on tracks and in sectors. The micro can locate the sectors either by software (for soft-sectored diskettes) or hardware (hard-sectored diskettes).

When diskettes do not provide enough storage space, you can attach one or two hard disks to some computers. The larger micros, such as the IBM PC XT and AT and the DEC Rainbow 100 + , come with a hard disk as a standard feature.

A large number of operating systems have been produced for micros, with the most popular being CP/M, PC-DOS, MS-DOS, and UNIX. CP/M was most popular with the earlier 8-bit word machines. PC-DOS and MS-DOS are popular with the current crop of 16-bit machines. All of the PC compatibles use the MS-DOS operating system. UNIX offers the ability to handle multiple users, and that feature is stimulating interest in the business area. There is such a large supply of MS-DOS application programs that a migration to UNIX will likely be slow.

BASIC has always been the most popular language for micros, and that popularity should continue. The more modern languages such as C, FORTH, and Pascal are not as well-suited for business needs.

Micros have an abundant supply of application software—accounting packages, statistical packages, graphics packages, electronic spreadsheets, and packages that integrate several functions. VisiCalc stimulated the use of the micro as a DSS, and other superior software sustained the trend. Lotus 1-2-3 quickly replaced VisiCalc as the most popular package by providing a graphics and file handling ability in conjunction with a spreadsheet.

It would be a misstatement to say that the micro is an integral part of the MIS. It is for some managers, but not for others. The manner in which the micro has been accepted by managers confirms the position that we have taken beginning in the first chapter—the computer can support part of the manager's information needs, but not all. The large numbers of micros presently being used for decision support indicate that, properly implemented, the micro can be a valuable tool. Organizations must recognize the micro and incorporate it into long-range plans for information resource management.

The process that an individual should follow in choosing a micro should be the same that a firm follows in choosing a computer of any size. The systems approach should be followed by first defining needs and then evaluating the various alternatives.

We will continue to weave the micro into the MIS as we describe the data base, data communications, computer applications, information systems, and the MIS life cycle. This chapter gives us the foundation that we need to proceed.

Key Terms

minicomputer, mini

small business computer

microcomputer, micro

microprocessor

personal computer

PC compatible

read-only memory (ROM)

random-access memory (RAM)

numeric keypad

function key

mouse

monochrome display

color monitor

single-, double-sided diskette drive

single-, double-density diskette drive

soft-sectored, hard-sectored diskette

write-protect notch

sector

hard disk, Winchester disk

CP/M (Control Program for Microprocessors)

word

PC-DOS, MS-DOS

UNIX

statistical package

graphics package

electronic spreadsheet

product family

file conversion utility

all-in-one applications package

operating environment

lap top

Key Concepts

The improving ratio of performance to both price and size for minicomputers and microcomputers

Reasons for the sales success of the IBM PC

How a micro fits the computer schematic

The difference between ROM and RAM

The manner in which a micro can be upgraded by additional components and circuitry

How data is recorded on a diskette

The manner in which operating systems have been tailored to particular microprocessors

The appeal of integrated software

The varying appeal of micros to managers, depending on the managers' individual characteristics

The need for a firm to establish a policy concerning micro use

The logical, step-by-step procedure of selecting and implementing a micro

Questions

1. What invention triggered the micro boom?
2. Name three innovative strategies that IBM used for the PC.
3. What are three ways that a manager can use a micro in an MIS?
4. What is the difference between ROM and RAM?
5. What distinguishes a soft-sectored diskette from a hard-sectored?
6. What does the diskette address 1234 specify? Use the sample format in the chapter.
7. What is a Winchester disk?
8. Name the three most popular operating systems. Which one would a "PC compatible" use? Which can handle multiple users at a time?
9. What is meant by an "8-bit word machine?"
10. How are the electronic spreadsheet columns usually used in a dynamic model?
11. Name the four approaches to integrating application software? Which is followed by 1-2-3?
12. Name four members of the "IBM PC family."
13. How does the screen size of the Tandy 2000 compare with the Macintosh?
14. How do the systems in question 13 compare with the IBM PC in terms of diskette capacity?
15. Which micro described in the chapter comes with only a monochrome display?
16. Is a "lap top" another name for "portable"? Explain.
17. According to John Dearden, which group of managers will not benefit significantly from using a micro? Which group of managers may benefit?
18. What are the three basic alternatives facing a firm as it sets micro policy?
19. What roles can a computer store play in the process of choosing a micro?
20. At which points in the computer selection process can a consultant be used?

Problems

1. Draw a computer schematic of a micro with a keyboard, two diskette drives, a monitor, and a graphics printer. Use standard flowcharting symbols.
2. The diskettes produced by early IBM operating systems contained data in 40 tracks and 8 sectors per side. Each track sector contained 512 bytes. What was the capacity of a single side? How much did the capacity increase by adding a 9th sector?
3. Visit a local computer store, book store, or library. Make a list of all the magazines aimed at the small computer market.

4. Use an electronic spreadsheet package to build a pricing model. Set it up so that you can key in price and quantity sold, and see the results for a 4-year period. Assume that the quantity will increase by 6 percent a year, after year 1. Include the following expenses:

Marketing—18 percent of sales revenue

Manufacturing—23 percent of sales revenue

Administration—5 percent of sales revenue, plus a fixed annual expense of $10,000.

Compute income tax as 48 percent of gross profit, yielding net profit. Simulate the effects of a volume of 100,000 units, and prices of $25, $30, and $35 per unit. Obtain hardcopies of your spreadsheet for each of the three simulations.

CASE PROBLEM: Tri-Cities Furniture

As part of your MIS course, you are expected to go into the community and study a data processing system. You are to document the present system and design a new, information-oriented one.

You remember that you once saw a small computer in a furniture store. You drive downtown to the white stucco building with a sign reading "Tri-Cities Furniture: Serving the Endicott, Binghampton, and Johnson City Area." You walk inside and ask to see the owner. There aren't many people in the store. You don't see anyone else who looks like a customer. The man you talked to looks like a sales clerk. An elderly woman sits behind a desk writing in a huge ledger. Three men are unloading a truck and bringing furniture into the store from the alley.

A man wearing a white shirt and tie comes out of an office and says, "Can I help you?" After you explain your situation and introduce yourself, he says, "I'm Albert Mendoza. I'm the owner, sales manager, part-time sales person, and bill collector. Ha ha."

Right away, you know Albert has a sense of humor. Before you stop smiling, he says, "Sure, you can study our operation. Come over here and let me introduce you to Alice and Ray."

You walk over to the woman with the ledger—Alice Cook, the bookkeeper. Alice has been with the firm for 23 years and has been the only person to keep the books. You turn to Albert and say, "I thought I saw a computer in here a couple of months ago."

"That's right," Albert replies. "We have a computer. It's over in this room next to my office. Come over here and I'll show it to you."

You walk into the computer room, and Albert turns on the light. There it is, smaller than you remembered it. But you recognize the parts—a keyboard, the CPU, a disk unit that can handle two floppies, a CRT, and a serial printer. The label on the CPU says "IBM System 5110." You don't remember studying that model, and Albert tells you it is one of IBM's earliest small systems.

About that time, the man you first talked to walks in. He is Ray Silva, and he divides his time between operating the computer and selling furniture. The computer work can be done in three or four hours a day. The computer is used to print tags that are placed on furniture arriving from the factory. It keeps inventory records on all items located in this store and in the Binghampton and Endicott stores. The computer also maintains records of installment payments. Tri-Cities caters to lower-middle-class trade, and much of the business is on credit. Albert handles the financing himself.

Albert tells you the story of his computer. On the advice of his accountant, he purchased it from a friend who operates a furniture store in Syracuse, some seventy miles away. The friend had purchased the unit from IBM and prepared all of the software himself. When the friend's business prospered, he installed a larger system. The friend made Albert an offer he couldn't refuse, so Albert plunged into the computer game.

As it turned out, it has been a sobering experience. The software doesn't really do the job. It is written to handle the accounts of a single operation, and the three locations of Tri-Cities present problems. Further, the software doesn't balance the accounts. That is why Alice still keeps the books by hand. Albert doesn't trust the computer. Ray processes the inventory and receivables transactions on the computer, and Alice also does them by hand. They have been hoping to cut over to the computer, but problems always come up. Albert hopes that eventually everything will work out so that he can start getting some return on his computer investment.

You ask if there is any documentation for the software (flowcharts, record descriptions, operating procedures, and so on), and find out that there is none. You also learn that anytime anything goes wrong, a systems analyst must come from Syracuse to solve the problem. He is the only person who understands the software. His daily rate is $350 plus mileage. To make matters worse, nobody at Tri-Cities knows anything about programming. Ray knows how to operate the system, but if anything goes wrong, he calls the analyst. Sometimes the trouble turns out to be hardware, and there is a local computer engineer who can fix the trouble.

Albert has problems. Alice is retiring at the end of the year, and Ray has given notice that he plans to leave at the end of the month. He is going into the aluminum siding business. Albert would like to hire a student part-time who knows enough about computers to debug the programs and to add a general ledger package that came with the system but has never been used. You tell him you'll think about it.

You ask Albert if he is getting any management information out of the computer. "No, I'm not," he says, "though I'd like to. You might think we don't have much business here, but we do. This is just a slack period. Weekends are our busiest time. I have trouble keeping up with everything. I'd like to know what's selling and what isn't, how much profit we're making on our different lines, and so forth. But we just don't know how to get that information out of our computer. And I'm not sure that it's in there. But I bought it with that objective in mind."

You tell Albert you'll get back to him about the term project. You are at a loss for words. You had expected a success story like the ones you heard in class.

This seems to be a real can of worms. You say good-bye to everyone, and as you start to walk out the door, Albert calls out, "Hey, I couldn't sell you a good water bed, could I?"

Questions

1. Does Albert need a computer?
2. Do you think that Albert should throw out the existing computer and start over?
3. If Albert chooses to stick with the existing system, what would you suggest that he do to solve his problems?
4. If Albert chooses to start over, what would you suggest that he do differently the next time?

Selected Bibliography

Microcomputer Systems

Allen, Randy L., and Michael Berkery, "Conducting the Cost/Benefit Analysis," *Small Systems World* 12 (October 1984): 38ff.

Benoit, Ellen, and Amy Bernstein, "Graphic Detail," *Business Computer Systems* 3 (April 1984): 40ff.

Bernstein, Amy, "Defining Integrated Software," *Business Computer Systems* 3 (June 1984): 56ff.

Brodwin, David R., and Miriam A. Hyman, "Lap-Top Computers—What Potential Users Should Know," *Office Administration and Automation* 46 (February 1985): 33ff.

Bryant, Susan Foster, "Integrated Software Gives You Functions Within Functions," *Computer Decisions* 16 (September 1984): pp. 104ff.

Carpenter, James, Dennis Deloria, and David Morganstein, "Statistical Software for Microcomputers," *Byte* 9 (April 1984): 234ff.

Commander, Jake, "MSDOS-Based Tandy 2000 Outperforms the IBM PC," *Business Computer Systems* 3 (October 1984): 136ff.

Cooper, Michael S., "Micro-Based Business Graphics," *Datamation* 30 (May 1984): 99ff.

Cowan, William M., "Business Graphics Add New Dimension To Decision Support," *Office Administration and Automation* 46 (April 1985): 32ff.

Dearden, John, "Will the Computer Change the Job of Top Management?," *Sloan Management Review* 25 (Fall 1983): 57–60.

DeVoney, Chris, *IBM's Personal Computer*, 2nd ed. (Indianapolis: Que Corporation, 1983).

Finger, Alan, "IBM PC AT," *Byte* 10 (May 1985): 270–277.

Flanagan, Patrick, "What I Use My PC For," *Office Administration and Automation* 45 (February 1984): 26ff.

Hearst, Marcia, "The Task of Managing PCs At Metropolitan Life," *The Office* 100 (September 1984): 105–106.

Karasik, Myron S., "Selecting a Small Business Computer," *Harvard Business Review* 62 (January-February 1984): 26ff.

Keen, Peter G. W., and Lynda A. Woodman, "What To Do With All Those Micros," *Harvard Business Review* 62 (September-October 1984): 142–150.

McLeod, Raymond, Jr., *Decision Support Software for the IBM Personal Computer* (Chicago: Science Research Associates, 1985).

McLeod, Raymond, Jr., and Alan D. Mazursky, *Decision Support Software for the IBM Personal Computer: Lotus Edition* (Chicago: Science Research Associates, 1986).

McNichols, Charles W., and Thomas D. Clark, *Microcomputer-Based Information and Decision Support Systems for Small Businesses* (Reston, Va.: Reston Publishing Co., 1983).

Nesbit, Irene S., "Evaluating Micro Software," *Datamation* 30 (July 15, 1984): 74ff.

Perrone, Giovanni, "A Multiuser Operating Systems Sampler," *PC Products* 2 (January 1985): 28ff.

Post, Dan W., "The Fate of UNIX," *Business Computer Systems* 4 (February 1985): 42ff.

Raho, Louis E., and James A. Belohlav, "Integrating Personal Computers into Organizations: Problems, Benefits, and Training Issues," *Journal of Systems Management* 36 (March 1985): 16–19.

Smith, Carlton L., "A PC Support Center," *Datamation* 31 (March 1, 1985): 138ff.

Taylor, R. L., "Low-End General-Purpose Systems," *IBM Journal of Research and Development* 25 (September 1981): 429–440.

Toong, Hoo-min D., and Amar Gupta, "Personal Computers," *Scientific American* 247 (December 1982): 86ff.

Walden, Jeff, "A New Formula for Spreadsheets," *Business Computer Systems* 3 (October 1984): 97ff.

Walsh, Myles E., "Will the Real IBM Personal Computer Please Stand Up!," *Journal of Systems Management* 35 (November 1984): 8–17.

Webster, Bruce F., "The Macintosh," *Byte* 9 (August 1984): 238ff.

Wozniak, Stephen, "Chips and Dips: The Homebrew Club and How the Apple Came To Be," *InfoWorld* 6 (October 8, 1984): 50–51.

Chapter 7

The Data Base

Learning Objectives

After studying this chapter, you should:

- Know the difference between a data base and a data base management system (DBMS), and the advantages and disadvantages of each
- Understand the objectives of data management
- Be familiar with the phases in the evolution from a pre-data base approach to a data base approach
- Understand how the physical organization of data can constrain the user
- Appreciate how linked lists and inverted files help overcome physical constraints
- Gain a working knowledge of DBMS terminology—schema and subschema, data dictionary, data description language, and data manipulation language
- See how the DBMS works with the application program and operating system to access, read, and write data
- Know the four parts of a DBMS and their functions
- Understand the objectives that the DBMS seeks to accomplish
- Be familiar with the three data base structures—hierarchical, network, and relational
- Appreciate the user friendliness of a micro DBMS such as dBASE III
- Be aware of the options for distributing both processing and the data base
- Be familiar with the role of the data base administrator (DBA)

Introduction

In Chapter 5 we studied the devices used for secondary storage. We recognized that the devices house the software library and the data base. The programs of the software library can be stored in secondary storage using a partitioned file organization. The operating system retrieves the programs and program segments when they are needed. The data base is also housed in secondary storage, and the contents are made available to application programs by means of either subroutines in those programs or by system software.

It is easy to see the importance of the firm's data resource. It provides the raw material from which the information product is created. Without data there could be no MIS.

The Data Base in the General Systems Model

In Figure 5-1 we positioned the information processor and the data base in the general systems model of the firm. Data and information from both the firm and the environment are entered into the data base by means of the input devices described in Chapter 5. Information from the data base is made available to the manager by means of the output devices.

Our interest in studying the data base is to understand how it is used in an MIS. In this chapter we will gain an understanding of how the data is arranged in secondary storage, and how the data base management software manages the data base. In later chapters we will see how the manager uses this valuable resource.

What Is a Data Base? A DBMS?

We have seen that data exists in a hierarchy. On the lowest level is the *data element*. The elements relative to a particular topic are assembled into a *record*. The space in a record where a data element is stored is called a *field*. All of the records together constitute a *file*. The *data base* consists of one or more files. Figure 7-1 shows several files comprising a data base.

The term *data base* can be defined broadly or narrowly. In a broad sense, a data base can include all of the data and information within an organization. Until now, we have used this definition. Narrowly speaking, we could limit a data base to include only that data and information stored in the computer. In this chapter and the remainder of the book, we use the narrow definition. In doing so, we recognize the potentially large amounts of data and information that are not stored in the computer.

During the past fifteen years, there has been much interest in a software system to manage the data base. This system is called a *data base management system (DBMS)*. DBMSs are available from a number of sources (computer manufacturers and software firms) at costs ranging from $100 to over $100,000.

We should make one point clear at the outset: a firm does not need a DBMS to have a good computer-based MIS. In large organizations the DBMS is almost a necessity, but when the data resource is relatively small and there is little sharing of common data within the organization, the DBMS is not needed. The firm's programmers can prepare programs to manage the data effectively. As computer use becomes more sophisticated and as the DBMS capabilities of minis and micros improve, the number of firms using a DBMS will increase.

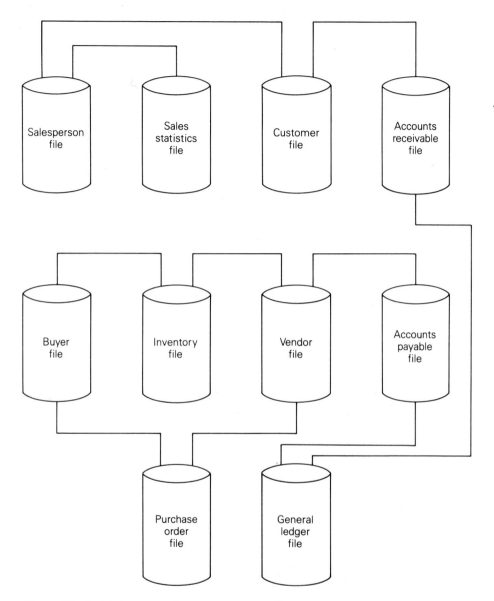

Figure 7-1 A data base consists of one or more files.

Objectives of Data Management

Data and information are resources and must be managed in the same manner as the physical resources of personnel, material, machines, and money. Data management involves acquiring the data resources, maintaining the resources so that they are available for use, and removing the resources when they are no longer needed.

This process of data management includes the *data management functions:*

- *Collect* Gather data and record it on a *source document*; enter data into the information processor either directly from the source document (MICR, OCR) or through keyboarding.
- *Organize* Prepare the data for storage by verifying its accuracy, arranging the records in sequence, adding necessary codes, and so on.
- *Store* Write the data to a secondary storage device (sequential or DASD) for later use.
- *Retrieve* Obtain the data from secondary storage when it is needed.
- *Manipulate* Perform certain processes on the data, such as rearranging and accumulating, to transform it into information.
- *Output* Make the information available to users, utilizing output devices such as printers, plotters, and screens.
- *Control* Maintain the accuracy of the data within specified tolerances, assure that the information output is available when needed, and assure that users receive only the information to which they are entitled.

All of these functions are performed by a person when the data base is not computer based. When a computer is used, it can perform all of the functions except for collecting and controlling. Those two functions are performed jointly by persons working with computing equipment.

Data Base Evolution

During the early years of computer use, more attention was given to the processing of data than to the data itself. The first programming language to give special recognition to data was COBOL, developed in 1960 by a joint government-industry group called CODASYL (Conference on Data Systems Languages). COBOL devotes one of its four divisions to data. In this division, files are subdivided into records, records into elements, and the characteristics of the elements are specified. One of the reasons for COBOL's continued popularity is the excellent manner in which it describes business data.

Other software advances in the sixties improved the performance of the computer as a data manager. *Utility programs* were provided to sort data files and perform other standard data tasks, and *report generators* were developed to minimize the effort required to produce printed output. The Report Program Generator (RPG) language added some file retrieval and updating features not found in COBOL.

The pre-data base approach

During the period 1955–1965, the major grouping of data was the file. The files were regarded as separate entities belonging to particular programs.

As an example, a firm might have a *customer credit file* containing data such as:

- Customer number
- Customer name and address
- Credit code
- Credit limit

Another file, called a *customer master file*, contains:

- Customer number
- Customer name and address
- Sales region number
- Salesperson number
- Customer class
- Shipping code
- Year-to-date sales this year
- Year-to-date sales last year

A third file, for *accounts receivable*, contains:

- Customer number
- Customer name and address
- First invoice data
    Invoice number
    Invoice date
    Invoice amount
- Second invoice data
    Invoice number
    Invoice date
    Invoice amount

        .

        .

        .

- *n*th invoice data
    Invoice number
    Invoice date
    Invoice amount

Each of these files has one or more purposes. The customer credit file is used for approving customer orders, the customer master file is used for invoicing customers, and the accounts receivable file represents the monies owed the firm by its customers. All are *master files*.

You will note some redundancy in the data elements contained within the files. All three files include customer number and customer name and address. This redundancy is necessary since each file is designed to provide all of the data needed by a particular program.

Let us assume that the sales manager wants a report showing the amount of receivables by salesperson. The firm's customers haven't been paying their bills promptly, and the sales manager wants to know which salespersons have neglected to follow up on past-due receivables. The sales manager wants the report to include the data listed in Table 7-1. You can see that the special report will require data from four files. A salesperson master file is needed to provide the salesperson name.

The report will list each customer by salesperson, following the process illustrated in Figure 7-2. In step 1 a program selects data from the three customer files that are maintained in customer number sequence. An intermediate file is created with the selected data (all of the data elements listed in Table 7-1 except salesperson name). This intermediate file is sorted into salesperson sequence in step 2. A sort is necessary since the salesperson master file is maintained in salesperson sequence. A second intermediate file is created and used with the salesperson master file to prepare the report in step 3. The programs for step 1 and step 3 would have to be specially written to satisfy this request.

This procedure is inefficient from the standpoints of both the user and the information services department. You can imagine how much time is involved. It could take weeks to program, debug, test, and run the programs that may be used only once. This inefficiency was a constraint on MIS performance during the pre-data base era. Managers wanted information but could not get it because the data resource was not in a readily usable form. The lack of software to produce the reports was another limitation.

Before we describe the next step towards a data base era, we should recognize that many firms are still following the pre-data base approach. The years identified with each step simply delineate a time period when the described methodology or technology represented the most advanced way to manage the data.

Table 7-1 Integration of report data from several files

Report Data	Customer Credit File	Customer Master File	Accounts Receivable File	Salesperson Master File
Salesperson Number		X		
Salesperson Name				X
Customer Data				
Customer number		X		
Customer name		X		
Credit code	X			
Year-to-date sales this year		X		
Total accounts receivable			X	

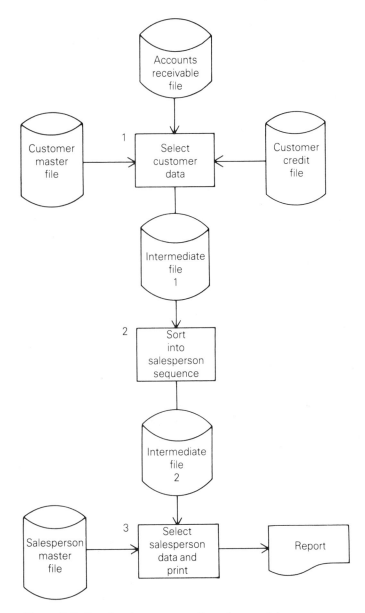

Figure 7-2 Pre-data base preparation of a special report.

Generalized file management systems (GFMS)

In the late sixties a new group of software products appeared. These products were called *generalized file management systems (GFMS)*, and they integrated all of the file handling, sorting, and reporting existing previously in separate packages. The term "generalized" means that they could be used by any type of organization.

The most popular GFMSs have been Informatic's Mark IV, Application Software's ASI-ST, and Program Products' Data Analyzer. These three packages accounted for approximately 80 percent of the 4000 GFMSs installed as of the early 1980s.[1] A Mark IV user simply fills out a form describing information to be retrieved from the data base. Specifications for the retrieval are entered into the computer using a terminal. The data is retrieved, manipulated, and printed. Figure 7-3 is a sample Mark IV retrieval specifications form, and Figure 7-4 shows the report that is produced.

A GFMS is superior to a programming language in its ease of retrieval but is limited in terms of the data manipulation that can be performed. The GFMS represents a step beyond programming languages, toward the more sophisticated

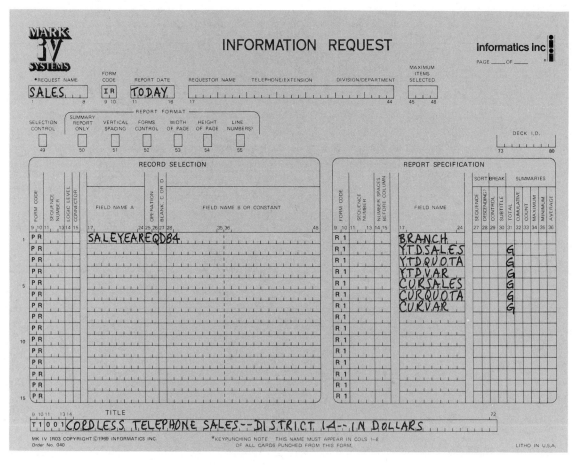

Figure 7-3   A MARK-IV retrieval specifications form.

[1] Alfonso F. Cardenas, *Data Base Management Systems* 2nd ed. (Boston: Allyn and Bacon, 1985), p. 160. This excellent text is very readable and is recommended if you wish to gain additional insight to the DBMS.

```
10/19/86        CORDLESS TELEPHONE SALES--DISTRICT 14--IN DOLLARS    PAGE 1
-----------------------------------------------------------------------------
                  YTD      YTD                     CURRENT  CURRENT
BRANCH           SALES    QUOTA     VARIANCE        SALES    QUOTA    VARIANCE
-----------------------------------------------------------------------------
ALLENTOWN        23715    25000      1285-          1856     2275      419-
ALTOONA          18556    20000      1444-          1432     1800      368-
HARRISBURG       46517    30000     16517           3348     2725      623
LANCASTER        32104    40000      7896-          3104     3625      521-

                120892   115000      5892           9740    10425      685-
-----------------------------------------------------------------------------
```

Figure 7-4   A report produced by MARK-IV.

software that is available today. Many firms still use a GFMS as an alternative to programming for retrieving information stored in their mainframe systems.

Higher-level data organizations

During this same time period, some large firms acted on their own to improve the retrieval of data and information from their data bases. These efforts were triggered, in part, by the interest in the MIS concept. Many of the computer systems used magnetic tape for secondary storage, and these systems could not offer fast response to information requests because of their batch orientation. Many firms, however, were implementing DASD-based computers, and these systems had the potential for rapid response. In many cases, this speed was not being realized. Even though the storage was direct access, the entire data base had to be searched.

For example, a manager might request a report showing the sales for salesperson 23. Assume that the firm assigns certain customers in a territory to a salesperson and that a customer file contains a record for each customer. The task is to select out those records for salesperson 23 and print the data on the report. Since the file is in sequence by customer, each record will have to be examined to determine if the salesperson field contains a 23. This could be a time-consuming process.

Information specialists realized that such special requests could be handled much more quickly if they could be anticipated and the data stored in a way that the records could be *selectively* retrieved. Two techniques were devised that proved especially effective—linked lists and inverted files.

Linked lists   A *linked list* is a group of data records arranged in an order based on embedded pointers. An *embedded pointer* is a special data field that links one record to another by referring to the other record. The field is embedded in the first record—that is, it is a data element within the record.

Linked lists often have a *head*, which is a pointer to the first record, and a *tail*, which points to the last record. You can start at the head and follow the list to the tail, or you can start in the middle and follow the list to the tail. You cannot, however, start in the middle and go back to the head. The linked list is a one-way street.

Figure 7-5 is a linked list of customer records. Each row is a record, and only the fields pertinent to our discussion are shown. The records are arranged sequentially using customer number as the key. Each customer record includes a data element identifying the assigned salesperson. In addition, in the rightmost field is a pointer (a *link*) that chains together all customer records for a particular salesperson—in this case salesperson 23. We can assume that customer 23694 is at the head of the list. The pointer links that record to the record for customer 25410 and so on until we reach the tail, at customer 30111. The asterisk in the link field identifies the tail.

This chaining ability is very powerful. The application program can initiate a search at the beginning of the file, looking for the first customer assigned to salesperson 23. When that record is found, the salesperson links enable the program to follow the chain and only process salesperson 23's records. This is much better than searching through the entire file.

The limitations of a one-way list can be overcome by including a second pointer field that points to the previous record in the chain. This *two-way list* is illustrated in Figure 7-6. In the two-way list there is no end-of-chain (tail) marker. Because the list forms a loop, it is sometimes referred to as a *circular* or *ring structure*. The ring structure permits the program to enter the list at any point and process all of the records.

It is possible to establish multiple linkages for a single file. In addition to the

Customer number				Salesperson number	Salesperson link
22504					
23694				23	25410
24782					
25409					
25410				23	30102
26713					
28914					
30004					
30102				23	30111
30111				23	*
30417					
31715					

Figure 7-5 A linked list.

Customer number			Salesperson number	Forward salesperson link	Backward salesperson link
22504					
23694			23	25410	30111
24782					
25409					
25410			23	30102	23694
26713					
28914					
30004					
30102			23	30111	25410
30111			23	23694	30102
30417					
31715					

Forward link   Backward link

Figure 7-6 A two-way linked list.

salesperson link in the customer file, for example, linkages can be established for customer class, sales region, credit code, and so on.

Inverted files The pointers establish the connections between records and are part of the data file itself. Often it is desirable to establish the logical connections apart from the data base—in the form of indexes or directories. An *inverted file* is a data file that includes an index arranged in a sequence different from the data records. The index can be used to extract file contents based on the index rather than the file sequence.

Figure 7-7 shows the index for a customer file inverted on salesperson number. The special report for salesperson 23 can be prepared by scanning the list of salesperson numbers in the index for "23." When found, the fields on the same row identify the customer records. The customer records can be retrieved directly, one at a time, using the customer number as the key.

Just as a single file can include multiple links, it can also be inverted on multiple keys. The customer file can have indexes relating to customer class, sales region, and so on.

Logically integrated files

General Electric is one of the firms that pioneered higher-level data organization. They carried the idea of linked lists one additional step—to link multiple files.

Salesperson number	Salesperson name	Customer 1	Customer 2	Customer 3	Customer n
16		17042	21096		
20		41854			
23		23694	25410	30102	30111
31		31002			
56		34107	13109		
92		20842			
98		61634			
104		10974			
110		16342	64210	51263	41782

Figure 7-7   An inverted file index.

Such files, connected by links, are called *chained files*. GE extended COBOL to allow chained files, and named their effort Integrated Data Store (IDS).

IDS is the first example of the *data base approach*, which is the logical integration of files intended to facilitate the retrieval of data without regard to the physical organization. Up until this point, all activity has been directed at single files.

Figure 7-8 illustrates how a combination of the inverted files and chained files techniques can be used to prepare the special report from our pre-data base example. To simplify the example, we will not include the salesperson master file. Data will be gathered from a customer credit file, a customer master file, and an accounts receivable file.

1. Using salesperson number as the key, the salesperson index is searched to identify the first (or next) customer number.
2. The customer number serves as the key to search the customer index to find the DASD address for the customer credit record.
3. The customer credit record is read into primary storage.
4. The customer master file link in the customer credit record directs the access mechanism to the DASD location of the customer master record.
5. The customer master record is read.
6. The accounts receivable link in the master record directs the access mechanism to the accounts receivable record.
7. The accounts receivable record is read.
8. The report data is assembled.

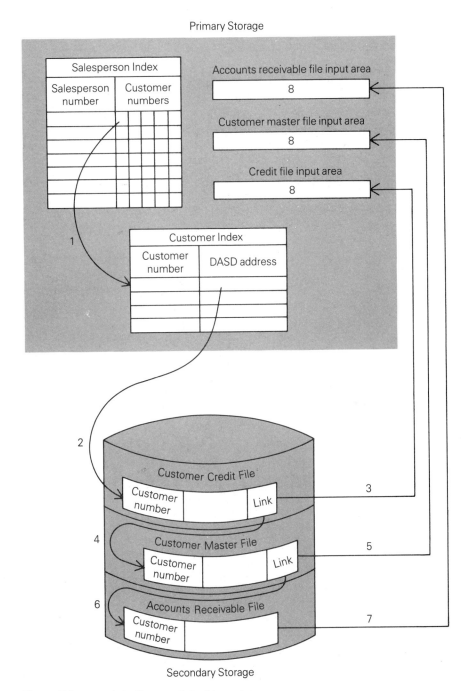

Figure 7-8 Multiple files are linked by pointers.

In this example, indexes are used to identify the initial record and its location. Then pointers are used to locate additional records.

In Figure 7-9, we see the system flowchart of the data base approach to report preparation. This approach is clearly much more straightforward than the pre-data base approach. The query is keyed into a keyboard terminal, the data is retrieved from the various files and assembled in the proper format, and the report is printed. The system is responsive, and *no* special programming is required. What makes all this possible? Three primary ingredients: an adequate computer configuration, the necessary software, and a data base containing records that are integrated logically.

Logical versus physical data organization

Until the development of higher level data organization such as linked lists and inverted files, the computer user was constrained by the physical organization of the data. Separate files and sequences of records in the files dictated what information could, and could not, be produced. This constraint even plagues the GFMSs.

The linked lists and inverted files are ways to overcome the *physical* constraints using *logical* organizations. The files are still maintained separately, and they can still be maintained in a certain sequence. But the links and indexes impose a logical organization on top of the physical that can be used for retrieval. For example, salesperson 23's records are physically scattered through the file, but the links make them appear, to the user, to be together. The *physical organization* is how the data appears to the computer; the *logical organization* is how the data appears to the user.

Generalized data base management systems (DBMS)

In 1961 an effort began that would eventually lead to the first generalized, commercial DBMS. North American Aviation (now Rockwell International) was named prime contractor for the Apollo moon project. North American management quickly recognized the need to computerize the spacecraft parts list, consisting of about two million parts. The resulting file occupied 18 reels of magnetic tape and was never up to date. IBM got involved, and the two firms produced a software package that offered a number of features that had never before been possible. The DASD-based system was named IMS (Information Management System). Users communicated with the system using 130 terminals, and 30 data

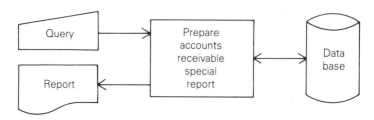

Figure 7-9 Preparation of a special report using a data base.

bases were stored on 32 disk stacks. Daily transaction volume was 17–20,000, and response time averaged two to five seconds. The system performed so well that IBM decided to market the design for use on their System/360 mainframe computer.

Since the introduction of IMS, other similar systems have appeared on the market, including Cincom's TOTAL, Software AG's ADABAS, Intel's System 2000, and Cullinet's IDMS. As of the early 1980s, there were approximately 10,000 of these systems installed worldwide. At the same time, micro-based DBMSs began making their appearance, with dBASE II being the most popular. By early 1985, over 300,000 copies of dBASE II had been sold.

This is how the current DBMS evolved. It evolved from the pre-data base era, to generalized file management systems, to higher-level data organizations, to logically integrated files, and finally to generalized data base management systems. We must understand that all computer-using firms have not progressed through these phases. There are many firms still in the pre-data base era, many firms still using generalized file management systems such as MARK IV, and many firms still using their own programs incorporating linked lists and inverted files. For one reason or another, these firms' management has elected not to embrace the newer approaches.

During the remainder of this chapter, we will describe what the DBMS can offer to firms that do elect to implement the data base approach.

DBMS Fundamentals

A DBMS is a sophisticated software system. However, there are a few fundamentals that enable us to understand what the DBMS does and how it is done. In this section, we address those fundamentals.

The data dictionary

The starting point in developing a data base is to specify the data elements that will be contained. The specification is named the *data element dictionary (DED)*, or simply *data dictionary*.

Figure 7-10 is a page from a *printed* data dictionary. The pages can be kept in a binder, and they provide the details about each data element. The details are called the *attributes*—or simply the characteristics such as type of data (numeric or alphabetic), number of positions, and number of decimal positions (if numeric). The data dictionary includes additional information about each element such as synonyms (other names used), a description of the element, application programs using the element, and perhaps a range of allowable values for numeric data.

The dictionary allows all persons designing and using an MIS to speak the same language. This common language enables all of the information specialists to work together as a coordinated team, and facilitates communication between information specialists and users.

You will soon learn one thing about computer people—they like to computerize everything. A manual system openly invites computerization. The printed

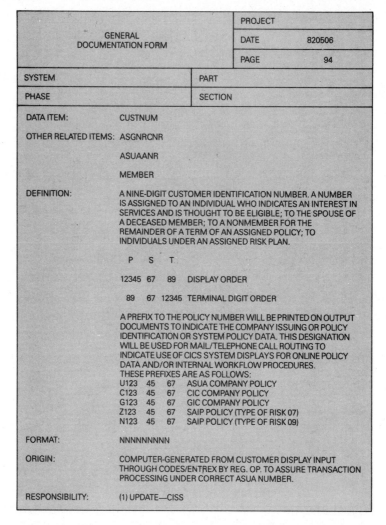

Figure 7-10 A page from a printed data dictionary.

data dictionary was quickly seen as something that could be maintained in computer storage. Large organizations (or organizations with large data bases) can purchase or lease system software called a *data dictionary system (DDS)* that keeps the dictionary current. Some of the DDSs are subsystems of DBMSs; some are standalone systems.

It is possible to prepare reports from a computer-based data dictionary. For example, the TOTAL DBMS provides for over a dozen types of reports such as a listing of application programs using each element. The reports enable a firm to monitor its data base—keep up to date on what it contains and who is using it.

Appendix C is devoted to the data dictionary. It contains a procedure that the information specialist can use, working with the user, to develop the dictionary entries.

The DBTG architecture

The DBMS concept has its roots in the COBOL language. The same group of government, industry, and academic representatives that was instrumental in developing COBOL also saw the need to establish data base standards. The CODASYL group established a Data Base Task Group (DBTG).

The DBTG recommended that firms implement the DBMS architecture pictured in Figure 7-11. The dotted line divides the architecture into the logical structure and the physical structure. The physical secondary storage devices are located at the bottom of the figure, and the users are at the top. The *DBMS users* can be persons or application programs. The users are far removed from the physical organization. In fact, the users need not be concerned with the physical organization.

Connecting the secondary storage with the logical organization is the *physical data base description*. The DBTG suggested a special language to describe how the data base is organized physically in secondary storage. This language is of no special interest to the user, and for that reason we will not discuss it.

The schema and subschema

The portions of the DBTG architecture that do concern the user are the schema and, more importantly, the subschema. The *schema* is the logical description of the entire data base contents. The schema is stored in the computer, and is derived from the data dictionary. The data dictionary is how the user sees the data base specifications, whereas the schema is how the computer sees them. The data dictionary specifications are communicated to the computer by means of a *data description language (DDL)*. The DBTG suggested a DDL for the schema and one for the *subschema*—a user's portion of the schema. You can see in the diagram that two users have their own subschema, and two users share a subschema.

The terms *schema* and *subschema* are important to an understanding of the DBMS. If you have experience with programming languages, you know that each data element has a name, and its attributes are specified. In COBOL, for example, all of the data elements for a record are listed in the data division specification in this manner:

```
01   PAYROLL-RECORD.
      02    EMPLOYEE-NUMBER PICTURE 99999.
      02    EMPLOYEE-NAME PICTURE X(20).
      02    DEPT-NO PICTURE 999.
      02    SOC-SEC-NO PICTURE 9(9).
      02    HOURLY-RATE PICTURE 999V99.
      02    YEAR-TO-DATE-PAY PICTURE 9(6)V99.
      02    YEAR-TO-DATE-TAX PICTURE 9(6)V99.
      02    YEAR-TO-DATE-FICA PICTURE 9(5)V99.
      02    YEAR-TO-DATE-NET PICTURE 9(6)V99.
```

In this example the 01 identifies the record name and the 02s identify the data elements. Each element has a name and a picture clause specifying the attri-

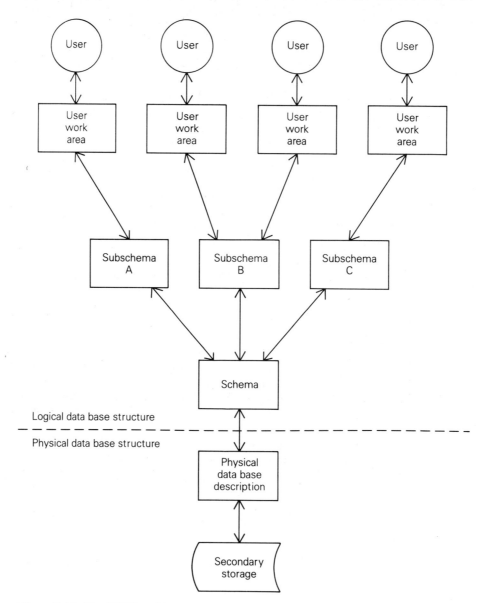

Figure 7-11 The DBTG architecture.

Source: Adapted from Alfonso F. Cardenas, Data Base Management Systems, *2nd ed.
(Boston: Allyn and Bacon, 1985), p. 184.*

butes. The 9s identify numeric positions, and the Vs identify decimal points. For example, the element HOURLY-RATE is a numeric value that can range from 000.00 to 999.99.

The DDL looks very much like the COBOL example above. The entire data base (the schema), as well as each user's portion (the subschema), is described to the computer in this manner.

The user uses a *data manipulation language (DML)* to obtain data specified by his or her subschema. The DBMS puts the data in the user's work area of primary storage, as illustrated in Figure 7-11. The application program performs the necessary processing at that point. When the user is ready to write data back to the data base, the DML is again used.

Using the DBMS

Assume that we have specified the data base contents in a data dictionary, and those specifications have been communicated to the DBMS using a data description language. Further, assume that data has been loaded into the data base in the prescribed format. Now we can use the data base. Figure 7-12 illustrates the steps, which are explained below.

1. An application program such as payroll is being executed. The program requires some data from the data base and contains a command that will cause the needed data elements to be retrieved. The control unit of the CPU causes each instruction of the application program to be executed in sequence. When the data manipulation language command is reached, the control passes from the application program to the DBMS.

2. The DBMS verifies that the data requested has been previously defined in the user's subschema, and that access should be permitted. The DBMS uses its access path mechanisms to identify where the needed elements are located in the data base. We will discuss those access path mechanisms later in the chapter.

3. The DBMS requests the operating system to execute an input operation.

4. The operating system causes the data to be accessed, read, and transmitted to a buffer storage area in primary storage. This is a special buffer storage used by the DBMS. Control passes from the operating system back to the DBMS.

5. The DBMS transfers the data from the buffer storage to the input area used by the application program.

6. The DBMS provides status information to the application program, such as "record found" or "record not found."

7. The application program processes the data.

This example recognizes the role of the DBMS in an input operation. A similar chain of events would occur for a write operation. *The DBMS provides a software interface between the application program and the operating system. The operating system in turn provides an interface between the software and the hardware.* All of these software and hardware elements work together as an information processor.

Primary Storage

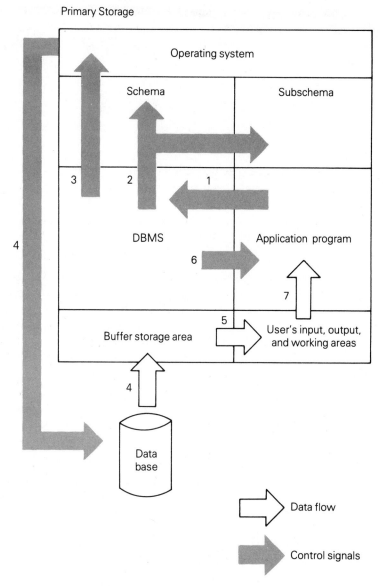

Figure 7-12 DBMS events.

A DBMS Model

Figure 7-13 is a graphical model of a DBMS. The model shows the four components listed below, and illustrates how they interact to perform the DBMS functions.

- The *data description language processor* creates the data base description (the schema) using the data description language (DDL). The input is the data description provided by the data dictionary.

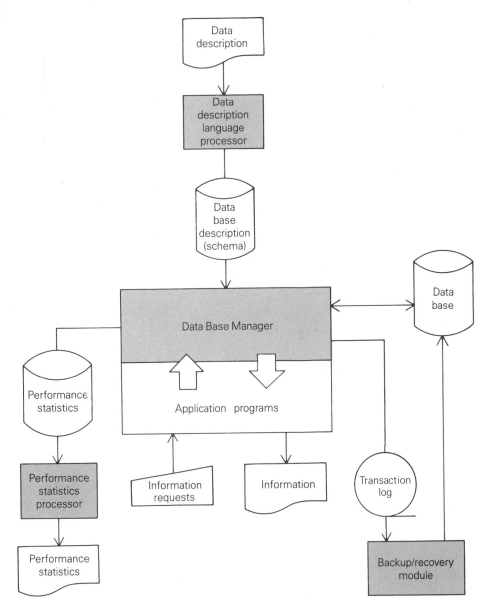

Figure 7-13 A DBMS model.

- The *data base manager* (also called the *data base supervisor*) resides in primary storage to handle requests from application programs. This element also produces performance statistics and a transaction log of data base activity.

- The *performance statistics processor* produces reports from the performance statistics identifying which data is being used and who is using it. The processor is brought into primary storage when the reports are to be prepared. The reports are used by managers in the information services department to manage the data base—identifying areas needing improvement and so on.

- The *backup/recovery module* reconstructs the data base in the event of a catastrophe. As the data base is updated, entries describing the changes are made in a transaction log. The transaction log can be recorded on magnetic disk or magnetic tape. These entries are used to reprocess a backup copy of the data base (created previously) to bring the copy up to date.

There is considerable variation among DBMS offerings on the market today, but most mainframe systems incorporate the basic elements in the model. The systems differ primarily in how the functions are performed. Micro-based DBMSs feature extremely user-friendly data description language processors and data base managers. However, these small-scale systems do not measure up to mainframe models in the performance statistics processor and backup/recovery module. Most micro-DBMSs offer neither statistics nor recovery features.

DBMS Objectives

Earlier in the chapter, we identified the objectives of data management. Those are the goal of any type of data base system—noncomputer as well as computer. When a firm purchases or leases a DBMS, there are certain objectives that the firm seeks to accomplish. The DBMS objectives are listed below. Some DBMSs do a better job of meeting these objectives than do others.

Reduce redundant data in storage

One of the benefits of implementing a DBMS is that it focuses attention on the firm's data resource. Shortcomings and inefficiencies become apparent. One of the most obvious inefficiencies is the redundancy in the data that is maintained. We recognized redundant data *elements* in the pre-data base approach records. In many cases, redundant *files* are also maintained. The redundant storage not only wastes space but valuable employee time as well in performing duplicate tasks. Another concern is the fact that it is difficult to keep all files synchronized or in balance—one file says that 125 widgets are on hand, and another file says 120. Which do you believe?

The intent is to consolidate these multiple files and create a single file that everyone can share. Most operational DBMSs fall short of this goal. Some redundancy cannot be avoided. Some users will insist on having their own files, and some data elements must be repeated within files. Therefore, the realistic objective of a DBMS is to *reduce* redundancy. The result of this effort benefits the firm in the form of lowered costs and increased data accuracy.

Increase data accuracy

Consolidated files are only one way to increase data accuracy. Other means are:

Validate data upon input As data is entered into the data base, the DBMS can ensure that the data attributes are as specified in the schema. Additional input validation is provided by application programs.

Coordinate multiuser access to data An error can occur when several users access a data element at the same time, update it, and put it back. The data base only reflects the last update, not all of them. One solution is to permit only one user with an update privilege at a time.

Update all file copies at a time If multiple files must be maintained, all copies should be updated with a transaction before another transaction is handled. All copies, therefore, are accurate conceptual representations of the physical system as of the last transaction processed.

Maintain an audit trail The term *audit trail* comes from the field of accounting. The idea is to keep a record of all transactions to a file. This record is helpful when reconstructing past history to correct an error or detect a security violation. Most mainframe DBMSs write one or more records on magnetic tape each time a record in the DASD is updated. This is the transaction log in Figure 7-13. Sometimes a *before and after image* of the updated record is written on tape, showing the record before it was updated and after.

Recover from failure

Each firm should plan for incidents that render the data base unusable. Any number of factors could cause the incident—acts of God (such as electrical storms), hardware or software failure, user error, and operator error, to name a few. The backup/recovery module reconstructs the data base in the event of a catastrophe.

Provide access

Approved users should be able to access the data base easily and quickly. Managers can access the data base from terminals utilizing a user-friendly *query language*. The DBMS offers this capability in the form of English-like commands. As an example, the ADABAS (pronounced "aid-a-base") DBMS includes the ADASCRIPT+ query language. Figure 7-14 illustrates the screen dialog when a manager wants a listing showing the employees named Davenport or Alexander with ages between 30 and 45. The manager only has to use two commands— FIND and DISPLAY.

In addition to the query language, the DBMS interfaces with programming languages such as BASIC and PL/I. The language programs include statements that obtain data from the data base and put data into the data base. Figure 7-15 contains a part of a COBOL program that inserts a record into an IMS data base. The instruction at line 2544 "calls" IMS using a "CBLTDLI" (COBOL to DL/I, the IMS language) routine to perform the insert function (ISRT). Line 2545 defines the input/output area to use, lines 2546 and 2547 define the path to be followed in inserting the record into the data base, and line 2548 contains key information used in determining where the record is to be inserted.

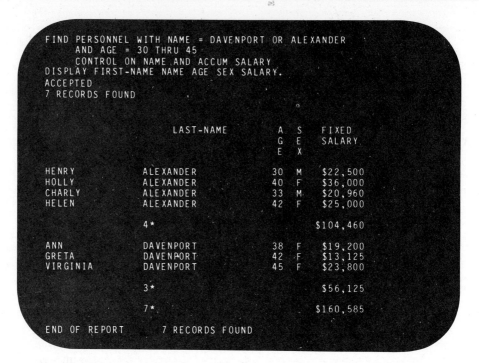

```
FIND PERSONNEL WITH NAME = DAVENPORT OR ALEXANDER
      AND AGE = 30 THRU 45
      CONTROL ON NAME AND ACCUM SALARY
DISPLAY FIRST-NAME NAME AGE SEX SALARY.
ACCEPTED
7 RECORDS FOUND


                           LAST-NAME          A   S    FIXED
                                              G   E    SALARY
                                              E   X

       HENRY          ALEXANDER              30   M   $22,500
       HOLLY          ALEXANDER              40   F   $36,000
       CHARLY         ALEXANDER              33   M   $20,960
       HELEN          ALEXANDER              42   F   $25,000

                      4*                             $104,460


       ANN            DAVENPORT              38   F   $19,200
       GRETA          DAVENPORT              42   F   $13,125
       VIRGINIA       DAVENPORT              45   F   $23,800

                      3*                             $56,125

                      7*                             $160,585

END OF REPORT       7 RECORDS FOUND
```

Figure 7-14 A data base query.

```
002530 9400-INSERT-SEGMENT SECTION.
002531
002532     MOVE ALL SPACES               TO DP-TIME-SEGMENT.
002533     MOVE MID-SCREEN-EMPLOYEE      TO DP-TIME-EMPLOYEE
002534     MOVE CONVERTED-SCREEN-DATE    TO DP-TIME-WORK-WEEK.
002535     MOVE CONVERTED-DATES (INDX)   TO DP-TIME-WORK-DATE.
002536     MOVE CONVERTED-HOURS (INDX)   TO DP-TIME-HOURS.
002537     MOVE DP-EMP-GROUP             TO DP-TIME-GROUP.
002538     MOVE MOD-SCREEN-LEV-REQ       TO DP-TIME-LEAVE-REQUEST.
002539     MOVE WORK-NONWORK-FLAG (INDX) TO DP-TIME-TYPE-PRJ.
002540
002541     MOVE MID-SCREEN-PRJ-CD (INDX) TO DP-PROJECT-ROOT-KEY.
002542     MOVE MID-SCREEN-PRJ-ID (INDX) TO DP-PROJECT-ID-KEY.
002543
002544     CALL 'CBLTDLI' USING ISRT DPPROJECT-PCB
002545                               DP-TIME-SEGMENT
002546                               DP-PROJECT-ROOT-SSA
002547                               DP-ID-SSA
002548                               DP-TIME-INSERT-SSA.
002549
002550     IF DPPROJECT-STATUS-CODE = SPACES
002551     THEN
002552         NEXT SENTENCE
002553     ELSE
002554         MOVE 'Y'      TO IMS-ERROR
002555         MOVE '9400-1' TO BSM-PARA
002556         MOVE 'PRJ'    TO BSM-DB
002557         MOVE DPPROJECT-STATUS-CODE TO BSM-STATUS
002558         GO TO 9400-EXIT.
```

Figure 7-15 Data base instructions imbedded in an application program.

Users should also be able to access data base contents using multiple keys. Thus far we have only identified a single key that identifies the record, such as employee number for an employee file. This is the *primary key*. The user might want to access the file using other keys; these are *secondary keys*. For example, secondary keys in a personnel file might include department number, job code, date-of-hire, and so on. DBMSs offer this multi-key capability.

Provide data independence

If a firm does not use a DBMS, and a change is made to the data format in the data base, changes must also be made to the application programs using that data. This practice can be expensive since firms are constantly adding new elements to their data bases. If a firm uses a DBMS, only the schema needs to be updated; no changes need to be made to the programs. This is termed *data independence*—the programs (or users using query language) are insulated from changes to the logical and physical organization of the data base.

Provide data security

When a firm implements a computerized data base, the issue of data security becomes important. The data base represents a very valuable reservoir of information, and the firm doesn't want it to fall into the wrong hands. The trend to more user-friendly DBMSs and data communications networks compounds the problem. If it is easy for the firm's employees to gain access to the data base, then it will be easy for others as well.

We will address the topic of security in Chapter 18 (Controlling the Operational MIS), but a few words can be included here. DBMSs offer varying degrees of security features. Some micro-based DBMSs offer hardly any, whereas some mainframe versions are well protected. In a well-protected data base, the user has to go through several *security levels* before access is granted.

First, the user must provide his or her *password*. The password uniquely identifies the user as someone with authorized access to the MIS. Next, the DBMS can check several directories to see exactly what kind of privileges the user has. A *user directory* (pictured in Table 7-2) lists all persons with authorized access, and possibly the computer resources available for use. For example, X. N. Leong can use as much as 120KB of primary storage, 5MB of secondary storage, and 2 tape units.

Another directory is the *field directory*, which lists each data element and identifies the authorized users. An example appears in Table 7-3. This directory identifies the users who have certain privileges relating to data elements. For example, user 01734 can read and update the employee number data element in the personnel file but cannot add a new number.

Another level of security is *encryption*, the coding of information stored in the data base. For example, a numeric field may be scrambled so that 123456 appears as 421635 when it is retrieved by an unauthorized user. Encryption is seldom offered as a standard DBMS feature. Two DBMSs that do offer it are ADABAS for mainframes and MDBS III for micros and minis.

Table 7-2 User directory

User Identification Number	Name	Accounting Reference Code	Systems Resources Allowed
01734	Smith, P. K.	21753-01	70KB primary 10MB secondary 3 tape units
36912	Leong, X. N.	14810-30	120KB primary 5MB secondary 2 tape units
40654	Zinsmeister, D.	22364-10	50KB primary 10MB secondary
82199	Herrera, M. A.	30412-00	110KB primary 50MB secondary 4 tape units
94076	Winfield, T. R.	60973-01	100KB primary 20MB secondary 2 tape units

Table 7-3 Field directory

Data Element	File(s)	Authorized Users	
		I.D. Number	R/W/U*
Employee Number	Personnel Payroll	01734 40654 94076	R/U R R
Employee Name	Personnel Payroll	01734 40654 94076	R/U R R
Date of Hire	Personnel	01734	R/U
Date of Last Salary Increase	Personnel	01734	R/U
Amount of Last Salary Increase	Personnel	01734	R/U
Current Annual Salary	Personnel Payroll	01734 40654	R/U R

* R—The user may read this data item.
   W—The user may add this data item to the file.
   U—The user may update this data item.

Data Base Structures

We have seen how linked lists and inverted files provided a means of logically overcoming constraints imposed by the physical organization of the data. Both of these techniques are used by DBMSs today, but they are used within larger, more basic frameworks or structures. The links can be used to *navigate* through the data base, going from one record to another. But how are the various records arranged? Keep in mind that the data base may include many kinds of records. These records must be interrelated in some way. The interrelationships or linkages enable us to select information from physically separate files.

In the brief history of DBMSs, three basic data base structures have been devised—hierarchical, network, and relational.

Hierarchical

When records are arranged hierarchically, they have the appearance of an organization chart. An example appears in Figure 7-16. Each box in the diagram represents a type of record or a file (customer, vendor, and so on). If the diagram were turned upside down, it would look like a *tree*, a name that is also used. The box labeled "1" in the figure is called the *root*.

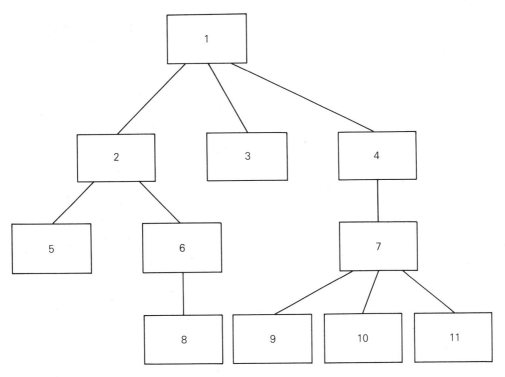

Figure 7-16 A hierarchical structure.

The structure represents records in a vertical hierarchy. An upper record (called the *parent*, or *owner*) is connected *logically* to a lower record (called the *child* or *member*). A parent can have one or more children, but a child can have only one parent. That is one of the constraints of the hierarchical structure.

Figure 7-17 provides an example of some types of business records that can exist in a hierarchy. There are multiple sales statistics records for each salesperson—one statistics record for each sales transaction. There are also multiple customer records for each salesperson—each salesperson has particular customers assigned. Each customer can have multiple accounts receivable records—one record for each unpaid purchase.

At the bottom of the figure are listed some of the data elements that could be contained within each record type. You will note that each record uses a pointer field that links that record to another. Both forward and backward links can be used.

It is important to understand that *all* files in a data base do not have to be linked—only those files that *are used together as a group* for an application. The records in Figure 7-17 have this logical relationship and are called a set. A *set* is simply a group of records connected logically.

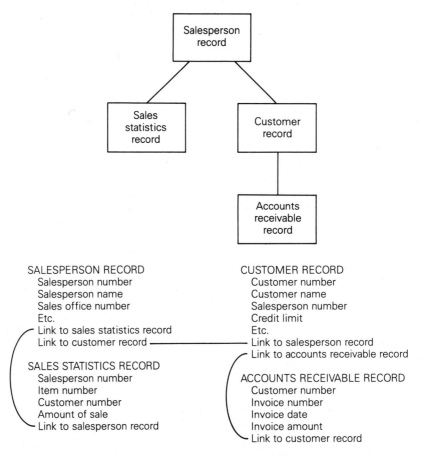

Figure 7-17 Example of a hierarchical or tree structure.

A data base employing the hierarchical structure therefore becomes a collection of files and logically connected sets of files. Figure 7-18 illustrates such a data base. Note that some files are not linked to other files. One of the sets is from Figure 7-17—with the salesperson record as the root. A user request for

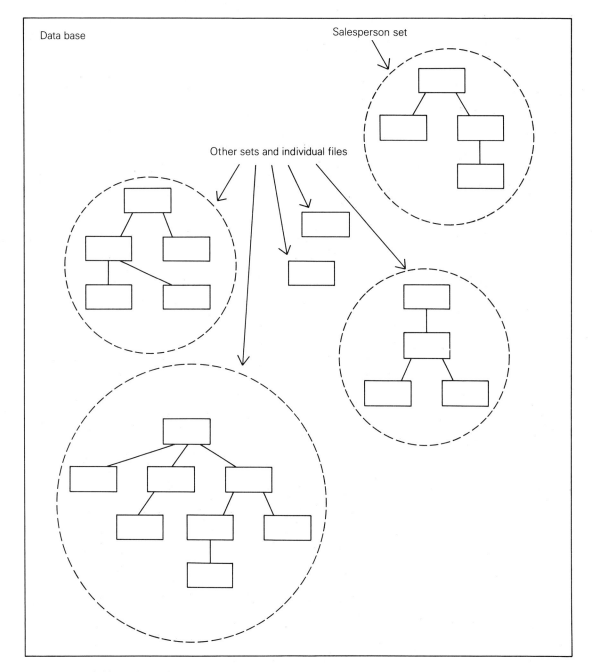

Figure 7-18 A hierarchical data base.

data elements included within the predefined set can be honored, but a request for elements from more than one set cannot. The important point is that the linkages must be established *in advance* of the query. The burden of responsibility is on the information specialist to work with the manager to identify the data sets. This understanding of information needs then forms the basis for the linkages incorporated into the data base as it is created.

IBM's IMS uses the hierarchical structure and is one of the largest and most complex DBMSs available. For this reason it requires a high level of expertise to install. However, it is powerful and has proven capable of handling very large data bases. It also offers good security and recovery procedures, plus an architecture that allows online use through a data communications network.

Network

The DBTG recommends the network structure. For that reason, this structure is often referred to as the *DBTG model*.

The network structure overcomes the constraint of the hierarchical structure that a child cannot have more than one parent. An illustration of a network structure appears in Figure 7-19. Note that record 4 has two parents—records 2 and 3. Figure 7-20 provides an example of networked business records. A buyer in the purchasing department is assigned certain inventory items. When it is time to reorder an inventory item, a field in the inventory record identifies the buyer responsible for making the purchase. Therefore, multiple inventory records can exist for each buyer record. An inventory record can refer to multiple vendor records since a firm usually has more than one source of supply for an item. A single vendor can be represented by multiple outstanding purchase orders (orders placed to the vendor but not yet filled by the vendor) and also by multiple records in the accounts payable file (payments due the vendor for purchases already received).

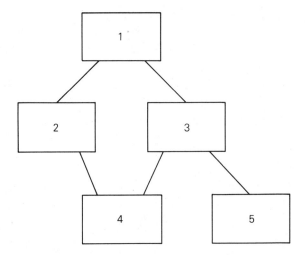

Figure 7-19 Network structure.

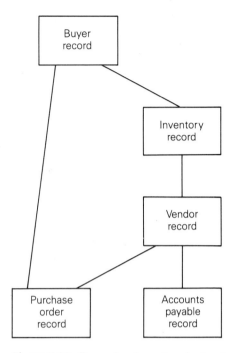

Figure 7-20 Example of a network structure.

In this example, the purchase order record has two parents—a buyer and a vendor record.

Again, it is not necessary that all files in the data base be networked—only the files in a set.

Cincom's TOTAL is an example of a network model. It and IMS account for about 40 percent of the installed mainframe DBMSs. TOTAL is based on the DBTG model but does not include all of the features. Because of its "no frills" architecture, it is very efficient—it is fast and conserves storage space.

The records in a network structure are linked in the same manner as illustrated for the hierarchical structure in Figure 7-17. TOTAL uses both forward and backward links to facilitate a bidirectional movement within the set. TOTAL directly accesses the root record using a hashing scheme (described in Chapter 5). Then, TOTAL can navigate from the root to the lower-level records and back again using the links.

Relational

The relational structure has received the most attention during the past few years. The interest stems from work performed by E. F. Codd in 1970. Codd published a mathematical approach to establishing interdependencies among data elements. One year later, C. J. Date published the textbook *Introduction to Database Systems* that included a hypothetical "relational" language. The work by Codd and

Date had an electrifying effect on an industry primed for a solution to its mounting data problems.

In a relational data base, the data is organized in two-dimensional tables. Each table can be considered to be a file. The term *flat file* is used since the file contents are arranged in the two-dimensional form.

A new set of terms has evolved for use in describing relational structures. These terms correspond to terms we have used to describe hierarchical and network structures. In the relational model, the term used instead of schema is *relational data model*. The term used instead of subschema is *relational data submodel*, or *view*. The term view is appropriate—it is the user's "view" of her or his portion of the data base.

In addition, special names are used to describe the parts of the flat files. A sample file is illustrated in Table 7-4. The columns of the table are referred to as *domains*, and the rows as *tuples*. A table is a collection of tuples pertaining to a particular topic. The table in Table 7-4 pertains to salespersons, and can be used to provide their names and their year-to-date sales.

At this point in our discussion we must make a confession. We have been referring to links and inverted files as logical structures. It is true that they do permit a view of the data different from the physical arrangement. But, as you may have already observed, the links and inverted file indexes *do exist physically*. So, those higher-level data organizations are actually a subtle intermingling of the logical and physical structures.

While the use of these quasi-logical approaches in hierarchical and network models is a big step forward, there are problems. The problems surface when there are many, many linkages and indexes. Then it becomes difficult to make changes—add and delete records, add fields, and so on.

We recognize these problems here because they are avoided with the relational approach. The relational structure is a purely logical one, employing *implicit*

Table 7-4   A flat file

Salesperson no.	Salesperson name	Year-to-date sales
112	ADAMS	12,682.94
128	WINKLER	9,223.60
153	HOUSE	575.00
159	FRANCIS	2,234.98
162	WILLIS	16,332.11
166	GROVETON	7,532.40

relationships, rather than the *explicit relationships* of both the hierarchical and network models.

The implicit relationships are established using Codd's relational calculus. We will not go into the details of that calculus here but will illustrate how it is used to bring together data from physically separate tables.

Assume that we have two tables in the data base—Table A and Table B. These tables are illustrated in Table 7-5. Table A identifies the sales territory (TERR) for each salesperson (SALESNO). Table B identifies each salesperson's name (NAME). The two tables exist separately—there are no physical linkages. The relationship is established implicitly by including the SALESNO domain in both tables.

Table 7-5 Implicit relationships between tables

Table A

SALESNO	TERR
112	1
128	3
153	2
159	1
162	1
166	2

Table B

SALESNO	NAME
112	ADAMS
128	WINKLER
153	HOUSE
159	FRANCIS
162	WILLIS
166	GROVETON

You would not require any special instructions to figure out that salesperson 112's name is Adams, and the territory is 1. Codd's calculus gives the DBMS the same logical power.

If a manager wants to know the names of the salespersons in territory 1, the relational calculus would be:

$$X(B.NAME): \exists \ (A.SALESNO = B.SALESNO \wedge A.TERR = '1').$$

In everyday English this says "Obtain the list of salespersons' names from Table B whose numbers are the same as those in Table A and territory number is 1."

It is not necessary for the manager to enter the query using the calculus form. Relational DBMSs have much more user-friendly query languages. Perhaps the query would be as simple as:

$$DISPLAY \ NAME \ WHERE \ TERR = '1'$$

The first mainframe relational DBMS was IBM's Query-by-Example (QBE) in 1980. Since then, additional mainframe and microcomputer DBMSs have been made available. Ashton-Tate's dBASE II was an early micro-based DBMS using the relational model.

QBE is extremely user friendly. As the name implies, the user only has to give an example of the information needed. The user does this by identifying on the terminal screen the domain values to be retrieved. Figure 7-21 illustrates the step-by-step process.

Step a. The user brings up a skeleton table on the screen.

Step b. The user identifies Table A data as being needed by typing an "A" in the first column of the skeleton table. QBE fills in the skeleton with the names of the Table A domains.

Step c. The user tells QBE that Table A data must be augmented with additional table data by typing a hypothetical salesperson number (123) in the SALESNO column. The salesperson number will establish the implicit relationship. Any salesperson number will do—it is only an example. The user also types a '1' in the TERR column indicating that the query will be restricted to tuples with a TERR value of 1.

Step d. The user brings up Table B by requesting another skeleton table and typing "B" in the first column.

Step e. Table A is linked to Table B by typing the common identifier (123) in the SALESNO column. The user specifies that the salesperson name is to be printed by typing P.SMITH in the NAME column. The "P" stands for "print." Again, SMITH is only an example.

Step f. The query response is displayed on the screen.

a. Bring up skeleton table.

b. Identify a table to be used.

A	SALESNO	TERR	

c. Identify the linkage (123) to Table B and the territory number (1).

A	SALESNO	TERR	
	123	1	

d. Bring up Table B.

B	SALESNO	NAME	

e. Identify linkage to Table A (123) and fields to be printed (P.SMITH).

B	SALESNO	NAME	
	123	P. SMITH	

f. QBE displays the response.

NAME
ADAMS
FRANCIS
WILLIS

Figure 7-21 A QBE example.

The relational structure offers three important advantages over hierarchical and network structures:

1. It is user friendly.
2. Relations are truly logical, providing greater insulation of the users from changes in the data base.
3. It is not necessary to predefine the linkages; they are established at the time the query is issued.

This third advantage greatly reduces the pressure on the information specialist and the manager to predetermine all future information needs so that explicit linkages can be built into the records.

dBASE III—A Micro DBMS

dBASE III from Ashton-Tate succeeded the popular dBASE II and is currently competing with two Microrim products, Rbase 4000 and Rbase 5000, for top spot in the micro DBMS market. Like its predecessor, dBASE III uses the relational model. In this section we will describe and illustrate how to perform several basic procedures using dBASE III.

dBASE III characteristics

The dBASE III data base consists of separate files. Each file contains only one *type* of record. For example, a payroll file contains only employee earnings records. There is no real limit on the *number* of records that can be included in a file—the only constraint is storage space (diskette or hard disk). Each record is limited to a maximum of 128 fields, and each field cannot exceed 254 bytes. You can work with a maximum of 10 files at a time. These limits are easy to live with—especially for a micro user.

Specifying the schema

Prior to creating a data base, you must specify the schema. The dBASE III DDL is invoked by typing CREATE. A screen display (Figure 7-22) includes a help menu at the top explaining cursor movement and how to correct errors in the specifications. You describe each record field by typing the field name, the type of data, its width, and the number of decimal positions (for numeric data). In the figure example, the user has described the first six record fields.

Entering data

After specifying the schema, you can enter data, one record at a time, using the screen provided in Figure 7-23. The size of each field is defined. When you fill up a field, an audible beep sounds and the cursor moves to the next field. When one record has been filled, a new, blank format is displayed for the next record. dBASE III assigns a number to each record in the file. This is the primary key. It is possible to have multiple secondary keys.

Maintaining the file

You can add records to the file by typing APPEND and then repeating the process just described for creating the file.

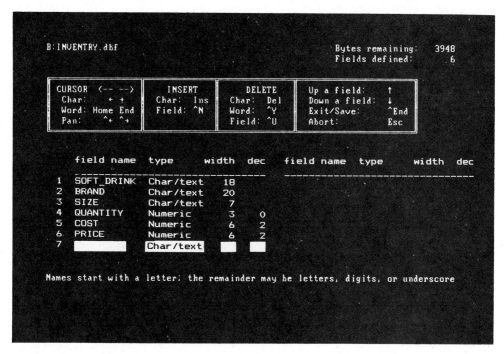

Figure 7-22   Specifying the schema.

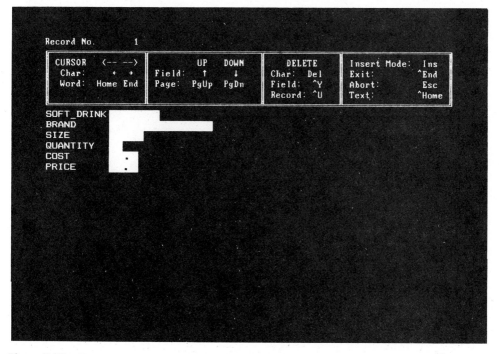

Figure 7-23   Entering data into the data base.

You can delete records by typing DELETE RECORD n, with n being the record number. Or, you can delete one or more records satisfying some condition such as DELETE FOR NAME = 'WIDGET'.

You can update, or change, fields by typing EDIT n. The record is displayed (Figure 7-24), and you move the cursor to the proper field and type the new data over the old, erasing the old.

Querying the data base

If you want to see an entire file displayed on the screen, you type DISPLAY ALL. The records are displayed in groups of 20. You display a new group by pressing any key, until all records have been displayed.

If you only want to display one or more records satisfying some condition, you type DISPLAY ALL FOR condition. For example, if you want to see all of the records for customer 123, you would type DISPLAY ALL FOR CUSTOMER = '123'. The DISPLAY command offers the micro user a powerful querying ability. Conditions can be quite complex, such as DISPLAY ALL FOR TERRI-TORY = '1' .AND. AMTOWED > 500. This would display all territory 1 customers owing the firm more than $500.

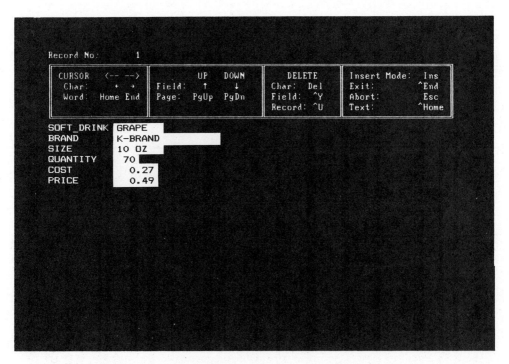

Figure 7-24 A record displayed for editing.

Sorting records

Records can be rearranged using either the SORT or the INDEX command. INDEX is faster but is restricted to ascending sequences. SORT permits ascending or descending sequences. Both SORT and INDEX permit the use of multiple sort keys. For example, if you want to sort records by salesperson number (minor key) within sales office number (major key), you type:

INDEX ON OFFICE + SALESPER TO INDEX1

The plus sign separates the two keys. INDEX1 is an index using the secondary keys. The reason the INDEX is faster than SORT is because the records are not rearranged physically; the index is used to retrieve the records in the desired order.

Printing reports

dBASE III includes a REPORT command that can produce printed reports. You have a number of options. The reports can be detailed listings or summaries, single- or double-spaced, with or without headings, with or without totals, and so on. An example of a detailed listing appears in Figure 7-25. A summary report produced from the same data appears in Figure 7-26.

The micro DBMSs cost only a fraction of what a mainframe version costs, $600 or so compared to around $100,000. But the micro versions only give you a partial data management capability. Even so, the micro DBMS permits the micro to function as an effective decision support tool.

Distributed Data Bases

In Chapter 5 we recognized that a popular trend during recent years has been toward distributed data processing. Low-cost minis and micros have encouraged this trend, and serve as distributed processing systems. We also recognized that firms have the option of distributing their data base.

Figure 7-27 illustrates the three options facing a firm. In 7-27a both programming and the data base are centralized. A firm headquartered in Pittsburgh, for example, would have a mainframe and its data base at that location. Outlying offices could timeshare the mainframe using remote terminals. In 7-27b the firm installs additional processors at the outlying offices but retains control over the data base. In 7-27c the firm permits the outlying offices to control their own data bases. Even in such a distributed environment, the firm would probably want to maintain a corporate data base at headquarters. Users in the network could have access to data bases located at headquarters or at other outlying offices.

Most DBMSs on the market today were intended for use with a centralized data base (7-27a and 7-27b). During the next few years, new DBMSs will appear that can manage the distributed data bases of 7-27c.

```
Page No.        1
07/01/86
                                   CIRCLE DRIVE-IN
                            MONTHLY SOFT DRINK INVENTORY

BRAND                        SIZE                        VALUE


**   COLA
  K-BRAND                    1 LITER                     45.03
  K-BRAND                    2 LITER                     37.52
  K-BRAND                    6 OZ                        36.18
  SCHUBERT'S                 10 OZ                       25.08
  SCHUBERT'S                 6 OZ                        26.88
** Subtotal **
                                                        170.69


**  GRAPE
  K-BRAND                    10 OZ                       18.90
  WELSH'S                    10 OZ                       64.74
  WELSH'S                    24 OZ                       91.30
** Subtotal **
                                                        174.94


**   ORANGE
  K-BRAND                    10 OZ                       33.22
  SUN MAID                   10 OZ                       18.76
** Subtotal **
                                                         51.98


**   ROOT BEER
  K-BRAND                    10 OZ                       20.09
  K-BRAND                    16 OZ                       23.76
  K-BRAND                    6 OZ                        24.90
  SCHUBERT'S                 16 OZ                       39.56
** Subtotal **
                                                        108.31

*** Total ***
                                                        505.92
```

Figure 7-25 A detailed listing.

Data Base Advantages and Disadvantages

The terms *data base* and *DBMS* are not synonymous. The data base is the conceptual resource of the firm, and the DBMS is the software system that manages that resource.

The *advantages* to a firm of having a data base are:

1. An organized and comprehensive means of recording the results of the firm's activities

```
Page No.        1
07-01-86
                                          CIRCLE DRIVE-IN
                                    MONTHLY SOFT DRINK INVENTORY

QUANTITY       COST       INVEST


**   COLA
** Subtotal **
       490                170.69

**   GRAPE
** Subtotal **
       319                174.94

**   ORANGE
** Subtotal **
       218                 51.98

**   ROOT BEER
** Subtotal **
       211                108.31
*** Total ***
      1238                505.92
```

Figure 7-26 A summary report.

2. A reservoir of data to be used in meeting the information requirements
   of the MIS users

The *disadvantages* stem from poor management of the data resource and
include:

1. An increased opportunity for persons or groups outside the organization
   to gain access to information about the firm's operations
2. An increased opportunity for persons to make unauthorized changes in
   the physical system of the firm through manipulations of the conceptual
   system; for example, by embezzling funds through computer theft
3. An increased opportunity for poorly trained persons within the organization to misuse the data resource unintentionally; for example, by mis-
   interpreting information output from the data base

The first two disadvantages are not so critical with a standalone micro (one
not networked to a host). The data base is usually in diskette form, which can be
easily duplicated and kept under lock and key. Also, micros are normally used
by only one person at a time. It is much easier to guard against unauthorized use
under such conditions. The third disadvantage does apply to micros; uninformed
users can misuse the output.

a. Centralized processing and data base

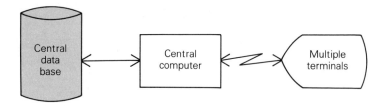

b. Distributed processing and centralized data base

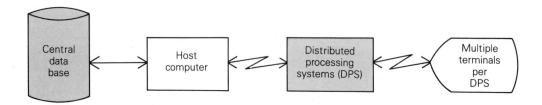

c. Distributed processing and data base

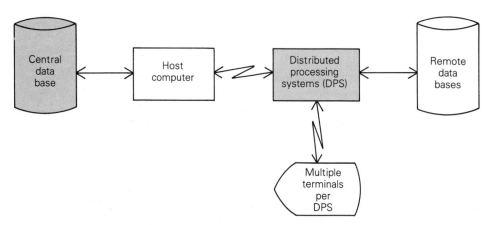

Figure 7-27   Processing and data base options.

As with any resource, the firm attempts to increase the value of the data base by improving both the quality and the quantity of its contents. The firm attempts to minimize the disadvantages by managing the resource better, which involves using a DBMS and improving security measures.

DBMS Advantages and Disadvantages

In general, the advantages of a DBMS relate to improvements in the management of the data base. The disadvantages relate primarily to the cost of the DBMS.

Specifically, the *advantages* of using a DBMS are:

1. Reduction in file and data redundancy
2. Integration of file contents, allowing data to be combined for improved information reporting
3. Ability to handle complex data structures
4. Rapid retrieval of data base contents
5. More accurate data base contents
6. Better security of the data base
7. Relatively easy recovery from unexpected catastrophe, such as equipment failure
8. Relatively easy creation and maintenance of the data base
9. Relatively easy preparation of information output, using query languages and report writers

Advantages 2, 3, and 6 are not nearly as strong for micro DBMSs. Integration usually exists only within a file, the data structures are usually not complex, and security is mostly left to the user. Advantages 8 and 9 are perhaps stronger for the micro DBMS since those packages are generally more user friendly than ones for mainframes.

Disadvantages of the DBMS include:

1. Expensive software
2. Greater hardware demands, requiring computers with larger primary and secondary storage capacities than would otherwise be necessary
3. Need for a technically trained staff to oversee the use of the data base and the DBMS

Disadvantages 1 and 2 apply to micro DBMSs as well as mainframe. To the micro user, $600 for a DBMS might be a large investment. The micro DBMS might also require more hardware than would otherwise be the case. Some dBASE III users, for example, feel that their micro should include a hard disk if the DBMS is to be used effectively. Disadvantage 3 can be bypassed in a micro shop, but the presence of technically qualified staff will increase the utility of the DBMS.

Most computer users apparently feel that the advantages of a DBMS outweigh the disadvantages. They recognize both the value of having a data base and using it efficiently. The DBMS helps achieve both goals.

The Data Base Administrator

Interest in data bases has opened up an entirely new job category—the *data base administrator*, or *DBA*. This person manages the data base. We included this position in the organization chart of the information services department in Chapter 5 (see Figure 5-26). In large organizations, more than one person is needed—a DBA staff. In small organizations (primarily micro users), a person usually is not given the title, but the duties are performed on a part-time basis.

The duties of the DBA fall into four major categories: planning, implementing, operating, and controlling.

Planning involves working with users to define the subschemas and the schema. In addition, the appropriate DBMS must be selected. The DBA evaluates the systems on the market and recommends a particular DBMS to top management.

Implementing consists of creating the data base to conform to the specifications of the selected DBMS and establishing and enforcing policies and procedures for data base use.

Operating includes teaching users how to work with the DBMS and providing assistance when needed. The DBA becomes the specialist in data base matters, relieving the systems analysts and programmers of much of this responsibility.

Controlling includes the monitoring of data base activity using statistics provided by the DBMS. In addition, the DBA remains alert to security threats and takes action to correct any weaknesses that appear.

In Chapter 1, we listed the ingredients of information resource management (IRM). One is a *data administrator*. This is *not* the DBA but someone on a higher level who is responsible for *all* of the firm's data—noncomputer as well as computer. If a firm has a data administrator, the DBA will report to that person. Thus far, few firms have established the data administrator role.

Putting the Data Base and the DBMS in Perspective

Data is the necessary ingredient of information. Most of the data exists in the form of accounting files such as payroll and inventory. Some files may be created solely for use in decision support. All of the information derived from the MIS by the manager—whether it be periodic reports, special reports in response to queries, or output from mathematical models—is derived from this data.

The DBMS has made it possible for firms to achieve the type of data base necessary for decision support. Very few firms have a programming staff that could achieve a software system to handle the data management tasks as well as a DBMS. During the late sixties and the seventies, only users of large- and medium-scale systems had the opportunity to obtain DBMSs. More recently, however, many such packages have been developed for mini and micro systems. During the decade of the eighties, the DBMS picture should improve even more, with more packages achieving better performance at lower prices.

A DBMS is a necessary requirement when the data resource is large and is shared by many users. The combination of the DBMS software, other system and application software, and the necessary hardware provides the firm with a valuable information processing capability.

Summary

As a firm seeks to manage its data resource, ways must be found to collect, organize, store, retrieve, manipulate, output, and control the data. The computer can be used to accomplish most of these objectives.

In the pre-data base era, data access was tied to the physical structure of the files. The first step toward removing the physical constraint was the development of generalized file management systems (GFMS). Another step forward was the discovery of higher-level data organizations such as linked lists and inverted files.

The Data Base Task Group established some guidelines for a generalized data base management system (DBMS). The guidelines recommended a network structure, and introduced new terms such as *schema, subschema, data description language,* and *data manipulation language.*

A data dictionary enables all users of the data base to use the same language by standardizing data element names and attributes. The dictionary can be printed, or it can be maintained in computer storage by a data dictionary system.

The DBMS is an interface between the users (application programs or online users) and the data base. The user issues a data base command. The DBMS verifies that the user has been approved for access, and passes the request along to the operating system. The operating system causes the data to be retrieved.

A DBMS usually has four basic parts—a data description language processor, a data base manager, a performance statistics processor, and a backup/recovery module. Micro-based DBMSs are usually deficient in the latter two parts.

The DBMS strives to reduce redundancy, increase accuracy, facilitate recovery from failure, and to provide access, data independence, and security.

In a hierarchical structure, a child can have only one parent, but that constraint does not apply to a network structure. Both structures use explicit linkages between logically related records in a set. This technique requires that the information specialist (DBA or systems analyst) and the manager specify the needed logical connections before the data base is created. This requirement can be overcome with the relational structure that uses implicit linkages. Most current attention is being directed at relational models.

dBASE III is a good example of a micro DBMS. It is very user friendly, yet powerful. A user can easily select records satisfying certain criteria, and display the records on the screen or print reports. System software such as dBASE III makes the micro a legitimate decision support tool.

A firm has a basic choice of whether to centralize or distribute its processing. Another choice pertains to the location of the data base. Work remains to be done in providing a DBMS to meet the needs of a distributed data base network.

There are no real disadvantages to having a data base that cannot be overcome with security measures. You don't have to have a DBMS to have a good MIS, but that situation is becoming more rare with low-priced micro DBMSs. The micro versions do not offer all of the advantages of the mainframe models, but they also do not have the disadvantage of high cost.

The person responsible for the firm's computer-based data resources is the data base administrator, or DBA. In some firms this person reports to a data administrator.

Data is the raw material of information. For that reason, the data base is an important ingredient of the MIS. In this chapter we have gained a good insight to the data base and how it functions in a computer-based MIS.

Key Terms

data base

data base management system (DBMS)

generalized file management system (GFMS)

linked list

embedded pointer

list head, tail

link

two-way list

circular, ring structure

inverted file

chained files

data base approach

physical, logical data organization

data element dictionary (DED)

attribute

data dictionary system (DDS)

DBMS user

physical data base description

schema

data description language (DDL)

subschema

data manipulation language (DML)

data description language processor

data base manager, supervisor

performance statistics processor

backup/recovery module

audit trail

before and after image

query language

primary key, secondary key

data independence

security level

password

user directory, field directory

encryption

hierarchical, tree structure

root

parent, owner

child, member

set

network structure

relational structure

flat file

relational data model

relational data submodel, view

domain

tuple

implicit, explicit relationship

data base administrator (DBA)

data administrator

Key Concepts

How linked lists and inverted files produce a logical data organization different from the physical

The data dictionary as the starting point of data base design

The schema as the description of all data in the data base; the subschema as a user's subset

Special languages for describing the data (DDL) and for manipulating it (DML)

How the DBMS serves as an interface between the query or application program, and the operating system

The basic parts of a DBMS

How the logical structure of the DBMS insulates the user from changes to the data base

Levels of data base security

The three primary data base structures

Sets of logically integrated files

Explicit versus implicit relationships

Questions

1. What is a data base? Provide both a broad and a narrow definition. What is a DBMS?

2. Must a firm have a logically integrated, computerized data base to have an MIS? Must it have a DBMS? Explain.

3. What are the objectives of data management? Which can be performed entirely by the computer?

4. How does the pre-data base approach differ from the data base approach?

5. What are two higher-level data organizations for expressing logical relationships between data? Provide a one-sentence definition of each.

6. In what form does the data dictionary exist?

7. What is an attribute? Give an example.

8. Is the schema the same as the data base? Explain.

9. What is meant by the term "DBMS user"?

10. What is the role of the DBMS in obtaining data from the data base to provide to an application program? What is the role of the operating system?

11. List the DBMS objectives.

12. What are some ways to increase data accuracy?

13. What is a query language?

14. How does the DBMS contribute to data security?

15. What structure is used by QBE? By TOTAL? By IMS? By dBASE III? Which of these DBMSs uses explicit relationships? Implicit relationships?

16. Are all files in a data base linked logically? Explain.

17. What two dBASE III commands are used to rearrange data? Name an advantage of each. A disadvantage.

18. What are the disadvantages of a firm having a computerized, logically integrated data base?

19. If you were to summarize all of the DBMS disadvantages into a single one, what would it be?

20. Which would a firm acquire first—a DBMS or a DBA? Explain.

Problems

1. Assuming that the following records constitute the customer master file, enter the forward and backward links.

Customer Number	Year-to-Date Sales	Salesperson Number	Forward Salesperson Link	Backward Salesperson Link
104	25000.00	12		
109	17500.00	24		
111	12500.00	12		
118	6000.00	12		
124	12000.00	36		
127	300.00	48		
132	18000.00	36		
138	24000.00	12		
142	26500.00	48		
149	120.00	24		
151	8000.00	48		

2. Construct an inverted file index in salesperson number sequence for the above customer file.

3. Your instructor will provide you with a list of records to enter into a data base named ACCREC. This is an accounts receivable file. Perform the following operations. Obtain a printout after each operation.
   a. Key the data into the file.
   b. Delete all records for West Motors.
   c. Add the following record:

Customer No.	3623
Customer Name	Arbuckle Motors
Customer Class	1
Order No.	88614
Days Past Due	60
Order Amount	127.50

   d. Display all records for customers with a class code = 1.
   e. Display all records with an amount over $100, and 120 days past due.
   f. Prepare a detailed report from the entire data base, with headings and a total order amount.

g. Rearrange the records into sequence by customer number (minor) within customer class (major).

h. Prepare a summary report from the entire data base, with order amount subtotals on customer class and a final total.

CASE PROBLEM: Maple Leaf Industries, Ltd.

You have one of the most successful computer consulting firms in Canada. Your first consulting jobs dealt with planning computer projects for energy companies, but you have since branched out into other industries.

Last week you presented a data base seminar in Toronto that was attended by over one hundred top executives in the country. The $250 tuition paid by each attending executive made the seminar a huge financial success, but you expect an even greater return in the form of follow-up consulting activity.

While enjoying your morning cup of coffee, you go through the stack of mail. You notice an envelope from Maple Leaf Industries, and you recall that they had a representative at the seminar. You open the envelope and read

> I greatly enjoyed the data base seminar. I was surprised to learn of the potential that a data base management system offers. It was a shock to my ego to realize that we are what you call a "pre-data base" company, but I want to change that.
>
> We are very interested in implementing a data base management system and would like to consider retaining you as a consultant on the project. At present, we have no in-house data base management expertise. Could you please prepare a short list of the basic steps that we should take in implementing a DBMS. Also, for each step, indicate the person, or persons, responsible. The list will give us a good idea of what we must do and an indication of the support we can expect from you in project planning. I am making the same request of two other computer consultants that I know.
>
> I look forward to receiving your response.
>
> Sincerely,
>
> Anthony Scarmodo, President
> Maple Leaf Industries, Ltd.

Assume that Maple Leaf has a good information services staff and is a prospect for a mainframe DBMS. Provide Mr. Scarmodo with the list of steps that he has requested. Identify the person (by title) who should be responsible for each step. Should you, as a consultant, have a role? Are there people within Maple Leaf Industries who should be responsible? Will Maple Leaf have to bring in new personnel to assume any of the responsibilities?

CASE PROBLEM: Blue Bell Plastics Manufacturing Company

Assume that you receive a letter from Ms. Adele Wasserman, president of Blue Bell Plastics Manufacturing Company. She attended the same conference as Mr. Scarmodo (above) and is interested in getting a DBMS for her micro. She has no information services staff and does not plan to add one. Her firm uses only prewritten programs, but she wants to be able to obtain more information on her operations.

Does an organization with only limited information services resources need a DBMS? If so, does such an organization go about DBMS implementation differently from a larger organization with a mainframe capability?

Write Ms. Wasserman a letter recommending what she should do. If you recommend that she get a DBMS, list the steps as Mr. Scarmodo requested.

Selected Bibliography

The Data Base

Bowerman, Robert, "Relational Database Systems for Micros," *Datamation* 29 (July 1983): 128ff.

Byers, Robert A., *Everyman's Database Primer: Featuring dBASE III* (Culver City, CA: Ashton-Tate, 1984).

Cardenas, Alfonso F., *Data Base Management Systems*, 2nd ed. (Boston: Allyn and Bacon, 1985).

Curtice, Robert M., and Paul E. Jones, Jr., "Database: The Bedrock of Business," *Datamation* 30 (June 15, 1984): 163ff.

Davis, Richard K., "New Tools and Techniques to Make Data Base Professionals More Productive," *Journal of Systems Management* 35 (June 1984): 20–25.

Grafton, William P., "IMS: Past, Present, Future," *Datamation* 29 (September 1983): 158ff.

Krakow, Ira H., "Powerful Data-base Manager Lacks Programming Capability," *Business Computer Systems* 3 (March 1984): 135ff.

Kroenke, David M., *Database Processing: Fundamentals, Design, Implementation*, 2nd ed. (Chicago: Science Research Associates, 1983).

Leigh, William, "Natural Language for Database Access," *Journal of Systems Management* 34 (November 1983): 22–24.

McGee, W. C. "Data Base Technology," *IBM Journal of Research and Development* 25 (September 1981): 505–519.

Mace, Scott, "Software Heavyweights Slug It Out," *InfoWorld* 7 (April 22, 1985): 29–33.

Martin, Janette, "Microrim's R:base 4000," *Business Computing* 2 (October 1984): 54–56.

Perry, Robert L., "Relational DBMS Takes Off," *Computer Decisions* 17 (February 12, 1985): 106ff.

Shah, Arvind D., "Data Administration: It's Crucial," *Datamation* 30 (July 15, 1984): 187ff.

Snyders, Jan, "DBMS: The More You Get, The More You Want," *Computer Decisions* 16 (February 1984): 124ff.

Spiegler, Israel, "MIS and DBMS: Where Does One End and the Other Start?," *Journal of Systems Management* 34 (June 1983): 34–42.

Sweet, Frank, "What, If Anything, Is a Relational Database?," *Datamation* 30 (July 15, 1984): 118ff.

Chapter 8

Data Communications

Learning Objectives

After studying this chapter, you should:

- Understand what is meant by the term *data communications*
- Know the objectives of data communications and how it is used in the MIS
- Be familiar with some of the alternatives in computing and communications equipment that can be integrated into a data communications network
- Understand a number of the more frequently used data communications terms
- Have a better knowledge of the different kinds of terminals
- Be familiar with some of the channel products offered by common carriers and other communications firms
- Appreciate the key role played by the front-end processor in the data communications network
- Understand what is meant by architecture standards, and why they are necessary
- See how protocols provide both logical and physical links in the data communications system
- Recognize the security problems of a data communications network, and ways of handling those problems
- Understand how a manager operates and uses a terminal

Introduction

In our discussion of the computer thus far, we have described the CPU, the input/output units, and secondary storage. In the preceding chapter, we presented the software used with the secondary-storage hardware. We have discussed all of the units that comprise an onsite computer configuration. In this chapter, we expand the scope of our study to include the communication of data from one location to another.

Data communications is the movement of encoded data and information from one point to another by means of electrical or optical transmission systems.[1]

Data communications is often referred to as *datacom*, and we will use that contraction in this book to save a little ink. You will also hear the terms *teleprocessing*, *telecommunications*, and *telecom*. All of these terms can be used interchangeably.

We have already encountered datacom in our discussion of information processor hardware. In Chapter 5 we identified several basic approaches to computer processing—online, time-sharing, and distributed—that make use of datacom. In our discussion of input/output devices, we described hardcopy and CRT terminals. In this chapter we will put these and other topics in perspective by describing the fundamentals of datacom. As we have noted, many firms are distributing their information processors throughout the organization. A datacom ability is an integral part of many modern MIS designs.

Datacom in the general systems model

Datacom can provide the link between the information processor on the one hand and the physical system of the firm and its environment on the other, as shown in Figure 8-1. The labeled rectangles represent hardware, and the arrows represent communication channels such as telephone lines. All of the channels are two-way flows of data and information. Data can be gathered throughout the firm and from the environment and entered in the information processor. Data and information can also be provided by management. In each situation, datacom facilitates input. Datacom can also be used to transmit information from the information processor to the user. For example, a graph can be prepared on a plotter located in a manager's office; a terminal in a factory can instruct a worker performing a production task; and a terminal in a buyer's office can print out a purchase order for needed materials. In all of these examples, datacom facilitates output. Datacom is needed when any of the inputs and outputs take place some distance from the information processor, such as across town, across the nation, or around the world.

Some of the rectangles in the figure contain new terms—host computer, front-end processor, and remote intelligent controller. These are all information processors that play a role in the datacom network. We will describe these units in the chapter.

---

[1] This definition is a minor modification of one found in Jerry FitzGerald, *Business Data Communications* (New York: John Wiley and Sons, 1984), p. 6. This excellent text explains a complex topic in a very readable style. It is recommended if you wish more detail than is provided in the chapter.

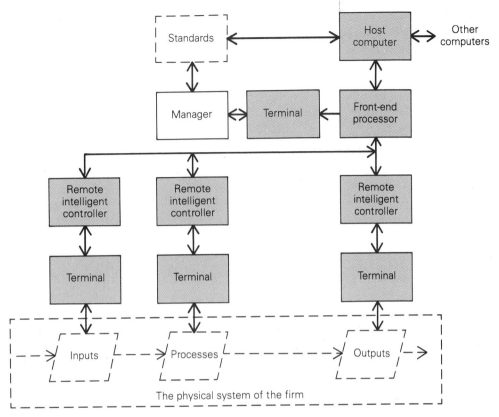

Figure 8-1 Data communications in the general systems model.

Objectives of datacom

Firms integrate datacom hardware and software into their MIS configurations to accomplish one or more of the following objectives.

- *Capture data at its source.* Datacom enables the data to enter the information processor sooner, and eliminates the unnecessary steps of recording and physically transporting data prior to entry.
- *Facilitate the rapid dissemination of information.* Datacom makes it possible to provide information to users without a delay in transport.
- *Contribute to improved management control.* Datacom makes it possible to get the right information to the right person at the right time. Managers can learn of activities as they occur or shortly thereafter. The managers can take remedial action before it is too late.
- *Facilitate organizational policies of either centralized or decentralized control.* Datacom makes it possible for a firm to achieve either objective. How the equipment is used depends on what the user seeks to accomplish.

- *Reduce time and effort needed to perform a task.* With datacom, an end user can completely handle a task by interacting with the information processor. For example, a manager can query the data base and receive a rapid reply, regardless of the distance separating the manager from the data base. Without datacom, the manager would have to wait hours or perhaps days to receive the report and complete the activity. The manager's desk would be piled high with semiprocessed work.
- *Reduce data transmission costs.* Datacom can be less expensive than using the mail or physically transporting data from one location to another.
- *Facilitate disbursed operations.* A firm can conduct its operations over a much wider geographical area with datacom. Datacom provides the electronic nervous system that enables far-flung operations to work in unison.
- *Facilitate company growth.* As a firm increases in size, it quickly outgrows its communications systems. Datacom enables the communication of large volumes of data and information among many participants at rapid speeds.

Uses of datacom in the MIS

Much datacom activity is directed at data rather than information processing. In online processing, order entry clerks enter sales order data using keyboard terminals. Claims adjusters verify policy coverage by querying the home office data base from claims office terminals. Factory workers record attendance and job completion from shop floor terminals. In each of these examples, a nonmanager is online to the information processor.

The datacom resources are usually economically justified based on the data processing applications. The resources are therefore available for use in decision support. In addition, the data processing activity produces an up-to-date data base that serves as a reservoir of data and information for the MIS. Were it not for datacom, such a data base would be impossible in large, geographically dispersed firms.

Datacom provides the link between the manager and the information processor, regardless of the distance separating them. *Reports* can be transmitted directly to the recipients—eliminating handling by intermediaries, and improving security. Management *queries* can be handled from any location in the firm, giving outlying managers the same level of information support as those at headquarters. Managers can key in the input data required by mathematical *models* and receive the results of the computations, even though the software and hardware are located elsewhere. In all of these examples, physical distance puts no constraint on management's use of the MIS.

Datacom evolution

Throughout the relatively short history of computers, their use has swung back and forth between centralized and distributed systems. Table 8-1 shows this pendulum-like behavior. The first computers were so costly that firms installed them

Table 8-1 Periods of centralized and decentralized computer use

	1951–1958	*1958–1965*	*1965–1975*	*1975–Present*
Headquarters	Large systems	Large systems	Large systems	Large systems
Outlying offices	No computing equipment	Small systems not connected to headquarters	Terminals connected to headquarters	Mini and microcomputers, often connected to headquarters
Overall emphasis	*Centralized*	*Decentralized*	*Centralized*	*Distributed*

only at their headquarters. Outlying offices mailed data to the central computer site and received output the same, slow way.

Lower-priced units became available in the late fifties, which the larger firms installed at their outlying offices. However, the outlying computers and the headquarters' computers were not interconnected in any way.

The mid-sixties brought newer and better datacom hardware and the first datacom software. The larger, more powerful CPUs offered "more bang per buck" than smaller models. Firms could process their data more economically on one large, centralized computer than on many smaller ones at outlying sites—economy of scale. Firms began to return the processor power to the central office and make that power available to the outlying sites by means of telephone communications facilities and terminals.

Then an unexpected series of events occurred. The minicomputer became popular in the mid-seventies and began to be applied to business data processing. The minis were so inexpensive that large, widespread firms benefited from distributing the processor power once again. The microcomputer boom only added to the trend. Today a common pattern is for a firm to have a large information processor—a *host*—at headquarters linked to distributed processors—usually minis—at outlying locations.

As Table 8-1 indicates, headquarters sites have always used large systems. Even though considerable computing equipment has been distributed throughout the organization, central control is maintained at headquarters. We can draw two conclusions from this situation. First, firms are not following a program of distributed processing, but rather of "semidistributed" processing. Second, distributed processing does not necessarily mean decentralized control.

The basic communication model

The fundamental parts of any communication can be represented by the *basic communication model*. The model, illustrated in Figure 8-2, contains five basic parts. A *sender* wishes to communicate, and uses some type of *encoder* to put the information in a form so that it can be communicated. For example, the sender

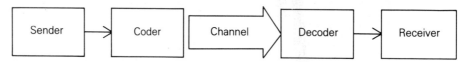

Figure 8-2 The basic communication model.

can encode the information by writing it on paper or speaking it orally. Once encoded, the information can travel along some *channel* to its destination. The channel might be the mail service, or a telephone line. The terms *circuit* and *line* are used interchangeably with channel. When the information arrives at its destination, a *decoder* is used by the *receiver* to understand the contents. The receiver may only have to listen to the spoken words or read the written words to decode them.

Figure 8-2 shows a one-way flow. When the receiver wants to communicate to the sender, the arrows are reversed.

A computer-based communications network

Figure 8-3 illustrates a basic datacom network. You can see the similarity to the basic model in Figure 8-2. Here a terminal and a CPU communicate with each other. Communication is achieved by transmitting a message. We will use the term *message* to describe the data or information transmitted through the network. A message can include one or more data elements, or it can include many records. A large file would most likely be represented by several messages.

Both the terminal and the CPU are attached to the data transmission channel (a telephone line, for example) with modems. *Modem* stands for *modulator-demodulator.* This unit converts a digital computer signal into an analog telephone signal (it *modulates* the signal) and converts an analog telephone signal into a digital computer signal (it *demodulates* the signal). The modem is required since the computer and the telephone equipment represent data differently. The computer represents data using a code of binary bits—zeros and ones. The telephone equipment represents data in an analog fashion—such as sound frequencies measured in cycles per second. The term *hertz* is often used to mean cycles per second. The different tones that you hear when you use a push-button telephone to dial a number are the different frequencies for the digits.

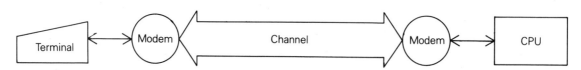

Figure 8-3 A basic datacom network.

The network pictured in Figure 8-3 can be used to transmit data in both directions. The terminal can send data to the CPU, and the CPU can send data to the terminal. The modem attached to each end of the channel either modulates or demodulates signals, depending on the direction of the data flow. This is a basic network configuration. The first networks in the mid-sixties looked like this. Since that time, a great many innovations in both hardware and software have improved the transmission of computer data. In the next few sections, we address that hardware and software.

Datacom Hardware

Figure 8-4 illustrates an overview of most of the types of hardware comprising a datacom network. Refer to this diagram as we discuss the various hardware units. We have expanded the basic network by adding several devices between the user's terminal and the CPU. These devices are intended to improve the performance of the network and relieve the CPU of much of the responsibility for managing the network. Since its inception in the 1950s, the computer has been intended to

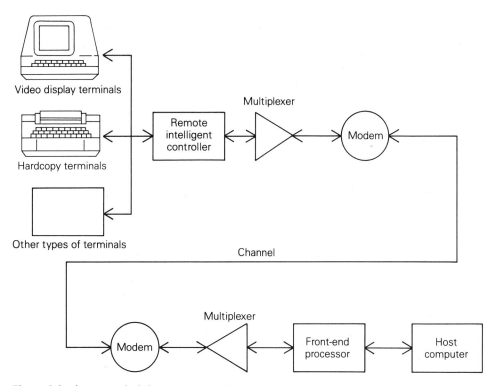

Figure 8-4 An expanded datacom network.

process data, not manage a datacom network. As a means of relieving the computer of much work that it was not intended to do, devices have been attached to the computer that are specifically designed for network management.

You will notice that we use the word *host* to describe the computer. The term *host* is appropriate in such a network where so many devices must be controlled by a central computer.

Terminals

We will begin at the user end of the network. Here, you find several different types of terminals—all designed to meet certain user needs. In Chapter 5 we discussed keyboard terminals—the CRT and hardcopy terminals. CRT terminals are also called *alphanumeric display terminals* and *video display terminals (VDT)*. The term VDT is increasing in use. Hardcopy terminals are also called *teleprinter terminals*, a term that is decreasing in use. These keyboard terminals are used by persons with relatively low volumes of input data. They also serve as output devices. The keyboard terminal is ideally suited to the manager. Other, nonmanager employees also use keyboard terminals.

Other types of terminals, in addition to the keyboard variety, are push-button telephone, remote job entry (RJE), point of sale, data collection, intelligent, and special purpose. Each of these types is discussed below. With the exception of the telephone, these terminals are not operated by the manager. Rather, they are operated by lower-level employees during the course of performing their daily activities. The transactions initiated by the employees using terminals keep the data base current. Thus a conceptual data resource that accurately reflects the physical system of the firm is continuously available to the manager.

1. *Push-button telephone.* The manager can use an ordinary push-button telephone to enter data into the computer by pressing the buttons, and can receive audible responses when the computer is equipped with an audio response device. An audio response device is attached to the host, and contains a limited vocabulary of words. The words are recorded magnetically, in much the same manner as words are recorded on magnetic tape. We described in Chapter 5 how a manager can query the data base for an inventory status report using a push-button telephone for input and the audio response device for output. When used in this manner, the telephone becomes the least expensive type of terminal.

2. *Remote job entry.* A *remote job entry (RJE)* terminal is used when a large volume of input and/or output occurs at a given location, such as in a timesharing network. A good example is an input/output center on a college campus. An RJE terminal, shown in Figure 8-5, includes a punched card reader and a line printer. If users submit their jobs in punched card form, the cards are read by the card reader, and the output is printed on the line printer. The card reader can read several hundred cards per minute, and the line printer can print several hundred lines per minute. If users submit their jobs using a keyboard terminal, the output is directed

Figure 8-5 A remote job entry (RJE) terminal.

to the RJE terminal for printing. In a business firm, the jobs can be weekly payroll calculations, personnel file changes, purchase orders, or other types of transactions that can be handled in batches.

3. *Point of sale.* Two basic types of *point of sale (POS) terminals* in popular use today are retail terminals, used primarily in department stores, and universal product code (UPC) bar code readers, used in supermarkets. The *retail terminal* (described in Chapter 5 and pictured in Figure 5-10) permits data entry from a keyboard or an OCR wand. The *UPC terminal* (also discussed in Chapter 5) is online to either a store mini or a larger system located some distance away.

4. *Data collection. Data collection terminals* are designed for use in factories but can be found elsewhere, as in libraries. The terminal permits data entry on a keyboard or from punched cards or plastic badges. Newer models can read documents optically. Factory workers use terminals such as the one in Figure 8-6 for *attendance reporting*—clocking on and off their shift. The terminals are also used for *job reporting*—clocking on and off each job performed. The workers identify themselves for both attendance and job reporting by inserting their badges in the badge reader. Jobs are identified using punched cards that accompany the materials. Variable data, such as the number of pieces rejected, is entered on a keyboard. Libraries use the same equipment to check out books. The units feature a rugged design that stands up well to rough treatment.

5. *Intelligent.* The terminals discussed up to now can perform only input/output operations. They are called *dumb terminals*. When a terminal includes a microprocessor, or when it is a microcomputer, it can perform

Figure 8-6   A data collection terminal.

certain operations independent of the host. This type is known as an *intelligent terminal.* When the intelligent terminal is a microcomputer, it frequently includes diskette drives for storing the user's data base. Some intelligent terminals rely on routines prerecorded in ROM. An example of an intelligent terminal application is order entry, where the terminal is able to edit input data for possible errors and conduct a credit check without interacting with the host.

6. *Special purpose.* Computing equipment manufacturers will frequently construct a terminal to meet the special needs of an industry or a firm. A good example is the terminal used at some McDonald's restaurants with keys representing the different products. You order an Egg McMuffin, and the clerk presses the appropriate key. The terminal automatically computes the bill and even updates the inventory of ingredients. Other examples of special-purpose terminals are nurses' station terminals in hospitals, teller terminals in banks, and automatic teller machines (ATMs).

You can see that there is a wide variety of terminal types. Regardless of the job, there is probably a terminal that can meet the varying needs.

Remote intelligent controller

If a firm has a large number of terminals in an area, such as the accounting department, all of the terminals can be connected to a *remote intelligent controller*. As the name implies, this unit is an intelligent device—executing its routines stored in primary storage or in ROM. The remote intelligent controller (usually a microcomputer) can control as many as 16 or so terminals at one time. The terminals can be different types. The controller achieves efficient use of the datacom channel by scheduling channel use by the terminals. The controller also permits a channel to transmit data in both directions at the same time (assuming that the channel has that ability). These routines performed by the remote intelligent controller have been downloaded from the host to relieve the host of the responsibility. The term *download* means to transfer something (data or processing) from a host to a lower-level device such as a micro.

Multiplexer

A multiplexer permits the channel to transmit multiple messages in one direction at a time. Various technologies are used, but we will not go into that detail. You can think of a multiplexer as a point in a highway where a single lane changes into multiple lanes. Up until this point, only one user's message at a time can travel over the channel. The messages are transmitted *serially*—one after the other. From this point on (until we encounter another multiplexer and the highway switches back to a single lane), multiple messages can be transmitted simultaneously—in *parallel*.

A clarifying note is in order at this time. Even though *messages* may be transmitted in *parallel* with a multiplexer, the *characters within* a message are *always* transmitted *serially*. Datacom channels transmit messages one character at a time.

Modem

We have already introduced the modem. At this point in the network, the modem modulates the message, converting it from the digital signals of the computing equipment to the analog signals used by the channel.

Most modems convert digital signals into sound frequencies. Other modems convert electrical signals from a terminal to pulses of light. These modems are used when the channel uses fiber optics. We will discuss fiber optics later.

Some few datacom channels use *digital signals*—the binary 0s and 1s of computing equipment. You still need a modem even when the channel is digital. The digital modem shapes the digital pulses.

Modems are built to operate at certain speeds—usually 300, 1200, 4800, 9600 bits per second, and up.

A common type of modem is the *acoustic coupler* (pictured in Figure 8-7), used with many micros. A cable attaches the acoustic coupler to the terminal or

Figure 8-7 An acoustic coupler.
Source: Courtesy of Novation, Inc.

micro. When you place the telephone handset in the specially shaped cradle of the coupler, you establish a datacom connection.

Up until this point, the responsibility for the datacom equipment and circuitry rests with the using firm. The firm provides the units and the cables that interconnect them. Now, the responsibility switches from the firm to a vendor that offers a local and/or long-distance communications facility. The vendor, regulated by the government, is referred to as a *common carrier*. Examples are AT&T, GTE, and Bell Canada.

The channel

We will use the telephone company as our example since it most often is the common carrier. The channel can be subdivided into three segments. The first segment, called the *local loop*, connects the firm's circuitry to the local telephone company's central office. This segment usually employs wires or cables. Four wires are necessary for each circuit, and they are usually twisted in pairs. The *twisted pair* is the most basic type of circuit. When there is a large number of circuits, such as within a large city, coaxial cables are used. A *coaxial cable* consists of a single wire covered with insulation, and contained within an outer cylindrical shell. Perhaps you have seen the coaxial cable that is used to receive cable TV transmissions. Very often several coaxial cables are bundled together. A bundle two inches in diameter can transmit 20,000 telephone calls simultaneously.

The next segment of the channel is designed to carry large volumes of traffic between cities. This segment is named the *interexchange channel*, sometimes called the *IXC circuit*. The telephone companies have just about completely converted from wire cables to some type of microwave transmission for the IXC circuit. Sometimes the transmission incorporates microwave towers, such as the one pictured in Figure 8-8. These towers provide line-of-sight transmission, so they have to be spaced 25–100 miles apart depending on the terrain. At other times the

Figure 8-8 A microwave tower.

microwave signal is bounced off of a satellite, 23,300 miles from earth. Dish-shaped transmitter/receivers are named *earth stations*. The earth stations can be very far apart, providing worldwide communication service. The transmission speed is very fast—in the 4 to 30 gigahertz (billion cycles per second) range.

The third segment of the channel is another *local loop* line, carrying the signals from the telephone company central office in the receiving city to the building where the message is to be received.

A channel provided by the telephone company to transmit data is the same one used for voice communication. For years the telephone company officials have been predicting that their channels will be used more for data than voice transmission. The volume of data traffic keeps increasing, but so does voice traffic. Currently, approximately three-fourths of the money spent to use these circuits is for voice, and one-fourth is for data.

In Figure 8-9, we have identified the basic elements in a datacom network. The firm is responsible for the cabling between the terminal and the modem on the user end, and between the modem and the host on the host end. Wire cables transmit the messages between the user modems and the telephone company central offices. The telephone company usually has a choice of IXC routes. The signal can be beamed along the earth's surface using microwave towers or bounced

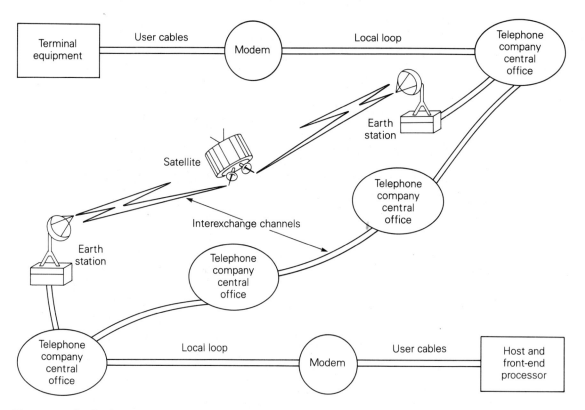

Figure 8-9 Basic elements in a datacom network.

off of a satellite. Or, the telephone company can use wire cables that interconnect the telephone company central offices.

The firm can establish a connection between the sender and the receiver in the same manner as a long-distance voice call is placed. This is called a *dial-up circuit*. Each time a dial-up connection is made, the telephone company selects the routing. If you place 10 calls between Los Angeles and Cleveland, the telephone company might select a different route each time. The selection is made by computer based on channel availability at the time. The firm pays for dial-up service the same way that you pay for long-distance calls—based on the number of calls, distance, and duration. A payment option that the firm has is *WATS (Wide Area Telecommunications Service)*. With a WATS line, the firm purchases a block of time each month for a flat fee. The number and distance of the calls have no effect on the cost.

The dial-up and WATS arrangements are best when the volume of data traffic is not large. A problem, however, relates to the quality of the service. Each time a message is routed through the switching equipment at the telephone company central office, noise is added to the signal. Noise is simply interference, such as static, that can garble an analog signal. The problem is not so severe with a digital signal. One way to get around the noise problem is to lease a *private circuit* to use 24 hours a day, 7 days a week. When you have a private line, the telephone company can specially *condition* the line to reduce noise, and they can route the line around their central offices. A line that has not been conditioned is termed a *voice-grade line*. Private circuits handle large volumes of traffic at a consistently higher quality than dial-up circuits.

Receiving multiplexer and modem

Refer back to Figure 8-4 to see the remaining parts of the datacom network.

The communication vendor's signal is made available at the receiving site where it is converted from analog to digital impulses by a modem—it demodulates the signal. The signal is then routed through a multiplexer that converts it from a parallel to a serial form.

The messages now travel along the circuit in a serial, digital form. Before entering the host computer, however, the messages are processed by the real workhorse of the datacom network—the front-end processor.

The front-end processor

The *front-end processor* can be any size computer but usually is a mini. Figure 8-10 shows the major parts. The front-end processor is an interface between the incoming channels from the multiplexers and the host. There can be 100 or more of these channels transmitting data to the host and receiving output from it. The front-end processor manages this network for the host.

The front-end processor is built with a certain number of channel connections, termed *ports*. Software in the processor converts the incoming data to a form acceptable to the host and enters the data into the host's input area. After the host completes the processing of a record to be sent out on the channel, the

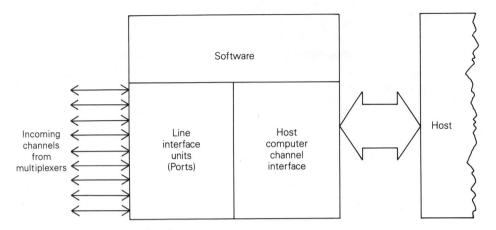

Figure 8-10 A front-end processor.

record is placed in the host's output area and then directed to the front-end processor. The processor prepares the message for transmission, and then sends it out on the proper channel to its destination.

The front-end processor may have a magnetic tape unit and a DASD attached. Some processors write an audit trail record on tape for each message handled. This tape provides a historical record of all datacom traffic. Some processors also write all incoming and outgoing messages on a DASD, for use in recovering from some type of disaster. Maybe only the last 20 minutes or so of traffic is kept in readily available DASD form.

Some of the more modern processors can perform a *message switching* function without involving the host. An incoming message is analyzed and its destination identified. The front-end processor sends the message back out again—on the channel leading to the destination. This type of message switching is performed when the computer is used to transport *electronic mail*—an office automation application that we will discuss in Chapter 10.

The host

We have finally arrived at the destination end of the datacom network. If we transmitted a message from a terminal, such as a data base query or a decision for a what-if model, then that message can be processed.

In such a complex network as we have described, it is easiest to think of the host as a mainframe computer. It could also be a mini, or even a micro. The size of the network, in terms of the number of channels and the necessary response times, influences the size of the host.

Datacom Software

When we discussed datacom hardware, we started at the user end of the network and worked our way toward the host. Since most of the datacom software resides at the host end of the network, we will start with the host.

Teleprocessing monitor

The system software of the host includes a *teleprocessing monitor*, along with an operating system and possibly a DBMS. The teleprocessing monitor controls the scheduling and movement of communication messages, or records, within the host. The teleprocessing monitor used in large IBM mainframes is CICS (Customer Information Control System). Burroughs systems use a Master Control Program (MCP). Each computer manufacturer has its own unique monitor. The specific functions performed by a monitor will vary from one package to the next but usually include most of the following:

- Putting messages in a queue based on some predetermined priority.
- Performing some type of security function such as logging types and volumes of transactions for each terminal, verifying that a terminal is authorized to handle a particular type of transaction, and so on.
- Establishing checkpoint and restart procedures so that the host can recover from a disaster. For example, the contents of primary storage are recorded on DASD periodically (a checkpoint). If a disaster occurs, the processing reverts back to the previous checkpoint and reconstructs all subsequently handled records.
- Maintaining statistics on network operation—volumes, response times, and so on.
- Maintaining the data base, depending on the teleprocessing monitor used.

Most DBMSs can be interfaced with a teleprocessing monitor. Cincom offers a monitor, ENVIRON/1, that can be used with its TOTAL DBMS. Some of the generalized file management systems have also provided their own interface models. For example, Informatics markets an IMS interface for its MARK IV GFMS. Some DBMSs have the teleprocessing monitor built in. IMS comes in a special *data base/data communications (DB/DC)* version that combines data base and network management. System 2000 includes a generalized teleprocessing monitor feature that can be interfaced with a variety of monitors.

Telecommunication access program

The *telecommunication access program* is frequently located in the front-end processor, although some of its functions may be performed by the host. IBM's TCAM (TeleCommunication Access Method) resides in the host, and the software in the front-end processor is called the NCP (Network Control Program). Regardless of where it is located, the telecommunication access program handles the polling, routing, and scheduling of terminals within the network.

We will assume that the telecommunication access program is located in the front-end processor, giving that device the following capabilities:

- *Poll terminals.* Determine if a terminal wants to use the channel. Three basic techniques are used. *Roll-call polling* is when the front-end processor checks the status of each terminal in a certain sequence. This technique can produce *wait time* for the user while other terminals are being polled. *Fast-select polling* attempts to reduce wait time by "asking" several terminals at a time if they want to transmit. The first one to respond gets the line. Then, another group is asked. Terminals that are not selected in the first group must wait until they are polled again. In *hub go-ahead polling*, the front-end processor passes a *poll character* to the farthest terminal on the line. The character asks the terminal if it wants to transmit. If not, the terminal passes the character up the line to the next terminal. In this manner, the terminals poll themselves. This technique requires intelligent terminals.

- *Assemble/disassemble messages.* Convert serial bits from the network to a parallel arrangement for transmission to the host. Perform a reverse conversion for bits received from the host to be sent out over the network.

- *Synchronize units with differing speeds.* Compensate for the differences in the transmission speeds of the various channels.

- *Establish controls.* Assign a date and time stamp to each message, along with a unique serial number.

- *Log messages.* Create magnetic tape and DASD records as previously described.

- *Edit messages.* Check for errors and perhaps rearrange the message format and add items.

- *Convert codes and protocols.* Compensate for differences in coding systems and protocols (communication conventions to be described later) that may exist between network equipment and the host. For example, DEC terminals and IBM mainframes code data differently, and they use different protocols.

- *Determine message transmission sequences.* Assign priorities to certain terminals and channels. Assemble both incoming and outgoing messages in queues based on their priority. Assemble several messages into a unit before sending them along to the host or the network.

- *Delete and add routing codes.* Incoming messages contain codes that cause the correct network path to be selected. These codes are deleted before sending the message to the host. Conversely, messages coming from the host must have the codes added.

- *Route messages.* Determine which terminal is to receive a message. Perform a *store and forward* service when a receiving terminal is not able to receive, by holding the message and transmitting it later.

- *Maintain statistics.* Keep a continuous record of all network traffic by channel, terminal, type of transaction, and so forth.

Other network software

Most of the software is stored in the front-end processor, and the remaining software is usually in the host. It is possible to download the software still farther—to remote intelligent controllers and the terminals themselves. When software is located at the user end of the network, it is used to select between alternate network paths. For example, in a distributed processing system, software in the remote intelligent controller can select the network leading to the proper information processor (since there are multiple processors).

Network Configurations

When we discussed distributed processing in Chapter 5, we recognized that the multiple information processors can be interconnected in either a star or a ring arrangement. Here, our interest is not limited to distributed processors, but also includes timesharing networks with only a single processor. Quite a variety of configurations have been developed to meet specific user needs. These configurations include point-to-point networks, multidrop networks, multiplexed networks, packet switching, local area networks (LANs), and private branch exchange/computer branch exchange (PBX/CBX) networks. We will describe each of these configurations below.

Point-to-point networks

A *point-to-point network* is one with only a single terminal or CPU on one end and a single terminal or CPU on the other.

Multidrop networks

When multiple terminals are attached to a single channel, the configuration is called a *multidrop network* or *multidrop line*—multiple terminals are dropped along the line. All of these units share the same channel under the control of the front-end processor. A multidrop network is illustrated in Figure 8-11.

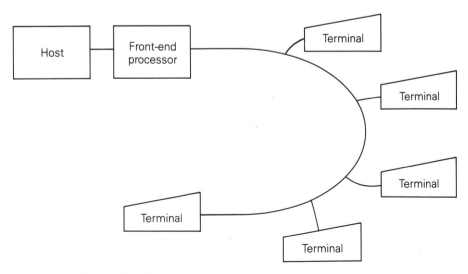

Figure 8-11 A multidrop line.

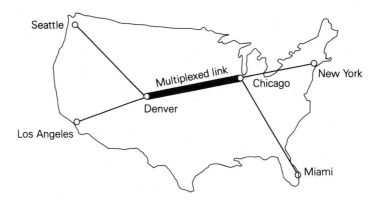

Figure 8-12   A multiplexed network.

Multiplexed networks

In a *multiplexed network*, there are two or more nodes that gather messages from multiple sources and transmit those messages in a group, using a multiplexer. A *node* is simply a location, or a point, within a network. This design is illustrated in Figure 8-12. In the figure, the Denver node gathers messages from the Los Angeles node and the Seattle node, and multiplexes the messages to Chicago. The Chicago node routes the messages on to the other nodes in the network. The messages can flow in the opposite direction as well. The idea is to design the network so that a segment can handle high-volume flow in a multiplexed fashion, reducing overall costs.

Packet switching

A *packet* is a fixed-length message block of perhaps 128 bytes. The packet is transmitted over a network consisting of multiple nodes, called *switching nodes (SN)*. In such a network, it is common for multiple IXC routes to exist between some of the SNs. Figure 8-13 shows a packet switching network with two inter-exchange channels connecting St. Louis, Dallas, and Houston.

Firms employ packet switching because it uses the channel very efficiently. To send a packet over a network, special *PAD (Packet Assembly and Disassembly)* software must be located in the front-end processor. This software subdivides the message into the packets, and routes the packets over the network. The front-end processor determines the first SN to receive the packet, and that SN routes the packet to another SN. This routing continues until the packet reaches its destination. Each SN also contains PAD software.

A firm can construct its own packet network (by buying IXC service between the SNs, furnishing PAD software, and so on), or it can lease service from a *public packet switching network*. When time is leased on a public network, lower costs

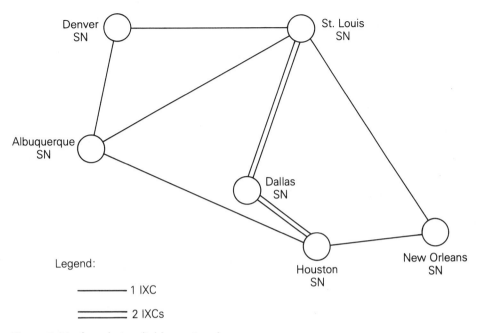

Legend:

——————— 1 IXC

══════ 2 IXCs

Figure 8-13 A packet switching network.

are usually realized since the charge is based on the volume of traffic (number of packets) rather than the distance. Another advantage is the improved reliability of the network. If an IXC or SN becomes inoperative, other routing is automatically initiated.

Local area networks (LANs)

A *local area network (LAN)* is constructed by the firm, and usually (but not always) consists of only a few hundred feet of circuitry within a building, or a few buildings. A common carrier is not involved unless the LAN is connected to an IXC, but even then the LAN is owned, maintained, and operated by the firm.

The LAN concept is receiving much attention since it could form the basis for interconnecting work stations in an office. The LAN is therefore central to office automation. For example, several word processors can share a letter quality printer if all of the units are a part of the LAN. Or, a manager can query a data base from her or his terminal or cause a graph to be prepared by a plotter. All of the units (terminal, data base storage, and plotter) are a part of the LAN. Figure 8-14 provides an idea of the mix of units that can be incorporated into a LAN. The sample configuration includes a *network server* that enables the users to share resources such as the server's hard disk unit, printers, plotters, and so on. The network server could be an IBM PC XT with a hard disk, capable of controlling from two to eight micros. Or, for a larger LAN, the network server could be a VAX 11/750, capable of supporting 100 micros.

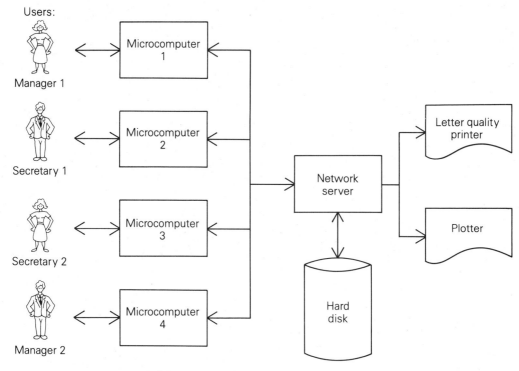

Figure 8-14 A local area network (LAN).

The four users in the figure include two managers and two secretaries, each with their own microcomputers. The managers use their micros for office automation applications such as electronic calendaring and electronic mail. The managers can also use their micros as decision support systems. The secretaries use their micros for word processing.

The first computer manufacturer to promote the idea of a LAN was Xerox, with its Ethernet system. Xerox has been joined by DEC and Intel in marketing hardware and software to be used in an Ethernet LAN, and other firms are also competing for the emerging LAN market. As of late 1985, IBM had not announced its LAN plans. This does not mean that a user cannot incorporate IBM products, such as the PC, into a LAN. IBM simply has not announced any special LAN software or hardware, or specified how its units are to be interconnected. Other firms, such as 3Com, offer LAN packages that can include IBM units.

One of the big questions concerning LANs is "What kind of cabling to use?" There are currently three basic technologies—twisted pairs, coaxial cables (coax), and fiber optics. Twisted pairs are the least expensive choice but only permit a single message to be transmitted at a time between any two nodes. Coaxial cable identical to that used by cable TV companies permits hundreds of messages to be transmitted at a time, but costs more than twisted pairs. The technology for both coaxial cable and twisted pairs currently exists; the same cannot be said for fiber optics.

Fiber optics is still an emerging technology, and the cost is very high. It is expected, however, that the cost will decrease significantly in the 1986–1988 period. Fiber optics offers several advantages over the other technologies that are important to computer users. One advantage is security. Because a fiber optic circuit consists of a hair-thin length of glass or plastic, it is very difficult to add a branch off of the main circuit. An unauthorized user, therefore, would have much more difficulty in tapping onto the circuit than if wire or coax were used. Other advantages include a practically unlimited number of messages that can be sent simultaneously, and potentially greater distances that can be linked. It is possible to construct a LAN using fiber optics that interconnects adjoining cities.

One of the advantages of a LAN constructed of coaxial cable and fiber optics is the ability to transmit video signals that could be used in teleconferencing. Teleconferencing is another office automation application that enables groups in different geographical locations to participate in a conference, linked by video and audio. A LAN constructed of twisted pairs does not have the capacity to handle such traffic.

PBX/CBX networks

You have probably seen photographs of old-fashioned telephone switchboards, with the wires plugged in by operators wearing headsets. The plugboard was a switching point where incoming calls were matched with the proper outgoing circuits. Larger firms with several telephone lines used these units, called *private branch exchanges (PBX)*. That level of technology represented the first PBX generation. The second generation used electromechanical devices to perform the switching. The third, current generation employs electronic computer circuitry and integrates voice and digital data. The current technology is often identified as *PBX/CBX*, with the *CBX* meaning *computer branch exchange*. Sometimes the term *digital PBX* is used.

There are several similarities between a PBX/CBX and a LAN. They both use the same circuitry—twisted pair, coaxial cable, and fiber optics. They both are usually used in a restricted setting of several hundred feet, and both are the responsibility of the firm, not the common carrier. They both permit the attachment of multiple units such as microcomputers, printers, and so on.

One big difference is the ability of the PBX/CBX to manage the firm's telephone system. The voice messages are converted from analog frequencies to a digital form, like that of computing equipment. Another difference is the advantage of the LAN over the PBX/CBX in terms of higher transmission speed and the ability to provide circuits for teleconferencing.

Figure 8-15 contains a schematic of a PBX/CBX, showing the types of devices that can be handled. The PBX/CBX can serve as the front-end processor, connecting a host computer to the other devices in the network such as computer peripherals (line printers, plotters, OCR readers, and the like), as well as multi-dropped micros and terminals. The PBX/CBX provides the connection between the telephone company's local loop lines and the firm's voice telephones. The PBX/CBX can also be connected to other PBX/CBX networks and to packet networks to form a network covering a larger geographic area than with a single

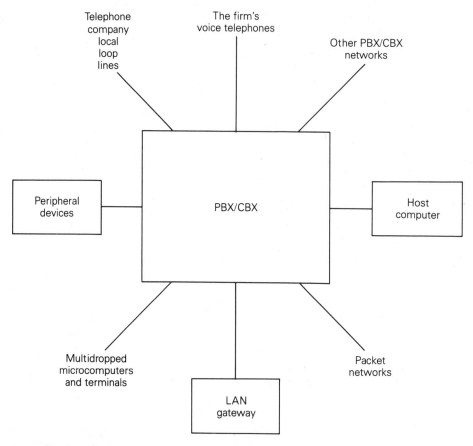

Figure 8-15 A PBX/CBX.

PBX/CBX. There is also considerable interest in incorporating one or more PBX/CBX networks in a LAN. The figure includes a LAN gateway. The term *gateway* is used in datacom to describe a connection between unlike parts—in this case a PBX/CBX and a LAN.

Much developmental work is going into the LAN and PBX/CBX areas, and the next few years will undoubtedly see a number of innovative technologies.

Datacom Standards

In the ten years or so since datacom became an important part of the computer field, a wide variety of hardware and software has been placed on the market. As an example, there are more than 15 firms selling expansion boards that allow an IBM PC to be used in a datacom network. When you add the wide variety of channels and networks that are available to interconnect the equipment, there is a mind-boggling set of network alternatives.

All of the possibilities also plague the manufacturers. In the early 1970s, for example, IBM alone was marketing more than 200 datacom products that were interconnected 15 different ways. In an effort to bring some standardization to their product line, IBM in 1974 announced something called SNA.

SNA

SNA stands for *System Network Architecture,* and it is an effort to separate the user and the information specialist from the datacom technology. Up until the time that SNA was announced, when a firm changed its datacom equipment configuration, its programs had to be changed, and perhaps its users had to be retrained. SNA was intended to insulate the people designing and using datacom systems from these changes.

IBM considered all of the activities that must be accomplished to transmit a message from a sender to a receiver, and grouped these activities into three *logical layers.* By "logical" we mean everything that causes the physical signals (0s and 1s) to be transmitted through the network. Figure 8-16 pictures this concept of layers spanning the datacom network.

Each box contains software that accomplishes some specific task in the transmission process. You will notice that the lower level of boxes spans the entire datacom network—from host node to user (terminal) node. This lower level of boxes contains the software causing the physical transmission to take place. This software is called the *transmission management layer.* Each node in the network (host, front-end processor, remote intelligent controller, and terminal) requires this software.

Additional software is required to interface both the host and the terminal user with the network. This additional software is represented by the second and third levels of boxes at both ends of the channel. The middle level, the *function management layer,* performs a formatting function—getting a message ready for

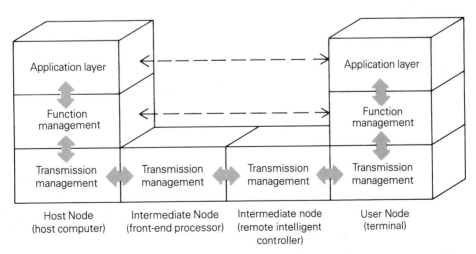

Figure 8-16 The three logical layers of IBM's System Network Architecture (SNA).

transmission on the sending end and preparing it for presentation to the user on the receiving end. The top layer, the *application layer*, represents the user's application program in the host, and actions of the terminal user or the terminal itself (if it is an intelligent terminal).

As an example of how the logical levels work together, assume that the application layer box at the host end represents a mathematical model that simulates the effects of a price change. The model is interactive, and asks the user for certain input data. The first request might be for the user to enter the new price. The message "ENTER NEW PRICE" is passed from the application layer to the function management layer at the host end. The function management layer formats the message so that it is compatible with the datacom network equipment, and passes the formatted message to the transmission management layer. There, software causes the message to be transmitted from node to node until it reaches its destination. The message is passed from the transmission management layer to the function management layer where it is formatted for display on the user's terminal. The formatted message is then passed to the application layer for display. The user keys in the response, and that message is passed down to the transmission management layer, where software causes the message to travel from node to node until it arrives at the host end. Then, the response message is passed upward to the application layer where it is used by the pricing model.

The dashed arrows in the figure represent corresponding levels of activity; they do not represent transmission of data or signals. All transmissions are controlled by the transmission management layer.

At this point, you may be asking why all of these layers are necessary. As we stated earlier, SNA was intended to insulate the users from the datacom hardware. A firm can completely change its datacom hardware, such as convert from a network of dial-up lines to a LAN, and the change will have no effect on the host or the terminal user. During the current era of frequent improvements in datacom technology, this insulation is very valuable.

The concept of logical layers was immediately picked up by other computer manufacturers. Sperry Univac and NCR both announced layered architectures. During the next several years, other architectures were added by DEC, Honeywell, Burroughs, and Xerox.

While the computer vendors were developing standards to be used with their own products (IBM's SNA was incompatible with DEC's Decnet, for example), there was a movement under way to establish an international standard that everyone could follow.

The OSI model

In 1979 the International Standards Organization announced a seven-layered network architecture and named it the *OSI (Open Systems Interconnection) model*. The layers are identified in Figure 8-17. The bottom layer is a physical layer where the data is transmitted. The upper six layers are logical.

The brackets at the left side of the figure identify where the software is *usually* located to perform the logical functions at the host node, and the brackets at the

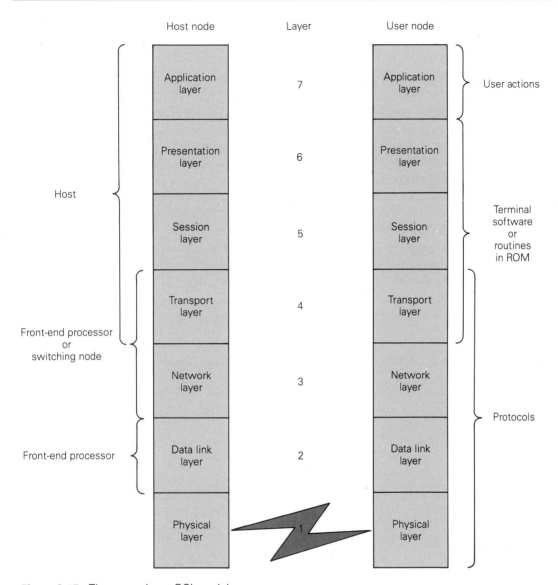

| Host node | Layer | User node |
| | | |

Figure 8-17 The seven-layer OSI model.
Source: p. 174, Jerry Fitzgerald, Business Data Communications *(Copyright © John Wiley & Sons, 1984).*

right show the same information for the user node. Like SNA, the host and user nodes of the network are the only ones with all of the layers. Intermediate nodes in the OSI model have only two or three layers depending on the situation.

Each of the seven layers is briefly described below:

1. *Physical layer.* Transmits the data in a digital or analog form from one network node to the next.

2. *Data link layer.* Causes the data to be formatted into a frame, or record, consisting of the data itself plus special identifying fields and addresses. Also performs an error detection function on the transmitted data.

3. *Network layer.* Causes the data to be transmitted from node to node until it reaches the destination. This layer manages the two lower layers.

4. *Transport layer.* Enables the host and the users to carry on a conversation. Controls the rate at which messages are sent so as to synchronize data movement between high- and low-speed units and between overburdened and idle units.

5. *Session layer.* Initiates, maintains, and terminates each session. A *session* is like a telephone call—it is a separate transaction with beginning ("Hello") and end ("Good-bye"). Sessions are initiated with standard log-on and user identification routines.

6. *Presentation layer.* Prepares data so that it will be in a usable format for the user. For example, data to be displayed on the terminal screen is formatted into the proper number of lines and characters per line.

7. *Application layer.* Performs the user's application by executing the application program in the host, or handling user input from the terminal.

A layer performs a service for the layer above. The bottom three layers are concerned only with transmission from one node to the next. Linked together sequentially, levels 1–3 move the message from the sender end of the network to the receiver end. Levels 4–7 are end-to-end functions that allow the sender and receiver to "talk" to each other.

The OSI model is a concept that datacom hardware and software vendors are urged to follow. It will take years for the vendors to incorporate the concept into their products.

Protocols

Both SNA and the OSI model specify the logical layers throughout the network. It is necessary that the layers communicate from node to node (layers 1–3 of the OSI model) and end to end (layers 4–7). A layer of one node communicates with the corresponding layer of another node. Layer 3 of the host node, for example, communicates with layer 3 of the front-end processor node. These layer-to-layer links are illustrated by the arrows labeled "P" in Figure 8-18. The P stands for protocol.

Protocol has been called "shaking hands." It is a way of establishing a working relationship between two persons—or nodes—in a network. An example of protocol is the routine that you follow when you place a telephone call ("Hello. This is Bobby. Is Sally there? Can I speak with her? Hello, Sally, this is Bobby . . .").

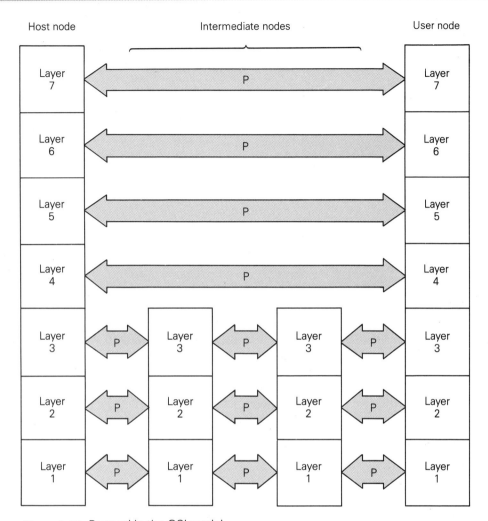

Figure 8-18 Protocol in the OSI model.

Protocols are necessary to put the OSI model and SNA and the other vendor architectures into operation. IBM has defined the protocol for all of its layers. Initially, there were the three layers of Figure 8-16, but improvements have blurred the layers. It is generally accepted today that the SNA layers, whatever their number, perform the same functions as the OSI model. IBM's protocol for SNA is called *SDLC (Synchronous Data Link Control)*.

While IBM and the other vendors have provided their customers with all of the protocols to make their architectures work, the international standards community is taking a slower approach. Protocols have been established for only the lower three layers of the OSI model.

An example of a protocol for the physical layer of the OSI model is the standardized plug that is used to interconnect the hardware. The *RS232c* plug is pictured in Figure 8-19. An example of a protocol for layer 2 (data link layer) is

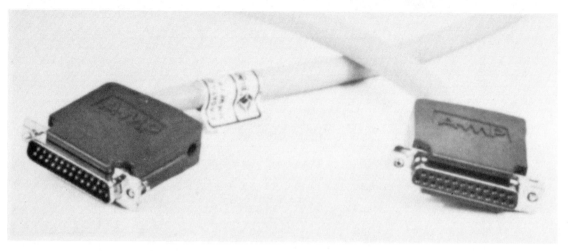

Figure 8-19 The standard RS232c cable connector.
Source: Black Box Corporation, a Micon Company,
© 1983.

the format for a message frame, pictured in Figure 8-20. The flags identify the beginning and end of the frame, and the address routes the frame to its destination. An example of a layer 3 (network) protocol is X.25, established by CCITT (Consultative Committee for International Telephony and Telegraphy). *X.25* defines the interface between data terminal equipment (DTE) such as the terminal and the host, and data circuit-terminating equipment (DCE) such as that found at intermediate nodes—front-end processors and remote intelligent controller.

Standardizing the standards

The situation today is much improved over the early seventies when there were no standards. The problem today is the multiplicity of "standards." Which one or ones do the users follow?

Beginning flag	Address	Control	Message	Frame check sequence	Ending flag

Figure 8-20 A message frame.

SNA has become a de facto standard, without international approval, simply by virtue of IBM's large base of installed mainframes. It is estimated that from half to three-fourths of IBM's mainframe users have adopted SNA. The other computer vendors' architectures have not fared so well. DEC's Decnet was well accepted, but the others were not.

We see the computer industry evolving to two standards—SNA and OSI. IBM has indicated that it will make SNA compatible with OSI so that a user can intermix datacom equipment from IBM and other vendors. OSI gateways will be built into SNA.

IBM is expected to continue to improve SNA, having it embrace LANs for example. CCITT or other international standards organizations are expected to continue to whittle away at OSI protocols, probably having all levels defined by the 1990s.

Datacom Security

The datacom portion of a firm's MIS is the most vulnerable. It is much easier to achieve security inside the computer room than in remote user locations and in the airspace where the data signals are sent. Practically anyone can tap into a firm's datacom network and help themselves to valuable information and even the firm's finances.

We address the general topic of security in Chapter 18, but we can devote special attention to datacom security here.

Encryption

We mentioned encryption in the data base chapter, describing how some DBMSs encrypt the data. The encryption makes the data meaningless to someone who isn't an authorized user.

Data transmitted through the datacom network can also be encrypted. Special devices can be attached to each end of the channel, as shown in Figure 8-21.

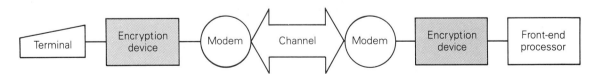

Figure 8-21 Encryption devices in the datacom network.

While data base encryption is normally accomplished through software, datacom encryption is normally accomplished through hardware.

The scrambling of the data to encrypt it is performed by an *encryption algorithm*. This is a formula that uses a *key*. The key can be changed to produce a different pattern of coded characters. The key can be changed as often as daily in order to keep possible intruders confused.

An overall datacom security plan

Encryption addresses only one type of potential datacom hazard. A firm should take a *systems approach* by looking at their overall network, from host to user, and identifying the potential hazards that exist at each point. Data communications consultant Jerry FitzGerald of Redwood City, California suggests that a firm construct a *control matrix* (see Figure 8-22) showing the network components at the left and the threats or hazards at the top.

The numbers in the matrix represent specific controls that have been defined by the firm. As an example, number 7 can mean "acknowledge the successful or unsuccessful receipt of all messages." Numbers are used simply to conserve space. The matrix provides the firm with a visual identification of secure areas (boxes with many numbers) and insecure areas (blank boxes).

The Network Manager

At this point, you should appreciate how complex the subject of datacom is. Datacom is a complete area, just like computing, with its own special language. It is unreasonable to expect anyone, user or information specialist, to be an expert in all aspects of both MIS and datacom. A firm with the need for a large network should have a full-time datacom specialist. That specialist is the *network manager*, also referred to as the *telecom manager*. We included the network manager in the information services organization chart in Figure 5-26. The network manager can have a staff of assistants in the case of a firm with a very large and complex network.

The duties of the network manager fall into four major categories: planning, implementing, operating, and controlling.

Planning consists of developing a datacom plan for the firm that is submitted to management for approval or modification.

Implementing includes recommending datacom hardware and software, as well as specifying procedures and standards for persons working with the datacom system.

Operating includes gathering statistics describing the system's operation to be used in managing the system, and solving problems that develop within the system.

Controlling involves continued surveillance of the network for the purpose of detecting weak points in security, and incorporating new security measures.

The network manager works with other information specialists such as systems analysts, programmers, and data base administrators to build and maintain a datacom network to support the MIS.

Figure 8-22 A datacom control matrix.

Source: p. 262, Jerry Fitzgerald, Business Data Communications (Copyright © John Wiley & Sons, 1984).

The Manager's Use of Terminals

When a manager wishes to establish a connection between a terminal and the CPU, he or she dials the telephone number of the computer center. When the manager hears a high-pitched tone, indicating that the connection has been made, he or she places the telephone handset in the acoustic coupler.

Some terminals do not utilize telephone circuits but are *hardwired* into the network using the firm's own circuitry. This is a common arrangement in a LAN. In this situation, the manager simply turns on the terminal and presses a key (such as RETURN) to alert the CPU.

The operating system in the CPU responds by displaying a request for identification. The manager keys in the identification, such as an account number (used by the operating system to charge computer use to the manager) and a password. When the operating system accepts the codes, it asks the manager to identify the nature of the job. If the manager wants to compile a program in BASIC, he or she may simply key in the word *BASIC*. If a particular program is to be executed that already exists in the software library, that program name is keyed in. The operating system retrieves the program from secondary storage and brings it into primary storage. The operating system may prompt the user by displaying a special character (such as a >) at the left margin.

Using the computer through terminal interaction is referred to as the *interactive mode* or *conversational mode*—the user and the computer converse with each other. There are three basic methods for achieving this interaction. First, the program can display a *menu* of items available for selection—such as models to execute. This is the *menu-display technique* shown in Figure 8-23. The cursor is positioned on the first selection. If the manager wishes to execute that model, he or she presses a certain key (such as the letter Y for yes). To select another entry, the manager presses the RETURN key. Each time the RETURN key is pressed, the cursor drops to the next item. Another methodology is to type the number or letter of the menu item chosen.

Once an entry from the menu has been selected, a second menu can be displayed, then a third, and so on. In this manner, the manager can communicate to the CPU which routine is to be executed as well as the input data for that routine. Menu display is designed for use with a CRT.

A second popular method for inputting data is the *form-filling technique*. An outline of a form can be displayed on the screen, and the manager types the needed data in the appropriate blanks. The cursor is moved from one blank to another by the user or by the program. Figure 8-24 illustrates this approach. This example displays data items needed by the pricing model selected from the previous menu. When the data has been entered, another form can be displayed, asking for additional items. Form filling also is best suited for a CRT.

The third method is the *questions-and-answers technique*. You can see in Figure 8-25 that the manager can respond by answering yes or no, or by providing data elements. The terminal prints or displays the question followed by a question mark. The question mark is the cue for the manager to respond. The response immediately follows the question mark. This technique works equally well with hardcopy and CRT terminals. On either terminal, the questions are asked one at

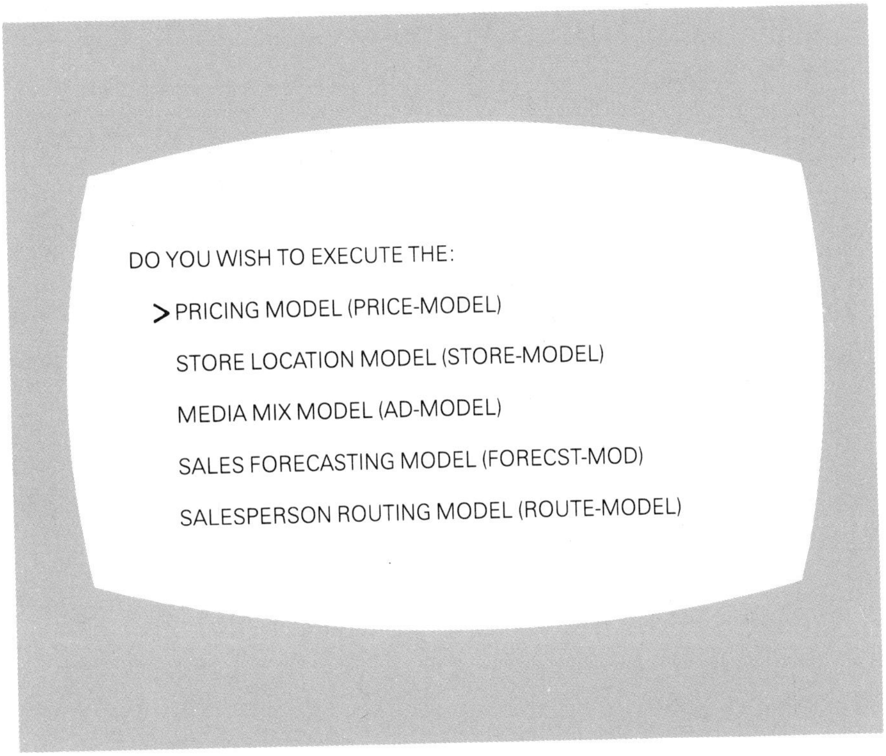

Figure 8-23 Menu-display technique.

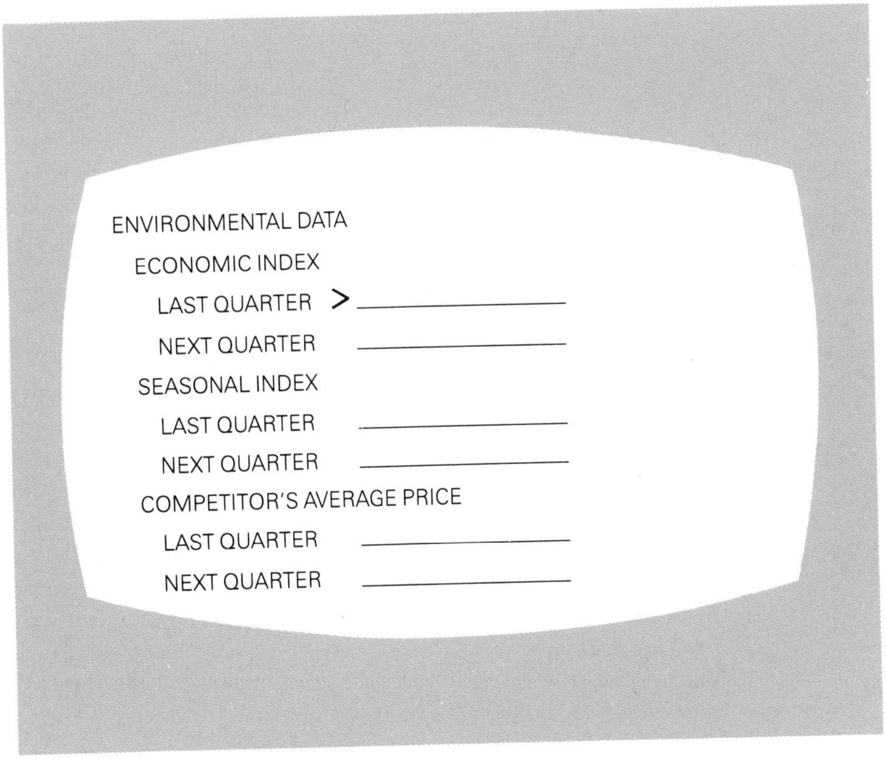

Figure 8-24 Form-filling technique.

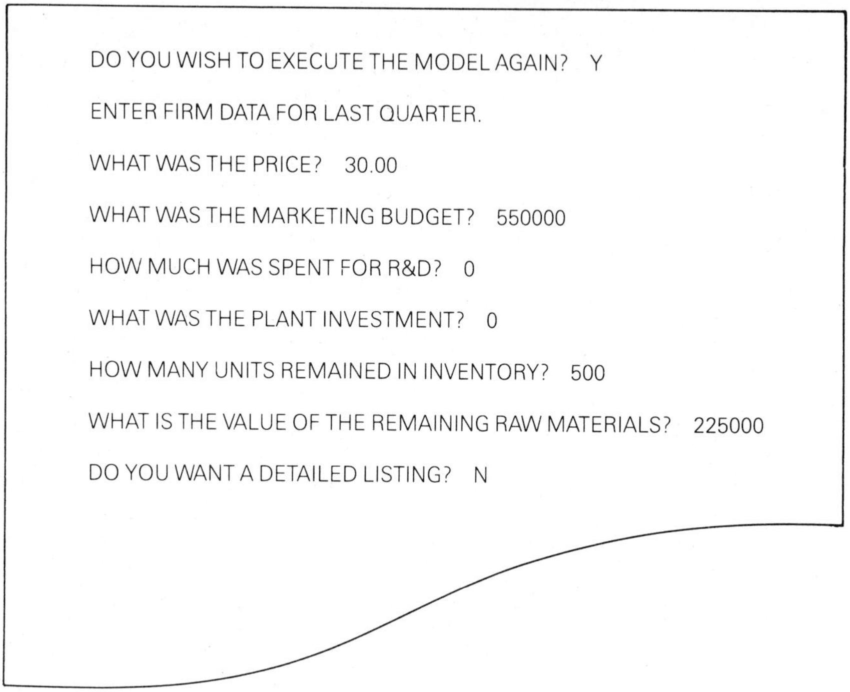

DO YOU WISH TO EXECUTE THE MODEL AGAIN?   Y

ENTER FIRM DATA FOR LAST QUARTER.

WHAT WAS THE PRICE?   30.00

WHAT WAS THE MARKETING BUDGET?   550000

HOW MUCH WAS SPENT FOR R&D?   0

WHAT WAS THE PLANT INVESTMENT?   0

HOW MANY UNITS REMAINED IN INVENTORY?   500

WHAT IS THE VALUE OF THE REMAINING RAW MATERIALS?   225000

DO YOU WANT A DETAILED LISTING?   N

Figure 8-25   Questions-and-answers technique.

a time. As soon as the manager responds, another question is asked. When all of the data and instructions have been entered, the data is processed.

Output can be displayed on the manager's terminal or directed to another device such as a line printer or plotter. The manager signs off by keying a command such as OFF and returning the telephone handset (if used) to its base.

Putting Datacom in Perspective

An MIS includes a datacom network when input/output units are not confined to the computing facility. These input/output units may be within the same building containing the computer, or they may be located much greater distances away.

The type of input/output equipment used does not depend on the distance to the CPU, but rather on the needs of the users. The distance to the CPU does influence the type of channel. Short distances can be spanned with twisted wire pairs or coaxial cables. Longer distances require microwave transmission, sometimes via satellite.

Batch processing does not require datacom unless the input origin or the output destination is separated by some distance from the CPU. If such a separation exists, an RJE terminal can transmit batched transactions to the host.

Online processing may or may not require datacom, depending on the size of the system. It is possible to use online processing with a mini or micro by using a CRT terminal attached to the CPU by a cable a few feet in length. But when a user is located elsewhere, online processing demands datacom. Timesharing and distributed processing all need datacom as well.

Datacom benefits geographically disbursed organizations in two ways. First, it improves the quality of the firm's operations by providing the necessary communications between units. For example, customer orders can be entered from area sales offices, and if one warehouse is out of stock, the order can be filled by another warehouse. The second benefit is an improved MIS. With datacom the data base is updated as each transaction occurs, regardless of location. Management can use this up-to-date data base for decision making. Most importantly, with datacom all managers in the organization have access to the MIS.

If it were not for datacom, the MIS concept would probably never have gotten off the ground. During the early years of MIS, datacom enabled firms to pursue the giant, centralized systems that were then in vogue. More recently, datacom has enabled firms to achieve distributed systems.

Summary

Data communications is also known as telecommunications, teleprocessing, telecom, and datacom. The equipment configurations that perform datacom are called networks.

Datacom captures data at its source to reduce the time and effort needed to perform a task and to facilitate the rapid transmission of information. Transmission costs can be lower than if other means were used, and a firm's communications network can keep up with organizational growth. Datacom supports either centralized or decentralized control of the information resource and contributes to overall management control.

A firm's datacom equipment is likely to be justified based on data processing tasks, but the equipment also contributes to a sophisticated MIS. Datacom facilitates data base querying, mathematical modeling, and the preparation of management reports without system degradation resulting from distance between the user and the information processor.

A manager interfaces directly with the datacom network using a keyboard terminal. Several terminals can be controlled by a remote intelligent controller. A multiplexer enables several terminals to share a channel at the same time. The modem converts signals to a form compatible with the channel. The channel is subdivided into three lengths—the local loop in the sending city, the interexchange channel, and the local loop in the receiving city. A front-end processor performs most of the network management functions, using a telecommunication access program. The host interfaces with the network using a teleprocessing monitor.

Networks can be configured several ways. The simplest is point to point, and a multidrop arrangement connects multiple terminals. Multiplexed networks and packet switching are designed for large volumes. Much current attention is being aimed at LANs, since they will likely tie together components of office automation systems. A PBX/CBX operates at a slower speed than a LAN but can handle both voice and data traffic. Large firms will likely integrate PBX/CBX networks within LANs.

IBM was the first to define overall standards for network architecture, with its SNA. Other computer vendors announced their standards, as did the International Standards Organization. The OSI model has been offered as a guideline for all firms to follow. However, to date protocols have been defined for only the three bottom layers. IBM and the other vendors, on the other hand, have defined all of the necessary protocols for their own architectures. Computer users appear to be migrating to either the OSI or SNA architectures.

A datacom network introduces many potential security problems. Specific hardware and software measures such as encryption can help, but an overall plan is needed. A matrix showing controls for each type of hazard at each point in the network is a good way to develop a datacom plan.

Large firms designate a network manager as the person responsible for planning, implementing, operating, and controlling the datacom network.

Managers use three basic terminal techniques—menu display, form filling, and questions and answers.

Datacom-based MIS designs help firms in two ways. First, widespread operations can be better controlled. Second, the data base can be updated as transactions occur throughout the firm, maintaining an accurate conceptual representation of the physical system.

This concludes our discussion of the information processor in Part Three. Our aim has been twofold in selecting and covering the topics. First, we have attempted to open up the "black box" of the information processor to provide a look at what is inside. This understanding should give the manager a strong sense of confidence when working with information specialists in designing management information systems. The manager will not know everything but will have an excellent foundation and framework from which to work. Second, if the manager is to successfully pursue end-user computing, he or she must have a good grasp of hardware and software fundamentals. Part Three, combined with an ability to use a procedural language and/or prewritten software packages are key ingredients of end-user computing.

Key Terms

data communications, datacom,
   teleprocessing, telecom,
   telecommunications

host

basic communication model

sender, receiver

encoder, decoder

channel, circuit, line

message

modem

modulate, demodulate

hertz

video display terminal (VDT)

teleprinter terminal

remote job entry (RJE) terminal

POS terminal

retail terminal

UPC terminal

data collection terminal

dumb, intelligent terminal

remote intelligent controller

download

serial, parallel transmission

acoustic coupler

common carrier

local loop

twisted pair

coaxial cable

interexchange channel (IXC)

earth station

dial-up circuit

WATS (Wide Area
   Telecommunications Service)

private circuit

voice-grade line

front-end processor

port

message switching

teleprocessing monitor

data base/data communications
   (DB/DC)

telecommunication access program

roll-call polling

wait time

fast-select polling

hub go-ahead polling

poll character

store and forward

point-to-point network

multidrop network, line

multiplexed network

node, switching node (SN)

packet

PAD (packet assembly and
   disassembly) software

public packet switching network

local area network (LAN)

network server

private branch exchange (PBX)

computer branch exchange (CBX)

PBX/CBX, digital PBX

gateway

SNA (System Network Architecture)

logical layer

transmission management, function
   management, and application
   layer

OSI (Open Systems Interconnection)
   model

session

protocol

SDLC (Synchronous Data Link
   Control)

X.25

encryption algorithm

encryption key

control matrix

network manager, telecom manager

hardwire

interactive, conversational mode

menu

menu-display technique

form-filling technique

questions-and-answers technique

Key Concepts

How datacom makes the information processor available to widely disbursed users

How the basic communication model forms the basis for all types of datacom networks

Basic components in a datacom network—host, front-end processor, remote intelligent controllers, and terminals

How the channel is subdivided into two local loop portions and one IXC portion

How tasks and software are downloaded from the host

The processes for polling terminals

Various network configurations made possible by different datacom hardware, software, and channel alternatives

How a LAN compares to a PBX/CBX network

Network architecture expressed as logical layers on top of one or more physical layers

Protocols as the way a layer at one node communicates with the corresponding layer at another node

How a firm's datacom security plan can be derived from a matrix showing system parts and hazards

Questions

1. What are five names that have been used to describe the transmission of computer data?

2. List the eight datacom objectives.

3. Explain how the modem acts as a coder and a decoder.

4. What is the least expensive type of terminal? What additional computing equipment is needed? (Hint: There are two types of devices.)

5. List eight types of terminals. Which would the manager likely use?

6. When do you need a remote intelligent controller?

7. What is a common carrier?

8. What two basic choices are open to a communications vendor in supplying an IXC?

9. What are two approaches for using microwave signals?

10. Why can't a user pay to have a dial-up circuit specially conditioned?

11. List the activities performed by a teleprocessing monitor.

12. List the activities performed by a telecommunication access program.

13. Which type of polling produces "wait time"? Requires an intelligent terminal?

14. How does packet switching increase system reliability?

15. What is the difference between a LAN and a PBX/CBX?

16. What are three technologies that can be used to connect units in a LAN or PBX/CBX? Name an advantage of each technology.

17. How does SNA relate to the OSI model?

18. Are protocols the same as architecture standards? Explain.

19. Name two places in the MIS where encryption is used. Is encryption accomplished by software or hardware in these two places?

20. If you had a teleprinter terminal, which technique would you use to interact with the computer?

Problems

1. Explain a telephone conversation between you and another person, using the basic communication model in Figure 8-2 as the structure for describing what happens.

2. Draw a diagram of a datacom network consisting of a host, a front-end processor, a remote intelligent controller, and three CRT terminals. The channel includes multiplexers, modems, and encryption devices. (Hint: Locate each encryption device between a multiplexer and a modem.)

3. Write a step-by-step procedure for logging on to your school's central computer. For each step describe the relationship, if any, to datacom security.

4. Assume that you have written a program to compute an economic order quantity (EOQ). Code the screen dialog that would be necessary to execute the program. Use the questions-and-answers technique. Arrange the dialog so that a variable number of EOQs (for different items) can be computed.

CASE PROBLEM: Northwest Paper

Bill O'Brien has just been hired as the new vice president of marketing for Northwest Paper, a large Oregon-based producer of both consumer and industrial paper products. O'Brien held a similar post with a smaller competitor and had built a top-flight marketing organization. During his job interview with the Northwest executive committee, Bill revealed that he believed the secret of good business operations was good communication. He emphasized that, if hired, he would need the resources to establish an effective communications system at Northwest.

During his first month on the job, Bill oriented himself to his new company, its resources, its limitations, and its opportunities. During the first four weekly executive committee meetings, Bill maintained a low profile and mostly listened to what Al DuPre, the president, Mal Volding, the vice president of finance, and Patricia Henson, the vice president of manufacturing, had to say. The purpose of the weekly meetings was to maintain open lines of communication at the top executive level—a practice that received Bill's complete approval.

At the fifth meeting, Al asked Bill how things were going, and Bill replied by saying that he was about ready to start work on his marketing communications system. He asked Mal to invite Don Bowen, the director of information services, to the next meeting so that they could all discuss the needed changes. Since Don reported to Mal, Mal was the logical person to extend the invitation.

When the next meeting rolled around, Mal asked Don to briefly describe the Northwest MIS. Don explained that they were using a large-scale CPU with eight disk drives, four magnetic tape units, two line printers, and a plotter. Accounting transactions were entered by means of CRT terminals, and similar terminals were located throughout headquarters for handling data base queries. A front-end processor polled all of the terminals on the multidrop line. System software included an operating system, a teleprocessing monitor, a telecommunication access program, and a DBMS.

After Don's explanation, Bill proceeded to tell the group what he needed. He wanted each of the company's thirty-one branch managers to be able to communicate with the computer on a daily basis from their offices located in twenty-six states. Daily sales report data would be transmitted to the computer, and responses to queries for sales statistics would be handled with very little delay. In addition, he wanted each of the firm's 250 sales representatives to be able to query the data base from a customer's office or a pay phone to check on the status of inventory items and unfilled orders. For himself, Bill wanted to be able to obtain summaries of the daily sales report data from a terminal in his office. The reports could be reproduced and distributed to the other members of the executive committee for the weekly meeting. Bill concluded his description by explaining that such a network would enable him, his branch managers, and his sales reps to keep up with their respective areas of responsibility. Information would flow freely, and the result would be an improved efficiency and sales level that would more than offset the cost of the equipment.

Bill clearly had the support of the other members of the executive committee. Mal turned to Don and said, "I want you to give us an idea of exactly what would be required in terms of added hardware, software, and communications facilities in order to meet Bill's request. Why don't you work that up and give us your answer at next week's meeting. I know you can't work up the costs on such short notice—just list the items. Do you need any more information from us?"

"I can't think of any," Don replied. "If I do, I'll make a note of it, and we can discuss it at the next meeting."

"That sounds good," said Mal. "See you next week."

Assignment

Provide Mal Volding with a list of the hardware, software, and datacom facilities that Bill O'Brien needs for his marketing communications system.

Selected Bibliography

Data Communications

Bolick, Lawrence, "Insight Into On-Site Telecom," *Datamation* 31 (March 1, 1985): 76ff.

Bryant, Susan Foster, "Micro-to-Mainframe Links," *Computer Decisions* 16 (July 1984): 162ff.

Coover, Edwin R., and Ali Eshgh, "Pairing for the Future," *Datamation* 29 (December 1983): 220ff.

Caswell, Stephen A., "Oil and Water?," *Datamation* 31 (April 15, 1985): 112ff.

Dickinson, Robert M., "Telecom Management: An Emerging Art," *Datamation* 30 (March 1984): 121ff.

Ferris, David, and John Cunningham, "Local Nets for Micros," *Datamation* 30 (August 1, 1984): 104–109.

FitzGerald, Jerry, *Business Data Communications* (New York: John Wiley & Sons, 1984).

Goeller, Leo F., Jr., and Jerry A. Goldstone, "The ABCs of the PBX," *Datamation* 29 (April 1983): 178ff.

Gordetsky, Gordon R., "Digital PBX—the Conduit for Integrated Offices," *The Office* 99 (April 1984): 140ff.

Gruhn, Marty, "Battle of the LANs," *Office Administration and Automation* 45 (March 1984): 26ff.

Haber, Lynn, "Fiber-Optic Technology Sheds Light on Local Area Networks," *Mini-Micro Systems* 17 (November 1984): 103ff.

Horwitt, Elisabeth, "Looking for the Promised LAN," *Business Computer Systems* 3 (June 1984): 112ff.

Jarema, David R., and Edward H. Sussenguth, "IBM Data Communications: A Quarter Century of Evolution and Progress," *IBM Journal of Research and Development* 25 (September 1981): 391-404.

Johnson, Jan, "IBM's Two-LAN Plan," *Datamation* 30 (February 1984): 120ff.

Kriebel, Charles H., and Diane M. Strong, "A Survey of the MIS and Telecommunications Activities of Major Business Firms," *MIS Quarterly* 8 (September 1984): 171–178.

Lowe, William H., Jr., "Local Area Networks: the Exploration Has Just Begun," *The Office* 100 (November 1984): 32ff.

Miller, Landon C., "Communications Planning," *Journal of Systems Management* 34 (October 1983): 18–21.

Moskowitz, Robert A., "IBM's Grand Design," *Computer Decisions* 17 (April 23, 1985): 82ff.

Moulton, James R., "Significant Network Standards," *Telecommunications* 19(March 1985): 88hff.

Passmore, L. David, "The Networking Standards Collision," *Datamation* 31 (February 1, 1985): 98ff.

Pyykkonen, Martin, "Handicapping LANs," *Datamation* 31 (March 1, 1985): 96ff.

Serlin, Omri, "Departmental Computing: A Choice of Strategies," *Datamation* 31 (May 1, 1985): 86ff.

Siegel, Eric D., "Your Pocket Protocol Primer," *Datamation* 30 (March 1984): 152–154.

Stenzler-Centonze, Marjorie, "IBM's LAN: To Wait Is the Question," *Mini-Micro Systems* 17 (August 1984): 125–126.

Stix, Gary, "Is There a PBX to the Promised LAN?," *Computer Decisions* 17 (March 26, 1985): 98ff.

"Telecom Manager: A New Career," *Small Systems World* 12 (October 1984): 29–30.

Webster, Roger, W., "Building a Microcomputer Local Network," *Data Communications* 14 (February 1985): 195ff.

Part Four

MIS COMPONENTS

The MIS includes all of the firm's computing activity. It serves as the framework for specialized subsystems that process data, automate office procedures, and provide decision support. In Chapter 1 we introduced this framework and illustrated it with the diagram in Figure 1-11. The diagram shows MIS as an outer box containing three inner boxes labeled data processing system, office automation, and decision support. This structure is one way to view the interrelationship between these systems. We will use this structure in this text, and in Part Four we address each of the main subsystems within the MIS.

Chapter 9 (Data Processing Systems) describes most of the accounting systems found in all firms. All firms have accounts payable, accounts receivable, and general ledger systems. In addition, firms that sell products have order entry, billing, inventory, purchasing, and receiving systems. Firms that provide services also have billing systems, and they must also purchase, receive, and inventory supplies used in performing their services. We use the term *distribution system* to describe the package of accounting systems that is found, in whole or in part, in a large number of both product and service firms. By studying the basic accounting systems used by these types of firms, we gain an understanding of data processing that can be generalized for practically all organizations.

Chapter 10 (Office Automation) addresses the fastest-growing area of computer application. Both hardware and software are available that enable firms to automate their office procedures. Triggered initially by word processing, office automation also includes electronic and voice mail, electronic calendaring, teleconferencing, and a host of other applications. Our objective will be to describe how these diverse applications relate to the MIS.

In Chapter 11 we describe the third MIS subsystem—DSS. We will see how managers obtain information for decision making in three basic ways—periodic reports, special reports, and mathematical model simulations. We will cover each of these information-producing techniques in detail.

In all three chapters, we will first present the concepts and then review the variety of hardware and software that is available. This material provides an up-to-date view of the components of an MIS.

Chapter 9

Data Processing Systems

Learning Objectives

After studying this chapter, you should:

- Know what makes data processing different from both office automation and DSS
- Understand the basic data processing functions in a distribution-type firm, and the related terminology
- Have an improved understanding of how data flow diagrams and data dictionary forms can be used to document processes and data
- Understand how systems are designed to minimize the amount of time spent in keying input data and accessing files
- Have an idea of how to go about adding processes to a data processing system to increase its information output
- Have an introductory knowledge of prewritten software that supports data processing functions on computers of all sizes

Introduction

What is a *data processing system*? The obvious answer is, "It is a system that processes data." That is true, but what distinguishes data processing from office automation (OA) and decision support systems (DSS)? OA and DSS process data as well. All three activities accept data as the input. The distinguishing feature is the output. OA and DSS are *always* supposed to produce information; that is their purpose. Data processing usually produces limited managerial information. That is the reason that the MIS concept caught on so quickly—there was a need for a system intended specifically to produce information.

The characteristic of data processing output that diminishes its information value is its *volume*. The output consists of hundreds or even thousands of documents such as payroll checks, invoices, statements, and purchase orders. There is so much of this output that it has no information value to persons within the firm, especially to managers.

The data processing systems are designed to perform the accounting functions of the firm. We use the terms *data processing system* and *accounting system* interchangeably. Firms have always had accounting systems. The first versions were *manual*; bookkeepers posted the entries to ledger books by hand. All of us have visions of Bob Cratchitt keeping Scrooge's books up to date. Bookkeepers such as Bob toiled long hours, sitting atop high stools, wearing green eyeshades, and using ink quills or fountain pens.

Shortly before the beginning of the twentieth century, about 1880 or 1890, inventors began to address the problem of slow, inaccurate, labor-intensive accounting systems. The first efforts produced strictly *mechanical devices*. Some of the data processing functions were performed mechanically, but the machines were powered by human muscle—the operator pressing keys and pulling levers. Electrical power was soon applied, giving birth to a variety of *electromechanical* devices that remained popular until the electronic computer came along.

Two basic classes of electromechanical devices were used during the first half of the twentieth century. These classes were (1) keydriven bookkeeping machines, and (2) punched card machines. Firms such as NCR and Burroughs dominated the market for keydriven machines, whereas IBM and Remington Rand (now Sperry Corporation) controlled the market for punched card machines. Both varieties of keydriven machines were used strictly for data processing—performing accounting operations. Larger firms used punched card machines in conjunction with bookkeeping machines because the punched card machines could handle large volumes of accounting transactions. Smaller firms could not afford the punched card machines. A group of such machines rented for a minimum of about $1,000 a month. Smaller firms wishing to mechanize their processing were restricted to bookkeeping machines.[1]

An important point to understand is the fact that accounting systems have undergone little change since the era of electromechanical devices. Although we are in an electronic age, the computer is still processing accounting data basically the same way as the electromechanical, mechanical, and even manual, systems of 25, 50, or even 100 years ago. The data processing concepts have changed little in the past and likely will change little in the future. This is an unusual, yet welcome, stability in a field that is known for change.

The Distribution System

There are many kinds of firms, but they all distribute something. They have customers who need products or services, and the firms are dedicated to meeting those needs.

---

[1] A number of large firms elected to use bookkeeping machines rather than punched card machines. This was common in the banking industry.

Product flow

It is easy to see the distribution systems of *product-oriented firms*. These firms include retailers such as supermarkets, hardware stores, fast-food restaurants, and so on. It is not so easy to see the distribution systems of firms that operate "behind the scenes" to furnish the retailers with products to sell. Wholesalers sell to retailers, and manufacturers, in turn, sell to wholesalers. These three types of firms (manufacturers, wholesalers, and retailers) form a *distribution channel*, illustrated in Figure 9-1. You, the consumer, are also a part of this channel, purchasing the products from the retailer.

The figure shows that *products* flow from the manufacturer through the channel to the consumer. In most cases, this is a one-way flow unless, for example, you or another channel member returns something that you bought.

Data and information flow

Another resource flow in the figure includes both data and information. The *data* flow is necessary because it *represents* the *physical resources* flowing through the channel. An invoice, for example, represents the items shipped to the customer. Without the data flow, the firm could not keep track of its incoming and outgoing physical flows.

Information must also flow between the channel members. The members must be able to function as a coordinated unit, and the information makes this possible. The information flow through a distribution channel is like the nervous system in the body, sending messages that explain what is happening.

A very important point is that the data processing system generally does not produce the information directly, but does so indirectly through its data base. The data processing system generates a data base from which information can be derived.

You will notice how some data and information links "leap frog" one or two intermediate channel members. Manufacturers often establish information links with retailers and consumers. You are familiar with warranty cards that you mail to the manufacturer when you buy a TV or stereo equipment. These cards typically ask questions such as "How did you learn about the product?" and "Where did you buy it?"

There is typically *not* an information link between the consumer and the wholesaler. Wholesalers rely on manufacturers and retailers for their information.

Flows in service-oriented organizations

It is not so easy to see *service-oriented organizations* as distributing something. These organizations include doctors, lawyers, rock bands, TV channels, churches, and the like. These organizations distribute services that people need—cures for ailments, legal assistance, entertainment, information, peace of mind, and so forth. If we think of these organizations as offering service *products*, then they become more similar to the product-oriented firms. For example, a hospital obtains medicine, equipment, and supplies from manufacturers and wholesalers. Doctors and nurses transform these inputs into service products—various medical treatments.

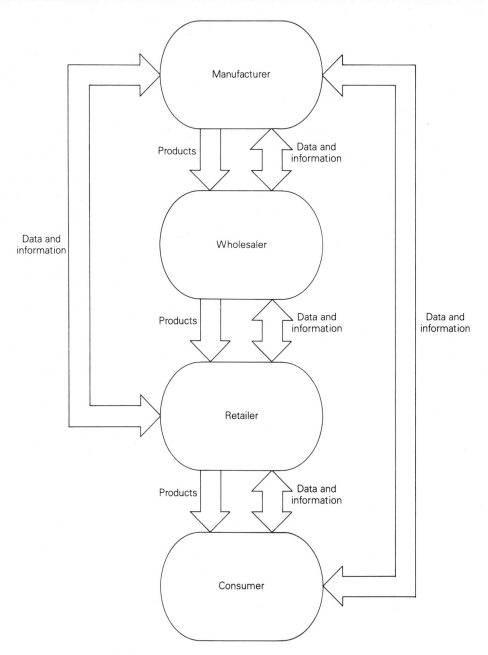

Figure 9-1 A distribution channel.

The hospital can be viewed as a type of retailer—selling its products to consumers. Like the product firms, there is a material flow to the service firms from their suppliers, and an information flow that connects the service organization with both its suppliers and its consumers. The channel pictured in Figure 9-1, therefore, fits a service organization as well as a product organization. The service organization plays the role of retailer.

The similarity of systems

Since both product- and service-oriented firms have similar data and information flows, the data processing systems of both types of organizations have much in common. Both have payroll systems to handle payments to employees, and inventory systems to control the products sold to customers or the supplies used in providing the services. Both types also have billing systems to charge customers for purchases, accounts receivable systems to collect monies due, purchasing systems to order more inventory, and receiving systems to handle the receipt of additional inventory. And, both types of firms use general ledger systems to tie all of the accounting transactions together.

This similarity in systems is important in two respects. First, it means that we do not have to learn many systems in order to understand data processing. We can learn one general system and then apply that system to various types of organizations—from supermarkets to libraries. Second, it means that packaged computer-based systems can be used by a wide variety of firms. Software vendors, quick to recognize the similarity in how the basic data processing jobs are performed in different types of firms, have aimed their products at companies in general. The same accounts receivable system, as an example, can be used by a drug store or a lawyer. All data processing systems, however, do not provide such a nice fit. Payroll is notoriously different from one firm to the next. Order entry procedures and the formatting of data on invoices also vary widely from one firm to the next. It is therefore doubtful that a package of prewritten data processing programs would fit *any* firm in an exact manner. There usually must be some "give and take"—either the packages or the company's procedures must be modified to some degree.

Most of this chapter is devoted to a description of a basic set of data processing subsystems used by distribution firms. As you study these systems, it will probably help to think of a product-oriented firm such as a manufacturer or a department store. But, keep in mind that the systems can also be found in service organizations and even the government—they are in the distribution business as well.

Also keep in mind that you probably can't find a firm processing their data in precisely the same way as described here. Our model is a general one—fitting most firms in a general way. Like the general systems model of the firm in Chapter 3, our data processing model can easily be adapted to a particular firm. It is an excellent base to build upon.

System Documentation

We will use data flow diagrams and the data dictionary to illustrate the data processing system. If you are unfamiliar with those techniques, you should first read Appendixes B and C before proceeding with this chapter.

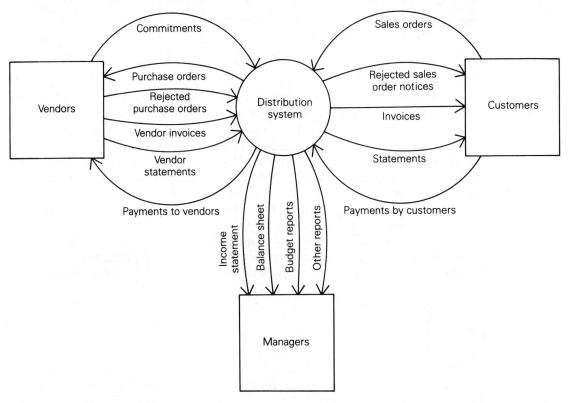

Figure 9-2 Context diagram of a distribution system.

System Overview

Figure 9-2 illustrates the set of data processing systems used by distribution firms. We will use the term *distribution system* to describe the data processing systems. The figure is a *context diagram* that shows the distribution system as a circle, connected to its environmental elements with arrows representing data flows. The environmental elements are shown as squares.[2] Physical flows of products, materials, and so on are not included. We are only concerned with the conceptual data flow of the data processing systems. Two of the conceptual flows are labeled *payments by customers* and *payments to vendors*. These are money flows, but we are assuming that payments are always made by check. The check is therefore a conceptual representation of the money. The firm's data processing system will prepare the checks to the firm's vendors.

We see that the only environmental elements with which the distribution system interfaces are customers, vendors, and management. The four flows con-

---

[2]The term "environmental element" is used to describe *all* elements interfacing with the system. These elements may be other systems or persons such as managers within the firm. In this case, "environment" does not mean "outside the firm," but rather "outside the system."

necting the firm with its customers are quite similar to the flows connecting the firm with its vendors. In fact, the firm is a "customer" to its vendors.

The inclusion of management as an environmental element receiving output recognizes that the data processing system has some information-producing capability. We include the reports in the distribution system because they are a major output from the general ledger subsystem. The line between the data processing system and decision support and office automation systems is often fuzzy, as illustrated by the general ledger reports. From a conceptual standpoint, the reports should be considered as decision support systems. From a practical standpoint, they are an output from the data processing system.

The diagram in Figure 9-2 fits a manufacturer, a wholesaler, or a retailer. They all have vendors, and they all have customers. Both the firm and its vendors use *invoices* (bills) to advise customers how much money they owe the firm, and use *statements* to collect unpaid bills. Orders received from customers are usually named *sales orders*, whereas the orders that the firm places to its vendors are named *purchase orders*. In some cases the firm will first obtain a verbal *commitment* from the vendor to supply the needed items and then prepare the purchase order. Very often the firms will have to send *rejected sales order notices* to its customers—perhaps their credit rating is bad. Also the firm must consider the possibility that their vendors will take similar action with *rejected purchase orders*.

The context diagram identifies *all* environmental elements with which the firm interfaces and *all* of the interconnecting data flows.

The context diagram is fine for defining the scope of the system—the environmental elements and the interfaces. But we need to learn more about what is contained in the circle labeled "distribution system." We accomplish that by identifying the major subsystems within the distribution system in Figure 9-3.[3]

Your first impression might be that the data flow diagram in Figure 9-3 is pretty disorganized. There are a lot of circles, with arrows going everywhere. As we get into the system, however, you will find that it is quite straightforward.

Figure 9-3 is a *top-level data flow diagram (DFD)*. It is the level showing the major subsystems, numbered 1.0 through 8.0. Our three environmental elements from Figure 9-2 are included, and notice that the arrows entering and leaving those boxes are exactly the same as the context diagram. All we have done is "explode" the single circle in Figure 9-2 into the eight interconnected circles in Figure 9-3.

We will explain each of the eight subsystems, using lower-level DFDs, but first we will explain the major functions of each subsystem. Notice that all subsystems are *integrated* with data flows (the arrows). All eight subsystems hang together in a nice, neat package. One system "feeds" data to another. This idea of integrated subsystems is nothing new—it was popular in punched card days.

---

[3]Some users of data flow diagrams restrict the identification of the processes (the circles) to a combination of a verb and an object. For example, the context diagram would be labeled "Distribute products" rather than "Distribution system." The circles in Figure 9-3 would likewise be labeled with verbs and objects. Although this approach is quite acceptable, we have elected to use system names. Over the years, the processes have been identified with system names, such as "inventory system." Since the names are used universally, we prefer the clarity with which they identify the processes.

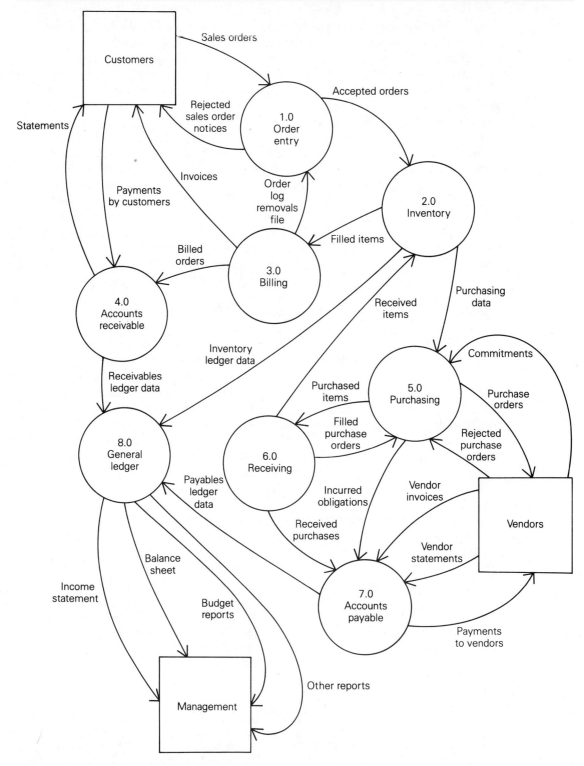

Figure 9-3 Major subsystems of the distribution system.

The *order entry system* does exactly what its name implies—it enters customer sales orders into the system. It can reject orders from customers for various reasons, including poor credit. Accepted orders are processed by the *inventory system* where the conceptual records of the firm's physical inventory resource are updated. When inventory is on hand to fill customer orders, the *billing system* prepares invoices and advises the accounts receivable system of the transaction. The *accounts receivable system* has the responsibility of collecting the money by sending statements. This data flow through the first four systems occurs during the process of filling customer orders and collecting payments.

Another data flow occurs when the inventory system recognizes a need to order more stock from the vendors. Perhaps the balance on hand reaches a predetermined reorder point. In that case, the inventory system notifies the *purchasing system* to prepare a purchase order.[4] After the purchase order is prepared, the purchasing system notifies the receiving system to expect the shipment, and advises the accounts payable system that the firm has incurred a future financial obligation—to pay for the stock when it is received. The *receiving system* notifies the inventory system when the replenishment stock arrives so that the conceptual inventory records can be updated. Receiving also notifies accounts payable so that the vendor can be paid. The *accounts payable system* receives invoices and statements from the vendor and makes payments.

Some of the above systems provide data to the general ledger system. The *general ledger system* maintains the account balances and prepares the income statement, balance sheet, and other reports.

There is another data processing system that we do not include in Figure 9-3. That is payroll. Payroll is not interconnected with distribution (unless salespersons are paid a commission on items sold), so it is omitted. Payroll does, however, tie in with the general ledger system.

Subsystem Descriptions

We will describe the distribution system in greater detail, using lower-level data flow diagrams.

Order entry

Figure 9-4 is a *second-level* DFD of the order entry system. Decimal positions are used in the process numbers to show that they are subsidiary to step 1.0 in Figure 9-3. We have simply subdivided step 1.0 into its four main parts. This is an example of a top-down, structured approach to system documentation and design. It is *top-down* since we start with the broad overview of the system as a whole and gradually make the picture more detailed. It is *structured* in that systems are

---

[4]Although the distribution system can also be used by a manufacturer, we are not incorporating the subsystems that enable a firm to produce its own inventory. That addition would unnecessarily complicate the description. We assume that all inventory is purchased from vendors.

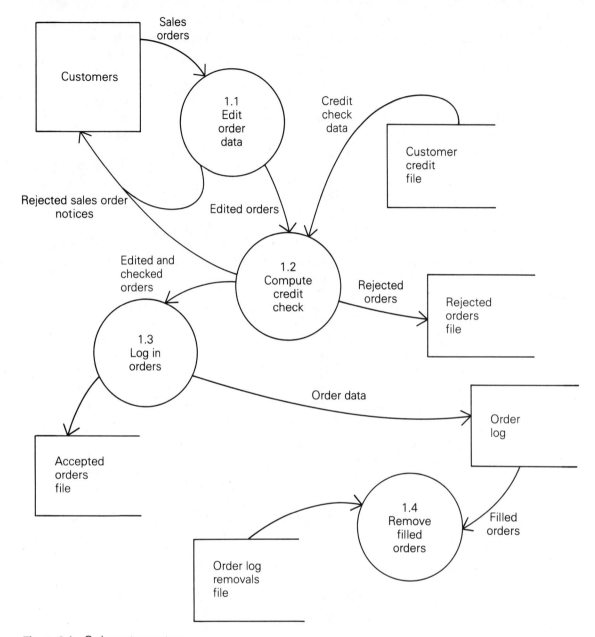

Figure 9-4 Order entry system.

recognized as existing in a hierarchy, and we can describe a system in terms of its subsidiary systems.

Data flow diagrams are only one example of structured documentation. Other examples are Warnier-Orr diagrams (Appendix F) and HIPO (Hierarchy plus Input Process Output) diagrams. HIPO is described in Appendix E, and Figure E-1 contains a HIPO diagram of the order entry system.

A unique feature of Figure 9-4 is the first-time inclusion of *data stores*, or files, (the open-ended rectangles). We did not include stores in the upper-level DFDs. We could have included stores in the top-level DFD, but did not in order to keep it as simple as possible. Stores are not included in context diagrams.

The first order entry process is 1.1—Edit order data. Here, the sales order is checked for missing or incorrect data. Maybe the order includes the customer name, but not the number. Or perhaps the item number doesn't match the item description. We will correct an error if we can (such as look up the customer number). But if we can't (such as reconcile the difference between item number and name), a rejected sales order notice is prepared and sent to the customer asking that the corrected order be resubmitted.

The other output from process 1.1 consists of the edited orders (including both rejected and accepted). These orders are input to step 1.2—Compute credit check. Here, the order amount is added to the amount of that customer's accounts receivable. The receivable amount is obtained from the customer credit file, a special file used for credit checking. The customer credit record also includes a credit limit. The data flow labeled "Credit check data" includes both the receivable amount and the credit limit. The amount of the current purchase plus the receivable amount is compared to the credit limit. When the credit limit is exceeded, the order is rejected. Orders that did not pass the edit check in steps 1.1 or 1.2 are recorded on the rejected orders file.

We can show the details of the credit checking operation with the third-level DFD in Figure 9-5. A lower-level DFD is drawn when there is a need to show more detail. Figure 9-5 shows the preparation of the rejected sales order notices (because of the credit check) and the writing of the rejected order records in the rejected orders file. This file is a temporary holding area pending solution of the rejection problem.

Another output from the credit check is the edited and checked orders that are input to step 1.3—Log in orders (refer back to Figure 9-4). When an order is accepted, we enter a brief identifying description in an order log, and write a record in the accepted orders file. The log is used to follow up on orders to make certain that they are filled. Orders in the file are *open*, or unfilled. The accepted orders file is input to the inventory system.

Steps 1.1, 1.2, and 1.3 form a connected chain. Step 1.4 is separate—taken when the billing system signals that orders have been filled. The order log removals file is created by the billing system to serve as the signal. In step 1.4 the filled orders are either removed from the log or marked in some manner to indicate that they are no longer open.

Inventory

We have accepted the customer orders. Now we must determine if we can fill them. Figure 9-6 is a second-level DFD of the inventory system.

Inventory is the hub of the distribution system—the other subsystems revolve around it. For that reason, we have quite a few inputs and outputs.

Two of the inventory processes are concerned with filling the customer orders (2.1 and 2.2). The other processes (2.3 and 2.4) have other concerns.

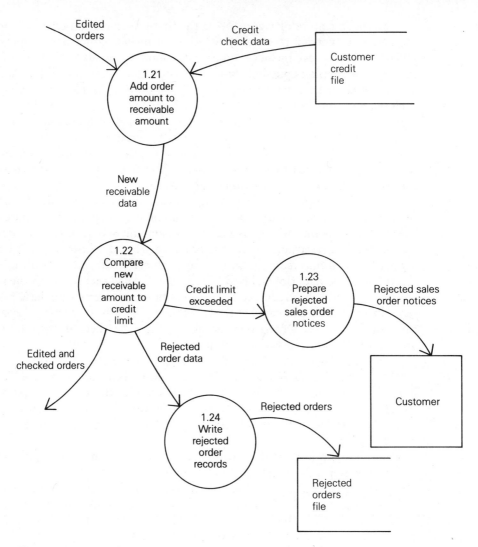

Figure 9-5 Compute the credit check.

The first process is 2.1—Check the balance on hand. The item record is retrieved from the inventory file. The *balance on hand* field is compared with the *order quantity* from the accepted order record to see if adequate stock exists to fill the order. If not, a backorder record is entered in the backorder file. A *backorder* means that "We can't fill the order now, but we will later when we replenish our inventory."

This is the point in the system where we pick up all of the data elements relating to the inventory item. The inventory record includes elements such as item description and warehouse location that will be needed later as we print the invoices and picking tickets. By retrieving that data here and carrying it along with the transaction data, we do not have to access the inventory file again later

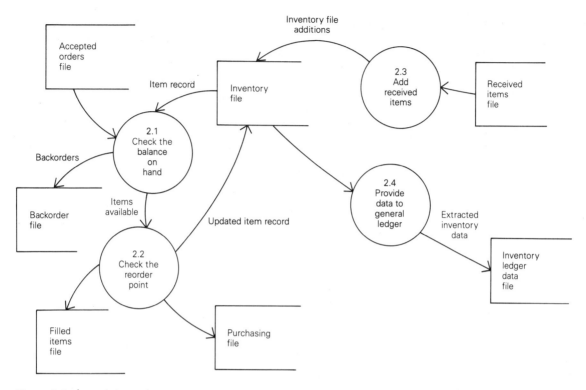

Figure 9-6 Inventory system.

in the procedure. The time to access records is usually a time-consuming part of any type of system.

When we *can* fill the order (balance on hand ≥ order quantity), we next check in step 2.2 to see if the new, lowered balance on hand caused the reorder point to be reached. Each item record contains a *reorder point* field. When the balance on hand drops to the reorder point, it is time to reorder. The reorder point is set high enough so that you hopefully will receive the new supply before you completely run out of stock—a *stockout*.

When the reorder point has been reached, reorder data is recorded in a purchasing file. The purchasing file is input to the series of processes to be taken to order and receive the stock (processes 5.0, 6.0, and 7.0 in Figure 9-3).

Records representing sold items are also written onto a filled items file for use by the billing system.

Before the processing of the sales order is completed, the updated item record is written back onto the inventory file. This updated record contains the new balance on hand (when the order is filled) and data describing the purchase, such as quantity ordered and date (when the reorder point is reached).

The above processes reduce inventory balances to fill orders. Another process is necessary to increase balances when the replenishment stock arrives. Step 2.3 handles the processing of receipts. This step takes data from the receiving system and updates the balance on hand fields of the received items in the inventory file.

As we mentioned earlier, several systems provide data to the general ledger system. Step 2.4 accomplishes that task by extracting from the inventory file the data that the general ledger system needs.

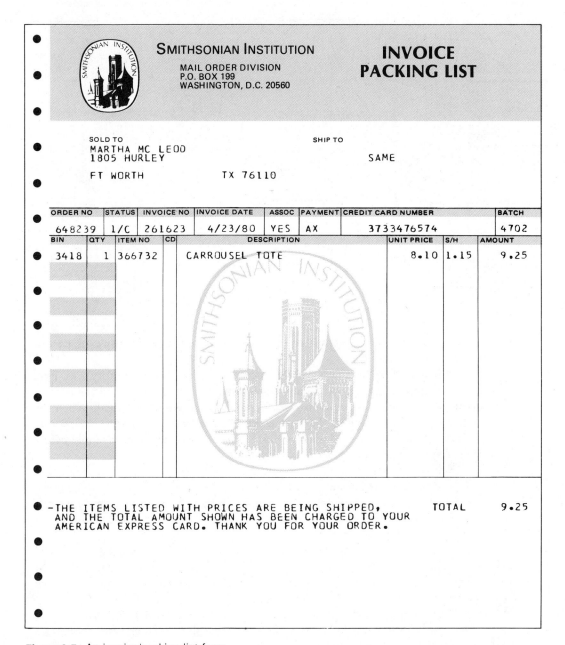

Figure 9-7 An invoice/packing list form.

Billing

Bills are called invoices by the firms preparing them. The system that prepares the invoices is the billing system. The billing system is second only to the receiving system in simplicity; it doesn't do much more than print and compute some amounts. Figure 9-7 pictures a typical invoice—complete with heading, body, and total areas. Figure 9-8 illustrates the three processes performed by the billing system.

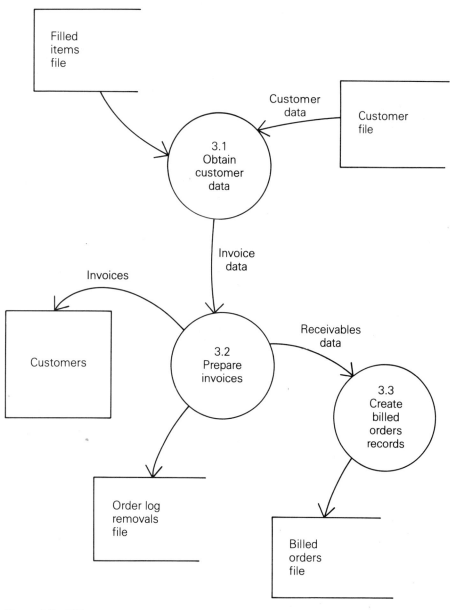

Figure 9-8 Billing system.

First, the inventory data from the filled items file is supplemented with customer data from the customer file. The customer data is needed for printing the invoices and for subsequent operations. The customer data includes name and address, shipping instructions, and salesperson number. This data is obtained in step 3.1.

The printing operation in step 3.2 includes some arithmetic—*extending* the *line items* (multiplying, for each item ordered, the price times the quantity), accumulating a total amount, and perhaps computing a sales tax. This detail could be shown in a lower-level DFD.

At this point we have filled the order and must notify the order entry system either to mark the entry in the order log as "filled," or to delete the entry. This notification is accomplished with the order log removals file.

The process in step 3.3 involves the "passing along" of data to be entered in the accounts receivable file by the accounts receivable system. This data summarizes the billing transactions—invoice number, invoice date, customer number, customer order number, salesperson number, and invoice amount.

Accounts receivable

The invoice is the official notification to the customer to pay for the merchandise ordered. Very often a firm will offer a discount (such as 2 percent) if the invoice is paid quickly (such as within 10 days).

It is common practice to give the customer 30 days to pay the invoice. During this time the receivable is *current*. The receivable becomes *past due* if payment has not been made within 30 days from the billing date. Firms remind their customers of past due invoices by mailing statements each month. The statement usually contains only a single line entry for each *outstanding invoice*—an invoice that has not been paid.

Figure 9-9 shows four processes performed by the accounts receivable system. Process 4.1 adds new receivables to the accounts receivable file, and is performed daily. Also on a daily basis, receivables records are removed from the file in step 4.2 when payments are made. The receivables file is a type of inventory file—an inventory of money owed to the firm by its customers. Records are added to the file when sales are made, and records are deleted when payments are made.

On a monthly cycle basis, the accounts receivable system prepares statements (step 4.3) that are sent to all customers with accounts receivable. The firm continues sending statements until the bill is paid or is written off as a bad debt. Some firms charge interest on the unpaid balance. Department and jewelry stores do this.

Also on a monthly basis, the receivables system feeds data to the general ledger system (step 4.4). This data includes payments made by customers during the month, plus unpaid receivables from the accounts receivable file. The general ledger system uses this data, for example, to prepare a balance sheet showing the accounts receivable as an asset. That figure comes from the accounts receivable system.

The accounts receivable system has a rather unusual structure. None of the processes are linked to form a chain—each stands alone. This situation occurs

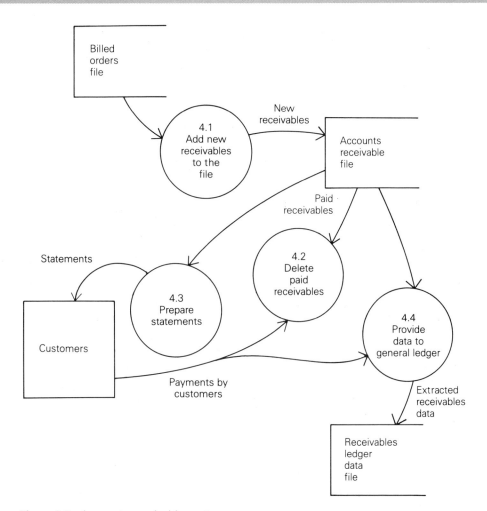

Figure 9-9 Accounts receivable system.

because this system has four *triggers* that cause processes to be initiated. The three previous systems have had one or two triggers (input arrows). The four receivables triggers are: (1) billed orders, (2) customer payments, (3) the statement preparation cycle, and (4) the general ledger reporting cycle.

At this point we have completed one circuit through the network. We have handled all of the activity dealing with customer orders. The next three systems procure replenishment stock as directed by the inventory system.

Purchasing

Most firms have purchasing departments. In manufacturing firms, these departments usually are a part of the manufacturing function since so many raw material purchases must be made. In wholesaling and retailing firms, the purchasing department often is a part of the marketing function.

The purchasing department consists of a number of *buyers,* who usually specialize in particular inventory categories. For example, one buyer might specialize in adhesives, and another in electronics. The inventory category is identified in the inventory record, so that when the reorder point is reached, it is easy to identify the responsible buyer. The inventory record can also identify vendors who previously provided the item.

The purchasing activity is triggered by the inventory system in step 2.2 of Figure 9-6 when the reorder point is reached. A record is written on the purchasing file, which serves as input to the purchasing system.

The first task of the buyer (step 5.1 in Figure 9-10) is to select the vendor to fill the order. There are usually several vendors for each item. The buyer can access the vendor file and obtain information describing past vendor performance. Factors receiving consideration are quality, the ability to meet promised delivery dates, and price.

Once a vendor is selected, the buyer frequently places a telephone call to the vendor to perhaps negotiate a lower price and to receive assurance that particular delivery dates can be met. This verbal commitment is included as step 5.2.

When the buyer is satisfied that the vendor arrangements are satisfactory, a purchase order is prepared and mailed to the vendor as indicated in step 5.3. A record is entered in an outstanding purchase orders file that represents purchase orders made but not yet filled. This file can be used by the buyers to assure that purchase orders do not get lost in the mail and that items are shipped when promised.

The purchasing system must notify two other systems at this time that the purchase order has been prepared. A data record is entered into the purchased items file for use by the receiving system. Another record is entered into the incurred obligations file for use by the accounts payable system. We will see shortly how these files are used.

One final transaction involving the purchasing system remains. It is necessary to remove records from the outstanding purchase order file when: (1) the order is filled, or (2) the vendor rejects the order. This close-out process is handled by step 5.4. The signal that the order has been filled comes from receiving in the form of the filled purchase orders file, and the signal that an order has been rejected comes from the vendor.

A sample purchase order appears in Figure 9-11. This sample was prepared by a computer. Many firms, including those using computers, still prepare purchase orders using typewriters. Of all the systems in our distribution system, purchasing is the least computerized. The role of the buyer is central to the entire process, and the computer plays a supporting role by providing the signal that it is time to reorder, providing vendor information, and perhaps printing the purchase order.

One reason that the computer has not been used to a greater extent in the vendor selection process is that the procurement scenario changes so frequently. Vendors come and go, prices change, vendors add and delete products, and so on. Since the buyer must review the scenario at the time of each procurement, there is little left for the computer to do.

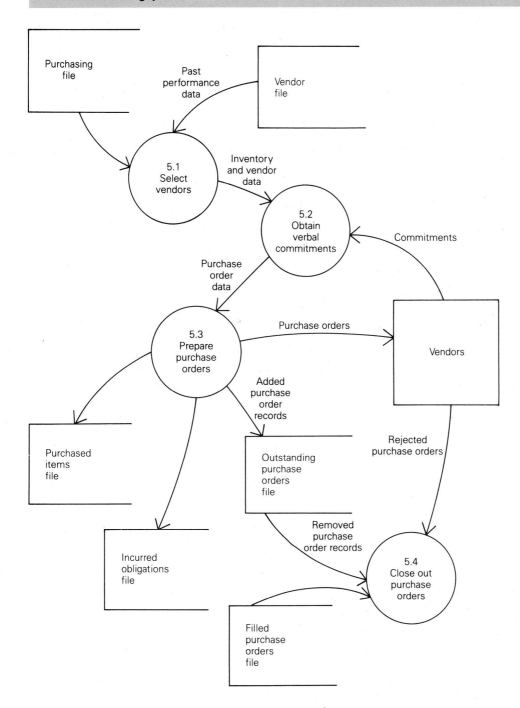

Figure 9-10 Purchasing system.

```
                        SCI  EQUIPMENT  INC.
1060 E. Providencia Ave.                    TWX #: 9104982757 GOLDWORD
Burbank, CA. 91501                          PHONE: (818) 848-1765

                        PURCHASE ORDER
                        NO.__8601_____

TO:                              SHIP TO:
     LogicSoft                        SCI Equipment Inc.
     (Dept J) 1101 Tri County Blvd.   1060 E. Providencia Ave.
     Farmingdale, NY 11335            Burbank, Calif. 91501

DATE         SHIP VIA     FOB.C&F.CIF     DATE REQUIRED     TERMS
1-03-86      UPS          ------          1-07-86           Visa
```

PLEASE SHIP THE FOLLOWING EXACTLY AS SPECIFIED:

ITEM	QUANTITY	DESCRIPTION	UNIT PRICE	AMOUNT
1	2	Epson FX-85 Dot Matrix Printer	$379.00	$ 758.00
2	1	AST Mega Pak (256K)	$369.00	$ 369.00
3	2	Hayes Smartmodem 2400	$719.00	$1438.00
4	1	Lotus Symphony Ver 1.1	$429.00	$ 429.00

Sub Total	$2994.00
Tax	NC
Shipping	NC
Insurance	59.88
Total	$3053.88

```
ACKNOWLEDGEMENT:

SHIPMENT WILL BE MADE                    ORDERED BY:

PARTIAL_____COMPLETE_____   SCI EQUIPMENT INC.

ACCEPTED
BY:_____DATE_____   _____
```

Figure 9-11 A computer-prepared purchase order.

Receiving

The conceptual part of the receiving system is quite simple and is illustrated in Figure 9-12. The first step is 6.1—Process receipts. Much of this processing is part of the physical system, which is not our concern here. A truck delivers cartons to a receiving dock. Receiving personnel obtain information from the purchased items file identifying the vendor, the firm's purchase order number, items ordered, and quantities. This information is used to inspect the contents of the cartons to assure that they are what was ordered and are in good condition.

When the physical processes of inspection and routing to other areas within the firm are completed, the receiving system notifies three other systems of the receipt. Inventory is notified with a received items file. We processed that file in step 2.3 of Figure 9-6. Purchasing is notified with a filled purchase orders file. We processed that file in step 5.4 of Figure 9-10. Accounts payable is notified with a received purchases file. We will process that file in the next section.

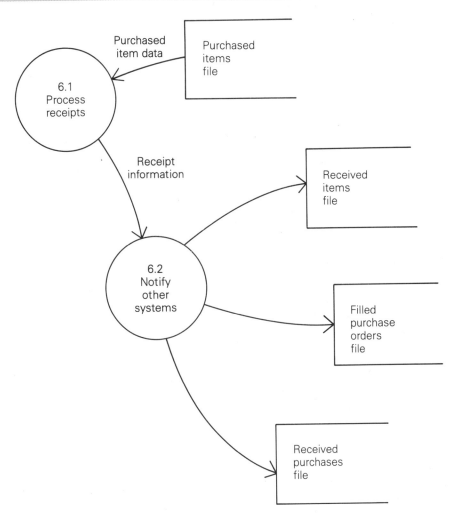

Figure 9-12 Receiving system.

Communication-oriented MIS designs do a good job of transmitting the three receipt notices. Terminals in the receiving area can signal the other systems almost immediately. In manual systems, it can take days for the notifications to make the rounds.

Accounts Payable

The accounts payable system is geared to waiting for all of the signals to come in saying that it is O.K. to pay the vendor. The purchasing system puts receiving on the alert that payments will eventually have to be made with the incurred obligations file prepared in step 5.3 of Figure 9-10. That file triggers the payables process in Figure 9-13. Records are added to the accounts payable file in step 7.1. Considerable time then might elapse before the items are actually received.

Most firms require two things to happen before a vendor payment is issued. First, the items must be received. That notification comes in step 7.2 in the form

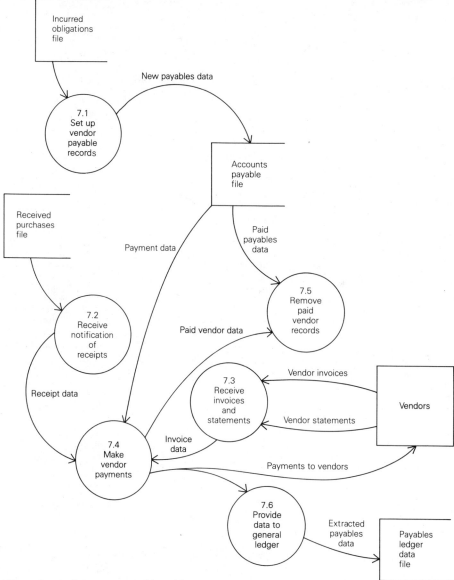

Figure 9-13 Accounts payable system.

of the received purchases file. Second, the vendor's invoice must be received. That action occurs in step 7.3. You notice that *both* step 7.2 and step 7.3 must be performed before the vendor payment is issued in step 7.4. As we mentioned earlier, some firms delay payment and also receive statements from the vendor. Also notice that data from the accounts payable file is used in making the payment. This data includes vendor number, the firm's purchase order number, date, and amount.

When a vendor payment is made, the corresponding record is removed from the accounts payable file as shown in step 7.5. Therefore, the accounts payable file is another inventory-type file (such as the order log and the accounts receivable file) that is added to and taken from.

The final responsibility of the accounts payable system is to provide data to the general ledger system in step 7.6. The data includes payments made to vendors during the month, plus unpaid payables from the accounts payable file. The data is used by the general ledger system to show, among other things, liabilities on the balance sheet.

General ledger

The general ledger system brings together the financial data describing the firm's activities. The system consists of the general ledger file that is composed of the individual accounts such as cash, accounts receivable, reserve for depreciation, and so forth. These accounts are maintained by making double-entry postings in the form of debits and credits.

As Figure 9-14 shows, the general ledger system is very simple in terms of what it does. It only does two things—maintains the general ledger (step 8.1), and prepares reports using the file data (step 8.2).

Three of the inputs to step 8.1 are familiar to us. They are generated by other systems in the distribution system. All systems do not generate inputs. The only ones generating inputs are those that have an effect on the general ledger accounts. In the distribution system, those systems are inventory, accounts receivable, and accounts payable. We recognized earlier that the payroll system also affects the general ledger. In step 8.1, the general ledger file is maintained by posting the transactions to it.

Reports are prepared on a cycle basis—usually monthly, quarterly, and annually. The reports include the "bread and butter" accounting reports such as the income statement and balance sheet. Budget reports can be prepared by integrating data from the general ledger (showing actual activity) with data from a budget file (showing budgeted, or planned, activity). A wide variety of other reports can be prepared from the general ledger data, depending on the managers' needs. The reports are directed to the third environmental element—management.

Most of the data presented in corporations' annual reports comes from the general ledger system. The data is displayed in both tabular and graphic form. Figure 9-15 contains two such displays of general ledger data from an annual report.

Processing Alternatives

You should be aware that the way the distribution system is described here is only *one* of many approaches. Also be aware that we have not shown all of the processes that are necessary. For example, we have not included *exception routines*—things that you do when something out of the ordinary happens. A good example is the billing system. The customer file is needed to supply the customer name and address. What happens when there is no record in the file for the customer identified on the order? Exceptions such as this must be addressed and described by lower-level DFDs. Also we have not included many processes that would only distract you from the main procedure flow. Such a process is the removal of an

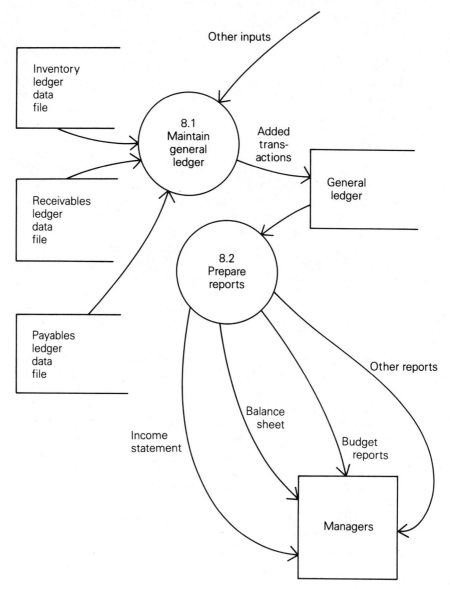

Figure 9-14 General ledger system.

order record from the rejected orders file when the reason for the rejection has been corrected.

System logic

As the systems analyst and managers design a new system, they are presented with many alternatives relating to the logical design. For example, in the order entry system, do we use a special customer credit file in making the credit check

*Millions Except Per Share Amounts

Consolidated Results	1985*	1984*	Percent Change
Net sales and operating revenues	$14,890	$14,449	+3%
Net income	631	716	−12
Preferred and preference stock dividends	61	62	−2
Net income to common stock	570	654	−13
Earnings per average share of common stock	4.01	4.75	−16
Average number of common shares outstanding	142	138	+3
Cash dividends per share of common stock	2.83	2.74	+3
Capital expenditures	1,748	1,609	+9
Total assets	18,205	17,994	+1
Return on average common stockholders' equity	9.5%	11.6%	−18

a. Tabular presentation

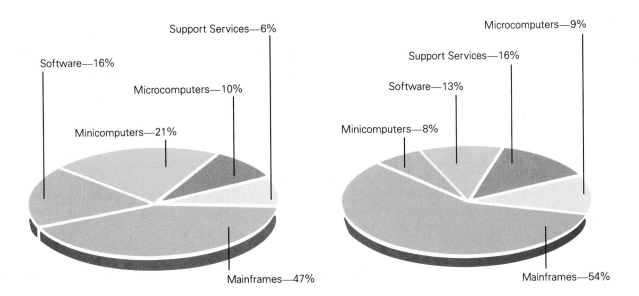

Average Net Assets Employed By Segment

Support Services—6%
Software—16%
Microcomputers—10%
Minicomputers—21%
Mainframes—47%

Capital Expenditures By Segment

Microcomputers—9%
Support Services—16%
Software—13%
Minicomputers—8%
Mainframes—54%

b. Graphic presentation

Figure 9-15 Annual report data from the general ledger.

in step 1.2, or do we use two files—the customer master file containing a credit limit, and the accounts receivable file? Within that same system, do we delete filled order records from the order log, or do we mark them as being filled? These examples give you an idea of the many choices of system logic. The systems analyst is skilled in evaluating these alternatives and recommending a design that most efficiently meets the firm's needs.

Technology

The DFDs provide no clue as to the technology used to perform the processes. The symbols are generic; they can describe manual, keydriven, or computer systems. The DFD is a good starting point in analyzing and designing systems. You can adapt the DFD to various technologies. For example, if a firm has DFDs describing their keydriven system, the same DFDs can provide the basis for a system incorporating a microcomputer. The DFDs show *logical*, not *physical*, design.

Batch versus online

Another option facing the system designers, in addition to the technology, deals with the choice of batch or online processing.

Most of the DFDs used here to describe the distribution system encourage batch processing. This effect is achieved by using files to communicate from one subsystem to the next. The top-level DFD in Figure 9-3 includes no files. Therefore, it *could* describe an online system. In such a system, *all* of the activities relating to one transaction would be handled before processing the next transaction. As an example, everything concerning a single sales order, from input editing to updating the receivables and general ledger files, would be performed before handling the next order. It is as if the DFD arrows and circles formed some type of electrical circuit, transmitting the current throughout all connected paths.

We have not described such an online system here. Rather, we have described a batch system. The second-level DFDs break up the "electrical circuit" into shorter segments by inserting files between the systems. One system communicates with another through the files, not directly. See the manner in which the order entry system in Figure 9-4 is connected to the inventory system in Figure 9-6. The connection is made with the accepted orders file. The same technique is used throughout.

The connections *within* each system make possible online processing. In the order entry system, for example, a data entry operator could key order data into the computer from a terminal as the data is being received over the telephone. The computer could edit the data as it is entered, check the customer's credit, log in the order, and write the data to either the accepted or rejected orders files.

It would be an easy task to convert the batch-oriented second-level DFDs to an online design by eliminating the connecting files. Of course, this assumes that secondary storage is DASD, not sequential.

The Data Base

The DFDs show the flow of the data through the system and show the files where certain data is retained.

The part of the data processing system that is of most value to the MIS is the data base. In our example, the data base consists of all of the data stores. These stores contain the conceptual representation of the physical system of the firm. The accuracy of the stores depends on the processes providing the data—how effectively they weed out errors, and how quickly they react to the physical system.

Table 9-1 lists the 24 files included in the system. There are two types of files—*master files* that are kept current by making additions and deletions, and *intermediate files* that connect the various systems. There are 11 master files and

Table 9-1 Distribution system files

Subsystem	File[1]	Type[2]
Order entry	Customer credit	M
	Rejected orders	M
	Order log	M
	Accepted orders	I
Inventory	Inventory	M
	Backorder	M
	Purchasing	I
	Filled items	I
	Inventory ledger data	I
Billing	Customer	M
	Billed orders	I
	Order log removals	I
Accounts receivable	Accounts receivable	M
	Receivables ledger data	I
Purchasing	Vendor	M
	Purchased items	I
	Incurred obligations	I
	Outstanding purchase orders	M
Receiving	Received items	I
	Filled purchase orders	I
	Received purchases	I
Accounts payable	Accounts payable	M
	Payables ledger data	I
General ledger	General ledger	M

[1] *Intermediate files are listed under system producing them.*

[2] *M = master file; I = intermediate file*

13 intermediate files. The intermediate files could be eliminated if the design were online.

Data documentation

We need to supplement the DFDs with additional documentation providing details about the data. We must be able to identify the record structures within files and the data elements within each record.

These data descriptions are contained in the data dictionary. Appendix C explains a set of three forms that describe files, records, and elements.[5]

DATA STORE DICTIONARY ENTRY

Use: To describe each data store, or file, on a data flow diagram.

DATA STORE NAME: Order log

DESCRIPTION: The record of all accepted sales orders. Used as a "tickler" file to follow up on orders. Each day the log is reviewed to determine if an order is taking too long being filled

DATA STRUCTURES: Order log record

VOLUME: 100–180 additions per day; like number of deletions

ACCESS: No restrictions

Figure 9-16 A data store dictionary entry.

---

[5]This set of forms is based largely on the system described by James Senn, *Analysis and Design of Information Systems* (New York: McGraw-Hill, 1984) pp. 125–134.

Figure 9-16 illustrates how the *data store dictionary entry* describes each data store, or file. The sample form describes the order log file from the order entry system. The log is briefly described, and the structures contained within it are identified. The log includes only a single data structure, or record—the order log record. The volume figures give some indication of the size and activity of the log. The access restrictions, if any, are specified at the bottom.

If we were describing the files of the distribution system with data store dictionary entries, we would need 24 forms—one for each file. The form describes both master and intermediate files.

The records within files can be specified with a *data structure dictionary entry*, such as that pictured in Figure 9-17. This sample describes the inventory record contained in the inventory file. Each data element in the record is listed in the "contents" area. The volume area indicates the size of the file in numbers of records.

DATA STRUCTURE DICTIONARY ENTRY

Use: To describe a formal data structure, such as a record or document.

STRUCTURE NAME: Inventory record

DESCRIPTION: A record of each item maintained in inventory

CONTENTS:
Item number
Inventory class
Item description
Warehouse location
Unit price
Unit of issue (each, pair, etc.)
Balance on hand
Reorder point
Economic order quantity
Quantity on order
Quantity backordered
Quantity available
Previous vendor
Previous price

VOLUME: 25,000 records; 35 percent active each month

Figure 9-17 A data structure dictionary entry.

We would need a data structure form for each structure or record in the system. The DFD does not specify how many structures are within each file. That information is listed on the data store form. If each file in the system contained the minimum of one structure, we would need 24 data structure forms.

The listing of data elements on the data structure form tells nothing about the data. That detail is contained on a *data element dictionary entry*. One appears in Figure 9-18. The data type can be numeric, alphabetic, or *alphanumeric—* mixed alphabetic and numeric. The length is the number of bytes or positions. Aliases are additional names used to describe the same element. Some examples

---

DATA ELEMENT DICTIONARY ENTRY

Use: To describe each data element contained within a data structure, data flow, and data store.

ELEMENT NAME: Warehouse location

DESCRIPTION: A code that identifies where the ordered merchandise is located in the warehouse. The code is printed on the picking ticket copy of the invoice.

TYPE: Numeric

LENGTH: 5 positions

ALIASES: Storage location

VALUE RANGE:

TYPICAL VALUE: 12083

LIST OF SPECIFIC VALUES (IF ANY):

OTHER EDITING DETAILS: The first two digits identify the aisle, and can range from 01 to 18. The next two digits identify the position on the aisle, and can range from 01 to 30. The units position identifies the shelf, and can range from 1 to 8.

Figure 9-18   A data element dictionary entry.

are often provided of data values, and editing details explain what to look for when checking for errors.

One data element form is needed for each data element used in the system. You only need one form per element even though that element appears several times in the system. The DFDs do not show how many elements are involved. We could get that information from the data structure forms.

The data dictionary and the forms described above enable the firm to manage its data resources.

The "snowball" effect

You know how a snowball gets bigger as you roll it through the snow. We have the same effect in a business system in terms of data accumulation. It is important that you understand this snowballing effect.

We have seen that many data elements are involved, but most of them are maintained by the system. It is not necessary to enter all of the elements for each transaction. We only enter *skeleton data*—the bare bones data needed to describe the transaction.

The distribution system is triggered by the receipt of a sales order in step 1.1 of Figure 9-4. We have to enter the following skeleton data to describe the order— *who* is ordering *how much* of *what*.

Customer number

Customer order number

Item number of each item ordered

Quantity of each item ordered

In addition, in order to compute the credit check in step 1.2, the total dollar amount of the order must be entered. This total is used only for the credit check; the billing system computes the invoice total.

The data entry portion of any system is an *input bottleneck*—processing occurs only as fast as the operator can press the keys. OCR and MICR are intended to ease this bottleneck, but they cannot be used for all input.

The snowballing effect occurs as we pick up data elements along the way that we will need to perform all of the system functions. We recognized this need earlier. In the inventory system, we pick up data elements describing the items ordered, and in the billing system, we pick up elements describing the customer. These added elements are carried through the system by the data flows. Table 9-2 shows how the sizes of the records increase as the system flow progresses.

Adding Information Output

We saw in Chapter 1 that the period preceding MIS is called the *data processing era*. Punched card and keydriven systems were used primarily for data processing, as were early computers. The term EDP (electronic data processing) described how early computers were used.

Table 9-2   The Snowballing Effect of Data Flow

| | Data flow | | |
Data element	Sales orders[1]	Filled orders[2]	Invoice data[3]
Customer number	X	X	X
Customer order number	X	X	X
Item number	X	X	X
Quantity ordered	X	X	X
Price		X	X
Item description		X	X
Warehouse location		X	X
Quantity filled		X	X
Quantity backordered		X	X
Customer name			X
Customer address			X
Salesperson number			X
Tax class			X
Shipping instructions			X

1—"Sales orders" data flow in Figure 9-4.
2—"Filled items" data store in Figure 9-6.
3—"Invoice data" data flow in Figure 9-8.

The data processing era has been criticized for *not* providing management information. This is not really true. The systems could, and did, provide information. In some cases, the information output was an absolute necessity—as with the income statement and balance sheet. In other cases, the information was what the systems analysts *thought* the managers wanted. The managers seldom participated in the design of the systems. The systems analysts could see that certain information output was possible, and incorporated these outputs into the design as a type of bonus extra. The term *automatic byproduct* was used to describe how the systems could produce information from data used by the data processing routines.

We can cite two places in the distribution system where such reports can be produced with little extra effort. The first place is the billing system. At this point in the processing, the invoice data includes everything describing the transaction. If we record that detailed data on a sales analysis file, as shown in Figure 9-19, then we can use the file to prepare reports for marketing management.

Figure 9-20 shows how the sales analysis file is sorted into different sequences to prepare reports analyzing sales by customer, by item, and by salesperson.

Another place where information output is possible is in the accounts receivable system. Here, we do not have to revise the processes; we only use the data already available. We can scan the accounts receivable file and prepare a special report for the firm's credit manager showing the status of each receivable. The report is the *aged accounts receivable report* shown in Figure 9-21. Since the

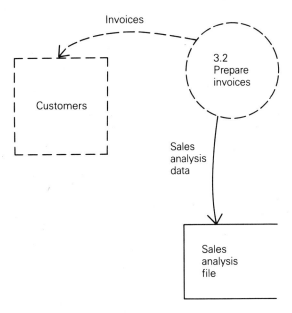

Figure 9-19 An added sales analysis file.

accounts receivable file identifies the billing date for each receivable, the information processor can identify (using the columns "30–60 days," and so on) the age of each receivable.

There is an important point to keep in mind regarding the addition of information output to a data processing system. The *manager* should determine what information she or he needs. The decision should not be made by an information specialist.

Packaged Data Processing Software

There are many prewritten software packages available to perform the data processing routines that we have described—and more. Most of the packages are written for micros (primarily the IBM PC and its "compatibles"). But there is much minicomputer and mainframe software as well. Most of the software is very general in nature, such as those systems we have described. But there is variety—some packages tailored to unique needs of banking, insurance, manufacturing, and other industries.

Microcomputer packages

The microcomputer market has received most of the attention during the past few years as software companies seek to profit from the micro boom. Most of the initial data processing packages were *standalone*, but more and more are integrated. The packages are designed so that the user will have to do no programming. The systems are intended to be used in a *turnkey* fashion—just turn

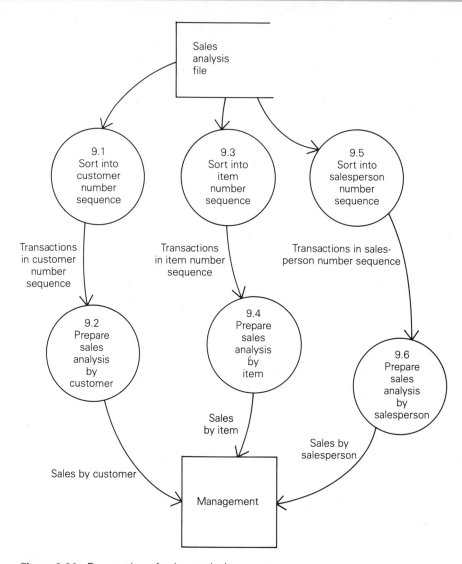

Figure 9-20 Preparation of sales analysis reports.

on the system. But in most cases, the packages are rather sophisticated and require considerable time and effort to implement. Some excellent educational tools have been produced to make the work as easy as possible.

IBM's initial strategy for the PC was to encourage other firms to produce the software. For a while IBM only marketed data processing packages from Peachtree and BPI. In 1984 IBM announced that it was getting into the PC software business, and its packages are now on the market. The group of packages includes order entry (which incorporates billing), payroll, accounts receivable, accounts payable, and general ledger. The packages can be used in an integrated fashion, or separately.

```
-----------------------------------------------------------------------
FOR WEEK OF 01/04/86                                          PAGE 3

CUSTOMER        CUSTOMER        CURRENT   30-60   60-90   OVER 90  BALANCE
 NUMBER          NAME                     DAYS    DAYS    DAYS
-----------------------------------------------------------------------
512-12-4    KELLY & MARLEY INC  1,003.10   20.26                   1,023.36
514-21-5    KENNEDY ELECTRIC      181.34                             181.34
524-72-7    KENYON MACHINERY      443.10                             443.10
532-04-4    KEPNER DANA CO                 153.26  114.14    1.12    268.52
542-33-8    KERITE CO             367.94   101.74                    469.68
545-74-9    KEYMAN ASSOCIATES                                .71        .71
550-81-7    KIMBULIANS             24.12   122.81                    146.93
554-30-7    KIRSH CO               26.30                              26.30
559-43-9    KOEBEL & CO                     49.42                      49.42
562-47-7    KOPECKY & CO           31.29   192.52                    223.81
571-63-7    KUNKLE INC            217.82                             217.82
582-96-9    LANDE MFG CO          106.95                             106.95
583-41-2    LANGE CO                       869.40                    869.40
586-54-1    LARRABEE INC          196.35                             196.35
593-55-2    LAURIENTI MFG CO       21.93     1.94                     23.87
602-40-1    LEBEN DRILLING INC      1.10   476.93  174.96           652.39
607-72-6    LEEMONT INC            35.87    35.95                     71.82
-----------------------------------------------------------------------
```

Figure 9-21 An aged accounts receivable report.

The accounts receivable system provides a good idea of how the systems work. The receivables system accepts input data directly from the order entry system or through the keyboard. Output data can be entered directly into the general ledger system. The system is set up to handle the irregularities of the real world—partial payments and overpayments of invoice amounts, and optional late charges. It prepares statements, such as the one pictured in Figure 9-22. It also prepares an aged accounts receivable report as illustrated in Figure 9-23. If a manager only wants the totals for the periods, a one-line summary can be printed. The user is limited to one current and four past-due periods.

Two other major micro manufacturers, Apple and Tandy, follow opposing strategies. Apple relies entirely on software firms such as BPI, Red Wing, State of the Art, and Great Plains Software. Tandy, on the other hand, offers software prepared by its own staff, augmented by that from software firms such as MAI/Basic Four. The MAI/Basic Four integrated package for the Tandy 2000 is illustrated in Figure 9-24. The packages are integrated as shown by the arrows. The financial statements system enables the user to prepare reports from general ledger data. The user can specify the format of reports that show summary activity and the net change from the previous period.

Minicomputer packages

The computer manufacturers who have been the most successful in marketing minis for business applications are IBM, Digital Equipment Corporation (DEC),

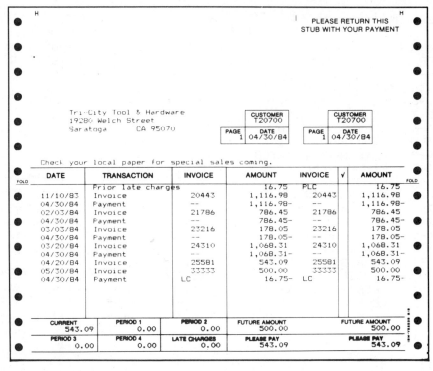

Figure 9-22   A statement printed by the IBM Business Management Series
accounts receivable system for the IBM PC.

and Data General. Therefore, most of the data processing software supports those
brands of computers.

Microscan SBC Corporation offers a data processing package designed especially for wholesalers using the IBM System/38. The package handles order
processing, inventory control, billing, accounts receivable, purchasing, accounts
payable, and general ledger.

MCBA, Inc. markets an accounting system for DEC PDP/11 and VAX systems
that performs a mixture of jobs, including payroll. MCBA claims 15,000 package
users. The package will run on systems other than DEC as well.

Mainframe packages

Most of the mainframe software is written to support IBM's line—System 360/
370, 303X, 308X, and 43XX systems. Firms catering to this market include MSA,
Walker Interactive Products, Data Design Associates, and McCormack & Dodge.

Since mainframe users have their own programming staffs, why would they
buy packaged software? There are several reasons. The staff is probably overworked and has a big backlog of waiting jobs. Or, perhaps there is not enough
time to create the system from scratch. Also, packages might exist that do the job
better than programs that the firm's programmers could produce.

A good example of how a mainframe user can benefit from packaged data
processing software is Crane Carrier Co. of Tulsa. They have an IBM 4341 installed,

```
Your Company Name                        Accounts Receivable                                Date 04/30/84   Page   7
00                          Ledger detail customer number                                  Time 15:55:54          AR50
                                          All customers
                                          All accounts balances
                                          All age period balances
                                          Change aging dates? N

Totals for accounts selected-

    Previous balance      17,968.33
    Current charges        8,386.76
    Current payments      15,962.54-
    Current adjustments       92.52-

                            Current*        Period 1      Period 2      Period 3      Period 4
                            04/30/84        03/31/84      02/29/84      01/31/84      12/31/83

    Amount due            10,300.03         1,571.06       314.79        143.37       1,429.48

    Future                 1,829.58

    Total account balance 12,129.61

                            *Current includes total late charges of          22.50
```

Figure 9-23 A summary aged accounts receivable report produced by the IBM accounts receivable system.

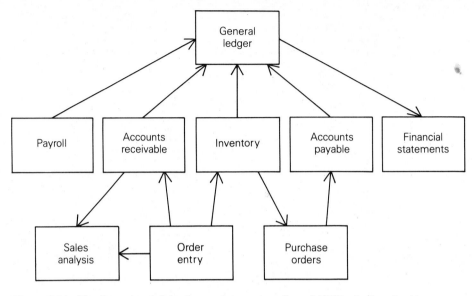

Figure 9-24 The integrated data processing system from MAI/Basic Four for the
Tandy 2000.

and it runs prewritten packages obtained from MSA. The payroll package handles
five separate payrolls for the 1,000 employees. The big advantage of the MSA
package is that it takes only two-and-a-half days to complete the payroll compared
to four days for the old system. The MSA package includes a report generator
that produces special payroll reports without the need for programming. MSA
also keeps Crane updated on changes to the software, such as changes in tax
tables. MSA will either send a listing of the changes to be made to the software
if 50 or less lines of code are required, or send a new program tape.

Putting Data Processing in Perspective

The data processing system is an integral part of the MIS. It could be considered
the foundation upon which the MIS is built. The data processing system must
exist before effective decision support systems can be achieved.

The other two components of the MIS—office automation and DSS—are
optional. A firm can take them or leave them. But the firm has no choice concerning data processing; it must be done. Data is processed so that the firm's
products and services can be delivered to its customers, so that it might acquire
needed raw materials, and so that it can pay its employees. As these tasks are
performed, a valuable data base is created. When the data processing system
handles the transactions quickly and accurately, the data base is a mirror image
of the firm that it represents. The data base provides the input to periodic reports,
makes itself available for manager queries, and forms the basis for future projections made by mathematical models.

The data processing system and its data base have been around for years, but previously they produced little management information. What is so different today compared to 20 or even 10 years ago? Two primary things. One, the data in the data base is much more accessible. Physical constraints have been all but eliminated with the logical structures of the DBMS. The data can be retrieved by a manager using query languages, and perhaps a data communications network. The technology is much improved today. The second point of difference is the manager. He or she is much more knowledgeable concerning the use of the computer. Each year's crop of new managers brings with it more computer expertise than the last. Many older managers have also learned how to use the computer as a tool. Today's managers know how to use the data resource, and the technology enables them to do it.

Summary

Data processing differs from both office automation and DSS mainly in relation to output. Data processing systems do not have information output as an objective, although it can easily be added. Data processing systems have been around for years—first manual systems, then mechanical, electromechanical, and now electronic. But the technology has had little effect. Processes have remained basically unchanged.

All firms distribute something, products or services, to meet the needs of their customers. Firms are arranged in a distribution channel that begins with the manufacturer and ends with the consumer. All firms within the channel, both product- and service-oriented, have the same basic flows of materials, data, and information. The similarity in data flows enables a general type of data processing system to fit most firms.

The network of data processing subsystems in a distribution firm is called a distribution system. It consists of eight integrated subsystems—order entry, inventory, billing, accounts receivable, purchasing, receiving, accounts payable and general ledger. When files are used to pass data from one subsystem to another, the system processes data in batches. Data can be processed online by removing the intermediate files, assuming that a type of direct access secondary storage is present. Most of the processing is triggered by an event, such as receipt of a sales order or reaching of a reorder point. Some processing, however, is triggered by a time schedule, such as end-of-the-month financial reporting.

The designers of data processing systems include systems analysts and users. These persons are presented with many alternatives as they assemble the system parts. The designers must have a good understanding of both processing needs and factors contributing to system efficiency as they consider the alternatives.

Data flow diagrams (DFDs) are one technique for documenting processes such as the data processing system. Data dictionary forms are one way to describe the data. The dictionary forms describe data in a hierarchy—from stores (files) to structures to elements.

Since data entry is slow compared to the speeds of the computer, and operator expense is high, every effort is made to minimize the amount of data entered from the keyboard. Skeleton input data is used to retrieve additional data from master files.

Information output can be added to the data processing system by using existing data in the data base or by adding extra processes. The data base represents a valuable resource, and the potential for information output is limited primarily by the ingenuity of the manager.

Prewritten data processing software exists for all computer sizes. Most micro packages support the IBM PC and its compatibles, but Apple and Tandy computers have impressive libraries as well. Most mini packages support DEC as well as IBM computers, and most mainframe packages support the IBM line. Other computer manufacturers' products are supported to a lesser degree.

The ability of the data processing system to support management decision making is much improved today over ten years ago. There are two reasons. First, DBMSs make the data base more readily accessible. Second, the users are more knowledgeable about computers.

The data processing system is the foundation upon which an MIS is built. In the next two chapters, we build the rest of the MIS by adding office automation and decision support systems.

Key Terms

data processing system	receiving system
accounting system	accounts payable system
mechanical, electromechanical device	general ledger system
product-oriented firm	structured documentation
distribution channel	data store
service-oriented firm	open order
distribution system	balance on hand
context diagram	order quantity
invoice	backorder
statement	reorder point
sales order	stockout
purchase order	invoice
data flow diagram (DFD)	line item, line item extension
order entry system	current, past-due receivable
inventory system	outstanding invoice
billing system	buyer
accounts receivable system	exception routine
purchasing system	data store dictionary entry

data structure dictionary entry

data element dictionary entry

alphanumeric

skeleton data

input bottleneck

data processing era

automatic byproduct

aged accounts receivable report

standalone package

turnkey system

Key Concepts

How data processing differs from both office automation and decision support systems in terms of its output

The relative immunity of accounting procedures to changes in data processing technology

The importance of data and information to members of the distribution channel

The similarity between product- and service-oriented firms in terms of their data and information flows

How the data processing system supports the office automation and decision support systems by providing a data base

Levels of data flow diagrams

How the subsystems of the distribution system are linked by data flows

The two separate networks within the distribution system—one for filling orders and the other for purchasing replenishment stock

How subsystem processes are triggered—either by a transaction such as a receipt of ordered stock, or a time period such as the end of the month

The many different alternatives confronting the designer of a distribution system

How a batch system can be converted to an online system by eliminating intermediate files

Different data dictionary forms for different levels of data organization

The snowball effect of picking up needed data while proceeding through the system

How information outputs can be added to the data processing system with little or no modification to the processes

The manner in which the bulk of prewritten software has been targeted for the most popular micros, minis, and mainframes

Questions

1. Does a data processing system produce information? Explain.

2. What effect has the introduction of the computer had on the performance of standard accounting functions?

3. Is a hospital a product- or service-oriented firm? What position does it occupy in the distribution channel?

4. What is used to integrate the subsystems of the distribution system? What effect does the form of integration have on whether data is processed in batches or online?

5. Could the order entry system be online and the rest of the systems be batch? Explain.

6. What data flow diagram symbols are used to indicate (a) an environmental element, (b) a data flow, (c) a data store, (d) a process?

7. What is the highest-level DFD called? The next-highest level? Are data stores included on these levels?

8. What is meant by "skeleton" input data?

9. How is the order log like an inventory file?

10. What triggers the purchasing system?

11. What is the difference between a backorder and a stockout? Could you have both at the same time?

12. What is the difference between an invoice and a statement? Which one is given to you by a department store clerk? A gas station attendant? A supermarket checker?

13. Which subsystems of the distribution system interface with environmental elements?

14. Which processes in the distribution system are triggered by a monthly cycle (end of the month)?

15. How can the computer support the buyer?

16. Why would a terminal in the receiving area be a good idea?

17. What two things must happen before a firm pays its bills?

18. How many data element dictionary entry forms would be needed to document the "sales orders" arrow in Figure 9-4? What are the elements?

19. Who would be interested in an aged accounts receivables report?

20. Which part of the data processing system is the most valuable to decision support?

Problems

1. Draw a second-level DFD to show the processes contained in process 2.1— Check the balance on hand, in Figure 9-6.

2. Complete a data store dictionary entry for the backorder file. Make reasonable assumptions about entries that you need. Your instructor will provide you with a blank form for this and the next two problems.

3. Complete a data structure dictionary entry for the data flow labeled "Sales orders" in the order entry system.

4. Complete a data element dictionary entry for the data element named "Reorder point."

Computer City is the largest computer store in Moorhead, Minnesota. One day the door opens and a well-dressed woman walks in and begins to walk around the showroom, looking at the computers. The salesclerk, a young man who looks like he might be a college student, walks up and says, "May I help you?"

The customer says, "I'm Freida Turnbull. I'm the administrator at Community Hospital, and I am interested in some software."

The young man responds to the word "software" like a cat to the sound of a can opener and replies, "Excellent. I'm Burt Wilson. What do you have in mind?"

"Well, I have been hearing a lot about management information systems lately, and I think that we could use one. We have a Compaq computer (an IBM PC compatible) and can't get any information from it. Do you have any hospital packages?"

"No," Burt answers, "We certainly don't. We just handle standard packages such as inventory, payroll, and so on."

"Oh, I see," says Freida. "We have inventory and payroll systems, but they aren't on the Compaq. We still handle them with our manual accounting system."

Burt asks, "What do you use the Compaq for?"

"We're using it in the typing pool for word processing. We want to use it for other things but just never got around to it."

"Is your accounting system very good?" Burt probes.

"Not really. Our CPA does it, but he says that it's hard to get the books to balance. Seems like we have too many errors."

"Like what?"

"Well, we don't always post all of the transactions. You know, somebody pays their bill, and we don't take it out of the accounts receivable file. We keep on sending statements. Very embarrassing."

"I can understand that," Burt says as he gets a small box off of the shelf. "I assume that you have heard of Lotus 1-2-3. Everybody has heard of Lotus. It's an excellent spreadsheet package that gives you a graphic capability, plus a little file management. Are you using Lotus?"

"No, but I've heard of it. It sounds like it would help since we need more management information. The graphs would be nice. But where does the data come from that it uses?"

"Oh, your data base. You do have a data base at the hospital, don't you?"

Freida answers, "Naturally, but most of it is manual. Just how do you think we could use Lotus?"

"It's excellent for spreadsheets. You can prepare income statements and balance sheets, and all kinds of financial reports on it."

"But those reports require accounting data, and we don't have that on the computer yet. Would that be a problem?"

"I don't think so. You could just key the data in directly from your manual accounting records."

"Well, we can give it a try," Freida says as she reaches in her purse for her checkbook. "We have a little money left in our budget for the year, and I guess that this would be a good way to use it. How much should I make the check out for?"

Questions

1. Is Burt a good salesclerk? Explain your answer.
2. Is Freida computer literate? MIS literate? Give your reasons.
3. What are some of the problems that Freida is likely to encounter as the hospital begins to use Lotus?
4. What does the hospital need? Make a list of actions that the hospital should take to provide better information for the managers. List the actions in the order that they should occur. Keep your list to about 6–10 items. Include "Obtain Lotus for use in producing management information" on your list.

Selected Bibliography

Data Processing Systems

"Applications Package Halves Processing Time for Truck Firm's Five-Part Payroll System," *Computerworld* (January 28, 1985): SR/30-SR/31.

Ceriello, Vincent R., "Computerizing the Personnel Department: Make or Buy?," *Personnel Journal* 63 (September 1984): 44–48.

Cole, Malcolm "A Three Ledger System for the Small Business," *Accountancy* 95 (May 1984): 96ff.

Cole, Malcolm, "Micro Accounting Software for the Small Business," *Accountancy* 95 (September 1984): 154–158.

DeVoney, Chris, *IBM's Personal Computer* (Indianapolis: Que Corporation, 1983), pp. 224–239.

Eliason, Alan L., and Kent D. Kitts, *Business Computer Systems and Applications* (Chicago: Science Research Associates, 1974), pp. 47–218, 267–284, 303–319.

Eliason, Alan L., *Business Information Processing* (Chicago: Science Research Associates, 1980), pp. 232–266.

Eliason, Alan L., *Online Business Computer Applications* (Chicago: Science Research Associates, 1983), pp. 85–481.

Forkner, Irvine, and Raymond McLeod, Jr., *Computerized Business Systems* (New York: John Wiley & Sons, 1973), pp. 421–445.

Kull, David J. "Strictly Software: Ledger Domains," *Computer Decisions* 16 (December 1984): 47ff.

McLeod, Raymond, Jr., and Irvine Forkner, *Computerized Business Information Systems*, 2nd. ed. (New York: John Wiley & Sons, 1982), pp. 453–486.

Post, Dan, "General Ledger's Bottom Line," *Business Computer Systems* 3 (July 1984): 68ff.

Rapp, John, "Reducing the Risks in Installing Packaged General Ledger Software," *CPA Journal* 54 (September 1984): 85–90.

"The Applications Software Survey," *Datamation* 31 (May 1, 1985): 118ff.

Wells, Robert P., Sandra Rochowansky, and Michael F. Mellin, *The Book of IBM Software 1984* (Los Angeles: The Book Company, 1984), pp. 185–223.

Wilkinson, Joseph W., *Accounting and Information Systems* (New York: John Wiley & Sons, 1982), pp. 63–164.

Chapter 10

Office Automation

Learning Objectives

After studying this chapter, you should:

- Recognize that office automation has a potential for improving management decision making as well as increasing productivity of secretarial and clerical workers
- Understand that the dividing line between office automation and the other MIS subsystems is often vague
- Be familiar with basic office functions—what they are and who performs them
- Know which applications comprise office automation, and the major functions of each
- Be familiar with the basic options for performing the applications—hardware, software, and commercially available services
- Understand how office automation contributes to data processing by adding new capabilities, and how it contributes to decision support by communicating information both to and from management
- Be familiar with one way to position office automation applications in the manager's information flow network
- See how both physical and behavioral considerations are important in the success of office automation systems
- Recognize both the potential and the limitations of office automation as a decision support tool

Introduction

Office automation offers a stark contrast to data processing in several respects. The contrast can be seen quite clearly in the amount of space given in the literature to each topic. Very little is being written today about data processing. The reason is that most of the data processing questions have been answered—long ago. Office automation, on the other hand, is just emerging, and there are many questions yet unanswered. Office automation offers great promise in solving some basic problems that have been bothering business for years, and it is getting much attention.

Our task in studying office automation is to synthesize the large volume of material and form a coherent picture of how office automation relates to the MIS.

What Is Office Automation?

Office automation, or *OA,* is the application of electronic and electromechanical devices to office procedures with the purpose of increasing productivity. The increased productivity is realized by improving the communication of information both within the office and between the office and its environment. Improved communications can benefit the manager by providing better information for decision making.

There are two views of office automation. One, the initial view that triggered the interest in the movement, is concerned primarily with increasing the productivity of clerical and secretarial workers. Any contribution to management productivity is essentially limited to the office manager level. This view was prompted by the historically low investment in office systems. During the 1970s, for example, the capital investment per office worker was $2,000–4,000, whereas the investment per manufacturing worker was approximately $25,000. During this same period, office productivity increased only 4 percent, and manufacturing productivity rose by 85–90 percent.[1]

The second view, which is just now emerging, includes an increase in management productivity in addition to clerical and secretarial productivity. The management productivity can occur on any level—from the departmental supervisors to the corporate executives. The productivity is reflected in improved decision making. This view is adopted in this book. We recognize the potential value of OA in capturing some of the informal information flows that have eluded the data processing and DSS components of the MIS. Our view recognizes office automation as one of the three MIS subsystems, along with data processing and DSS. In our view, the formal systems that perform the accounting functions of the firm are called *data processing.* The formal and informal systems that have the primary purpose of producing management information are called *decision support.* The formal and informal systems that are concerned with communication of information to and from persons in the firm are named *office automation.*

The line separating these MIS subsystems is often not distinct. For example, when a manager asks a secretary to retrieve a document from the files for use in decision making, is it OA or DSS? If the document is a computer report designed for decision support, it is probably DSS. If, on the other hand, the document is

---

[1] Nancy B. Finn, *The Electronic Office* (Englewood Cliffs, NJ: Prentice-Hall, 1983), pp. 8–9.

not intended for use by management in decision making, such as a correspondence file, then the application should be considered OA. This fuzzy dividing line between OA and data processing and DSS is likely to get even fuzzier as OA capabilities increase.

What Is an Office?

As we begin our study of office automation, a good place to start is the office itself. The office can be a paneled board room, a large open area where many personnel of all kinds have their desks, or a cubbyhole in the warehouse where the clerks keep their relatively primitive records. The *office* is the place where the management and administrative activities of a firm are performed. The office houses the components that comprise the conceptual system of the firm—the people, the equipment, the furniture, and the supplies.

Office functions

What work is performed in an office? The varied activities fall within three categories: storage, manipulation, and communication.

Storage Office workers must create and maintain some of the files that are the conceptual representations of the physical system. This activity includes capturing data by making entries on paper forms, preparing the forms for storage by adding and arranging data elements in an acceptable format, and entering the data into a storage unit such as a file cabinet. The maintenance activity that keeps the files current and the retrieval of the data when it is needed are also considered part of the storage activity.

Manipulation When data is retrieved from storage, there is usually some need to perform operations that convert the data into a usable form. Perhaps totals are accumulated, descriptions are added, computations are made, and so on.

Communication Much information is communicated in offices. It is estimated that office workers spend up to 46 percent of their time in meetings and on the telephone.[2] Very often special conference rooms are set aside to facilitate communication.

Figure 10-1 illustrates how the three basic office functions can be linked. Sometimes information can be communicated without the need for storage or manipulation. In some cases, storage is required but not manipulation, and vice versa. In one pattern, all three functions are linked. You will note that communication is always included as the last function. There is no reason to store or manipulate data and information unless they are communicated.

---

[2] Elisabeth Horwitt, "Confronting the Communications Quandry," *Business Computer Systems* 3 (September 1984): 40.

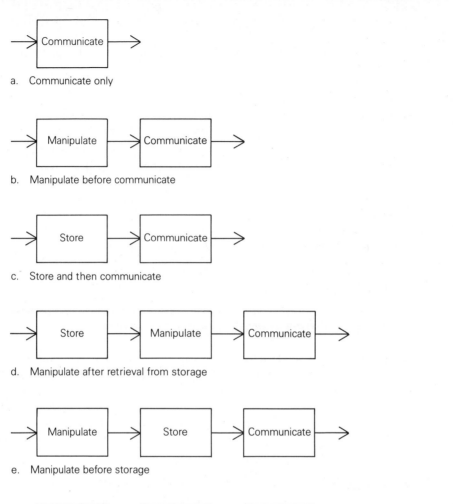

a. Communicate only

b. Manipulate before communicate

c. Store and then communicate

d. Manipulate after retrieval from storage

e. Manipulate before storage

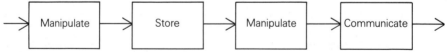

f. Manipulation both before and after storage

Figure 10-1 Office functions.

Office workers

Who works in offices? We can identify four categories of personnel: professionals, managers, secretaries, and clerical employees.

The *professionals* include persons such as buyers in the purchasing department and salespersons in the marketing department who perform key jobs that directly relate to the activity of the firm. Also included in this category are managers' assistants who perform a variety of duties ranging from conducting sophisticated quantitative analyses to handling travel arrangements. The factor distinguishing these persons from *managers* is that the professionals do not manage other persons. The term *knowledge worker* is often used to describe both professionals and managers.

   Secretaries are usually assigned to provide the administrative support to one or more managers. The work responsibilities of secretaries are varied, including typing, filing, answering the telephone, maintaining an appointments calendar, and so on.

   Clerical employees are not usually assigned to particular managers; they support the entire office. Duties consist mainly of typing and filing. In a small office, one person may perform the duties of professional, secretary, and clerk.

The electronic office

The term *electronic office* is frequently used to describe an office where office automation has been applied. The implication is that some of the functions are performed electronically. Other terms are *office of the future*, first coined about 1978, and *paperless office*. There are no standard definitions of these terms. The term electronic office is often used to mean office automation, whereas the term office of the future implies a combination of technology not yet available or widely adopted. The term paperless office implies that all paper documents have been replaced by electronic media. While this objective is possible, it is not an immediate goal of office automation.

Office Automation Applications

In this section, each of the OA applications is explained. There are ten of them. Specific examples of hardware, software, and commercially available services are given where applicable.

Word processing

Word processing can be defined as the use of a keydriven device with an electronic storage capability for the preparation of printed documents. The device, called a *word processor*, performs a variety of functions—some automatically.

   Just exactly what functions are included in word processing? Changes can be made easily by viewing the document on the CRT and inserting, deleting, and moving characters, words, and even whole paragraphs. You can rearrange the sequence of paragraphs and even assemble a letter by retrieving previously stored paragraphs. It is easy to make changes to page format—changing the spacing and margins. An advanced feature is called *search and replace* that enables you to scan a document automatically to find each point where a certain word (such as "manager") is used and replace it with another word (such as "executive"). Very often the word processor will have a *spelling checker*, can merge name and address with document files for mass mailings, and automatically build an index (with page numbers) for key words. In short, word processing is excellent for making corrections and handling high-volume typing in a manner that appears to be personalized to the receiver. These capabilities have made word processing the first office automation application to achieve widespread use.

One advantage of word processing is the fact that it lends itself to a wide variety of documents. It is excellent for letters and memos but also can be used for lengthy reports, procedure manuals, price lists, and policy manuals. A second advantage is its ability to facilitate communications between two firms. It is not necessary for both firms to have the same hardware or software to exchange word processing documents. A third appeal of word processing is the fact that it produces a hard copy; many managers prefer the traditional paper document over more modern electronic media.

In Chapter 1 we recognized that word processing can be performed three ways—with a device designed specifically for word processing, with a keyboard terminal connected to a mainframe, and with a micro. All three approaches include the same basic types of components—an operator-controlled keyboard, the word processor or computer, some type of electronic storage, and a printer. These components are pictured in Figure 10-2.

The device designed specifically for word processing has been termed a *standalone word processor*. The Wang Wangwriter pictured in Figure 10-3 is such a standalone system. Since the standalone is intended for word processing only, it performs functions efficiently and easily. Special keys enable the operator to initiate certain functions with only a single keystroke.

In terms of the MIS, the big disadvantage of the standalone is that it is not connected to the corporate data base, making it impossible to retrieve data electronically for inclusion in documents. This data base limitation coupled with stiff competition from micro-based word processing software packages has prompted some authorities to predict that the standalone will shortly become obsolete. While sales are already dropping, there are so many standalones in use that they will be around for quite some time.

The other two approaches to word processing (mainframe terminal and micro) are similar in that general purpose computing equipment is used. The word processing functions are performed by software. The data base is accessible, and

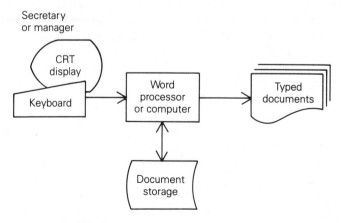

Figure 10-2 Word processing.

Figure 10-3   The Wang Wangwriter.

the equipment can also be used for computing. This approach appeals especially to firms that cannot afford specialized word processor units.

The first micro word processing software package to successfully emulate the standalones was WordStar, released by MicroPro in 1978. Since that date, over one million copies have been sold. WordStar's success triggered many other similar packages—EasyWriter, Volkswriter, Word Perfect, and more. MicroPro has countered this competition by bringing out improved products—WordStar 2000 and WordStar 2000 Plus. The micro area is where most of the word processing action is. At least 50 word processing packages are available for the IBM PC alone.

As we conclude the discussion of word processing, one point must be made clear. It is not necessary that the manager operate the equipment. Many managers do, typing short messages or drafts. But many managers believe typing to be a waste of their time. Even if the secretary does the typing, word processing still contributes to the communication flow by improving the quality of the documents and speeding their preparation.

Electronic Mail

Computer-based word processing has been so successful that other OA applications have sought to extend the scope of the computer beyond data processing. One of the first areas to be exploited was *electronic mail*. The computer and its keyboard terminals were seen as a giant communications network. By utilizing the secondary storage of the computer, and its store-and-forward capability, it became possible to key a message into the terminal keyboard and direct that message to someone else who also has access to a terminal. The message can be entered into storage, and the recipient can retrieve it when he or she wants. A diagram of an electronic mail system appears in Figure 10-4.

Electronic mail is an extension of communications networks established by Western Union before the computer era. First there was TWX and then Telex. Electromechanical keyboard devices called *teletypewriters* or *teleprinters* were used to produce a hardcopy. Many firms still use Telex, and a smaller number still use TWX. When computer manufacturers began promoting the use of remote terminals connected to a central computer in the mid-1960s, *message switching* was billed as an application. The idea of using networked computer terminals for communication has gradually eroded the TWX and Telex market.

When a person sends an electronic message to another person, the message is not immediately transmitted to the receiver but instead is stored in the computer's secondary storage. The storage is segregated into separate areas for each mail user, and the areas are known as *electronic mail boxes*. Users check their electronic mail boxes at times convenient to them by querying the system. The electronic mail software causes a list to be displayed of all the items in a user's mail box. The user selectively retrieves items for review, and the messages are displayed on the screen. The user can retain or delete an item in the mail box. Most systems also enable the user to send a received message to another party—a way to "route" a message through the organization.

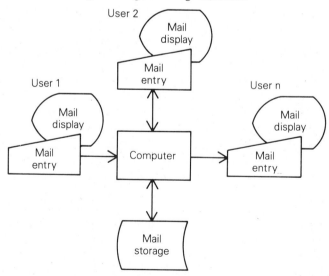

Figure 10-4 Electronic mail.

It is possible to send a message to more than one person, such as to all members of a committee or to all sales region managers. It is also possible to enter messages into the system that *all* users can read, a technique called an *electronic bulletin board*. The bulletin board can be used for news items of general interest.

The acceptance, to date, of electronic mail has been slow, but there are indications that the concept is catching on. Expenditures for electronic mail increased from $80 million in 1983 to $200 million in 1984, and the level is expected to reach $2.1 billion by 1988.[3]

Initially there were no standard protocols for transmitting electronic mail between users of different hardware and software, but now there are two standards. In 1981, IBM modified its system network architecture (SNA) to handle electronic mail, and the modification is called DIA (document interchange architecture). The other standard is from the Consultive Committee for International Telephony and Telegraphy (CCITT), and it is called X.400. Both standards are expected to survive, and there will likely be gateways for communicating between DIA and X.400 systems. The gateways will enable a person whose organization has adopted one standard to send messages to a person whose organization has adopted the other standard. The standards and the gateways should stimulate the use of electronic mail by persons in different organizations, broadening the scope of use to include environmental information.

There are three basic ways for a firm to use electronic mail. They can subscribe to a commercial electronic mail service, they can buy electronic mail software, or they can buy integrated OA packages that include an electronic mail capability. We will discuss the integrated packages later in the chapter.

There are about two dozen firms offering an electronic mail service. The U.S. Post Office offered a service called E-COM but discontinued it in 1984 due to slow sales. After two and a half years, they had only 983 subscribers. The major services being offered today are MCI Mail, and Easy Link from Western Union. Other services include GTE's Telenet, ITT's Dialcom, and RCA Mail. Message cost depends on message length, and is about twice that of regular postal service but less than a telephone call.

The MCI Mail system organizes your messages just as they would be in hardcopy form on your desk. You have an *inbox* for incoming messages and an *outbox* for messages sent. Received messages are on your *desk*, and the *draft folder* contains messages written but not yet sent. The opening MCI Mail menu appears in Figure 10-5.

Electronic mail offers two advantages to the manager for communicating rather brief messages. First, the other party does not have to be "on the line" at the same time—eliminating telephone tag. *Telephone tag* is the "game" that you and someone else play when you alternately return calls and the other person is out. As a second advantage, electronic mail offers a degree of security greater than that of typed messages. A message can be sent without even the manager's secretary being involved. Users must supply passwords to gain access to their mail boxes.

---

[3] Francis X. Kenney, "Electronic Mail Is Both Effective and Efficient," *The Office* 101 (February 1985): 26.

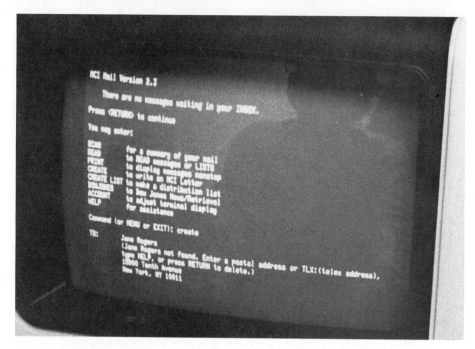

Figure 10-5   An MCI Mail menu.

Source: Courtesy of MCI Communications Corporation.

The major disadvantage of electronic mail to the manager, other than its one-way nature, is that the users must type the messages.

Voice mail

A way to get around the typing problem is voice mail. Voice mail is very similar to electronic mail, only you speak your message into a telephone. Figure 10-6 illustrates the types of equipment involved. When you want to send a voice message, you enter the number of the receiver's voice mail box, using the telephone buttons. Then you dictate the message, which can be up to 5 or 6 minutes in length. The voice message is stored in a digitized form in the computer's secondary storage. The recipient can retrieve voice mail messages in the same manner as electronic mail messages. The recipient can use the telephone buttons to cause portions of the message to be replayed, to skip over portions, or to route the message to another person. The system is very user friendly, guiding the user with verbal instructions.

Voice mail appeared on the market in 1980 in the form of commercial voice mail services. Pioneering firms included VMX, Inc. of Richardson, Texas, VMI of Santa Clara, California, and Wang. In 1982 the first Wang system was installed, and in 1984 GTE announced its Telemessager service.

If a firm wants to install their own system, they can do so using a mainframe or a micro. Microtel Inc. of New York offers an IBM PC/XT-based system called Micro-Talker I that can support up to 100 users. Microtel provides the software plus a necessary expansion board for the XT.

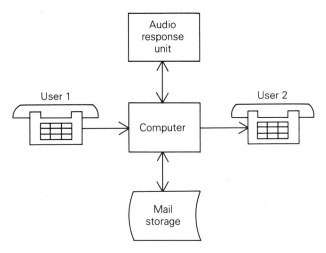

Figure 10-6 Voice mail.

The "no typing necessary" appeal of voice mail may result in widespread adoption. VMI alone has over 4,000 subscribers. Data communications consultant Jerry FitzGerald believes that "voice mail will be the overall glue that holds together and controls the automated office of the future."[4]

Electronic calendaring

Another use of the computer terminal is *electronic calendaring*. The manager or secretary can enter the manager's appointments schedule using a keyboard terminal as pictured in Figure 10-7. Once stored, the calendar can be retrieved easily by the manager using her or his own terminal. The calendar can be updated easily, and one manager can access another manager's calendar to identify a common free time for a meeting. It is also possible to "protect" an appointment from viewing by others.

Electronic calendaring is unique among the OA applications since it is not intended as a vehicle to communicate information; rather it is a time organizer. It is easy to implement, but is seen by some managers as having marginal utility. Some managers have simple daily schedules, perhaps seeing only half a dozen people. Other managers see as many as 20 or 30 people per day in individual or group sessions. One would intuitively expect the more complex schedules, and the greatest utility of electronic calendaring, at the upper-management levels.

Audioconferencing

Innovations in electronic mail and also video technology have stimulated efforts to link a group of people electronically. The product of these efforts is known as teleconferencing.

---

[4]Jerry FitzGerald, *Business Data Communications* (New York: John Wiley & Sons, 1984), pp. 161–162.

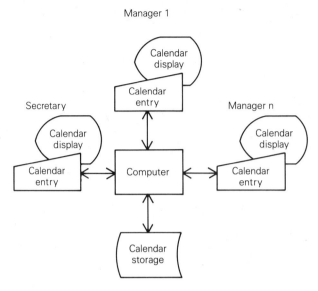

Figure 10-7 Electronic calendaring.

Teleconferencing may be defined as two or more remote locations communicating by means of electronic and/or image producing facilities. Teleconferencing exists in three forms based on the facilities used—audioconferencing, videoconferencing, and computer conferencing. Neither audio- nor videoconferencing requires the use of computers.

Audioconferencing, illustrated in Figure 10-8, provides audio communication only, most often two-way. Audioconferencing can be traced back to the *conference call* using telephones, where an operator can make connections enabling more than two persons to share the line at one time. Modern telephones are able to make these connections without operator intervention.

Bank of America has been using an audioconference hook-up between San Francisco and Los Angeles since 1974. Executives at both locations sit in corporate conference rooms and use a switch to establish a high-quality audio connection.

Videoconferencing

Videoconferencing involves the addition of video to the audio network. The video can be communicated in either a one- or two-way direction, as illustrated in Figure 10-9. *One-way videoconferencing* has been in use for some time. For example, many large firms have used it to announce new products to their field sales organizations. The term *closed-circuit TV* has been used to describe this approach.

One-way video combined with two-way audio can be used to control projects involving persons at widely scattered locations. For example, the video can update persons on the status of a computer implementation project by displaying charts and graphs. Then, the project can be discussed using the audio network.

Of all the OA applications, *two-way videoconferencing* appeals to managers the most. Managers love meetings, and they like to be able to look the other

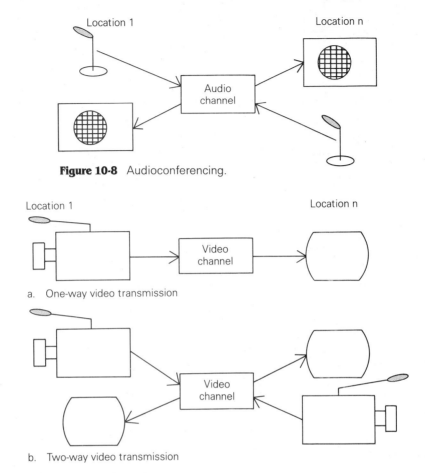

Figure 10-8 Audioconferencing.

a. One-way video transmission

b. Two-way video transmission

Figure 10-9 Videoconferencing.

person in the eye and observe body language such as facial expressions. The two-way videoconference is the only OA application that comes close to the intimate arrangement that managers prefer.

There are two choices in how the video will be handled. *Full-motion video* is what we see on our home TV—movement and action. *Still video* involves the use of snapshot-like images. In early 1984 it was estimated that approximately 20 North American firms had permanently installed full-motion systems, and another 100 used still video.[5]

Figure 10-10 illustrates a typical videoconferencing room layout. Microphones are positioned to pick up all conversation. Several TV cameras are used—one to show all of the participants, and others to show each participant separately. Some camera setups are voice actuated—focusing on a person when he or she begins to speak, and focusing on the group when no one is speaking. Wall-

---

[5] Robert Johansen and Christine Bullen, "What to Expect from Teleconferencing," *Harvard Business Review* 62 (March–April 1984): 165.

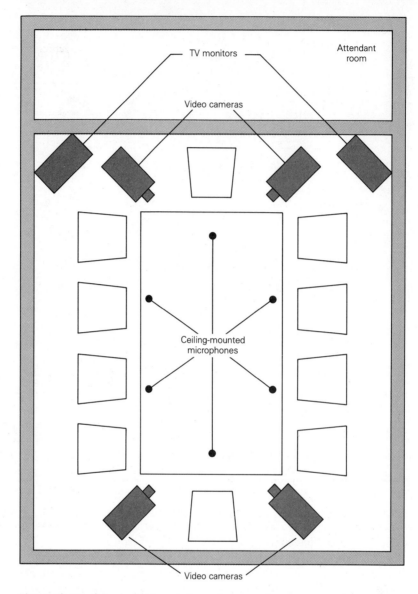

Figure 10-10 A typical videoconferencing room layout.

mounted TV monitors permit the participants to view activity at other locations and possibly themselves as well.

In 1982 Satellite Business Systems (SBS) and the National Opinion Research Center surveyed 10 firms using videoconferencing. They found that 70 percent of the participants felt that their productivity had increased because of the conferencing. Faster decisions, more effective meetings, and less travel were cited as additional advantages.[6] It has been found that participants are better prepared

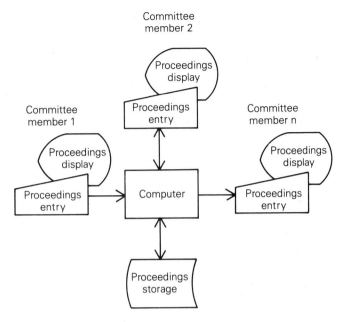

Figure 10-11 Computer conferencing.

for videoconferences than regular face-to-face meetings. This situation could change after the newness of the medium wears off.

Computer conferencing

The third form of teleconferencing is *computer conferencing*, where conference sites are linked by a computer network as illustrated in Figure 10-11. Regular CRT terminals can be used, or the images can be projected onto a giant wall screen. All communication between the sites is via the digital and graphic images produced by the computer system.

Computer conferencing is very similar to electronic mail. Note the similarity between Figures 10-11 and 10-4. The main difference is that computer conferencing involves a well-defined group of participants who address specific topics. The emphasis is on a two-way discussion.

Computer conferences permit an arrangement not possible with audio- and videoconferences—all participants do not have to be assembled at the same time. Audio- and videoconferences are conducted in *real time*, in a *synchronous* manner with all participants in attendance at once. A computer conference can be conducted in an *asynchronous* manner—a participant keys a narrative into the terminal and the narrative is added to the cumulative proceedings in the computer storage. At any time a conference member can retrieve the proceedings, review them, and add his or her own comments. While it seems like this method would

---

[6]David Green and Kathleen J. Hansell, "Videoconferencing," *Business Horizons* 27 (November–December 1984): 60.

Figure 10-12 AT&T's Picture-phone Meeting Service.

cause a conference to drag on indefinitely, the approach has received a favorable response. Some persons do not like the regimentation of regularly scheduled meetings. There have been instances where a conference member will enter a comment at 3 a.m. or on a Sunday afternoon. In mid-1984 approximately 100 U.S. firms were using computer conferencing.[7]

Firms interested in installing teleconferencing can obtain the help of a large number of support organizations. If audioconferencing is being considered, organizations such as Darome, Kellogg Communications, and Comex International will link the various sites using sophisticated equipment so that communication can be established by dialing a central number or flipping a switch. If videoconferencing is believed to be the answer, there are several options. Holiday Inns provides the needed facilities at some of their hotels, as does Hilton. The common carriers such as Western Union and AT&T have added videoconferencing services. AT&T's Picture-phone Meeting Service, shown in Figure 10-12, provides fully equipped conference rooms in major U.S. cities. If computer conferencing is being considered, vendors such as Participation Systems provide the needed software. The PARTICIPATE package operates on IBM, DEC, Prime, and Honeywell computers. Infomedia and New Era Technologies provide similar software.

Videotex

Another OA application involving a TV set or the CRT of a terminal or micro is *videotex*. Here, the objective is not an interchange of information, but rather a receipt. The communication is one-way; information in the secondary storage

---

[7]Dennis Livingston, "Computer Conferencing," *Datamation* 30 (July 15, 1984): 111.

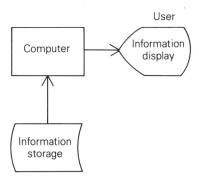

Figure 10-13 Videotex.

can be retrieved and displayed on the user's screen as shown in Figure 10-13. The display can be digital or graphical.

You may wonder how videotex differs from querying a data base from a terminal. The data base contains files and records, and often the output must be summarized and formatted in a special way. In videotex, textual information is stored so that it might be retrieved in its whole form. For example, it is possible to subscribe to a videotex service and receive the *New York Times*. IBM markets a system, SVS/1, that provides access to Dow Jones information and the *Official Airline Guides Electronic Edition*. DEC uses their own VAX VTX systems to make available directories, parts catalogs, personnel manuals, and newsletters to every terminal in the company.

Any need that a manager has to view textual information can be satisfied with videotex. In addition, the application can be used to communicate information to employees in a broadcast manner.

Document retrieval

It is often necessary to retrieve a document, or an image of a document, rather than only the data. An example is the requirement to view a copy of a policyholder's application form when an insurance claim is filed. The person processing the claim verifies that the signature on the claim form matches the signature on the application. Data stored in a digital form in a computerized data base does not satisfy this requirement.

Document retrieval, sometimes called *image retrieval*, is the use of one or more devices that facilitate the location and copying of stored document images. The images are typically recorded on microfilm. *Microfilm* is the name used to describe the miniaturization of document images onto roll photographic film. Microfilm has been around a long time, used by organizations with large volumes of archival storage. The problem comes when retrieval is attempted. Where is the particular microfilm located? The computer has been employed to help in the search.

See Figure 10-14 for an illustration of the document retrieval processes. The microfilm can be produced by the computer—computer-output microfilm (COM), as shown in process "a." A standard microfilm recorder can also be used. Process "b" illustrates how the microfilm address (such as reel number and frame number)

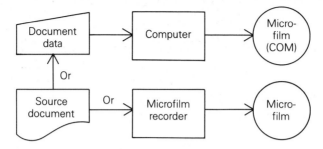

a.   Recording process

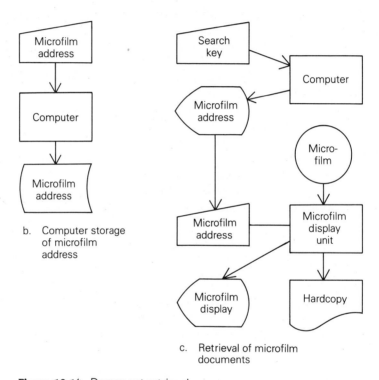

b.   Computer storage of microfilm address

c.   Retrieval of microfilm documents

Figure 10-14   Document retrieval.

is entered into the computer along with a search key (such as invoice number). Later, as shown in process "c," the operator keys the search key into the computer and obtains the microfilm address. The operator selects the proper reel from a storage cabinet and places the reel in the microfilm display unit. Perhaps you have used a similar unit in the library to view periodicals stored on microfilm. The address is entered into a keyboard, and the display unit locates the image and displays it on the screen. The operator can print a hardcopy if desired. In this system, the computer simply advises the operator where a microfilm image can be found.

Union Carbide uses document retrieval equipment in their accounts payable system. Purchase order documents are microfilmed after six months of inactivity. The ability to quickly retrieve historical purchasing information eliminates the costly error of paying twice for the same purchase. Union Carbide uses the popular Kodak IMT-150 micro image terminal pictured in Figure 10-15 to make approximately 100 retrievals per day. Users at the South Charleston, WV plant and as far away as Louisiana use computer terminals to identify microfilm addresses and request hardcopies. The copies are sent to the requestors in the mail.

Document retrieval equipment will invariably be installed and justified to support data processing applications such as the Union Carbide payables system. But, once installed, the equipment is available for use in decision support. In such firms the managers should evaluate how the equipment can be used to provide historical information.

Facsimile transmission

Facsimile transmission, often called *fax*, does not require a computer. The process can best be described as "long-distance copying." You have a document and you want someone else, in another location, to have a copy. You have a special facsimile machine that scans the document and sends the image signals over an

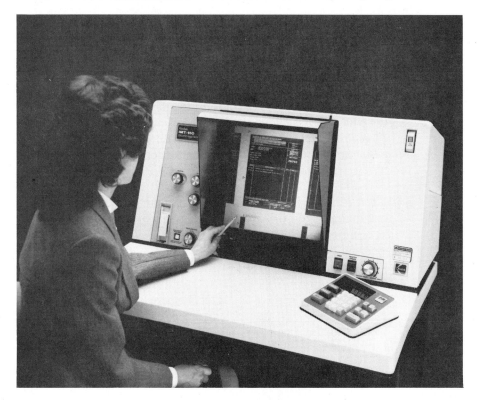

Figure 10-15 A microfilm viewing and printing terminal.
Source: Courtesy of Eastman Kodak Company.

Figure 10-16 Facsimile transmission.

ordinary telephone line to the receiving location. There, a second facsimile machine converts the analog signals to a copied image. The same type of machine is used at both ends of the line as illustrated in Figure 10-16. Each machine has a sending and a receiving capability. Graphical as well as text material can be transmitted.

Fax technology has improved greatly in the past few years. The early machines required constant operator attention and could take as long as eleven minutes to transmit a page. Modern units do not require such attention and can transmit a page in less than a minute. The Canon FAX31, pictured in Figure 10-17, can transmit a document image from Atlanta to New York City in 22 seconds.

The CCITT has defined standard protocols to be used in fax transmissions. These protocols, combined with the improved and lower-priced technology, account for the currently high level of interest. In 1984 there were approximately 450,000 fax units installed in the U.S., and this number is expected to reach 850,000 by 1987.[8]

The CCITT has classified fax machines into four categories. The Group 1 machines are the older ones no longer being produced. Most machines on the market today belong in Groups 2 and 3. Group 2 machines require 2 or 3 minutes to transmit a page using analog signals. Group 3 machines use digital signals and require less than 1 minute per page. Group 4 machines are just now coming onto the market and are capable of transmitting a page in less than 1 second.

If a company has a low document transmission volume, say less than 10 per day, there are a number of commercial fax services. RCA's Q-Fax is one of the oldest, initiated in 1978, and can transmit a document to the Pacific, Europe, or South America in less than 30 seconds. Air Couriers International offers a service called The Beam that provides service to every major U.S. city and over 2,500 cities internationally. In 1984, Federal Express initiated ZapMail—delivery promised within 2 hours within the continental U.S.

All efforts at establishing commercial fax services, however, have not been successful. ITT's Faxpax attempted to set up a network of customers that were using different machines, but encountered tremendous difficulties.

Many large firms have successfully implemented their own fax networks. TRW Systems believes their 150-unit fax network to be better than electronic mail, Citibank uses fax to transmit document data to any of their branches around the world, and the Zale Corp. uses a network of 1,200 desk-top machines for credit approval.

---

[8] Dennis L. Anderson, "Facsimile in the Integrated Office," *The Office* 100 (November 1984): 70.

Figure 10-17 A facsimile transmission device.

A composite view of the OA applications

Table 10-1 lists the OA applications that we have discussed and compares them on several basic characteristics. Looking at the table entries from the left, the first two columns identify whether the basic medium is visual, oral, or both. Eight of the ten applications feature visual media; the only two restricted to oral media are voice mail and audioconferencing. Videoconferencing is the only application featuring both visual and oral media.

Table 10-1 Comparison of OA Applications.

Application	Basic Medium		Medium Enhancements			Likely Used By:			Network Scope		Focused?
	Visual	Oral	Graphics	Animation	Color	Manager or Professional	Secretary	Clerk	Internal	Environmental	
Word processing	X						X		X	X	X
Electronic mail	X					X			X		X
Voice mail		X				X			X		X
Electronic calendaring	X					X	X		X	X	
Audio-conferencing		X				X			X		X
Video-conferencing	X	X	X	X	X	X			X		X
Computer conferencing	X		X		X	X			X		X
Videotex	X		X		X	X		X	X	X	
Document retrieval	X		X					X	X		
Facsimile transmission	X		X					X	X		X

The next three columns indicate features that can enhance the communication—graphics, animation, and color. Five applications can convey graphical information—two in the form of computer graphics (videotex and computer conferencing), and three in any graphic form (facsimile, document retrieval, and videoconferencing). Only videoconferencing features animation, or motion, and only videotex, videoconferencing and computer conferencing can selectively employ color. In terms of these media features, videoconferencing is clearly the most flexible. Computer conferencing and videotex are slightly less flexible, being restricted to computer-stored material. The remaining applications are tailored to rather narrow media use.

The next three columns show whether the manager/professional, secretary, or clerical employee are the likely users. Only word processing is tailored to the secretary, and a clerk would operate the facsimile, videotex, and document retrieval machines. A manager could operate his or her own videotex machine to retrieve predefined decision support material. Most of the applications lend themselves to manager use.

The next two columns recognize the application scope—whether use is restricted to internal communications, or can bring in environmental information. Only two applications can be relied on to convey environmental information—word processing and videotex. Electronic calendaring can facilitate the flow of environmental information by maintaining appointment schedules with external contacts.

The far right column indicates whether the medium is focused—i.e., can be restricted to specific items of interest. For example, if the manager is attempting to solve a problem, can information bearing directly on that problem be acquired—without sifting through a volume of nonrelated information or data? The only applications that do not have such focus are videotex and document retrieval; all other applications can be aimed at particular subject areas.

In addition to the fact that videoconferencing stands out as the most flexible and robust medium (as well as the most expensive), some basic patterns emerge from Table 10-1. OA offers primarily visual communications, and most of these are in a written form. Most of the applications can be used by the manager to obtain primarily internal information. Practically all of the applications can be focused on specific items of manager interest.

OA will not replace all informal communication, but it can improve a portion. Electronic mail, for example, will not replace all telephone calls, but it may replace some. Teleconferencing will not eliminate the need for face-to-face meetings, but it may replace some. There are undoubtedly areas where OA will do a better job than current procedures. The task of the manager and the information specialist is to identify these areas and design OA systems to meet specific manager needs.

Integrated OA Packages

You can see that there are many OA applications. A firm can assemble its own application mix by evaluating the various alternatives and selecting those best suited to its needs. Or, a second option exists. The larger computer firms have assembled selected OA applications that can be implemented as a package. Three such packages are IBM's PROFS, DEC's ALL-IN-1, and Sperry's Sperrylink.

PROFS was developed by the AMOCO Research Center in Tulsa working in conjunction with IBM. It evolved through no grand plan by IBM, but user support gradually increased. In 1983, IBM decided to market it in earnest and had 300 installations within six months. PROFS runs on IBM mainframes and features electronic mail. Also available are electronic calendaring and some sophisticated word processing features like a spelling checker that can even detect errors where words are used in the wrong context—such as "affect" instead of "effect."

DEC's ALL-IN-1 integrates four OA applications—word processing, electronic mail, voice mail, and electronic calendaring—plus an ability to integrate their videotex system (VAX VTX) and user-designed applications. Voice mail requires the use of the sophisticated DECtalk audio response unit.

The Sperrylink Office System also features word processing, electronic and voice mail, and electronic calendaring. The installation at the City of Scottsdale, Arizona, won the first-place award in the 1985 OA competition sponsored by *Office Administration and Automation* magazine. The Scottsdale system's success has been due to two main factors. First, a large number of people were involved in the project. A committee of employees from throughout the city was involved in early planning, and the city council supported the project from the beginning. Second, an elaborate employee training program was designed—some key employees had terminals installed in their homes so that they could learn at their own pace, and a special classroom (resembling an office) was built. System designers paid special attention to the behavioral aspects of the system—producing a special newsletter to keep employees informed, holding an open house, and installing a "help line" for employees. Between April and September of 1984, 220 employees were trained, and 147 computer terminals were installed.

It is important to pay special attention to behavioral considerations when implementing OA since it affects so many employees. A good knowledge of behavioral management theory can be put to good use. The Scottsdale story provides a good guide to follow.

Ergonomics

Like the rest of the computing field, too little attention has been directed at the behavioral impact of office automation. However, OA is the only area where there has been a legitimate interest in the *physical* impact of the equipment. The term *ergonomics* describes the study of factors that affect the welfare, satisfaction, and performance of people working with man-made systems and equipment. The terms *human engineering* and *human factors considerations* are also used.

Ergonomics got its start during World War II as designers grappled with the problem of adapting weapons systems such as tanks and planes to the wide range of people who would use them.

The subject has never been a factor in computer systems design until recently, when attention began to be aimed at the use of CRT terminals by clerical workers. When the workers sit in a constrained position for long periods looking at the screen, they often complain of headaches, tiredness, back pain, and eye trouble. Thus far, in studies both in Sweden and the U.S., such problems have been found to be temporary and do not pose a health hazard.

Manufacturers of office equipment have responded to this interest in the physical well-being of office workers by designing chairs, tables, lighting, and CRT units to minimize the strain and fatigue of using the equipment. For example, CRT terminals have been designed with nonglare screens and detachable keyboards that can be relocated on the work surface. Chairs have been designed with an adjustable backrest and seat height. Desks have been designed so that the height can be adjusted, and holders for source documents are constructed so that the documents can be positioned near the screens to minimize eye movements.

Managers do not typically spend long periods of time at terminals or micros. For this reason, ergonomics only affects the managers in an indirect way. The office workers are an important part of the MIS, and if they are fatigued and strained, they cannot perform at their best. Such problems reduce the overall efficiency of the system, and the system cannot provide the information support that the managers need.

Studies have shown increases in productivity when attention is paid to ergonomics. The National Institute of Occupational Safety and Health has stated that productivity can be enhanced by 25 percent just by paying attention to posture and vision. A Norwegian study revealed a 50 percent reduction in absenteeism when ergonomically designed furniture was provided to CRT operators. A study by the American Productivity Center showed a 12 to 14 percent increase in work output by properly designing the office environment.

These figures justify the inclusion of ergonomics in OA implementation projects. In order for a system to be considered ergonomic, it must satisfy the following criteria. The system must be:

- Supportive of the task performed by its operators
- Safe and acceptable to its operators
- Reliable and dependable
- Easy to learn and use
- Adjustable and adaptable to the operator's body and mind.[9]

These criteria relate not only to the hardware used in OA systems but also to software, training, and documentation.

---

[9] Richard P. Koffler, "Ergonomic Office Systems Design," in Constance U. Greaser, ed., *1984 Office Automation Conference Digest* (Los Angeles: AFIPS, 1984), p. 258.

OA as an MIS Subsystem

We have seen that OA evolved from a number of unrelated technological developments in the fields of computing, office equipment, and communications. There was no central plan to guide this evolution. As a result, the manager sees the OA applications as pieces of a jigsaw puzzle. Perhaps the view is not so disorganized when OA is viewed very broadly as everything intended to increase office productivity. But a narrower view, regarding OA as a subsystem in the MIS, raises some questions that have not been answered as yet. We encountered some of these questions when we earlier attempted to draw lines dividing OA from data processing and DSS.

In the following sections, we will describe how OA supplements data processing applications and communicates management information.

How OA supplements data processing

OA equipment and applications can be used to supplement data processing applications such as those of the distribution system. OA either performs tasks better than they were performed previously or performs entirely new tasks. Listed below are four examples of how OA supplements data processing.

Facsimile transmission in order entry   Some firms require a signed copy of a credit history form before an installment purchase is approved. This policy is difficult to enforce in a widespread operation such as a jewelry store chain. If the approval must be granted by headquarters, the sale could be lost as the customer waits for several days. This problem can be solved with facsimile transmission. As soon as the customer fills out the credit form in the retail store, the form image is transmitted to headquarters. There, the credit decision is made and the legally binding, signed duplicate is filed. The credit decision is transmitted back to the retail store by telephone. The entire process may take no longer than ten minutes.

Videotex in purchasing   As an example of how OA offers a new capability, consider the task of the buyer in selecting a vendor. We saw in Chapter 9 that this process has received very little computer support since it is difficult to keep an up-to-date vendor price list in the computer. It is possible to use videotex to obtain a copy of the vendor's price list directly from the vendor. This application requires the vendor and the firm to work together, but such a relationship should not be difficult to arrange since it benefits both parties. A vendor can make its price list and even its product catalog available in a videotex form. A buyer can then key in the necessary codes to have the vendor data transmitted to her or his terminal.

Word processing in accounts receivable   Word processing can be used to prepare customized collection letters for past due accounts. Customer name and address can be keyed in by the operator or typed automatically from data in the accounts receivable file. Paragraphs can be selected from storage based on the age of the receivable. As an example, polite reminder paragraphs can be selected for current receivables, and more stern paragraphs can be selected for those past due. By being more personal, these letters are expected to be more effective than ordinary form letters.

Electronic mail in production expediting   Manufacturing applications were not included in the previous chapter's data processing discussion, but they provide a good opportunity to use electronic mail. The production control office of a factory is responsible for ensuring that production work progresses according to schedule. Professionals, called expediters, stay in communication with production area personnel to keep the work moving. An expediter learns that a job has just completed a step in the production process and is ready to move to the next step. The expediter learns of this job status from a terminal located in the production control office. Using electronic mail, the expediter can send a message to the next work station advising those persons to prepare for the upcoming step. The same type of message can be sent to personnel in stockrooms who must keep the needed materials flowing to the production areas. Electronic mail adds a new dimension to intraplant communications.

These are only a few examples, but they provide an idea of how OA can work in conjunction with data processing systems to achieve improved performance.

How OA communicates management information

OA plays an important role in the MIS by communicating informal information that supplements the formal output of the data processing and DSS components. Before OA came onto the scene, these informal flows could be handled only manually—often in a slow and inaccurate way. OA not only improves existing flows but provides some entirely new means of communication.

Word processing in policy decisions   If a firm has its policy manual in a word processing form, such as stored on diskettes, changes can be made quickly and easily. Assume that an executive committee is considering changes to the retirement policy. Using word processing, the policy manual can be scanned for all references to retirement. These sections can be printed for executive review. When the decisions are made, word processing can be used to update the appropriate manual sections and prepare a letter to employees advising them of the change. In this example, word processing improves the information flow *to* the manager *before* the decision is made and improves the flow *from* the manager *after* the decision is made.

Electronic calendaring and electronic mail in scheduling meetings
One of the problems in scheduling meetings is finding a time that is mutually convenient to everyone. If everyone has an electronic calendar, the person scheduling the meeting can review the calendars to find a time when everyone can attend. A notice can then be sent to each person, using electronic mail, advising the time, place, and agenda.

Voice mail in internal communications The beauty of voice mail is that a terminal is not required as is the case with electronic mail. Not all managers have terminals, but all have telephones. When a manager wants to send a message to someone else in the organization, he or she need only dial the call and speak the message. This means of communication is much more convenient than trying to reach the other party by telephone, and by manually writing messages on a yellow pad for the secretary to type—a procedure followed by many managers.

Videotex in obtaining environmental information Environmental information, such as economic statistics and competitor activity, can be entered into the secondary storage of a computer and made available in videotex form. Anyone in the organization can retrieve the information from a CRT terminal, assuming that they are authorized to have access. The information can be displayed in a numeric or graphic form. A loan officer in a bank, for example, can use videotex to stay up to date on changing interest rates, and a marketing manager can use videotex to review competitive activity as reported in annual reports and press releases. Videotex is an effective way to quickly retrieve relatively large bodies of data and information such as tables and reports.

Document retrieval in obtaining archival data It is not economically feasible to keep all of the firm's data in readily accessible computer storage. Most firms archive their records after a certain length of time. Perhaps only records for the current year are kept in the computer or in departmental file cabinets. After that time the records are located elsewhere, possibly in a warehouse. This method of archival storage has two major disadvantages: (1) it takes up too much space, and (2) it makes retrieval difficult. Both of these disadvantages are overcome with document retrieval of microfilm records. Microfilm affords space savings of 98 or 99 percent, and retrieval is facilitated by computer identification of the microfilm location. The manager or secretary can enter the search key into the computer and receive the microfilm location. That location is given to a microfilm equipment operator who obtains the appropriate microfilm reel and produces a hard copy image of the requested document. Computer-assisted microfilm retrieval can reduce the time for obtaining archival data from days to hours or even minutes.

In these examples, OA is used to expedite the flow of information both to and from the manager. OA therefore has an application scope greater than increasing clerical productivity; it can provide information for decision making. Managements' information needs should first be identified and then OA systems implemented to satisfy those needs in all or in part.

An Office Automation Model

There are several approaches to designing OA systems to provide decision support, but they all tie back in some way to the management or organization theory that we discussed in Part Two. For example, we can design OA systems to support managers as they carry out Fayol's functions, to provide support to each of Anthony's management levels, or to solve problems of varying structure as defined by

Simon. In each of these cases, we take some interpretation of management and adapt OA to it. This approach gives OA some overall plan or direction.

We will use Henry Mintzberg's managerial roles as the basis for structuring the OA subsystem of the MIS. You recall from Chapter 2 that Mintzberg classifies management activity into ten roles. We can use nine of these roles for the OA framework. The diagram in Figure 10-18 provides the starting point.

The figure includes all of the roles except figurehead since it is not dependent on an information flow. The other roles (the rectangles) are linked by arrows showing the direction of the flow. The information sources (the circles) include:

- Other operating units—units other than the manager's own unit within his or her firm.
- Environment—everything (organizations and individuals) outside the manager's firm.
- Internal support units—units within the manager's firm dedicated to gathering and providing information. The accounting and computing departments are good examples.
- Superiors—persons on organizational levels above the manager.
- Subordinates—persons on lower levels.

You can see that there is a top-to-bottom information flow, originating with four of the sources and flowing into the liaison and leader roles. From there, the information flows to the monitor role. As monitor, the manager remains alert to any information that may benefit the unit or the firm. The manager can take two actions with this information. One, the information can be passed along to others—the spokesperson and disseminator roles. Two, the manager can use the information in playing the four decisional roles as the bottom of the figure.

The arrows represent the task of the MIS designer. Systems must be put in place that facilitate the flows. Figure 10-19 identifies the points where the systems can be added. The systems are identified in boxes overlaying the arrows. The systems are mixes of OA applications. See the legend box for an explanation of the OA abbreviations.

You will note that all OA applications are not included for each information flow. Only those applications are included that *can* communicate the information, considering current technology, in a form that managers indicate that they prefer. As we have recognized, incompatibility between different brands of computing equipment severely limits the use of OA to link the firm with its environment. Also, managers have preferences for information in particular forms, depending on a number of factors such as the source, the situation, and characteristics of both the manager and the organization. As an example, the manager of a firm with operations restricted to the local area would not consider teleconferencing or facsimile transmission.

The basis for the managers' preferences in the figure is data gathered by the author in a study of information systems of five executives. The study will be described in Chapter 12—Executive Information Systems. *The mix of OA applications presented in Figure 10-19 fits the preferences of the five study executives, but likely would be altered by other managers based on their own individual styles.*

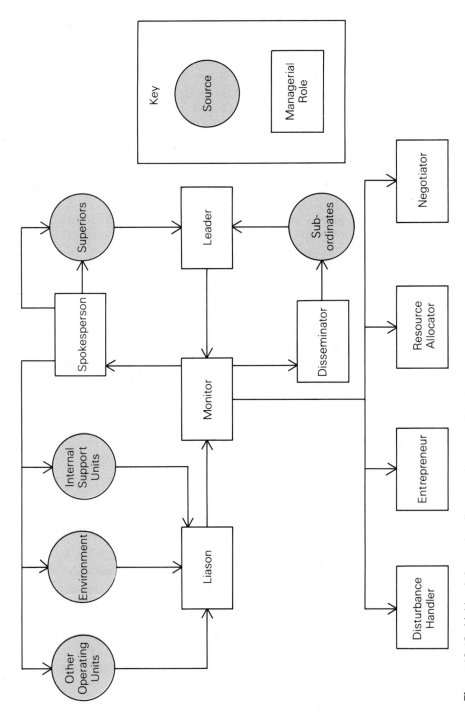

Figure 10-18 Linking information flows and managerial roles.

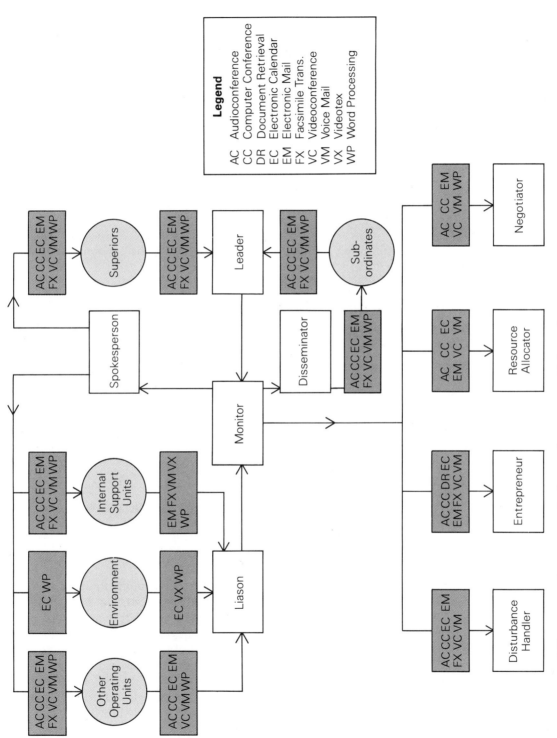

Figure 10-19 Office automation as a communicator of management information.

The purpose of including the OA mix in the figure is to illustrate that a particular OA application will fit some flows better than others. Such is likely the case for all managers.

Flows from the environment

The manager can use electronic calendaring, videotex, and word processing to obtain environmental information. Electronic calendaring assists in keeping appointments with persons in the environment, whereas videotex provides information in the form of catalogs, price lists, financial data, and so on. Word processing facilitates the incoming flow when used by the external contact to improve his or her own communication ability.

Flows to the environment

Only two OA applications are used in communicating to the environment—electronic calendaring and word processing.

Flows from superiors, peers, and subordinates

Persons within the firm can communicate information to the manager using eight of the OA applications. Messages can be transmitted using electronic and voice mail, as well as word processing. In some situations, facsimile transmission can be used for messages—those containing graphics for example. All three forms of teleconferencing can be used when groups of people are involved, and electronic calendaring can keep track of scheduled face-to-face meetings. The applications getting the heaviest workout are electronic calendaring, electronic and voice mail, and word processing.

Flows to superiors, peers, and subordinates

The manager can use the same applications to communicate *to* persons in the firm that are used to receive information *from* them.

Flows to the decisional roles

The manager can use several of the applications to provide information for all four decisional roles. All three forms of teleconferencing, electronic mail, and voice mail provide information in the form preferred by the study managers for all four roles. Each role also has unique information requirements. Facsimile transmission can be used in handling disturbances and making entrepreneural decisions. Document retrieval also can be used in the entrepreneural role. The roles of resource allocator and negotiator are more selective in their information needs. Fax, document retrieval, and videotex are not preferred. The preference for oral information diminishes the value of word processing while allocating resources, and the unscheduled nature of negotiating decreases the value of electronic calendaring.

Again we urge caution in interpreting Figure 10-19. A particular manager will likely show a different preference. The task of the information specialist is to identify the manager's needs, and design an OA system to meet those needs.

Putting OA in Perspective as an MIS Subsystem

OA is better suited to stimulating information flows within the firm than between the firm and its environment. This is because many of the OA applications require the sender and the receiver to use compatible equipment and/or communications protocols.

We should recognize at this point that OA will not handle *all* communications. Managers will still use the telephone, take tours, have face-to-face meetings, and read periodicals. OA is a way to improve certain communications, but managers will continue to favor the informal media and continue to use them. OA is largely a formal system defined by procedures, to be used in conjunction with the other formal systems—data processing and DSS.

The appeal of OA is that it more closely resembles the informal media than do data processing and DSS. OA is more user friendly. For this reason it is more likely to be used by managers. A manager has to have both a computer and an MIS literacy to use some of the more sophisticated DSS tools. OA tools, on the other hand, are very forgiving in this regard—for the most part not even requiring computer literacy.

If management embraces OA, it will be due primarily to the informal nature of OA. Both MIS and DSS have had an uphill battle in gaining management acceptance. OA may succeed in places where MIS and DSS have not. Time will tell.

Summary

OA was initially viewed as only a means of increasing office productivity, but improved management decision making recently has been recognized as an advantage. The decision-support capability of OA makes it one of the three MIS subsystems.

An office is any place where administration and management activity occurs. The processes performed in offices are storage, manipulation, and communication. The persons performing these functions are managers, professionals, secretaries, and clerical employees.

OA evolved from word processing, and the applications largely took the form of computer technology finding new uses over and above data processing. As a result of this diffuse beginning, the present task is to integrate the various applications into systems that satisfy user needs.

OA applications in addition to word processing include electronic and voice mail, electronic calendaring, three forms of teleconferencing (audio-, video-, and computer), videotex, document retrieval, and facsimile transmission. These applications supplement data processing and/or communicate management information.

Word processing can be performed using a standalone system dedicated to word processing, a keyboard terminal connected by a datacom channel to a central computer, or a microcomputer. Electronic mail requires a central computer, with all users sending and receiving mail through their terminals. Voice mail is similar to electronic mail, only push-button telephones are used as terminals. Electronic calendaring does not communicate information, but enables the manager to arrange his or her daily schedule so that communication by other media occurs. Audioconferencing provides a two-way audio connection between remote sites, whereas videoconferencing offers either a one-way or a two-way video connection plus two-way audio. Both audio- and videoconferencing require that all members participate at the same time—in a synchronous manner. Computer conferencing permits members to both enter and receive dialog using their terminals, at their own convenience—in an asynchronous manner. Videotex is a one-way transmission of video signals that can be received using a CRT terminal or a TV set. The feature distinguishing videotex from data base querying is the bulk nature of the videotex material—narratives, complete tables, and so forth. Document retrieval permits the storage and location of microfilm images of documents. This ability becomes necessary when it is not sufficient to only retrieve the data from a document. Fascimile transmission enables the sending of a document image over an ordinary telephone line—"long-distance copying."

Eight of the ten OA applications feature visual material, and videoconferencing is the only application offering both visual and oral media. Five of the applications can provide graphical as well as tabular data. Only three make use of color, and only videoconferencing includes animation. Most of the OA applications lend themselves to direct use by the manager or professional. A secretary would operate a standalone word processor, and a clerical employee would likely operate videotex, document retrieval, and facsimile transmission machines. The big disadvantage of OA is the fact that only two applications communicate information from the environment—word processing and videotex. The establishment of datacom standards will be necessary before the other OA applications can link multiple firms.

Some computer manufacturers offer integrated packages of OA applications. Examples are IBM's PROFS, DEC's ALL-IN-1, and Sperry's Sperrylink. The Sperrylink installation at the City of Scottsdale is a good example of how to incorporate behavioral considerations into an OA project.

Ergonomics is the study of factors affecting the physical impact of equipment on operators. To date, most of the interest has been directed at operators of keyboard terminals—primarily the CRT variety. The studies have concluded that the effects are not long-term, but manufacturers of terminal equipment and office furniture have redesigned many of the products to make them easier to operate.

OA can supplement data processing by performing certain tasks better than conventional equipment. OA enables higher quality communications within the firm, in many cases more rapidly than would otherwise be possible. Transmission of credit applications for a jewelry purchase and of messages expediting the flow of work through a factory are examples. OA can also supplement DSS by providing improved communications. The communications can be *to* the manager, as in the case of using word processing to scan the policy manual, and also *from* the manager, as in the case of using word processing to communicate the policy change to the employees.

Henry Mintzberg's concept of managerial roles provides a good starting point for defining how OA applications can be used for decision support. OA can provide *some* of the information flows connecting the roles.

As with other MIS applications, some managers will incorporate OA into their decision-making activity and others will not. OA has the inherent appeal, however, of a less formal electronic system than managers have been expected to accept in the past.

Of all the areas of MIS, office automation will see the greatest expansion during the next few years.

Key Terms

office automation (OA)

office

professional

knowledge worker

electronic office, office of the future, paperless office

word processing

standalone word processor

electronic mail

electronic bulletin board

telephone tag

voice mail

electronic calendaring

teleconferencing

audioconferencing

videoconferencing

computer conferencing

real time, synchronous conferencing

asynchronous conferencing

videotex

document retrieval, image retrieval

microfilm

facsimile transmission (fax)

integrated OA package

ergonomics, human engineering, human factors considerations

Key Concepts

The potential of OA as a decision support tool

How OA can supplement data processing

The capability of OA to closely approximate much of the informal communication that managers prefer

How word processing can route information to the manager before a decision is made, and route information from the manager

after the decision is made

How word processing is a part of the MIS regardless of whether the manager operates the equipment

The current OA focus on primarily visual material communicated within the firm

The synchronous characteristic of audio- and videoconferencing

The importance of including both behavioral and ergonomic considerations in OA projects

Questions

1. How can OA increase management productivity?
2. What is the relationship between the office and the conceptual system of the firm?
3. What are the three basic office functions? Which one would most likely be performed by a manager?
4. What are the four categories of office workers? Who are the knowledge workers?
5. Is an electronic office the same as a paperless office? Explain.
6. Name a primary disadvantage of a standalone word processor. Name an advantage.
7. Explain how word processing can improve management decision making if the manager doesn't operate the keyboard.
8. How could a manager use an electronic bulletin board?
9. What types of computing equipment are needed for electronic mail? What about voice mail?
10. What is telephone tag? Which OA applications eliminate it?
11. Which OA application does not communicate information itself, but rather facilitates communication by the other applications?
12. Is computing equipment needed to perform teleconferencing? Explain.
13. Why do managers like two-way videoconferencing?
14. Describe how a teleconferencing system composed of still video and two-way audio can be used to control geographically dispersed projects.
15. Explain the difference between videotex and using a terminal to query the data base.
16. What hardware units are required to perform computer-assisted document retrieval?
17. List the things that the City of Scottsdale did to stimulate acceptance of their OA system by the employees.
18. Is ergonomics concerned primarily with behavioral or physical aspects of a system?
19. Is ergonomics of direct or indirect interest to management? Explain.
20. List the characteristics of an ergonomic system.

Problems

1. If you have access to a word processor, type the following part of a report. Obtain a hardcopy printout, double spaced.

IMPLEMENTATION PROCEDURE

To prepare for the implementation of a computer, it is necessary to accomplish the following steps:

1. Prepare the physical facilities. Perhaps a new room must be built to house the computer. Or, an existing room must be remodeled.
2. Educate users. All persons who will use the computer output must understand how to interpret that output.
3. Select the computer. The proposals from the various hardware vendors must be evaluated, and the one is selected that best enables the firm to meet its objectives.
4. Plan the implementation. A schedule must be prepared, showing what is to be done, who is to do it, and when it is to be done.

2. If your word processor has a search and replace feature, use it to change each use of the word "computer" to "information processor." Obtain a printout.
3. If your word processor includes block move commands, use them to rearrange the paragraphs so that they are in the following order: 4, 3, 2, 1. Change the numbers so that they read 1, 2, 3, 4. Obtain a printout.

CASE PROBLEM: Great Sequoia Life Insurance Company

Great Sequoia Life (GSL) is a mid-sized life insurance company with its home office in Memphis. The president is Jim Hall, and his father is the chairman of the board. Jim's grandfather founded the company to provide life insurance coverage to military personnel. The company has grown by also writing policies for civilians. All of the administrative work is performed in the home office. GSL is licensed to do business in 34 states, and sales are made by independent insurance agents who represent several companies. Therefore, there is no network of regional or branch sales offices. The agents communicate with the home office primarily by mail; in very rare instances is there a need to use the telephone.

The Hall family is very active socially in Memphis. Jim belongs to many organizations, both social and civic, and has many friends in the community. He estimates that approximately half of his daily contacts, face-to-face and over the telephone, are with persons outside GSL—bankers, hospital administrators, charity fund-raisers, and so forth.

One summer, two professors from an area university were engaged in research concerning the information sources and media used by top-level executives. The professors, Mildred Orsak and Howard Mayfield, contacted Jim and asked him to participate. Jim agreed, and an appointment was made for the initial interview.

The three met in the conference room next to Hall's office, where he prefers to meet with groups. The interview was very informal, and Mildred and Howard just let Jim talk. They first asked Jim about his management philosophy, and he described how he tries to guide GSL with a very soft hand. He prefers to cultivate decision-making skills among his management staff and put them in positions of responsibility for their decisions. He encourages his staff to lend support to someone making a decision, rather than "letting them saw off a branch that they are sitting on."

When asked about his computer use, Hall revealed that he spent two years as a COBOL programmer while working his way up the corporate ladder. But this high degree of computer literacy has not resulted in a great reliance on the computer as an information source. He has neither a terminal nor a micro in his office. Jim feels a responsibility to place a computing resource in the hands of his staff, rather than use that resource himself. All of his managers have terminals in their offices. He sees his role as providing overall, long-term strategic guidance.

Hall likes to rely on his managers one and two levels down in the organization for information. He leaves his office door open as an invitation for anyone to visit him when he is not busy. He also answers his phone when he can; his secretary answers it when he is out of the office or in conference. Jim explained that he likes to be available to persons both inside GSL and in the community. This openness to communicate results in a heavy schedule, with an average of 4 meetings and about 20 unannounced "walk-ins" each day. Very often he will be so busy during the day that he must come to work before anyone else, often at 5 o'clock in the morning, to catch up on his paperwork. He likes to write all of his letters and memos using a notepad. He believes that even though the method is slow, it gives him time to select his words carefully. He prides himself in being able to write warm, personal letters and memos.

Mildred asked Jim about the importance of written communications within the company, and Jim explained that he isn't a stickler for grammar when it comes to interoffice memos. He doesn't care whether a person misspells a word or uses wrong punctuation as long as the purpose is to communicate internally. He said "What the heck." When pressed, however, Jim revealed that he doesn't receive many memos or telephone calls from persons inside GSL. He reasoned that since it is so easy to see him in person, his people don't bother to use the phone or the mail.

GSL is a progressive computer user. A marketing information system was implemented a couple of years ago, and word processing has been thoroughly implemented at the secretarial level. All of the company's typewriters were removed, and the secretaries had to use their terminals linked to the central computer for typing. The SCRIPT package, obtained from the University of Waterloo (Canada), provides the word processing software support. Arrangements were made for all managers to attend a word processing course at a local university, but attendance was slim. Only a few managers use word processing themselves, but GSL uses it extensively, producing camera-ready copy for preparation of sales brochures, policy manuals, and the annual report to the board of directors.

As the interview drew to a close, Jim said, "I think I should do a better job of explaining my feelings about computers. I sense that you expected me to rely on the computer a lot in my decision making. I *do* feel that the computer is an indispensable part of our operation. We couldn't get along without it. And as far as my own personal use of the computer is concerned, I doubt that I'll ever use it. As you know, we have pioneered word processing, and I might be tempted to use that."

Question

Knowing nothing more about Jim than what you learned from the interview, which OA applications do you think he needs? Prepare a list, and for each application include a single example of how it would be used.

Selected Bibliography

Office Automation

"A Marriage Made in Charleston," *Modern Office Technology* 30 (February 1985): 90ff.

Anderson, Dennis L., "Facsimile in the Integrated Office," *The Office* 100 (November 1984): 70.

Austin, Sandy, "Word Processing Programs: Bundles of Functions," *Business Computer Systems* 4 (March 1985): 85ff.

Bernstein, Amy, "Putting Out the Words," *Business Computer Systems* 3 (March 1984): 123ff.

Boczany, William J., "Justifying Office Automation," *Journal of Systems Management* 34 (July 1983): 15–19.

Canning, Bonnie, "Options in Electronic Records Management," *Office Administration and Automation* 45 (January 1984): 48ff.

Chol, Warren E., "The Role of Ergonomics in Aiding Productivity," *The Office* 101 (March 1985): 17ff.

Coumou, C. J., "Should the Office Be Automated?," *Journal of Systems Management* 35 (April 1984): 14–16.

Crawford, A. B., Jr., "Corporate Electronic Mail—A Communication-Intensive Application of Information Technology," *MIS Quarterly* 6 (September 1982): 1–13.

Curley, Kathleen Foley, "Are There Any Real Benefits from Office Automation?," *Business Horizons* 27 (July-August 1984): 37–42.

Galitz, Wilbert O., "Video Display Terminals: A Controversy Continues," *The Office* 100 (September 1984): 131–132.

Goldfield, Randy J., "Aiming OA Towards the Top," *Modern Office Technology* 30 (February 1985): 55ff.

Green, David, and Kathleen J. Hansell,"Videoconferencing," *Business Horizons* 27 (November-December 1984): 57–60.

Gremillion, Lee L., and Philip J. Pyburn, "Justifying Decision Support and Office Automation Systems," *Journal of Management Information Systems* 2 (Summer 1985): 5–17.

Gruning, Carl F., "VDTs and Vision—New Problems for the '80s," *The Office* 101 (February 1985): 19ff.

Hammer, Michael, "The OA Mirage," *Datamation* 30 (February 1984): 36ff.

Jarrett, Dennis, *The Electronic Office* (Aldershot, Hampshire, England: Gower, 1984).

Johansen, Robert, and Christine Bullen, "What to Expect from Teleconferencing," *Harvard Business Review* 62 (March-April 1984): 164ff.

Kenney, Francis X., "Electronic Mail Is Both Effective and Efficient," *The Office* 101 (February 1985): 26ff.

Livingston, Dennis, "Computer Conferencing," *Datamation* 30 (July 15, 1984): 111ff.

McCartney, Laton, "Teleconferencing Comes Down to Earth," *Datamation* 29 (January 1983): 76ff.

McLeod, Raymond, Jr., and Donald H. Bender, "The Integration of Word Processing Into a Management Information System," *MIS Quarterly* 6 (December 1982): 11–29.

McLeod, Raymond, Jr., and Jack W. Jones, "The Potential Role of Office Automation in Decision Support Systems: Some Empirical Evidence," in John Goldthwaite, ed., *1985 Office Automation Conference Digest* (Atlanta: AFIPS, 1985), pp. 149–156.

Marshak, Ronni, "Words to the Wise," *Business Computer Systems* 3 (May 1984): 102ff.

Meyer, N. Dean, "The Office Automation Cookbook: Management Strategies for Getting Office Automation Moving," *Sloan Management Review* 24 (Winter 1983): 51–60.

O'Keeffe, Linda, "Assessing PROFS," *Datamation* 30 (February 1984): 185ff.

Opper, Susanna, "Keep Corporate Teams on Target," *Computer Decisions* 16 (November 15, 1984): 100ff.

Opper, Susanna, and A. David Boomstein, "Corporations Conquer Distance," *Computer Decisions* 16 (November 15, 1984): 62–68.

Panko, Raymond R., "Electronic Mail: The Alternatives," *Office Administration and Automation* 45 (June 1984): 37ff.

Panko, Raymond R., "Electronic Mail," *Datamation* 30 (October 1, 1984): 118ff.

Panko, Raymond R., "EMS: Electronic Mail for Managers," *Office Administration and Automation* 46 (March 1985): 40ff.

Poppel, Harvey L., "Who Needs the Office of the Future?," *Harvard Business Review* 60 (November-December 1982): 146–155.

Portway, Patrick S., "What Teleconferencing Adds, Not Eliminates," *The Office* 99 (April 1984): 101ff.

Rash, Wayne, Jr., "E-Mail for the Masses," *Byte* 10 (February 1985): 317ff.

Roman, David, "Electronic Mail: Faster Than a Speeding Bulletin," *Computer Decisions* 16 (July 1984): 146ff.

Seaman, John, "Voice Mail: Is Anybody Listening?," *Computer Decisions* 16 (May 1984): 174ff.

Schmitt, Robert J., Jr., "Information Systems Help to Reach Corporate Goals," *The Office* 100 (November 1984): 94ff.

Siragusa, Gail, "Instant Document Delivery: The Next Phase," *Office Administration and Automation* 45 (August 1984): 34ff.

Sova, Dawn, "An Old Technology Takes on a New Shine," *Computer Decisions* 16 (November 15, 1984): 92–97.

Steinbrecher, David, "Stand-Alone WP: Seeking an OA Niche," *Office Administration and Automation* 45 (November 1984): 45ff.

Wolfe, John, "Tuning in to Videotex," *Datamation* 29 (November 1983): 225ff.

Chapter II

Decision Support Systems

Learning Objectives

After studying this chapter, you should:

- Have an expanded theoretical base for understanding decision making and the design of decision support systems (DSS)
- Know how the DSS concept evolved
- Understand the objectives of DSS
- Be aware of some of the controversy surrounding DSS such as how it compares with MIS, the necessity for online devices, and whether the manager should personally use the DSS
- Understand one model of the DSS and its major features—the data base, basic methods of providing information, and the software library
- Know the basic characteristics of reports, how reports are used by managers, and how to incorporate management by exception into reports
- Have an introductory knowledge of how the INQUIRE DBMS provides a querying ability
- Understand how managers use queries to identify and understand problems
- Know the different attributes of mathematical models
- Understand how linear programming and the Monte Carlo method can provide decision support
- Know the main advantages and disadvantages of modeling
- Appreciate that graphics and color are effective only in certain situations, and know some ways that their use can be improved
- Understand what kinds of software provide decision support, and which ones facilitate end-user computing
- Know when a DSS implementer should be used, and the role that he or she plays

Introduction

We have discussed two of the three MIS subsystems—data processing and office automation. In this chapter, we address the third subsystem—decision support. We have seen that managers obtain information from the data processing and OA systems. Standard management reports, such as the balance sheet and income statement, are byproducts of the data processing system. Much informal information is communicated by the OA system. In this way, the data processing and OA systems contribute to decision support. This contribution, however, is not their main objective. The unique feature of the decision support system (DSS) is the fact that it is dedicated to decision support. It has no other objective.

In the previous ten chapters, we have built the foundation for this discussion of DSS. We have reviewed the underlying theory, the hardware, and the software. This chapter is the only one remaining where our objective is to answer the question "What is an MIS?" We have saved the DSS for the final area, and that strategy is fitting since we view all of the MIS as intended for decision support. The remaining chapters of the text will be concerned with providing examples of how firms have built their information systems along functional lines and how the systems should be implemented.

Decision Making

A good starting point in our discussion of DSS is the decision-making process. We began the discussion earlier, in Chapters 2 and 4, when we laid the theoretical groundwork. In Chapter 2 we recognized the decision theory school of management and gave Henry Mintzberg credit for including a decisional category in his description of managerial roles. In Chapter 4 we distinguished between problem solving and decision making and described both systematic and intuitive approaches. We also recognized Herbert A. Simon for his classification of decisions based on the degree to which they can be programmed, i.e., made according to a procedure. Here we will expand on the explanations of these contributions and add some additional theoretical constructs. With this foundation, we will then be able to build a model of this part of the MIS, just as we have done for the other two parts.

Simon's types of decisions

Simon, in his 1977 book, elaborated on the terms "programmed" and "nonprogrammed" decisions. He claimed that the terms had been used in management literature for some time, so he didn't take credit for coining them. He did, however, describe the terms in a manner that has become a widely accepted basis for studying decision making.

According to Simon, decisions exist on a continuum with programmed at one end and nonprogrammed at the other. He said that *programmed decisions* are "repetitive and routine, to the extent that a definite procedure has been worked out for handling them so that they don't have to be treated *de novo* (as new) each time they occur."[1] *Nonprogrammed decisions* are "novel, unstructured, and unusually consequential. There is no cut-and-dried method for handling the problem because it hasn't arisen before, or because its precise nature and structure are elusive or complex, or because it is so important that it deserves a custom-tailored treatment."[2]

Simon explained that the terms programmed and nonprogrammed are only the black and white ends of the continuum, and that the world is mostly gray. But he felt that the distinction between programmed and nonprogrammed decisions was important because each calls for a different technique.

Simon's phases of decision making

Simon is also credited with identifying four phases that the manager goes through in making a decision. These phases are also frequently cited when describing the theory of decision making. Simon's phases are:

- *Intelligence activity*—searching the environment for conditions calling for decision.
- *Design activity*—inventing, developing, and analyzing possible courses of action.
- *Choice activity*—selecting a particular course of action from those available.
- *Review activity*—assessing past choices.

These activities account for most of what managers do, in Simon's opinion. He felt that the most time is spent in design activity, with a lesser amount in intelligence. Choice and review were believed to account for very little of the manager's time.

Simon's four phases relate directly to the steps of the systems approach that we described in Chapter 4. His intelligence activity relates to our steps of analyzing system parts in sequence and proceeding from a system to a subsystem level in search of problem signals. His design activity corresponds to our step of identifying and evaluating alternatives, and his choice activity relates to our step of selecting the best alternative. Finally, his review activity relates to our step of implementing the solution and following up. Simon's phases, therefore, are another interpretation of the systems approach.

We will continue to reference Simon's phases in this chapter since they have often served as the theoretical basis for studying the DSS.

Mintzberg's decisional roles

Our OA model in the previous chapter was based on Mintzberg's managerial roles. Information is used in decision making. As the manager makes decisions,

---

[1] Herbert A. Simon, *The New Science of Management Decision*, revised ed. (Englewood Cliffs, N.J.: Prentice-Hall, 1977), p. 46.

[2] Ibid.

she or he plays four decisional roles—entrepreneur, disturbance handler, resource allocator, and negotiator.

Mintzberg paid special attention to the possible influence of management level on the roles. He felt that all managers perform all of the roles, but differences might exist in the orientation and relative importance of the roles from level to level. In explaining orientation, he gave as an example an upper-level manager negotiating the acquisition of a firm, and a lower-level manager negotiating a delivery date with a supplier. Both managers are negotiating, but with a different orientation. In explaining the difference in importance of the roles, he stated that the disturbance handler and negotiator roles might be more important at the lower levels.

Melcher's degrees of decisional responsibility

Another management author, Robert Melcher, classified the manager's decision-making activity in a different way. He recognized that managers often do not shoulder all of the responsibility for making a decision. The managers can have differing degrees of responsibility based on relationships with other managers. He used the term *responsibility relationships* and identified seven categories:

- *General responsibility*—the person who provides overall guidance and direction to an activity, working through the person who has operating responsibility.
- *Operating responsibility*—the person directly responsible for executing an activity.
- *Specific responsibility*—the person responsible for executing a portion of an activity.
- *Must approve*—the person other than the ones holding general and operating responsibility who must approve or disapprove the decision before it is implemented.
- *Must be consulted*—the person who *must* be called upon for advice or information *before* a decision is made.
- *May be consulted*—the person who *may* be called upon for advice or information *before* a decision is made.
- *Must be notified*—the person who must be notified of a decision *after* it has been made.[3]

These relationships recognize that decision making is often a group activity, involving people with varying degrees of responsibility. As an example, assume that a company is designing a new computer-based MIS. The executive vice pres-

---

[3] Robert D. Melcher, "Roles and Relationships: Clarifying the Manager's Job," *Personnel* 44 (May–June 1967): 35.

ident has *general responsibility* for the project, but the vice president of information services has *operating responsibility*. Persons reporting to the vice president of information services, such as the programming manager, DBA, and so on, have *specific responsibility* for their areas. Assume also that the president has let it be known that she or he *must approve* the design before it is implemented. Further, the president has directed that the firm's management consultant *must be consulted* as the design is put together. Other individuals and groups such as the firm's CPA and computer vendors *may be consulted*. Those persons who will have to implement the design, the analysts and programmers, *must be notified* after the design decision has been finalized.

Melcher's responsibility relationships appear to form a hierarchy—the person with general responsibility has the most at risk in a decision, and the person who must be notified has the least.

An integrated decision model

Simon recognized both the structural differences in decisions and the way decision making evolves over time—from intelligence to review activity. Mintzberg saw organizational and environmental influences producing different types of decision-making behavior, and Melcher recognized the varying degrees of responsibility that might exist.

These three views of decision making can be combined into a single model, as drawn in Figure 11-1. The model is a three-dimensional box incorporating Mintzberg's roles as vertical slabs, Simon's phases as sections across the top, and Melcher's responsibility hierarchy along the side. The shaded cells identify the persons with responsibility as the decision process unfolds. The shaded pattern applies to decisions in all four roles.

Only those persons with general and operating responsibility would ordinarily be involved in intelligence activity—looking for problems to solve. All of the persons except those who only need be notified of a decision after it is made are involved in design activity (identifying alternatives) and choice activity (selecting an alternative). Finally, once a decision is made, those persons who were only consulted in the process of making the decision are not involved in review activity.

We can relate the model to the MIS design example. The executive vice president and the vice president of information services recognize a need for the project. Once the project gets underway, managers with specific responsibilities (such as the DBA) are involved through the review phase. Although the president must only approve the decision, he or she would likely be kept up to date during the design phase and also the review phase.

You should recognize that Figure 11-1 is a general model. In some situations, a consultant might be involved in review activity, for example. The model is important to our discussion of DSS because it recognizes the group nature of decision making and the fact that certain persons have differing responsibilities during a project. These persons need decision support systems at the points in the project where they are involved—the shaded cells in the model.

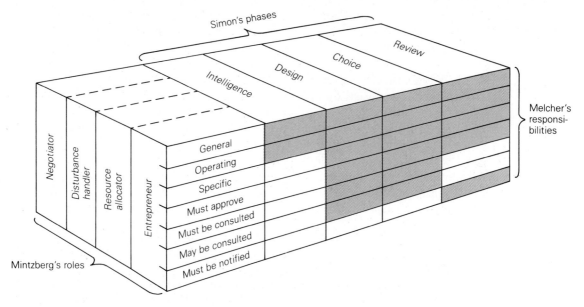

Figure 11-1   An integrated decision model.

The Decision Support System Concept

The DSS concept came about, in part, because of the misuse of the term MIS. MIS initially meant something different from data processing—a use of the computer oriented toward helping the manager make decisions. But, over time, MIS began to mean *all* computer activity. Therefore a need was seen for a term once again addressing *only* the manager's need for information.

Evolution of the DSS concept

DSS got its start in the late sixties when computer timesharing became popular. For the first time, the power of the computer became available to a person, to manipulate and use as she or he saw fit. Timesharing opened up new opportunities for computer use.

     It was not until 1971, however, that the term DSS was used in a formal sense. G. Anthony Gorry and Michael S. Scott Morton, both MIT professors, co-authored an article for the *Sloan Management Review* titled "A Framework for Management Information Systems."[4] The authors felt a need for a framework to channel computer applications toward management decision making. They used Simon's decision types and Anthony's management levels as a basis for creating the framework pictured in Figure 11-2. The management levels form the columns, and the

---

[4]G. Anthony Gorry and Michael S. Scott Morton, "A Framework for Management Information Systems," *Sloan Management Review* 13 (Fall 1971): 55–70.

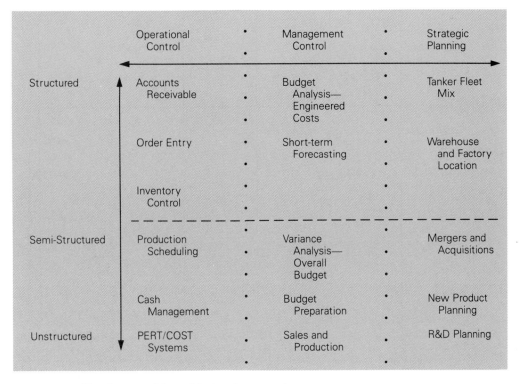

	Operational Control	Management Control	Strategic Planning
Structured	Accounts Receivable	Budget Analysis— Engineered Costs	Tanker Fleet Mix
	Order Entry	Short-term Forecasting	Warehouse and Factory Location
	Inventory Control		
Semi-Structured	Production Scheduling	Variance Analysis— Overall Budget	Mergers and Acquisitions
	Cash Management	Budget Preparation	New Product Planning
Unstructured	PERT/COST Systems	Sales and Production	R&D Planning

Figure 11-2 The Gorry and Scott Morton framework.

Source: G. Anthony Gorry and Michael S. Scott Morton, "A Framework for Management Information Systems," Sloan Management Review 13 (Fall 1971): 62. Reprinted with permission.

degrees of problem structure form the rows. Instead of using Simon's programmed and nonprogrammed decisions, they used structured and unstructured decisions. *Structured decisions* are those that are made according to specified procedures or rules. *Unstructured decisions* are made in the absence of such procedure. Like Simon, Gorry and Scott Morton recognized the vast gray area in between—*semi-structured decisions*, those partially described by procedure.

Gorry and Scott Morton entered types of business problems into their table. As an example, accounts receivable is solved by managers on the operational-control (lower) level making structured decisions. R&D planning is accomplished by strategic-planning (upper-level) managers making unstructured decisions.

The dotted line across the middle of the table is significant. The line separates those problems that had been successfully solved with computer assistance (above) from those problems that had, at that time, not been subjected to computer processing. The upper area was named *structured decision systems (SDS)*, and the lower area was named *decision support systems (DSS)*.

Gorry and Scott Morton initially regarded DSS as describing only future computer applications. Subsequently, the term has been applied to *all* computer applications dedicated to decision support—both current and future.

The next major contribution to an understanding of DSS was made by Steven L. Alter, who conducted a study of 56 decision support systems as a part of his

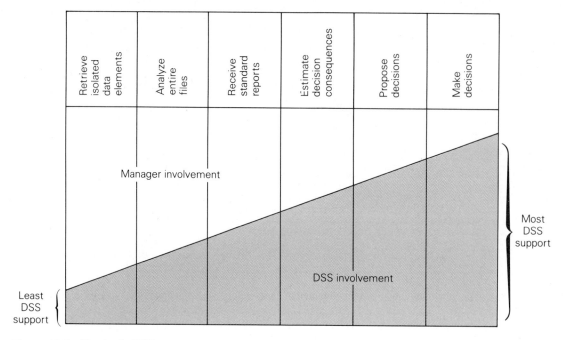

Figure 11-3 Alter's six DSS types.

Source: Raymond McLeod, Jr., and Irvine Forkner, Computerized Business Information Systems, *Second Ed. (Copyright © John Wiley & Sons, 1982) p. 493.*

doctoral work at MIT. The study enabled him to identify six DSS types.[5] The types are illustrated in Figure 11-3. The feature distinguishing the types is the degree of support provided, and this support is illustrated by the shaded area.

The DSS offering the least support is one enabling the manager to *retrieve isolated data elements.* The manager might query the data base to obtain a return on investment (ROI) figure for some aspect of the firm's operations. Slightly more support is provided by a DSS permitting an *analysis of entire files.* The manager might request a special report using data from the inventory file. Slightly more support is provided by *standard reports* such as the income statement.

Up to this point, DSS support comes in the form of data base queries and reports. The final three types involve the use of mathematical models. A model that only *estimates the consequences* of a decision provides less support than a model that actually *proposes decisions.* For example, one model might say, in effect, "If you lower the price to $25, the net profit will increase by $5,000." The model is unable to determine that $25 is the *best* price, only what *might* happen if such a decision is made. More support is provided by a model that can say, "The *best* price is $37.50." The DSS type providing the most support is one that *makes decisions* for the manager. Alter used the example of a computer determining rates to be charged by an insurance company.

---

[5] Steven L. Alter, "How Effective Managers Use Information Systems," *Harvard Business Review* 54 (November–December 1976): 97–104.

The Alter study is important because it was the first study of DSSs actually used by business firms.

DSS objectives

Another DSS pioneer at MIT, Peter G. W. Keen, teamed with Scott Morton to define DSS in terms of its objectives:

- Assist managers in their decision processes in *semi-structured* tasks.
- *Support*, rather than replace, managerial judgment.
- Improve the *effectiveness* of decision-making rather than its efficiency.[6]

The focus on semi-structured tasks aims at a large area, as illustrated in Figure 11-4. If a problem is completely structured, the computer can solve it. An example is the EOQ (economic order quantity) formula. If, on the other hand, a problem has no structure, the manager must solve it with no help from the computer. Semi-structured problems are solved by the manager with computer support. The computer serves as a decision support system.

In terms of the second objective, the DSS is not intended to replace the manager. The manager concentrates on the unstructured portion of the problem—applying judgment or intuition, and conducting analyses.

The third objective, improve effectiveness rather than efficiency, has more meaning today than it did in 1978. DSS strives to help managers make *better* decisions. Decision-making *efficiency* is fine, but that is not the real objective. The objective of *effectiveness* is especially meaningful today as the concept of

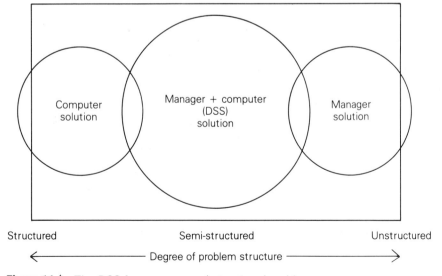

Figure 11-4 The DSS focuses on semi-structured problems.

---

[6] Peter G. W. Keen and Michael S. Scott Morton, *Decision Support Systems: An Organizational Perspective* (Reading, MA: Addison-Wesley, 1978), p. 1.

artificial intelligence and expert systems receives more attention. Artificial intelligence is concerned with using computers to reason through problems without human aid. Expert systems is a subset where the intent is to provide the computer with the same capabilities as an expert, such as a consultant. By incorporating the notion of expert systems into the DSS, the computer can advise managers in better decision-making processes. The DSS must be programmed so that it can innovate new decision-making processes rather than simply repeat the same ones over and over.

We are not far enough along in the integration of expert systems into the DSS to be able to cite many real accomplishments. We will pay particular attention to the future potential of expert systems in Chapter 19—the Future of the MIS.

A DSS definition

With this background of how DSS evolved and its objectives, we can define a *DSS* as a system that supports the manager seeking to solve a semi-structured problem by providing information and suggestions. The suggestions can take the form of recommended decisions and also recommended processes to follow. This inclusion of recommended processes enables the DSS to function as an expert system.

Notice that use of a computer is not specified. Like MIS, we define DSS broadly—including all forms of support. In our view, a manager's use of a weekly scheduled meeting is viewed as a decision support system, for example. Not everyone views DSS in such a broad way.

Must the DSS be interactive?

Early descriptions of DSS frequently included mention of a terminal used by the manager. In a 1976 *Sloan Management Review* article, Keen listed the *interactive* nature of problem solving as one of three DSS assumptions. (The others dealt with supporting the manager's judgment and semi-structured tasks.)[7] A more recent description of DSS by Richard Denise in *Datamation* included a desktop terminal on the list of "ideal" hardware and software.[8]

The interactive requirement seems to be less of a current issue. In a 1984 *Datamation* article, Michael Davis commented that the need for a terminal had been rejected by real-world practitioners as too restrictive.[9]

The position taken in this text is that an interactive ability is *not* required, although it is desirable. Our position is based on the fact that much problem solving in business moves very slowly, and the fast response of an interactive system is not always necessary.

---

[7] Peter G. W. Keen, "'Interactive' Computer Systems for Managers: A Modest Proposal," *Sloan Management Review* 18(Fall 1976): 1-17.

[8] Richard M. Denise, "Technology for the Executive Thinker," *Datamation* 29 (June 1983): 208.

[9] Michael W. Davis, "Anatomy of Decision Support," *Datamation* 30 (June 15, 1984): 208.

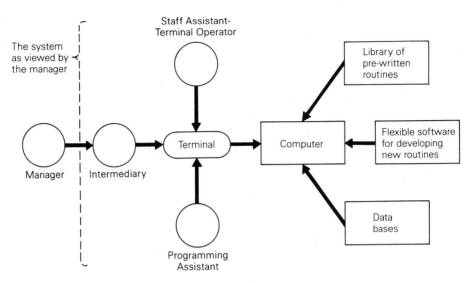

Figure 11-5 Keen's model of an interactive DSS.

Source: Peter G.W. Keen, " 'Interactive' Computer Systems for Managers: A Modest Proposal," Sloan Management Review 18 (Fall 1976): 9. Reprinted with permission.

There is no question, however, about the trend of DSS technology. It is definitely toward interactive systems—using terminals and microcomputers.

Must the manager be online?

In those cases where an interactive DSS is available, is it a requirement that the manager personally use the terminal or micro?

Keen included an *intermediary* in his diagram of an interactive system used for strategic planning.[10] The model appears in Figure 11-5. In this view, the manager does not operate the terminal; the intermediary serves as the interface between the manager and the DSS. The term *chauffeur* is also used—the person who "drives" the DSS for the manager.

Ralph H. Sprague, Jr., a professor at the University of Hawaii, also included an intermediary in his list of role players in the DSS. He defines the intermediary as "the person who helps the user, perhaps merely as a clerical assistant to push the buttons of the terminal, or perhaps as a more substantial 'staff assistant' to interact and make suggestions."[11]

This inclusion of an intermediary is now being seen by some as not only unnecessary but undesirable. In his 1985 keynote address to the Fifth International Conference on Decision Support Systems, Eric Carlson, vice president of Convergent Technologies, emphasized that there should be only two groups of

---

[10] Keen, op. cit., p. 8.

[11] Ralph H. Sprague, Jr., "A Framework for the Development of Decision Support Systems," *MIS Quarterly* 4 (December 1980): 1–26.

people involved with the DSS—users (the managers and their staffs) and the computer people (those performing data processing and maintaining the data base). Carlson conceded that the manager doesn't have to personally be online; the manager's line or staff managers can provide that service. Figure 11-6 shows these acceptable interfaces. The figure also includes an unacceptable arrangement where an information specialist such as a management scientist or operations researcher is used as an intermediary. Carlson acknowledges the power of the intermediary to inject his or her own views. If an intermediary is used, the person should be someone who thoroughly understands the problem. This understanding is most likely to be found in a subordinate in the manager's unit.

The question, therefore, is not whether to use an intermediary. Such use is perfectly acceptable. The question deals with the type of person to fill that role.

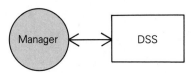

   a.   The manager can personally use the DSS.

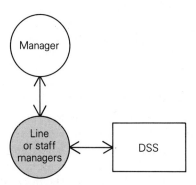

   b.   The manager's subordinate managers can serve as intermediaries.

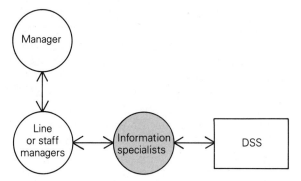

   c.   The manager should not use information specialists as intermediaries.

Figure 11-6   Ways for the manager to interface with the DSS.

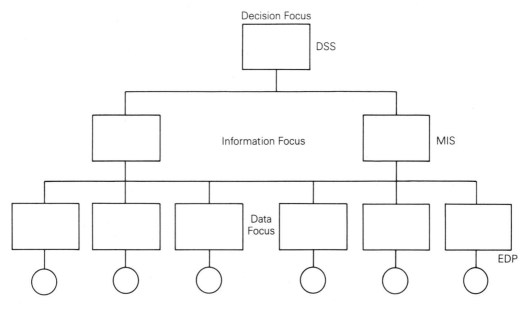

Figure 11-7 Sprague's model comparing DSS, MIS, and EDP.

> *Source: Ralph H. Sprague, Jr., "A Framework for the Development of Decision Support Systems,"* MIS
> Quarterly *4 (December 1980): 3.*

DSS Versus MIS

We established in Chapter 1 that our view of DSS is as a subsystem within the
MIS. There has been considerable controversy in the computer field concerning
the status of DSS versus MIS.

Ralph Sprague addressed the issue in his effort to establish a DSS framework.
He used the diagram in Figure 11-7 to position MIS between DSS and EDP. DSS
was seen as having a decision focus, MIS an information focus, and EDP a data
focus. He recognized that, *in practice*, MIS had been aimed at middle-level managers and DSS at top-level executives, although that is not a distinguishing characteristic. He maintained that MIS emphasized reports and data base queries,
whereas DSS stressed quick response, user control, and tailored support for individual managers.

Davis used an almost identical structure—viewing the hierarchy of information processing systems as a pyramid.[12] His structure has been redrawn in
Figure 11-8. Davis regarded DSS as being nearer to the decision process than is
MIS. He recognized the stronger analytical capabilities of the DSS compared to
the MIS.

---

[12]Davis, op. cit., p. 202.

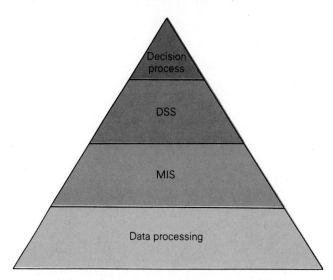

Figure 11-8   Viewing DSS as providing a higher level of decision support than does MIS.

The issue was still being addressed in 1985. Carlson compared DSS and MIS using the data in Table 11-1. The MIS provides indirect support since the manager must interpret the information, whereas DSS can provide a specific decision recommendation. MIS helps the manager only during Simon's intelligence phase, whereas DSS provides support throughout all phases. MIS has been aimed at "management" problems in general, whereas DSS has always been restricted to semi-structured problems. Finally, MIS has been concerned mainly with providing information, and DSS has been aimed at the decision-making process.

Our definition of DSS is compatible with Carlson's table. We include reference to semi-structured problems and recommended decision processes.

DSS *is* different from MIS—even the MIS that was originally conceived some 20-odd years ago as being something different from data processing. Two things account for this basic distinction between MIS and DSS. First, more is known about problem solving and decision making now than at the time MIS got its start. We have the work of Simon and others to pinpoint the types of management problems where support is needed. MIS had no such theoretical base. Second, computing technology is much more advanced today. The hardware and software available to today's manager opens up many more opportunities for decision support than was possible in the early years of MIS.

The terms MIS and DSS are likely to be around for quite some time; they are both well established in the vocabulary of business computing. As long as both terms are in use, there will be controversy about what each means and how one relates to the other.

Table 11-1 Comparing MIS and DSS

Criteria	MIS	DSS
Support for the decision maker	Indirect	Direct
Phases of decision making supported	Intelligence	All
Types of decisions supported	Management	Semi-structured
Emphasis	Information	Support the decision process

A DSS Model

We presented models of the data processing and office automation systems in the two previous chapters. A model of the DSS appears in Figure 11-9. The manager and the decision process are at the right, and the DSS is at the left. The DSS provides support in the form of information to each step of the decision process. The steps are those of the systems approach, with Simon's four phases also noted. The decisions enable the manager to play the four decisional roles.

The DSS consists of three major components:

- A data base containing data and information gathered internally and from the environment
- An information processor that produces reports, responds to data base queries and simulates business phenomena
- A software library containing the various types of software needed to satisfy the manager's information needs.

The information provided to the manager includes not only facts and figures, but also recommended decision strategies as the DSS serves as an expert system.

In the following sections, we will recognize the importance of the data base to the DSS and will pay attention to the acquisition of data. We will describe the three basic methods of obtaining information and how computer graphics can be used. We will also describe the DSS software library and how it facilitates end-user computing.

The DSS Data Base

There are two basic sources that provide data and information essential to the DSS. These sources are: (1) internal—within the firm, and (2) environmental—outside the firm.

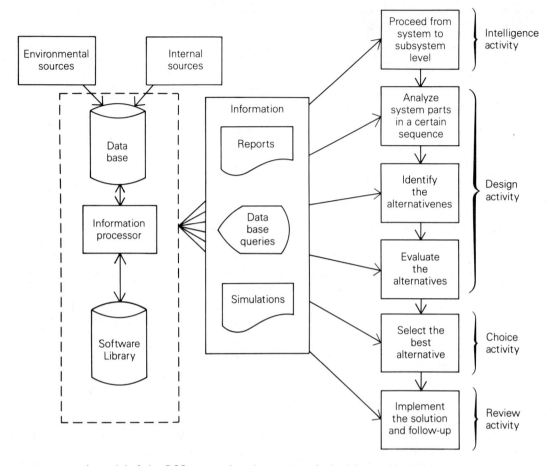

Figure 11-9 A model of the DSS supporting the manager's decision-making process.

Data is very important to the DSS. Keen says that data is the fuel that drives the DSS. He feels that this is an area needing improvement—that most firms are facing an "energy crisis" by not having enough fuel (data).

Another aspect of data that needs more emphasis is data from environmental sources. DSS designers currently recognize the need to aim the DSS at upper-management levels where the critical decisions are made. There is general agreement that upper-level managers have greater needs for environmental information than do managers on lower levels.

Firms have two options as they build their data bases of both internal and environmental data. They can gather the data themselves, or they can obtain data that other organizations have gathered. The data that firms gather is called *primary data*, and the data obtained from others is called *secondary data*. The firm's vast reservoir of accounting data is an example of primary data. Most of this data describes the firm's internal workings. A survey conducted by the firm's marketing research department of customer attitudes is an example of primary data describing the firm's environment. A firm will rely on secondary data primarily to shed light on the environment. This data can be purchased from firms that specialize in such a service. The data can be acquired in either hardcopy or computer-readable media such as magnetic tapes. Very seldom will a firm be able to obtain secondary data describing its own internal operations.

Gathering primary data

Firms that gather much of their own data will hire specially trained employees who usually are located in marketing research and financial research departments. Firms without an inhouse research ability can receive help from several sources. Washington Researchers, Ltd. publishes books that can be helpful—with titles like *How to Find Information About Companies*, *Understanding the Competition*, and *Developing Industry Strategies*. Washington Researchers also conducts seminars describing how to gather data. In late 1985, they offered a two-day course on "researching company information" and a one-day course on "researching foreign firms."

The firm gathers some data by conducting *field projects*—mail surveys and the like. Other data is gathered through *library research* with assistance provided by the business reference librarian and also online data bases. Three firms (Bibliographic Retrieval Services, DIALOG/Lockheed Information Services, and SDS Search Service) offer online access to hundreds of data bases. One firm, Information USA, claims that there are over 5,000 computerized data bases. That firm will conduct a search for you for a price of $50 per subject.

It is also possible to buy micro software especially designed for search of computer data bases. Menlo Corp. markets a package called In-Search for the IBM PC and the TI Professional. The package allows you to browse through any of the 240 data bases available from Dialog Information Services Inc. You pay for each search based on the amount of online time required. For a small extra charge, you can subscribe to a Selective Dissemination of Information (SDI) service where your research project is automatically rerun periodically, using the up-to-date data base.

The manager and the information specialist should work together in defining data and information needs and sources. College graduates with experience in conducting library and field research are valuable to their firms in acquiring the data needed for the DSS.

Gathering secondary data

Much secondary data is available from the federal government free of charge, but some must be purchased. As an example, the Department of Commerce sells international market research surveys for prices ranging from $50 to $200. A survey provides information about the market for a product in a given country. The reports contain statistics, plus interpretations made by the department's analysts.

Printed matter can be purchased from private sources as well. FIND/SVP sells reports on a variety of subjects—U.S. pesticides markets, the ice cream market, the soft drink industry, the U.S. Hispanic market, and so on. Prices range from a few hundred dollars to several thousand. Another firm, Trinet, Inc., sells computer reports dealing with sales by firms in a particular industry. An example of a report of pumping equipment sales by geographic area appears in Figure 11-10. Information is listed for each firm, including their percentage of U.S. sales. Trident says that the reports can be used to develop sales strategy, find competition, and understand the industry.

Some DSS experts would argue that simply supplying information to the manager, such as the pumping equipment report, is an example of an MIS rather than a DSS. Our perception is Alter's—that querying and reporting systems are examples of DSS.

Methods of Obtaining Information from the DSS

There are three basic methods that the manager can use to obtain information from the DSS: reports, data base queries, and mathematical simulations. Figure 11-11 shows how these methods provide the means of interaction between the manager and the MIS.

Reports come to the manager automatically; they do not have to be requested. They can be *repetitive*—prepared daily, monthly, quarterly, and so on. Some people use the terms *periodic* and *scheduled* to describe a repetitive report. Alternatively, reports can be *special*, prepared in the event of an extraordinary occurrence such as an accident. Some procedure is established that triggers the reporting process.

As Figure 11-11 indicates, some reports are printed, and some are displayed on a CRT. While it is tempting to envision a terminal or micro sitting on each manager's desk, that day has not yet arrived. The majority of reports are produced by line printers and delivered to the manager through the firm's mail service. In some cases a hardcopy or RJE terminal is located in a department for use by all managers in the area.

Queries are made from a terminal, and the response usually comes back to that same terminal. It is possible, however, to make a query from a terminal and receive the response in a report format printed by a line or serial printer. This would be the case when the manager wants a hardcopy and the terminal is a CRT, or when the report is too big to be accommodated easily on a slow-speed hardcopy terminal.

A query response can look just like a report. Therefore, what distinguishes a report from a query response? If the manager receives the printout automatically, it is a report. If he or she has to ask for it, it is a query. This is another area in computing where the dividing line is fuzzy.

Simulations involve the use of mathematical models to represent the behavior of a real phenomenon. Our specific interest is the simulation of a business system. The objectives of the simulation are to provide the manager with a greater understanding of the system being modeled and to predict how that system might behave, given certain influences. The scenario of the simulation along with trial decisions are entered through a terminal or the keyboard of a micro. The *scenario* is the situational data that provides the setting for the simulation—the firm, its

DATE 10/24/84

S H I P M E N T S   R E P O R T
FOR SIC 3561 PUMPS & PUMPING EQUIPMENT

PAGE 1

NAME OF ESTABLISHMENT	ADDRESS	CITY	ZIP	PHONE	1983 SALES MIL$	SALES PCT US	PARENT COMPANY
ALABAMA							
DALLAS							
LABOUR PUMP CO INC	SELMA INDUSTRIAL PK	SELMA	36701	205 875-4100	3.2	.07	KATY INDUSTRIES INC *
		COUNTY TOTALS			3.2*		
JEFFERSON							
FLUID DYNAMICS INC	1920 27TH AVE S/BOX 6127	BIRMINGHAM	35209	205 871-4673	1.8	.04	FLUID DYNAMICS INC
		COUNTY TOTALS			1.8*		
MARSHALL							
HEIL CO	PO BOX C	ARAB	35016	205 586-8152	1.9	.04	HEIL CO
		COUNTY TOTALS			1.9*		
		STATE TOTALS			6.9**		
ARIZONA							
COCHISE							
SIMMONS MACHINE & PUMP INC	754 E MALEY/BOX 520	WILLCOX	85643	602 384-2273	1.8	.04	SIMMONS MACHINE & PUMP INC
		COUNTY TOTALS			1.8*		
MARICOPA							
SOUTHWEST PIPE & SUPPLY CO	7600 W OLIVE AV	PEORIA	85345	602 979-3211	5.9	.12	SOUTHWEST PIPE & SUPPLY CO
		COUNTY TOTALS			5.9*		
YAVAPAI							
AQUARIUM PUMP SUPPLY	314 WHIPPLE ST	PRESCOTT	86301	602 445-4202	4.4	.09	AQUARIUM PUMP SUPPLY
		COUNTY TOTALS			4.4*		
		STATE TOTALS			12.1**		
ARKANSAS							
ARKANSAS							
LAYNE ARKANSAS CO	2015 SOUTH MAIN	STUTTGART	72160	501 673-1591	2.6	.05	MARLEY COMPANY
RICELAND MACHINE & SUPPLY	3102 S MAIN/P O BOX 833	STUTTGART	72160	501 673-3000	2.2	.05	RICELAND MACHINE & SUPPLY
		COUNTY TOTALS			4.8*		
FAULKNER							
AERMOTOR CO	INDUSTRIAL PARK	CONWAY	72032	501 329-9811	12.9	.27	VALLEY INDUSTRIES INC *
		COUNTY TOTALS			12.9*		
GREENE							
JET SCREEN INC	HWY 1 NORTH/P O BOX 832	PARAGOULD	72450	501 236-8772	2.2	.05	JET SCREEN INC
		COUNTY TOTALS			2.2*		
LONOKE							
JACUZZI BROS INC	500 JACUZZI LANE	LONOKE	72086	501 676-6506	8.5	.18	KIDDE INC *
		COUNTY TOTALS			8.5*		
PULASKI							
ARK INDUS MACHINERY INC	3804 NORTH NONA	N LITTLE ROCK	72118	501 758-2745	2.2	.05	ARK INDUS MACHINERY INC
JACUZZI BROS INC	11511 NEW BENTON BOX 3533	LITTLE ROCK	72203	501 455-1234	17.1	.35	KIDDE INC *
		COUNTY TOTALS			19.3*		
UNION							
PUMPS & POWER INC	P O BOX 1716	EL DORADO	71730	501 862-6679	2.3	.05	PUMPS & POWER INC
		COUNTY TOTALS			2.3*		
		STATE TOTALS			50.0**		
CALIFORNIA							
ALAMEDA							
AR GO PUMP CO	10007 SAN LEANDRO	OAKLAND	94603	415 632-4075	3.7	.08	AR GO PUMP CO

CONFIDENTIAL - THIS REPORT IS NOT TO BE REPRODUCED WITHOUT THE WRITTEN PERMISSION OF TRINET, INC.

Figure 11-10 A purchased report of product sales by geographic area.
Source: Courtesy of Trinet, Inc.

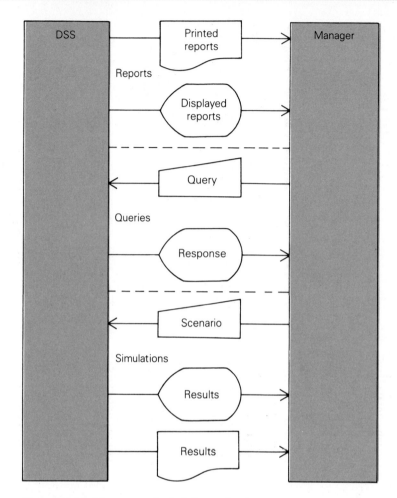

Figure 11-11 Managers obtain information by report, query, and simulation.

customers, its suppliers, the economy, and so on. Simulation results can come back to the terminal or be printed on the computer printer.

Evolution of the three methods

The oldest method of obtaining information is the report. Business reports have been popular since the first days of commerce. Keydriven, punched card, and now computer systems have all used the report as the primary means of output. Although more attention is currently being directed toward the other two methods—queries and simulations—the report is the most widely used method of transmitting *computer* information to the manager.

The dominance of the report method can be seen in the conceptual representation in Figure 11-12. The increasing use of the computer in the mid-fifties spawned a corresponding increase in the use of reports. At the same time, simulation became a much-discussed though infrequently used method. Managers

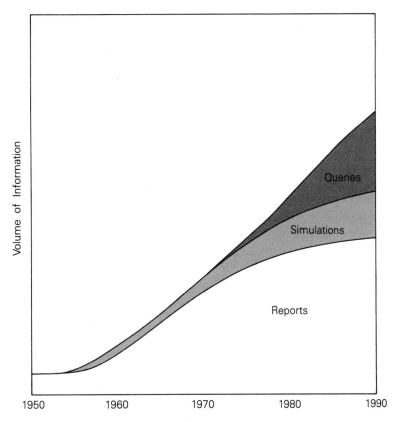

Figure 11-12 Evolution of information-producing methods.

still have not embraced simulation to a great degree, mainly because of the demand it places on mathematical skills. This hostile attitude will erode as more computer-literate managers enter business and the modeling software becomes more user friendly.

At the present time, the query method is stimulating a great deal of interest. Of the three methods for obtaining information, querying is the newest—getting its start in the early seventies with the advent of mainframe DBMSs. From all indications, this is the method of the future.

Two basic uses of information

Managers make two basic uses of information. First, they use information to identify and define problems. This is the *definition effort* phase of the systems approach. It corresponds to Simon's *intelligence* phase. Next, managers use information to solve the problems that have been identified. This is our *solution effort* and Simon's *design* and *choice* phases.

As a general rule, reports and queries are used primarily in definition effort, and simulations are used in solution effort. Figure 11-13 illustrates this condition. Primarily through reports and secondarily through queries and simulations, the

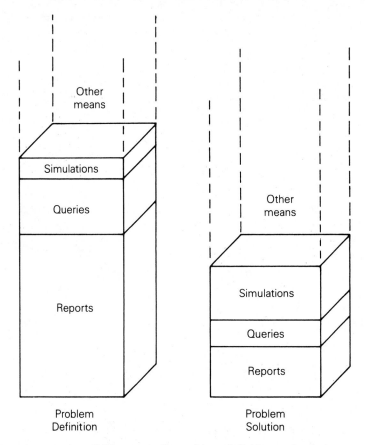

Figure 11·13   DSS support for problem definition and solution.

DSS handles much of the problem identification and definition workload. Managers also use other means (such as informal information contacts) to identify and define problems. In fact, more problems are probably identified from informal cues than from those provided by the computer-based DSS.

Reports can be designed to identify problems or potential problems. Managers can also query the data base to find problems or to learn more about problems that have already been identified. Simulations frequently uncover hidden problems, because weaknesses tend to stand out when part of the firm's operation is manipulated mathematically.

Reports and queries can also help the manager solve problems by identifying alternatives, providing information to be used in evaluating and selecting alternatives, and providing follow-up information. But this is the area where simulation really shines. Mathematical models enable the manager to play the "what-if" game—trying out strategies mathematically to predict their consequences.

The next sections of the chapter explain in greater detail these three basic methods of obtaining computer information—reports, queries, and modeling.

Reports

In addition to being either repetitive or special, reports can also be detailed or summary. A *detailed report* provides specifics, usually a line of data, about each transaction. For example, a payroll register lists each employee and shows earnings information. This type of report is also called a *detailed listing*.

When a report contains entries that are distillations of multiple transactions, the report is a *summary report*. A departmental earnings report, showing one line of data for each department, is a summary report. Generally, detailed reports are used at lower-management levels, and summarized reports are used at upper levels.

Report organization

A general pattern provides a format for all reports. A report consists of three main areas—*heading*, *body*, and *footing*. In the heading area, centered at the top of the page, is *fixed heading material* such as the name of the report. Immediately below is *variable heading material* such as date and page number. In the body area are *column headings* that identify the vertical *columns of data* immediately below. The generally accepted convention is to place identification data (such as employee number) on the left, descriptive data (such as employee name) in the center, and quantitative data (such as earnings amounts) on the right. In the footing area are *column total* amounts accumulated for each column and also an *overall total* or group of totals. Not all reports contain the three main areas. Some are printed without headings, and some do not have totals.

Reports are typically printed in some sequence. An *ascending* sequence is the most popular with the lowest control number printed first and the highest printed last. A *descending* sequence can often direct the manager's attention to key items. As an example, a retail store president might receive a sales report with the highest-selling items listed first. The report lines would be in descending sequence based on sales amount.

How managers use reports

Most accounting systems have been designed to produce a set of repetitive reports. Balance sheets and income statements are examples. Both have companywide interest. Other reports have a narrower focus. An aged accounts receivable report is of interest to the credit manager, a sales-by-salesperson report is prepared for the sales manager, and a report of overtime earnings is used by the plant superintendent.

Most of these reports perform a valuable service. Balance sheets and income statements are greatly distilled summaries of hundreds or thousands of separate transactions that show at a glance the financial position of the firm. Reports such as this are read by upper-level managers and are even included in annual reports to stockholders.

Other reports are used by lower-level managers to monitor the performance of their areas. The credit manager uses the aged accounts receivable report (refer back to Figure 9-21) to identify poor-paying customers and to direct the firm's collection efforts. The sales manager uses the sales-by-salesperson report (Figure 11-14) to identify those representatives performing in an extraordinary manner—either very well or very badly. The sales manager makes this identification by examining the variance-from-quota columns. The plant superintendent uses the overtime earnings report (Figure 11-15) to identify those departments adding the most to production costs by paying extra premiums for labor. This analysis can relate to the current period or to the cumulative status for the fiscal year.

All of these reports are easily prepared by the computer. Accounting data stored in the data base describes the period's transactions—sales, payments, hours worked, and so on. At the end of the period, programs extract data from the data base, sort it into appropriate groupings, summarize the transactions, compute measures of variation, and print the reports. It is also possible to store the report data in the data base for display on a manager's terminal when desired.

The reports in Figures 9-21, 11-14, and 11-15 reflect *management by exception*. The aged accounts receivable report classifies the exceptions (the past-due receivables) in terms of their age. The overtime earnings report provides less support by not classifying the exceptions in any way. The sales-by-salesperson report provides the least amount of support by reporting everything, and leaving it up to the manager to analyze the variance and determine whether it falls outside the acceptable range. The manner in which a report is designed determines the degree of decision support that it can provide the manager.

One problem with many repetitive reports is that they were not designed by a manager. Instead, they were designed entirely by an information specialist. The manager receiving the report tosses it into the wastebasket. Perhaps the manager doesn't know how to interpret it, or perhaps the report deals with an unimportant aspect of the manager's job.

```
                    SALES BY SALESPERSON REPORT
                         MARCH 31, 1986

---SALESPERSON------     ---CURRENT-MONTH------    ---YEAR-TO-DATE------
 NO.      NAME           QUOTA   ACTUAL  VARIANCE  QUOTA ACTUAL  VARIANCE

 0120   JOHN NELSON      1200    1083     -117     3600   3505     -95
10469   LYNN SHERRY      1000    1162     +162     3000   3320    +320
19261   DARVIN UPSHAW     800    1090     +290     2400   2510    +110
20234   JANIE EVANS      1500    1305     -195     4500   4110    -390
61604   TRAVIS BURKE     2000    2333     +333     6000   6712    +712
62083   CATHY HAGER      1000     990      -10     3000   2319    -681
63049   STEVE JENNER     1100    1250     +150     3300   2416    -884
64040   SAM MOSELEY      1050     985      -65     3150   3020    -130

        TOTALS           9650   10198      548    28950  27912   -1038
```

Figure 11-14   A sales-by-salesperson report.

```
                    OVERTIME EARNINGS REPORT
                       AUGUST 31, 1986

                                          OVERTIME HOURS
  DEPARTMENT NO.    DEPARTMENT NAME    CURRENT MONTH   YEAR-TO-DATE

      16-10          RECEIVING            2305.00         5319.20
      16-11          INSPECTION           1025.60         4386.12
      16-12          MATL'S HANDLING      3392.50        12629.00
      16-13          TOOLING                78.00         1049.00
      16-14          ASSEMBLY                 .00          792.80
      16-15          PLATING              3504.90        12635.20
      16-16          SHIPPING             5219.16        18294.16

                     TOTALS             15525.16        55105.48
```

Figure 11-15 An overtime earnings report.

Data Base Queries

You can imagine how appealing the idea of a query ability is to a manager. With a query ability, if you want to know something, you just ask for it. It's a more convenient and responsive information service than you get with a repetitive report.

Actually, the query ability requires a great deal of preplanning, perhaps more than reports do. To have a query ability, you need two ingredients—a data base, and a way to get at the data. Data must be converted to a computer storage medium such as a DASD and then organized logically to conform to a particular DBMS. Then, a retrieval is possible by using a query language. The language can be part of the DBMS or it can be a separate software package. In Chapter 7 we discussed how a micro DBMS, dBASE III, can be used to query the data base and how a generalized file management system, MARK-IV, can be used to produce special reports from the data base. Here we will include an example of a mainframe DBMS query language.

INQUIRE

INQUIRE is a DBMS for large-scale IBM systems that is marketed by Infodata Systems, Inc. Its query language permits selective retrieval of data, design of report formats, and computation of report data. The user forms a query by using one or more *commands*. These are listed in Table 11-2. Read the descriptions of the commands now, so that you might understand the examples that follow. Each *command statement* begins with a command verb. For example, the statement below causes the retrieval of all personnel records with an occupation title of PROGRAMMER and a current salary (CURSAL) greater than (GT) $10,000.

FIND PROGRAMMER AND CURSAL GT 10000

Table 11-2 INQUIRE Retrieval and Report Generation Commands

Commands	Function
Retrieval tasks	
FIND	Directly accesses data in the data base
SCAN	Sequentially reads each record in the data base, searching for items
Report generation tasks	
TAB	Enables the user to specify positioning and formatting of data on a report
LIST	Permits vertical listing of all data fields in a record, without formatting
TITLE	Allows the user to print headings over each column of data
FOOTER	Allows the user to print a footer at the bottom of data columns
HEADER	Allows the user to print a title at the top of a report
ONPAGE	Enables the user to print variable information, such as page number, at the top of the report, just below the heading and above the titles
COUNT	Counts the number of records meeting the search criteria
SAVE	Saves selected records for later use
COMPUTE	Permits the user to compute values from retrieved data
TOTAL	Enables the user to print totals at the end of the report or to compute values such as averages, maximums, or minimums
SORT	Permits data sorting for report preparation
BREAK	Allows the users to specify computing, totaling, and printing actions at control breaks

Once this data has been retrieved, it can be printed with the statement

TAB NAME CURSAL ($D) SKIP

The $D causes the salary data to be printed with a decimal point separating dollars and cents, preceded by a dollar sign. SKIP inserts a blank line between the detail lines. The report appears in Figure 11-16.

There are two *retrieval commands*—FIND and SCAN. FIND is used with direct access (indexed sequential and direct organization), and SCAN is used when the data base is organized sequentially. There are three *printing commands*—LIST, TAB, and COUNT. If you instruct

FIND SKILLS = ENGINEER,
TAB NAME 1 EDTYPE 35 DEGREE 45 SKILLS 54.

you will receive the report in Figure 11-17. The numbers in the TAB command identify print positions.

```
        NAME                              CURSAL

        ---------------------------------------------

        FRED JAMES                        $23,500.00

        WALLACE COLLINS                   $17,285.00

        DONALD LEHNERT                    $19,278.00

        ALTON FUCHS                       $25,000.00

        TERRY BARANSY                     $21,627.70
```

Figure 11-16   A query response in a simple report format.

We might want to dress up the report with headings and to sort the records. The following statement produces the report in Figure 11-18.

SCAN, TAB NAME CURTITL CURSAL CURDEPT, HEADER 'EMPLOYEES GROUPED BY DEPART-MENT' " 'AND ORDERED BY SALARY', TITLE 'EMPLOYEE NAME' NAME (JOB TITLE) CURTITL 'SALARY' CURSAL (CURRENT DEPT) CURDEPT, SORT CURDEPT (A) CURSAL (D).

The sequential file is scanned. Data elements to be printed in columns are NAME, CURTITL, CURSAL, and CURDEPT. The title of the report is EMPLOYEES GROUPED BY DEPARTMENT, followed by a blank line (") and then the words AND ORDERED BY SALARY. The column headings are printed by indicating what is to be printed (such as EMPLOYEE NAME) followed by the data base identifier (such as NAME). Enclosing words in single quotes—'EMPLOYEE NAME'—causes the words to be printed on the same line. Enclosing words in parentheses—(JOB TITLE)—causes the words to be printed on


```
                                                            PAGE    1
                                                            09/15/86


        NAME                         EDTYPE    DEGREE   SKILLS
        -----------------------------------------------------------------

        PAULA F. SMITH               COLL      BEE      ENGINEER
                                     GRAD               INSTRUMENTATION
                                                        PRODUCTION CONTROL
                                                        ELECTRICAL
                                                        TELEPROCESSING
                                                        SUPERVISORY

        ROBERT R. JONES              COLL      BEE      ENGINEER

        JAMES GLEASON                COLL      BEE      ENGINEER
                                     GRAD      MBA      SYSTEMS DEVELOPMENT
                                                        PROPOSAL WRITING
                                                        SUPERVISORY
                                                        SYSTEMS ANALYST
```

Figure 11-17   Formatted data records.

```
                    EMPLOYEES GROUPED BY DEPARTMENT        PAGE   1
                                                          09/15/86
                        AND ORDERED BY SALARY

        EMPLOYEE NAME          JOB              SALARY     CURRENT
                               TITLE                      DEPT
        --------------------------------------------------------------

        JEAN CHING             SR STATISTICIAN          $24,500.76   201

        SAM JACKSON            GRP LDR SYS DEVELOPMENT   $24,000.00   201

        RICHARD HOPKINS        SR SYSTEMS PROGRAMMER     $23,584.75   201

        JANICE PARKS           SR PROGRAMMER            $22,055.79   201

        PAT FLEMING            PROGRAMMER-ANALYST       $19,759.31   201

        JOHN H. WHITE          MGR-CUSTOMER SUPPORT     $27,895.34   316

        BILL APPLE             PERSONNEL MANAGER        $25,485.50   316

        JANET WILLIAMS         SR SYSTEMS ANALYST       $23,500.00   316

        NANCY W. MOORE         SR SYSTEMS PROGRAMMER    $22,565.77   316

        GEORGE MILLER          COST ANALYST             $21,800.00   316

        JAMES GLEASON          ASST MGR-CUST. SUPP.     $21,475.85   316

        SALLY SCHUSTER         SYSTEMS ANALYST          $19,480.00   316

        JAMES P. HILL          APPLICATIONS GRP LDR     $19,259.99   316

        ROBERT P. KELLY        PROGRAMMER               $13,600.00   316

        FRED SMITH             RECEPTIONIST              $9,000.00   316

        JOE DECKER             CHEMIST                  $16,445.00   384

        WAYNE RUIZ             MGR PERSONNEL TRAINING   $27,845.50   401
```

Figure 11-18   A query response including headings and sorted records.

separate lines. Before the report is printed, the data is sorted into descending (D) sequence by salary within ascending (A) sequence by department.

A mainframe query language such as INQUIRE is much more powerful than the query ability afforded by a micro DBMS such as dBASE III or Rbase 5000. Of course, the mainframe version costs much more than the micro version.

How managers use queries

In Chapter 4 we recognized that managers differ in their problem-solving styles. The *problem avoider* tries to block out problems and assume that everything is fine. This type of manager makes little use of the DSS for problem identification and definition. The *problem solver* does not look for problems but solves them when they arise. This person most likely relies on reports to identify problems or potential problems. The *problem seeker* makes full use of the DSS as a problem identification tool. Data base queries provide a convenient vehicle for searching out problems to solve. Reports signal areas for attention, and then queries can probe for specific problems.

Once a manager's attention is called to a problem area, the DSS permits the manager to focus on the source. This can be a step-by-step process, starting with a large area and gradually narrowing down. For example, a sales manager with poor sales for a new product can start out by reviewing sales for a sales region, then sales for a sales office within the region, and finally sales for a salesperson within the office. This method of logically identifying problems is known as *heuristic searching*.

The query ability enables the manager to take an aggressive problem-solving stance—searching out problems to solve. The manager can ask for single data elements or a complete report. With queries, the firm's data base becomes a window through which the manager sees what is happening in the firm. Query information tends to explain the present, whereas reports describe the past. Simulation predicts the future.

Simulation

Simulation is excellent for helping the manager identify alternatives, evaluate them, and select the best. The essential ingredient is a set of mathematical expressions or formulas that describes some essential aspect(s) of the phenomenon being modeled.

Attributes of mathematical models

In Chapter 3 we recognized four basic types of models: physical, narrative, graphical, and mathematical. Here we are concerned only with mathematical models. Mathematical models can be static or dynamic. A *static* model represents the entity being modeled at a specific point in time. A firm's balance sheet is an example; it shows the financial condition at a particular time, such as at the close of business on December 31. A firm's income statement, however, is a *dynamic* model since it represents the behavior of the entity (the firm) over a period of time such as a year.

Mathematical models can also be optimizing or nonoptimizing. An *optimizing* model identifies the single best solution to a problem. A *nonoptimizing* model is one that simply projects an outcome of a particular activity—not necessarily the best outcome.

A final classification deals with the degree of certainty with which the elements or parts of the model can be specified. A *deterministic* model is one where all of the elements are known to act in a specific way. The EOQ (economic order quantity) model is a good example.

$$EOQ = \sqrt{\frac{2AS}{R}}$$

The model has only three elements, or variables. *A* represents the acquisition cost, or the cost to prepare a purchase order, such as $20. *S* is the annual sales amount for the inventory item. Assume this is 1000 units. *R* is the retention cost of maintaining the item in inventory, say $0.16 per unit per year.

These numbers are "plugged into" the model to compute an economic order quantity of 500 units.

$$EOQ = \sqrt{\frac{2 \times 20 \times 1000}{0.16}} = \sqrt{250{,}000} = 500$$

There is no other answer. The variables always interact in the same way.

The other form of model is one where the behavior of the variables cannot be predicted accurately. It is known as a *probabilistic* model. This form uses the probability of things happening. Weather forecasters use this approach, for example, when they say that there is a 30 percent chance of rain.

Probabilities are expressed in percentages. If you are 100 percent certain something will happen, the probability is 1.00. If you are certain it will not happen, the probability is .00.

Since it is impossible to discuss all of the model types, we have singled out two that provide good illustrations of decision support—linear programming and Monte Carlo.

Linear programming

Linear programming, or *LP*, is an optimizing technique that identifies the best solution to a static situation. The word *programming* means that a solution can be identified with a certain amount of precision. The word *linear* means that there is a constant ratio between the variables. For example, if $20,000 in advertising produces $100,000 in sales, then $40,000 in advertising should produce $200,000 in sales.

LP has been a popular computer application since the late 1950s. It focuses on a common management problem—achieving a particular goal with limited resources. In LP, the limited resources are called *constraints*, and the goal is the *objective function*. The objective can be to maximize something, such as profits, or to minimize something, such as costs. LP problems can be solved without a computer, but it is a slow process.

Assume that the owner of a furniture store has a problem in how to allocate warehouse space to the most profitable items. The warehouse has 6500 square feet, of which 3672 are used for minimum quantities of the seven furniture items carried. The items, the floor space required for each item, the minimum quantities, and the total floor space for the minimum quantities are shown in Table 11-3. The question is how best to use the remaining 2828 square feet to maximize profit.

The manager, or an information specialist, prepares a mathematical expression representing the objective function. To do this, profit figures are assembled for each of the seven furniture items (Table 11-4). A variable name (X_1 through X_7) is assigned to each item to represent the *quantity* of each to be located in the available warehouse area. The LP model will compute the value of each of these variable names.

The manager knows that the total profit from the sale of a certain mixture of items will be the sum of the quantity of each times its profit figure. This is the objective function.

Maximum profit $= 20X_1 + 40X_2 + 75X_3 + 170X_4 + 60X_5 + 150X_6 + 65X_7$

Table 11-3 Floor space for minimum quantities

| | Floor Space (Sq. Ft.) | | |
Item	Each	Minimum Quantity	Total
Mattress	9.7	4	38.8
Chair	10.7	50	535.0
Sofa	26	40	1040.0
Dining room suite	32.4	25	810.0
Coffee table	12.2	50	610.0
Bedroom suite	32.9	15	493.5
Bookcase	5.8	25	145.0
Total			3672.3

Table 11-4 Item profit figures

Item	Name of Quantity Variable	Profit (Each)
Mattress	X_1	$ 20
Chair	X_2	40
Sofa	X_3	75
Dining room suite	X_4	170
Coffee table	X_5	60
Bedroom suite	X_6	150
Bookcase	X_7	65

For example, the $20X_1$ means that profit from mattresses will be the product of the unit profit ($20) times the number of mattresses (X_1). The LP model can assign any non-negative value to X_1, including zero. Zero means that none of that item is to be included in the solution.

The remaining task for the manager is to identify any constraints that may exist. One constraint is floor space. Only 2828 square feet are available for the seven items. This contraint can be stated mathematically, using the floor space figures for each of the items from Table 11-3.

$$9.7X_1 + 10.7X_2 + 26X_3 + 32.4X_4 + 12.2X_5 + 32.9X_6 + 5.8X_7 \leq 2828$$

The floor space area for each item multiplied by the quantity of each, added together, cannot be greater than 2828.

Other constraints are expressed in a similar mathematical fashion. The constraints can be more complex than the one of floor space. We can, as an example, instruct that the solution will include twice as many chairs as sofas, and no more dining room suites than coffee tables. In this way, the manager can use her or his judgment to temper the results of the modeling.

The mathematical expressions can be entered into a terminal. The manager must first specify that the linear programming model is to be used by typing in the model name, such as LINPR. The model will be called from the software library by the operating system and entered into primary storage. Execution of the model begins, and the instruction MAXIMIZE is displayed. The manager responds by typing in the objective function. The model responds with the instruction SUBJECT TO. The manager then types in each of the constraints, followed by the word END. The model performs the computations and displays the optimal value of the objective function and the quantities of each furniture item that produce the optimal value. In our example, the model determines that only two items should be located in the available area: chairs and sofas. If 113 chairs ($X_2 = 113$) and 57 sofas ($X_3 = 57$) are stocked, the profit from the use of the available area will be $8783.

LP is a *static* model. Time is not a variable. Only one solution is produced, and it is expected to be used until at least one of the factors changes and a new solution must be computed. LP is an *optimizing* model. The furniture arrangement provided by LP is the best in terms of accomplishing the maximum profit objective. No other arrangement will produce a higher profit. LP is also a *deterministic* model in that it includes no probabilities. The variables are expected to interact in the prescribed manner with 100 percent certainty.

LP is designed to handle problems with a great deal of structure. Invariably, however, the manager will want to evaluate the LP decision before it is implemented. LP is good for addressing the structured portion of the problem, but the manager will want to apply judgment or intuition in addressing the unstructured portion.

A probabilistic model: Monte Carlo

We will conclude our discussion of computer-based decision support with a model that simulates an activity over time (it is dynamic), doesn't identify the single best answer (it is nonoptimizing), and deals in probabilities. This model illustrates the Monte Carlo method of simulating randomly occurring events.

Assume in this case that the manager of a department store doesn't know how many sales clerks to assign to a department because the volume of customer activity varies. Different numbers of customers enter the department at different times throughout the day and make purchases of different values. Data describing these variations in customer activity can be gathered, and a model can be constructed to simulate the effect of assigning different numbers of sales clerks.

The store hours can be divided into ten-minute intervals (9:00–9:10,

9:10–9:20, and so on) and a record kept of the number of customers arriving during each interval. The distribution of customers might look like this:

Number of intervals with zero customers	6
Number of intervals with one customer	12
Number of intervals with two customers	20
Number of intervals with three customers	6
Number of intervals with four customers	4
	48

Of the 48 ten-minute intervals during the eight-hour day, six intervals had no customers, twelve had one customer, and so on.

This distribution of arrivals can be converted into a *probability distribution* by calculating percentages (or probabilities) for each customer group.

$$
\begin{aligned}
\text{Zero customers} &= 6/48 = .12 \\
\text{One customer} &= 12/48 = .25 \\
\text{Two customers} &= 20/48 = .43 \\
\text{Three customers} &= 6/48 = .12 \\
\text{Four customers} &= 4/48 = .08 \\
&\qquad\qquad\quad 1.00
\end{aligned}
$$

The same technique can be used for the dollar values of the 86 customers' purchases.

$$
\begin{aligned}
\text{No purchase} &= 18/86 = .20 \\
\$5 \text{ purchase} &= 20/86 = .23 \\
\$10 \text{ purchase} &= 22/86 = .26 \\
\$15 \text{ purchase} &= 16/86 = .19 \\
\$20 \text{ purchase} &= 10/86 = .12 \\
&\qquad\qquad\quad 1.00
\end{aligned}
$$

The problem is how many sales clerks to assign to the department to maximize profit. If one sales clerk is required to serve one customer during a ten-minute interval, the number of clerks can range from one to four (since a maximum of four customers is in the department at one time). If only one clerk is assigned, customers will frequently not be served and sales will be lost. On the other hand, if four clerks are assigned no sales will be lost, but there will be some idle clerk time and expenses will be higher.

An important assumption of the model is that there is no pattern to either customer arrivals or purchases. They are both strictly random. A technique that can be used to simulate the random activity is *Monte Carlo*, and it is based on the selection of random numbers. The numbers range from 00 through 99. The chance of selecting one of these 100 numbers at random is 1 percent or .01.

Series of the hundred numbers can be assigned to each entry in the two probability distributions. For example, the distribution of arrival times looks like this:

Number of Customers	Probability (P)	Number Series
0	.12	00–11
1	.25	12–36
2	.43	37–79
3	.12	80–91
4	.08	92–99

The computer can randomly generate numbers from 00 through 99, and the chance of generating one from 00 through 11 is 12 percent, corresponding to the first probability of .12. Similarly, the chance of generating a number from 12 through 36 is 25 percent (since this series represents 25 of the 100 numbers), corresponding to the second probability of .25. In this manner, the computer can simulate the random arrival pattern of the customers. Any number generated will fall within one of the five number series. The series within which the random number falls determines the number of customers arriving during a given ten-minute interval. Other numbers can be assigned to the customer purchases, and that activity too can be simulated randomly.

The model simulates the effect of assigning a certain number of sales clerks. In the example in Figure 11-19, only one clerk is assigned, and the activity of only a single hour is simulated. In practice, a much larger number of hours would be simulated. The computer randomly selects the number 23 to represent the number of customer arrivals in period 1. When matched to the number series of customer arrivals, 23 falls within the range of 12–36. This means that one customer arrives in period 1. The computer then selects the number 45 to determine the value of that customer's purchase. The number falls within the range of a $10 purchase. One random number is selected for each time period to represent the number of arrivals. Then a single random number is selected for each customer arriving in that period to represent the value of each purchase. Since only one clerk is available, only the first customer arriving in a ten-minute interval can be served. Other customers could have made purchases in the amounts shown, but they leave the store and those sales are lost.

In a similar manner, the other numbers of clerks can be simulated. The nonoptimizing model doesn't identify which alternative is the best. The model only supplies the results that can be expected from each.

The manager can select the best alternative by comparing costs and benefits, as shown in Table 11-5. Costs are calculated by adding the hourly cost of the clerks to a fixed cost. The benefits are the sales. According to the example, three clerks produce the most profit.

The model supports the manager by processing data representing the structured portion of the problem. But there are other factors—the unstructured por-

INTERVAL	RANDOM NUMBER-- ARRIVALS	NUMBER OF ARRIVALS	RANDOM NUMBER-- PURCHASES	VALUE OF PURCHASE	CLERK NO. 1 SALES	IDLE TIME	LOST SALES
1	23	1	45	$10	$10	0	
2	64	2	14	$ 0		0	
			59	$10			$10
3	79	2	11	$ 0		0	
			28	$ 5			$ 5
4	49	2	46	$10	$10	0	
			47	$10			$10
5	99	4	60	$10	$10	0	
			25	$ 5			$ 5
			97	$20			$20
			41	$ 5			$ 5
6	50	2	81	$15	$15	0	
			31	$ 5			$ 5
			TOTALS	$105	$45	0	$60

Figure 11-19 Simulation of assigning one sales clerk to the department.

Table 11-5 Cost benefit analysis

Number of Clerks	Sales	Costs	Profit (Loss)
1	$395	$400	$(5)
2	$460	$435	$ 25
3	$515	$470	$ 45
4	$520	$505	$ 15

tion—for the manager to consider. These unstructured factors include the store's image, the competitive situation, the sense of community responsibility, marketing strategies, and so on. Together the model and the manager solve a semistructured problem.

The Monte Carlo retail salesclerk model is a *dynamic* model in that it simulates activity over time—each ten-minute interval during a day, week, month, or even year. The Monte Carlo model is a *nonoptimizing* model; it does not point out the best solution. The model simply says, "If you decide to use three clerks, this is a likely outcome." Since the Monte Carlo model uses probabilities, it is a *probabilistic* model. We do not know exactly when an event will occur, but we know the likelihood based on past history.

Like the linear programming model, the Monte Carlo model would be initiated from a terminal. The model is stored in the software library and is called into primary storage. The manager is asked to input the necessary scenario and decision data. When all of the data has been entered, the model is executed and the results displayed or printed. The manager examines the output and then decides whether to run another simulation. The manager can enter new data, such as a different number of clerks, and execute the model again. The manager continues to simulate alternate strategies until he or she feels that all of the feasible ones have been explored. Then the manager makes the decision.

You can see the basic difference between the Monte Carlo model and the linear programming model. The linear programming model provides a greater amount of decision support by identifying the optimal solution. But LP requires a greater degree of problem structure than does Monte Carlo. The nature of the problem dictates the choice of the model and, to a great extent, the amount of decision support that the model can provide.

Modeling advantages and disadvantages

Models offer some real advantages to the manager. They provide a *predictive power*—a look into the future—that no other information-producing method offers. Also, the modeling process can be a *learning experience* for the participating manager, and models are *less expensive* than the trial-and-error method. The modeling process is costly, but not nearly as costly as a bad decision. Finally, the *speed* of the simulation enables decisions to be evaluated in a short period of time. In less than an hour, a manager can simulate the effects of several strategies on several simulated years of operation.

There are also some disadvantages to models. Most important is the *difficulty of modeling a business system*. Many business operations are influenced by environmental impacts that the firm doesn't control or completely understand. Additionally, a business organization is a social system composed of one or more people—each with his or her own unique motives, goals, problems, and so on. The resulting system is extremely difficult to quantify. Therefore, models only approximate the business system. A second disadvantage is the *high degree of mathematical skill* that can be required. This is a good work area for graduates of business schools. A blend of business and mathematical knowledge, along with computer literacy, is a valuable resource to a firm engaged in modeling activities.

Modeling in perspective as a DSS tool

The mathematical model has always been central to the concept of a decision support system. This key role should increase in importance as DSS designers work to incorporate features of expert systems. If the DSS is to function as an expert system, it will do so by virtue of its modeling ability—not reports and data base queries.

The fact is, however, that modeling has probably been oversold as a DSS tool from the beginning. We have seen that managers base decisions on intuition as well as analytic data. Many managers have never used models, and those who have used them have tempered their output with their own judgment. But this is the DSS concept—the manager and DSS work together to jointly solve problems. This reality, that the DSS does not make the decision, explains much of the success that the DSS concept has enjoyed compared to early MIS ideals.

Another reason why modeling has been oversold is the factor of speed. Managers typically do not have to make decisions in a few minutes. The pressure to make quick decisions may occur occasionally at lower-management levels, but rarely at the top. A manager will take her or his time when making a crucial decision. Very often, a group will interact for weeks or months before agreeing on a solution. The need, therefore, for a DSS tool that responds in seconds or minutes is of less value than first thought.

Perhaps the reasons for managements' reluctance to embrace the model are being overcome with the new breed of modeling tools. When micro software such as VisiCalc, Multiplan, and 1-2-3 are included as modeling tools, a different picture emerges. We see thousands of managers, many with minimal computer skills, using these packages with apparent success. Without question, this is the area of modeling where the most interest, and success, is being seen. This activity is stimulating newer and more powerful spreadsheet packages such as Framework, Symphony, and Visi On. Also, as managers gain confidence in using micro-based spreadsheet software, they will be stimulated to engage in more sophisticated modeling projects. Maybe the spreadsheet is exactly what was needed to get managers involved in modeling.

Computer Graphics

Each of the three information-producing methods (reports, queries, and simulation) lends itself to graphical output.

Much attention is currently being directed at computer graphics, but the research to date comparing graphics to tabular output has been disappointing. We commented in Chapter 5 on the review of graphics research by DeSanctis that showed mixed results. Seven projects showed graphics to be better than tables, twelve showed tables to be better, and ten showed no difference. Blake Ives, a Dartmouth professor, came to the same conclusion in a similar review in 1982. Ives concluded that

> The empirical literature examining the impact of graphics and color on various indicators of success offers scarce support for the widely held notion that graphics, and especially color graphics, will contribute substantially to decision maker effectiveness.[13]

---

[13] Blake Ives, "Graphical User Interfaces for Business Information Systems," *MIS Quarterly* (Special Issue 1982): 23.

Ives urged caution in believing the claims of graphics firms that their products will lead to improvements in decision quality.

Perhaps graphics will not be the panacea that is often claimed, but that has been the case with every MIS and DSS tool that has been developed, as well as the overall concepts themselves. The variability among decision makers causes the tools and concepts to work better for one manager than another. The fact that uniformly positive research findings have not been achieved should not cause us to dismiss graphics as a possibly valuable DSS tool. The fact that 7 projects out of 29 showed graphics to be better than tables indicates that in *certain* situations graphs may do a better job of conveying information and therefore contribute to better decision making. The task then becomes the identification of (1) the situations lending themselves best to graphical representation, and (2) the characteristics of managers best able to utilize graphical information. This understanding would enable the information specialist to recommend graphics in those situations where they would do the most good.

Since the level of interest in graphics is high, and is expected to go higher, we will briefly review the graphics options facing the modern manager.

Graphics hardware

Graphics can be produced on any size computer. Figure 11-20 identifies 5 options. The first two employ a mainframe or minicomputer. The plotter can be either online or offline. We described the basic types of plotters in Chapter 5. The three remaining options apply to a micro. The graphics can be displayed on the screen, printed on a serial printer with a graphics capability, and printed on a plotter. According to a 1984 survey of almost 200 organizations by the University of Minnesota, microcomputer configurations are the most popular.[14]

Graphics software

The Minnesota study revealed that SAS/GRAPH is the most popular mainframe graphics package followed by TELL-A-GRAF and DISSPLA. Figure 11-21 is a graph printed using DISSPLA. The sample combines a map with a bar graph and a three-dimensional effect. With a mainframe graphics package, there are practically no limits to how the data can be displayed.

The same study revealed 1-2-3 to be the most popular micro graphics package. Although 1-2-3 is not limited to graphics, it was being used by about 65 of the organizations. Chartmaster and Visi Trend (both graphics packages) were next most popular but were each used by less than 10 organizations. These figures support what many persons have believed all along—that 1-2-3 is largely responsible for the current interest in graphics. 1-2-3 provides for fewer options than a mainframe package but is very easy to use. The graphics capability is built into the spreadsheet model.

---

[14]John A. Lehman, Doug Vogel, and Gary Dickson, "Business Graphics Trends," *Datamation* 30 (November 15, 1984): 119–122.

a. Online mainframe or mini plotter.

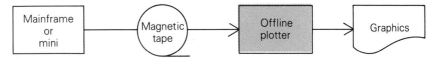

b. Offline plotter.

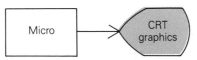

c. Microcomputer screen graphics.

d. Microcomputer serial printer.

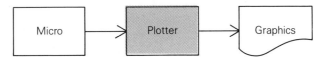

e. Microcomputer plotter.

Figure 11-20 Graphics hardware options.

Graphics design tips

Ives makes a number of suggestions concerning graphics design. Some of the suggestions appear in a reworded form below.

Bar charts

- Avoid crossing bars with grid lines.
- Leave adequate space to separate groups of bars.

Pie charts

- Don't include too many slices.
- Arrange slices in sequence according to size.

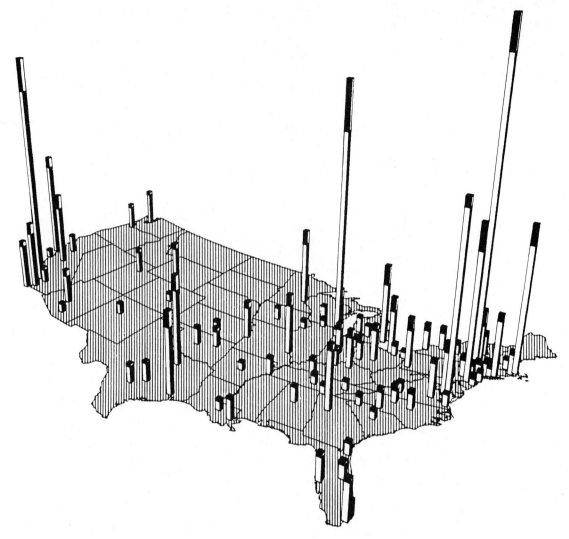

Figure 11-21 A computer graphic employing multiple charting techniques—three dimensions, a
map, and bars.

Source: Produced using DISSPLA, a proprietary software product of ISSCO, San Diego, CA.

Grids

- Avoid unnecessary or overly prominent grid lines.
- Avoid labeling grids at too fine a level of detail.

Titles, labels, and text

- Locate chart title at the top and outside the grid.
- Use horizontal labels, even for vertical axes of bar charts and scatter diagrams, and for slices of pie charts.

- Avoid using legends or keys if the chart can readily accommodate direct labeling.
- Type size should indicate hierarchical level, but keep the type style consistent.
- Don't use all capital letters or right justification for long titles or text.
- Locate the titles in the same position on multiple charts.
- Avoid lines of text greater than 60 characters.
- Avoid abbreviations.

Color

- Multiple lines on a line graph are more easily distinguished using different colors than using different types of lines such as dots, dashes, and so on. But do not use color combinations that are difficult to distinguish, such as yellow and orange.
- Use color on the parts of the chart to be emphasized.
- Avoid combinations of foreground and background colors that clash, such as red and blue.
- Maintain consistency in color assignment between multiple charts.

Presentation graphics

Firms are finding that the utility of computer graphics goes beyond the screen display or the hardcopy plot. It is possible to make color slides of the graphs for use in group presentations.

The early approach was to mount a camera on a tripod in front of the CRT. More modern, specially designed video slide output devices do a better job. The Computer Camera from Celtic Technology plugs into the micro between the CPU and the monitor. As signals are sent to the monitor, they are converted by the Computer Camera to a film image. A similar device is the Lang Videoslide 35 featuring a Polaroid 35mm Instant Slide System. With this setup, it is possible to create a slide in five minutes.

Coca-Cola USA has used the Videoslide 35 with much success. They previously paid about $60 per slide to have them professionally made. Now the cost is only 50 cents each. Although the quality is not quite as good, the computer-produced slides are "very satisfactory."

Presentation tips

When making a graphics presentation, keep the following suggestions in mind:

- Let the graphics serve as your notes
- Don't read labels and text—the audience is capable of doing this
- Keep the lights on as much as possible to minimize the opportunity for snoozing
- Place the projection screen to the side of the room so that you do not interfere with the image

Who uses graphics?

The Minnesota study revealed several important findings concerning graphics usage:

- Almost 90 percent of the surveyed organizations have a computer graphics capability
- The information services, finance, and marketing areas are the big users
- Very few end users of all computer output have business graphics experience
- Managers and professionals have the most business graphics experience
- Graphics are used as a DSS tool more at the lower and middle levels than at the top

The survey respondents, predominantly information services managers, believed that the major growth area for graphics will be decision support. Twenty-six percent of the respondents shared this view. Other areas (that can be considered DSS when defined broadly as we have done) are written reports (18 percent), oral presentations (14 percent), replace computer reports (10 percent), and informal communications (2 percent).

Putting computer graphics in perspective

It is easy to see the attraction that managers have for computer graphics. The graphics can be very impressive and cost little to prepare. Combine this natural vulnerability with strong sales efforts by the some 700 firms selling graphics hardware, software, and supplies, and we will definitely see an increase in graphics use.

If the users' experiences follow the research findings, there will be many situations where graphics add little or nothing to the communication of information. But even if graphics are not contributing to decision support, the users will likely be satisfied—as the Minnesota researchers found. This satisfaction will stimulate heavier use.

This concludes our description of the methods that the manager can use to obtain information from the computer—reports, queries, and modeling. Graphics is an option for all three methods.

One element of the DSS model remains. It is the DSS software library.

The DSS Software Library

The DSS software library contains all of the software needed to provide the manager's information. Three categories of software are included—application programs, statistical packages, and fourth-generation languages.

Application programs

The application programs coded by information specialists using programming languages mainly produce repetitive reports. Some of the reports are byproducts of the data processing system. Examples are the balance sheet and the aged receivables report.

Statistical packages

Packages of statistical routines have been available for a number of years. Examples are SAS and SPSS. These packages include most of the standard statistical techniques such as t-test, regression, time series, factor analysis, and so forth. Most likely you have used one of these packages in a statistics course.

The first packages were written for use on mainframe computers. During the past few years a new group of packages has been designed specifically for use on micros. We listed some of these packages in Table 6-1.

Historically, managers have not personally used these packages even though their firms had the necessary hardware and software. The packages have been used instead by management science and operations research specialists. This situation has already begun to change for two reasons. First, managers are becoming more skilled in the use of statistics, and second, micro-based statistical software makes the tools more accessible.

Fourth-generation languages

During the early years of the computer, it was popular to categorize hardware developments by generation. That practice is no longer popular since technology innovation leveled off, and the mini/micro boom blurred the picture. Today, software is getting the generation treatment. The term *fourth-generation language (4GL)* has been coined to represent the assortment of user-friendly software that has hit the market.

The term nonprocedural language is often used interchangeably with 4GL. A *nonprocedural language* is one where the programmer need not code the instructions in the same sequence that the computer will follow. The user can concentrate on the problem to be solved rather than the process that the computer will follow in solving it. Most 4GLs are nonprocedural, but a few are not.

A 4GL gives the user much more power than does a conventional programming language such as BASIC or COBOL. The increase in productivity, measured in the number of lines of code written per day, has been estimated to be a factor of 10 or more.

James Martin, a computer visionary who has been promoting the use of 4GL for several years, estimates that by 1990 users will be doing 50 percent of their own program development. This level of self-sufficiency has already been met, and exceeded, by some firms. The sales forecasting department at Pet Foods, for example, develops 80 percent of their projects.

A 4GL includes one or more of the following components:[15]

- A data base query language
- A modeling language
- A report writer
- A very high level language
- A graph generator
- An application generator

Our earlier discussions should provide us with an understanding of data base query languages, report writers, and graph generators. We will discuss the other components here. *Modeling languages* are intended for use in developing mathematical models. Conventional programming languages can be used, but special simulation languages make the task easier.

One of the oldest simulation languages is GPSS (General Purpose Simulation System), developed by IBM in the early 1960s. It is still popular, and versions are available for many popular mainframes and minis. Other simulation languages include DYNAMO, SLAM, SIMSCRIPT, GASP, and MODEL.

MODEL is intended for use by the manager in a variety of ways. It can produce a spreadsheet, a forecast, a project network, or a simulation of future activity. An example of the MODEL language is printed in Figure 11-22. This model can be used to conduct a what-if type of analysis for the coming five-year period. An example of the output appears in Figure 11-23. The manager keys in the instructions and receives the output using a terminal.

The manager views the output and may elect to simulate the effect of some changed inputs. Figure 11-24 shows the effect of changing the "net sales" and the "other expense."

The electronic spreadsheet packages such as Symphony, Jazz, 1-2-3, and Framework are used in simulation, but they are not really languages as such. You can see that the MODEL instructions in Figure 11-22 have the appearance of a program produced by a procedural language. You do not get such a program when you use a spreadsheet package.

The term *very high level language* is often used to describe a programming language, such as APL, that offers a succinctness and power (but not necessarily user friendliness) over and above that of conventional languages. A number of 4GL packages include the very high level capability—FOCUS, MANTIS, and NOMAD 2 are examples.

An *application generator* enables the user to produce an application program, such as payroll, without programming. An early example was MANTIS. MARK V (a descendant of MARK IV) is a current example.

FOCUS, from Information Builders, Inc., has proven to be very attractive as a 4GL. It provides all six of the components and is available for the IBM 370, PC, DEC VAX, and Wang VS computers. Because of its comprehensiveness and user friendliness, FOCUS is often the main software package offered by information centers. Figure 11-25 includes the FOCUS instructions necessary to produce the output in Figure 11-26.

---

[15] This classification comes from Dipankar Basu, "Cleaning Up the Language," *ICP Data Processing Management* 9 (Winter 1984): 44ff.

```
DESCRIPTION                              Describe what you want to see
  COLUMNS
    RESERVE 5 YR
      HEAD BY YEAR FROM 1985
  ROWS                             You implicitly control the order of your
    NET SALES                                      report output here
    COST OF SALES
    GROSS PROFIT
    OPERATING EXPENSE
    DEPRECIATION
    OPERATING PROFIT
    OTHER INCOME
    OTHER EXPENSE
    NET BEFORE TAX
    TAX
    NET PROFIT
    CASH COMMON
    NET AFTER DIVIDEND
    RET EARN BEGIN
    RET EARN END
    SHARES
    EPS
  VARIABLES                              For single elements of data
    PRESENT VALUE

  MATH                             Describe formulas and logic here
    GROSS PROFIT   NET SALES   COST OF SALES
    CALL DEPSIMPLE (DEPRECIATION,1000,0,4,12,12,200)    Depreciation
    OPERATING PROFIT   GROSS PROFIT   (OPERATING
      EXPENSE + DEPRECIATION)
    NET BEFORE TAX   OPERATING PROFIT + OTHER INCOME   OTHER
      EXPENSE
    TAX   NET BEFORE TAX*.48
    NET PROFIT   NET BEFORE TAX   TAX
    NET AFTER DIVIDEND   NET PROFIT   CASH COMMON
    RET EARN END   RET EARN BEGIN + NET AFTER DIVIDEND
    FOR COLUMNS YR2 THRU YR5         Column by column calculations
        RET EARN BEGIN   RET EARN END (COLUMNS-1)
        RET EARN END   RET EARN BEGIN + NET AFTER DIVIDEND
    NEXT
    EPS   NET PROFIT/SHARES
    CALL NPV (PRESENT VALUE,EPS,18,12)              NPV on EPS
REPORT DETAILS                             The detailed report
    TITLE
      'ABC COMPANY'
      ' '                                     Cause a blank line
      RIGHT 'PREPARED:' DATE                    Date the report
    UNDERLINE AFTER COST OF SALES, DEPRECIATION, OTHER
    EXPENSE
    UNDERLINE ' ' BEFORE NET PROFIT
    SUBTITLE BEFORE CASH COMMON
      ' '

    LEFT 'PER SHARE ANALYSIS:'
REPORT SUMMARY                             The summary report
    SHOW NET SALES, NET PROFIT, EPS           Show only select
    TITLE                                      rows (or columns)
      'SUMMARY'
      ' '

    SUBTITLE AFTER EPS
      LEFT 'PRESENT VALUE AT 18% IS:'PRESENT VALUE
INSTRUCTIONS                        This controls the sequence of events
    GET 'ASSUMED' DATA                The file that has the assumptions
    PERFORM MATH                       Use the MATH section statements
    PRINT REPORT DETAILS                        Select detailed report
    WHATIF
```

Figure 11-22 Example of the MODEL simulation language.

Source: Courtesy of Lloyd Bush.

ABC COMPANY

PREPARED: 10/15/84

	1985	1986	1987	1988	1989
NET SALES	$7,000	$7,300	$7,600	$7,900	$8,200
COST OF SALES	5,528	5,667	6,000	5,769	5,997
GROSS PROFIT	1,472	1,633	1,600	2,131	2,203
OPERATING EXPENSE	1,032	659	1,070	918	1,011
DEPRECIATION	500	250	125	125	0
OPERATING PROFIT	(60)	724	405	1,088	1,192
OTHER INCOME	56	48	47	47	51
OTHER EXPENSE	9	10	21	15	19
NET BEFORE TAX	(13)	762	431	1,120	1,224
TAX	(6)	366	207	538	588
NET PROFIT	$ (7)	$ 396	$ 224	$ 582	$ 636
PER SHARE ANALYSIS:					
CASH COMMON	200	300	275	400	500
NET AFTER DIVIDEND	(207)	96	(51)	182	136
RET EARN BEGIN	653	446	542	492	674
RET EARN END	446	542	492	674	810
SHARES	31	31	31	31	31
EPS	(0)	13	7	19	21

Figure 11-23   Sample output from a MODEL simulation.
Source: Courtesy of Lloyd Bush.

The Manager and End-User Computing

In the previous chapter we noted that we can expect the manager to personally use some OA applications, but not all. What about DSS? Are there some DSS tools that the manager is more likely to adopt than others?

Application programs

The manager can call up application programs using a terminal and have reports displayed or printed. The reports that the manager is likely to trigger in this manner are those that he or she feels are important, and possibly worked with the information specialist to develop.

Statistical packages

The manager is likely not to personally use statistical packages. These packages have been around for a long time and have never stimulated manager use. Even

```
WHATIF: NET SALES = 7500 GROW BY 3%          Use convenient data
WHATIF: OTHER EXPENSE = 12 INCREASE BY 5       generation aids
WHATIF: PERFORM MATH
WHATIF: PRINT REPORT SUMMARY                  Select your report
```

	SUMMARY				
	1985	1986	1987	1988	1989
NET SALES	7,500	7,725	7,957	8,195	8,441
NET PROFIT	(8)	484	344	665	755
EPS	(0)	16	11	21	24

PRESENT VALUE AT 18% IS: 39

Figure 11-24 Input and output for a "what-if" simulation.
Source: Courtesy of Lloyd Bush.

if the manager has the necessary mathematical skills, she or he would rather have someone else, such as a management scientist or operations researcher, do the work.

Now that these packages are available for micros, we will see greater use in smaller organizations, but not by the managers.

Fourth-generation languages

Manager use of 4GL depends on factors unique to the manager and also characteristics of the 4GL tools and the problem to be solved. We discussed the personal factors influencing problem solving in Chapter 4. Characteristics of the problem include the degree of structure, the number of variables, whether probabilities are involved, the need for optimization, whether time is a variable, and so on.

```
DEFINE FILE SALES
REGION/A12=DECODE REGION(NE 'NORTH EAST'
            SE 'SOUTH EAST' MW 'MID WEST'
            MA 'MID-ATLANTIC' ) ;
END
TABLE FILE SALES
HEADING CENTER
"PRODUCT UNIT SALES ANALYSIS </1 "
SUM UNITS AND ROW-TOTAL AND COLUMN-TOTAL
ACROSS REGION
BY PRODNUM AS 'PRODUCT,NUMBER'
END
```

Figure 11-25 Example of FOCUS instructions to produce a printed output of a selected portion of a data base.

PAGE1

PRODUCT UNIT SALES ANALYSIS

REGION PRODUCT NUMBER	MIDWEST	MID-ATLANTIC	NORTH EAST	SOUTH EAST	TOTAL
10524	164	181	184	115	644
10526	40	126	150	45	361
11275	189	219	133	168	709
11302	179	130	288	172	769
11303	99	121	220	30	470
11537	90	260	110	124	584
11563	297	245	520	371	1433
11567	86	80	.	20	186
12275	.	.	.	30	30
12345	.	10	.	.	10
13737	.	.	29	.	29
13797	110	160	65	389	724
13938	324	186	441	164	1115
13979	.	12	.	.	12
14156	200	538	120	169	1027
15016	94	257	156	245	752
16394	252	210	187	40	689
16436	.	132	52	20	204
16934	.	50	.	.	50
17434	166	378	84	174	802
17905	164	70	108	199	541
34562	25	.	.	.	25
34567	100	.	.	.	100
56267	146	190	910	255	1501
TOTAL	2725	3555	3757	2730	12767

Figure 11-26 Printed output produced by FOCUS.

The tool characteristics can be viewed as user friendliness on one hand and something that might be called "DSS power" on the other. The power includes all of those factors producing decision support. The power is a measure of what the manager gets out of the DSS; user friendliness is a measure of what he or she puts in.

The six 4GL tools are positioned in Figure 11-27 using the factors of user friendliness and power. The dotted line labeled "Efficiency Line" is a type of breakeven point; tools above the line offer better ratios of power to ease of use than do the tools below the line. The purpose of the figure is to illustrate the

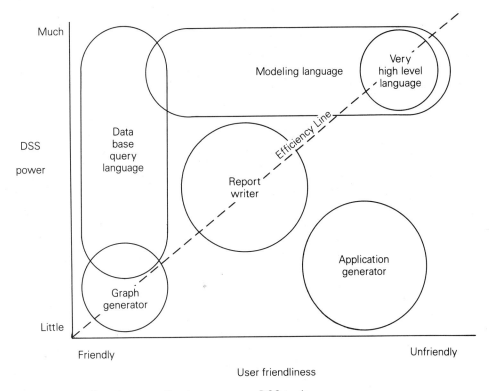

Figure 11-27 Fourth-generation languages as DSS tools.

general appeal that the tools have for manager use. It is only a conceptual diagram and would not apply equally to all managers or all DSS tools.

The two ovals in the figure, data base query language and modeling language, indicate considerable variation within each category. The upper part of the query language oval includes mainframe DBMS and the lower part includes micro DBMS. The left-hand part of the modeling language oval includes the micro spreadsheets, and the right-hand part includes languages such as GPSS. The right-hand end of the modeling oval overlaps the circle of very high level language such as APL. This means that a user would have two tools such as APL and GPSS that could offer approximately the same power and user friendliness for certain classes of problems.

DSS Implementation

The manager will be able to do his or her own implementation for small DSSs. For example, a manager can use INQUIRE to prepare a report of selected data base contents or use 1-2-3 to build a spreadsheet model and graph the results. If, however, a DSS is too large for the manager to handle, then an information specialist must help. Keen uses the term *implementer* to describe the information specialist with the necessary DSS skills.[16]

If the manager elects to use an implementer, then it is important that the implementer understand the decision-making process. Keen regards that understanding as the key to DSS implementation.

A DSS Example

Eastman Kodak spent two years and $1.2 million implementing their Market Intelligence DSS (Midss).[17] The information services staff interviewed 30 people from various parts of the company to generate a primary list of user needs. The needs were then transformed into information and software requirements. Available packaged software was evaluated, and the decision was made to build the Midss around Management Decision Systems' 4GL named EXPRESS. The decision was made to also provide SAS, SAS/GRAPH, IFPS, and APL in order to meet a wide variety of needs.

The Midss consists of several systems. The first one implemented was a model that supports decisions relating to advertising strategy. Kodak feels that this model alone has saved $5 million in unnecessary advertising costs. The largest system tracks consumer buying behavior and matches film purchasing and processing to that behavior. This model is believed to have produced savings 10 times greater than the cost of the Midss—in the first year alone.

Months of soul-searching concerning just what the Midss should accomplish preceded the actual implementation. The implementers seem to have had the skills that Keen recognized as necessary for DSS success.

Summary

The DSS concept originated because of the failure of early MISs to provide managers with information for decision making. Gorry and Scott Morton built upon Simon's decision types and Anthony's management levels to construct their grid. They used the term DSS to describe all of the problems that had not received support from the computer. The DSS concept gradually picked up support, and by the late seventies was rivaling MIS for followers.

DSS is most certainly different from MIS, but how do the two relate? Some experts such as Sprague regard DSS as something providing a higher level of support than the MIS. In this text we regard DSS as a part of MIS, just as Gorry and Scott Morton did in their grid.

There has always been general agreement that the DSS is intended to solve semi-structured problems. But there has been disagreement concerning whether a terminal is required, whether the manager must personally use the DSS, and whether information-producing methods in addition to mathematical modeling

---

[16] Peter G. W. Keen, "Decision Support Systems: Translating Analytic Techniques into Useful Tools," *Sloan Management Review* 21 (Spring 1980): 33–44.

[17] "Kodak's Midss Zooms in on DSS Role," *Computerworld* (January 21, 1985): 41, 52.

are used. Our view is that a terminal is not required and that an intermediary can "drive" the DSS for the manager. We view the DSS broadly, as did Alter, by including reports and data base queries.

A DSS includes a data base, an information processor, and a software library. The key to developing a good DSS is not hardware or software, however, but a good understanding of the decision process necessary to solve the problem at hand. This is where management theory comes into play. We can use theoretical constructs such as Mintzberg's roles, Simon's decision phases, and Melcher's responsibility relationships to better understand the needs to be supported.

As firms build their DSS data base, they can gather their own primary data or obtain secondary data from government or private organizations. As a general rule, primary data describes internal operations and secondary data describes the firm's environment.

There are three basic methods that the manager can use to obtain information from the DSS—report, query, and simulation. These methods are used in definition and solution. Reports and queries contribute most to definition; simulation contributes most to solution.

Reports are prepared according to a schedule or in response to a special event. Reports can be detailed or summary, and contain three basic parts—heading, body, and footing. Managers use reports primarily to review past performance. Management by exception can be built into the report formats to increase their utility.

Queries require a data base and a query language. With INQUIRE, statements are formed using commands. The commands permit data retrieval and report generation. Managers use queries to obtain current information. Successive querying—narrowing the scope of a potential problem area—is called heuristic searching. A manager can use queries to seek out problems and to better understand them.

Simulation permits the manager to look into the future, although with less than 100 percent accuracy. Mathematical models provide this predictive power and can be classified based on the inclusion of a time element, the degree of optimization, and the use of probabilities. Linear programming is a static, optimizing, deterministic model. The Monte Carlo sales clerk model is the opposite—dynamic, nonoptimizing, and probabilistic. Models enable the manager to predict and to learn with economy and speed. But modeling is difficult, and it requires skill in both development and use.

Each of the three methods for obtaining information (reports, queries, and simulations) can employ graphical output. Although research findings recognize that graphics do not contribute to improved decision making in every instance, there are certain situations where graphics should be used. Graphics can be produced by plotters or printers with a graphics capability, either online or offline, and utilizing a mainframe, mini, or micro. The decision support capability of graphics can be enhanced by employing several suggestions relating to art, labels, and color. Computer output of presentation graphics enables the manager or information specialist to integrate graphics into group presentations.

The DSS software library includes application programs, statistical packages, and fourth-generation languages (4GL). There are six possible components that can be incorporated into a 4GL—data base querying, modeling, report writing, very high level language, graph generating, and application generating. A manager can be expected to use those 4GL that offer enough DSS power to compensate for the amount of effort required to learn and use them.

When a DSS becomes large or complex, an information specialist can assist the manager by playing the role of implementer.

Key Terms

programmed, nonprogrammed decisions

intelligence, design, choice, and review activity

entrepreneur, disturbance handler, resource allocator, negotiator

responsibility relationships

structured, unstructured, semi-structured decisions

structured decision system (SDS)

decision support system (DSS)

intermediary, chauffeur

primary, secondary data

repetitive, periodic, scheduled report

special report

simulation

scenario

detailed report, listing

summary report

ascending, descending sequence

heuristic search

static, dynamic model

optimizing, nonoptimizing model

deterministic, probabilistic model

linear programming (LP)

constraint

objective function

Monte Carlo method

probability distribution

presentation graphics

statistical package

fourth-generation language (4GL)

nonprocedural language

modeling language

very high level language

application generator

implementer

Key Concepts

Simon's phases of decision making as an illustration of the systems approach

Mintzberg's decisional roles

Melcher's responsibility relationships

How decisions, and the problems that they solve, can be viewed on a continuum ranging from structured to unstructured with a vast semi-structured area in between

The synergistic relationship between

the manager and the computer in solving semi-structured problems

How the responsibility of the DSS to function as an expert system distinguishes the DSS from the early MIS concept

How the DSS provides decision support at each step of the problem-solving process

The special abilities of reports and queries to support problem definition effort and of simulations to support solution effort

How reports can be designed to facilitate management by exception

Use of a query language in heuristic searching

Model types and attributes

The relatively structured nature of problems solved with linear programming

The semi-structured nature of problems solved with Monte Carlo

How the Monte Carlo method simulates randomly occurring activity

The ability of graphics to contribute improved communication of information in particular situations

The variety of software labeled fourth-generation language

The relative contributions that the various categories of 4GL can make to end-user computing

The necessity of a DSS implementer for complex systems

Questions

1. What terms did Simon use to describe the different types of decisions? What terms did Gorry and Scott Morton use?

2. How do Simon's decision-making phases relate to the systems approach?

3. Which decisional role is being played when a manager settles a labor dispute? Approves the fiscal budget for the coming year? Decides to beef up the sales force upon learning of intensified competition? Decides to phase out a product line over the next three years due to low sales?

4. Which of Simon's decision-making phases are performed by someone with operating responsibility? By someone who must approve the decision? By someone who must be notified?

5. Which theorists did Gorry and Scott Morton draw upon in building their grid?

6. List Alter's six DSS types. Which one, or ones, would function as an expert system?

7. If a terminal is used, who should operate it? Who should not?

8. Is an intermediary the same as a chauffeur? As an implementer?

9. Specify whether it is MIS or DSS that (1) provides direct support for the decision maker, (2) supports all phases of the decision process, (3) addresses management problems, (4) emphasizes information.

10. What are the three main components of the DSS?

11. What are the two basic kinds of data? Which type is represented by (1) accounting data, (2) marketing research conducted by the firm, (3) marketing research reports purchased from a research organization?

12. What are the three basic methods that the manager uses to obtain information from the DSS?

13. What are the two basic kinds of reports?

14. How would a "problem solver" type of manager use heuristic searching?

15. How would Alter classify linear programming? The Monte Carlo salesclerk model? Which provides the most decision support? Why?

16. How can a mathematical model provide a learning experience for the manager?

17. What are the five ways to prepare computer graphics?

18. What is the most popular mainframe graphics software? Micro graphics software?

19. What is meant by 4GL? Is INQUIRE an example? What about MODEL? An electronic spreadsheet? FORTRAN? QBE? dBASE III? BASIC?

20. What DSS software is included in Kodak's Midss?

Problems

1. Redesign the sales-by-salesperson report in Figure 11-14 to increase the level of decision support that it provides. Achieve this by strengthening how it facilitates management by exception. Use the data in the figure for your example.

2. Code the INQUIRE command to prepare a revised version of the report in Figure 11-18. Assume that the data resides in a file with direct organization. Rename the report "DEPARTMENTAL PAYROLL EXPENSES." Print the column heading "JOB TITLE" on one line. Print the body lines in ascending sequence based on both salary and department number.

3. Determine the five number series for the distribution of customer purchases in the Monte Carlo example. Start with 00. Use your number series to determine the total amount for the following purchase:

Purchase Number	Random Number	Purchase Amount
1	28	
2	01	
3	35	
4	88	
5	37	
6	45	
7	70	
8	31	
9	39	
10	87	
Total amount		

CASE PROBLEM: Dairy Dreem, Inc.

Dairy Dreem is a national chain of fast food restaurants featuring soft ice cream. Their main competitor is Dairy Queen. A mainframe computer is located in the Cincinnati headquarters and is used primarily for data processing. A DBMS is not used, although MARK-IV is used to prepare some special reports. Minicomputers are located in warehouses across the country that supply the 1,850 restaurants.

The president of Dairy Dreem is Moe Schwartz, age 33, who inherited the company two years ago. He attended a private Eastern college, where he was an all-conference baseball star. He dropped out of school and played major-league ball until the death of his father placed the leadership of Dairy Dreem on his shoulders.

The first two years for Moe were hectic, learning the ropes in basically a trial-and-error fashion. A total lack of business preparation made it necessary to learn everything from the bottom up. Now, most of the initial crises have been solved, however, and Moe is settling into a routine of looking into the future for opportunities.

One day he telephones his computer manager, Angela Harris, and asks her to come to his office for a chat. When Angela arrives, Moe asks how things are going in the computer department. Angela reviews the current projects and assures him that everything is under control.

Moe leans back in his chair, puts his feet up on his desk, and begins to talk.

"You know, Angela, Dairy Dreem is in a very sound financial condition. My father laid a good foundation for expanding the scope of our business. I envision that during the next five years we will open enough new stores to surpass Dairy Queen. The problem is that we really are not geared up to do a lot of things in a large-scale manner. We are going to have to acquire an ability to make more decisions, quicker, than we are in the habit of doing."

Moe looks at Angela. Angela nods. Moe continues.

"One of our big decisions is where to locate stores. It's a long-term decision— we sign a lease on some property and we have to live with it for 20 or 25 years. Not only is it long-term, it's expensive. We're talking big bucks."

"We have tried to minimize the risk of bad location decisions with our real estate department. When we decide to open up a new store in an area, we send out a team of three or four people to meet with realtors, look over the sites, and decide where to build. This has worked out well, but I can't see how we can continue the practice if we get involved in a heavy expansion program. What I want to do is use the computer to tell us where to locate a store."

Angela asks, "Do you want the computer to just tell us which towns are the best ones of a bunch, or do you want the computer to pick a specific location in a town such as 503 South Main?"

"Both," Moe replies. "It could first tell us which towns are best and then which site in each town. We can provide local realtors with a form including space for all of the information that we need—land cost, taxes, and so on. What they can't provide, they can get from the Chamber of Commerce. I'll bet they would even give us a count of how many cars pass by each day. We feed the numbers into the computer, and bingo—it tells us which locations are best. What do you think?"

"Well, I'll have to admit, it sounds intriguing. It's an example of what we in the computer trade call a decision support system—"

"That's great," says Moe. "I love it. A decision support system. That's just what we need. Now, tell me. How do we get started? What can I do to help? I want to open 1,000 new stores next year. We've never opened more than 175, so we need some decision support fast. Just tell me what you need in the way of a budget and it's yours. We have to move fast. Oh, I'm so excited."

Questions

1. Make a list of the variables entering into the decision that can easily be measured quantitatively.
2. Make a list of the variables that are difficult to quantify.
3. Would you characterize this problem as being structured, unstructured, or semi-structured?
4. Will it be possible to obtain all of the data needed for the model? Explain.
5. Will the store location model be able to make the decision, recommend a decision, or advise what is likely to happen if a decision is made?
6. Will Moe need an intermediary? An implementer? Explain your reasoning.
7. Assuming that the project gets under way, which of Melcher's responsibility relationships will Moe have? What about Angela?

Selected Bibliography

Decision Support Systems

Alter, Steven L., "How Effective Managers Use Information Systems," *Harvard Business Review* 54 (November-December 1976): 97–104.

Alter, Steven, *Decision Support Systems: Current Practice and Continuing Challenges* (Reading, MA: Addison-Wesley, 1980).

Appleton, Daniel S., "Law of the Data Jungle," *Datamation* 29 (October 1983): 225ff.

Basu, Dipankar, "Cleaning Up the Language," *ICP Data Processing Management* 9 (Winter 1984): 44ff.

Beaver, Jennifer E., "End Users—DP's Dilemma—Bend or Be Broken," *Computer Decisions* 16 (December 1984): 130ff.

Bennett, John L., ed., *Building Decision Support Systems* (Reading, MA: Addison-Wesley, 1983).

Bronson, Richard, "Computer Simulation: What It Is and How It's Done," *Byte* 9 (March 1984): 95ff.

Cowan, William M., "Business Graphics Add New Dimension to Decision Support," *Office Administration and Automation* 46 (April 1985): 32ff.

Davis, Michael W., "Anatomy of Decision Support," *Datamation* 30 (June 15, 1984): 201ff.

DeSanctis, Gerardine, "Computer Graphics as Decision Aids: Directions for Research," *Decision Sciences* 15 (Fall 1984): 463-487.

Fuerst, William L., and Merle P. Martin, "Effective Design and Use of Computer Decision Models," *MIS Quarterly* 8 (March 1984): 17–26.

Gorry, G. Anthony, and Michael S. Scott Morton, "A Framework for Management Information Systems," *Sloan Management Review* 13 (Fall 1971): 55–70.

Huang, Philip Y., and Parviz Ghandforoush, "Simulation Language Selection," *Journal of Systems Management* 34 (April 1983): 10–15.

Huber, George P., "Issues in the Design of Group Decision Support Systems," *MIS Quarterly* 8 (September 1984): 195–204.

Ives, Blake, "Graphical User Interfaces for Business Information Systems," *MIS Quarterly* (Special Issue 1982): 15–47.

Jones, Jack William, "Making Your Decision Support System Pay Off," *Computer Decisions* 11 (June 1979): 46–47.

Keen, Peter G. W., " 'Interactive' Computer Systems for Managers: A Modest Proposal," *Sloan Management Review* 18 (Fall 1976): 1–17.

Keen, Peter G. W., "Decision Support Systems: Translating Analytic Techniques into Useful Tools," *Sloan Management Review* 21 (Spring 1980): 33–44.

Keen, Peter G. W., "A Walk Through Decision Support," *Computerworld* (January 14, 1985): ID/3ff.

Keen, Peter G. W., and Michael S. Scott Morton, *Decision Support Systems: An Organizational Perspective* (Reading, MA: Addison-Wesley, 1978).

Lehman, John A., Doug Vogel, and Gary Dickson, "Business Graphics Trends," *Datamation* 30 (November 15, 1984): 119–122.

McLeod, Raymond, Jr., Jack W. Jones, and Joe L. Poitevent, "Executives' Perceptions of Their Information Sources," in Robert W. Zmud, ed. *Fourth International Conference on Decision Support Systems* (Dallas: IADSS, April 1984): 2–14.

McLeod, Raymond, Jr., Jack W. Jones, and Joe L. Poitevent, "How Can Executives Improve Their Decision Support Systems?," in Joyce Elam, ed. *Fifth International Conference on Decision Support Systems* (San Francisco: IADSS, April 1985): 67–76.

Meador, Charles Lawrence, and David N. Ness, "Decision Support Systems: An Application to Corporate Planning," *Sloan Management Review* 15 (Winter 1974): 51–68.

Meador, C. Lawrence, and Peter G. W. Keen, "Setting Priorities for DSS Development," *MIS Quarterly* 8 (June 1984): 117–129.

Melcher, Robert D., "Roles and Relationships: Clarifying the Manager's Job," *Personnel* 44 (May-June, 1967): 33–41.

Milutinovich, Jugoslav S., "Business Facts for Decision Makers: Where to Find Them," *Business Horizons*, 28 (March-April 1985): 63–80.

Reimann, Bernard C., and Allan D. Waren, "User-Oriented Criteria for the Selection of DSS Software," *Communications of the ACM* 28 (February 1985): 166–179.

Ridington, Richard W., Jr., "Menlo's In-Search Simplifies Dialog Access, Saves Money," *Business Computer Systems* 4 (February 1985): 105ff.

Roman, David, "Presentation Graphics: Producing a Hit Show," *Computer Decisions* 16 (September 1984): 150ff.

Shim, Jae K., and Randy McGlade, "Current Trends in the Use of Corporate Planning Models," *Journal of Systems Management* 35 (September 1984): 24–31.

Simon, Herbert A., *The New Science of Management Decison*, revised ed. (Englewood Cliffs, NJ: Prentice-Hall, 1977), pp. 40–44.

Sprague, Ralph H., Jr., "A Framework for the Development of Decision Support Systems," *MIS Quarterly* 4 (December 1980): 1–26.

Part Five

MIS SUBSYSTEMS

At this point in the book we have reached a milestone. We have covered all of the basic MIS concepts. You could stop reading at this point (if your instructor would allow you) and have all of the fundamentals necessary to begin using a preexisting MIS, designing a new one for yourself, or helping a manager design a new one. The remainder of the book is devoted to two basic topics that are really icing on the cake. The two topics deal with MIS subsystems and the MIS life cycle. In Part Five, which deals with the subsystems, we will update ourselves on examples of what companies are actually doing in the MIS area. We will divide the MIS into manageable subsystems so that we can gain a better understanding of how the fundamentals from the first part of the book are applied. In Part Six we will trace the steps that are taken to implement an MIS—either a completely new one or a modification of an existing one. Part Six will be especially valuable in providing a suggested outline for you to follow on that day when you become involved in an MIS implementation project.

The most important point concerning this part dealing with MIS subsystems is that we are *not* suggesting that a firm can implement a *part* of an MIS. From the beginning, the MIS concept has assumed one integrated system for use by all of the managers in the organization. It is neither necessary nor desirable that the MIS be a single, giant system. But it should be designed so that all of its parts, the subsystems, work together.

If the requirement of an integrated system holds true, then perhaps you are not clear about what we call "MIS subsystems." Actually, the MIS is not *physically* divided into the subsystems. The subsystems exist only *conceptually*. The idea of a subsystem is simply that the designers recognize the special information needs of groups of managers, and the MIS satisfies those needs. Take, for example, marketing managers who need special types of information. The contents of the data base and the software library enable the MIS to produce those outputs. The designers similarly provide the necessary data and software to support managers in the manufacturing, finance, and other areas.

You can see why a firm cannot have just one of the information subsystems, such as marketing. Much of the marketing data comes from the finance and manufacturing areas. If those areas do not attempt to achieve the same high quality in their data bases and software libraries, then they cannot provide the type of support that marketing needs. This situation is analogous to one home-owner keeping his or her home and yard in good shape while the neighbors let their property run down. Everybody's property values are higher when all home-owners maintain their property. There is a synergism among the parts—the whole is greater than the sum of the parts. The utility of the overall MIS is maximized only when all of the subsystems are present and functioning in an integrated manner.

In the above example, we use functional areas as the subsystems. This is the most popular approach since firms typically are organized along functional lines. But it would be possible to view MIS subsystems as levels of management (strategic planning, management control, and operational control) or as flows of resources (personnel, money, material, machines, and information).

In Part Five we recognize the need for an MIS subsystem to support the managers on the strategic-planning level. We call this the executive information system, and it is the subject of Chapter 12. We also recognize the strong influence of functional information systems, and devote Chapters 13 through 15 to marketing, manufacturing, and financial information systems.

In studying the chapters on functional information systems, be aware of an important fact. The descriptions are presented in a normative, or ideal structure. This note of caution does not apply to the chapter on executive information systems, where the material is strictly descriptive. The functional information system examples represent, for the most part, what very progressive organizations are doing. Do not get the idea that all firms have developed their information systems to such an extent. The value of presenting a normative view is the preparation that it provides for your career. When you become a part of an organization, you will have a blueprint of how firms *ought* to be using their MIS. When you see examples where the organization's MIS does not match your blueprint, then you can determine the reason why. In some cases you might find that your organization has found a way to improve the blueprint.

Chapter 12

Executive Information Systems

Learning Objectives

After studying this chapter, you should:

- Understand what is meant by the term "executive"
- Recognize the need for a special information system to satisfy the information needs of executives
- Appreciate how the executive's responsibilities and activities differ from those of lower-level managers
- Recognize that the computer is only one means of providing executive information
- Have a good understanding of how five sample executives obtain and use information
- Recognize that there are two major dimensions of an executive's information system—volume and value
- Know what the major sources of executive information are, and what media are used
- Recognize that many basic questions remain unanswered concerning how executives and other managers use information
- Have some good ideas about how computers can be used more effectively on the executive level using the three traditional ways of obtaining information from the computer—reports, queries, and simulations—plus new opportunities offered by office automation

Introduction

> "A rich man is not just a poor man with more money."
> Pierre Martineau[1]

Pierre Martineau, in his study of social class in America, recognized inherent differences between the rich and the poor, differences that could not be measured by the amount of money that each did or did not have. As we address the special information needs of executives, we recognize that there is something that distinguishes them from managers on lower levels. Executives *are* different. Perhaps it is not so much an inherent personal difference as it is a difference in the job. We could paraphrase Martineau's quote and say: An executive is not just a lower-level manager on a higher level. The job changes drastically when the manager reaches the top, and the manager must change to fit it. In this chapter we describe how the MIS can lend support.

---

[1] Pierre Martineau, director of research and marketing for the *Chicago Tribune,* quoted in Stuart U. Rich and Subhash. C. Jain, "Social Class and Life Cycle as Predictors of Shopping Behavior," *Journal of Marketing Research 5* (February 1968): 41.

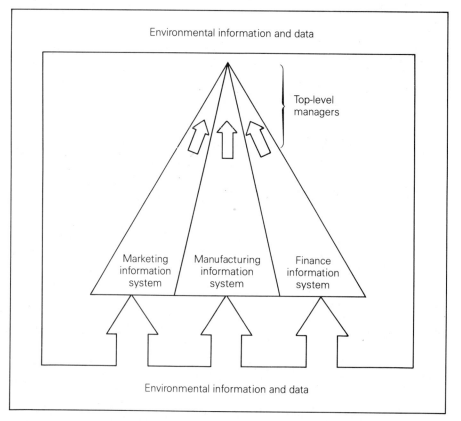

Figure 12-1 A firm without an executive information system.

If we did not include a special MIS subsystem for the managers at the top, and only included functional subsystems, the MIS would have the appearance of the model in Figure 12-1. The top-level managers would receive all of their information from the functional subsystems. It would be necessary for these managers to distill and synthesize this data into a form that would be meaningful to them. Managers on the top level should not have to do this type of work, and for that reason a special MIS subsystem is established for them—the *executive information system,* or *EIS.*

The executive information system sits atop the functional systems as shown in Figure 12-2 and processes lower-level data into a form usable by top-level managers. You will notice that the executive information system also gathers data and information from the environment. It has long been believed that the higher you are in the organization, the more important the environmental data and information become. If this is true, and there is every reason to believe that it is, then this environmental data and information is especially important to the executive information system.

By including an executive information system, we are simply recognizing that the firm's top-level managers, or executives, have special information needs, and a portion of the MIS is dedicated to provide this support.

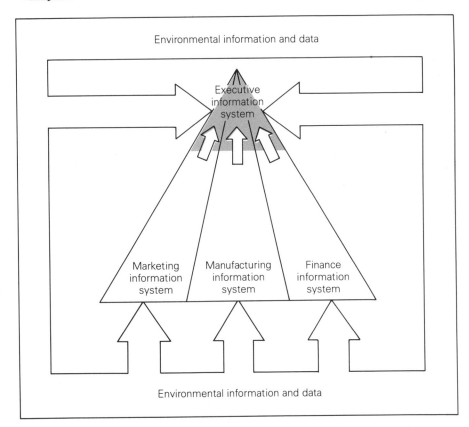

Figure 12-2 A firm with an executive information system.

Who Are the Executives?

The term *executive* is rather loosely applied. There is no clear line that distinguishes the executive level from the next lower one. The term is used to identify managers at the top who exercise a strong influence on the firm. The term executive could apply to all of the managers on the strategic-planning level. In Chapter 2 we defined the strategic-planning level in terms of its planning horizon. We said that managers on that level plan five or more years into the future. Actually, there is nothing sacred about the five-year figure; it might be more or less in a particular firm. What is important is that these managers have the responsibility for keeping the firm on the correct course, and this course should be mapped out for several years into the future.

In recognizing the planning horizon, we must not make the mistake of believing that these strategic-planning managers, or executives, have no interest in the current happenings of the firm. That is not true. Even the highest level executives, including the President of the nation, spend much of their day thinking about and acting on matters of a current nature. Executives are interested in what is happening now, but they also want to know what the situation is likely to be one, five, or even ten years into the future.

Several levels of managers can be included in the executive category, and are illustrated in the organizational chart in Figure 12-3. The top-level executive is the chairperson of the board. Next come the individual members of the board of directors. These top levels assume that the organization is a corporation. Reporting to the board is the president, and reporting to the president are the vice presidents. Very often, a president will establish special vice president positions, such as executive vice president and vice president of administration. It is also very common for the president to establish a top-level committee, called the *executive committee* or simply the *management committee* to jointly consider important issues. All of these persons are generally considered to be executives.

The size of the organization plays a big part in determining whether a position is on the executive level. In a very large organization such as a Fortune 500 firm or a federal government agency, the person at the top would be considered an executive even though there are many levels of managers above. For example, the manager of the General Motors assembly plant in Arlington, Texas is an executive because of scope of responsibility, not nearness to the top. In a very small firm, such as a local hardware store, perhaps there is only one executive—the owner.

The term *CEO (chief executive officer)* is used to identify the single person at the top of the organizational hierarchy. Usually this person is the chairperson of the board. In some organizations, the president and the CEO will be the same person.

In addition to their long-term planning horizon, executives can often be distinguished from managers on lower levels by their attitude. Executives tend to have the attitude that the welfare of the firm is more important than the welfare of units within the firm. Executives are "company oriented." Some, but by no means all, managers on lower levels tend to put the welfare of their own units ahead of that of the firm. A functional vice president is torn between these two

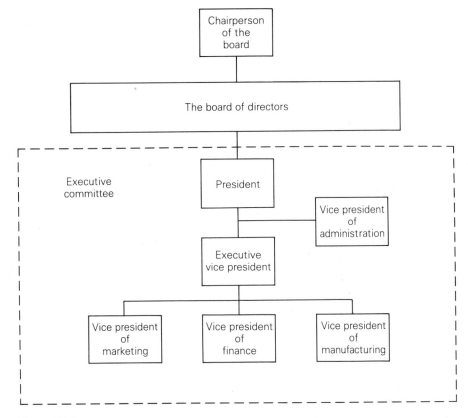

Figure 12-3 The executives.

forces. As an executive, he or she believes in the supremacy of the interests of the firm, but as a functional leader, he or she senses a responsibility to the people within his or her own functional area.

What Do Executives Do?

The classical management theorists, led by Henri Fayol, addressed the question of what managers on all levels do. Modern management theorists still seek to answer this very elusive question.

Fayol's management functions

Fayol believed that all managers perform the same management functions—plan, organize, staff, direct, and control. The widespread belief is that executives allocate more time and devote more emphasis to planning than to the other functions. The idea is that the executives leave most of the other functional activity to managers on lower levels. We recognized this belief in Chapter 2 and illustrated it with Figure 2-2. The importance of planning to the top level is emphasized by naming it the strategic planning level. Very often the executive information system is named the *strategic planning information system*.

Mintzberg's managerial roles

We could also define the executive's duties in terms of Mintzberg's managerial roles. He believes that all managers perform all roles, but that the orientation is different on each level. One of the decisional roles is that of negotiator, and Mintzberg gave the example of a top-level manager negotiating a merger, and a lower-level manager negotiating a delivery date with a supplier. Both negotiate, but with different orientations. In Mintzberg's study of five CEOs, he found that they did not spend equal amounts of time in discharging the decisional roles. They concentrated on making long-range entrepreneurial improvements to the firm and responding to unanticipated disturbances, while leaving much of the resource allocating and negotiating to managers on lower levels.

Kotter's agendas and networks

Harvard professor John P. Kotter believes that executives cope with the challenges of their jobs by following a three-step strategy.[2] First, they establish the _agendas_ that are in effect objectives for the firm to achieve. Agendas vary from short to long term. The long-term agendas tend to be vague estimates, such as a general idea of what kinds of products that the firm should be selling 5 to 20 years from now. The short-term agendas are more specific, such as the market share that each of the firm's current products should achieve.

Second, the executive builds _networks_ of cooperative relationships among those people who are needed to accomplish the agendas. Network members can be found throughout the firm and in the firm's environment. Kotter says that there can be hundreds or thousands of network members.

Third, the executive works to establish the right kind of _environment_ consisting of norms and values so that the network members can work to achieve the agendas. The environment is created primarily through face-to-face interactions. The executive interacts with all of the network members but concentrates on subordinates—persons on lower levels in the executive's own unit.

It is important that new executives be given the opportunity to establish agendas and networks. Once established, the effort to keep their agendas current and their networks intact occupies executives' attention throughout their careers.

How Do Executives Think?

Most of the research aimed at learning about managers focuses on observable behavior. Very little attention has been directed at what goes on inside a manager's mind while this behavior occurs. The manager's mind is often regarded as a black box, not to be opened.

Harvard professor Daniel J. Isenberg studied the thought processes of more than a dozen executives over a two-year period to gain insight into what execu-

---

[2]John P. Kotter, "What Effective Managers Really Do," *Harvard Business Review* 60 (November–December 1982): 156–167.

tives think about and how they apply their thinking.[3] Isenberg's research probes deeper into the executive's mind than does Kotter's; managers have certain thoughts as they establish their agendas and networks.

What executives think about

Isenberg found that executives think about two general classes of problems—how to get things done, and how to deal with a few overriding concerns or general goals. In thinking about how to get things done, executives are more concerned with the organizational and personal issues in getting subordinates to solve a problem rather than what the specific solution will be. Executives are certainly concerned with decision outcome, but their thoughts tend to be more occupied by the mechanics of producing the decision than the decision itself. In tackling the organizational and personal issues, the executive is very aware of the individual agendas of the subordinates, and he or she works to make the agendas compatible with those of the organization.

Although the executive may be facing a large number of issues or concerns at any one time, he or she tends to be preoccupied by a few major ones. The major ones may take months or years to solve and are always on the executive's mind. As an example, an executive might see the need for greater discipline in the organization. Everything that the executive does is influenced by the perceived need for greater discipline; that passion weaves its way in and out of all daily activities.

The role of intuition

Executives usually have many projects ongoing at one time, and their daily activity often appears disorganized. Much of the disorganization is caused by the need to handle disturbances. It appears to the observer that the manager is not following any rational problem-solving process, such as the systems approach. After the problem has been solved, it might be possible to see that the manager defined the problem, evaluated alternatives, and selected the best solution. While the problem is being solved, however, these steps may be obscure.

More and more researchers are coming to the conclusion that managers do not follow the steps of the systems approach—one after the other. Isenberg observed that the executive will often skip from problem definition forward to solution implementation, and then back to alternative evaluation, for example. Executives do make rational decisions, but the decisions might not come as the result of always following a series of well-defined steps in the same order.

Isenberg observed the need for both rational thinking and intuition. We defined intuition and recognized its role in decision making earlier—in Chapter 4. There are several reasons why executives use intuition. Intuition is used to (1)

---

[3]Daniel J. Isenberg, "How Senior Managers Think," *Harvard Business Review* 62 (November–December 1984): 81–90.

identify problems, (2) respond without thinking to make "programmed" decisions, (3) synthesize isolated bits of data and experience, (4) check on the accuracy of quantitative analysis, and (5) respond quickly when necessary.

Intuition is not the opposite of analysis; the two go hand-in-hand. Isenberg believes that the executive uses intuition at each step of the problem-solving process. Intuition probably plays a more important role at the executive level than on lower levels because of the unstructured nature of the problems and also the vast reservoir of experience that the executive can bring to bear on a problem.

Unique Information Needs of Executives

Gordon B. Davis, an MIS professor at the University of Minnesota, was among the first to recognize the manager's need for informal information. In his 1974 MIS textbook, he included the diagram in Figure 12-4.[4] Part of the MIS is public, available for use by anyone in the organization, and part is private, restricted to only the person establishing it. The computer resource is a part of the *public MIS*, whereas the information that an executive receives from telephone calls, letters and memos sent only to her or him, are examples of the *private MIS*. Likewise, part of the MIS is formal, and part is informal. The *formal MIS* is prescribed by

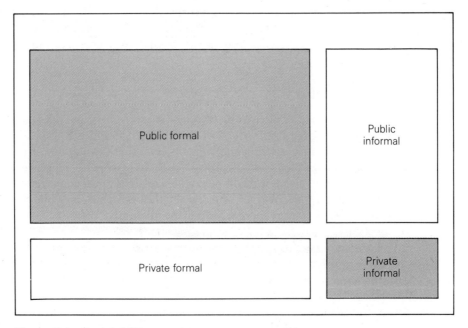

Figure 12-4 Davis's MIS components.

Source: Gordon B. Davis, Management Information Systems: Conceptual Foundations, Structure and Development (New York: McGraw-Hill, 1974), p. 198.

[4]Gordon B. Davis, *Managing Information Systems: Conceptual Foundations, Structure and Development* (New York: McGraw-Hill, 1974), pp. 197–200.

procedure, such as computer programs. The *informal MIS* has no spelled-out routine. Davis intended the size of the four boxes to illustrate their portion of the MIS—the largest being public formal, and the smallest being private informal.

There is growing support for the belief that the informal part of the MIS is the largest. John Dearden, in evaluating the executive's need for the computer, stated that "most of the important information required by top management is never on the computer."[5] While this feeling is not shared by everyone, there is little argument that executives need both computer and noncomputer information.

Noncomputer information

Mintzberg identified five basic media that communicate information to the manager—the mail, the telephone, the unscheduled meeting, the scheduled meeting, and the tour. He kept time records on his five CEOs' activities and learned how they allocated their time to the various media. His findings appear in Figure 12-5. Personal interaction accounted for 78 percent of the executives' time (the shaded slices in the figure). Mintzberg did not specifically include computer output in his study. Instead, he emphasized the role of the informal systems that communicate oral information. He concluded: "It would appear that it is more

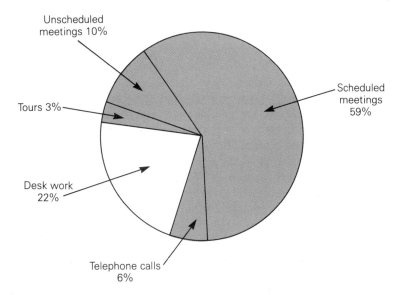

Distribution of Hours

Figure 12-5 How Mintzberg's CEOs spent their time.
Source: Henry Mintzberg, The Nature of Managerial Work (New York: Harper & Row, 1973), p. 39. Reprinted with permission.

[5]John Dearden, "Will the Computer Change the Job of Top Management?" *Sloan Management Review* 25 (Fall 1983): 58.

important for the manager to get his information quickly and efficiently than to get it formally."[6]

Of course much has changed concerning the use of computers as decision support systems since Mintzberg gathered his data in the early 1970s. No doubt today's CEOs place more importance on computer output than they did 15 years ago. However, Mintzberg's findings have value as we consider modern MIS designs. He emphasized the role of the informal information system, and this is an area where office automation (OA) can be applied as we recognized in Chapter 10. One advantage that is frequently cited for OA is that it will reduce the manager's wasted time. In his book on office automation, Dennis Jarrett quotes a survey by *Fortune* magazine that lists time wasters as including "phone calls interrupting work and train of thought, unexpected callers in person interrupting work, and over-long meetings."[7] Mintzberg recognized that when the phone rings or someone walks into the manager's office, it is not an interruption of the manager's work. It *is* the manager's work. The manager gets much, perhaps most, of her or his valuable information from these "interruptions." The last thing that the manager wants to do is to eliminate them. To present OA as a substitute for telephone calls and face-to-face contact is not the way to sell OA to management.

Computer information

Nobody is saying that computer information is unimportant. Some, like Mintzberg and Dearden, are saying that it is just not the *most* important. Dearden's article, deemphasizing the potential role of the micro at the executive level, prompted the president of a British company, David Davis, to respond with a description of how he personally uses the micro as a DSS.[8] The micros in his firm are used strictly for DSS work, and he believes that they perform computations for the managers in 20 percent of the time required by manual calculation. Over 50 percent of the programs were written by users, and took less than five hours to develop. He feels strongly that the micro is useful, citing four projects that he worked on during an eight-month period where the micro was used as a DSS.

It is easy to find descriptions of how executives use computers. In 1982, John F. Rockart and Michael E. Treacy of MIT described their study of executives' use of computers in 16 companies.[9] In each company, at least one of the top three officers, most often the CEO, personally used computers on a regular basis. One of the most dedicated computer supporters was Ben W. Heineman, CEO of Northwest Industries, who had a terminal in his office, one at home, and took one with him on vacations. Another executive, George N. Hatsopoulos, president of Thermo Electron, was writing programs in APL to conduct analyses. The executives were all enthusiastic about the support that they were receiving from the computer.

---

[6]Henry Mintzberg, *The Nature of Managerial Work* (New York: Harper & Row, 1973), p. 47.

[7]Dennis Jarrett, *The Electronic Office,* 2nd ed. (Aldershot, Hampshire, England: Gower), p. 23.

[8]David Davis, "Computers and Top Management," *Sloan Management Review* 25 (Spring 1984): 63–67.

[9]John F. Rockart and Michael E. Treacy, "The CEO Goes On-Line," *Harvard Business Review* 60 (January–February 1982): 82–88.

Heineman stated that "There is a huge advantage to the CEO to get his hands dirty in the data because the answers to many significant questions are found in the detail." Another executive commented that "You learn the nature of the real question you should have asked when you muck around in the data."

Rockart and Treacy identify three reasons why executives use computers:

- User-oriented terminal facilities are available at an affordable price
- Today's executives are better informed concerning what the computer can do
- Today's volatile competitive conditions demand the speed and power of the computer

One key to successful use of the computer by the executive is to provide her or him with the needed technical support. Many of the executives studied by Rockart and Treacy had received assistance from *EIS (executive information system) coaches*. These EIS coaches were often former consultants and were not affiliated with the firm's information services department. This type of assistance is not always needed. Owen B. Butler, chairperson of the board for Procter & Gamble, taught himself how to program. His motivation was to learn it well enough to be able to converse with information specialists. He is convinced of the value of the computer, calling it a "mind expander."[10] He has used a terminal, and purchased an IBM PC as soon as it was available.

Perhaps one reason why computers are not more widely used by executives is that the top computer manager often does not have a more personal relationship with the other executives and their activities. Pennsylvania State University professor Mehdi Khosrowpour surveyed Fortune 500 company CEOs to learn their feelings about the use of the MIS in setting corporate goals.[11] The information provided by the CEOs revealed that they seldom involve the top computer manager in the firm's goal-setting process. With such little understanding of the process, the computer manager is unable to provide the needed support.

In another study, Blake Ives of Dartmouth and Margrethe Olson of New York University surveyed 150 companies in 1981 to learn that the top computer managers spent only 8 percent of their time with users on any level, and only 7 percent with their superiors.[12] At the time of the Ives–Olson study, only two computer managers had terminals in their offices, and the units were used primarily for demonstration purposes. Clearly, if the information services unit is to provide computer support to executives, the information specialists must have a clear understanding of the executives' information needs and how the computer can, and cannot, be used.

---

[10]Owen B. Butler, " 'A Computer is a Mind Expander,' " *Business Computer Systems* 3 (February 1984): 74.

[11]Mehdi Khosrowpour, "Are MIS Capable of Setting Goals?" *Journal of Systems Management* 34 (October 1983): 25–29.

[12]Blake Ives and Margrethe H. Olson, "Manager or Technician? The Nature of the Information Systems Manager's Job," *MIS Quarterly* 5 (December 1981): 49–63.

Putting the computer in perspective

Some managers place great emphasis on computer-generated information, and some do not. Some executives prefer that the computer output go to their staff and subordinate managers, who then communicate the relevant points in face-to-face conversation. The executives therefore receive the benefit of computer processing without actually receiving the outputs.

There is probably a smaller proportion of heavy computer users on the executive level than on any other. Two reasons prompt this belief. First, the problems at the executive level are less structured and therefore more difficult to support with computer processing. Second, executives tend to be older and more likely have had no benefit of formal computer training. Age in itself is not an issue, as proven by CEO Butler who has been at Procter & Gamble since 1945. Also, the lack of training is something that can be easily overcome. Persons at the executive level got there by overcoming many obstacles of a more serious nature.

Perhaps it is mainly the personal bent of the executive—how analytical he or she is. If the executive emphasizes rational problem solving, then he or she will make good use of computer information.

The important points in this discussion are that (1) computer use is a personal thing, and (2) computer information is only a portion of all of the information reaching an executive. All executives want to receive good information from any source. Heineman, as strong a computer advocate as you will find on the executive level, expressed this feeling when he said that he believed in "not being the captive of any particular source of information."

Executive Information Systems—An Exploratory Study

There has been a surprisingly small amount of research directed at the total information set that executives use for decision making. Practically all of the research has been restricted to computer information. The author, working with professor Jack W. Jones of Texas Christian University, recognized a need to learn more about all of the information sources and media. We were influenced by the work that Mintzberg had done, but felt that a more focused study was in order—building on the concept of decisional roles.

The study plan

The basis for the study was the model illustrated in Figure 12-6. The model depicts the two major sources of executive information, environmental and internal, as well as two major media types, written and oral. You recall that Mintzberg lumped all written media into a "documents" category. We identified five different types of written media—computer reports, letters, memos, periodicals, and noncomputer reports. Mintzberg identified four oral media—telephone conversations, scheduled meetings, unscheduled meetings, and tours. We augmented this list with social activities and business meals.

The model shows these eleven media coming from the two environmental sources and being used by the executive in performing the four decisional roles.

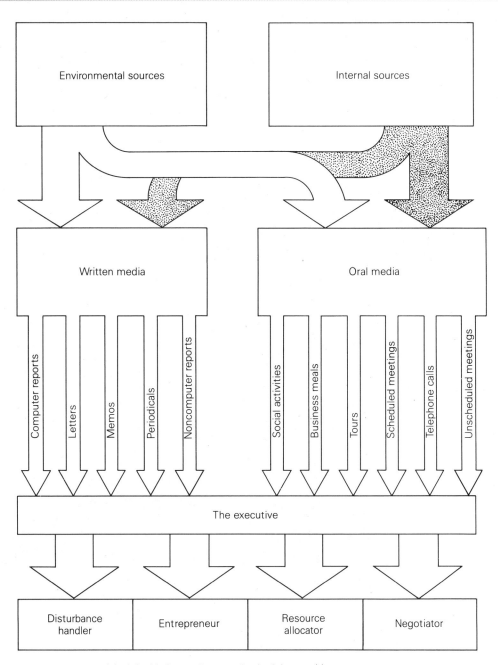

Figure 12-6 Model of information use in decision making.

We decided to limit our study to executives since so little is known about information flow at that level. We identified our task as keeping tallies of the number of information "transactions" of each media type coming to the executives from specific sources both within the firm and the environment. These tallies would provide an idea of the sources of information that executives draw upon and the types of media that link the executives with the sources. We additionally planned to relate the information received to the decisional roles. The data would provide an idea of the types of information that the executives prefer when playing each of the roles.

We knew that because of such a small sample we could not generalize our findings to all executives. The important thing for you to keep in mind is that *different findings would be encountered with a different group of executives*. However, the study *does* provide an insight to the information systems of the five executives who logged all of their information inputs.

Figure 12-7   The bank CEO and president. Joseph M. (Jody) Grant is chairperson of the board and president of Texas American Bank/Fort Worth, the flagship bank of Texas American Bancshares Inc. Grant's bank has assets in excess of $2 billion. He sees his role as an organizer and a stimulator. Habits formed while earning a Ph.D. in economics influence his leadership style. He provides direction by staying alert to what is happening in the banking industry and by seeing to it that his committees have the information that they need for decision making. He strongly believes that "the best decisions that can be made are made with a full hearing and a lot of inputs and a great deal of information."

Figure 12-8 The insurance company president. Peter J. Hennessey III is president of Government Personnel Mutual Life of San Antonio, a firm with insurance in force exceeding $1 billion. Before he became president, he worked as a COBOL programmer, work measurement analyst, and salesperson. His programming background enables him to understand what goes into his computer reports and to help plan his company's computer efforts, his work measurement experience gives him an awareness of the firm's administrative systems, and his sales experience makes it easier to establish a rapport with his sales force— "They know I carried a rate book."

The executives

Brief biographical sketches of the executives appear in Figures 12-7 through 12-11. The executives included Joseph Grant, a bank CEO and president; Peter Hennessey III, an insurance company president; John Easton, an energy company vice president of tax; Bill Guthrie, an energy company vice president of finance; and Bob Camp, a CEO and president of a retail chain.

The data gathering

During the two-week period, a total of 1,454 transactions were logged. A transaction is a communication involving any of the media—business meal, social activity, observational tour, telephone call, letter, memo, meeting, report, and periodical. An analysis of the data produced the findings that are described below.

Figure 12-9 The vice president of tax. John Easton is vice president of tax at
Tenneco's corporate headquarters in Houston. Tenneco is one of the
nation's largest industrial firms with sales over $15 billion. As a former
partner in a Chicago public accounting firm, Easton frequently finds
himself as special problem solver. He sees his task as bringing into focus
for Tenneco management the key factors bearing on a problem, and
compares his job to that of a chef by explaining "If you go into a
restaurant and order a filet, you don't want someone to bring out a cow
and then cut the filet out of it. In some cases, I guess I'm a fileter of
information."

Information volume

The executives averaged receiving 29 information transactions per day. There
was considerable variation from executive to executive and considerable fluctuation from one day to the next for the same executive. Figure 12-12 shows these
variations.

The retail CEO Camp and the bank CEO Grant had the largest volumes and
almost identical patterns. Camp's transactions varied from a daily low of 28 to

Figure 12-10 The vice president of finance. At the time of the study, Bill Guthrie was vice president of finance for Baker Production Services of Houston, an autonomous division of Baker International Corporation, a $2.5 billion firm providing products and services to the petroleum and mining industries. In 1985 he resigned his position to accept a similar position with Elder Oil Tools of Victoria, Texas. While at Baker, Guthrie performed two primary functions—planning and control. He put together the strategic plan for his division, and then served as a watchdog by monitoring actual performance. Using computer reports, he once detected an $800,000 scam in a foreign operation.

a high of 60 with an average of 41. At the other extreme, vice president of finance Guthrie's average was 14, with a low of 8 and a high of 19.

The two CEOs had the highest volume, and the two vice presidents the lowest, with the president in between. The information volume for these five executives varied directly with management level, but it would be a mistake to assume that such is always the case. Another study might find that lower-level managers receive higher volumes than do managers on upper levels.

Figure 12-11 The retail store CEO and president. At the time of the study, Bob Camp was president of Pier 1, a retail chain of 240 stores specializing in imported merchandise, headquartered in Fort Worth. He has since resigned to open his own chain of retail stores in the Pacific Northwest. As "a marketing man down to my socks" his primary interest is the customer, and sees the computer as a means of improving customer service. But, he recognizes that the real key to that service is his employee force—from the top down to the bottom. In commenting on Pier 1's plans to install a new computerized point-of-sale system, he said "We're going to have the best system in the land. We will be better merchants. That just cannot be your only god. It won't know what an eyebrow looks like when it goes up."

Information value

The executives' task of assigning a value to each log entry was not easy since the assignment was made at the time the transaction was received. In many cases it was not clear how, if at all, the information would be used. Quite likely the value

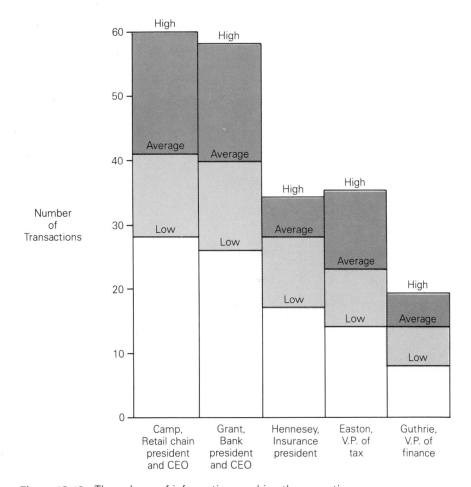

Figure 12-12 The volume of information reaching the executives.

changes over time as use becomes clearer. However, the recorded value is a good measure of the executives' perceptions at time of receipt.

The bar graph in Figure 12-13 illustrates the distribution of transaction values for all of the executives combined. Thirteen percent of the transactions were given a value of zero—the most frequently assigned value. Another 13 percent received a value of only 1 or 2. The executives possibly assigned a low value when they had no idea of how the information would be used.

The bars in the exhibit show a plateau of mid-range values from 3 to 8; 67 percent of the transactions fit into this category. The executives sparingly assigned higher values—only 6 percent of the transactions were given a 9 or a 10.

There was also a variation in the level of values assigned by each executive. Easton's average was only 2.9 and Grant's was 5.5. The other executives fell between these extremes. The overall average was 4.5. Lines have been superimposed on the bars in Figure 12-13 to show how Easton and Grant distributed their ratings. Easton most often assigned a value of zero and never assigned a 10.

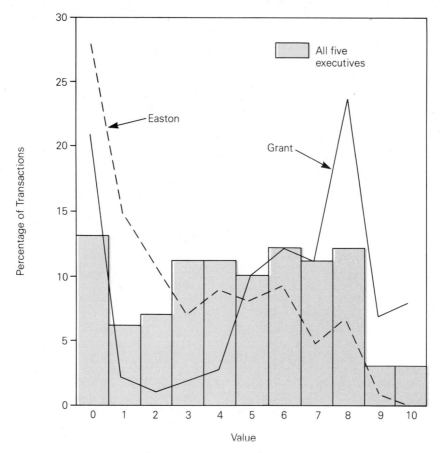

Figure 12-13 The value of information reaching the executives.

Grant's most frequent value was 8, and 15 percent of his transactions were 9s or 10s.

The reason for the fluctuation in value is likely due to a combination of things—personal differences in grading style and the information quality, among others. Quite possibly the position of the executive in the organization had an influence. The two vice presidents again had the lowest averages. They perceived their information to have less value than the presidents. Perhaps, because of the narrower scope of their roles, it was easier for the vice presidents to see that incoming information had little value.

The cause of the differences in value cannot be determined. However, the data does show that the executives were exposed to much information (roughly one-fourth) that was perceived to have little or no value, and that less than 10 percent was perceived to have very high value.

One could easily get the idea that when you reach the top you will have built an information system that lets managers on lower levels filter out all of the worthless transactions. The executive could be seen as one who receives a small volume of very highly filtered and refined information. The study executives did not fit this pattern. They received a large volume of information, much of which they regarded as having absolutely no value.

Information sources

Figure 12-14 is a map positioning the executive at the center of the information sources. Each box represents a source category. The upper number in the box is the percentage of total transactions represented by that category, and the lower number is the average transaction value. The left-hand box represents sources outside the executive's firm, and the boxes to the right of the dashed line represent sources within the firm.

The environment.   One of the most popular tenets of management information systems is that "the higher you are in the organization, the more important environmental information becomes." With 43 percent of the transactions coming from the environment, this study indicates that such is likely the case. A large portion of the executives' information did come from the environment.

Fifty-six percent of Grant's transactions originated outside his bank, and 49 percent of Hennessey's inputs were external. Of the five executives, Grant and Hennessey have the deepest outside commitments, and this has an influence on the information that they receive. Grant especially has strong external ties, not only to the city of Fort Worth, but to the banking industry and the management profession as well. In commenting on the time he spends as chairman of the Fort Worth Chamber of Commerce, he explained, "There's little I can do that is more important to the long-term future of this organization than to help mold what is happening in this city." In addition, he is a national board member of YPO (Young Presidents Organization), and these duties add up to large volumes of messages from the environment. During the two-week data gathering period, for example, he handled 22 transactions concerning YPO alone. Hennessey has this same heavy external commitment, belonging to some 15 civic, social, and industry organizations.

Of the three presidents, Camp had the lowest proportion of environmental transactions—35 percent. This was slightly lower than Easton's (39 percent) but higher than Guthrie's (23 percent). Easton has a definite external focus, interfacing with a number of accounting firms on all of Tenneco's tax matters.

Forty-six percent of the presidents' transactions came from the environment, whereas the percentage was 33 for the two vice presidents. The presidents averaged 168 environmental transactions for the 2-week period compared to the vice presidents' 61.

Upper and lower levels.   Since executives were involved in the study, only 5 percent of the information originated from above—from board chairpersons, board members, and officers of holding companies. However, 38 percent came from the bottom—as far as 4 levels down, with the volume decreasing at each level.

All executives except Easton obtained more information from one level down than from two levels down. Nineteen percent of Camp's and Hennessey's data

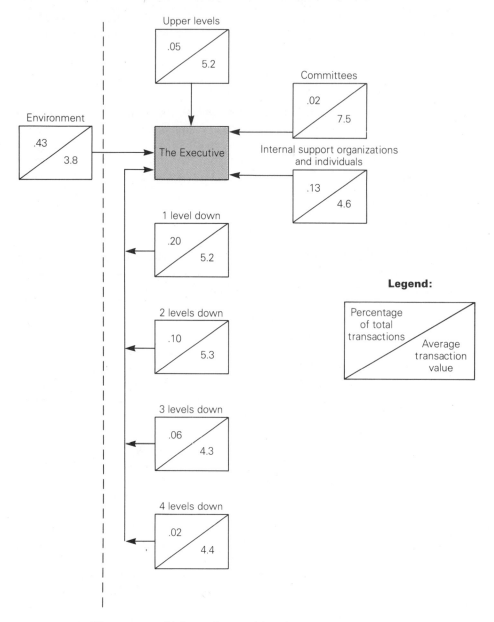

Figure 12-14 The sources of information reaching the executive.

came from the level immediately below—their vice presidents. Guthrie had the highest proportion of contacts with persons reporting to him—22 percent. He relied heavily on his controller and the persons in charge of accounting at Baker's Eastern and Western Hemisphere offices.

Easton demonstrated a different style, obtaining 6 percent from one level down in his tax department and 8 percent from two levels down. During the study, he was chairing a task force seeking a solution to some problems that had developed in a South American country. A devaluation of the local currency in relation to the U.S. dollar had made it difficult for Tenneco to inject capital to support a manufacturing operation. The currency problem had also made it difficult for the South American government to pay for an offshore drilling operation. The staff analyst assigned to the project team was located two levels down from Easton, and the two spent considerable time together. On two occasions they met in the analyst's office, there were two telephone calls, one scheduled meeting, one memo, and one business meal.

Camp and Grant were also adept at cultivating information sources in the ranks below. Camp got 12 percent of his information from 3 and 4 levels down, and Grant got 5 percent. Hennessey's volume diminished considerably with each lower level, and he had only 1 percent below the second level down. Clear differences can be seen in the depth of the executives' data gathering within their own units.

Very often an executive will go outside of his or her unit to gather information in lower ranks. This is especially common for vice presidents. Of the 544 transactions from the lower levels, 100 (18 percent) originated outside the executive's unit. The percentages in Figure 12-14 are for all lower-level transactions—both inside and outside the unit.

Committees. Grant made the most frequent use of committees. His 13 meetings put him far ahead of Hennessey's 6 and Camp's 4. Although Grant sits on several committees, he chairs only one, saying "I like to work through other people." He provides direction to his committees by getting his items on the agenda and then pushing to see that they get a full hearing. He likens his persistence to "water on a stone." Camp uses basically the same tactics in getting his ideas approved, although much of his promoting is done informally—in the halls, at coffee, and before meetings begin. He thinks of himself as a percolator or coffee pot—"I've always had more ideas than I have time."

People and support organizations outside the executive's unit. This category includes persons on the same level as the executive, plus other organizations within the firm such as the accounting, computer, and personnel departments. Camp and Hennessey received 16 percent and 15 percent respectively of their information from internal organizations, mainly their accounting and computer departments. Both Camp and Hennessey believe that their computer operations are top-flight. Hennessey's company has pioneered applications since the early years of the computer, and Camp's company was implementing a new retail point of sale system at the time of the study. None of the other executives spoke of their computer departments in such glowing terms.

The value of information sources. Figure 12-15 illustrates the contrast between quantity and quality. The sources are arranged from left to right based on their volume. The bars above the zero line show the sharp differences in volumes. The bars below represent average transaction value and differ from volume in two respects. First, the variation in value is not great—six of the eight sources have an average between 4.3 and 5.3. Second, there is no clear relationship between

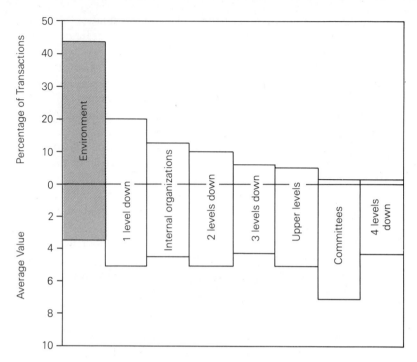

Figure 12-15 Comparison of sources by volume and value.

the value and the volume. For committees, upper levels, and the environment, there seems to be an inverse relationship. Not many transactions involve upper levels and committees, but their information is valued highly. The environment, in contrast, provides the executive with a large volume of messages that are perceived to have the least value.

This inverse relationship does not hold for both one and two levels down. These levels provide a large number of high value inputs. It is easy to see the importance of these two lower levels to the executive.

The executives exhibited individual differences in assigning values to their sources. Camp and Hennessey both assigned high values to their committees and to their sources on the first two levels down. Easton gave highest value to his information coming from the second level down in his department—the level of his task force analyst. Guthrie valued inputs from his president and from internal organizations slightly higher than inputs from the level immediately below—his controller and the two Hemisphere accountants. Grant's values revealed a horizontal and an upward focus. Most highly valued were his committees and his inputs from levels above him and from other bank presidents. These differences emphasize the personal nature of an executive's information system.

Management of information sources. To a certain extent an executive can select his or her information sources. The executive can decide which levels below are to provide information, as well as the internal organizations and individuals. If the executive is on committees, he or she can influence the degree of information support that they provide. The executive usually has less control over upper levels and the environment. Many of their inputs come without being requested. Since the executive does not have complete control, a large quantity of inputs must be accepted that have little value.

The goal of information management is to minimize the proportion of information received from low-value sources and maximize the proportion received from high-value sources. This is a good goal, but it is difficult to achieve. The executive doesn't know the value of an item until it is received. There is always a chance that a source that ordinarily provides low-value information will unexpectedly provide a real gem. One strategy that the executive can follow is to assign a staff member or perhaps a secretary the responsibility to screen inputs, especially those from traditionally low-valued sources. That person could allow only the high-valued items to get through. Such a procedure would give the person doing the screening a great deal of responsibility, to say nothing of the influence over what information the executive receives.

Information media

The media provide the connecting link between the sources and the executive. Some of the media are oral—social activity, business meals, telephone calls, observational tours, and scheduled and unscheduled meetings. Some are written—computer and noncomputer reports, letters, memos, and periodicals.

Media volume.   Figure 12-16 shows how the media pie was sliced for all of the executives. Written media are grouped in the shaded portion and accounted for

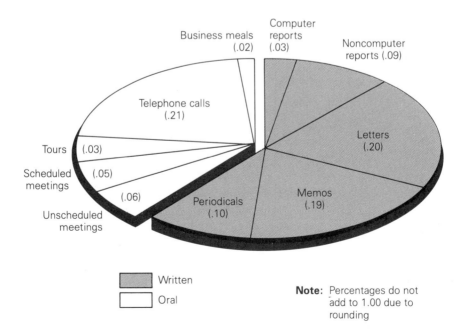

Figure 12-16   The media pie (in percentages of total transactions).

61 percent of the number of transactions. Telephone calls were the only oral communication that accounted for a large volume. Unfortunately for the executive, the three media that he or she controls the least (letters, memos, and telephone calls) have heavy volumes. These three media accounted for 60 percent of the transactions. In terms of volume, the information systems of the executives were geared primarily to provide written information.

Media value. If executives do indeed prefer oral media, then those media should have received higher values than the written media. Figure 12-17 shows that this is essentially the case. The oral media are the unshaded bars, and they occupy the top four positions based on average value. Telephone calls and business meals are the only oral media outranked by written media.

It is not clear why telephone calls fared so poorly. Mintzberg reported that his executives preferred the phone. Perhaps it is because it is not a face-to-face medium, or because the volume is so large that the perceived value of a single call is low. Or, perhaps the telephone is not used to convey much information, but rather as a means of alerting the executive to some impending problem or to simply set up meetings where information can be relayed. Whatever the reason, the executives did not value telephone information highly.

It is not such a mystery why business meals were ranked the least valued oral

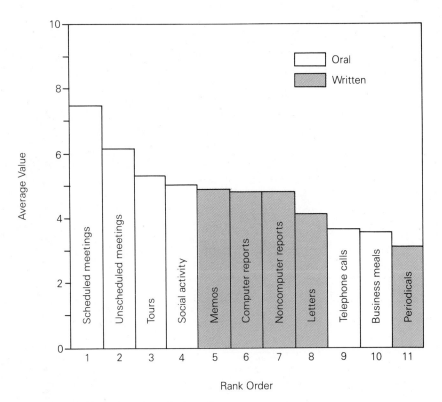

Figure 12-17 Ranking of media by value.

medium. The study revealed that this type of activity is frequently used as a ceremonial device rather than a means of gathering information. For example, Hennessey takes his home office employees to lunch on their anniversary with the company.

Individual media preferences. Each executive had a unique mix of media volumes. As with the sources, the executive can exercise some control over the media that he or she receives. The only uncontrolled media are those that are unsolicited from the environment—letters and telephone calls. The media preferences provide some indication of the leadership styles of the executives. For example, Grant's external orientation is reflected in the large number of letters and telephone calls. Eighty-six percent of his letters and 74 percent of his telephone calls originated outside his bank. In contrast, Guthrie used memos and the telephone to obtain information from sources inside Baker.

Each of the media is addressed in the sections below, in order based on the average value. Unique ways in which the executives employ them are pointed out.

Scheduled meetings. The value of information communicated at scheduled meetings averaged 7.4, making them the most highly valued medium. Twenty-two percent of the meetings were with committees, and 31 percent were with people on the three lower levels. Twenty-nine percent were with outsiders, and 9 percent were with upper-level sources. The upper-level meetings were valued the highest—8.6.

Unscheduled meetings. An *unscheduled meeting* occurs when one or more people call on the executive without an appointment or when the executive summons one or more people to address a special issue. The executive can let others know whether he or she is receptive to such meetings and thus control their volume. All executives except Easton have an *open-door policy*—an expressed willingness to receive input. Hennessey literally leaves his door open so that anyone can walk in if he is not in conference. Unscheduled meetings accounted for 16 percent of his volume, and the information was graded very high—6.4.

Tours. A *tour* occurs when the executive leaves the office for the purpose of gathering information. All executives except Hennessey toured, and information value averaged 5.3—the third highest medium. Hennessey explained that he tours but just didn't do it during the study. The big tourers were Camp, Guthrie, and Easton. Easton tries to tour his department twice a day. By establishing a touring schedule, he uses it as a formal system, whereas it is typically used in an informal way.

Camp estimates that he spends 30 percent of his time "sniffing around, looking for innuendo and comment." He believes that the purest input comes that way. He maintains "I would be worried if I had to sit up here and read somebody's interpretation of what was wrong downstairs or what was right." Guthrie relies on the tour to put him in contact with his subordinates. He specifically mentioned visiting his controller, who is "just down the hall," and his Western Hemisphere accountant, who is "just down the road."

Three executives—Hennessey, Camp, and Easton—recognized the value of the tour in terms of maintaining a high visibility with lower-level employees. Hennessey said, "They know you're here." The tour also is an effective way to gather information on upper levels and from the environment.

Social activity. Only two social transactions were recorded, one by Camp and one by Easton, and the value of only one transaction was high. Perhaps executives don't rely on social events as information sources to the extent that is popularly imagined. At least, that was the behavior of the study executives.

Memos. Memos provided the highest valued written input—higher than either computer or noncomputer reports. Over one-third of Guthrie's inputs were memos, yet he gave them the lowest value of all the executives—3.3. Grant relied on them the least and valued them the highest—6.5. These inverse ratios between volume and value indicate the difficulty of managing the media. If an executive values information in memo form, he or she should be able to encourage sources to use that medium. Conversely, if the executive does not prefer memos, he or she should be able to discourage their use. Apparently this degree of control is difficult to achieve, as the figures for Guthrie and Grant show.

Half of the memos came from one and two levels below the executive, and these were valued higher than average. High values were also assigned to memos coming from outside the firm and from people in internal support organizations.

Hennessey views the memos as "sort of like a pop test." He pays more attention to a memo than to other media such as periodicals because he knows from experience that the sender will later ask him about it. He encourages his subordinates to use memos, frequently saying "Put that in a memo" as a way to get the person to crystallize his or her thinking on a subject.

Computer reports. Computer reports did not emerge as a key medium. Grant said, "I seldom see them," and Easton didn't receive a single one during the two-week period. At the time of the study, Easton had a Corona microcomputer in his office and an Apple at home. He was also teaching himself to use the Multiplan electronic spreadsheet. In addition to the micros, he also had access to Tenneco's timesharing network. During the eighteen months after the data was gathered, Easton began using his office micro for financial analyses. At the same time, the number of micros in his tax department increased from two to ten, and they are in use constantly. One of the applications that he values the most is a datacom service that communicates changes in the tax laws on a daily basis. The information is printed on one of the micros and arrives several days earlier than the previous system that used the mails.

The other executives expressed varying opinions concerning computer use. Hennessey's opinion stands out for several reasons. For one thing, his background is unique, having worked as a programmer on his way to the top. He is, therefore, very computer literate. During the study, he received a higher percentage of computer reports than did the other executives, and received many more computer than noncomputer reports. At that time, he had neither a terminal nor a micro in his office, but later acquired a terminal. However, his plans for the terminal involved mostly OA applications rather than decision modeling. He is a firm believer in the computer as a decision-support tool, but is more interested in putting that tool in the hands of his management team than using it himself.

Camp revealed an interest in getting a terminal but, like Hennessey, expressed no particular preference for the computer as a decision support system. He seemed more interested in the computer as a means of providing improved customer service. When explaining why he didn't get involved with the computer end of his company's entry into the mail order business, he described the computer portion as a "nuts and bolts kind of thing."

The executives clearly preferred noncomputer media. Guthrie explained his hesitancy to rely more on computer output: "I could sit there and I could spend seven hours a day looking at those computer runs. If I did I couldn't talk with anybody."

Noncomputer reports. Grant and Camp relied heavily on noncomputer reports. This input accounted for 15 percent of each executive's volume; however, neither assigned a particularly high value. Although all of the firms have impressive computer resources, almost three-fourths of the executives' reports were prepared some other way.

Letters. Letters represented a high-volume input but relatively modest value. Only two of the managers, Grant and Guthrie, have their secretaries screen incoming mail. In Grant's case, it is clear that he needs help. His volume was the highest of all the executives—123 letters in two weeks. Guthrie's volume, on the other hand, was very low—only 4 letters. Guthrie's volume by itself doesn't warrant the screening, but he feels that that is one job that he can delegate, freeing him for more important responsibilities.

Telephone. Hennessey, Guthrie, and Camp take many of their calls directly, whereas Grant and Easton have them routed through their secretaries. Grant is the only executive keeping a record of his calls, and none of the executives uses the telephone as a formal system with scheduled calls. Guthrie uses the Telex to communicate with his Eastern Hemisphere office in London and with other subsidiary offices around the world.

Although Camp and Easton rely on the telephone the most, they both rated it below the average of 3.7. Hennessey used the telephone the least and rated it the lowest (2.5), but he specifically mentioned how he wants to be available by telephone to persons both within and outside the company. Perhaps his open-door policy makes him so available for unscheduled meetings that his sources use that medium rather than the telephone.

Fifty-seven percent of the calls to the executives came from the outside, but a large proportion (35 percent) came from the four lower levels. Calls from the two levels immediately below were valued higher than those from upper levels.

Business meals. Grant's management committee meets for breakfast once a week, and they developed the bank's long-range plan in those sessions. It does not appear, however, that he regularly relies on business meals as an information-gathering device since he recorded only two such transactions during the study. Although the volume was low for all of the executives, the average value was high—between 5.0 and 6.0 for Camp, Grant, and Easton. Hennessey used the medium the most but valued it the least—1.3. We commented earlier how Hennessey uses meals for ceremonial purposes.

Periodicals.   Grant maintains his own clipping file relating to the economy and bank management. Only Hennessey has implemented a formal procedure for others to screen and clip periodicals and forward them to him. He relies on two of his vice presidents to monitor specific topics.

In terms of average value, periodicals ranked lowest, yet they represented a large portion of the volume for all executives except Camp and Grant. Hennessey received the most and ranked them the highest (5.8). Easton received the second largest volume but ranked them the lowest (1.0). Perhaps Easton's specialized interests enable him to be very discerning concerning his information inputs.

A few publications were forwarded to the executives from the two levels immediately below and from internal support organizations, but 89 percent came from the outside. Periodicals from the inside had a higher average value (4.4) than those from the outside (3.0). This stands to reason. The periodicals forwarded to the executives had been previously screened by the sources and found to contain information of possible value.

Managing the media.   The study revealed the difficulty of managing the media. Large volume media often are perceived to have low value. It is neither realistic nor possible to eliminate these low-value inputs entirely. The best that an executive can do is identify those sources and media that he prefers, and develop and refine those systems. Each executive evidenced an ability to do this.

The two vice presidents have a different challenge in managing their flows than do the presidents. The vice presidents serve as information monitors for their executives above and must personally handle a large number of inputs with low information content. Both have sought to develop mechanisms to cope with these volumes. Guthrie's secretary screens his mail, and Easton has not opened his door to unannounced walk-ins. Both executives use the tour because it is a medium that can be controlled, and it provides information of high value.

Grant seems to have devoted the most time to systematizing his media flows with his clipping file, screened telephone calls and mail, and written records of committee assignments and proceedings. These systems did not come about by accident. During the interview he said, "I believe that organization is the key to the whole thing." In fact, none of the executives' information systems has come about by accident. The executives are all aware of the importance of information and have worked to cultivate their systems.

Information use in the decisional roles

Each transaction was coded with the decisional role where the information would likely be used. Figure 12-18a is a pie chart showing how the transaction volume

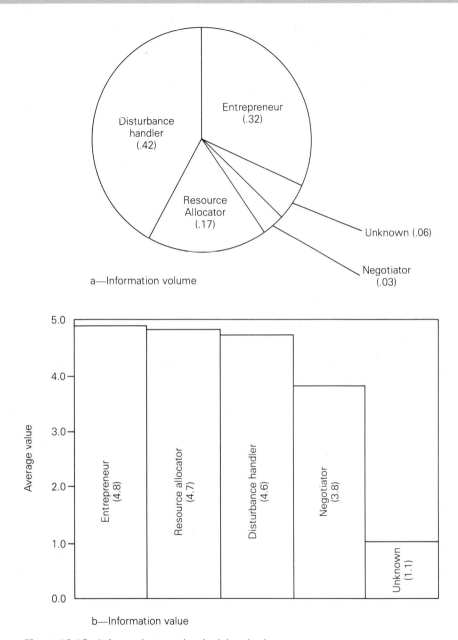

a—Information volume

b—Information value

Figure 12-18 Information use by decisional role.

was allocated to the four roles. More transactions were identified with disturbance handler than any other role. Close behind was entrepreneur. These roles accounted for 74 percent of the transactions. It appears that the study executives had built information systems primarily to handle these two roles.

Only 17 percent of the transactions were earmarked for resource allocator, but the vice presidents had higher percentages than the presidents. Forty-nine percent of Guthrie's transactions and 23 percent of Easton's were of the resource allocation type.

None of the executives had a large volume of negotiation transactions. The number of transactions ranged from Hennessey's 1 to Camp's 24. The fact that Hennessey had the most longevity as president (8 years), and Camp the least (1 year) might have had an influence. Perhaps, with time, the executive can delegate most negotiating duties to lower-level managers.

These findings are compatible with what Mintzberg and other researchers have found. Of the four decisional roles, disturbance handler and entrepreneur appear to be the most important at the executive level.

Value of decisional information. The bar chart in Figure 12-18b shows an almost identical value level for the three roles that the executives seem to emphasize the most—entrepreneur, disturbance handler, and resource allocator. There is a noticeable difference in value between the information intended for these three roles and the role of negotiator. It appears that the executives place less value on negotiation information because they are less involved with that activity.

The bar chart also reveals another interesting point concerning information value. Six percent of the transactions could not be identified with any role, and the value of those transactions is very low. If, upon receipt of a piece of information, the executive cannot easily associate that information with one of the decisional roles, then that information is perceived to have little value.

The sources of decisional information. The manner in which information from the sources is used to support the decisional roles is illustrated in Figure 12-19. The width of the arrows approximates the volumes of information flowing from the sources to the roles. You can see how the environment and lower levels dominate the sources and how the disturbance handler and entrepreneur roles utilize most of the transactions. You can also see three major "arteries" of information flow:

1. Environment to disturbance handler
2. Environment to entrepreneur
3. Lower levels to disturbance handler

These three flows account for 54 percent of all of the transactions. As the executive goes about assembling her or his information system, it would appear that these three flows form the foundation.

In recognizing the importance of the major arteries, we should not lose sight of the necessity for having the many other smaller flows. None of the executives complained about having too much information; rather, they seemed interested in obtaining all that they could. It is as if they are saying, "I know where most of my information comes from, but I am going to try to get as much as I can from other sources as well."

We must also keep in mind that the flows in Figure 12-19 are based only on volume. We know that much information of high value comes from the three low-volume sources.

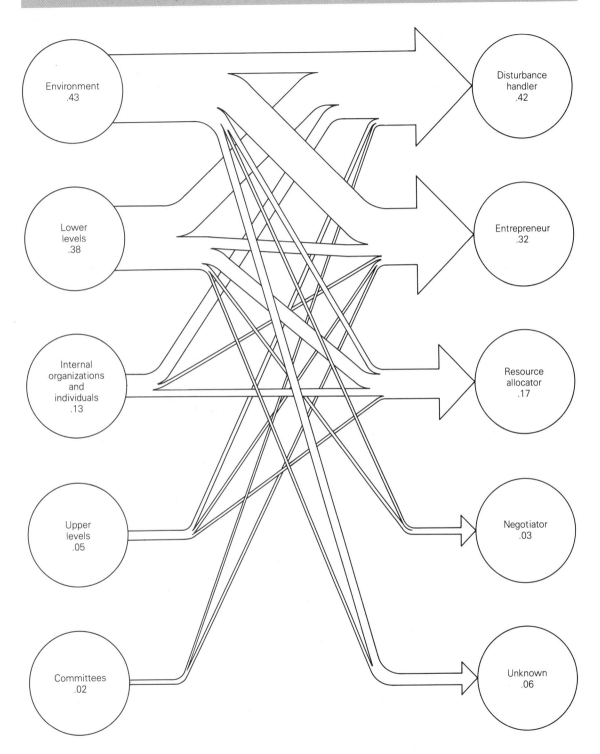

Figure 12-19 Sources of decisional information.

Media used in decisional roles. Which media are used to communicate information to the various roles? Table 12-1 lists the number of transactions flowing to each decisional role by means of each medium. The dark shading identifies the flows with the heaviest volume, whereas the lighter shading identifies flows of medium volume. You can see the dominance of a few flows. Letters and telephone calls convey information used in all four roles. Many of these transactions originate in the environment. Memos are used mainly in the disturbance handler, entrepreneur, and resource allocator roles, and these messages originate primarily on lower levels. Noncomputer reports provide much of the information volume used in handling disturbances and allocating resources. Information from periodicals is intended almost entirely for use in making entrepreneural improvements.

It is interesting to see how the executives used meetings. The executives relied on scheduled meetings the most in making entrepreneurial improvements and relied on unscheduled meetings the most in handling disturbances. Each type of meeting has its own special value, depending on the type of decision being made.

Table 12-1 Media Used in Decisional Roles (In Number of Transactions)

| Media | Decisional Role | | | | | |
	Disturbance Handler	Entrepreneur	Resource Allocator	Negotiator	Unknown	Total
Scheduled Meetings	27	43	7	1		78
Unscheduled Meetings	50	11	25	4	1	91
Tours	19	11	17	1	1	49
Social Activity	2					2
Memos	160	47	61	7	3	278
Computer Reports	19	10	19		1	49
Noncomputer Reports	77	15	39	2	3	136
Letters	108	109	26	10	31	284
Telephone Calls	131	92	43	18	28	312
Business Meals	4	14	2	1	3	24
Periodicals	17	118	5		11	151

Legend:
   ■ *Heavy volume*
   ▥ *Moderate volume*
   □ *Light volume*

Executive preferences for decisional information. A statistical technique, analysis of variance (ANOVA), was used to determine whether source and medium had a significant influence on the values that the executives assigned. For purpose of the analysis, the source was considered to be either internal or environmental, and the media were considered to be either oral or written. The analysis concluded that the following influences are statistically significant. They could have occurred by chance no more often than 3 times in 10,000 (P = .0003).

- When handling disturbances, the executives valued internal information higher than external.
- When handling disturbances, the executives valued internal information higher if it was oral, and valued environmental information higher if it was written.
- When making entrepreneurial improvements, the executives valued internal information higher than environmental, and valued oral information higher than written. However, internal information was not valued higher just because it was oral, and environmental information was not valued lower just because it was written.
- When allocating resources, the executives valued internal information higher than environmental.

The statistical analysis is important in that it provides strong evidence that source and medium influence information value in different ways based on the decisional role where the information is intended to be used.

Significance of the study findings

Three findings of the study appear to be the most significant:

- Most of the executives' information came from environmental sources, but they preferred the information coming from internal sources.
- Most of the executives' information came in a written form, but they preferred the information in an oral form.
- The executives received very little information directly from the computer.

You can see the difficulty of the information management task for the executive. Most of the information transactions to which the study executives were exposed were neither from the preferred sources nor in the preferred form. Even at the top level, the manager must sift through many transactions with little or no value in search of the relatively few that convey something meaningful.

The executives did not perceive the computer as one of their main media. Most of their reports did not come from the computer, but many most likely contained information that had been produced by the computer originally. As a group, the executives seemed to be content with this arrangement. They viewed computer information coming to them in a two-step flow. Members of their management team obtain information from the computer, and then pass that information along to the executives in another form—a written noncomputer report or perhaps an oral report in a meeting.

None of the executives expressed a desire to use the computer directly. Although the computer resources were there in each case, the executives were not attracted to them. Perhaps the executives had no real feel for how the computer could be used as a decision-support system. Even in Hennessey's case, his background of writing data processing programs might not have provided him with an appreciation of the different ways that a computer can provide information. All of the executives relied on reports to convey the computer information. None of the executives were querying the data base or simulating decision strategies—even through intermediaries. Should certain of the executives gain a better exposure to computer-based decision support, their usage habits might improve. However, that is only supposition.

The situation of the five study executives might be typical. Some executives would use the computer if they had a good understanding of how to use it as a DSS, whereas others would not. Not all executives are potential computer users, but many are. It would seem that the challenge to the information specialist is to identify the potential users and provide them with the understanding and the tools that they need to become (1) self-sufficient end users, and/or (2) users of decision-support output produced by the information services unit.

Many important questions concerning management use of the computer remain unanswered, but there are significantly more answers today than there were just three or four years ago. The literature of MIS is growing both in size and quality. Today's managers and information specialists have much information available that should make it possible to implement valuable information systems at each management level.

Suggestions for Improving Computer Use

Some executives utilize the computer more than do the study executives, and some utilize it less. Based on the *Harvard Business Review* article, for example, we would expect Ben Heineman to receive a larger volume of computer transactions and perhaps value them higher. But there must be many executives who make no effort to incorporate computer output into decision making. One can't help but feel that the computer represents an untapped information resource for a large number of executives. Exactly how can computer use be improved? Some suggestions are described below that apply to managers on all levels.

Computer reports

Information specialists should work with managers to learn why computer reports are not used more often and valued higher. If noncomputer reports are preferred, what characteristics do they have that computer reports do not? Perhaps the computer reports can be redesigned, incorporating the features that the managers value. Information specialists should make suggestions of ways that the reports can be improved, such as incorporating management by exception, graphics, and color.

Data base queries

Companies without a DBMS should determine whether decision support can provide a justification for acquiring one. The executives, and lower-level managers as well, should be interviewed to determine if there is a need for a querying ability. These fact-finding sessions will likely take a long time to complete in firms where the managers have little appreciation for the role that queries can play.

In firms that already have a DBMS, the main barrier to manager use would seem to be education. Special sessions should be conducted by the information specialists for all of the managers who are interested, explaining and demonstrating how to make different types of queries and how to perform heuristic searches with sequences of queries.

Simulations

It is possible that some managers in the firm are using mathematical models, and some are not. In that case, there might be modeling packages in the software library that are readily available to the nonusers. An example is Lotus 1-2-3. Education again seems to be the main obstacle. Perhaps the using managers can provide some insight regarding modeling that can be passed on to the nonusers.

In those firms where modeling is not being used at all, the task is much more difficult. Sufficient interest must be stirred up to justify the purchase of modeling software. A good strategy might be to begin with micro software such as 1-2-3, Framework, and Jazz. Good experience with these inexpensive packages can stimulate interest in more sophisticated software.

Office automation

OA might offer more untapped potential for increased computer use than the three approaches described above. The reason is that OA is so new that managers likely have not had an opportunity to evaluate its contribution.

One way to apply OA is to regard it as a substitute for certain media that the manager receives. For example, word processing, electronic mail, and voice mail might be used for *some* of the letters and memos that the manager receives. In a like manner, the three forms of teleconferencing might take the place of *some* of the scheduled meetings.

Figure 12-20 is a grid showing the most logical relationships. Note that electronic calendaring contributes to oral communications, but not to written. Also note that OA can be considered as a substitute for only a portion of a manager's communications.

This approach of regarding OA as a substitute is the most straightforward, but it overlooks a key point. In some situations, OA can be regarded as a *new* form of communication. A good example is computer conferencing. Its asynchronous nature permits a way to conduct a conference that has never before been possible. The real value of OA as an MIS subsystem might be the new communication abilities that it offers.

A good way to stimulate management interest in OA is an in-house educational program. One or two OA applications such as word processing and elec-

Media	Electronic calendaring	Word processing	Electronic mail	Voice mail	Image storage and retrieval	Facsimile transmission	Videotex	Videoconferencing	Audioconferencing	Computer conferencing	
Scheduled meetings	■							■	■	■	
Unscheduled meetings	■										
Tours											
Social activity	■										
Memos		■	■	■	■						
Computer reports			■		■						
Noncomputer reports		■	■		■						
Letters		■	■	■	■						
Telephone calls	■	■	■	■	■						
Business meals	■										
Periodicals					■	■	■				

Figure 12-20 Communication media and corresponding OA applications.

tronic mail can be implemented in the executive suite and then expanded to include the lower levels. This is the approach that TRW took at their executive offices in Cleveland. In addition, the OA applications can increase in sophistication, including noncomputer technologies as well. For example, a firm can start with audioconferencing, build up to still-picture videoconferencing, and finally to two-way, full-motion video.

An effort should not be made to force computer use on executives or anybody else when the use is not justified. But if the reason for the nonuse is a lack of understanding on the part of the manager for what the computer can contribute, then an effort should be made to stimulate that understanding.

Summary

An executive information system is a subsystem of the MIS designed to support the executives of the firm as they play their decisional roles.

Executives exist on several levels, with the lowest level generally including vice presidents. Persons below the vice presidential level are considered to be executives when they are responsible for a large amount of resources. Executives are believed to emphasize the planning function, as well as the roles of disturbance handler and entrepreneur. They cope with the challenges of their jobs by identifying agendas for their firms to achieve and building networks of people to work toward achieving the agendas. The executives also create a stimulating environment for their networks, mainly through face-to-face contact with their subordinates. Executives are concerned more with how to get their networks to work toward the agendas, than with specific decisions made along the way. Executives use intuition as well as rational analysis; the intuition is applied at each step of the problem-solving process. A well-defined series of steps is not always followed in solving a problem.

The MIS consists of both public and private portions, as well as formal and informal portions. Although the formal, public portion has received most of the attention because of its use of the computer, the informal, private portion may be the largest and most important to the executive. The formal, public portion consists of computer and noncomputer reports, as well as scheduled meetings. The informal, private portion consists of telephone calls, letters, memos, unscheduled meetings, tours, business meals, and social activities. Periodicals are considered a part of the informal, public portion.

Some executives emphasize the use of the computer in decision making. If a manager prefers an analytical style rather than intuitive, he or she can overcome learning barriers to operate the computer himself or herself. Some executives prefer to let their subordinates use the computer and pass the information along using other media.

Eight major sources supply the executive with information, using 11 basic media. Data from a study of five executives indicates that daily volumes vary from executive to executive, and from day to day for the same executive. Executives value their information using different criteria, but probably obtain much information that they consider to be of little or no value.

The environment supplies a large volume of information usually having a low value, whereas committees and upper levels supply small volumes of high-value information. The two levels immediately below the executive are special in that their information is both high value and high volume.

Almost two-thirds of the transactions reaching the study executives were written, but the top four media, based on average transaction value, were oral. An unanswered question is why the telephone calls ranked so low in perceived value. It may be because such calls are frequently used to make arrangements for communicating information using other media, such as meetings and tours.

Most of the information reaching the study executives was to be used in handling disturbances and making entrepreneurial improvements. Information for these two roles, plus that intended for use in resource allocation, was valued about the same. Information to be used in negotiating was valued somewhat lower, and information that could not be associated with any role was valued very low. The environment and lower levels provide a large volume of information used in handling disturbances. The environment also provides a large volume for making improvements. The high-volume media are letters, memos, telephone calls, noncomputer reports, and periodicals.

While executives exhibit many preferences for different types of information in different situations, the only statistically significant preferences based on the study data were for: (1) internal information when handling disturbances, making entrepreneurial improvements, and allocating resources; (2) internal information in an oral form and environmental information in a written form when handling disturbances; and (3) oral information when making entrepreneurial improvements.

We should not attempt to increase manager use of the computer unless such use can make a contribution. The key is to educate the manager concerning the potential benefits that the computer can offer. Redesigned reports, DBMS query languages, inexpensive microcomputer simulators, and office automation are all possible avenues for increasing computer use at the executive level and lower levels as well.

With this look at the information needs of executives, we turn our attention in the next three chapters to MIS subsystems that support lower-level managers in functional areas of marketing, manufacturing, and finance.

Key Terms

executive information system (EIS)

executive

executive committee, management committee

CEO (chief executive officer)

strategic planning information system

agenda

network

public MIS, private MIS

formal MIS, informal MIS

EIS coach

unscheduled meeting

open-door policy

tour

Key Concepts

How executive responsibilities, duties, and information needs differ from those of lower-level managers

The fact that some executives rely heavily on computer information

The uniqueness of each executive's information system—molded to fit her or his particular interests, plus the demands of the organization and its environment

The inverse relationship between

volume and value for many of the executive's information sources and media

How subordinates, one and two levels below the executive, provide large volumes of high-value information

The reality that an executive can manage some but not all of his or her information sources and media

How the volume of information reaching the executive is dominated by written media originating in the environment, but the preference appears to be for oral media originating inside the firm

The manner in which the study executives have built information systems primarily to support the disturbance handler and entrepreneurial roles

The possibility that an executive might value information less when it cannot be easily associated with a decisional role, or if the role is not one that the executive emphasizes

Education as the key to improved manager use of the computer

Questions

1. Are executives concerned with what is happening now or what might happen in the future? Explain.

2. Which of Fayol's management functions are (is) emphasized by executives? Mintzberg's managerial roles?

3. How does Kotter's use of the term "environment" differ from how we have been using it?

4. Do executives follow the systems approach? Explain.

5. Why are telephone calls and unexpected visitors not considered to be interruptions by the executive?

6. What is an EIS coach? When is one used?

7. Name the three reasons for increased executive use of the computer, as identified by Rockart and Treacy.

8. List the eight major sources of executive information identified in the chapter.

9. Why would a president be expected to receive a larger volume of information than would a manager on a lower level?

10. Why might a vice president value his or her information less than does a president?

11. How could a president eliminate or reduce the volume of information that has no value? Do you see any problems if this is done?

12. Which source provides the highest volume of information according to the study? Which the highest value?

13. How can an executive manage the information sources?

14. Which form of media did the study executives prefer—oral or written? Support your answer.

15. Explain the difference between a tour and an unscheduled meeting.

16. Although not explained in the chapter, why do you think an executive would value a memo higher than a report?

17. Why were periodicals received from internal sources valued higher by the study executives than those received from the publishers?

18. How can an executive manage the media?

19. Which two decisional roles are supported the most by the study executives' information systems? Is this support in terms of volume, value, or both?

20. What are four major avenues to increasing manager use of the computer?

Problem

Draw a diagram similar to Figure 12-4, showing the public/private and formal/informal parts of an MIS. Enter into the appropriate part the information media (computer reports, and so on) that we have discussed in the chapter. For example, computer reports would go into the public formal part.

CASE PROBLEM: New World Consultants

Upon graduation from college you formed your own firm—New World Consultants. You plan to specialize in implementing executive information systems. You decide that your first contacts will be the executives identified in the chapter and that you will limit your recommendations to office automation.

A good approach seems to be to relate the OA applications to the information media and to recommend specific OA applications in those instances where the media volumes are large. You use the grid in Figure 12-20 as a basis for the relationships. You also obtain from the executives the individual media volumes from the study. These figures appear in Table 12-2.

Practically all of Grant's internal sources are located in the main bank building, and all of Hennessey's are located in his company's home office building. Camp communicates with managers in his firm's 240 stores by telephone, but each store's computer is linked to the mainframe at headquarters. Easton and Guthrie frequently communicate with their firm's subsidiary operations (most of them very large with either mainframes or minis). Most of Easton's communications are restricted to the U.S., using the telephone. Guthrie's communications span the globe, using Telex.

Your task is to recommend for each executive: (1) how OA might be used, and (2) a brief implementation strategy for each OA application. Support your

Table 12-2 Media volumes for each of the executives

Media	The Executives				
	Camp	Easton	Grant	Guthrie	Hennessey
Scheduled Meetings	19	5	37	2	15
Unscheduled Meetings	23	6	14	3	45
Tours	19	13	3	14	
Social Activity	1	1			
Memos	80	51	47	50	50
Computer Reports	13		10	6	20
Noncomputer Reports	60	10	59	5	2
Letters	58	33	123	5	65
Telephone Calls	105	70	77	31	29
Business Meals	6	6	2		10
Periodicals	22	37	26	24	42

plan with the above information, plus that from the chapter. Note: Solution of this case assumes an understanding of the material presented in Chapter 10—Office Automation.

Assignments

1. Recommend an OA plan for Grant.
2. Recommend an OA plan for Camp.
3. Recommend an OA plan for Hennessey.
4. Recommend an OA plan for Easton.
5. Recommend an OA plan for Guthrie.

Selected Bibliography

Executive Information Systems

Alavi, Maryam, "An Assessment of the Concept of Decision Support Systems as Viewed by Senior-Level Executives," *MIS Quarterly* 6 (December 1982): 1–9.

Baker, Vicki F., and M. Lynne Markus, "Understanding Managerial and Professional Office Automation Preferences," in John Goldthwaite, ed. *1985 Office Automation Conference Digest* (Atlanta: AFIPS, February, 1985): 141–148.

Butler, Owen B., "A Computer Is a Mind Expander," *Business Computer Systems* 3 (February 1984): 74–75.

Davis, David, "Computers and Top Management," *Sloan Management Review* 25 (Spring 1984): 63–67.

Davis, Gordon B., *Managing Information Systems: Conceptual Foundations, Structure and Development* (New York: McGraw-Hill, 1974), pp. 197–200.

Dearden, John, "Will the Computer Change the Job of Top Management?," *Sloan Management Review* 25 (Fall 1983): 57–60.

Isenberg, Daniel J., "How Senior Managers Think," *Harvard Business Review* 62 (November-December 1984): 81–90.

Ives, Blake, and Margrethe H. Olson, "Manager or Technician? The Nature of the Information Systems Manager's Job," *MIS Quarterly* 5 (December 1981): 49–63.

Kotter, John P., "What Effective General Managers Really Do," *Harvard Business Review* 60 (November-December 1982): 156–167.

Kurke, Lance B., and Howard E. Aldrich, "Mintzberg Was Right!: A Replication and Extension of *The Nature of Managerial Work*," *Management Science* 29 (August 1983): 975–984.

McLeod, Raymond, Jr., Jack W. Jones, and Joe L. Poitevent, "Executives' Perceptions of Their Information Sources," in Robert W. Zmud, ed. *Fourth International Conference on Decision Support Systems* (Dallas: IADSS, April 1984): 2–14.

McLeod, Raymond, Jr., Jack W. Jones, and Joe L. Poitevent, "How Can Executives Improve Their Decision Support Systems?," in Joyce Elam, ed. *Fifth International Conference on Decision Support Systems* (San Francisco: IADSS, April 1985): 67–76.

McLeod, Raymond, Jr., and Jack W. Jones, "The Potential Role of Office Automation in Decision Support Systems: Some Empirical Evidence," in John Goldthwaite, ed. *1985 Office Automation Conference Digest* (Atlanta: AFIPS, February, 1985), pp. 149–156.

Millar, Victor E., "Decision-Oriented Information," *Datamation* 30 (July 15, 1984): 159–162.

Mintzberg, Henry, *The Nature of Managerial Work* (New York: Harper & Row, 1973), pp. 38–53.

Nolan, Richard L., and James C. Wetherbe, "Toward a Comprehensive Framework for MIS Research," *MIS Quarterly* 4 (June 1980): 1–19.

Rockart, John F., and Michael E. Treacy, "The CEO Goes On-Line," *Harvard Business Review* 60 (January-February 1982): 82–88.

Ryans, John K., Jr., and William L. Shanklin, "Improving Corporate Communications with Members of the Board," *Strategy and Executive Action* 1 (Summer 1984): 8ff.

Vancil, Richard F., and Charles H. Green, "How CEOs Use Top Management Committees," *Harvard Business Review* 62 (January-February 1984): 65–73.

Waldo, Charles N., "Information Packages for Directors," *Business Horizons* 27 (November/December 1984): 77–81.

Chapter 13

Marketing Information Systems

Learning Objectives

After studying this chapter, you should:

- Understand how functional organization structure can influence the design of an MIS
- Appreciate the high level of interest in marketing that has provided structural models to be used in designing functional information systems
- Visualize a functional information system as a group of input and output subsystems
- Understand how the input subsystems gather data and information both internally and from the environment
- Recognize that the output subsystems are tailored to meet the information needs of the functional managers
- Understand how data and information are gathered by the marketing intelligence and marketing research subsystems
- Be familiar with some of the programs in the software library that support decisions relating to product, place, promotion, price, and the integrated mix
- Appreciate strengths and weaknesses in marketing information systems currently used by Fortune 1000 companies

Introduction

In the previous chapter we saw how the executive information system sits atop the functional information systems, providing information support to the executives. In this chapter we introduce the concept of functional information systems and describe the one that has received the greatest amount of attention—the marketing information system.

Functional Organization Structure

Business firms have traditionally been organized along functional lines. These are not the same management functions that Henri Fayol identified (plan, organize, staff, direct, and control). Rather, they are the major jobs that the firm performs, such as marketing, finance, and manufacturing. All types of organizations—government, private industry, and nonprofit organizations—have a finance function. Most types of firms have a marketing function, even if it does not appear as a separate division on the organization chart. Only the organizations that produce the products that they sell have a formal manufacturing function. Other functions, depending on the particular organization, include engineering, information services, personnel, and research and development. Some industries have their own unique functions. For example, banking functions include demand deposit (checking account), time deposit (savings account), and mortgage loan.

A functional organization chart of a manufacturing firm can be seen in Figure 13-1. The executives include the president, vice presidents, and director of personnel. Both middle- and lower-level managers are listed for each of the four functional areas shown. Notice that we have included information services.

In this and the next two chapters we focus our attention on the marketing, manufacturing, and finance functions. These functions are important because they include most of the users of the information system. In Part Six we devote attention to the information services function.

Functional organization and the flow network concept

In Chapter 2, a systems theory of management and organization was presented that stressed the flows of the basic resources of personnel, material, machines, money, and information. Although the flow network approach has not been embraced by the real world of business as an organizational method, it can be used to explain the roles of the three functions.

The two concepts are not completely different. The financial function is concerned with the money flow. The manufacturing and marketing functions represent most of the material flow. The material includes both products and services. The marketing function determines what material should flow from the firm to its customers, and the manufacturing function creates that material.

The personnel, information, and machine flows lack separate representation in the functional structure. This is because all of these resources are used in all of the functional areas. A firm's personnel department specializes in personnel-related activities but does not perform them all. The same can be said for the information services department—it performs some of the information-related activities, but not all. It is also unlikely that a firm would establish a separate unit to handle the machine flow. The personnel, information, and machine flows diffuse throughout all functional areas. This diffusion creates problems when the firm attempts to work together as a system.

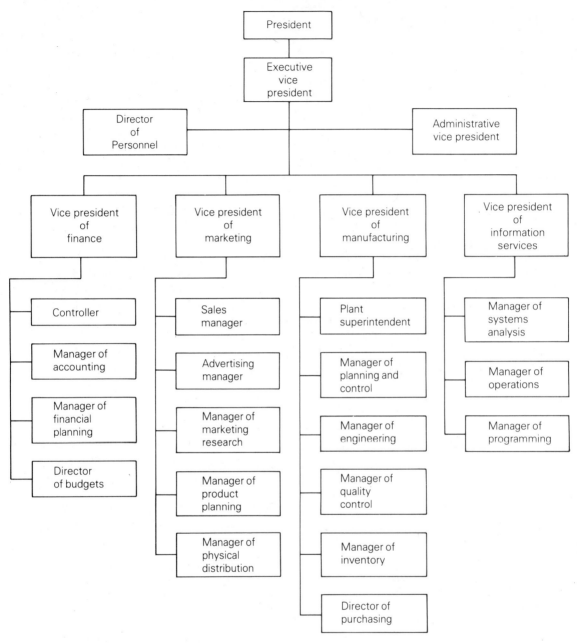

Figure 13-1 A functional organization chart.

Functional Information Systems

When trying to implement a conceptual information system that will reflect the physical system, it is difficult to ignore the functional influence. The easiest approach is for the information system to be organized functionally as well, as illustrated in Figure 13-2. The conceptual information system representing the physical marketing system has been named the *marketing information system*. The same logic has created a *financial information system* and a *manufacturing information system*.

Human resource information systems

As we introduce functional information systems in a general way, we should recognize one that is becoming increasingly prominent. It is the *human resource information system (HRIS)*. The HRIS is the information system that supports the personnel function. It has been estimated that in 1983 nearly 80 percent of all U.S. corporations with over 5,000 employees had a formal HRIS, and that by the year 2000 all major corporations will have one.[1]

In 1985, Professor Gerardine DeSanctis of the University of Minnesota conducted a study of 171 members of the Association of Human Resource System Professionals.[2] Professor DeSanctis found the personnel area of the firm to be fairly sophisticated in its use of the MIS. This area is a regular user of the firm's mainframe computer, micros, and both statistical and graphical software.

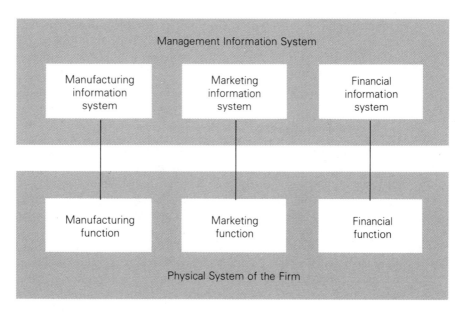

Figure 13-2 Functional information systems represent functional physical systems.

---

[1] Marguerite Zientara, "New Job Links DP, Personnel Management," *Computerworld* (February 28, 1983): 8.

[2] Gerardine DeSanctis, "Functional Area Information Systems: The Case of HRIS," in *Proceedings of the 1985 Annual Meeting of the American Institute for Decision Sciences,* Las Vegas, NV, November 11–13, 1985, pp. 311–313.

Although the HRIS is quite prevalent in large organizations, its popularity is recent. Very few firms had an HRIS prior to 1975. The major applications performed by the HRIS are:

- Reporting information relating to benefit, compensation, and insurance programs, as well as employee demographics and position descriptions to both internal and external (government) users
- Reporting employee background and skills information to management for use in recruiting, selection, assignment, and promotion
- Reporting economic and industry forecasts to management for use in making personnel projections

DeSanctis also found that the most frequent users of the HRIS are located in the personnel function, followed by the compensation, benefits, and equal employment/affirmative action sections. Next come line and staff managers, followed by top managers. Other users include members of the employee/labor relations department, and persons involved with recruiting and training.

Perhaps since the HRIS is such a recent development, top management has yet to fully appreciate its value. The personnel professionals responding to the questionnaire believed that only about 30 percent of their top managers valued the HRIS highly, about 50 percent valued it somewhat, and about 18 percent were indifferent. One would expect a more favorable attitude among lower-level managers who are the primary users of the HRIS output. One way to improve the attitude among top managers will be to provide better decision support for strategic personnel planning.

Potential problems with functional systems

The key to the effectiveness of functional information systems is the attitude of management. If management has a *functional attitude* of putting the function before the organization, then the MIS will be a disjointed assembly of parts that do not work together. It is necessary that those managers influencing the design of the functional systems have a *company attitude* of putting the interests of the organization before those of the functions.

This influence of attitude has existed from the very beginning of functional computer-based systems. Another factor is emerging today, however, that may have more influence. This is the trend to end-user computing. As users in the various functions become more computer literate and acquire their own hardware and software resources, there is a danger of separate functional "islands" being formed. Each island could stand alone and not communicate with the others. If this happens, the value of an integrated MIS will be lost. The best way for the firm to prevent the islands from forming is to address the issue in their information resource management (IRM) plan.

It is important to remember that functional information subsystems do not diminish the importance of an integrated system for the firm—the MIS. The functional subsystems must work together. They must share a common data base, and decisions made in one area must be compatible with those made in others and with the overall objectives of the firm.

The remainder of the chapter will be devoted to the marketing information system.

Marketing Principles

We start with the marketing information system, not because it is the most important, but because its composition is better defined than the others. Marketers have spent considerable time studying the subject of information systems and have developed some excellent models showing how the systems should be constructed.

What is marketing?

Many people think of marketing in very narrow terms—selling and advertising only. Marketers, however, define it very broadly. William J. Stanton, professor of marketing at the University of Colorado at Boulder, defines marketing as

a system of business activities designed to:	plan, price, promote, and distribute
something of value:	want-satisfying goods and services
to the benefit of:	the market—present and potential household consumers or industrial users.[3]

Recently a large number of firms has moved toward a *marketing orientation*. This means that the entire organization is dedicated to the objective of marketing—the satisfaction of customer wants and needs at a profit. This is called the *marketing concept*. The marketing concept is important in terms of the opportunity that it offers the firm to contribute to the improving standard of living and also to meet its social obligations. More importantly here, the marketing concept has a special significance to the subject of MIS.

Much has been said in previous chapters about the importance of the firm's acting as an integrated system. This integration is very difficult to achieve. One of the most demanding tasks of the CEO is to integrate the functional elements of the firm into a smoothly operating unit. The marketing concept implies that the integration is best achieved through marketing goals. This does not mean that the marketing function should dominate the company. But it does mean that everyone in the organization should work toward the basic goal of the marketing function—satisfying customer needs.

The marketing concept could provide the rallying point for the integration of information systems within the firm. In order for all parts of a firm to work together and to share information resources, there has to be some all-encompassing sense of purpose. The marketing concept could provide this unity of

---

[3] William J. Stanton, *Fundamentals of Marketing,* 7th ed. (New York: McGraw-Hill, 1984), p. 7.

direction. All other things being equal, achieving an MIS is easier in a firm that has implemented the marketing concept than in a firm that has not.

The marketing mix

Like managers in other areas, marketing managers recognize that they have a variety of resources with which to work. The objective of the marketing manager is to develop strategies that enable these resources to be used in marketing the firm's products and services. The marketing strategies consist of a mixture of ingredients that has been termed the marketing mix.

The *marketing mix* is the package of products and/or services presented to the prospect or customer as a means of satisfying needs and wants. The marketing mix consists of *the four Ps*—product, promotion, place, and price. *Product* is what the customer buys to satisfy the perceived need or want and can also be some type of service. *Promotion* is concerned with all the means of encouraging the sale of the product, including advertising and personal selling. *Place* deals with the means of physically distributing the product to the customer. This ingredient includes transportation, storage, and distribution on the manufacturing, wholesaling, and retailing levels. *Price* consists of all the elements relating to what the customer must pay for the product or service, including discounts and bonuses.

Evolution of the Marketing Information System Concept

Marketers were quick to adapt the MIS concept to their own needs. The computer was already being used to analyze customer and prospect data gathered through the use of marketing research techniques such as surveys. The marketing information system was seen by some of its early supporters as an extension of marketing research.

The marketing nerve center

In 1966 Professor Philip Kotler of Northwestern University used the term *marketing nerve center* to describe a new unit within marketing to gather and process marketing information. He identified three types of marketing information:

- *Marketing intelligence*—information that flows into the firm from the environment
- *Internal marketing information*—information that is gathered within the firm
- *Marketing communications*—information that flows outward to the environment.[4]

---

[4]Philip Kotler, "A Design for the Firm's Marketing Nerve Center," *Business Horizons* 9 (Fall 1966): 63–74.

Kotler recognized the decision-support intent of the nerve center—"complex marketing decisions such as dropping a price, revising sales territories, or increasing the advertising expenditure level can be preevaluated and postevaluated through the scientific analysis of available data."

The Brien–Stafford model

It didn't take marketers long to use the marketing mix as a basis for structuring the marketing information system. In a 1968 article, University of Houston professors Richard H. Brien and James E. Stafford explained the diagram that is illustrated in Figure 13-3.[5] This was one of the first schematic diagrams of a marketing information system.

The model showed how the system could support the marketing manager in developing planned programs for each of the ingredients of the marketing mix. Names slightly different from the ones defined earlier for the four Ps were used in the four large center boxes. The model showed both information flows (dashed arrows) and decision flows (solid arrows).

The planning process starts with the dark arrow at the left of the diagram. Strategies are developed for each of the four Ps, and then the program is executed. The dark arrow at the right of the diagram represents the effect of the program on consumer behavior. Feedback from this behavior results in changes to individual mix strategies or to the entire program.

The Kotler model

During the period 1967–1974, no fewer than five additional models were described in the literature. One was prepared by Kotler, and it is reproduced in Figure 13-4.[6] Kotler's model divided the marketing information system into four subsystems—internal accounting, marketing intelligence, marketing research, and marketing management science. These subsystems take data from the environment and transform it into information for the marketing executive.

By including the *internal accounting system,* Kotler recognized the symbiotic, or dependent, relationship among the functions of the firm. In fact, it is the internal accounting system that provides a common bond throughout the firm, gathering data describing actual operations and using that data to prepare basic accounting documents and management reports.

The *marketing intelligence system* is concerned primarily with disseminating information to alert the manager to new developments in the marketplace. This system differs from the accounting system in that the output information is oriented toward the future, rather than the present or the past.

The systems that evaluate alternative strategies and either decide which alternative is best or provide information to the manager so that he or she can make that decision are the marketing research system and the marketing management

[5] Richard H. Brien and James E. Stafford, "Marketing Information Systems: A New Dimension for Marketing Research," *Journal of Marketing* 32 (July 1968): 19–23.

[6] Philip Kotler, *Marketing Management: Analysis, Planning and Control,* 2nd ed. (Englewood Cliffs, NJ: Prentice-Hall, 1972), p. 295.

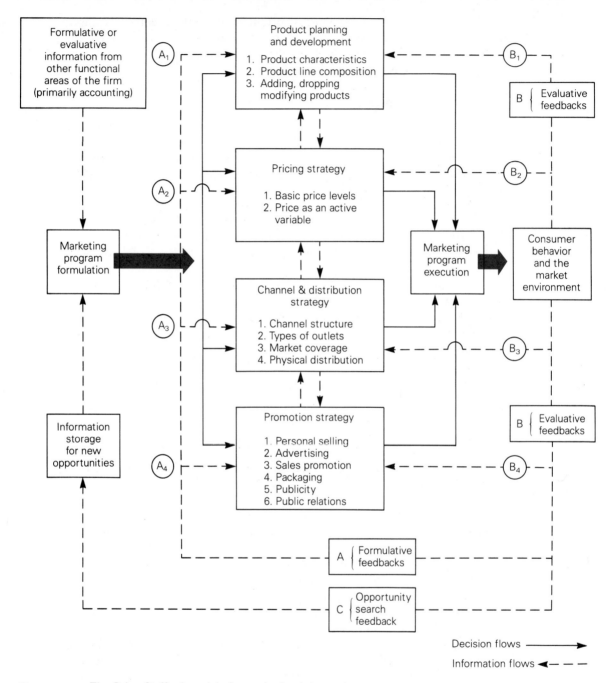

Figure 13-3   The Brien-Stafford model of a marketing information system.

Source: Richard H. Brien and James E. Stafford, "Marketing Information Systems: A New Dimension for Marketing Research," Journal of Marketing *32 (July 1968): 20. Reprinted with permission.*

MARKETING INFORMATION SYSTEM

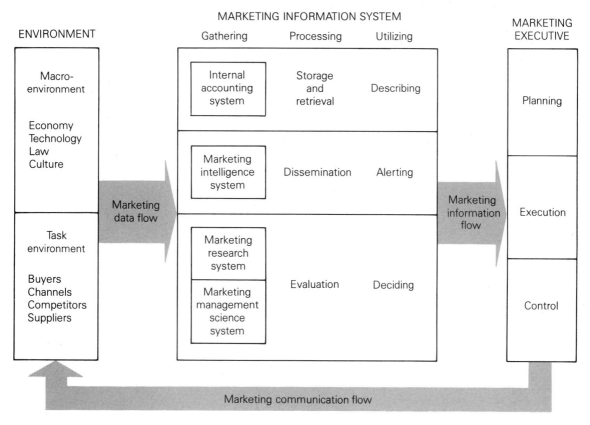

Figure 13-4 The Kotler model of a marketing information system.

Source: Philip Kotler, Marketing Management: Analysis, Planning, and Control, © *1972, p. 295. Reprinted by permission of Prentice Hall, Englewood Cliffs, New Jersey.*

science system. *Marketing research* is a twofold activity carried on in many firms. It involves (1) gathering current data describing all parts of the marketing operations, and (2) presenting the findings to management in a form that facilitates decision making. The emphasis is on the timeliness of the information; it is usually necessary to design and conduct special projects that will gather data describing what is currently happening. The techniques used for analyzing the data are most frequently quantitative in nature, although qualitative analysis is becoming more popular. The quantitative techniques can be either basic or complex.

In *marketing management science,* the emphasis is on the use of only sophisticated quantitative techniques, such as simulation. The data sources can be either the marketing research system or the internal accounting system.

The marketing research and marketing management science systems therefore represented the most modern methods of analyzing data to assist the manager in problem solving. Kotler saw the marketing manager using the information output for planning, executing, and controlling.

Kotler produced a good structure for identifying the primary methods of generating marketing information. His model assigned most of the sophisticated problem-solving techniques to the marketing research and marketing management science systems. For our purposes, we need a finer breakdown so that we can see the different types of decision support provided by a marketing information system.

A Marketing Information System Model

All of the decisions that a marketing manager makes relate to one or more of the mix ingredients. Since the ingredients are a good way to categorize marketing decisions, they are also a good way to categorize the activities of the marketing information system. Each part, or subsystem, of the marketing information system can support a particular group of decisions. This is the approach that we will take. Our marketing information system will be divided into subsystems that produce output describing each of the mix ingredients.

Output subsystems

The mix subsystems in Figure 13-5 provide the interface between the manager and the data base. Each subsystem provides information about its part of the mix. The *product subsystem* provides information about the firm's products. The *place subsystem* provides information about the firm's distribution network. The *promotion subsystem* provides information about the firm's advertising and personal selling activities. The *price subsystem* helps the manager make pricing decisions.

In addition, there is a fifth subsystem labeled the *integrated-mix subsystem*. This subsystem enables the manager to develop mix strategies by considering the effect that each ingredient has on the others. For example, a manager might want to know the effect of lowering the advertising budget while also raising the price of the product. The integrated-mix subsystem enables the manager to understand how the mix ingredients interact.

Each of the five *output subsystems* consists of programs in the software library. Programs can include application programs such as report writers and mathematical models, and also system programs such as fourth-generation languages.

Input subsystems

A model of the marketing information system should also recognize the *sources* of the data used to provide the needed information. Kotler's model identified the three main sources: the internal accounting system, the marketing intelligence system, and the marketing research system. (The marketing management science system emphasizes information processing rather than data gathering.) When the three data *input subsystems* are added to the basic mix subsystems, the result is a model that views the marketing information system in terms of its input data sources, its data base, and its output information. The model can be seen in Figure 13-6. We will use the name *data processing subsystem* rather than *internal accounting system*.

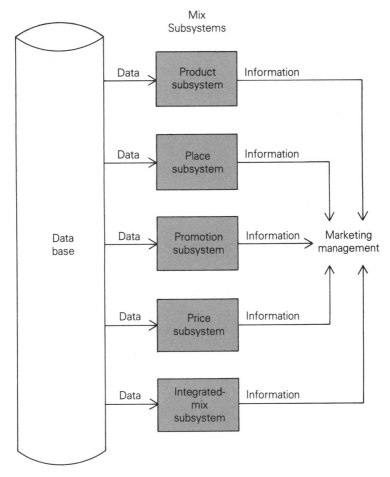

Figure 13-5   Marketing mix subsystems provide information output.

This model provides for a fine breakdown of how information systems help solve marketing problems. It will serve as the basis for our discussion of the marketing information system. We will first describe the input subsystems.

Data Processing Subsystem

The data processing subsystem was the subject of Chapter 9. It provides data to all of the functional information systems. We recognized in Chapter 9 that the data processing subsystem also produces some information output. In Figures 9-19 and 9-20, we illustrated how a special sales analysis file can be created to produce reports presenting the data in various sequences. Figure 13-7 shows such a report—a detailed listing of sales by customer, within sales district, within product class. The data can also be presented in a summary form, as shown in Figure 13-8.

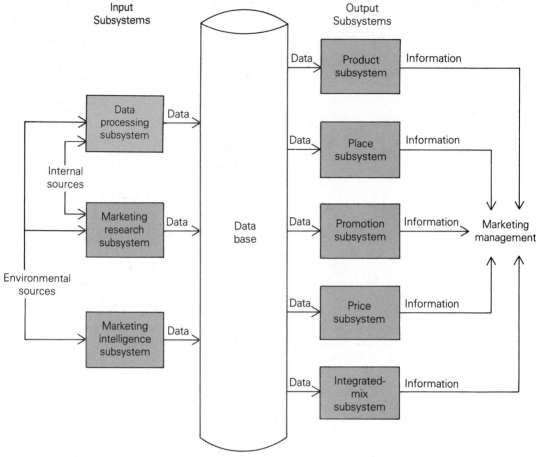

Figure 13-6 The McLeod model of a marketing information system.

The marketing manager can use the sample reports to determine which customers are buying which product classes. The manager can spot exceptionally good sales district performance (such as district 23's sales of product class 12) as well as poor performance (such as district 18's sales of the same class).

Notice that the two reports do not incorporate management by exception. Too often the "automatic byproduct of data processing" report is designed by information specialists based on what *they think* the manager needs. If the manager requests the reports and participates in their design, then the chance that they will be used increases.

Marketing Intelligence Subsystem

Marketing has the responsibility to provide the firm's interface with two elements in the environment—customers and competition. The data processing and marketing research subsystems both gather data and information describing the firm's customers. The marketing intelligence subsystem gathers data and information describing the firm's competitors.

```
                    SALES FOR MONTH OF SEPTEMBER

                    PETROPLEX OFFICE SUPPLY

PRODUCT      SALES       CUSTOMER         CUSTOMER              SALES
 CLASS      DISTRICT      NUMBER            NAME               DOLLARS
---------------------------------------------------------------------
   12          14         102236     WOODY'S AUTO SUPPLY      $1250.00
                          134532     NATIONAL CENTER            454.50
                          226793     ABO'S GALLERY              723.75
                                                             $2428.25*

               18         099235     ALEXANDER & CO.         $   10.00
                                                             $   10.00*

               23         452988     BOULDER LABS            $ 373.95
                          672098     HEINZMAN HARDWARE         5623.00
                                                             $5996.95*

                                                             $8435.20**

   20          08         236759     NIWOT ARCH. SUPPLY      $ 334.30
                          441434     MOUNTAIN SYSTEMS           17.45
                          569809     MIDLAND LIFE INS.        4377.85
                          789467     ODESSA GAS CO.            985.24
                                                             $5714.84*

               16         234745     JOHN NASH               $   8.95
                          678300     WEBA SOLAR CO.           1255.95
                                                             $1264.90*

                                                             $6979.74**

   24          32         957620     VARION METALS           $ 245.00
                                                             $ 245.00*

                                                             $ 245.00**

   28          20         592641     VALLEY WATER            $ 240.00
                          879303     MODULAR ICE                79.95
                          889045     NILES FIXTURES           3450.23
                                                             $3770.18*

               42         349566     ZALES DATA SYSTEMS      $1233.33
                          542863     MIDWEST HOME              890.90
                          694029     METRO NEWS CENTER          12.50
                          737322     SHANE COMPANY              5.00
                                                             $2141.73*

                                                             $5911.91**

***COMPANY TOTAL***                                      $21,571.85***
```

Figure 13-7 A detailed listing of accounting data.

```
+-----------------------------------------------------+
|                                                     |
|            SALES  SUMMARY  REPORT                   |
|                                                     |
|             MONTH  OF  SEPTEMBER                    |
|                                                     |
|          PETROPLEX  OFFICE  SUPPLY                  |
|                                                     |
|      PRODUCT        SALES           SALES           |
|       CLASS        DISTRICT        DOLLARS          |
|      ------------------------------------------     |
|        12            14        $  2428.25*          |
|                      18              10.00*         |
|                      23            5996.95*         |
|                                                     |
|                                $  8435.20**         |
|                                                     |
|        20            08        $  5714.84*          |
|                      16            1264.90*         |
|                                                     |
|                                $  6979.74**         |
|                                                     |
|        24            32        $   245.00*          |
|                                                     |
|                                $   245.00**         |
|                                                     |
|        28            20        $  3770.18*          |
|                      42            2141.73*         |
|                                                     |
|                                $  5911.91**         |
|                                                     |
| ***COMPANY  TOTAL***           $21,571.85***        |
|                                                     |
+-----------------------------------------------------+
```

Figure 13-8 A summary report prepared from accounting data.

Marketing has no responsibility to establish a communication flow *to* the competition, but it must establish an incoming flow. The term *marketing intelligence* may bring to mind visions of spying—an activity called *industrial espionage*. A certain amount of undercover work surely goes on in the competitive world of business, although few instances have been reported. Firms are hesitant to report thefts of proprietary information for fear of damaging their corporate image. Also, such violations are difficult for authorities to prosecute.

One of the most highly publicized cases occurred in 1982 when two Japanese computer firms, Hitachi and Mitsubishi Electric, were charged with stealing trade secrets from IBM. In November of 1981, IBM began noticing that confidential technical information was disappearing. IBM called in the FBI, which set up a "front" operation in the Silicon Valley called Glenmar Associates. Glenmar's first customers were 14 employees of the two Japanese firms. Glenmar collected $622,000 and promised to turn over technical details of the IBM 3380 disk drive unit. IBM began to get nervous about the "bait" that the FBI was using, and the seven-month undercover operation was terminated with the indictment of all of the employees and the arrest of six. Hitachi claimed that it thought it was purchasing information legally, and had entered the payment in its books as being for "memory technology."[7] The following year, IBM reached an out-of-court settlement with Hitachi, obtaining access to Hitachi marketing and technical documents, plus reimbursement for court costs.

Some accusations of unethical data gathering involve computerized data bases. Frontier Airlines accused United of monitoring competitors' activity as recorded in the APOLLO reservation system, and then using the information to either lower prices or broadcast special messages to travel agents.[8] Braniff, at the time they filed for bankruptcy, made similar charges against American.

Such stories make interesting reading, but there probably isn't as much of this type of industrial espionage as one would imagine. There is no reason to break the law to obtain information that is so easy to obtain legally. Marketing intelligence refers to the wide range of *ethical* activities that may be used to gather information about competitors, and not to the unethical or clandestine.

Informal systems

Much information about competitor firms is revealed by the communications media, especially those specializing in business news. An executive can glean a wealth of information on the activities of competitors by reading *The Wall Street Journal*. The trade press of the various industries provides additional, and usually more detailed, descriptions of such activities.

In addition to exposure to mass-circulation media, information-gathering efforts can take the form of attending competitor stockholder meetings and reading stockholder announcements such as the annual report, attending competitor open-house celebrations to dedicate new facilities or announce new products, purchasing competitor products for engineering and design analysis, and visiting competitor stores to learn what is being sold and what prices are being charged.

The sales force of the firm is also expected to play an important role in this feedback of competitive information. When the salesperson establishes a good relationship with a customer, it is possible to learn much about competitor activity. The customer can pass along information just obtained from competitor salespersons.

Formal systems

Unfortunately, in the few reported instances of companies' monitoring feedback from their sales staff, the system didn't work very well. Some firms have planted competitor information so that it would be obtained by their sales reps. Either the information was never reported to headquarters, it took forever to get there, or it was greatly distorted during the feedback process. If a firm wishes to rely

---

[7]"Inscrutable Computer Scam," *The Economist* 283 (June 26, 1982): 74. See also "Hitachi and Mitsubishi Electric Employees Are Indicted," *Fortune* 106 (July 26, 1982): 7.

[8]James I. Cash and Benn R. Konsynski, "IS Redraws Competitive Boundaries," *Harvard Business Review* 63 (March–April 1985): 135.

on salesperson feedback, an effort should be made to install a formal system. The formal system should include forms and procedures for reporting competitor information.

It is also possible for a firm to establish a special marketing intelligence office, although a few have done so. One exception is Mitsubishi, which has an entire staff devoted exclusively to poring through U.S. technical and trade literature.[9]

A formal system can also be established for purchasing competitive data. Data in computer-readable form (such as magnetic tape) can be purchased from firms such as A. C. Nielsen, Market Research Corporation of America, and Brand Rating Index Corporation. This data usually consists of grocery and drug store sales statistics.

One of the most elaborate formal systems is Defender, a computer model that enables a firm to select the best strategy to counter a competitive move. Defender was created by Professors John Hauser of MIT and Steven Shugan of the University of Chicago, working with Steve Gaskin of Information Resources of Waltham, Massachusetts.

Just as soon as a firm learns of new competitive activity, a Defender analysis can be initiated. The process begins with consumer interviews designed to learn preferences for existing products. The consumers are then exposed to ads for all of the products including the new one, and are allowed to shop in a simulation store where all products are displayed. After "purchases" are made, the consumers are interviewed again. The consumers are given time to use the new product and are then contacted by telephone to learn their reactions.

All of this data is entered into the Defender model and a map is printed showing the relative positions of the competitors based on product features that the consumers believe to be important. Figure 13-9a positions the analgesics market competitors before Datril was introduced. This map shows Tylenol having a slight advantage by offering less side effects per dollar but being at a disadvantage by offering less effectiveness per dollar as a result of high price. Tylenol is thus vulnerable to a competitor matching the "lack of side effects" advantage at a lower price, which is exactly what Datril did. A second map is then printed, as shown in Figure 13-9b, that includes the new competitor Datril. This visual understanding of the competitive situation enables a Tylenol manager to play the what-if game, varying mix ingredients and seeing the results in minutes. Tylenol decided to match Datril's low price, plus launch a massive promotion campaign. Their strategy was to reposition Tylenol as shown in Figure 13-9c. Their strategy was effective, enabling Tylenol to remain the leading brand.[10]

Normally the manager using Defender does not personally enter the scenario and decision data, but instead uses an intermediary. So far, the reception to Defender has been good—with 15 or more firms using it. It runs on a mainframe computer, a Prime 850.

---

[9]Leonard M. Fuld, "Competitive Intelligence: It May Be Right Under Your . . . ," *Marketing News* 19 (January 4, 1985): 7.

[10]John R. Hauser, "Theory and Application of Defensive Strategy," Massachusetts Institute of Technology Working Paper No. 1642–85, September 1984.

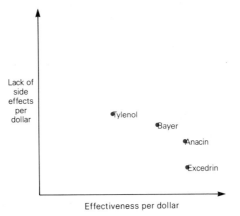

(a) A computer-generated map showing the analgesics market prior to the introduction of Datril.

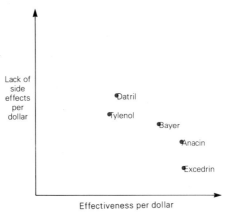

(b) The analgesics market shortly after the introduction of Datril.

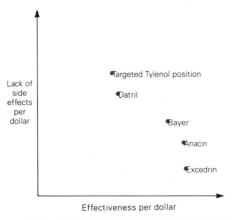

(c) The new position in the analgesics market targeted by Tylenol to counter the Datril introduction.

Figure 13-9 Defender—a formal system for gathering and using competitor data.

Defender is unique for two reasons. First, it enables a firm to take an aggressive stance relative to its competition—mapping out strategies immediately after a competitive move. Second, it is an example of how modeling can be used in an area dominated by less sophisticated formal systems and, primarily, informal systems.

Marketing Research Subsystem

The marketing manager can use marketing research to gather information and data about his or her own marketing system, or about customers and prospects. In practice, very little research effort is directed internally.

As presented here, the marketing research subsystem does not have an output responsibility. Marketing research is used to gather data and enter it into the data base. The preparation of research reports using the data is the responsibility of the various output subsystems.

Marketing researchers are interested in the customer and why the customer buys the firm's products. Marketing research is a common business activity, in practice since about 1911. Large firms have marketing research departments, and an increasing number of marketing research firms perform the service for their clients. The research process is much more formal than gathering marketing intelligence.

The marketing researcher works with both primary and secondary data. You recall that we distinguished between primary and secondary data in Chapter 11. Secondary data is used when possible because it is much less expensive and can be acquired more quickly than primary data. A great deal of secondary data is available from the federal government in the form of statistics. Some of this government data is purchased; some is free. Secondary data can also be purchased from commercial sources. Mailing lists are probably the most frequently purchased marketing research data. These lists are available on magnetic tape and can be prepared for special consumer groups, such as retired military officers living in the Southwest.

Means of gathering data

It is difficult to find a person who is unfamiliar with marketing research. When asked about marketing research, the common response is, "Oh yes, you mean surveys." Almost everyone has been approached at one time or another, in person, by mail, or by telephone, for information about shopping habits, product preference, brand loyalty, and so on.

Actually, the survey is only one method of gathering data through marketing research. A *survey* is conducted when the same questions are asked of a number of persons, by whatever method (personal interview, telephone, or mail). The number of persons surveyed may be relatively small, say thirty, or quite large, say several thousand. Figure 13-10 shows a personal interview being conducted in a shopping mall—a convenient place to contact shoppers and ask them questions about their shopping habits.

Figure 13-10 A personal interview.

When different questions are asked of a small number of people, such as three or four, the technique is known as an *in-depth interview*. The time devoted to the interview is much longer than that spent with any single survey participant. Also, the emphasis is on probing for information explaining why customers behave as they do. This approach is based on similar techniques developed in psychology.

Another technique from the behavioral sciences is *observation*. It presumes that the best way to learn about a behavior is either to observe that behavior occurring or to obtain indications that it has occurred. The technique has been used quite effectively in anthropology and sociology and has been adopted by marketers. Marketing researchers note license plate numbers in a shopping center parking lot in order to learn how far people have driven to patronize the center. Or they set up movie or video cameras in supermarkets to record the response of shoppers to displays.

Marketers have even adopted the technique of the *controlled experiment* from the physical and behavioral sciences, and both the real marketplace and the classroom serve as laboratories. Very often college students serve as subjects in experiments designed to measure the effect of a particular treatment (say a certain type of ad) on behavior (the ability to recall the ad).

Computer-assisted telephone interviewing

Today's large marketing research firms use microcomputer systems in conducting telephone interviews. The application is called *CATI (computer-assisted telephone interviewing)*. The computer controls the sequence in which the questions are asked, displaying them on the CRT for the interviewer to read over the telephone. The interviewer keys in the response, and the next question is displayed.

The sequence in which the questions are asked can be complex, depending on the responses. In this respect, the sequence is similar to the logic paths of a computer program. The control that CATI provides in assuring that the proper paths are followed is a valuable contribution. In addition, the computer can also keep a record of callback attempts, take into account time zone differences, and keep statistics on each question and each interviewer. The statistics enable researchers to reword questions that are causing difficulty and to counsel interviewers who are having problems.

The research firms can provide their clients with computer tapes of the research data that the clients can process on their own computers. Or, the research firms can process the data and provide the clients with printed reports.

Marketing research software

Up until a few years ago, only the largest organizations could conduct their own marketing research. The smaller organizations had to rely on marketing research organizations or do without. Now, there are a large number and variety of marketing research software packages on the market. Most of the packages are written for micros.

The packages perform a variety of research-related tasks. Some, like Question-Writer, provide the CATI software. Some simply tabulate responses to questionnaires. An example is TABULYZER, available for several IBM PC and Apple II models. Other packages, such as SPSS/PC, conduct sophisticated statistical analyses. There are also several packages that enable the user to prepare graphics of the research findings. For example, the Atlas package produces color maps.

Developing an independent research capability

The micro hardware and software make marketing research available at a price that the smallest organizations can afford. The key, however, is not the hardware or software. Rather, the firm must have the expertise available to design their research projects and interpret the findings. This expertise can come from consultants or from the firm's own employees. An undergraduate major in marketing or, preferably, an MBA degree provides the foundation in analytic skills necessary for the work.

For employees who did not have the benefit of formal training, and for those who did but want to sharpen their skills, there are short courses in various research topics. The Burke Institute offers between 20 and 30 different seminars at various locations across the U.S. Sample seminar titles are "Fundamentals of marketing research," "Questionnaire construction workshop," "Tabulation and interpretation of marketing research data," and "Computer packages and applications for marketing research."

A qualified marketing research staff combined with hardware and software are the necessary ingredients for the firm that wants to do its own research.

This concludes our description of the three input subsystems. We now turn our attention to the output subsystems.

Product Subsystem

The product is usually the first specified ingredient in the marketing mix. The firm decides to provide a product to satisfy a particular market need. Subsequently, the remaining ingredients (place, promotion, and price) are identified and described.

The product life cycle

The marketing manager is concerned with developing strategy and tactics for each ingredient in the marketing mix and then integrating these into an overall marketing plan. A framework called the *product life cycle* guides the manager in making these decisions. As its name implies, the product life cycle charts the development of the product from introduction, or birth, through various growth and developmental stages, to deletion, or death. Names have been given to four stages in the life cycle: introduction, growth, maturity, and decline. The cycle and its stages are shown in Figure 13-11.

Although the product life cycle consists of four stages, there are three time periods during which the marketing information system helps the marketing manager make product-oriented decisions. The first period precedes the introduction of the product, when a decision must be made whether to develop and market the product. The second period is during the introduction, growth, and maturity stages, when the product is healthy. The final period is during the decline, when product deletion must be considered. These three decision periods also appear in Figure 13-11.

A number of techniques have been developed to provide the manager with the information needed for making product-oriented decisions. The technique discussed below helps the manager decide which product should be selected for introduction to the market. Techniques such as this, plus others relating to product decisions, constitute the product subsystem of a firm's marketing information system.

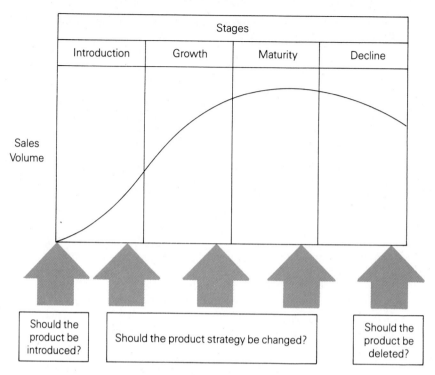

Figure 13-11 The product life cycle and related decisions.

A new-product evaluation model

The decision to develop a new product should be carefully considered, have a sound financial basis, and be made by top corporate management. Prior to the decision, information should be available to indicate, with a high degree of certainty, the profit potential of the proposed product. Many firms have developed an orderly and systematic approach to the consideration of new products that considers a variety of factors, such as profitability and utilization of resources. Scores can be computed for products under consideration, and management attention can focus on products with the best scores.

Figure 13-12 illustrates this quantitative approach to new-product evaluation.[11] In this example, new products are evaluated on both their marketing and their production features. A product selected for introduction scores high in both categories. The decision criteria are listed for both production and marketing considerations along with a weighting (criteria weight) that reflects the relative importance of each. The center portion of the tables consists of ratings that each criterion receives, from very good to very poor. The ratings all have values, from a high of 10 for very good to a low of 2 for very poor. In the column beneath

---

[11]Based on Stewart H. Rewoldt, James D. Scott, and Martin R. Warshaw, *Introduction to Marketing Management,* 3d ed. (Homewood, Ill.: Richard D. Irwin, 1977), pp. 253–262. The technique is not new—an early description appeared in John T. O'Meara, "Selecting Profitable Products," *Harvard Business Review* 39 (January–February 1961): 83–89.

A--UTILIZATION OF PRODUCTION RESOURCES (PROPOSED NEW PRODUCT JXL5005)

DECISION CRITERIA	CRITERIA WEIGHT	VERY GOOD (10)		GOOD (8)		AVERAGE (6)		POOR (4)		VERY POOR (2)		TOTAL	CRITERION EVALUATION (TOT. EV X WEIGHT)
		P	EV	P	EV	P	EV	P	EV	P	EV		
PLANT CAPACITY	.20	.2	2.0	.6	4.8	.2	1.2	0	0	0	0	8.0	1.60
LABOR SKILLS	.30	.2	2.0	.7	5.6	.1	.6	0	0	0	0	8.2	2.46
ENGINEERING KNOW-HOW	.30	0	0	.2	1.6	.2	1.2	.6	2.4	0	0	5.2	1.56
EQUIPMENT AVAILABILITY	.10	0	0	0	0	.7	4.2	.3	1.2	0	0	5.4	.54
MATERIAL AVAILABILITY	.10	0	0	0	0	.1	.5	.6	2.4	.3	.6	3.6	.36

TOTAL PRODUCTION RESOURCES VALUE · 6.52

(a) Utilization of production resources

B--UTILIZATION OF MARKETING RESOURCES

DECISION CRITERIA	CRITERIA WEIGHT	VERY GOOD (10)		GOOD (8)		AVERAGE (6)		POOR (4)		VERY POOR (2)		TOTAL	CRITERION EVALUATION (TOT. EV X WEIGHT)
		P	EV	P	EV	P	EV	P	EV	P	EV		
PRODUCT COMPATABILITY	.20	0	0	.2	1.6	.5	3.0	.2	.8	.1	.2	5.6	1.12
SALES KNOWLEDGE	.20	.1	1.0	.5	4.0	.3	1.8	.1	.4	0	0	7.2	1.44
DISTRIBUTION FACILITIES	.30	.3	3.0	.5	4.0	.2	1.2	0	0	0	0	8.2	2.46
LONG-TERM DEMAND	.30	0	0	.2	1.6	.6	3.6	.2	.8	0	0	6.0	1.80

TOTAL MARKETING RESOURCES VALUE · 6.82

(b) Utilization of marketing resources

C--UTILIZATION OF FIRM RESOURCES

RESOURCE	VALUE	WEIGHT	WEIGHTED VALUE
PRODUCTION	6.52	.40	2.61
MARKETING	6.82	.60	4.09
TOTAL · · · · · · · · · · · · · · · ·			6.70

(c) Utilization of firm's resources

Figure 13-12 Quantitative evaluation of a possible new product.

each rating is listed the probability (P) of the new product scoring the indicated rating on each specific criterion. For example, the probability of the new product receiving a rating of very good on the criterion of plant capacity (in Figure 13-12a) is .20. This probability is multiplied by the rating value of 10 to obtain an "expected value" (EV) of 2.0. The second column from the right contains a summation of the expected values for each criterion, and these are multiplied by the appropriate criterion weight to obtain the figures in the rightmost column. The total of these figures represents a "total production resources value" of 6.52 for the new product. The table reflecting the marketing consideration (Figure 13-12b) is constructed in the same manner. Both the production and marketing resource utilization scores are multiplied by respective weights (to reflect the relative importance of production and marketing considerations for the new product), and the weighted values are added. The final score of 6.70 represents the company production and marketing resource utilization for the new product (Figure 13-12c). Similar scores are developed for the other products under consideration to aid management in selecting the new product to be produced and marketed. The products with the highest scores receive the highest consideration.

In order to use such an approach, it is necessary to quantify a number of essentially subjective measures. Numbers must be assigned to criteria weights, probabilities of performance, and relative weights of production and marketing. It is extremely difficult to quantify these estimates. Very often they will be made by a new product evaluation committee who also assigns the ratings to each new product candidate. Even in light of the various difficulties, such an approach has an inherent value. It forces the manager, or managers, to identify the factors influencing the decision and to consider the relative significance of each.

This new-product evaluation model is a static, probabilistic, nonoptimizing model. Using a model like this is justified only in firms that develop a large number of new product possibilities. The model supports the manager by providing a quantitative analysis of the possibilities. The new product decision has very little structure, and the model output must be combined with a great deal of judgment.

Place Subsystem

Firms must make their products and services available to their customers through channel systems. For some firms the channels are short—the Fuller Brush Company, for example, sells door-to-door. For others, the channels are quite long—farmers' products reach the supermarket through a number of intermediaries, including wholesalers, brokers, and distributors.

The method by which the firm makes its products available to the customer is identified as the "place" ingredient in the marketing mix. Place decisions fall into two basic categories: (1) the establishment of channel systems, and (2) the performance of the distribution functions.

Establishing channel systems

A firm takes two steps in establishing channel systems. First, the firm must decide which other firms will be members. This decision is made by the most dominant member of the channel, usually the manufacturer but possibly a strong retailer such as Sears. Next, the necessary resource linkages must be established to facilitate the product flow.

Selection of channel members is basically an informal process. It is possible to make the process more formal by gathering data describing potential channel members and processing that data on the computer. Sometimes the output is displayed graphically, especially when the selection process includes geographic location. Figure 13-13 is a map of Houston showing motorcycle sales that was used by Yamaha in establishing the number and location of dealers. Each dot represents a past sale, and the heavy lines are the dealer boundaries.

In establishing the necessary resource linkages, attention must be paid to both the flow of physical and information resources. Figure 13-14 shows the resources and the directions of the flow. The material and money flows present no real challenges. Firms have demonstrated an ability to establish the necessary transportation, storage, and data processing procedures. The information flow is more difficult to achieve. The information must flow in both directions—toward the consumer and toward the manufacturer.

The manufacturer must know the details of the product flow at each point in the channel. For example, the manufacturer needs to know the rate at which wholesalers are buying the product, the rate at which retailers are buying from wholesalers, and the rate at which consumers are buying from retailers. It

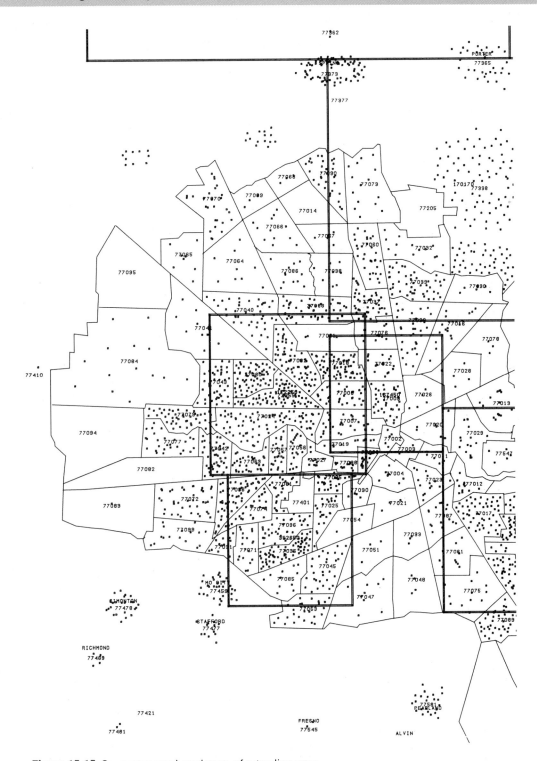

Figure 13-13 Computer-produced map of a trading area.

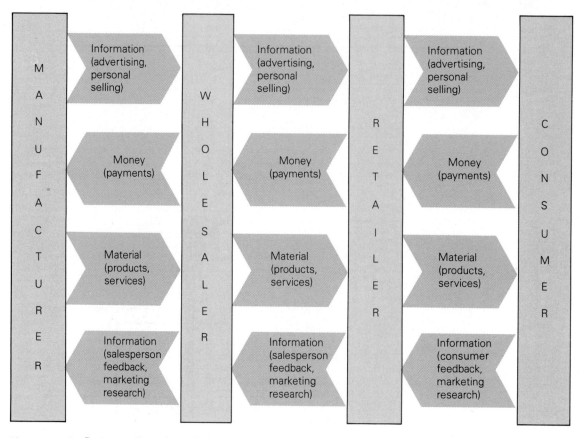

Figure 13-14   Resource flow through the distribution channel.

would be a mistake for the manufacturer to continue production of a product that the wholesalers were buying but the retailers and consumers were not.

If the manufacturer expects feedback from the channel members farther down the line, something must be offered in return. Quite possibly this need only be information—a type of *feedforward information* to the wholesaler and the retailer. Just as the manufacturer needs information *after* the physical product flow occurs, the wholesaler and the retailer need information *before* the flow begins. Feedforward information from the manufacturer to the channel members can include announcements of new products, sales and promotion aids, and forecasts of demand. If the participants in the channel system realize the value of the information flow and the improved performance that it offers, then an efficient interfirm information system is possible.

The information flows are accomplished in various ways. Sales representatives of the channel members are responsible for preparing written reports and for communicating information by word of mouth. Very often information or data is transmitted by a data communications network. A channel system that permits information to flow freely among the firms provides an edge over competitive systems without that capability.

Performance of distribution functions

Once the channel members have been selected and arrangements made for the flows, the channels can go into operation. This is the area of marketing where the computer has the potential for being applied most effectively. The problems of physical distribution, or logistics, are essentially structured and deterministic. The variables such as shipping and storage costs are known and are measured quantitatively. The computer can be used to keep the distribution costs to a minimum, as illustrated in the two following examples.

Wholesale example: Graham Electronic Supply Inc. Graham Electronic Supply of Indianapolis carries an inventory of some 167,000 items. The items include everything from diodes to microprocessors, and are stored in nine warehouses. The sales territory includes electronics retailers stretching from Michigan to Florida.

A Sperry 1160 mainframe computer with 137 terminals and 27 printers online was installed in 1980 to handle the basic data processing systems such as inventory and billing. About 29,000 invoices are generated per month, and picking lists are printed on printers located in the warehouses. Items are printed on the lists in a sequence that minimizes the distance that the warehouse workers must travel in filling the order.

Two uses of the computing equipment make the Graham application special. First, six of the terminals are located in customer offices, permitting the customers to generate queries concerning inventory status and even to enter orders. Second, Graham also uses terminals connected to some of its own vendors' computers. Both Graham and its vendors have seen the benefit of providing their customers with access to their own computer systems, thereby facilitating the flow of information through the channel.

Retail example: Kinney Shoe Corp. Kinney Shoes is a chain of 2,400 retail stores, each with an IBM 3680 POS terminal. During the day, as sales are made, records are written onto disks attached to the terminals. During the evening, the central computer in Camp Hill, Pennsylvania, polls the terminals and receives the sales data. Forty-eight telephone lines are used, and the polling takes about four hours.

The sales data is entered into the accounting system data base and is also used to generate orders for replenishment merchandise. The store managers are therefore relieved of the responsibility of determining when and how much to order to replace sold stock. One of the main advantages of the system is the time that it saves the managers, who can concentrate on managing rather than bookkeeping.

Promotion Subsystem

Comprising both personal selling and advertising, promotion is an important ingredient in the marketing mix. But it has been extremely difficult to harness the power of computerized information systems in this area. Companies have had salesperson-reporting systems for years, but these systems provide only a record of past performance. Even less has been accomplished in advertising.

Advertising is more an art than a science. Creativity plays a big role and marketers actually know little about why some ads encourage purchases whereas others do not. An ad may have a high entertainment value but be ineffective in stimulating sales. For years, marketers have tried to create *media planning models* to support generally unstructured advertising decisions. These models are typically developed by academicians and see only limited use by advertising agencies. The models select combinations of media for campaigns and develop a time schedule for their use.

The computer has also helped firms decide how much to spend for advertising, and how to allocate it, by relating advertising to certain indicators such as population trends, birth rates, income levels, and interest rates. These *econometric models* typically utilize canned statistical software and data bases of economic data.

Generally speaking, it has been difficult to apply the computer to any phase of advertising—either decisions made in planning a campaign or measuring its effectiveness. One form of advertising, public relations, has been especially difficult. *Public relations (PR)* is the conveying of a promotional message by a third party. Examples are newspaper columns that critique movies and TV programs.

Public relations firms assist clients in getting their names before the public in a favorable light. The PR campaign is approached in much the same way as an advertising campaign. One organization, Ketchum Public Relations of New York, decided on computer modeling as a way to evaluate a particular PR campaign after it has been completed. They developed the Publicity Tracking Model to measure the extent to which objectives have been met. To appreciate Ketchum's goals, you have to understand that specific objectives are not always set for PR campaigns. The Ketchum model forces client firms to set objectives—in itself a real accomplishment.

The Ketchum computer has a data base containing audience statistics and demographic data for virtually every magazine, newspaper, and TV and radio station in the nation's top 120 markets. The data describing the results of the campaign is entered into the computer, and a report similar to the one in Figure 13-15 is printed.

The media are listed in the left-hand column, along with their target audience sizes—the number of readers, listeners, and viewers. In this example, the audience is located in the Orlando, Florida, market. The next column (Avg. Size/Length) specifies the size or length of the achieved promotions. The campaign achieved one-ninth of a newspaper page, one-half of a magazine page, 5 hours and 10 minutes of network TV time, and so on. The next column (Avg. Media Units) converts all of the media to a standard numeric measurement. Ketchum has conducted research to determine that 10 hours of local radio offers slightly more (2.60) media units than 6 hours and 5 minutes of local TV (2.13). The media units simply provide a common denominator for the size of the message.

The media units are multiplied by the target audience to obtain the "Publicity Exposure Units." These units measure the quantity of material reaching the target audience. These units are next multiplied by an "Average Impact Factor," which represents the quality of the material that was communicated. When the cam-

SAMPLE TRACKING REPORT FOR PR CAMPAIGN IN ORLANDO, FLA., MARKET

Placement Type	DMA Target Audience*	Avg. Size/ Length	Avg. Media Units	Publicity Exposure Units	Avg. Impact Factor	Publicity Value Units
Newspapers	4,552,000	1/9 page	.93	4,233,000	1.26	5,334,000
Magazines	268,000	1/2 page	1.69	455,000	1.44	656,000
Network TV	95,000	5:10 min.	1.93	183,000	.81	149,000
Local TV	504,000	6:05 min.	2.13	1,073,000	1.81	1,946,000
Local radio	200,000	10:00 min.	2.60	520,000	1.40	728,000
Totals	5,619,000		1.15	6,464,000	1.36	8,813,000

Publicity Exposure Norm, Orlando DMA
5,960,000
Publicity Exposure Index—6,464/5,960   1.08
Publicity Value Index—8,813/5,960   1.48

The publicity Exposure Index suggests that the campaign's exposure was 1.08 as good as expected on a normal* (= 1.00) basis.

The Publicity Value Index suggests that the impact value of the campaign was 1.48 times as good as expected on a normal* (= 1.00) basis.

The Publicity Exposure Norms are established by estimating the target audiences (adults 18–49, weighted 60% male, 40% female) exposure of a "good" hypothetical placement schedule.

SOURCE: Ketchum Public Relations

Figure 13-15   Evaluation of a publicity campaign.

Source: "Computer-Based 'Publicity Tracking Model' Evaluates Performance of Campaign," Marketing News 18 (January 6, 1984): 1/10.

paign is planned, objectives are set for this material. The objective impact factor is 1.00. In the example, the local TV exceeded the objective by 81 percent (1.81), and the network TV missed the objective by 19 percent (.81). Overall, the campaign exceeded the objective by 36 percent (1.36).

The model then computes two indexes. The total Publicity Value Units (8,813,000) are divided by the total target audience (5,619,000) to get a "Publicity Value Index." This index measures the *quality* of the material that was communicated for the entire campaign. The second index (publicity exposure units divided by target audience) is the "Publicity Exposure Index." It evaluates the campaign on strictly a *quantity* basis—how much material was communicated.

The value of the model is that it provides both the client and the agency with a way to plan publicity campaigns and to evaluate their effectiveness.

Personal selling decisions

Decisions relating to personal selling are more structured than those of advertising or public relations because they depend less on the whims of the buying public. Sales managers perform all of Henri Fayol's functions, but the MIS provides the greatest support in planning and controlling.

Many firms use computer-based planning techniques to plan activities for the coming year. These plans, based on a sales forecast, provide a basis for determining recruiting and training needs. Personnel plans can schedule new hires and training programs throughout the year in order to meet annual sales objectives. We saw a good example of such planning in Figures 1-9 and 1-10, where the insurance company projected its needs for new agents and recruiters.

A sales manager can use an electronic spreadsheet for both planning and controlling. The spreadsheet makes two main contributions. First, it enables the manager to play the what-if game, varying certain critical decisions. Second, it brings to light some rather subtle characteristics of the data that might otherwise go unnoticed.

Take, for example, the spreadsheet in Figure 13-16. This is an analysis of three customers—Boulder Labs, Mountain Systems, and Midwest Home. The manager enters the data highlighted in color—each customer's total demand for the previous period, our sales, the expected change in the demand for the next period, our projected share of the demand, and the number of sales calls needed to obtain that share. The spreadsheet model computes the remaining figures— our share last period, the total projected demand for the next period as a percentage of the prior period, our projected sales, and the sales dollars per sales call.

According to this example, the revenue per call will be highest ($26.25) for Mountain Systems. However, this figure is for only one future period. When more periods are simulated, by entering the number of periods at the top of the sheet, Boulder Labs produces more sales per call because of its higher growth rate (1.2 compared to 1.05 for Mountain Systems).

The manager can play the what-if game by manipulating any of the scenario items. For example, what will be the effect if Boulder Labs' sales increase at a rate of 1.10?

This example is only a simple model, but it illustrates how an electronic spreadsheet enables a sales manager to control the level of sales coverage in a territory taking into account various future projections.

The value of promotion decision support

The promotion system supports the advertising decisions by enabling the manager to come to grips with a generally unstructured problem. Models such as the Ketchum PR campaign evaluation model force the manager to think in terms of objectives and the contribution of various media toward those objectives. The promotion system supports personal selling decisions by relieving the sales manager and the salesperson of time-consuming clerical and computational duties, freeing them for more direct sales activity.

Pricing Subsystem

The pricing area runs a close second to promotion in terms of DSS difficulty. For years the marketing manager received very little support for pricing decisions.

```
                    SALES COVERAGE PROJECTION


              NUMBER OF PERIODS:    1

    _____


                   BOULDER    MOUNTAIN    MIDWEST
                    LABS       SYSTEMS      HOME       TOTAL
    _____

   LAST PERIOD

     TOTAL DEMAND       500       1250        713       8708

     OUR SALES          200        125        214       1788

     OUR SHARE         .400       .100       .300       .205


   NEXT PERIOD ESTIMATES

     DEMAND LEVEL      1.20       1.05       0.95       1.01

     OUR SHARE         .475       .200       .300       .226

     NO. OF SALES CALLS  11         10         20        880


   FORECAST

     TOTAL DEMAND       600       1313        677       8795

     OUR SALES          285        263        203       1988

     SALES PER CALL   25.91      26.25      10.16       2.26
```

Figure 13-16 Projected sales revenue per sales call.

Source: This example is based on one presented in G. David Hughes, "Computerized Sales Management" Harvard Business Review 61 (March-April 1983): 104.

Companies tended to follow a *cost-based pricing* policy of determining their costs and then adding some desired markup to arrive at the price. This approach is a rather cautious one. You make your desired profit when you sell the items, but there is a chance that the customer would have paid more.

Another approach is less cautious. It is a *demand-based* policy that establishes a price compatible with the value that the buyer places on the product or service. It is possible to make a higher profit from a sale with this approach than with the more conservative cost-based policy. The marketer is constrained from setting the price too high, however, because of competition.

The MIS can support the manager in both pricing policies. With the cost-based approach, the MIS can provide accurate cost-accounting data upon which to base a decision. With the demand-oriented approach, the MIS enables the manager to engage in what-if modeling to locate the price level that maximizes profit yet retards competitive activity.

A pricing model

A mathematical model can simulate the effect of a firm's pricing strategy on profits. The model in our example is dynamic—it simulates the effect of the price over a period of time, such as a year. It is nonoptimizing, telling the manager what the results of a strategy might be rather than selecting the best price. It is also deterministic. You must understand that it would be possible to develop a model with opposite characteristics—static, optimizing, and probabilistic.

Our model is designed to consider both environmental and internal influences.

Environmental influences

- National economy
- Seasonal demand
- Competitors' pricing strategy
- Competitors' marketing budget

Internal influences

- Plant capacity
- Raw materials inventory
- Finished goods inventory
- Marketing budget

Data representing each of these influences is entered into the model. The data represents the scenario that, along with a particular price, will produce a likely output. The pricing model is designed for interactive use—it prompts the manager to input the scenario items and the price. Either a procedural language or a spreadsheet can be used to create the model. The simulation is performed, and the results are printed or displayed on the terminal or micro in the form of an income statement. Figure 13-17 shows the dialog between the model and the manager. The model can be designed to obtain the needed scenario from the data base or other models, as shown in Figure 13-18. The manager only has to enter the price decisions.

The model consists of a number of mathematical equations. For example, one equation multiplies price times sales volume to get sales revenue. Another equation multiplies plant value times a depreciation percentage to get depreciation expense. The results of the simulation are printed as an income statement, shown in Figure 13-19.

```
ENTER THE FOLLOWING ENVIRONMENTAL DATA
   ECONOMIC INDEX--LAST QUARTER? 1.10
   NEXT QUARTER? 0.95
   SEASONAL INDEX--LAST QUARTER? 0.75
   NEXT QUARTER? 1.10
   AVERAGE COMPETITOR PRICE--LAST QUARTER? 120
   NEXT QUARTER? 115
   AVERAGE COMPETITOR MARKETING BUDGET--LAST QUARTER? 500000
   NEXT QUARTER? 750000

ENTER THE FOLLOWING FIRM DATA
   PLANT CAPACITY (IN FINISHED GOOD UNITS)? 325000
   RAW MATERIALS AVAILABLE (IN F.G. UNITS)? 1375000
   FINISHED GOODS INVENTORY (UNITS)? 15000
   MARKETING BUDGET FOR NEXT QUARTER? 375000

ENTER YOUR ESTIMATE OF NEXT QUARTER'S DEMAND (UNITS)? 425000

ENTER NEXT QUARTER'S PRICE? 125
```

Figure 13-17 Pricing model dialog.

Since the model is nonoptimizing, the manager must try several pricing strategies. During this iterative process, the manager has only to enter the new price, and another income statement is printed. If desired, the manager can also manipulate the marketing budget to see what effect it, in conjunction with the price, will have on profit.

Figure 13-20 illustrates graphically how the iterative modeling process can lead to an optimal price. The manager starts with a price of $125 and gradually raises it on the second, third, and fourth iteration. Each time, profit also increases. During iteration 5, the price of $145, when compared with the competitors' price, causes sales to be lost and profit to drop. The manager sees that a price of $145 is too high, so the price is gradually decreased during repetitions 6 through 9 until profits increase to the earlier level. A price somewhere between $141 and $142 is optimal. In iterations 10, 11, and 12, the model identifies $141.75 as the price yielding the most profit.

A word of caution should accompany the illustration in Figure 13-20. A model is only as good as the mathematics and the data. In this example, the manager has to estimate some values such as the competitors' expected price and marketing budget, along with the national economy. As the manager uses the model output, he or she must keep these estimates in mind. The model most likely isn't accurate enough to pinpoint a price of exactly $141.75. The manager can use the output, however, to establish a price *range* (say, from $138.00 to $145.00). The model gives a certain structure to the problem, but the manager must respond to the unstructured portion.

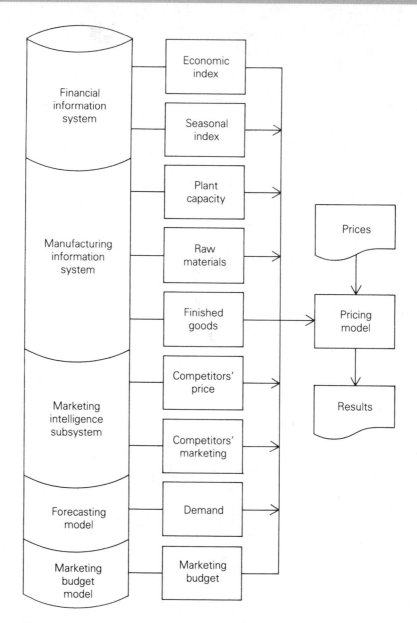

Figure 13-18 The pricing model.

Integrated-Mix Subsystem

The manager creates a marketing mix that includes all of the ingredients. It is, therefore, necessary for some portion of the marketing information system to integrate the separate ingredients and consider how they interact as a package. This is the purpose of the integrated-mix subsystem.

```
SALES REVENUE                                       $15,542,580

EXPENSES
     MARKETING                                          500,000
     RESEARCH & DEVELOPMENT                             500,000
     ADMINISTRATION                                     275,000
     MAINTENANCE                                         82,005
     LABOR                                              675,725
     MATERIALS                                          683,379
     REDUCTION, FINISHED GOODS                          180,000
     DEPRECIATION                                       614,687
     FINISHED GOODS CARRYING COSTS                            0
     RAW MATERIALS CARRYING COSTS                        68,750
     ORDERING COSTS                                      52,000
     PLANT INVESTMENT EXPENSES                              490
     FINANCE CHARGES                                          0
     SUNDRIES                                           260,900

PROFIT BEFORE INCOME TAX                             11,649,643

     INCOME TAX                                       5,588,453

PROFIT AFTER INCOME TAX                               6,061,189
```

Figure 13-19   Pricing model output.

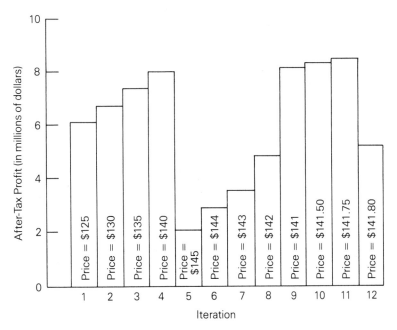

Figure 13-20   Iterative simulation of different pricing strategies.

Descriptions of integrated mix subsystems are hard to find in literature. Perhaps firms jealously guard their versions, recognizing the competitive edge that the systems provide. This argument seems unlikely since firms have generally not concealed their accomplishments with the individual mix ingredients. A more likely reason for the lack of publicity is the modest level of accomplishments that has been achieved. An integrated mix system is more complex than systems for the separate ingredients. An integrated-mix model appears very similar to the giant models attempted during the early years of MIS. Failures of these giant models prompted the DSS movement, and more modest modeling efforts are currently in vogue. This is not to say, however, that firms do not, or should not, attempt to model complex phenomena.

BRANDAID

The integrated mix model receiving the most publicity is BRANDAID, developed by Professor John D. C. Little of MIT.[12] The model is more than an academic exercise and has been implemented with good success. The graphs illustrated in this section represent use of BRANDAID to integrate the mix strategies of a well-established brand of packaged goods sold through grocery stores.

BRANDAID is an online model consisting of submodels for advertising, promotion, price, personal selling, and retail distribution. BRANDAID simulates the activities of a manufacturing firm selling to customers through retailers in a competitive environment. This environment, including the main elements and the influences that interconnect them, is shown in Figure 13-21. The solid arrows represent the influences flowing from the manufacturer to the other elements, and the dashed arrows represent influences flowing back through the channel based on consumer response to the various marketing strategies.

The basic approach of the model is to estimate the effect of the various influences on the firm's sales. Four categories of influences are considered—those of the manufacturer, the retailer, the competition, and the general environment. Manufacturer-controlled variables include product characteristics, wholesale price, advertising, personal selling, packaging, and production capacity. Retailer-controlled variables include retail price, promotions (such as coupons and stamps), and advertising. Competitor-controlled variables are the same as for the retailer. Environmental variables include seasonality, trends, and other influences.

Each influence is modeled with one or more mathematical expressions. The results of the influences do not simply add together but interact multiplicatively. For example, if packaging is expected to increase sales by 20 percent (from 1.00 to 1.20) and retailer promotion is expected to increase sales by 20 percent (from 1.00 to 1.20), the combined influence will be 44 percent (1.20 × 1.20 = 1.44) rather than 40 percent (.20 + .20 = .40). This feature recognizes the synergism among ingredients in the marketing mix.

[12]John D. C. Little, "Decision Support Systems for Marketing Managers," *Journal of Marketing* 43 (Summer 1979): 9–26. For a detailed description of BRANDAID, see John D. C. Little, "BRANDAID: A Marketing-Mix Model, Parts I and II," *Operations Research* 23 (July–August 1975): 628–673.

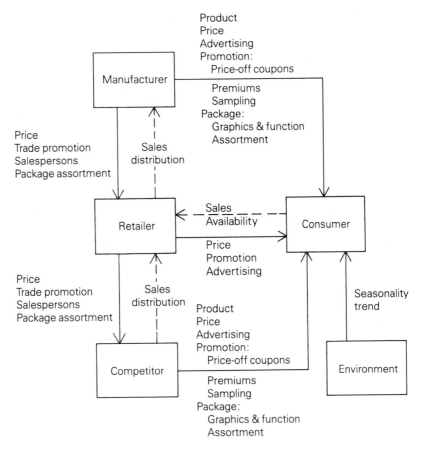

Figure 13-21 The BRANDAID integrated-mix model.

Figures 13-22 and 13-23 illustrate this interaction. Figure 13-22 shows the behavior over time of four of the influencing variables. If only one of these variables were present, sales would fluctuate as shown. The combined influences can be seen in Figure 13-23. The graph shows sales projected by the model along with actual sales.

As you can see, BRANDAID does a good job of projecting sales based on an integrated-mix strategy. However, the model is only able to consider built-in factors. If some unexpected event occurs, the model cannot handle it. This is what happened when the company using BRANDAID was hit by a strike, followed by an unexpectedly good sales response from a change in packaging. The effect of these influences is pictured in Figure 13-24.

BRANDAID was initially intended for use in annual planning, to be put on the shelf during the interim. What happened, however, was that the firm's managers began to use the model during the year for strategy decisions. In one case, a brand manager heard a rumor that his advertising budget was going to be cut in half. By 5 o'clock he had a complete analysis of what the effect of the cut on

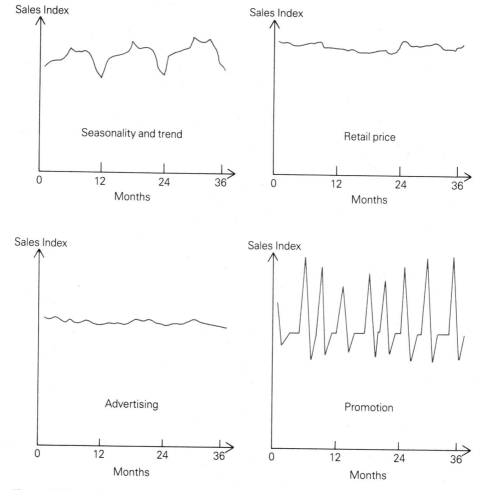

Figure 13-22 Influences of four vairables considered separately.

sales and profits would be. In other cases, managers have used the model to simulate the effect of certain anticipated competitive actions.

An integrated-mix model such as BRANDAID can be a powerful tool, not only for marketing managers but for other managers in the firm as well. But such a tool is not created overnight. Work on BRANDAID started in 1969 and efforts to improve it have continued. A firm implementing BRANDAID can anticipate a start-up period of two or more years.

Current Status of Marketing Information Systems

The author, working with marketing professor John C. Rogers of Montana State University, conducted a study of the status of marketing information systems in

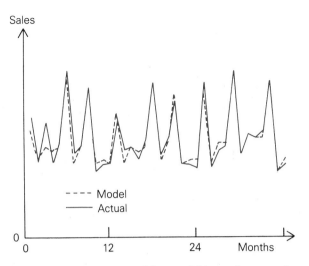

Figure 13·23 Influence of four variables, taken together.

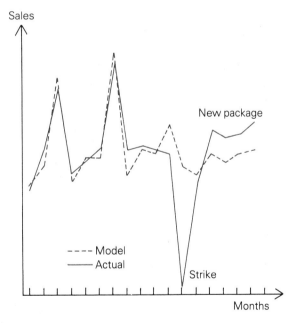

Figure 13·24 A model cannot cope with unexpected events.

large U.S. organizations. Ninety-nine firms in the Fortune 1000 supplied the data. The respondents were primarily heads of their firms' marketing research departments. Seventy-six percent of the firms have a marketing information system, and 89 percent of these are computer-based.

Terminal use

Fifty-three percent of the managers responding to the questionnaire use a terminal daily, and 11 percent use one at least weekly. Only 16 percent do not use a terminal. The terminals are used primarily to query the data base but also for running programs, obtaining reports, and executing models. As one would expect, the levels of terminal usage are considerably higher than those reported several years ago in similar studies.

Input subsystems

The managers were asked to rank the three input subsystems that we have studied based on the importance of the data supplied. The rankings appear in Figure 13-25. The three bars do not add up to 100 percent because some respondents did not rank all three systems. You can see that 60 percent of the managers rank the data processing system as their number 1 input system, about 12 percent rank it number 2, and about 16 percent rank it number 3. About 36 percent of the managers put marketing research in second position. Marketing intelligence was ranked about equally in all three positions.

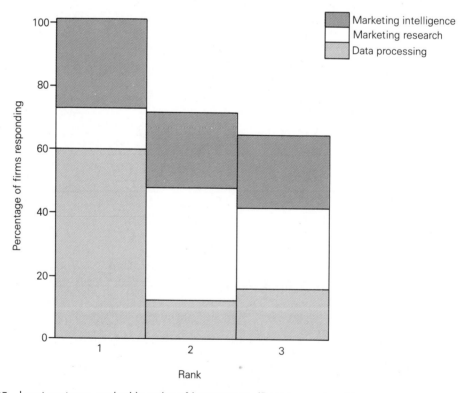

Figure 13-25 Input systems, ranked in order of importance. (Best support = 1)

Source: Raymond McLeod, Jr., and John C. Rogers, "Marketing Information Systems: Their Current Status in Fortune 1000 Companies," Journal of Management Information Systems 1 (Spring 1985): 64. Reprinted with permission.

It is important to recognize the influence of the firm on the rankings. If, for example, a firm wants to emphasize marketing intelligence, then that subsystem can be the most important. On the whole, however, most of the marketing information systems emphasize accounting data.

The data base

Most of the firms (91 percent) store customer data in the data base. Fewer firms store data on competition (33 percent), prospects (25 percent), national economy (25 percent), and the federal government (12 percent). The low percentage for economic data is surprising. One would expect the nation's largest firms to make better use of the computer to monitor economic influences on their marketing operations.

Support for management levels

The marketing information system is being used most often to support top- and middle-management levels, as pictured in Figure 13-26. The MIS concept has

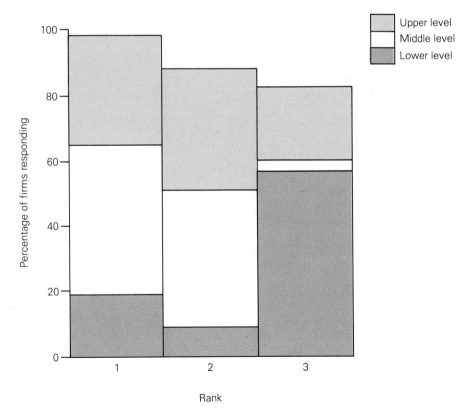

Figure 13-26 Management levels, ranked in order of support from the marketing information system (best support = 1).

Source: McLeod and Rogers, page 68. Reprinted with permission.

been criticized in the past for not providing better support to upper-level managers, but this is not the case for marketing information systems in Fortune 1000 companies. The most support appears to be at the middle level, and the least at the lower level.

Support for management functions

It is widely believed that the MIS provides best support for planning and control and less support for the other management functions. This is true for the Fortune 1000 marketing information systems. Figure 13-27 shows both planning and control dominating the top three positions. Staffing clearly is most often perceived as receiving the least support and organizing fares little better. The strong showing of directing is surprising. It is receiving good support in most firms.

These rankings by management functions conform to the rankings by level. Since top- and middle-level managers do a lot of planning and controlling, they are supported very well by the information system. Since lower-level managers do a lot of organizing and staffing, the information support is less. If the information system is to provide better support to lower-level managers, it must do a better job of supporting organizing and staffing. Perhaps the marketing managers can look to other systems for better support of certain functions. As an example, the human resource information system should facilitate staffing.

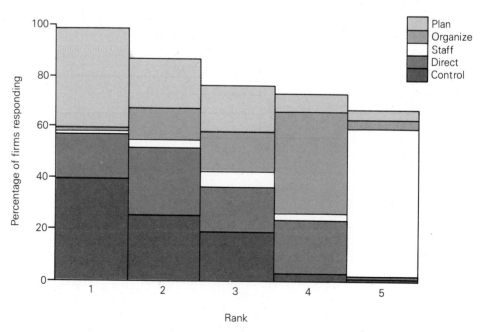

Figure 13-27   Management functions, ranked in order of support.

Source: McLeod and Rogers, page 71. Reprinted with permission.

Support for marketing mix decisions

The marketing information system provides the strongest support for decisions relating to product, as shown in Figure 13-28. The other rankings were not anticipated. Both promotion and price receive good support, and place does not. The firms have achieved more success with the difficult pricing and promotion systems than with the more deterministic place systems.

The study reflects only what the larger firms are doing. Much less is known about smaller firms. Most of the current activity is in smaller firms, implementing micro-based systems. The situation in the larger firms is much more settled. The larger firms are fine-tuning their systems to provide better decision support. The areas needing attention are staffing and organizing, as well as decisions relating to place.

Putting the Marketing Information System in Perspective

We have developed a basic structure for an information system consisting of input subsystems entering data into the data base, and output subsystems taking data from the data base and converting it into information for management. This structure is a product of the considerable activity in marketing to describe a marketing information system—its composition and its uses.

Marketers have shown much more interest in defining an information system tailored to meet their own needs than have managers in manufacturing and finance.

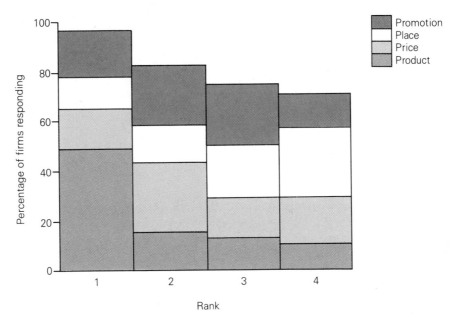

Figure 13-28 Marketing mix ingredients, ranked in order of support.
Source: McLeod and Rogers, page 72. Reprinted with permission.

It is not clear why this has happened. Certainly marketing managers' appreciation for the importance of information is no greater than their counterparts' in the other functional areas.

One possible explanation is that the current literature of business tends to focus on unsolved problems. Once a problem is solved, it has less interest to the readers. Perhaps the information systems in manufacturing and finance are much more developed than those in marketing. This is possible because of the primarily internal and quantitative focus of manufacturing and financial activity. Marketing, on the other hand, has an environmental and subjective focus. Marketing activity is keyed to the customer—an environmental element over which the marketer exercises little control.

Because it is so difficult to quantify the relationship with the customer, implementing a marketing information system is a real challenge. This is not to say that implementing an information system in manufacturing and finance is easy, but it is relatively easier to computerize those areas than to computerize marketing. The generally higher level of computer use in manufacturing and finance tends to bear this out.

How managers use the information system

Marketing managers use the information system to learn about needs and wants in the marketplace that can be satisfied with new or improved products and services. Their planning horizon is usually quite long. Marketing managers must

Table 13-1 Users of the Marketing Information System.

	Subsystem				
User	Product	Place	Promotion	Price	Integrated mix
Vice president of marketing	X	X	X	X	X
Other executives	X	X	X	X	X
Brand managers	X	X	X	X	X
Sales manager			X	X	
Advertising manager			X	X	
Manager of marketing research	X	X	X	X	X
Manager of product planning	X				
Manager of physical distribution		X			
Other managers	X	X	X	X	X

make many decisions from the time a need or want is recognized until the product or service appears on the market. The marketing information system makes it possible for firms to react more quickly to consumer needs.

Once the product or service has been provided, marketing managers use the information system to follow up on how well the consumers' needs are being satisfied. The marketing information system provides feedback information from the marketplace, and this information is used to modify, improve, or delete products and services.

There are no set rules concerning which managers use which subsystems, but some general pairings can be made. This is done in Table 13-1. Note that all of the firm's executives are included. Even though there is a separate executive information system, the executives obtain information from the functional systems as well.

The marketing information system recognizes the specialized needs of many different managers for information concerning the ingredients of the marketing mix. In addition, the information system recognizes the need to provide support to each management level and management function or role to the maximum extent possible.

Summary

The objective of this chapter has been to provide a structure for studying the MIS. Since organizations and managers are grouped according to the functional areas of finance, manufacturing, and marketing, the uses of the MIS can also be grouped this way. Constructing the MIS as a composite of these functional subsystems, however, should not imply that an integrated MIS is unnecessary. The end objective of every firm's IRM program should be the attainment of an integrated MIS in which all parts work in harmony. If parts of the system do not work together, the MIS will not be effective. In this case, it is doubtful that the physical system of the firm can be any more efficient. The two systems must work together: an efficient physical system demands an efficient information system, and vice versa.

The main functional areas identified in this chapter are marketing, manufacturing, and finance. It is assumed that all managers except the CEO, board members, and the executive and administrative vice presidents fit within one of these three areas. Functional information systems are developed for each area, and all of the managers—including the executives—derive information from them.

Our model of the marketing information system is based on the pioneering work of several marketing theorists. Input subsystems gather internal and environmental data and enter it into the data base. Output subsystems convert data into information for decision making. The input subsystems include data processing, marketing intelligence, and marketing research. The data processing system interfaces with the firm's vendors and customers and gathers internal data as well. Both the marketing intelligence and marketing research systems have an environmental focus—on customers and competition. The marketing intelligence system features primarily informal data and information, but some firms establish formal systems. Marketing research is typified by short, concentrated studies to obtain answers to specific questions. A variety of data-gathering techniques is used, but the survey is the most popular. More firms are doing their own marketing research, using micro hardware and software.

The output subsystems represent the four ingredients of the marketing mix, plus an integrated-mix subsystem. The product subsystem supports the manager as decisions are made throughout the product life cycle. The place subsystem enables the manager to build and operate distribution systems linking the manufacturer, wholesaler, and retailer. Computers are used in some channels to link the members by means of two-way information flows. The promotion subsystem assists the manager in making decisions relating to advertising and personal selling. The advertising decisions are the most difficult to support with the computer because of their lack of structure. The computer assists salespersons and sales managers by relieving them of clerical duties and performing sophisticated analyses. Sales managers can use electronic spreadsheets to model key decisions relating to management of sales territories. The price subsystem provides support to either cost-based or demand-based policies. Cost-based policies are supported with accurate accounting data, and demand-based policies are supported with mathematical models that take into account multiple variables—many environmental. Theoretically, the marketing information system should also include an integrated-mix subsystem that treats all of the ingredients as a package. In practice, such integrated-mix subsystems have been difficult to achieve.

Marketing managers in Fortune 1000 firms make frequent use of terminals, and their information systems provide best support at the upper levels. The systems also are used primarily in planning and control. Product decisions are supported the most, and place decisions the least. Little is known about the status of marketing information systems in smaller organizations.

We will use the same basic system architecture of input and output subsystems in the next two chapters as we study manufacturing and financial information systems.

Key Terms

marketing information system

financial information system

manufacturing information system

human resource information system (HRIS)

functional attitude, company attitude

marketing orientation, marketing concept

marketing mix (the four Ps)— product, place, promotion, price

marketing nerve center

marketing intelligence

marketing communications

marketing research

marketing management science

product, place, promotion, price subsystems

integrated-mix subsystem

output, input subsystems

industrial espionage

survey

in-depth interview

observation

controlled experiment

CATI (computer-assisted telephone
  interviewing)

product life cycle

feedforward information

media planning model

econometric model

public relations (PR)

cost-based pricing

demand-based pricing

Key Concepts

Functional organization structure

The similarities and dissimilarities
between functional and flow
network structures

The development of functional
information systems
corresponding to the functionally
organized physical resources of
the firm

How nonintegrated functional
systems diminish the effectiveness
of the MIS

The manner in which the marketing
concept can unify the various
functional areas so that they work
together as a single system

How the marketing mix provides an
effective means of both classifying
marketing decisions and
subdividing information outputs

Input and output subsystems

How the firm's data processing
system is an input subsystem of
the marketing information system

How marketing intelligence
subsystems can be made more
formal

The product life cycle

Resource flow through the
distribution channel

The subjective nature of
promotional decision making

Uneven levels of support provided by
marketing information systems in
Fortune 1000 companies in terms
of management levels and
functions, and also mix
ingredients

Questions

1. If the MIS is an integrated system that meets the information needs of the entire firm, how do you explain the existence of functional information systems?

2. Does a military branch, such as the army, have a marketing function? Explain your answer.

3. Would a nonprofit organization like the United Way have a financial function? Explain.

4. What functional area of the firm is responsible for the personnel flow?

5. In a firm with information systems organized functionally, where do the executives get their information?

6. What did Philip Kotler contribute to the concept of functional information systems?

7. Which environmental element is the primary responsibility of the marketing intelligence subsystem? The marketing research subsystem?

8. What is the difference between industrial espionage and marketing intelligence?

9. List five legal things that a firm can do to keep informed of competitive activities.

10. How does the marketing research subsystem differ from the marketing intelligence subsystem?

11. What are the four basic means of gathering marketing research data? Which has been computerized? What is it called?

12. What are the three time periods in the product life cycle in which information support is provided?

13. What type of firm would use the quantitative new-product evaluation model? What should a manager keep in mind when using the model?

14. What is feedforward information? Which channel member, or members, should provide it?

15. As the sales manager carries out Fayol's management functions, which receive the most support from the MIS?

16. What are the two basic approaches to pricing? Which receives support from the MIS? How?

17. Why did profit fall when the manager raised the price from $140 to $145 in Figure 13-20?

18. What are the four categories of influences on consumer behavior in the BRANDAID model?

19. Is a good data processing system a requirement for a good marketing information system in a Fortune 1000 company? Explain.

20. Which management function is supported the least by the Fortune 1000 marketing information systems? How could the HRIS help?

Problems

1. Go to the library and make a list of periodicals that provide information about specific industries. Hint: *Chain Store Age* provides information about chain stores.

2. Your instructor will identify for you a successful business establishment near campus. Identify which of the marketing mix ingredients are key to the firm's success. How has the firm's management emphasized the key ingredients? Do not contact the firm's management without first checking with your instructor.

3. Design a telephone interview form to obtain the following information. Arrange the format of the questionnaire so that it can be administered easily by someone else.
   a. age?
   b. education?
   c. if college, which degree?
   d. if no college, how many years?
   e. if business degree, which major?
   f. if computer major, which programming languages studied?
   g. current job?
   h. worked way through college?
   i. name?

CASE PROBLEM: Great Lakes Boat and Marine

Your career is progressing nicely—six successful years with a Big Eight accounting firm in its management service division. Your performance as a computer consultant was so outstanding that you got a job offer from one of your clients. You managed the conversion from a batch to an online data processing system for Great Lakes Boat and Marine so well that the company offered you the position of vice president of information services. Sue Rankin, the president, told you that the next step was to develop an MIS and that she needed someone to implement it. The system you installed earlier does all of the essential data processing tasks—order entry, inventory, billing, accounts receivable, purchasing, and receiving. You know that Great Lakes has a sound data processing system, which should make it possible to achieve an excellent MIS.

During your first day on the job, you meet with Rankin to learn more about her expectations. She tells you that she has formed an MIS committee consisting of Rick Guenther (vice president of manufacturing), Don Lehnert (vice president of marketing), Cheryl Mitchell (vice president of finance), and you. Rankin wants you to call on each member, introduce yourself, and set a date and time for the first planning meeting.

You already know Mitchell, having worked with her on the installation of the data processing system. You know that she is extremely computer literate and anxious to expand the scope of the computer applications. You have heard of Guenther and Lehnert but haven't met them. As you leave, you ask Rankin, "Aren't you going to be on the MIS committee?"

"No," Rankin replies, "I'm too busy planning our entry into the New England market. I just don't have time. That's why I hired you."

Your first stop is Guenther's office. You find him extremely likeable—a warm handshake, boundless energy, contagious optimism, and a great sense of humor. You spend two hours in his office, getting to know him and talking about the computer. Guenther wants to get started immediately. "We've just been waiting for someone like you," he says. "We've known about MIS and how it can help us in manufacturing but haven't had anyone to get things moving. I want data collection terminals in every work area. I need good data to establish production standards. I want all manufacturing managers to have terminals in their offices, and I want each to attend a course on how to use the computer. I've seen what a good MIS can do in manufacturing, and I can't wait to get started."

Neither can you. You are so excited after talking with Guenther that you almost run down the hall to Lehnert's office. When his secretary ushers you into his office and his greeting is, "Well, what do *you* want?" you suspect rough sailing. You introduce yourself and explain your purpose. You feel uncomfortable when Lehnert nervously jingles coins in his pocket as you talk. When you pause to catch your breath, he says, "Listen, I don't have time to get involved with Sue's MIS. We're planning to expand our market area and I have to find eight new distributors by the end of the month. I can't do that sitting around talking about computer programs. If I can't get my marketing job done, there won't be any company to put an MIS in."

"Now, I have to go. Why don't you talk with my manager of marketing administration, Willie Campbell. The MIS would really be in Willie's area. He'll get you fixed up. Just a minute, and I'll have my secretary take you to his office. I've appreciated meeting you, and I wish you all the luck in the world. I'm sure you'll give us a good MIS."

Questions

1. What is the problem here?
2. Assuming that Rankin insists on going ahead with the MIS project, what would you suggest that they do to assure that they get a "good MIS"?

CASE PROBLEM: National Foods, Inc.

National Foods is one of the leading manufacturers and distributors of food products, competing directly with firms like General Mills, General Foods, and Nestlé. A mainframe computer is installed at headquarters in Minneapolis, with distributed processing systems at plant and distribution centers across the country. Each of the firm's 625 sales representatives is equipped with a portable keyboard terminal that can be attached to an ordinary push-button telephone. At the end of each day, the sales reps transmit sales call data to headquarters using the WATS line. The data includes sales figures (products and units) plus reports of special promotions such as ads, coupons, and contests. They call the application a "sales tracking system."

The computer operation at National is managed by Dan Kennedy, vice president of information systems. It's the Friday afternoon before Memorial Day weekend, and Dan is just about to leave the office when the phone rings. Fred Enden, vice president of marketing, is on the line.

Fred congratulates Dan on the new sales tracking system that has just been installed. "It's absolutely fantastic," Fred says. "We're able to track the sales volume of any of our products throughout the life cycle. The reps are following the procedure and reporting their data daily. We can even see the effect of our advertising and promotional campaigns—something we've never been able to do before."

This is all sweet music to Dan's ears, but he is anxious to get on the road. He interrupts, saying, "Listen, Fred, I'm on my way out the door to pick up Alice so that we can head for the lake. If this can wait until Tuesday, I'd rather discuss it then."

Dan thinks Fred will take the hint and is surprised to hear, "I understand, Dan, but just let me tell you what's on my mind. It'll only take a minute, and I'd like you to think about it over the weekend. Then we can talk more on Tuesday.

"I have a great idea. Why don't we install a sales tracking system that will track competitive sales? We could limit it to only selected items at first. Maybe we could start off with a single line, like dog food. I'd like to know about the competition's plans to put a new brand on the market before it actually hits. Then I'd like to track the sales during the life cycle. When we see the volume dropping off, we can anticipate a new product to take its place. Then we can increase our intelligence activity. Doesn't that sound like a good idea? Now, I'd like you to give me your suggestions about the data inputs we'll need and where they can come from. Why don't you think it over, and we can get together first thing Tuesday morning."

Dan's feelings are a mixture of surprise, flattery, and dejection. He manages to say, "Sure, Fred. That sounds like a good idea. I'll think it over." With that, he hangs up the phone, dials a number, and says, "Alice, about that trip to the lake—."

Questions

1. Is Fred's idea of a competitive tracking system feasible?
2. How could National learn of competitive products before they are introduced?
3. How could they track competitive product sales?
4. Could a system be designed using secondary data only?
5. Would the National sales reps be involved in any way?
6. Which subsystems of the marketing information system would be involved in the new system?

Selected Bibliography

Marketing Information Systems

Benjamin, Robert I., John F. Rockart, Michael S. Scott Morton, and John Wyman, "Information Technology: A Strategic Opportunity," *Sloan Management Review* 25 (Spring 1984): 3–10.

Brien, Richard H., and James E. Stafford, "Marketing Information Systems: A New Dimension for Marketing Research," *Journal of Marketing* 32 (July 1968): 19–23.

Cash, James I., Jr., and Benn R. Konsynski, "IS Redraws Competitive Boundaries," *Harvard Business Review* 63 (March-April 1985): 134–142.

Gladstone, Susan, "Vital Statistics," *Business Computer Systems* 3 (May 1984): 92ff.

Hertz, David B., and Howard Thomas, "Decision and Risk Analysis in a New Product and Facilities Planning Problem," *Sloan Management Review* 24 (Winter 1983): 17–31.

Hughes, G. David, "Computerized Sales Management," *Harvard Business Review* 61 (March-April 1983): 102–112.

Hughes, G. David, "Pricing for Profit," *Business Computer Systems* 3 (April 1984): 31–33.

Hughes, G. David, "When Inventory Means Sales," *Business Computer Systems* 3 (July 1984): 33ff.

Hutt, Michael D., and Thomas W. Speh, "The Marketing Strategy Center: Diagnosing the Industrial Marketer's Interdisciplinary Role," *Journal of Marketing* 48 (Fall 1984): 53–61.

Ives, Blake, and Gerard P. Learmonth, "The Information System as a Competitive Weapon," *Communications of the ACM* 27 (December 1984): 1193–1201.

King, William R., and David I. Cleland, "Environmental Information Systems for Strategic Marketing Planning," *Journal of Marketing* 38 (October 1974): 35–40.

Kotler, Philip, "A Design for the Firm's Marketing Nerve Center," *Business Horizons* 9 (Fall 1966): 63–74.

Little, John D. C., "BRANDAID: A Marketing-Mix Model, Part 1: Structure," *Operations Research* 23 (July-August 1975): 628–655.

Little, John D. C., "BRANDAID: A Marketing-Mix Model, Part 2: Implementation, Calibration, and Case Study," *Operations Research* 23 (July-August 1975): 656–673.

Little, John D. C., "Decision Support Systems for Marketing Managers," *Journal of Marketing* 43 (Summer 1979): 9–26.

McFarlan, F. Warren, "Information Technology Changes the Way You Compete," *Harvard Business Review* 62 (May-June 1984): 98–103.

McLeod, Raymond, Jr., and John C. Rogers, "Marketing Information Systems: Uses in the Fortune 500," *California Management Review* 25 (Fall 1982): 106–118.

McLeod, Raymond, Jr., and John C. Rogers, "Marketing Information Systems: Their Current Status in Fortune 1000 Companies," *Journal of Management Information Systems* 1 (Spring 1985): 57–75.

Montgomery, David B., and Glen L. Urban, "Marketing Decision-Information Systems: An Emerging View," *Journal of Marketing Research* 7 (May 1970): 226–234.

Sharman, Graham, "The Rediscovery of Logistics," *Harvard Business Review* 62 (September-October 1984): 71–79.

Wood, Lamont, "Directing the Flow of Goods," *Computer Decisions* 16 (September 15, 1984): 62ff.

Chapter 14

Manufacturing Information Systems

Learning Objectives

After studying this chapter, you should:

- Understand how the manufacturing information system can be used in making plant location and layout decisions
- Appreciate the essentially informal nature of the system that gathers labor information
- Appreciate how a formal procedure for gathering vendor information contributes to meeting manufacturing schedules and achieving desired levels of quality
- Recognize that the industrial engineer (IE) is concerned with both physical and conceptual manufacturing systems
- Appreciate the contribution that a data collection network can make to gathering attendance and job data
- Understand the basic mechanics of inventory management
- Recognize how management can influence the quality level of the firm's products
- Understand the concepts of material requirements planning (MRP) and manufacturing resource planning (MRP-II)
- Be able to follow a job through a factory from the time that it is scheduled until the finished goods are available for sale
- Appreciate the potential for providing the manufacturing manager with specific and up-to-date information on production costs
- Be up to date concerning efforts to automate the factory, including CAD/CAM and robotics
- Understand the basic features of a technique that might revolutionize production—JIT (Just-In-Time)

Introduction

In the previous chapter we saw that marketing is concerned with more than distributing the product; marketing also has the responsibility of determining what the consumers want and need. Once the wants and needs have been determined, it is the responsibility of the manufacturing function to produce the products. The production process is our topic in this chapter. We will look at the physical manufacturing system and identify the basic responsibilities of manufacturing management. Then we will describe the subsystems that comprise the manufacturing information system—the conceptual information system that enables manufacturing management to manage the physical manufacturing system. We will conclude the chapter with a discussion of some of the revolutionary changes that are taking place in manufacturing today—manufacturing resource planning, CAD/CAM (computer-aided design and computer-aided manufacturing), robotics, CIM (computer-integrated manufacturing), and JIT (just-in-time) manufacturing. As we study these new production methods, the application of systems theory from Chapter 2 will be evident.

The Physical System

The general systems model of the firm (see Chapter 3) describes a manufacturing organization in a general way. At the bottom of the model is the physical system. The physical system is composed of system inputs received from the environment, transformation processes, and systems outputs directed to the environment. Manufacturing management is responsible for (1) constructing this physical system, and (2) using the system to produce the firm's products. Our discussion here will focus on products, not services.

Constructing the physical system

The decision to construct a physical manufacturing system such as a plant is made at the top level because the decision has long-term effects and represents a sizable investment. Once the decision is made, the firm must determine where to locate the plant, and this involves the middle-management level as well. First, management must select a particular *region* of the United States or another country. Some of the factors influencing the selection of a region include the concentration of customers, availability of a labor supply, land costs, availability of raw materials, climate, and strength of unionization.

Once the region has been selected, management must decide on a particular *city*. This decision considers customer concentration, labor supply, land, taxes, transportation, community services (police, fire, and so on), community attitudes, cultural resources, and management preferences.

Finally, management must choose a particular *area* of the selected city. Factors influencing this decision include customer concentration, land costs, transportation, utilities, and zoning restrictions.

These are *semi-structured* decisions. Some factors, such as land costs, taxes, and transportation facilities, can be measured quantitatively. Other factors, such as community attitudes and cultural resources, are difficult to measure.

The MIS can help the manufacturing manager make any of the location decisions. A model can consider both quantitative and subjective factors, or quantitative factors only. *Linear programming (LP)* is frequently used to consider quantitative factors to identify the best location.

A plant location model.   Assume that a firm has three plants, one in Denver, one in St. Louis, and one in Pittsburgh. These plants manufacture ice chests that are shipped to distribution centers in Los Angeles, Seattle, Atlanta, and New York. Figure 14-1 shows the site locations and indicates the unit shipping charges from each plant to each distribution center.

The firm attempts to minimize shipping costs by shipping from the plant closest to each distribution center. This is not always possible because the plants have different capacities and the distribution centers serve market areas with different demand levels.

Plant capacities are:

Pittsburgh	10,000 units
St. Louis	15,000 units
Denver	23,000 units

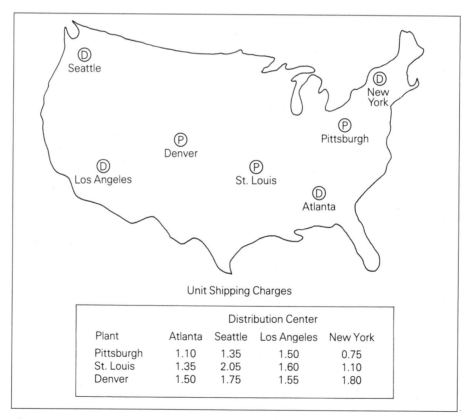

Unit Shipping Charges

	Distribution Center			
Plant	Atlanta	Seattle	Los Angeles	New York
Pittsburgh	1.10	1.35	1.50	0.75
St. Louis	1.35	2.05	1.60	1.10
Denver	1.50	1.75	1.55	1.80

Figure 14-1 A production and distribution network.

Distribution center demand levels are:

Atlanta	12,500 units
Seattle	10,000 units
Los Angeles	8,000 units
New York	17,500 units

The company uses LP to allocate plant output according to distribution center demand. Using an interactive model, the shipping costs, capacities, and demands are entered into a terminal or micro. The model dialog and entered data appear in Figure 14-2. The model asks for data by typing ENTER. . . . The data entered appears on the line below and to the right of the [ ]: cursor symbol.

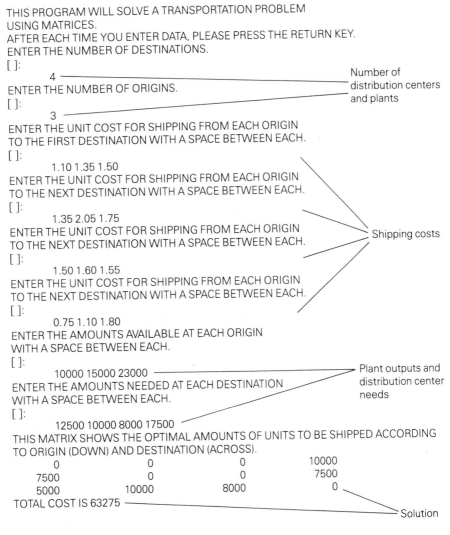

THIS PROGRAM WILL SOLVE A TRANSPORTATION PROBLEM
USING MATRICES.
AFTER EACH TIME YOU ENTER DATA, PLEASE PRESS THE RETURN KEY.
ENTER THE NUMBER OF DESTINATIONS.
[ ]:
    4 —————————————————————— Number of
ENTER THE NUMBER OF ORIGINS.   distribution centers
[ ]:   and plants
    3
ENTER THE UNIT COST FOR SHIPPING FROM EACH ORIGIN
TO THE FIRST DESTINATION WITH A SPACE BETWEEN EACH.
[ ]:
    1.10 1.35 1.50
ENTER THE UNIT COST FOR SHIPPING FROM EACH ORIGIN
TO THE NEXT DESTINATION WITH A SPACE BETWEEN EACH.
[ ]:
    1.35 2.05 1.75
ENTER THE UNIT COST FOR SHIPPING FROM EACH ORIGIN
TO THE NEXT DESTINATION WITH A SPACE BETWEEN EACH.   Shipping costs
[ ]:
    1.50 1.60 1.55
ENTER THE UNIT COST FOR SHIPPING FROM EACH ORIGIN
TO THE NEXT DESTINATION WITH A SPACE BETWEEN EACH.
[ ]:
    0.75 1.10 1.80
ENTER THE AMOUNTS AVAILABLE AT EACH ORIGIN
WITH A SPACE BETWEEN EACH.
[ ]:
    10000 15000 23000 ———————————————— Plant outputs and
ENTER THE AMOUNTS NEEDED AT EACH DESTINATION   distribution center
WITH A SPACE BETWEEN EACH.   needs
[ ]:
    12500 10000 8000 17500
THIS MATRIX SHOWS THE OPTIMAL AMOUNTS OF UNITS TO BE SHIPPED ACCORDING
TO ORIGIN (DOWN) AND DESTINATION (ACROSS).

0	0	0	10000
7500	0	0	7500
5000	10000	8000	0

TOTAL COST IS 63275 ———————————————————————
                                                 Solution

Figure 14-2 Model dialog—three plants.

The model uses the term *origin* for the plants and the term *destination* for the distribution centers.

At the bottom of the printout is a matrix showing the number of units to be shipped from each plant to each distribution center to produce the minimum cost. Just below the matrix is the total cost amount—$63,275.

The solution matrix is reproduced in Table 14-1 showing the plant and distribution center names. Pittsburgh ships all of its output to New York. St. Louis ships 7,500 units to Atlanta and 7,500 units to New York. Denver ships 5,000 units to Atlanta, 10,000 units to Seattle, and 8,000 units to Los Angeles.

The model printout in Figure 14-2 does not show how the cost figures are computed; that detail appears in Table 14-2.

The firm is considering the construction of a new plant in the southeast United States as part of a long-range plan to expand that market area. Top-level management first decides on Florida and then picks Orlando as a possible city. The LP model is executed a second time, entering new shipping costs from the Orlando site, and the capacity of the Orlando plant (4,000 units are to be trans-

Table 14-1 Optimal Shipping Allocations—Three Plants

	Distribution Centers			
Plant	Atlanta	Seattle	Los Angeles	New York
Pittsburgh	0	0	0	10,000
St. Louis	7500	0	0	7,500
Denver	5000	10,000	8000	0

Table 14-2 Shipping-Cost Computations—Three Plants

	Distribution Centers			
Plant	Atlanta	Seattle	Los Angeles	New York
Pittsburgh				.075 × $10,000 = $7500
St. Louis	1.35 × $7500 = $10,125			1.10 × $7500 = $8250
Denver	1.50 × $5000 = $7500	1.75 × $10,000 = $17,500	1.55 × $8000 = $12,400	

ferred from Pittsburgh). The number of destinations and their demand levels remain the same. Figure 14-3 illustrates the model dialog.

The addition of the Orlando plant will not reduce shipping costs very much—only by $1,000 (to $62,275). That savings alone would not justify the plant; but perhaps other, subjective factors would. Better customer service and long-range market expansion must also be considered.

The managers can consider other options. They can simulate other Florida locations, or they can consider another area, such as the Midwest. They can even consider adding a new distribution center—perhaps in Florida. These are all possibilities, and the LP model can quickly provide cost information. In this fashion, the MIS helps management make the long-range decision of plant location.

```
THIS PROGRAM WILL SOLVE A TRANSPORTATION PROBLEM
USING MATRICES.
AFTER EACH TIME YOU ENTER DATA, PLEASE PRESS THE RETURN KEY.
ENTER THE NUMBER OF DESTINATIONS.
[ ]:
        4
ENTER THE NUMBER OF ORIGINS.
[ ]:
        4
ENTER THE UNIT COST FOR SHIPPING FROM EACH ORIGIN
TO THE FIRST DESTINATION WITH A SPACE BETWEEN EACH.
[ ]:
        1.10 1.35 1.50 0.75
ENTER THE UNIT COST FOR SHIPPING FROM EACH ORIGIN
TO THE NEXT DESTINATION WITH A SPACE BETWEEN EACH.
[ ]:
        1.35 2.05 1.75 2.00
ENTER THE UNIT COST FOR SHIPPING FROM EACH ORIGIN
TO THE NEXT DESTINATION WITH A SPACE BETWEEN EACH.
[ ]:
        1.50 1.60 1.55 1.40
ENTER THE UNIT COST FOR SHIPPING FROM EACH ORIGIN
TO THE NEXT DESTINATION WITH A SPACE BETWEEN EACH.
[ ]:
        0.75 1.10 1.80 1.15
ENTER THE AMOUNTS AVAILABLE AT EACH ORIGIN
WITH A SPACE BETWEEN EACH.
[ ]:
        6000 15000 23000 4000
ENTER THE AMOUNTS NEEDED AT EACH DESTINATION
WITH A SPACE BETWEEN EACH.
[ ]:
        12500 10000 8000 17500
THIS MATRIX SHOWS THE OPTIMAL AMOUNTS OF UNITS TO BE SHIPPED ACCORDING
TO ORIGIN (DOWN) AND DESTINATION (ACROSS).
        0               0               0            6000
     3500               0               0           11500
     5000           10000            8000               0
     4000               0               0               0
TOTAL COST IS 62275
```

Figure 14-3 Model dialog—four plants.

General layout of the plant.   After the plant site has been selected, the next step is to determine the details of the plant layout. Primary attention is given to efficiency of operations—moving the materials the shortest possible distance to keep costs down and eliminate bottlenecks and delays. Lower-level managers become involved in the plant layout decision, since they will be using the arrangement on a day-to-day basis.

A plant typically includes the areas shown in Figure 14-4. The portion corresponding to the input element in the general systems model consists of a *receiving* area, a *receiving inspection* area, and a *raw-materials storeroom.* The *shop floor* area corresponds to the transformation element in the general model. The shop floor consists of several *work stations*—areas where different types of processes are performed. The area corresponding to the output element in the

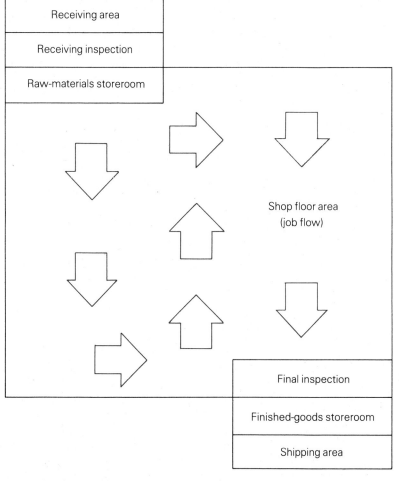

Figure 14-4   General plant layout.

general model includes a *final inspection* area, a *finished-goods storeroom*, and a *shipping* area.

The key to a profitable production operation is timing. Vendors' raw materials should arrive at the plant precisely when they are needed. Too early means unnecessary inventory-carrying costs. Too late means missed production schedules. Materials also should arrive at the work stations precisely when they are needed, and the finished goods should be shipped to the customer immediately after passing final inspection. The MIS can play a key role in achieving this precise timing.

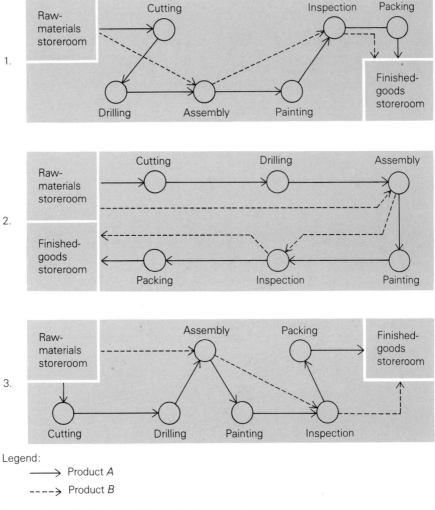

Figure 14-5 Evaluation of alternate plant layouts.

A plant layout model. Figure 14-5 illustrates how several different layouts can be considered. All three consist of the same work stations; only the arrangements differ.

There have been a number of *plant-layout models* available for quite some time. Manufacturers spotted plant layout as a possible use of linear programming and similar optimizing models early in the computer era. There are some 30 or 40 models on the market, designed specifically for plant layout. Two of the earliest, and most widely known, are CORELAP (COmputerized RElationship LAyout Planning) and CRAFT (Computerized Relative Allocation of Facilities Technique).

Even though you would consider plant layout to be a structured problem, the output from these models must be checked and reviewed before a decision is made to implement a layout. The logic of the layout must be verified, and some manual fine tuning can almost always achieve additional efficiencies.

Operating the physical system

The task of the manufacturing manager is to make the best use of available resources to accomplish production objectives. Managers ordinarily are constrained by their resources— personnel, machines, material, and money. At any given time, certain resources are in short supply, while others are overabundant.

The manufacturing function is largely an operational level activity. All of the employees and most of the managers are concerned primarily with meeting short-term production goals. Most attention focuses on what is to be accomplished today, this week, and this month. Few managers in the manufacturing area address long-range planning and control. This short-term horizon is changing somewhat due to the requirements of the more modern computer models to plan one or more years into the future. Of the three main functional areas that we are studying, however, manufacturing managers spend the greatest proportion of their time solving current problems.

The Manufacturing Information System

The manufacturing manager is concerned mainly with material flow from vendors, through the transformation process, and to marketing for distribution. Both personnel and machines are used to expedite and facilitate this flow. In a manufacturing firm, most of the employees work in the manufacturing function. Also, much use is made of machines that move material by conveyors, cranes, and trucks, and transform raw materials into finished goods. Many of these machines, oftentimes robots, are controlled by computers.

In both creating the physical production system and operating it, the manufacturing manager needs information. The MIS subsystem that provides the needed information is the *manufacturing information system*. A model of such a system is illustrated in Figure 14-6.

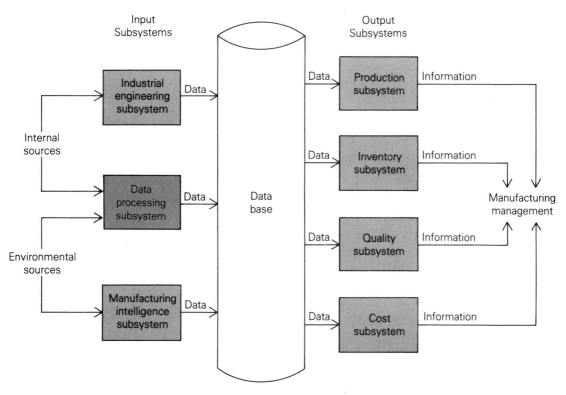

Figure 14-6 Model of a manufacturing information system.

You can see the similarity between this model and the one used for the marketing information system. Both models consist of a structure comprising input subsystems, a data base, and output subsystems.

Input subsystems

Three subsystems gather data and enter it into the manufacturing information system. They include data processing, industrial engineering, and manufacturing intelligence.

The *data processing subsystem* gathers internal data describing the manufacturing operation by means of data collection terminals located throughout the manufacturing area. Manufacturing management uses information produced from this accounting data for planning and controlling its operations. The *manufacturing intelligence subsystem* gathers data from the environment. The two environmental elements of particular interest to the manufacturing manager are vendors and labor. The vendors provide both material and machine resources; they also provide information such as catalogs and price lists. Data describing the labor element in the environment is much less formal and specific. Such data rarely finds its way into the computerized portion of the MIS but instead is communicated by word of mouth and in the form of typed documents. The *industrial engineering subsystem* is like the marketing research subsystem in that it involves primarily special data-gathering projects. The two subsystems are dissimilar in that the industrial engineering subsystem gathers data from inside the firm rather than from the environment. The industrial engineering subsystem is the direct descendant of Frederick W. Taylor's scientific management group.

Output subsystems

The *production subsystem* describes each phase of the transformation process, from the ordering of raw materials from a vendor to the release of the finished goods to marketing. A great many activities are tracked by this subsystem—purchasing, receiving, material handling, and the production process itself. This subsystem reports on the processes that are performed as the material flows through the firm.

As the material flows, the manager wants to know how well the work is progressing. The production subsystem monitors the timing, and three other subsystems measure quantity, quality, and cost. The *inventory subsystem* reports on quantity by keeping a record of how much material flows from one step to the next—from raw materials to work in process and finally to finished goods. A special *quality subsystem* is used to assure that the quality level of raw materials received from vendors meets the required standards. Then this subsystem reports on the quality level at each critical step of the transformation process. The *cost subsystem* tells the manufacturing manager exactly what the transformation process is costing. The costs of labor, materials, and machines can be reported very specifically in production units or even in seconds of time. The data collection terminals record the exact time that a worker or a machine starts a job and the exact time that the job is finished. The same devices can also report exactly how much material is used. The data can be compared with predetermined standards. Excessive costs call for decisions that make the material flow and transformation process more efficient.

We will now discuss the subsystems in greater detail.

Manufacturing Intelligence Subsystem

All production organizations make some use of personnel. Even in highly automated processes, people are needed to initialize, maintain, and monitor the automated machinery. All organizations also use material resources acquired from vendors. The manufacturing manager should remain aware of the status of these personnel and material sources so that they are available to the firm as needed.

Labor information

Labor is not the most expensive ingredient going into the finished product. That honor goes to materials, currently representing about 55 percent of the cost of goods sold. Labor, on the other hand, represents only about 2 to 14 percent. If you were to ask a manufacturing manager which resource is the most important, however, the answer would be labor. The manufacturing manager recognizes the value of highly skilled, resourceful, and loyal employees.

The manufacturing manager does not have all of the responsibility for the flow of the personnel resource through the firm. It is the responsibility of the firm's personnel department to advertise for applicants, screen and test them, and arrange for interviews with the managers of the areas where the openings exist.

There is one condition, however, that causes manufacturing managers to become actively involved with the labor element of the environment. That condition is unionization. In many firms the personnel resource is organized into labor unions. A contract is established between the firm and the union, describing the expectations and obligations of both the firm and the union members. Information describing the actual performance of both the firm and the union members must be gathered so that management can ensure that the terms of the contract are being met. This information is usually obtained by supervisors as part of their daily contact with union members. The supervisors forward this information to higher-level managers by personal contact or written report. The firm's industrial relations department can play a role in this information flow, initiating and expediting it throughout the manufacturing organization. Very seldom does this information enter the computer, but the information must be available for effective management.

Figure 14-7 shows the flow of labor information from the several environmental elements to the personnel department. The two-way formal flow between manufacturing management and the personnel department consists of (1) written requests for personnel, and (2) data sheets on applicants. A formal flow can also exist from manufacturing management to upper-level corporate management. This flow consists of reports detailing the degree to which the contractual terms are being followed.

Vendor information

Substantially more data and information are gathered about the firm's environmental sources of material than about personnel. For one reason, firms usually have many vendors, and transactions involving the vendors occur each day. Another reason is that several of the firm's employees gather and use vendor data and information. These employees are called *buyers*, and they work in the purchasing department. Most purchasing departments have several buyers, and they usually specialize in contacts with certain classes of items. For example, one buyer will specialize in procuring electronic components, and he or she will be well informed about the electronics suppliers. Another buyer will specialize in adhesives, another in maintenance supplies, and so on.

The selection of reliable vendors is an important step toward production quality and efficiency. Ordered raw materials must arrive on schedule, at the expected quality level. One approach to building reliable vendor relationships is to screen possible vendors before making a purchase commitment. This screening can be a two-step process. First, a firm asks a prospective vendor to complete a questionnaire inquiring about such topics as production resources and the importance placed on quality control. Data from these forms is stored in the data base and updated periodically.

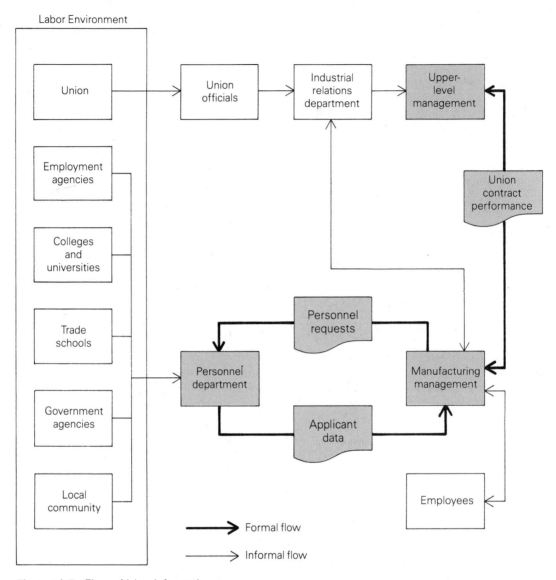

Figure 14-7 Flow of labor information.

The second step involves an in-depth financial analysis of the vendor. For large vendors, data can be obtained from annual reports or from Securities and Exchange Commission reports. For small vendors, managers must request information directly from the organizations. An analysis of balance sheet and income statement items will indicate the long-term ability of the vendor to perform as a reliable supply source.

These two data-gathering steps can be augmented by personal visits to vendor plants by purchasing personnel. This degree of screening is especially important for the vendors of critical materials.

Once a vendor has been selected, buyers should remain current on the vendor's capabilities. The buyers get much information directly from the vendor. The vendor's sales representatives make personal calls on the buyers and furnish manuals and catalogs. Also, buyers frequently contact the vendor by telephone to ask specific questions.

Each time a firm obtains materials from a vendor, a record is created describing the results of the transaction. The record is kept in the data base along with data obtained from the vendor survey forms and the financial analyses. Additional data is provided by quality control inspections during the production process and by repairs and replacements of customer units after sale. A complete vendor record will provide an analysis of the organization as well as the performance of its materials from receipt to end-product use. Figure 14-8 illustrates these three sources of vendor information.

Industrial Engineering Subsystem

Industrial engineering can be traced back to Frederick W. Taylor and his scientific management, but it has come a long way since those days. *Industrial engineers* (or *IEs*) study the manufacturing operation and make recommendations for improvement. The modern IE is not just an "efficiency expert" with stopwatch and clipboard, shaving seconds off production processes. The IE is a systems analyst—a specialist in the design and operation of physical systems who is knowledgeable in conceptual systems as well. Much of the work of the IE concerns conceptual systems, such as order quantities and reorder points in inventory systems. It is difficult to distinguish between the work of the IE in the manufacturing area and the work of the systems analyst. Both work with conceptual systems, but the IE also works with physical systems.

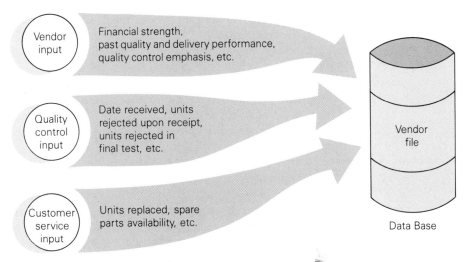

Figure 14-8 Input to vendor records.

IEs support the manufacturing managers as they make the plant location and layout decisions described earlier. The IEs are skilled in the use of modeling techniques such as linear programming. IEs also spend a great deal of time assisting manufacturing management in the establishment of production standards. These standards are a critical ingredient in management by exception. Actual performance is compared with the standards, and any exceptional variance is reported to management. The data describing actual performance comes from the third input subsystem—data processing.

Data Processing Subsystem

Even though data processing is usually identified with the financial function, a significant portion relates directly to the manufacturing function. This portion is the data collection network—the main source of input data describing production activities.

Data collection terminals accept input from punched cards, plastic badges, magnetic-strip cards, or keyboard entry, and then transmit the data to a computer. Each time a step in the production process is initiated or completed, an entry can be made in a nearby terminal. The central computer uses this input to update the data base so that it reflects the current nature of the physical system. This is *job reporting*.

Figure 14-9 shows twelve data collection terminals located throughout a factory. Terminal 1 is in the receiving area. When raw materials are received from vendors, receipt data is entered in the terminal. All material receipts then undergo a quality control inspection, and the results are recorded on terminal 2. As the accepted receipts enter the raw-materials inventory, that action is logged on terminal 3. The same terminal is also used to record the release of materials to the production process. Terminals 4 through 10 are used by production employees to signal the start and completion of each step of the production process. When the final product is finished, terminal 11 is used to show that the goods are now in the finished-goods inventory. Terminal 11 also signals the release of finished goods to the shipping department. When the goods are shipped to customers, that action is recorded on terminal 12.

The data collection terminals track the flow of materials through the plant every step of the way. In addition to reporting material flow, the terminals also record the use of personnel and machine resources. The same terminals can be used for *attendance reporting*, with workers using their plastic badges to "punch in" in the morning and "punch out" in the afternoon. Also, as production steps employing machines are started and completed, the computer can determine how long the machines are in use. Since the data collection system records the use of the three main manufacturing resources (material, personnel, and machines), it effectively records every important production action. Manufacturing management can use this information to monitor the activities of the entire production system.

This concludes the discussion of how data is entered into the manufacturing

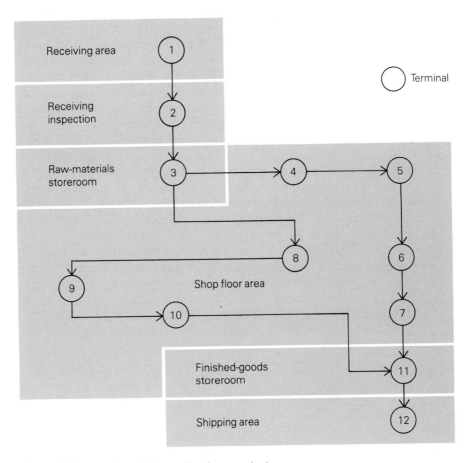

Figure 14-9 Location of data collection terminals.

information system by the three input subsystems. The remaining discussion will deal with the output subsystems.

Inventory Subsystem

Manufacturing management has always been responsible for the raw materials and work-in-process inventory. Marketing, in some instances, is responsible for the finished goods inventory. Records show the on-hand balance, and physical counts assure that the conceptual and the physical inventory systems are in balance.

The annual cost of maintaining or carrying an inventory can be as much as 30 percent of its value. This *maintenance cost* includes factors such as spoilage, pilferage, obsolescence, taxes, and insurance. If the raw-materials storeroom contains $1 million in inventory, the inventory can run up an annual maintenance cost as high as $300,000. These maintenance costs (also called *carrying costs*) vary directly with the inventory level—the higher the level, the higher the costs.

The inventory level of an item is influenced primarily by the number of units ordered from a vendor at one time. The average inventory level can be estimated at half of the order quantity plus any safety stock. *Safety stock* is an extra quantity that is maintained to minimize stockouts and backorders. A *stockout* is a condition when no items remain in inventory—the cupboard is bare. A *backorder* is an order from a customer that cannot be filled because of a stockout.

The model in Figure 14-10 shows the effect of order quantity on average inventory level. In the upper example, a quantity of 20 is ordered from the vendor. Sometimes (just after receipt) there are 25 units in inventory. Sometimes (just before receipt) there are only 5. On the average, there are 15 units in inventory.

In the lower example, a quantity of 16 is ordered and the average level drops to 13. This effect would seem to identify lower order quantities as the best goal for the manager. That conclusion would be true were it not for another cost that *increases* as the order quantity decreases. This is the *purchasing cost*. It costs a fixed amount to prepare a purchase order, perhaps $45, regardless of the number of units ordered. Therefore, the fewer the units, the higher the *per-unit* purchasing cost. If the firm orders one unit at a time, the per-unit purchasing cost is $45. This cost can be reduced to $22.50 per unit when two are ordered, to $15 when three are ordered, and so on.

The *EOQ (economic order quantity)* formula balances these two inventory costs and identifies the lowest combined cost. The graphical model of this tech-

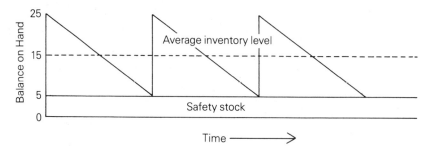

(a) Order quantity of 20; average level is 15.

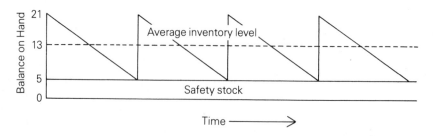

(b) Order quantity of 16; average level is 13.

Figure 14-10 The effect of order quantity on the average inventory level.

nique is included in Figure 14-11. An EOQ can be established for each item in raw-materials inventory.

Another economic quantity can be used for the finished-goods inventory. This is the *economic manufacturing quantity (EMQ)*, also called the *economic lot size*. The EMQ balances the costs of carrying the inventory with the costs of production inefficiencies. These quantities—EOQ and EMQ—are optimum. They cannot be improved upon without changing the values of the variables. The manager, therefore, need not decide how much to order.

In a similar fashion, the MIS can decide when to reorder replenishment items. A *reorder point* can be calculated for each item to trigger a purchase order to the vendor (in the amount of the EOQ) or a production order to the factory (in the amount of the EMQ).

The formula for the reorder point is:

$$R = LU + S$$
where: R = reorder point
L = vendor lead time (in days)
U = usage rate (number of units used or sold per day)
S = safety stock level (in units)

For example, if it takes the vendor 14 days to provide the ordered materials, and you use ten units per day, you will use 140 units while waiting for the vendor to fill the order. Add to this a safety stock of 16, and the reorder point is 156.

These two decisions—*when* to order and *how much* to order— represent the two key decisions in inventory management. The inventory subsystem can make both with little or no management intervention.

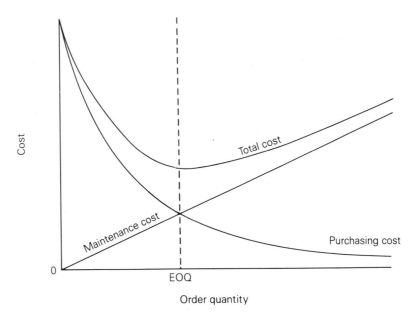

Figure 14-11 The EOQ represents the lowest total cost.

If you are looking for two examples of structured decisions in business, these are the ones that you want. They represent Steven Alter's highest-level DSS, the one that makes the decision for the manager as discussed in Chapter 11.

Quality Subsystem

A firm normally establishes quality standards for its products. It is not sufficient, however, to simply check the quality of the products as they come off of the assembly line. It's really too late at that point to influence quality. Instead, quality control checks are incorporated into the production process beginning with the receipt of raw materials.

Harvard Professor David Garvin studied the quality control systems of U.S. and Japanese manufacturers of room air conditioners.[1] He found that the companies with the highest quality were also earning the highest return on investment (ROI). In other words, quality is good business. In studying the firms with high quality products (fewer rejects and fewer service calls), he identified the following practices:

- Top management was actively interested in the question of quality. At the U.S. firm with the lowest service call rate, the president met weekly with the vice presidents to review service call statistics.
- Annual targets were set to reduce field failures. U.S. firms with the lowest failure rates established targets for each inspection point on the assembly line.
- Information describing assembly line rejects and field failures was made available to management quickly, and in a form that told the whole story.
- Production machinery was well maintained, the work areas were kept clean and orderly, and the workers were well trained.
- The quality department participated in vendor selection, and the importance of raw material quality was emphasized.

It is common practice for Japanese firms to subject raw materials from a new vendor to 100 percent inspection. When quality performance is demonstrated, then all inspection stops and the raw materials are sent directly to the assembly line upon receipt. At the first sign of quality deterioration, the 100 percent inspection rate is reinstated.

Of all the topics receiving current attention as possible reasons why Japanese products often outsell U.S. products, quality appears to be the key. The Japanese have been able to achieve a high level of quality not strictly through a practice of close inspections, but rather through an overall emphasis. We will return to the Japanese approach later in the chapter.

---

[1]David A. Garvin, "Quality on the Line," *Harvard Business Review* 61 (September–October 1983): 64–75.

Production Subsystem

The production subsystem is the most complex of the output subsystems. It is concerned with all of the processes performed on the flow of material resources. These processes are performed by two other basic resources: personnel and machines. The production subsystem is, therefore, a conceptual representation of how these three resources (material, personnel, and machines) are used together to create finished products.

Managers on all levels make production decisions. The decisions of where to locate plants and how to arrange them are made on the upper levels. These are production decisions, and the production subsystem provides support as described earlier. Managers on the lower levels are given the authority to make decisions relating to day-to-day operations.

Material requirements planning (MRP)

A good example of system operation decisions is *material requirements planning (MRP)*. MRP is a technique of managing production inventories that takes into account the specific timing of material requirements. MRP is a schedule of material required in each time period covered by the firm's production schedule. The production schedule is determined by the sales forecast provided by the marketing information system.

MRP is a positive approach to materials management— anticipating material needs and planning their acquisition. This is in contrast to the old technique (still used in many firms) of waiting for customer orders to arrive and then reacting to those orders with material requisitions.

MRP interacts with two other systems—production scheduling and capacity requirements planning—as pictured in Figure 14-12.

In step 1, the sales forecast is used to create a *master production schedule (MPS)*. The sales forecast identifies the quantities of the various finished goods to be sold. The time period covered by the schedule can be a year or more. The schedule should be able to accommodate the longest vendor lead time plus the time needed to produce the item when all of the materials are available.

In step 2, the material requirements planning system uses the MPS to determine the types and quantities of raw materials needed to produce the finished goods. This determination is made by "exploding" the bill of material. The *bill of material* is simply a list of all raw materials and their quantities needed to produce one item of finished goods. The bill of material is like a recipe. The exploding is accomplished by multiplying the number of units of finished goods to be produced by the quantities of needed raw materials. We will see an example of this process later in the chapter.

The total quantities of raw materials needed are called the *gross requirements*. It will probably not be necessary to purchase the gross requirements from vendors, since many (perhaps all) of the raw materials are already on hand. The raw material inventory file is checked, and the quantities subtracted from the gross requirements. The balance, identifying the materials that must be purchased, is

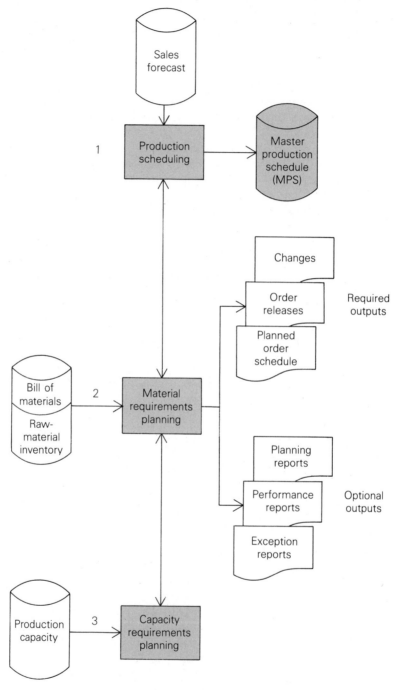

Figure 14-12 Scheduling production and determining raw material needs.

called the *net requirements*. The net requirements are allocated to the different time periods to reflect vendor lead times and specific steps during the production process when the materials will be needed.

Before the MPS is finalized, a check is made in step 3 to ensure that sufficient capacity is available to produce the needed items according to the schedule. By capacity, we mean the quantity and type of production machines, employees, and supplies to perform the transformation process. MRP has the ability to schedule this capacity on an overtime basis if management wants to produce more than the regular capacity will permit.

When the capacity constraint has been satisfied, the MPS in step 1 is finalized. Note that two-way arrows connect the three steps of the figure; all three work as a system.

Although we have been using the word "finalized" to describe the MPS, keep in mind that this schedule can be, and is, changed frequently to reflect changes in the business. This ability to quickly and easily reschedule is a big advantage of advanced MRP systems.

The outputs from the MRP system include those that are required to carry out the production schedule along with some optional management reports. The required outputs include (1) a *planned order schedule* that lists needed quantities of each material by time period and is used by buyers to negotiate with vendors; (2) *order releases*, which are authorizations to produce the products on the planned order schedule; and (3) *changes to planned orders*, which reflect canceled orders, modified order quantities, and so on.

Optional outputs include (1) *exception reports*, which flag items requiring management attention; (2) *performance reports*, which indicate how well the system is performing in terms of stockouts and backorders; and (3) *planning reports*, which are used by manufacturing management for future inventory planning.

MRP in a nutshell

We use the sales forecast to identify the finished goods that manufacturing must produce during the future period. Next, we identify the raw materials needed, and check to see if they are already on hand. If not, they will be purchased to arrive at the time they are needed. Our materials plan is based on the sales forecast. To appreciate the positive, future orientation of MRP, consider the traditional method. The traditional method relies on a reorder point for each raw material item to trigger a purchase order. When the balance on hand drops to the reorder point, a signal is issued indicating that it is time to reorder. The traditional *reorder-point method* is a reactive strategy, whereas MRP is a proactive strategy anticipating material needs before they occur.

A Production Subsystem Example

As an example of how the production subsystem supports the day-to-day activities of the manufacturing organization, let us assume that a company manufactures bicycle flashlights—the type that you strap onto your leg so that the light bobs up and down as you pedal. A clear lens mounted on the front provides some light ahead, and a red lens at the rear warns motorists behind you.

An MPS is produced that supports the sales forecast. The MPS identifies the optimal quantity of flashlights for a single production run by using the economic manufacturing quantity (EMQ). The production run quantity is called the *lot size*. The MRP system determines the quantities of materials required for a lot size of, say, 2,200 flashlights.

The lights are constructed from a number of separate parts. The plant purchases all of the parts from vendors and simply assembles them into finished products. An exploded view of the flashlight, along with its bill of material, appears in Figure 14-13. Only single quantities of each part are used, except for batteries. Each light uses two batteries.

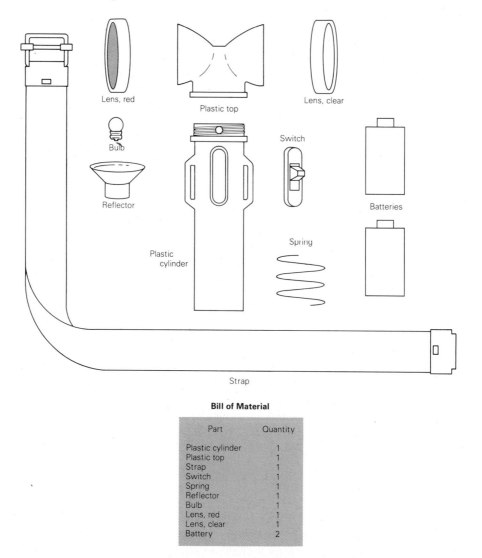

Bill of Material

Part	Quantity
Plastic cylinder	1
Plastic top	1
Strap	1
Switch	1
Spring	1
Reflector	1
Bulb	1
Lens, red	1
Lens, clear	1
Battery	2

Figure 14-13 The bicycle flashlight and its accompanying bill of materials.

If the plant is to produce 2,200 flashlights, raw materials sufficient for 2,200 bills of material will be required. The process of exploding the bill of material is illustrated in Figure 14-14. The gross requirements appear in the right column.

The production subsystem checks the inventory status of each part to determine the net requirements. This process is shown in Figure 14-15.

You can see that all of the parts are available in the needed quantities except two: switches and bulbs. The firm has only 800 switches on hand, and it needs 2,200. The firm also needs to order bulbs, since there are no bulbs in raw-materials inventory.

It is possible that additional purchase orders will be triggered by the net requirements computation. These orders are for items still in stock, but with a balance below the reorder point. The reflector is one of these items. There are enough reflectors on hand, but only four will be left after the flashlights are produced. The requirement for the flashlights will drop the balance on hand below the reorder point.

Part	Qty. per Final Product		Number of Final Products		Gross Require-ment
Plastic cylinder	1	x	2200	=	2200
Plastic top	1	x	2200	=	2200
Strap	1	x	2200	=	2200
Switch	1	x	2200	=	2200
Spring	1	x	2200	=	2200
Reflector	1	x	2200	=	2200
Bulb	1	x	2200	=	2200
Lens, red	1	x	2200	=	2200
Lens, clear	1	x	2200	=	2200
Battery	2	x	2200	=	4400

Figure 14-14 An exploded bill of material.

Part	Gross Requirements	Inventory on Hand	Net Requirements
Plastic cylinder	2200	3000	0
Plastic top	2200	2250	0
Strap	2200	6000	0
Switch	2200	800	1400
Spring	2200	2999	0
Reflector	2200	2204	0
Bulb	2200	0	2200
Lens, red	2200	3625	0
Lens, clear	2200	5500	0
Battery	4400	5005	0

Figure 14-15 Net raw-material inventory requirements for flashlight parts.

The production subsystem uses the raw-materials file in the data base to determine the net requirements. The inventory subsystem then uses the EOQ in determining the quantity to order. The specific vendor is selected with information provided by the quality subsystem. In this manner, all three subsystems work together to requisition needed materials, as illustrated in Figure 14-16.

Production cannot start until all of the parts are available. When the switches and bulbs arrive, the production subsystem notifies manufacturing management, by transmitting data to the central computer from terminals located in the receiving and the receiving inspection areas. The computer then notifies the appropriate managers, such as the schedulers and dispatchers, by transmitting messages to terminals in their offices.

Scheduling production

The flashlights are assembled one step at a time from the required parts. The items move from one work station to another as the assembly process proceeds. Figure 14-17 shows this flow through the plant.

The production flow starts by releasing the raw materials from inventory. In this example there are two main flows: one for assembling the cylinder and one for the top. Work can be done simultaneously on the cylinder and the top to

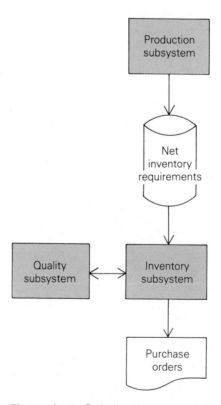

Figure 14-16 Ordering the raw materials.

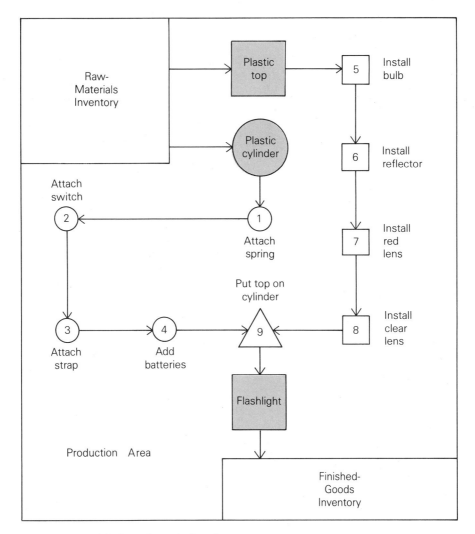

Figure 14-17 Job flow through the plant.

reduce the length of time required for the job. The steps in the cylinder flow are numbered 1 through 4 and are circled. The steps for the top are numbered 5 through 8 and are enclosed in squares. In step 9 the top assembly is attached to the cylinder assembly, and the result is a finished flashlight that enters the finished-goods inventory.

The production schedule determines when the flashlights will be produced. To determine the schedule, the lot quantity must be multiplied by the performance standards for each step. For example, if the first step is the attachment of a battery spring to the plastic flashlight cylinder (step 1 in Figure 14-17), a special spring insertion machine can be used. The machine must have an operator. The standard insertion time of 0.16 minute means that 352 minutes of both machine and operator time will be required to attach 2,200 springs. Similar computations can be made for each remaining step of the process to identify the total machine and personnel requirements.

The computations can be seen in Figure 14-18. Some steps (1, 2, 5, 7, and 8) require machines and operators. The others are assembly processes performed manually. Specific types of machines and employees are identified.

Once the machine and labor requirements have been determined, the job can be scheduled. The production scheduling program schedules the various jobs for the best use of plant capacity. Determining when a job should be done hinges on a number of factors, such as job priority, time already waiting in the queue, availability of resources, and so on.

A production schedule appears in Figure 14-19. The date and time of day are printed for the release of each of the 10 parts from raw-materials inventory. The parts are not released until they are needed. When they are released, they are transported to the work station where they will be used.

The nine production steps are also listed, along with a start date and time for each. A production step is scheduled to begin no later than 30 minutes after the raw materials have been delivered to the work station. Steps 5 through 8 require a total of 1,892 minutes of production time, compared with 1,408 minutes for steps 1 through 4. The start time for the cylinder assembly (steps 1–4) is therefore delayed so that the tops can be attached (step 9) as soon as the cylinders are assembled.

The production process

The production subsystem triggers the production process. Information is prepared for employees in the inventory and production areas, telling them what to do, when to do it, and (if necessary) how to do it. One approach is for the computer to transmit signals to the appropriate terminals as the actions are scheduled to

```
                 MACHINE AND MANPOWER REQUIREMENTS

PRODUCT--BICYCLE FLASHLIGHT
PRODUCTION QUANTITY--2200


                   --------MACHINE------        -------EMPLOYEE-------
      STEP         TYPE  STD.  TOT. TIME        TYPE   STD.  TOT. TIME

 1--ATTCH SPRG     129   .16    352            0-129   .16    352
 2--ATTCH SW       402   .30    660            0-402   .30    660
 3--ATTCH STRP     ---   ---    ---            ASSY    .10    220
 4--ADD BATTS      ---   ---    ---            ASSY    .08    176
 5--INST BULB      202   .16    352            0-202   .16    352
 6--INST REF       ---   ---    ---            ASSY    .30    660
 7--INST LNSR      602   .20    440            0-602   .20    440
 8--INST LNSC      604   .20    440            0-604   .20    440
 9--ATTCH TOP      ---   ---    ---            ASSY    .16    352
```

Figure 14-18 Computation of machine and personnel requirements.

```
                        PRODUCTION SCHEDULE

JOB NAME        BICYCLE FLASHLIGHT
JOB NO.         79-133

  RAW             RELEASE       PRODUCTION        START          COMPLETION
 MATLS          DATE   TIME        STEP        DATE   TIME       DATE   TIME

CYLINDER        10-24  0800
SPRING          10-24  0800    1-ATTCH SPRG   10-24  0838     10-24  1430
SWITCH          10-24  1430    2-ATTCH SW     10-24  1500     10-26  0900
STRAP           10-26  0930    3-ATTCH STRP   10-26  0950     10-26  1330
BATTERY         10-26  1345    4-ADD BATTS    10-26  1404     10-26  1700
TOP             10-23  0900
BULB            10-23  0900    5-INST BULB    10-23  0930     10-23  1522
REFLECTOR       10-23  1530    6-INST REF     10-23  1600     10-25  1000
LENS RED        10-25  1030    7-INST LNSR    10-25  1100     10-26  0920
LENS CLEAR      10-26  0930    8-INST LNSC    10-26  1000     10-26  1620
                               9-ATTCH TOP    10-27  0800     10-27  1352
```

Figure 14-19 Example of a production schedule.

begin. Another approach calls for the computer to print all of the information on forms that are put in a folder called a *shop packet*. The shop packet accompanies the job as it moves through the plant. The timing of the actions is specified on a separate printed production schedule.

As work begins on a step in the production process, the worker uses the terminal at his or her work station to advise the computer of:

- Job identification
- Step number
- Work station
- Employee identification
- Start time

The first three items are entered from a punched card or a plastic card like a credit card with a magnetic strip. Or, the items can be keyed into a keyboard. The employee can be identified by inserting his or her plastic identification badge. Start time is recorded by the computer as the message is received.

When the job step is completed, the worker advises the computer by using the terminal. Again the computer enters the time of day. In this way the computer can calculate the time required to complete the step (stop time minus start time).

The production subsystem can keep the manager informed of job progress by means of exception reporting. If a step took too long to complete, subsequent steps may be delayed. Perhaps management can take action to prevent the delay. If a step is completed earlier than scheduled, it might be possible to speed up the completion of the job in order to make an earlier shipping date.

The computer has relieved managers of many decisions on the operational-control level. Formerly, people in the production planning and control office made all of the decisions based on little more than wall charts and keyboard calculators. Now these people are able to concentrate on handling disturbances that arise.

The production subsystem tracks the physical system as each process is performed. It is possible for manufacturing management to know the status of the physical system at all times. This is a good example of the value of a conceptual information system.

Cost Subsystem

Inventory costs can be minimized through the use of economic order and manufacturing quantities. Production costs can be controlled through the use of accurate cost standards. On a periodic basis the manufacturing manager can receive a report showing how the actual production costs compare with the standards. An example is shown in Figure 14-20.

The manager can key a query into a terminal or a micro, and cost data for each department can be displayed. The computer program compares total standard hours with total actual hours and calculates the variance. When the actual hours exceed the standard, the job numbers contributing to that excess are printed. In the figure, the painting department exceeded the standard by 35 hours on jobs 79-283 and 79-291.

```
                  PRODUCTION COST REPORT
                      BY DEPARTMENT

             WEEK ENDING 10-22-86

  DEPARTMENT      STD.      ACT.     VAR.    SEE JOB      JOB
                  HRS.      HRS.             NUMBERS      VAR.

  WELDING         1090      1085      -5

  PAINTING         330       365      35     79-283       10
                                            79-291       25

  PLATING          523       522      -1

  INSPECTION        78        85       7     79-303        7

  ASSEMBLY        2027      2423     396     79-292       23
                                            79-295      107
                                            79-298       47
                                            79-313      219

  CLEANING         293       278     -15
```

Figure 14-20 Production cost report.

If the manager wants more information on the excess, another query can be made and the data can be reported by employees. Figure 14-21 is an example. Analysis of this data indicates that employee 8514 accounted for a six-hour overage on job 79-283. Now the manager has the information needed to determine the cause. The supervisor of the painting department can meet with the employee to discuss what happened on job 79-283. Once the causes are identified, action can be taken to eliminate or minimize them in the future.

The required ingredients for an effective cost control program are (1) standards of comparison and (2) accurate reporting of actual costs. The data collection network of the production subsystem helps meet both requirements. Data describing actual job performance is collected, and over a period of time this data is used to set standards. When start and stop times are recorded for each step of the production process, accurate actual times can be computed. When the conceptual system is able to track the flow of resources through the physical system in the manner described, the manager is able to control all dimensions of acceptable performance: quality, time, quantity, and cost.

Manufacturing Resource Planning

Companies were keeping track of their inventories and exploding bills of material when the computer came onto the scene in the mid-1950s. Some systems were manual and some used punched cards. The first computers were applied to do these jobs the same way—only faster.

The honor of originating the MRP concept goes to Joseph Orlicky of the J. I. Case Co., a Racine, Wisconsin tractor manufacturer. In the early 1960s, Orlicky devised an elemental MRP package. Another person, Oliver Wight, is given credit for expanding the idea of MRP. Wight recognized that MRP didn't just involve manufacturing, but interconnected with the rest of the firm.

```
              PRODUCTION COST REPORT
           BY DEPARTMENT AND BY JOB

           WEEK ENDING 10-22-86

DEPARTMENT      JOB       EMP.      STD.      ACT.      VAR.
                NO.       NO.       HRS.      HRS.

PAINTING      79-283      3124       11        13        2
                          3309       18        18        0
                          4119       62        65        3
                          7218       42        40       -2
                          7301       10        11        1
                          8514       73        79        6

              TOTALS . . . . . .   216       226       10
```

Figure 14-21 A second production cost report.

The first commercial MRP package was PICS (Production Information and Control System) from IBM. It became available in the late 1960s. PICS stressed inventory control and production planning. It wasn't until the early 1970s that MRP, as we described it earlier, was conceived. The capacity requirements planning feature was added, along with feedback from the shop floor to produce a *closed-loop MRP*. The status of both the capacity and the performance of the plant in terms of the schedule could be updated as the production occurred. Data collection terminals facilitated the feedback from the shop floor.

MRP was the talk of the manufacturing world during the 1970s. Many companies tried it; they were mostly the large companies since the software was available only for mainframes and minis. These companies saw MRP as a way to achieve goals of reduced costs, increased efficiency, and improved responsiveness to changes in consumer demand as reflected in the sales forecast.

All users did not achieve their goals, an especially disheartening result since the costs of installing MRP are high. For the successful firms, MRP was a good investment since they recovered their installation costs in as little as two years. A study of the successful MRP users revealed that they did not rely on MRP alone to achieve their goals. Rather, they made changes throughout the company. The changes began at the top-management level and even involved the relationships of the firms with their customers and vendors. This company-wide view of MRP has been named *manufacturing resource planning—MRP-II*. Most likely, after the new wears off, the "II" will be dropped, and the concept will be simply MRP. The letters will mean "manufacturing resource planning," however, to recognize its new company-wide scope.

Management actions to achieve MRP success

Professors John Anderson and Roger Schroeder of the University of Minnesota believe the key to MRP success to be "that each of the plans, priorities, and actions of manufacturing, marketing, finance, engineering, and personnel must be linked to the closed-loop production and inventory control system, and, in turn, information must flow back to each of these functions to accomplish management goals and objectives for the firm."[2]

Anderson and Schroeder identify 8 actions that top management can take to implement a successful MRP system:

1. Recognize that MRP is just a more disciplined way of conducting the business of the firm, and learn firsthand the concepts and the technology.
2. Appoint a task force, led by an executive, to implement MRP.
3. Provide the necessary resources by assigning people full time to MRP and making MRP a top priority for all managers.
4. Develop a formal implementation plan, covering about two years into the future, before work actually starts.

---

[2]John C. Anderson and Roger G. Schroeder, "Getting Results from Your MRP System," *Business Horizons* 27 (May–June 1984): 58.

5. Insist that vendor-supplied MRP software be used, since it will usually work with little or no modification.
6. See to it that everyone involved gets a good education in what MRP can do and their role in it.
7. Require that marketing, finance, manufacturing, and personnel jointly engage in the implementation process.
8. Be patient. Although some results can be expected in the first year, it might be from two to five years before the system is completely implemented.

Two similar companies in the same industry can implement MRP using the same hardware and software. One project will be a success and the other a failure. Anderson and Schroeder believe that the determining factor is top management's commitment and its willingness to make changes throughout the firm so that it operates as a smoothly functioning system.

MRP software

Approximately 72 percent of the MRP installations use minis, 20 percent use mainframes and 8 percent use micros. As you would expect, the micro segment is the fastest growing.

Most of these systems, from mainframe to micro, use packaged software. It was realized from the very beginning that most firms, even the very large ones, could not afford to create their own custom systems. As a result, a wide variety of MRP software is on the market. At the end of 1984 there were approximately 165 MRP packages available, and 30 to 40 were for micros.

The prices of the micro packages range from $10,000 to $36,000, and most are written to interface with MS-DOS or PC-DOS. A wide variety of micros are used, with the IBM PC model XT being very popular. In some cases, several micros are networked so that multiple users can access the system. A hard disk is invariably required to store large files.

The most popular MRP package is MAPICS (Manufacturing Accounting and Production Information Control System)—marketed by IBM to run on their System/34 mini. It is estimated that 35 percent of the installed MRP systems use MAPICS. Gulf and Western Manufacturing Co. of Southfield, Minnesota has installed more than 10 MAPICS systems since 1980 at an average cost of $300,000 each. They have also installed four of IBM's mainframe MRP systems (called COPICS [Communications Oriented Production Information and Control System]) at a cost of about $500,000 each.

Studies have shown that the average MRP installation cost is around $400,000 with 73 percent going to hardware and 27 percent to software. The software cost appears low, but it is increasing—having doubled during the 1982–84 period. The reason for the higher overall expense is the fact that today's MRP systems are much more sophisticated than those of a few years ago. As an example, practically all of the MRP packages for micros include a scheduling system, whereas the minicomputer packages of the early 1980s did not.

If a firm wants to use MRP but doesn't want to invest in their own hardware and software, they can subscribe to an MRP timesharing service. ASK Computer

Systems of Los Altos, California makes its MANMAN and PLANMAN systems available for about $1,200 for the first terminal and $750 to $1,000 for additional terminals. You also have to pay for the time that you are connected to the central computer. Total costs run about $6,000 a month.

Environmental impact of MRP

The firm's customers benefit the most from MRP by receiving their products on time and possibly at a lower price if the cost savings are passed along. The customers are generally unaware, however, that MRP is providing these benefits.

The firm's vendors, on the other hand, become aware very quickly of the firm's MRP efforts. MRP causes a major change in how the using company orders its raw materials. This change can place a strain on its vendors. Under the traditional reorder-point method, an order is placed with a vendor at the time the material is needed. MRP, on the other hand, looks into the future and triggers orders far in advance. Since MRP enables frequent changes to the production schedule (such as weekly), it is common to issue change orders to vendors several times before the material is actually shipped. Some vendors are not equipped to respond to these changes as quickly as necessary. The result is an inefficient system.

The best solution is for the vendor to also use MRP. Then, the input to the vendor's MRP system is the output from the customer's system. The two systems work together as one.

If the vendor cannot also use MRP, the next best solution is to keep the vendor informed concerning the MRP-using firm's inventory status. A good example of how this is done is provided by Steelcase Corporation. Steelcase contacted all of its vendors before installing MRP and educated them in how the system worked and the effect that it would have on orders. When the system became operational, Steelcase began mailing their vendors both weekly and monthly reports, providing information about orders— total purchases, quantity received last week, and quantity past due. A copy of the production schedule was also provided. The vendors were therefore better able to anticipate Steelcase's orders and to respond to those orders when they were received. This example shows that a datacom network is not an absolute necessity for achieving a coordinated performance between the vendor and the MRP user.

MRP as an integrating force

In the previous chapter we identified the marketing concept as a means of overcoming the functional attitude that frequently exists in a firm. MRP is another, perhaps more effective, means of achieving the same integration. Robert W. Dintinger, vice president of materials and manufacturing at Best Industries of Houston, explains it this way: "Within six months of the day we began installing the system, inventory dropped $2 million, and turnover jumped to 3.75 times a year. Sales grew 30 percent to 40 percent annually over the next three years.

Without MRP, it wouldn't have happened. The key accomplishment of the system was to give the entire company a business objective."[3]

Putting MRP in perspective

The literature of business has been practically void of any mention of "manufacturing information systems." It's not that computers have not been used to generate information; the term just never caught on. During the early years of computer use, manufacturers (unlike the marketers) had no overall framework upon which to build their systems. Manufacturers had a molecular view—focusing on the separate applications like inventory management, scheduling, routing, and so on rather than the system as a whole.

MRP was the first step toward integrating all of these manufacturing subsystems. In fact, MRP became *the* manufacturing information system. MRP-II has expanded the concept to apply outside of manufacturing as well. The term *business resource planning (BRP)* has been used to convey the idea of a company-wide scope.[4]

As with any such complex endeavor, the results from MRP have been mixed. There seems to be general agreement that management support is the key. In the successful firms, like Best Industries, the results have been impressive. But perhaps the infatuation of U.S. industry for MRP goes beyond the bottom line of the income statement. David Biggs, vice president of manufacturing for Bently Nevada, Minden, Nevada, explains: "Prior to MRP, working in production at my company was not very pleasant because wrong decisions were *always* being made. Decisions are only as good as the information on which they're based. The company was giving the production-control clerks bad information and asking them to make some pretty important decisions. MRP gives them accurate information—and they now make smart decisions. The rest of the organization no longer looks down on them as 'those clerks who can't get anything right.' They became important; others started listening to their ideas. Almost every department has gained this kind of credibility. Everyone is making better decisions. There is an epidemic of trust."[5]

Factory Automation

Much has been accomplished in the use of machines, often computer controlled, in the production area. The machines can do jobs that were formerly done by workers. The machines cost less than the workers and are capable of performing better in some cases. As one might expect, factory automation has met with

---

[3]David Kull, "MRP: The Industrial Revolution Meets the Information Age," *Computer Decisions* 15 (October 1983): 128.

[4]Anderson and Schroeder, p. 58.

[5]Kull, p. 240.

considerable resistance from organized labor. Over time, however, this resistance has worn away as firms seek ways to compete better in the marketplace.

In the sections below, we will recognize the major types of factory automation. All of these examples relate primarily to the physical system of the firm. Since our main interest is the conceptual information system, we will not attempt a detailed explanation.

CAD/CAM

The term *CAD/CAM* is quite popular. *CAD (computer-aided design)* involves the use of a computer to assist in the design of everything from buildings and bridges to individual parts such as those used in automobiles. CAD first appeared in the aerospace industry around 1960. It was then adopted by the auto makers as a way to cope with the task of redesigning body panels so as to achieve a different appearance for each model year. Figure 14-22 shows a design engineer using a CRT terminal equipped with a special *light pen*, used for input. The engineer only has to "sketch" the design on the screen using the pen, and the CAD software will refine the drawing by smoothing and/or straightening the lines. Once the design is entered into the computer, the engineer can subject the design to various tests to detect weak points. The CAD software can even make parts move as they would when in use. For example, windshield wipers can move across an automobile windshield so that engineers can ensure that federal regulations specifying minimum vision area are met.

CAM (computer-aided manufacturing) is the application of the computer to those tasks that come *after* design—the production of the item. This activity can be traced back to the late 1950s and early 1960s when computers were used to

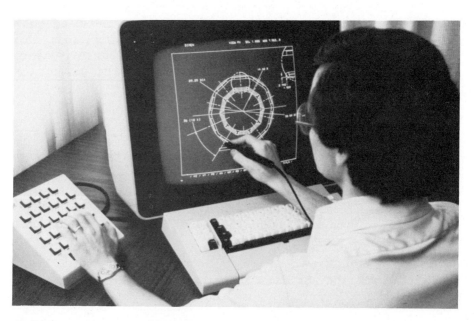

Figure 14-22 Computer-aided design.
Source: Courtesy of International Business Machines Corporation.

create punched paper tape that could then guide a production machine such as a drill press or cutting tool. This application was called *NC (numeric control)*. The numeric codes punched into the tape controlled the machines. Take, for example, a ship manufacturer using NC to cut multiple parts from a piece of sheet steel. The computer could determine a much better arrangement of the parts on the sheet in order to minimize scrap than could a human. And, the numerically controlled cutting tool could do a more precise job than a worker using a cutting torch.

The advent of the minicomputer in the 1970s enabled manufacturers to bypass the intermediate paper tape step and connect the computer directly to the tool or tools being controlled. This application was named *DNC (direct numeric control)*. The mini is online to the tools and can control several simultaneously.

Robotics

Industrial robots (IR) fill the gap between automation such as DNC and the worker. A robot incorporates much of the adaptability and responsiveness of the worker.

Robots, such as the one pictured in Figure 14-23, got their start in the automobile industry about 1974. The auto industry was the first to embrace *robotics*,

Figure 14-23 A factory robot.

Source: *Minimater Industrial Robot by Fairey Automation, Ltd. courtesy Mobility Systems, distributor.*

the use of robots, but other industries have since followed. At the end of 1985, the number of U.S. robots was estimated at 14,500, and it is forecasted that it will jump to 65,000 by 1990. Currently, there are more robots being used in Western Europe and Japan than in the U.S.

Robots come in many sizes (as small as a breadbox and as large as a car) and in many prices (from $7,000 to more than $100,000). Companies use robots primarily to cut costs, but they often use them for hazardous work, such as working in areas where temperature is very high. One state prison decided to use robots to patrol cell blocks at night, using sensors to detect open doors and unauthorized persons in the area.

Robots can be programmed either offline or online. In *online programming*, a person sequentially moves the robot to the various positions that it must take as it performs its task. Each position is recorded in the robot's "memory" by using a *teach packet* with buttons on it. In *offline programming*, the program is created while the robot is doing something else. The program is then transferred into the robot's memory. Offline programming is preferred since the production area where the robot is working does not have to be shut down.

Future improvements in IR technology can be expected in two areas—visual sensors and tactile sensors. Visual sensors will be devised that give the robots a sense of sight, enabling them to identify parts laid out on a work bench, for example. Tactile sensors will enable a robot to apply just the needed pressure to grip an object, depending on what that object is. Also, future robots will be smaller and lighter, made with more plastic parts, yet able to perform heavier work.

Computer integrated manufacturing (CIM)

You can see that a manufacturing manager is like a kid in a candy store, trying to decide which modern technology to adopt— MRP, CAD, CAM, or robotics. This technology has been conceived and marketed by a wide variety of vendors. Over the years, manufacturing managers have usually reacted to each new technology without regard for an overall master plan. The result is "islands" of technology, often incompatible with each other.

CIM (computer-integrated manufacturing) is a concept, not a technology. It is a management philosophy that all of the technologies must work together. CIM is a way of looking at the firm's production resource as a single system and defining, funding, managing, and coordinating all improvement projects in terms of how they affect the entire system. CIM is a systems view of production rather than a molecular view of only dealing with the parts separately.

Just-In-Time (JIT)

Just-In-Time, or *JIT*, is a new approach in the U.S. for performing the production function, but it has been in use in Japan since the early 1950s. JIT is exactly opposite to the approach traditionally practiced in the U.S.—mass production of large quantities of products at one time. The process that we described earlier for the assembly of the bicycle flashlight is an example of the traditional U.S. approach. U.S. firms have followed the mass-production approach to minimize setup and production costs and to get quantity discounts from vendors. In reality, mass production also carries with it high inventory costs. In the bicycle example, the firm would have considerable funds tied up in raw materials inventory waiting for the production run to start. Then, during production, considerable investment would be tied up in work-in-process inventory as the job lot moves from work station to work station. Finally, the large lot size would represent a big investment in finished-goods inventory until the items are sold.

JIT attempts to minimize the inventory costs by producing smaller quantities. Ideally, a lot size would be only a single item, moving from work station to work station. Timing is the secret. A supply of raw materials arrives from the vendor "just in time" for the production run; there is no raw materials inventory to speak of. Small quantities of raw materials are received at a time; perhaps a single vendor's trucks arrive several times a day.

The raw materials start down the assembly line. As soon as the first worker finishes his or her task with the first item, the item is set aside. The next worker picks up the item and begins his or her work. The workers are often positioned close together, although this is not a requirement, so that the items can easily flow from worker to worker.

If a worker spots a defect caused by a previous worker, the entire assembly line is shut down until the cause of the defect is identified and corrected. You can imagine how this practice motivates each worker to do good work. The result is improved quality of the items produced—a big advantage of JIT.

When a worker is ready for the next item, he or she signals the previous worker. The term *kanban*, Japanese for "card" or "visible record," is used for the signal. The worker might display a card, as shown in Figure 14-24. Or, perhaps a system of flashing lights is used. Other forms reveal an even higher level of ingenuity, such as rolling golf balls down a pipe.

The kanban signals enable the work to flow rapidly. The kanban "pulls" the items through the assembly process, as opposed to the manner in which the traditional, large-quantity job lot "pushes" its way from station to station. Since there is less material in the work flow, the amount of work space is reduced. Firms using JIT find that they can use more of their space for production and less for inventory. The work area is neater, one of the factors contributing to improved quality recognized earlier.

The initial reaction to JIT is that the practice of frequent deliveries of raw materials in small quantities will increase purchasing costs. Recall that in the EOQ formula, unit purchasing costs go up with more frequent ordering. JIT users have found a way to get around these higher purchasing costs. JIT users do not place separate purchase orders each time they request a shipment. Instead, they usually place a *blanket purchase order* to cover a period of time such as a year. Then, specific orders can be placed simply with a phone call or a form letter.

JIT is most widely used in Japan, but U.S. firms are implementing it as a means of better competing in the world market. Implementation is usually phased. NBI first implemented it in 1984 with 10 people building a display module for a word processor. Hewlett-Packard first tried JIT with 120 workers assembling a

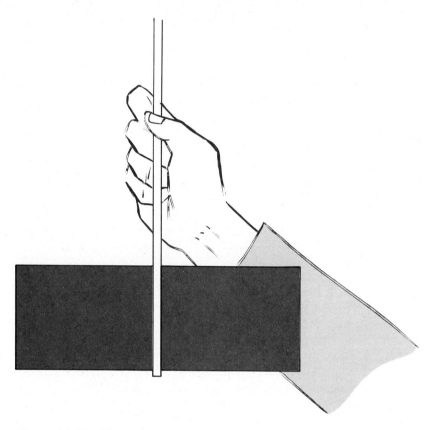

Figure 14-24 A "kanban."

diskette drive. JIT is being used on a wider scale at U.S. factories that are Japanese subsidiaries. The Kawasaki plant in Lincoln, Nebraska, installed JIT in 1980. Similar efforts have occurred at a Sony plant in San Diego and a Honda plant in Marysville, Ohio, proving that JIT is not something that will work only in Japan.

Effect on vendors

Earlier we recognized how MRP puts added strain on vendors. The strain by JIT is much greater. Vendors must be able to deliver exactly the desired quantities, at exactly the right time, at the expected level of quality. Vendors are usually located close to the factory so that they can make frequent, quick, and small shipments.

Vendors benefit in many ways, but perhaps the most meaningful is the long-term relationship that is established with the customer. Customers do not use a large number of vendors, changing frequently from one to another. The vendor is assured of the business as long as the requirements of quality and responsiveness are met.

JIT and MRP

You can see the contrast between JIT and MRP. MRP emphasizes long-term planning and the use of computers. JIT emphasizes timing and the use of non-computer signals. U.S. firms have been investing heavily in MRP, and along comes JIT. Can the two concepts co-exist?

MRP can provide the overall planning and coordination effort, and JIT can fit within this framework. At points where the two concepts differ, such as the purchasing horizon, it appears that MRP is being adjusted to fit JIT. That strategy has been used at Harley-Davidson and at Deere & Co.

It is too early to prescribe exactly how MRP and JIT will interact. That issue will receive a lot of attention during the next few years. It must. Firms have invested too heavily in MRP, and JIT appears to be too good to pass up.

Putting the Manufacturing Information System in Perspective

Manufacturing managers have a shorter planning horizon than marketing managers. Manufacturing managers are concerned with maintaining the steady flow of materials through the plant. They focus primarily on the current year's operations, with special attention to the current month, week, and even day.

The manufacturing information system enables manufacturing managers to plan and prepare for the production process and then to monitor that process to assure that the schedule is met. It provides a means by which they can view the production operation as it occurs.

Although technology and methodology are changing rapidly in manufacturing, the model of the manufacturing information system presented earlier can withstand such change. The reason is that the model relates to the basic manufacturing processes, not the technology or methodology by which they are performed. The production subsystem, for example, implies that information will accompany the flow of materials. Whether that information is conveyed by a kanban or a CRT terminal is irrelevant.

How managers use the manufacturing information system

The manufacturing information system can be used in both the design and the operation of the production system. The information is used by different managers in the manufacturing area, and by others as well. This usage is shown in Table 14-3.

As with the marketing information system, the executives receive information from all output subsystems in summary form. The plant superintendent also uses summarized output describing the entire operation.

Managers in marketing and finance will probably also make use of the output. Marketers will be interested in all aspects of production (cost, quality, and availability) since these factors influence the product that is to be sold. Financial managers will have a special interest in output from the cost subsystem.

Table 14-3 Users of the Manufacturing Information System

User	Subsystem			
	Inventory	Quality	Production	Cost
Vice president of manufacturing	×	×	×	×
Other executives	×	×	×	×
Plant superintendent	×	×	×	×
Manager of planning and control	×		×	
Manager of engineering		×	×	×
Manager of quality control		×		
Director of purchasing	×	×		×
Manager of inventory control	×			
Other managers	×	×	×	×

Summary

The manufacturing function of the firm primarily involves the flow of material resources. Managers in this area must design and operate a system to handle this flow.

Computers have been applied in two basic ways: to control production processes, and to serve as information systems. The manufacturing information system can be used in both the design and the operation of the production system. Design decisions are made infrequently, but they are important in that they commit large sums of money for long periods of time. These semistructured decisions are made on upper-management levels. Although the information system probably cannot supply all of the information that the manager would like when making these decisions, it does provide a good deal of information and can help structure some parts of the decision.

Operational decisions are of a different type. They are made on a daily basis and can be structured to a great extent. This is because most of the important variables can be identified and measured in quantitative terms. The feature making manufacturing systems complex and difficult to control is their dynamic nature. The systems must react quickly to changes in consumer demand. Change is the name of the game, and any information system must be able to respond to this change.

The manufacturing information system includes three input subsystems. Manufacturing intelligence gathers environmental data describing vendors and labor. The industrial engineering subsystem gathers internal information describing the physical production system. The data processing subsystem, primarily through the use of data collection terminals, gathers internal data but can also record certain environmental data such as receipts from vendors.

Four output subsystems track the flow of material through the production area. The production subsystem provides measures of time, the inventory subsystem provides measures of quantity, and the quality and cost subsystems address those two measures.

For the past 10 years, MRP has been the hottest topic in manufacturing. First it was restricted to integrating production systems, and later it was expanded to also involve systems in marketing, finance, and personnel. This broader view has been named MRP-II. MRP is a way for firms producing large quantities of items in batches to schedule their capacity and material needs far into the future. MRP provides better control over material flow but puts a strain on vendors. One way to ease the strain is to keep vendors informed concerning the firm's current inventory position and future needs.

We can regard a firm's MRP system as their manufacturing information system. They both contain the same subsystems.

While many firms have been implementing MRP, a movement has also been under way to automate the factory. CAD and CAM, along with robotics, are intended to reduce production costs by replacing workers with machines. As firms consider these technologies, they are caught between a pressure to appease organized labor and a necessity to compete in a world market. The firms usually elect to compete.

CIM is a management philosophy that attempts to integrate all of the separate computer-based information systems plus automation. Manufacturing managers have their work cut out for them in putting all of the pieces of the puzzle together.

The newest innovation is JIT, a revolutionary concept that goes against the mass-production nature of U.S. business. JIT developers disregarded computer technology altogether in concentrating on the material flow. JIT will have an impact for two reasons—it is exceedingly simple, and it works. The next few years will see firms attempt to integrate the best features of MRP and JIT.

Key Terms

linear programming (LP)	data processing subsystem
origin, destination	manufacturing intelligence subsystem
receiving area, receiving inspection area	industrial engineering subsystem
raw-materials storeroom	production subsystem
shop floor area	inventory subsystem
work station	quality subsystem
final inspection area	cost subsystem
finished-goods storeroom	buyer
shipping area	industrial engineer (IE)
plant-layout model	job reporting
manufacturing information system	attendance reporting

maintenance cost, carrying cost

safety stock

stockout

backorder

purchasing cost

EOQ (economic order quantity)

EMQ (economic manufacturing quantity), economic lot size

reorder point

material requirements planning (MRP)

master production schedule (MPS)

bill of material

gross requirements

net requirements

reorder-point method

lot size

shop packet

closed-loop MRP

manufacturing resource planning (MRP-II)

BRP (business resource planning)

CAD (computer-aided design)

light pen

CAM (computer-aided manufacturing)

NC (numeric control)

DNC (direct numeric control)

IR (industrial robots)

robotics

online, offline robot programming

teach packet

CIM (computer-integrated manufacturing)

just-in-time (JIT)

kanban

blanket purchase order

Key Concepts

The use of quantitative techniques to support semistructured decisions of plant location and layout

The design of physical manufacturing systems along flow network lines

A manufacturing information system as a combination of input and output subsystems

The informal nature of labor information

The potential for developing a formal vendor data-gathering system

The role of the industrial engineer (IE) in analyzing and designing both physical and conceptual manufacturing systems

The structured nature of inventory management

Components of inventory costs, and means of optimizing them

The relationship of order quantity to average inventory level

The relationship of the reorder point to stockouts and backorders

Management influence on the quality of a firm's products, and how that influence is achieved

The integrated nature of production scheduling, material requirements planning, and capacity requirements planning

The step-by-step manner in which a production schedule evolves—considering inventory, machine, and personnel constraints

The ability that data collection terminals provide a manufacturing information system of monitoring processes as they occur

How the manufacturing information system facilitates cost control by providing data for setting standards, and data describing actual operations

Manufacturing resource planning (MRP-II) as a step beyond material requirements planning (MRP)

The importance of management support to MRP success

MRP as a means of integrating the major functions of the firm

The demand that MRP places on coordination with vendors

CAD/CAM and robotics as means of improving the physical rather than the conceptual system

The simplicity of JIT, and its revolutionary nature

Questions

1. What types of decisions do manufacturing managers on the top and the middle management levels make? What about managers on the lower level?
2. What is structured about a plant location decision? What is unstructured?
3. What areas of a plant layout correspond to the input element of the general systems model? The transformation element? The output element?
4. What two environmental elements are the focus of the manufacturing intelligence subsystem?
5. What are the two steps of gathering vendor data?
6. How does the work of the IE contribute to management by exception?
7. How are data collection terminals used for attendance reporting? For job reporting?
8. How do firms minimize stockouts?
9. What two costs are incorporated in the EOQ formula?
10. When would an EMQ be used instead of an EOQ?
11. What is the relationship between the manufacturing intelligence subsystem and the quality subsystem?
12. What is MRP?
13. How are gross requirements computed? How are net requirements computed?
14. How are production performance standards used to prepare the production schedule?
15. What is the relationship between the data processing subsystem and the cost subsystem?
16. How can a manager influence the success of MRP in her or his firm?
17. How does CAD contribute to the firm's physical system? Does it contribute to the conceptual information system? How? What about CAM?
18. Which places the most severe strain on vendor relations—MRP or JIT? How can that strain be eased in each case?
19. Name two ways that JIT contributes to improved product quality.
20. Can a firm use both MRP and JIT? Explain.

Problems

1. Use an LP model to allocate plant output using data from Figures 14-2 and 14-3. Obtain a hardcopy printout. Do you get the same answer?

2. Using the formula in the chapter, compute the reorder point for the following items.

Item	Vendor lead time	Usage rate	Safety stock	Reorder point
1	8	4	6	
2	12	3	7	
3	24	8	20	
4	5	1	2	
5	38	19	40	

3. Using the formula in Chapter 11, compute the economic order quantity for the following items.

Item	Acquisition (purchase) cost (dollars)	Annual sales (units)	Retention (maintenance) cost (dollars)	EOQ
1	40	12,000	2.50	
2	40	500	5.00	
3	40	2,500	12.50	
4	40	100,000	.25	
5	40	150	10.00	

CASE PROBLEM: Interstate Hydraulic Manufacturing Co.

Interstate Hydraulic Manufacturing Co. is an established, family-owned manufacturer of hydraulic devices used in automobile suspensions and forklift trucks. From the factory in Muncie, Indiana, products are shipped to customers throughout the United States and several foreign countries. All data processing is performed by a service bureau, which uses a computer to handle payroll, billing, accounts receivable, inventory, and cost accounting. Workers clock on and off the job using time clocks, and they report job progress by filling out a forms packet that accompanies each job lot. Data from the time cards and forms packets is keyed into the computer by service bureau employees, using terminals.

Ben Lambert is in charge of customer service, handling complaints, conducting plant tours, and providing information to the plant manager on product performance. One day Lambert is sitting at his desk, handling the backlog of correspondence he has accumulated. He picks up his office recorder and dictates:

Ms. Ellie Nostrom
Purchasing Director
McCullin Enterprises

Dear Ms. Nostrom,

Thank you very much for being so understanding last week when you called to inquire about your order. As I explained, we have a large number of jobs in process at any one time, and many more waiting in line. It is simply impossible to locate where one is without spending considerable time looking through our records.

I later learned that your order was held up due to a lack of materials. We have been having difficulty obtaining the nylon bushing that attaches the actuating arm to the housing. We have had only one supplier that could meet our high quality standards, and we have recently learned that their factory has been on strike for almost half a year.

We finally located another supplier in California and placed an order with them. But when the bushings arrived, the receiving report was misfiled, and we didn't know that they were here. The receiving report, which is normally sent to our accounting department, was sent to purchasing by mistake.

After your call, I talked with the supervisor of receiving, and he said he remembered seeing the shipment. We finally located it in raw-materials inventory and have issued a production order. The job is presently in process and should be completed either by the end of next week or early the following week.

Again, thank you for calling attention to your order. Our customers are our most valuable asset, and we appreciate your business. You have our pledge that we will continue to be responsive to your needs and supply you with the same high level of service that has been our trademark. Please do not hesitate to call on me at any time.

Sincerely,

Ben Lambert, Manager
Customer Service Department

Questions

1. Which manufacturing information subsystems were involved with Ms. Nostrom's problem?

2. What types of computing equipment would be necessary to help prevent this problem from recurring?

3. What is the fundamental problem at Interstate, as reflected by the mishandling of Ms. Nostrom's order?

4. Will the problem be solved with the equipment specified in your answer to question 2? Explain your answer.

CASE PROBLEM: Polar Bear Refrigeration, Inc.

Freeway Ford (remember them from the Chapter 1 case?) went bankrupt since it could not compete with the Japanese imports. The president, Phil Rains, decided to get out of the automobile business, and started a company manufacturing room air conditioners. One of the first things that Phil did was to enroll in an executive seminar sponsored by the American Production and Inventory Control Society (APICS). The one-week seminar was titled, "How to Compete with the Japanese on Their Own Terms." The title caught Phil's eye.

Phil arrived home from the seminar on Friday night and was in the office early Monday morning. As you walk into your office, the phone is ringing. It's Phil. He asks you to come down to his office right away. You walk down the hall and go through the open door. Phil is sitting on the sofa in the corner and motions for you to sit next to him.

"You wouldn't believe how great the APICS seminar was. I learned so much. We spent most of our time learning about JIT. I think that we should try it. We have held off from investing in MRP, and that appears to be a wise move right now. JIT is the coming thing."

"Now you are familiar with my college training in systems theory. I want you to take a look at JIT and give me your impression of how it will affect us in systems terms. We didn't get a systems view at the seminar."

Questions

1. How does JIT affect the firm's interfaces with its environment?
2. How does JIT affect the flow of resources through the firm?
3. Is JIT a physical system, a conceptual system, or both?

Selected Bibliography

Manufacturing Information Systems

Anderson, John C., and Roger G. Schroeder, "Getting Results from Your MRP System," *Business Horizons* 27 (May-June 1984): 57–64.

Appleton, Daniel S., "The State of CIM," *Datamation* 30 (December 15, 1984): 66ff.

Bernstein, Amy, "MicroMRP Gets It Together," *Business Computer Systems* 3 (October 1984): 82ff.

Biggs, Joseph R., Donald C. Bopp, Jr., and William M. Campion, "Material Requirements Planning and Purchasing: A Case Study," *Journal of Purchasing and Materials Management* 20 (Spring 1984): 15–22.

Cox, James F., and Steven J. Clark, "Problems in Implementing and Operating a Manufacturing Resource Planning Information System," *Journal of Management Information Systems* 1 (Summer 1984): 81-101.

Csere, Csaba, "Cars by Computer," *Car and Driver* 28 (April 1983): 103ff.

Eblen, Pam, "The Robots Are Coming!," *ICP Manufacturing Software* 9 (Winter 1984): 20–22.

Froehlich, Leopold, "Mighty Oaks Take Time," *Datamation* 29 (January 1983): 113ff.

Foulkes, Fred K., and Jeffrey L. Hirsch, "People Make Robots Work," *Harvard Business Review* 62 (January –February 1984): 94–102.

Gand, Harvey, and Milt E. Cook, "Choosing an MRP System," *Datamation* 29 (January 1983): 84ff.

Garvin, David A., "Quality on the Line," *Harvard Business Review* 61 (September-October 1983): 64–75.

Green, Gary I., Chang S. Kim, and Sang M. Lee, "A Multicriteria Warehouse Location Model," *International Journal of Physical Distribution & Materials Management* 11 (Number 1, 1981): 5–13.

Green, Gary I., and Leonard B. Appel, "An Empirical Analysis of Job Shop Dispatch Rule Selection," *Journal of Operations Management* 1 (May 1981): 197–203.

Hughes, G. David, "Vendor Selection: No Game of Chance," *Business Computer Systems* 3 (May 1984): 33ff.

Marks, Peter A., "The Strategic Importance of CAD/CAM," *Information Strategy* 1 (Winter 1985): 4–10.

Manoochehri, G. H., "Improving Productivity with the Just-In-Time System," *Journal of Systems Management* 36 (January 1985): 23–26.

Meal, Harlan C., "Putting Production Decisions Where They Belong," *Harvard Business Review* 62 (March-April 1984): 102–110.

Morecroft, John D. W., "A Systems Perspective on Material Requirements Planning," Decision Sciences 14 (January 1983): 1–18.

Schonberger, Richard J., and James P. Gilbert, "Just-In-Time Purchasing: A Challenge for U.S. Industry," *California Management Review* 26 (Fall 1983): 54–68.

Stix, Gary, "Building in Efficiency—Computers Accelerate Manufacturing," *Computer Decisions* 16 (September 15, 1984): 44ff.

Stix, Gary, "Manufacturing-Resource Planning Keeps You on Time, on Target," *Computer Decisions* 16 (October 1984): 142ff.

Teicholz, Eric, "Computer Integrated Manufacturing," *Datamation* 30 (March 1984): 169ff.

Chapter 15

Financial Information Systems

Learning Objectives

After studying this chapter, you should:

- Have an improved understanding of the role played by the data processing system in the MIS
- Understand how a corporation gathers information from its stockholders
- Know one example of how the gathering of financial intelligence information can be formalized
- Appreciate the necessity for including internal auditors in the MIS
- Understand the two basic types of forecasts—short-term sales and long-term environmental
- Have an introductory understanding of how forecasting can be accomplished with a packaged software system
- Be aware of forecasting support that can be provided by econometric service bureaus and national data services
- Be familiar with a process followed by a large conglomerate in preparing a consolidated forecast
- Understand how a nonoptimizing model can be used for cash flow decision making
- Appreciate the value of the budget and performance ratios to the financial control of a firm

Introduction

Business people have been developing mechanized financial information systems for fifty or more years. Punched card machines were used primarily by the financial function. Actually, their use was restricted to the processing of accounting data, and little attention was paid to the information needs of managers—even financial managers. When computers came onto the scene, they too were applied to the same accounting problems. It wasn't until the mid-sixties that financial information systems were developed beyond the basic accounting tasks.

The financial function is concerned with the money flow through the firm. First it is necessary to acquire enough money to support the manufacturing and marketing activities. Then it is necessary to control those funds to assure that they are used in the most effective way.

Information describing the money flow—both anticipated and actual—permits managers in all functional areas to meet their financial responsibilities. This information is provided by the financial information system. This system has three basic tasks: (1) to identify future money needs, (2) to assist in the acquisition of those funds, and (3) to control their use.

Model of the Financial Information System

The three basic tasks are represented as output subsystems in the financial information system. The model of this system is illustrated in Figure 15-1. This system has the same structural arrangement of input and output subsystems that we used for the marketing and manufacturing information systems.

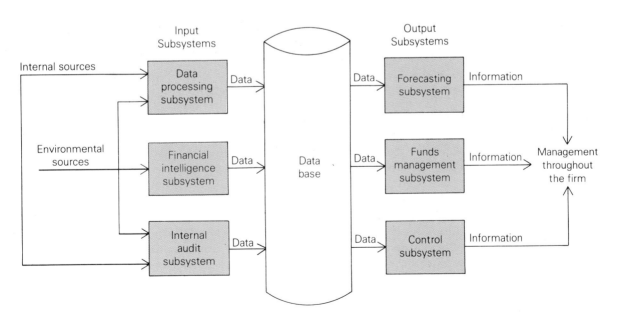

Figure 15-1 Model of a financial information system.

Input subsystems

There are three input subsystems: the data processing subsystem, the financial intelligence subsystem, and the internal audit subsystem. The *data processing subsystem* gathers both internal and environmental data. We have seen how data collection terminals in the manufacturing area provide much of this data. Other data captured from source documents is entered into the data base using a micro, or from keyboard terminals located throughout the firm.

The data processing subsystem also gathers environmental data as a result of business transactions with other firms. The environmental data provides a basis for analyzing vendors' performance and customers' purchasing habits. Both manufacturing and marketing managers use the information produced from this accounting data.

The *financial intelligence subsystem* gathers data from the financial community—banks, government agencies, securities markets, and the like. This subsystem monitors the pulse of the nation's economy and informs the firm's executives of trends that can affect the financial condition of the company. Within the past few years, the environment that this subsystem monitors has broadened from national to international in scope. The interdependence of U.S. and foreign economies requires that attention be given to international conditions.

The *internal audit subsystem* is similar to the marketing research and the industrial engineering subsystems in that it is designed to conduct special studies of the firm's own operations. Internal auditors are employees of the firm, usually reporting to the CEO, who can become involved in the design and evaluation of conceptual information systems throughout the firm.

Output subsystems

The *forecasting subsystem* projects the activity of the firm for a period of up to ten years or more. The activity of the coming year is influenced primarily by market demand and internal constraints, such as the size of the sales force, production capacity, and available finances. As the forecast period lengthens, the importance of the environment increases. The changing needs of consumers must be anticipated, as should the economic climate. Forecasting models have been developed that include both internal and environmental data to provide a basis for immediate and long-term planning. These models serve as DSS tools for solving a problem that becomes less structured as the forecasting horizon lengthens.

The *funds management subsystem* uses projections of company activity to determine the flow of money into and out of the firm. The manager can simulate several strategies designed to achieve the best balance in the inflow and outflow during a future period, such as the coming year. Balanced flows reduce the need to borrow operating capital and increase the return on invested surplus funds. Cash flow models can be created using a procedural or modeling language or an electronic spreadsheet.

The use of available funds is controlled by the *control subsystem*. This subsystem primarily uses data gathered by the data processing subsystem to produce reports showing how monies are being spent. The reports compare actual financial performance to a budget and provide ratios between financial figures as a measure of good performance. As business becomes more competitive and the costs of operations increase, good budget performance becomes increasingly important. The control subsystem enables managers to track their cost control activity.

More packaged software has been developed for the financial area than for any other. These are mostly data processing packages such as payroll, inventory, and accounts receivable. Financial managers and analysts also make good use of electronic spreadsheets. The spreadsheet rows are excellent for representing financial data such as sales and cost of goods sold, and the columns are excellent for showing time periods such as months, quarters, or years. The spreadsheets seem to be more applicable to the financial function than any other.

These packaged software systems enable small firms to achieve good financial control without investing in large information services staffs. The systems are also popular in large firms, where their ease of use makes them an attractive alternative to procedural or modeling languages.

Output information from the financial information system in the form of management reports and traditional accounting statements keeps management and members of the firm's environment informed of the firm's financial condition. The firm's stockholders, members of the financial community, the government, and vendors require different kinds of information describing the firm's financial condition. Much of the financial information is directed to groups and organizations that never have been, and never will be, directly associated with the firm—securities analysts, educators, and potential investors.

Data Processing Subsystem

We described the data processing system, or subsystem, in Chapter 9. In this and the two previous chapters, we have identified data processing as an input subsystem in the functional information systems. The data processing subsystem also provides input to the executive information system. The data processing subsystem is the only one appearing in all of the information systems—it is the foundation upon which the information systems are built.

Relationship to accounting

We are using the terms *data processing system* and *accounting system* interchangeably. Both terms refer to the resources and procedures that process the firm's data so as to maintain an accurate record of the firm's operations. Most of the personnel resources that are used to process this data are located in the accounting department, which is a part of the financial function. Most of the machine resources in the form of computers and peripheral equipment reside in the information services department. However, much computing equipment is located throughout the firm in the form of micros and terminals. It is important to realize that the data processing system, or accounting system, is not restricted to the accounting department. It is a company-wide activity.

Basic roles of the data processing system

The data processing system performs three basic roles in the MIS. First, it produces information output for managers on all levels. We have commented earlier on the limited nature of this output—it is often regarded as an automatic byproduct of the data processing rather than something to satisfy a specific information need. Nevertheless, the data processing system can, and does, produce information. Second, the data processing system serves as a DSS for lower-level managers. The data processing system makes many decisions of a programmed nature—when to reorder, how much to reorder, when to send a late notice, and so on. Third, the data processing system provides the primary source of data for the data base. This data base is the conceptual representation of the firm, and it enables each separate information subsystem—executive and functional—to know what has happened in the past and, to a certain extent, what is happening now. Online data gathering devices such as data collection and POS terminals enable the data processing subsystem to monitor current operations as they occur. The data also permits a look into the future by providing the input to mathematical models. *The real value of the data processing subsystem to the MIS is the accounting data that is made available.*

Accounting data

Accounting data provides a record of everything of monetary importance that happens in the firm. A record is made of each transaction, describing the important facts—what happened, when it happened, who was involved, and how much money was represented. This data is useful in that it can be analyzed in various ways to meet management's information needs. If a wholesaler wants to learn more about customers who have bought more than $25,000 worth of merchandise in the past month, those accounting records can be selected for analysis. If a retailer wants to know how sales fluctuate by day of the week, that information, too, can be obtained. Virtually any type of information can be produced from this accounting data.

There are three key features of accounting data. First, it deals only with the firm and the activities of environmental elements dealing with the firm. The firm must be directly involved. If information is needed about environmental elements never involved in the firm's business transactions, the data processing subsystem cannot provide it.

Second, the data represents thousands of facts, which, presented separately, would only confuse management. This data must be processed to convert it into information. This is the task of the MIS.

Third, the data is historical. An accounting transaction is not generated until after an event occurs. Modern data-gathering techniques utilizing online terminals are doing much to make accounting data more current.

Each day, hundreds or thousands of transactions occur within a firm. Even though there are a lot of these transactions, many of them result from chain reactions, with one or more triggered by a single activity. A large number are triggered by a customer order as we saw in Chapter 9.

Accounting reports

The two basic accounting reports are the income statement and the balance sheet. The *income statement,* such as the one in Figure 15-2, summarizes income and expenses for a period of time. The time period is usually one year, although an income statement can be generated more often, such as quarterly or monthly. It is also possible to prepare income statements for subsidiary organizations within the firm. For example, the Los Angeles office of a nationwide insurance company could have its own income statement.

The other basic report, the *balance sheet,* is illustrated in Figure 15-3. The balance sheet provides a look at the firm's assets and liabilities at a specific point in time, such as December 31.

Corporations include income statements and balance sheets in their annual reports to stockholders as a way of communicating basic financial information. The two samples were taken from the annual report of Quotron Systems, Inc. Firms also use these reports internally, as a way to keep management informed. Because of their summary nature, the reports are of most value to the firm's executives.

Consolidated Statements of Income
(Dollars in thousands except per share amounts)

Years Ended December 31,	*1984*	*1983*	*1982*
Revenues:			
Financial Information Services	**$171,921**	$140,867	$110,436
Sales	**17,878**	12,943	10,482
Total	**189,799**	153,810	120,918
Costs and Expenses:			
Cost of Financial Information Services	**90,822**	75,440	64,434
Cost of Sales	**11,745**	9,329	7,507
Engineering, Research and Development	**15,940**	10,773	7,343
Selling, General and Administrative Expenses	**20,888**	17,478	12,529
Interest Expense (Income)	**1,640**	(1,391)	1,477
Total	**141,035**	111,629	93,290
Income before Income Taxes	**48,764**	42,181	27,628
Provision for Income Taxes	**21,941**	18,200	10,593
Net Income	**$ 26,823**	$ 23,981	$ 17,035
Earnings Per Share	**$ .78**	$ .69	$ .52

Figure 15-2 An income statement.

Source: Quotron Systems, Inc. 1984 Annual Report, p. 17. Reprinted with permission.

Consolidated Balance Sheets
(Dollars in thousands)

December 31,	1984	1983
Assets		
Cash and Short-Term Investments	$ 817	$ 6,420
Accounts and Notes Receivable, less allowance for doubtful accounts of $259 and $211 in 1984 and 1983, respectively	19,905	10,096
Inventories, at the lower of average cost or market:		
Raw materials and purchased parts	30,033	11,963
Work in process	16,771	12,510
Finished goods	6,375	934
Total inventories	53,179	25,407
Service Equipment, at cost	226,316	180,744
Less—Accumulated depreciation and amortization	113,261	87,198
Service equipment—net	113,055	93,546
Property and equipment, at cost	58,251	39,975
Less—Accumulated depreciation and amortization	8,350	5,425
Property and equipment—net	49,901	34,550
Other Assets	4,535	1,340
Total	$241,392	$171,359
Liabilities and Stockholders' Equity		
Accounts Payable	$ 8,235	$ 4,971
Accrued Liabilities:		
Salaries and wages	7,141	6,485
Income taxes	—	2,791
Other	6,650	9,466
Long-Term Debt	39,696	718
Deferred Income Taxes	12,067	7,718
Total liabilities	73,789	32,149
Stockholders' Equity:		
Common stock, par value $.10 per share		
50,000,000 shares authorized		
34,344,041 shares and 34,018,282 shares		
outstanding in 1984 and 1983, respectively	3,434	3,402
Additional paid-in capital	64,495	62,476
Retained earnings	99,674	73,332
Total stockholders' equity	167,603	139,210
Total	$241,392	$171,359

Figure 15-3 A balance sheet.

Source: Quotron Systems, Inc. 1984 Annual Report, p. 16. Reprinted with permission.

Financial Intelligence Subsystem

The financial intelligence subsystem is responsible for gathering data and information from stockholders, the financial community, and the government. Since the financial function controls the money flow through the firm, information is needed to expedite this flow. This system seeks to identify the best sources of additional capital and the best investments of surplus funds.

Stockholder information

All but the smallest corporations have a stockholder relations department within the financial function. This department maintains the flow of information between the firm and its stockholders. Most of the information flows from the firm to the stockholders in the form of the annual and quarterly reports. Both current and potential stockholders use this information to appraise the investment opportunity offered by the firm. Stockholder reports are prepared by the stockholder relations department working closely with top management. The reports contain information in a highly summarized form. In Figure 9-15, we illustrated the graphic form that information often takes in stockholder reports.

Stockholders have an opportunity to communicate information (complaints, suggestions, and ideas) to the firm through the stockholder relations department. Also, once a year an annual stockholders meeting is held where stockholders can learn firsthand what the firm is doing. Very often, stockholders take the opportunity to communicate directly with the corporate executives as shown in Figure 15-4.

Financial community information

The relationship between the firm and the financial community also receives attention from financial management. It is the responsibility of the financial intelligence subsystem to compile information on sources of funds and investment opportunities.

An important indirect environmental effect influences this money flow through the firm. The federal government controls the money market of the country through the Federal Reserve System. There are various means of releasing the controls to expedite the money flow and of tightening the controls to reduce the flow.

The firm, therefore, must gather information from both financial institutions and the Federal Reserve System. This information permits the firm to remain current on national monetary policies and trends, and possibly to anticipate future changes. A variety of publications can be used for this purpose. Examples include *Bondweek, The Wall Street Transcript,* the Salomon Brothers Inc. *Bond Market Roundup,* and the *Federal Reserve Bulletin* prepared by the Federal Reserve System.

In addition to the need to acquire funds, the firm frequently must invest surplus funds on either a short- or long-term basis. These funds can be invested in a number of different ways—in United States Treasury securities, commercial

Figure 15-4 An annual stockholders' meeting.
Source: Recognition Equipment, Inc.

paper, or certificates of deposit (CDs). Since the terms and rates of return for some of these vary over time, it is necessary to monitor these investment opportunities continually so that the investment portfolio will include the mix producing the greatest return.

Gathering information from the financial environment is the responsibility of the financial intelligence subsystem. As with the other two functional intelligence subsystems, the information is usually handled outside the computer system.

Example of a formal financial intelligence system

A good example of how the computer has been applied in this area is the dissemination of information relating to taxes that businesses must pay. The Bureau of National Affairs, Inc. of Washington, D.C., publishes a newsletter called the *Daily Tax Report*. It contains tax-related news such as congressional bills, court decisions, interpretations of tax laws, and so on. The "BNA," as it is called, varies in size depending on the volume of news for a particular day but is usually in the 30–50 page range. Companies subscribe to the BNA and receive it through the mails.

When regular mail service is used, the BNA may arrive 2 or 3 days after it is published. For an extra fee, the BNA can be delivered on the afternoon of the publication day by using one of the special overnight delivery services. For those companies that feel they need the information earlier, it can be obtained by computer.

When a firm subscribes to the computer service, a designated employee can come to work 30 minutes before the others arrive and use a micro to establish a datacom link with the BNA computer in Washington. A summary report, such as the one shown in Figure 15-5, is printed and circulated to those persons interested in tax matters. If greater detail is needed, the number of the news item can be keyed in, and the full text will be printed. The full text is the same material contained in the printed newsletter. The charge for the service is based on the time that the micro is connected to the BNA computer.

This example illustrates the time value of information. A company will go to considerable expense just to get the tax information at 8 a.m. rather than 3 p.m. In one company, a vice president wants the information in time for an 8 a.m. staff meeting on Monday morning. The computer-transmitted BNA makes this possible.

Internal Audit Subsystem

Firms of all sizes rely on outside organizations called *external auditors* to conduct an audit of the accounting records for the purpose of verifying their accuracy. Annual reports of corporations contain a "Statement to the Stockholders" that this audit has been conducted.

Larger firms have their own staffs of *internal auditors,* persons who can perform the same type of analysis as external auditors, but who also can have a broader range of responsibilities. We include internal auditing as an input subsystem of the financial information system because of its ability to independently appraise and influence the firm's operations from a financial standpoint.

In some firms the internal auditing department consists of only a single employee, usually a *certified public accountant (CPA).* In very large firms, the department can consist of many employees—CPAs, other auditors with other professional backgrounds such as computer science, and support staff consisting of junior analysts and secretaries.

Figure 15-6 shows a popular way to position internal auditing in the organization. In this example, the board of directors includes an audit committee that defines the responsibilities of the internal auditing department. The department director reports to the CEO.

Types of auditing activity

There are four basic types of internal auditing activity— financial, operational, concurrent, and control system design. One internal auditor can engage in all four types.

Financial auditing   A *financial audit* verifies the accuracy of the firm's records and is the type of work performed by external auditors. Internal auditors can also

```
BNA Daily Tax Advance
Friday    Sept. 6, 1985


SUMMARY


1    DAILY TAX ADVANCE SUMMARY

GENERAL NEWS

2    DISC:   IRS GIVES TRANSITION-PERIOD GUIDANCE ON INITIAL PSC
     TAX-YEAR DATES, DEEMED DISTRIBUTIONS (173 DER LL-1)

3    TAX REFORM:   REAGAN VISITS NORTH CAROLINA IN BID TO WIN
     PUBLIC SUPPORT FOR HIS TAX REFORM PLAN (173 DER G-1)

4    ENVIRONMENT:   HURDLES FACING SUPERFUND REAUTHORIZATION SEEN
     MAKING CONGRESSIONAL ACTION UNLIKELY BY DEADLINE (173 DER G-3)

5    PENSIONS:   IRA VERSUS 401(k) PLAN DEBATE DOMINATES HOUSE
     HEARING ON RETIREMENT POLICY (173 DER G-4)

6    TAX CREDITS:   COMMENTS TO IRS ON REHABILITATION PROJECT
     RULES SEEK LIBERALIZATION OF RELOCATION PROVISIONS (173 DER G-7)

7    TAX REFORM:   AIRPORT OFFICIALS HIT REAGAN PLAN TO END
     TAX-EXEMPT FINANCING (173 DER G-8)

8    TAX REFORM:   TENTATIVE MARKUP SCHEDULE SLIPS; HOUSE
     WAYS-MEANS PANEL LIKELY TO BEGIN SEPT. 24 (173 DER G-9)

9    TAX LEGISLATION:   ADMINISTRATION HOPES TO DOUBLE DIESEL FUEL
     TAX PAID BY INLAND WATERWAY USERS BY 1997 (173 DER G-9)

10   TAX REFORM:   TREASURY STUDY SHOWS NEW YORK TAXPAYERS WOULD
     BE HIT HARDEST BY REPEALING STATE-LOCAL TAX DEDUCTION (173 DER G-11)

11   CORRECTION (173 DER G-15)

12   IRS:   HAYES RESIGNS AS
     CHIEF SPOKESMAN TO JOIN FAA (173 DER G-15)

NEW TAX DECISIONS AND RULINGS

13   LEVY:   THREAT OF LIEN, WITHOUT LEVY, DOES NOT WAIVE
     SOVEREIGN IMMUNITY (173 DER H-4; CA5, Interfirst Bank Dallas, N.A.)

14   RETURNS:   IRS AGENT LIABLE
     FOR DISCLOSURE TO BANK (173 DER H-9; CA8, Rorex)

TEXT

15   JOINT COMMITTEE ON TAXATION STAFF PAMPHLET ON REVENUE PROVISIONS OF
```

Figure 15-5 Tax information received daily from a computer network.

Source: The Bureau of National Affairs, Inc. Washington, D.C. 20037. Reprinted with permission.

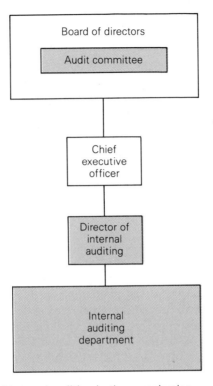

Figure 15-6 Position of internal auditing in the organization.

conduct special financial audits separate from those of the external auditors, or they can work in conjunction with the external auditors. Many firms reduce the cost of external auditing by making their internal staff available for tasks such as data gathering. This is considerably less expensive than paying the $25–35 per hour billing rate for the external firm's junior staff.

Operational auditing An *operational audit* is not one conducted to verify the accuracy of records, but rather to validate the effectiveness of the procedures. The systems studied are almost invariably conceptual in nature and include both computerized and noncomputerized types. The auditors working with computerized systems are called *EDP auditors*.

When internal auditors review an existing operational system, they look for three basic features: adequacy of controls, efficiency, and compliance with company policy.[1] Systems analysts should also have these goals in mind as they design computer-based systems.

---

[1] For an example of an operational audit, see Dale L. Flesher, "An Operational Audit of Marketing," *The Internal Auditor* 40 (February 1983): 23–29.

Concurrent auditing   A *concurrent audit* has the same objective of verifying system effectiveness as does an operational audit, but an operational audit is a special study whereas a concurrent audit is ongoing.

An example of concurrent auditing is provided by Newport News Shipbuilding. Some 20,000 hourly workers are employed, and they are scattered over a wide geographic area as they perform their duties. Some of the employees work below decks, while others work high up on scaffolding. Some may even be in submarines. In such a situation, it would be possible for an unscrupulous supervisor to add a fictitious name to the payroll, and then accept the check, promising to "pass it along." To minimize the chance of this happening, internal auditors randomly select work units and personally hand the checks to the employees, even if it means going into a submarine.

Internal control systems design   In operational and concurrent auditing, the internal auditors study existing systems. However, there is no reason why an auditor must wait until a system is implemented to exert an influence on its design from a control standpoint. From the very beginning, internal auditors should be a part of the team that designs and implements conceptual systems. This includes computerized as well as noncomputerized systems. In performing this task, the auditors assure that proper controls are built into the system.

When internal auditors become involved in design work, they make it clear that they do not want operational responsibility for the system once it is installed. They work strictly in an advisory capacity. They make the relevant facts known to management, but it is management's decision whether to respond to the advice. In this fashion, internal auditors perform exactly the same as systems analysts.

Internal auditors use a variety of documentation techniques as they design new systems and evaluate existing ones. They often use the same techniques as systems analysts. (See Appendices A through F.) In some cases, however, the standard documentation tools do not offer the degree of detail that the auditors prefer, and they have devised their own types. One is called a *control flowchart* and is illustrated in Figure 15-7. You can see that the symbols are not the same as the system flowchart. Such a chart might best suit internal auditors and be used for that purpose. It does not, however, facilitate communications with information services personnel because of the special symbols used.

Putting internal auditing in perspective

The scope of internal auditing depends on the skills of the auditors and the desires of management. Management can look upon internal auditors as "trouble shooters" and assign them to all types of projects. Internal auditors can do the same work as external auditors, consultants, and systems analysts. The feature making internal auditors unique when compared to the other analysts is their independence. They owe their allegiance only to the CEO. They cherish this independence and refrain from activities that would threaten it.

This ability to cut across departmental boundaries is seen by internal auditors as a reason to employ them as communicators of information. Some even see the

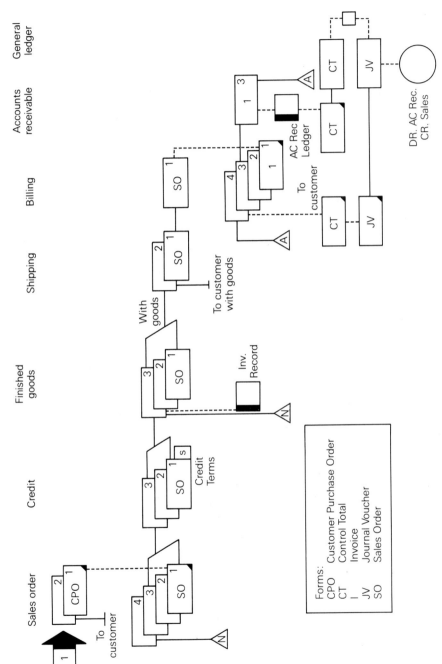

Figure 15-7 A control flowchart used by an internal auditor.

Source: This figure was reprinted, with permission, from the August 1983 issue of The Internal Auditor, published by The Institute of Internal Auditors, Inc.

scope of their data gathering as including the firm's environment.[2] This view of internal auditing as a gatherer of external intelligence is new, and it is too early to predict whether it will be incorporated into the company's MIS. The view does recognize, however, that internal auditing can play a greater role in the MIS than it has in the past. We recognize this broad interpretation of internal auditing in the Figure 15-1 model by including environmental as well as internal sources.

This concludes our discussion of the input subsystems of the financial information system. We now turn our attention to the output subsystems. As we describe these output subsystems, we should remain aware that they provide information to managers throughout the firm—not just within the financial function.

Forecasting Subsystem

A large variety of forecasting techniques has developed over the years.[3] Many of these techniques are informal and depend to a great extent on the knowledge, experience, and intuition of the manager. Others involve the use of quantitative methods. A firm will frequently use a combination of several techniques, both quantitative and nonquantitative, in seeking the best prediction of the future.

Quantitative methods were used in forecasting long before they were applied to other areas of the firm's operations. But the power of the computer and more sophisticated quantitative methods such as simulation have enabled the consideration of a larger number of influencing factors.[4]

Who does forecasting?

Forecasting is performed by the marketing function to project the level of sales for the near future, such as the coming year. Each functional area uses the sales forecast as a basis for determining the resources needed to support the level of projected sales activity. We saw in the previous chapter that manufacturing uses the sales forecast as a basis for scheduling production several months into the future. Thus, the sales forecast serves as the basis for short-term planning.

Many firms, however, need to plan activity for a longer period of time—perhaps ten years into the future. Long-range forecasting of this type can belong to the financial function or to a special long-range planning group.

---

[2] See, for example, Wade S. Williams, and Bill C. Wilson, "Environmental Analysis—the Strategic Response," *The Internal Auditor* 41 (October 1984): 34–35.

[3] For an analysis of eighteen different forecasting techniques, see John C. Chambers, Satinder K. Mullick, and Donald D. Smith, "How to Choose the Right Forecasting Technique," *Harvard Business Review* 49 (July–August 1971): 45–74.

[4] For a description of simulation in forecasting, see Terry W. Rothermel, "Forecasting Resurrected," *Harvard Business Review* 60 (March–April 1982): 139–147.

Forecasting methods

There are two categories of forecasting methods—quantitative and nonquantitative. Since forecasting is a semistructured type of activity, we can assume that nonquantitative methods are used to some degree in all forecasts. It is also important to recognize that all forecasting methods, even the most sophisticated quantitative ones, are based on projections of what has happened in the past.

Nonquantitative methods. A nonquantitative approach does not involve computations of data. The manager follows reasoning such as, "We sold 2,000 units last year, and we should be able to improve on that. So I think we will sell 2,500 next year." Forecasts such as this can have little or no basis, or they can result from an informed firsthand knowledge of the situation. Many managers are very good at the nonquantitative approach.

Some firms have established formal procedures for making forecasts using nonquantitative methods. The *panel consensus* technique consists of a group of experts openly discussing the factors bearing on the future and arriving at a single projection based on these inputs. The *Delphi method* involves a group of experts who do not meet in person but submit responses to a series of questionnaires prepared by a coordinator. Each round of questionnaires incorporates inputs from previous rounds, thus gradually refining the content.

Quantitative methods. The structured portion of the decision can be handled by a wide variety of quantitative methods that range from very simple to very complex. One technique that has remained popular for the past 25 or so years is *regression*. It involves the relationship of the activity to be forecast, such as sales, to some other activity, such as the number of salespersons. This relationship is shown in Figure 15-8.

Seven points are plotted on the graph. They represent the relationship between the two variables during previous periods, say the past seven years. For example, in one year twenty salespersons were employed, and sales were approximately 2,300 units (dashed lines). It is apparent from the plot of points on the graph that a positive relationship exists between the two variables—the more salespersons that the firm employs, the higher the sales.

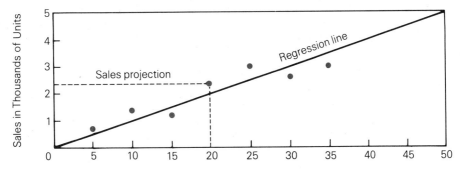

Figure 15-8 Using the number of salespersons to project sales.

Regression analysis permits the use of a mathematical model to specify the relationship very exactly. When the model is executed, a *regression line* can be extended through the points so that the total distance from each of the points to the line is at a minimum. This line is the "best fit" to the points. The management can then use the regression line to forecast sales based on a particular number of salespersons. For example, if the firm employed fifty salespersons, it could assume that sales would approximate 5,000 units.

This example involves only two variables: an *independent variable* (salespersons) and a *dependent variable* (sales). Sales depend on the number of salespersons. This type of regression is known as *bivariate regression* or *simple regression*—only two variables are involved.

Many business activities, such as sales, are sufficiently complex to defy predictions based on a single independent variable. In those cases more than one can be used; this technique is called *multivariate regression* or *multiple regression*. For example, it might be necessary to relate sales to (1) the number of salespersons, (2) the advertising budget, (3) the number of retail outlets, and (4) the number of customers.

The calculations required for bivariate regression can be easily made on a pocket calculator. The calculations for multivariate regression are much more tedious and require the use of a computer.

Prewritten programs are used to perform regression analysis on the computer. Usually these programs are part of a set that performs different types of statistical analyses. Some of the more popular sets, or *stat packages,* are BMDP 77, OMNI-TAB 80, SAS®, and SPSS. Some of the packages are written especially for micros. Examples are ENCORE for the IBM PC and its compatibles, Interstat for the Apple II, and Statistics Pac for the TRS-80 and Apple.[5]

One of the most popular stat packages is SAS (for Statistical Analysis System).[6] We will use it as an example of forecasting with a stat package. Assume that you own a creamery that sells ice cream to supermarkets. You have been in operation for ten years and have accumulated some statistics on your operation. The statistics presented in Table 15-1 represent your annual sales (Y) in thousands of dollars, your advertising budget (X_2), also in thousands of dollars, and a ratio (X_3) of your price compared with your competitors' average price. To compute the ratio, your price is divided by the competitors' average price.

Both the data and the SAS instructions can be entered through a terminal or with punched cards. It is possible to use data already stored in the data base, in which case you only have to enter the SAS instructions. We will assume that the historical data in Table 15-1 is *not* in your data base, so you must enter it from a terminal.

You would like to use SAS to develop a regression equation that expresses

---

[5] For a brief description of the different packages, see Gillian Rice, Essam Mahmoud, and Susan Margaret Pick Vadivel, "A Directory of 132 Packages for Forecasting and Planning," *Journal of Business Forecasting* 3 (Spring 1984): 11–23.

[6] SAS is the registered trademark of SAS Institute, Inc., Cary, N.C.

Table 15-1 Sales Forecast Data

| Year | Sales (Y) | Historical Data | |
		Advertising (X₂)	Price ratio (X₃)
1	24	4	80
2	27	4	80
3	31	5	90
4	29	5	100
5	33	6	100
6	38	7	110
7	37	8	120
8	40	8	100
9	45	9	90
10	49	10	100

the slope of the regression line. The equation will be based on the historical data. All you need to do is enter the data and the SAS instructions as follows:

```
DATA;
  INPUT SALES 1-2 ADVER 4-5 PRICE 7-9;
  CARDS;
  24    4    080
  27    4    080
  31    5    090
  29    5    100
  33    6    100
  38    7    110
  37    8    120
  40    8    100
  45    9    090
  49   10    100
PROC GLM;
  MODEL SALES = ADVER PRICE;
```

The word DATA tells SAS to create a file. The word INPUT is used to define the format of the input record. The first field is SALES, which appears in the first two positions. The next field is ADVER, which is in positions 4 and 5. PRICE appears in positions 7 through 9. The word CARDS is used when the data is entered in card form or through a terminal. The ten data records follow.

The instruction PROC (pronounced "prock") is a request for SAS to process your data. GLM stands for general linear model, the part of SAS that performs the regression. The MODEL expression first identifies the dependent variable

(SALES) and then the independent variables (ADVER and PRICE). In this model, sales depend on advertising and price.

The SAS output appears in Figure 15-9. The equation data is in the lower left-hand corner. The equation is:

$$Y = 16.51 + 3.93X_2 - 0.07X_3$$

Sales for a given year can be expected to be the sum of $16,510 plus 3.93 times each thousand dollars invested in advertising minus 0.07 times the price ratio.

Econometric models

The most complex type of forecasting model is the *econometric model* that uses a large number of equations to process economic data. The term *macro economic model* is also used since the models simulate the entire nation's economic activity rather than that of only a single firm (a micro model). The first econometric models were used by the federal government for drafting fiscal and monetary policies. Only recently have they been adopted by private industry. Their use is generally restricted to only the larger firms, however, because of their high cost. Also a staff of economists is necessary to interpret the output in terms of how it affects the firm.

The basic equation for an econometric model is:[7]

$$GNP = C + I + G + NE$$
where:
$$\begin{aligned}
GNP &= \text{gross national product}\\
C &= \text{personal consumption expenditures}\\
I &= \text{business investment}\\
G &= \text{government purchases}\\
NE &= \text{exports minus imports}
\end{aligned}$$

Each independent variable in this equation is derived from a number of other equations. As an example, personal consumption expenditures is computed from equations dealing with income earnings, expenditures, taxes paid, and savings. The variables in these equations are computed from still another lower level of equations, and so on. The model, therefore, is a network of equations with the GNP equation above serving as the root.

Most firms, even the largest, cannot afford to create their own econometric models. For this reason, several *econometric service bureaus* have sprung up around the world. Three basic services are offered. First, the service bureaus use their models to make periodic forecasts, which are distributed in the form of a subscription service. Second, they make their extensive data bases of economic data

---

[7]This model is explained more fully in A. Migliaro, "The National Econometric Model—A Layman's Guide," in A. Migliaro and C. L. Jain, eds., *An Executive's Guide to Econometric Forecasting* (Flushing, NY: Graceway, 1983) pp. 5–8.

S T A T I S T I C A L   A N A L Y S I S   S Y S T E M   14:07 WEDNESDAY, MAY 12, 1982   2

GENERAL LINEAR MODELS PROCEDURE

DEPENDENT VARIABLE: SALES

SOURCE	DF	SUM OF SQUARES	MEAN SQUARE	F VALUE	PR > F	R-SQUARE	C.V.
MODEL	2	556.41542632	278.20771316	110.12	0.0001	0.969196	4.5027
ERROR	7	17.68457368	2.52636767			STD DEV	SALES MEAN
CORRECTED TOTAL	9	574.10000000				1.58945515	35.30000000

SOURCE	DF	TYPE I SS	F VALUE	PR > F	DF	TYPE IV SS	F VALUE	PR > F
ADVER	1	551.00594059	218.10	0.0001	1	443.50691568	175.55	0.0001
PRICE	1	5.40948572	2.14	0.1868	1	5.40948572	2.14	0.1868

PARAMETER	ESTIMATE	T FOR H0: PARAMETER=0	PR > |T|	STD ERROR OF ESTIMATE
INTERCEPT	16.50961065	3.94	0.0056	4.18787189
ADVER	3.92557910	13.25	0.0001	0.29627964
PRICE	-0.07338590	-1.46	0.1868	0.05015139

Figure 15-9 Sales forecast produced by SAS.

available to firms that want to conduct their own analyses. Third, they provide forecasting consulting service.

Three popular service bureaus are Data Resources, Inc. (DRI), Chase Econometrics, and Wharton Econometrics. These three organizations have approximately 2,000 subscribers to their monthly forecasts.[8] There are about eleven such organizations in the U.S., plus approximately seven located in England, Canada, France, and China.[9]

Table 15-2 summarizes the key features of the three popular U.S. models. You will note that all use a combination of techniques, including judgment. All of the models derive their data from government sources plus special surveys, and they release their projections on a monthly basis. All of the forecasts are subdivided into individual sectors of the economy and specific industries.

Commercial data bases

In addition to the econometric service bureaus, other firms have made data bases available to be accessed via datacom networks.[10] These *national data services* provide files of numeric data that can be used in quantitative forecasting systems and also files of textual information that can be used in nonquantitative systems. Five such services are The Source, CompuServe, Dow Jones News/Retrieval Service, Dialog, and DRI/VisiLink.

Table 15-2   Key Features of Three Econometric Models

	Model		
Features	*DRI*	*Chase*	*Wharton*
Number of variables	1000	700	10,000
Number of equations	1000+	455	669
Horizon	2–8 yrs.	2–8 yrs.	10 yrs.
Techniques used and weights			
Econometrics	55%	70%	60%
Judgment	30%	20%	30%
Time series	10%	5%	—
Current data analysis	5%	5%	10%

Source: Thomas P. Chen, "A Quick Glance at Four Econometric Models," in A. Migliaro and C. L. Jain, eds., An Executive's Guide to Econometric Forecasting *(Flushing, NY: Graceway, 1983), p. 32. Reprinted with permission.*

[8]Thomas P. Chen, "A Quick Glance at Four Econometric Models," in Migliaro and Jain, p. 32.

[9]C. L. Jain, "A Guide to Selecting an Econometric Service Bureau," in Migliaro and Jain, p. 51.

[10]This section is based on Pamela K. Coats, "Business Data Sources Grow with Personal Computer Usage," *Journal of Business Forecasting* 2 (Spring 1983): 22–24.

The Source, begun in 1978, consists of over 45 data bases, news stories that can be retrieved by key words, abstracts to 27 business journals, and historical data on 3,100 common stocks. CompuServe includes mostly financial data such as data on 40,000 stocks and bonds and Standard and Poor's General Information File. Dow Jones features financial data on some 6,000 companies as well as current and historical quotes for the major stock exchanges. Dow Jones also markets its own line of software to be used in processing the data. Dialog is a bibliographic retrieval service that draws from 150 data bases, representing more than 55 million references. DRI/VisiLink is a special offering of the DRI econometric information to smaller firms. Users receive a catalog and can order predetermined reports.

A forecasting example

A large Southern U.S. corporation provides a good example of how an econometric forecast is prepared. This corporation is a conglomerate comprised of several large subsidiary firms. The parent corporation places such emphasis on forecasting that a special corporate planning staff, managed by a vice president, has been established. The staff consists of nine professionals, each with superior quantitative and computer skills. Terminals in the department enable the staff to timeshare the corporate mainframe. An IBM PC is also available, and it is used mainly for electronic spreadsheet analysis.

The forecasting process consists of three steps, as illustrated in Figure 15-10. Each year, the staff assembles all of the information that it has available on the economic outlook for the coming five years, and condenses that material into a five-year guideline. The guideline reflects a variety of inputs such as the opinion of experts both within the parent corporation and outside, publication data such as the Chase monthly subscription service, and computer data bases.

The staff does not rely completely on the Chase model data, even though it is available. The staff injects much of its own experience and expertise. Forecasting is approached as a semistructured problem.

The 5-year guidelines are distributed to the subsidiaries in step 2 of the figure. The subsidiaries have access to all of the information available to the corporate planning staff, plus their own inputs. Each subsidiary develops its own 5-year plan, reflecting the influence of the overall forecast on its operations.

When the subsidiary 5-year plans are returned to corporate planning in step 3, the staff reviews the plans to verify that they are compatible with the economic outlook. All of the plans are then consolidated into a plan book that is distributed to key executives in the corporate headquarters and the subsidiaries. This consolidated plan book includes tables of numeric data, explanations, and computer-produced graphics.

This corporation can put more resources on the forecasting process than most companies because of its large size, but the forecasting challenge is greater than most. Since their operations span the globe, they must consider influences outside the U.S. as well as within. It is interesting that computers do not play a greater role, considering that the hardware and data are available. There are no

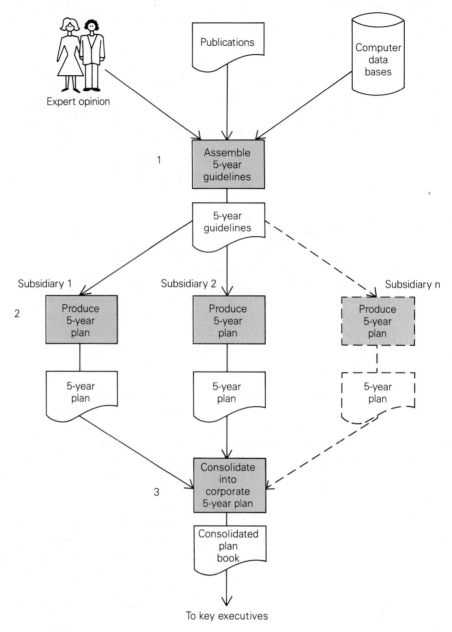

Figure 15-10 Producing a long-range operating plan.

plans to build a giant mathematical model to make the projections.[11] The feeling among the planning staff is that the executives would feel uneasy about the assumptions built into such a model, perhaps by low-level employees not fully

---

[11]For an example of such a model, see George W. Gershefski, "Building a Corporate Financial Model," *Harvard Business Review* 47 (July–August 1969): 61–72.

understanding the situation. In referring to the executives, one of the planners said, "They have a gut-feel. Most of the time it is pretty accurate based on 20 years of understanding how things are put together."

Putting forecasting in perspective

All firms forecast in one manner or another. In very small organizations, the forecast may simply be the intuition of the owner. As the size of the operation increases, forecasting techniques become more complex in order to cope with the many influences. The most complex forecasting device is the econometric model.

Short-term forecasting is done throughout the firm. Marketing forecasts sales, and manufacturing forecasts production. Long-term forecasting must consider the influences of the national and possibly international economies. Very often the group responsible for making long-term forecasts is located within the financial function. In very large firms, the group may exist as a separate function.

Funds Management Subsystem

The general systems model of the firm shows how resources flow from the environment, through the firm, and back to the environment. One of these flows is money. Money flow is important in that it makes possible the other resources.

The money flow can be managed to achieve two goals: (1) to assure that the inflow of sales revenue is greater than the outflow in the form of expenses, and (2) to assure that this condition remains as stable as possible throughout the year. A firm could show a good profit on the year's activities, yet have periods during the year when expenses exceeded revenues. This situation can be seen in Figures 15-11 and 15-12, where a manufacturer of garden equipment enjoys high sales in the fall and low sales in the spring. From March through May, the monthly sales of $300,000 are not high enough to cover the monthly manufacturing expenses of $360,000. Money outflow during March through May exceeds inflow by $262,000, even though profit for the year is $1,908,000.

The funds management subsystem can be used to track the inflow and outflow by month. The graph in Figure 15-11 as well as the report in Figure 15-12 was produced by Lotus 1-2-3. Spreadsheets are excellent for this type of analysis.

Although the annual results of the garden equipment manufacturer are good, the money flow throughout the year is anything but stable. Since the sales to wholesalers are made mostly in the winter months, there is a big inflow of money from September through February. But the plant operates at a fixed output throughout the year, and this policy puts a drain on money from March through August. This feast-or-famine condition presents problems for financial management. What can be done with the surplus during the winter months? What about the deficit during the summer?

The model that the manager uses to solve the money flow problem is called a *cash flow model*. The cash flow model in this example is dynamic, deterministic, and nonoptimizing.

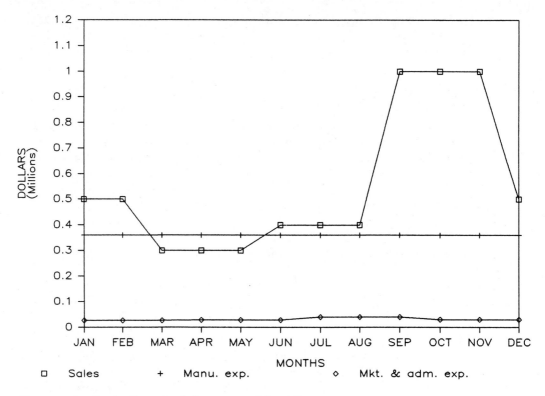

Figure 15-11   Fluctuating sales influence monthly profit.

PROJECTED MONEY FLOW													
	JAN	FEB	MAR	APR	MAY	JUN	JUL	AUG	SEP	OCT	NOV	DEC	TOTAL
MONEY INPUT													
SALES	500	500	300	300	300	400	400	400	1000	1000	1000	500	6600
MONEY OUTPUT													
MANUFACTURING													
EXPENSES													
WAGES	82	82	82	82	82	82	82	82	82	82	82	82	984
MATERIALS	220	220	220	220	220	220	220	220	220	220	220	220	2640
OTHER MFG.													
EXPENSES	58	58	58	58	58	58	58	58	58	58	58	58	696
TOTAL MANU-													
FACTURING													
EXPENSES	360	360	360	360	360	360	360	360	360	360	360	360	4320
MARKETING AND													
ADMIN. EXP.	26	26	26	28	28	28	40	40	40	30	30	30	372
NET CHANGE IN													
MONEY	114	114	-86	-88	-88	12	0	0	600	610	610	110	1908

Figure 15-12   An unbalanced money flow.

First simulation—variable production schedule

One alternative is to develop a new product that would increase revenues during the first part of the year. But because such a development program normally spans a period of several years, it is not a feasible immediate solution.

Another way to achieve a better balance between sales and expenses is to match production to sales rather than spend constant amounts for wages, materials, and manufacturing expenses. The financial manager considers the effect of scheduling production for one month to equal the sales forecast for the next. Of course this change would have to be approved by the manufacturing manager. This new strategy is illustrated with the graph in Figure 15-13 and the printout in Figure 15-14. The new strategy shows a peak manufacturing period during the summer, with a slack period during the winter.

Second simulation—delayed materials payments

The above change helped the situation during the first four months, but the money drain during May through August actually increased. The main reason for these negative balances is the high materials expenses for May–July of $400,000 per month. If the manager can shift these expenses to months with high sales revenues, the negative balances can be eliminated or reduced. It probably would not be

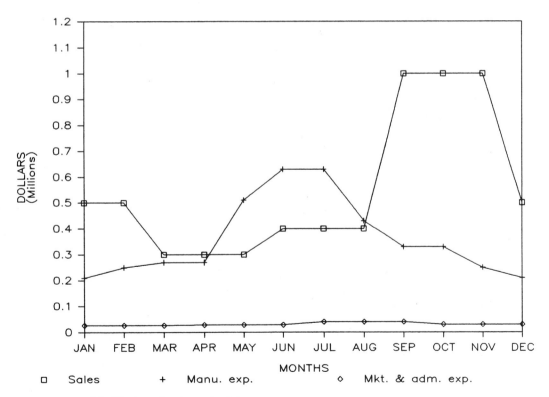

Figure 15-13 Modified production schedule.

```
                              PROJECTED MONEY FLOW

               JAN   FEB   MAR   APR   MAY   JUN   JUL   AUG   SEP   OCT   NOV   DEC  TOTAL


MONEY INPUT
  SALES        500   500   300   300   300   400   400   400  1000  1000  1000   500  6600

MONEY OUTPUT
  MANUFACTURING
  EXPENSES
    WAGES        44    44    60    60    60   150   150   150    74    74    74    44   984
    MATERIALS   120   160   160   160   400   400   400   200   200   200   120   120  2640
  OTHER MFG.
    EXPENSES     46    46    50    50    50    80    80    80    56    56    56    46   696

  TOTAL MANU-
  FACTURING
  EXPENSES      210   250   270   270   510   630   630   430   330   330   250   210  4320
  MARKETING AND
  ADMIN. EXP.    26    26    26    28    28    28    40    40    40    30    30    30   372

NET CHANGE IN
  MONEY         264   224     4     2  -238  -258  -270   -70   630   640   720   260  1908
```

Figure 15-14 Effect of production changes on money flow.

practical to shift the acquisition of materials to an earlier or later period, but the payment might be delayed. Materials could be acquired for the May–July production peak, and payment delayed until September–November. Vendors would have to approve a 120-day delay in payment. Vendors would be especially receptive to such an arrangement if (1) the customer's purchases represent a large portion of the vendor's business, and (2) interest can be charged on the delayed payments. Assuming that vendors would be receptive, the finance manager can simulate this solution. The results are illustrated in Figures 15-15 and 15-16. A four-month interest charge of 4 percent has been added to each month's material expenses to reflect the delayed payments.

You can see that there is a positive cash flow each month except for very small negative flows from June through August. If this flow is satisfactory to the financial manager, no further simulations are performed.

The cash flow model enables the manager to simulate the effect of various strategies to achieve the best use of available money. The finance manager can use the model to evaluate strategies and then work cooperatively with other functional managers to select and implement the optimal strategy.

Putting funds management in perspective

The sales forecast reveals the month-by-month input of revenue. Financial management must ensure that this inflow is sufficient to cover the projected costs of manufacturing and selling the products. A situation of surplus cash also merits attention—the firm will want to make interest-bearing investments.

The cash flow problem appears to be very structured, but you must not overlook the subjective nature of some of the inputs, such as the monthly sales projection. Many environmental factors can also influence the costs paid for labor and materials.

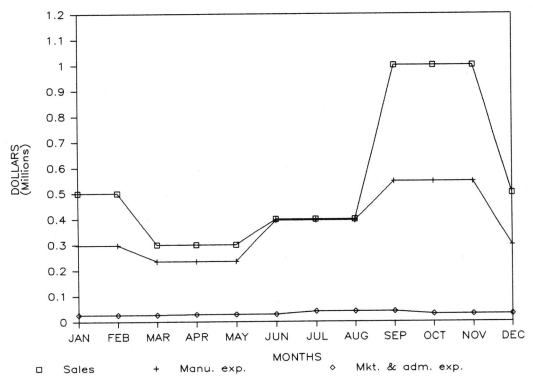

Figure 15·15 Effect of delaying payments to vendors.

```
                              PROJECTED MONEY FLOW

                  JAN   FEB   MAR   APR   MAY   JUN   JUL   AUG   SEP   OCT   NOV   DEC   TOTAL

MONEY INPUT
  SALES           500   500   300   300   300   400   400   400  1000  1000  1000   500   6600

MONEY OUTPUT
MANUFACTURING
EXPENSES
  WAGES            44    44    60    60    60   150   150   150    74    74    74    44    984
  MATERIALS       208   208   125   125   125   166   166   166   416   416   416   208   2745
  OTHER MFG.
  EXPENSES         46    46    50    50    50    80    80    80    56    56    56    46    696

  TOTAL MANU-
  FACTURING
  EXPENSES        298   298   235   235   235   396   396   396   546   546   546   298   4425
MARKETING AND
ADMIN. EXP.        26    26    26    28    28    28    40    40    40    30    30    30    372

NET CHANGE IN
  MONEY           176   176    39    37    37   -24   -36   -36   414   424   424   172   1803
```

Figure 15·16 Effect of delayed materials payments on cash flow.

The financial function is not at the complete mercy of its environment, taking the situation as given. Considerable influence can be exerted on incoming revenue flows and outgoing expense flows through the use of DSS tools such as the cash flow model. Another strong influence over expenses is exerted by the third output subsystem—the control subsystem.

Control Subsystem

We know that one of the basic management functions is control. Managers compare actual performance with predefined standards to assure that overall objectives are being met. This occurs on all management levels.

Managers have operational objectives to achieve, such as producing or selling a certain value of items. Managers are given an amount of money to use in meeting these objectives; this money is called the *operating budget* (often simply called the *budget*). The budget provides the operating funds for a *fiscal year*, or financial year.

Establishing a budget is a semistructured decision. Managers enter into the process and prepare a budget that will be realistic, yet will stimulate efficient operations.

Each organizational unit has its own budget. Together, these budgets constitute the budget of the entire firm. Managers on all levels are evaluated not only on how well they meet their operational objectives, but also on how well they stay within their budgets.

The budgeting process

Because firms have paid so much attention to the budgeting process, it is now very refined. Firms have learned that the best budget is developed jointly by all participants. A purely *top-down* budgeting approach is likely to fail when it is imposed on lower-level managers by those above. The lower-level managers feel that it is not their budget, but their superiors'. A purely *bottom-up* approach would offer little improvement. Lower-level managers would tend to play the "Army game" of asking for much more funding than they think they need, knowing that their requests will be cut. Also, a budget comprised of separate budgets prepared by each of the units might not support the firm as it works toward its objectives.

The most effective budgeting approach combines the participation of both lower- and upper-level managers. In the absence of a widely used term to describe such an approach, we will call it an *integrative budget*. The integrative budget combines the advantages of overall, informed guidance from top-level managers with the specific knowledge of resource needs from managers on the lower level. Coordination of these inputs is performed by managers on the middle level who have the responsibility for developing the budget.

Figure 15-17 illustrates the process of developing a budget using the integrative approach. The numbered paragraphs of the following description correspond to the numbers in the figure.

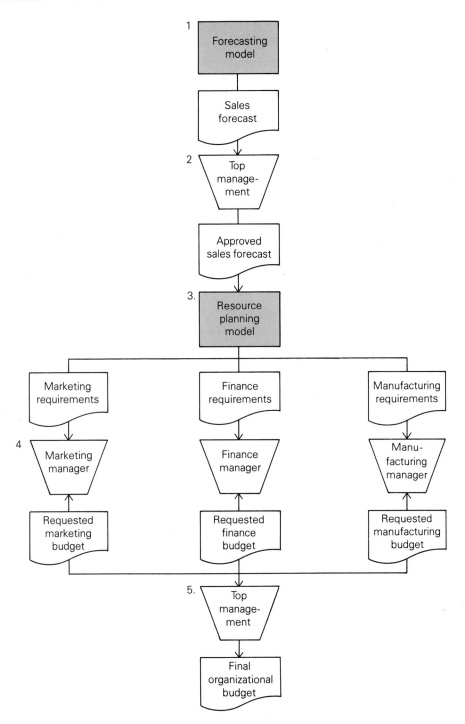

Figure 15-17 The budgeting process.

1. The starting point is the sales forecast. This forecast can be prepared by a forecasting model, perhaps using multiple regression.

2. Top management examines the forecast and makes adjustments based on their subjective evaluations plus other inputs.

3. The approved forecast data is then entered into a resource-planning model that converts the sales objectives into resource requirements for each functional area. For example, if the firm is to sell 230,000 units next year, eight new salespersons must be hired, a new drill press must be purchased, two new accounting clerks must be added, and so on.

4. The resource-planning model's programmed projections are then evaluated by each of the managers of the units to which they apply. These managers use their knowledge of the business to increase or (very infrequently) to decrease the budgeted amounts. Each manager works in conjunction with his or her superior to arrive at an acceptable budget. The two-way arrows connecting this and the next step illustrate the give and take between top management and functional management before the budget is finalized.

5. The combined approved functional budgets represent the organizational budget. Once budgets are established, they may or may not be changed based on management policy. Changed budgets, revised during the fiscal period, provide poor yardsticks for control purposes. Changes may be justified, however, in firms with extremely dynamic environments.

Budget reports

The operating budget for a unit, such as a department or division, usually consists of amounts for each of the basic expense items (salaries, telephone, rent, supplies, and so on). These expense items are usually allocated monthly throughout the budget period.

Each manager with budget responsibility receives a monthly report showing actual expenditures compared with the budget. An example of such a report appears in Figure 15-18. Managers pay considerable attention to these reports. In some firms, management compensation plans are based, in part, on budget performance. Perhaps bonuses are paid when performance is within budget. The important goal is to meet the total budgeted amount for the year. The manager works toward this objective by monitoring the monthly reports and responding to unusual variances.

The manager can use a budget report to identify areas for follow-up and then can query the data base to obtain more detailed information. For example, if the office has exceeded its telephone budget, the manager may be able to determine who is responsible. Of course, the detailed information must be in the data base in order to answer this query.

Upper-level managers receive reports that summarize the budget performance for the entire firm. Figure 15-19 is one of the reports that goes to the board of directors of a major conglomerate company. At the board level, the use of graphics as a form of communication is more prevalent than at lower levels.

```
                    BUDGET REPORT
                AS OF JANUARY 31, 1986
                    MIDWEST REGION

                CURRENT MONTH                    YEAR-TO-DATE
   ITEM       BUDGET    ACTUAL   DOLLARS     BUDGET    ACTUAL   DOLLARS

SALARIES      $23,500   $22,000  $1,500-     $59,000   $54,250  $4,750-
TRAVEL          8,250     9,000     750+      23,500    28,100   4,600+
ENTERTAINMENT   1,400     1,635     235+       4,200     5,100     900+
TELEPHONE         200        85     115-         600       225     375-
RENT              535       535       0        1,605     1,605       0
FURNITURE           0         0       0          420       505      85+
SUPPLIES          625       410     215-       1,875     1,320     555-
MISC.             400       620     220+       1,200     1,963     765+

TOTAL         $34,910   $34,285     625-     $92,400   $93,070     670+
```

Figure 15-18 A budget report.

Performance ratios

In addition to the budget, the control subsystem produces a number of *performance ratios* that enable managers on all levels to compare their performance with internal standards and also with those accepted as desirable by financial analysts. Many industries also have standards that member firms seek to attain in order to remain competitive. These ratios are computed using summary totals of accounting transactions.

There are quite a few ratios. Among the most popular is the *current ratio*, which measures the extent to which a firm can cover its short-term debts with assets easily converted into cash.

$$\text{Current ratio} = \frac{\text{current assets}}{\text{current liabilities}}$$

A ratio of 1.0 or greater is desirable since it means that the firm can cover its debts without having to sell some of its assets.

Another popular ratio is *inventory turnover*.

$$\text{Inventory turnover ratio} = \frac{\text{cost of goods sold}}{\text{average inventory value}}$$

Generally, the higher the ratio, the better. The ratio is an indication of the managers' abilities to "keep that stock moving." Firms that have implemented MRP point to higher inventory turnover as one of the advantages.

Ratios such as these are used by managers and by outsiders (such as financial analysts, potential investors, and stockholders) to monitor the performance of the firm. Figure 15-20 shows a typical report of ratios and other meaningful measurements that is prepared for senior executives. The ratios represent highly

STATEMENT OF INCOME
(Expressed in Millions Except Per Share Amounts)

	1986 Budget	1985 Estimate	1985 Budget	1984 Actual
REVENUES	$16,963.6	$15,531.0	$16,977.1	$15,648.5
COSTS AND EXPENSES:				
Cost of sales and operating expenses	12,505.3	11,098.4	12,342.0	11,270.5
Excise tax on oil production	144.9	167.0	287.3	225.2
Depreciation, depletion and amortization	1,160.0	1,030.0	1,052.6	845.1
Selling expenses	734.1	795.7	840.1	849.9
Administrative and general-direct	404.2	394.9	406.5	425.2
Corporate overhead	100.6	90.2	83.1	79.2
	15,049.1	13,576.2	15,011.6	13,695.1
INCOME before interest and federal income taxes	1,914.5	1,954.8	1,965.5	1,953.4
INTEREST EXPENSE:				
Incurred	769.9	922.6	876.0	895.7
Capitalized	(229.4)	(196.2)	(236.9)	(212.5)
	540.5	726.4	639.1	683.2
FEDERAL INCOME TAXES	446.7	378.0	461.7	456.4
INCOME FROM CONTINUING OPERATIONS	927.3	850.4	864.7	813.8
INCOME (LOSS) FROM DISCONTINUED OPERATIONS NET OF INCOME TAX	–	3.1	–	(.9)
LOSS ON SALE OF DISCONTINUED OPERATIONS NET OF INCOME TAX	–	(33.7)	–	–
	–	(30.6)	–	(.9)
NET INCOME	927.3	819.8	864.7	812.9
PREFERRED AND PREFERENCE STOCK DIVIDENDS	61.7	62.1	61.9	62.5
NET INCOME TO COMMON STOCK	$ 865.6	$ 757.7	$ 802.8	$ 750.4
AVERAGE SHARES OUTSTANDING	138.5	131.8	129.5	124.9
EARNINGS (LOSSES) PER AVERAGE SHARE:				
CONTINUING OPERATIONS	$ 6.25	$ 5.98	$ 6.20	$ 6.02
DISCONTINUED OPERATIONS	–	(.23)	–	(.01)
	$ 6.25	$ 5.75	$ 6.20	$ 6.01

Figure 15-19 Consolidated budget reports are used by the firm's executives.

distilled representations of accounting data. They provide a handy way to come to grips with the data.

The MIS cannot take credit for making these ratios possible. Most of the ratios were around long before the computer— laboriously cranked out by manual, keydriven, and punched card systems. Computers have simply made it easier to calculate the ratios. The ratios can be computed and stored in the data base, waiting for a manager to ask for them. Or the ratios can be computed at the time a query is made.

FINANCIAL MEASUREMENTS

	1986 Budget	1985 Estimate	1985 Budget	1984 Actual
Return on net assets employed	12.9%	13.7%	13.9%	15.1%
Return on common equity	14.9%	14.4%	15.2%	16.3%
Book value per share	$43.57	$40.27	$42.34	$39.05
Common dividend payout	43.5%	44.4%	43.8%	43.5%
Current ratio	1.06	1.03	1.04	1.08
Effective tax rate	32.5%	30.8%	34.8%	36.0%
Capitalization (including short-term debt):				
Short-term debt	5.5%	7.0%	6.9%	9.1%
Long-term debt	40.2	41.8	41.7	43.1
Total debt	45.7	48.8	48.6	52.2
Preferred and preference stock	4.8	5.0	5.0	5.1
Common and other stockholders' equity	49.5	46.2	46.4	42.7
	100.0%	100.0%	100.0%	100.0%

Figure 15-20 Financial ratios measure several key dimensions of the firm's performance.

Putting the Financial Information System in Perspective

Financial managers use the financial information system to manage the money flow. The managers must look into the future and identify the monetary needs of the firm. Sources of these funds must be identified, and relationships must be established so that the funds flow into the firm as needed. These activities are long-range and environmental in nature. The financial managers use the information system to keep current on the financial environment and to cultivate that environment so that it represents an asset of the firm rather than a constraint.

Funds flowing through the firm are managed so that they are used as effectively as possible. This management activity is guided by the operating budget. The data processing subsystem gathers data describing the financial transactions of the firm. The control subsystem reports, in a summarized form, the results of those transactions to managers throughout the firm. This feedback information enables managers to adjust their systems and procedures in order to meet the financial objectives.

Financial managers also use the information system to identify the best places to invest surplus funds. Like the acquisition of funds, investment activity involves the financial community and requires that future financial environments be anticipated.

How Managers Use the Financial Information System

Table 15-3 identifies the users of the financial information system. The CEO makes use of selected information from each of the output subsystems. Top managers in the financial area, such as the vice president of finance and the controller,

Table 15-3 Users of the Financial Information System

User	Subsystem		
	Forecasting	Funds management	Control
Vice president of finance	X	X	X
Other executives	X	X	X
Controller	X	X	X
Manager of accounting			X
Manager of financial planning	X		X
Director of budgets			X
Other functional managers	X	X	X

also use all of the subsystems. Lower-level financial managers tend to favor those subsystems relating directly to their area of responsibility. It is important to note that managers in other functional areas use the financial system's output. Every day, managers throughout the firm use financial information.

Summary

The heart of the financial information system is the data processing subsystem, providing detailed data concerning everything of a monetary nature happening in the firm. The financial intelligence subsystem monitors the economic environment of the financial community and also interfaces with the firm's stockholders. The internal audit subsystem participates in both the design and evaluation of conceptual information systems throughout the firm. Some internal auditors see their responsibility as including the gathering of environmental information as well.

Marketing and manufacturing conduct short-range forecasts of their own activity, but someone must take a more distant view. The responsibility for long-range forecasting often is assumed by the financial function. Both quantitative and nonquantitative techniques are used. Quantitative techniques can use canned programs such as SAS, sophisticated econometric models, and data bases of economic and industry data.

The funds management subsystem assists financial management not only in tracking the flow of money through the firm, but in influencing that flow as well. A nonoptimizing, what-if cash flow model simulates the effect of alternate decisions on the flow. These models can be written using a procedural or modeling language or by keying the formulas into an electronic spreadsheet.

Managers throughout the firm use the output of the control subsystem. Monthly budget reports during the fiscal year advise managers how well they are performing compared to their budgets. Financial ratios distill a volume of data into meaningful measures of financial performance. Both budget reports and ratios are used by managers on all levels, including the board of directors.

We have now concluded our study of subsystems within the MIS. We have seen how these subsystems support the unique information needs of executives and of managers on all levels in marketing, manufacturing, and finance.

Next we turn our attention to the process that is followed in implementing an MIS. That is the subject of Part Six.

Key Terms

data processing subsystem

financial intelligence subsystem

internal audit subsystem

forecasting subsystem

funds management subsystem

control subsystem

income statement

balance sheet

external auditor

internal auditor

certified public accountant (CPA)

financial audit

operational audit

EDP auditor

concurrent audit

control flowchart

panel consensus

Delphi method

regression analysis

regression line

independent variable

dependent variable

bivariate regression, simple regression

multivariate regression, multiple regression

econometric model, macro economic model

econometric service bureau

national data service

cash flow model

operating budget, budget

fiscal year

top-down budgeting approach

bottom-up budgeting approach

integrative budgeting approach

performance ratio

current ratio

inventory turnover

Key Concepts

The focused attention of financial management on money flow

The value of accounting data,

transformed into basic accounting reports by the data processing system, and stored in the data base

How the data processing subsystem supports lower-level managers by making programmed decisions, and supports managers on all levels by producing basic reports and maintaining a data base

The responsibility of the financial intelligence subsystem for gathering information from stockholders and the financial community

The manner in which internal auditors contribute to the integrity of conceptual systems

The incorporation of nonquantitative methods into all forecasts

The importance of good historical data to forecasting

The dynamic nature of a firm's cash flow, caused by influences both within and outside the control of the firm

The manner in which upper and lower management levels work together in developing an operating budget

Questions

1. What are the three basic tasks of the financial information system in terms of the money flow?

2. Which type of packaged software seems to be especially well suited to financial analysis? How is it generally used?

3. Where in the firm are the resources located that process accounting data?

4. What three basic roles are played by the data processing system in the MIS?

5. Name three key features of accounting data.

6. Is an income statement a static or dynamic model? Explain. What about a balance sheet?

7. Distinguish between an internal and an external auditor.

8. Distinguish between a financial audit and an operational audit.

9. What tools do internal auditors use in designing and evaluating systems?

10. Which organizational function usually prepares the sales forecast? The long-range economic or environmental forecast?

11. What are the two categories of forecasting techniques?

12. What is regression analysis? What is the regression line?

13. What distinguishes multivariate regression from bivariate regression?

14. What are the three ways of providing data to a SAS forecasting model?

15. What are the three services offered by an econometric service bureau?

16. What are the two goals of money flow management? Does a cash flow model help achieve these goals? Explain.

17. Is a budget the same as an operating budget? What time period is usually covered by a budget?

18. What are the three basic approaches to budgeting? Which works best? Why?

19. What is the relationship between sales forecasting and the budgeting process?
20. Who uses financial performance ratios?

Problems

1. Go to the library and obtain the most recent annual reports for three firms in the same industry. Compute the current ratio and the inventory turnover ratio for each firm using data contained in the reports. Interpret your findings in a brief report.

2. Use a stat package such as SAS to develop a regression equation using the following historical data.

Year	Sales revenue (in thousands)	Number of salespersons	Advertising budget (in thousands)	Sales promotion budget (in thousands)
1	12.1	25	0.5	0.2
2	12.4	25	0.9	0.2
3	12.9	26	1.1	0.2
4	12.7	26	1.0	0.3
5	13.2	26	1.2	0.3
6	13.6	27	1.2	0.3
7	14.1	27	1.5	0.0
8	13.8	28	1.5	0.3
9	14.1	28	2.0	0.3
10	14.0	30	2.0	0.4
11	14.5	29	1.5	0.4
12	14.6	30	2.0	0.5
13	15.3	31	2.5	0.5
14	15.5	31	2.2	0.5

What sales revenue would be expected if the firm has 30 salespersons, invests $2,000 in advertising, and $500 in sales promotion?

3. Redesign the budget report in Figure 15-18 to show the variance of the budget from the actual as a percentage. The percentage is computed by dividing the actual by the budget. Use the numbers in the figure. Which version of the report do you think would be the best? Explain your answer.

CASE PROBLEM: Laser Technology, Inc. (A)

You are the manager of marketing planning for Laser Technology, Inc., a manufacturer of high-speed laser printers. One day your boss Ted Andretti, the vice president of marketing, calls you into his office. He tells you that he would like for you to design a report that can show the current month's budget performance for each of the divisions within marketing—sales, advertising, and marketing research. He would like for you to prepare a sample showing the sales division performance during August, 1986. During that month, the sales division had the following budget amounts:

Salaries	$40,000
Travel	12,500
Entertainment	3,250
Telephone	1,625
Rent	9,250
Furniture	2,500
Supplies	1,000
Miscellaneous	9,000
Total	$79,125

Knowing how important it is to get the problem specifications right the first time, you ask Ted questions about the report layout. He tells you that he wants the title "Monthly Budget Report" centered at the top, with the organizational unit, such as "Sales Division," immediately below. Then, on the next line is the date, such as "For the Month of August, 1986." There are five columns of data and each has a column heading. Starting at the left is the "Account" (salaries and so on). Next is the "Monthly Budget Amount" (the amounts listed above), followed by the "Monthly Actual Expenses." For the month of August, the following actual expenses were incurred: salaries $38,625; travel $13,450; entertainment $4,720; telephone $1,460; rent $9,250; furniture $725; supplies $1,863; miscellaneous $8,426.

The two rightmost columns show the variance of actual to budgeted expenses. The rightmost column is labeled "Variance Percent." In it, the percent is listed for the actual expense divided by the budgeted amount. For example, if the budget is $10,000, and the actual is $12,500, the variance percent is 1.25. A manager would say "I'm 125 percent of budget" or "I'm 25 percent over budget."

The second column from the right is titled "Variance Amount." In it, the budget is subtracted from the actual, and the variance (plus or minus) is printed. Ted also tells you that he wants totals for all of the quantitative columns, and he adds "Dress it up any way that you like—you know, underlines, spaces, and such."

You sketch out a rough drawing of the report format, frown, and ask, "Do you want a total on the variance percent column also?" Ted replies that that wouldn't make a whole lot of sense and asks your opinion. You think a while and say, "Well, we could either average the eight variance percent figures, or we could divide total actual by total budget." Ted says that he likes the second idea the best.

You tell Ted that you will give him a sample report of the August 1986 data for the Sales Division. He says, "Great, I'll be looking forward to seeing it. If this works out okay, I would like to consider some more applications."

Assignment

1. If you have an electronic spreadsheet available, use it to prepare the sample report.
2. If you do not have an electronic spreadsheet available, prepare the sample report on a typewriter. (Hint: First sketch it out in pencil.)

CASE PROBLEM: Laser Technology, Inc. (B)

You are sitting in your office reading *The Wall Street Journal* when the phone rings. It's Ted. He says it's urgent that you come into his office—right now.

When you walk in, you are greeted by a big smile. "That budget performance system is working like a charm," he says. "All of the offices are on it, and I just got the last of the monthly reports this morning. I'm ready to talk about the next application. Sit down."

Ted begins to explain: "I have always wanted to formalize our resource planning activity. As you know, each year the marketing division projects the sales activity for the corporation for the coming fiscal year. This sales forecast is used by all of the organizational units in planning their resource needs for the year. It's ironic. We prepare the forecast that everybody else uses for their planning, but we probably do the poorest job of using it ourselves. I would like for you to create another sample system."

You respond that you think it's an excellent idea, and that you will get right on it. You ask Ted to explain more about what he wants.

"The key to everything is personnel. We have to have a certain personnel mix and level in order to meet our sales objectives. All of our budgeted expenses— salaries, travel, entertainment, and so forth—are based on the number of personnel that we have."

"What about rent?" you interrupt.

Ted answers, "In the short run rent is a fixed expense—so much per month. But, in the long run, it also varies with personnel. The more people we have, the larger our sales offices must be."

You press Ted for some guidelines that you can use in designing the system. "Just what is the relationship between personnel and our objectives?" you ask.

"One sales team—a sales representative and two systems analysts—can sell one laser printer system per month. And, after they sell it, they can install it. We can use a figure of $225,000 for the revenue derived from one sale. So, a sales team should be able to sell 12 systems at $225,000, or about $2,400,000 in annual revenue."

"$2.7 million," you reply.

Ted says, "If we want to sell $27 million, then we need 10 teams working the entire year. I figure a sales rep costs about $2,000 per month in salary (not counting commission, which we're not concerned with here), and a systems analyst goes for about $2,250. To determine personnel needs, we start with our sales forecast, which is in numbers of systems per month. That tells us how many sales teams we need. Then we use a cost-per-person approach in coming up with all of the budget items."

"What does our sales forecast look like for the next fiscal year?" you ask. "It's April now, and our fiscal year starts in November. That gives us 7 months to get geared up."

Ted pulls out a typed forecast for fiscal year 1986–87, which lists:

Month	Number of Systems
November	8
December	9
January	10
February	10
March	12
April	13
May	15
June	17
July	19
August	21
September	21
October	22

"If we're going to sell 8 units in November, then we have to have 8 sales teams, right?" you ask.

"Right," Ted responds. "But we can't just hire them on November 1 and expect them to start selling immediately. I estimate that a team must be on board 6 months before we can expect an order."

"So, we have to have 8 teams on board in May if we are to meet the November target. That means we better start hiring, as we have only 6 teams now."

"You've got it," Ted says.

"Let me see if I've got this straight," you say. "We take the number of forecast systems and convert that into a head count. Then we compute the salaries—"

Ted interrupts, "Exactly. Then we use some dollar amounts per person for the remainder of the expenses."

"Do you know what those are?" you ask.

"Not really. I think you had better come up with some," Ted says. "Why don't you do that and then get back with me."

You dig through old expense account forms and bills and develop the following average monthly expenses per person:

Telephone	$42.25
Travel	563.70
Entertainment	84.65
Supplies	38.10

During an employee's first month, approximately $910 is spent on furniture—a desk, chair, wastebasket, and file cabinet. All of these expenses vary directly with the number of personnel. The rent figure does not. Rather, it remains at a level of $8,450 per month for all of the office locations within the division. The final budget item, miscellaneous, includes everything not included in the other accounts, such as education and fringe benefits. During the past year, the miscellaneous category was about $450 per person per month.

You present these figures to Ted. "These look good. You've done a good job. On these expenses that vary with the head count, let's round them off—use $50 for telephone, $600 for travel, $60 for entertainment, $40 for supplies, and $450 for miscellaneous. Let's use $8,500 per month for rent, and a one-time expense of $925 for furniture. That should just about do it, shouldn't it?"

"Are you sure about the $60 for entertainment? They've been spending $84 . . ."

Ted interrupts, "That's too much. I'm going to clamp down on that. The $60 is fine."

You ask, "What about salaries?"

"For the sales rep let's use $2,125, and for the analyst let's use $2,400. These are a little high, but I would like to allow some room for raises. Now, does that do it?"

You look over your notes and respond, "I think I need to know the system forecast for the first six months of fiscal year (FY) 1987 and 1988 if I am to give you a resource projection for FY 86/87. You see, we must hire sales reps and analysts during the last six months of FY 86/87 to meet the sales forecast for the next year."

"You're right," Ted concedes. "I just happen to have those figures. Here they are."

November 1987	22 systems
December 1987	23 systems
January 1988	23 systems
February 1988	24 systems
March 1988	24 systems
April 1988	25 systems

Ted asks, rather impatiently, "Now do you have everything that you need?" You reply that you believe you do, and, as a final check, summarize your task. "I'll prepare a projection for the next 18 months of these expenses for the sales division. The first six months, May through October 1986, will get us geared up to meet the FY 86/87 sales forecast. The last 12 months, November 1986 through October 1987, will be the budget projection that you need. Do you want all 18 months, or just the last 12?"

"Give me all 18. I'd like to be able to see what we have to do during the next 6 months in order to meet next year's goals. But, let me have totals for both the 6-month period and the 12-month period. I want to be able to see the figures separately by fiscal year. Any more questions?"

"Only one," you reply. "What about format? What do you want the report to look like?"

"I'll leave that up to you. Just be sure and give me monthly totals on everything, and I would like to see totals for each budget item. Let me know when you have something." With that, Ted returns to the papers on his desk, and you check your mailbox to find today's issue of *The Wall Street Journal* with a headline "More Firms Turn To Formal Planning."

Assignment

1. If you have an electronic spreadsheet available, use it to prepare the resource projection.
2. If you do not have an electronic spreadsheet available, prepare the projection using a typewriter. (Hint: First sketch it out in pencil.)

Selected Bibliography

Financial Information Systems

Casey, Cornelius J., and Norman J. Bartczak, "Cash Flow—It's Not the Bottom Line," *Harvard Business Review* 62 (July-August 1984): 61–66.

Chambers, John C., Satinder K. Mullick, and Donald D. Smith, "How to Choose the Right Forecasting Technique," *Harvard Business Review* 49 (July-August 1971): 45–74.

Churchill, Neil C., "Budget Choice: Planning vs. Control," *Harvard Business Review* 62 (July-August 1984): 150ff.

Coats, Pamela K., "Business Data Sources Grow With Personal Computer Usage," *Journal of Business Forecasting* 2 (Spring 1983): 22–24.

Flesher, Dale L., "An Operational Audit of Marketing," *The Internal Auditor* 40 (February 1983): 23–29.

Gale, Bradley T., and Ben Branch, "Cash Flow Analysis: More Important Than Ever," *Harvard Business Review* 59 (July-August 1981): 131–136.

Gershefski, George W., "Building a Corporate Financial Model," *Harvard Business Review* 47 (July-August 1969): 61–72.

Goyal, Suresh K., Essam Mahmoud, and Gillian Rice, "How to Choose the Forecasting Software Package You Need," *Journal of Business Forecasting* 2 (Summer 1983): 3–5.

Hayen, Roger, "Applying Decision Support Systems to Small Business Financial Planning," Execucom Systems Corporation White Paper (1982).

Lacob, Miriam, "Managing the Float—Computers Put Corporate Cash to Work," *Computer Decisions* 16 (September 15, 1984): 108ff.

Li, David H., "Control Flowcharting for Internal Control," *The Internal Auditor* 40 (August 1983): 28–33.

Migliaro, A., and C. L. Jain, eds., *An Executive's Guide to Econometric Forecasting* (Flushing, NY: Graceway, 1983).

Oliverio, Mary E., and Bernard H. Newman, "Sharpen the Focus of Your Internal Auditing Function," *The Internal Auditor* 42 (February 1985): 30–33.

Rice, Gillian, Essam Mahmoud, and Susan Margaret Pick Vadivel, "A Directory of 132 Packages for Forecasting and Planning," *Journal of Business Forecasting* 3 (Spring 1984): 11–23.

Ridington, Richard W., Jr., "OZ: Just the Ticket for Managing Company Finances," *Business Computer Systems* 3 (October 1984): 109ff.

Rothermel, Terry W., "Forecasting Resurrected," *Harvard Business Review* 60 (March-April 1982): 139–147.

Viscione, Jerry A., "Small Company Budgets: Targets Are Key," *Harvard Business Review* 62 (May-June 1984): 42ff.

Wallace, Wanda A., "Internal Auditors Can Cut Outside CPA Costs," *Harvard Business Review* 62 (March-April 1984): 16ff.

Williams, Wade S., and Bill C. Wilson, "Environmental Analysis—the Strategic Response," *The Internal Auditor* 41 (October 1984): 34–35.

Part Six

MANAGING THE MIS

At this point, five important topics have been covered: an overview of the entire MIS area, the theoretical basis of MIS, computing hardware and software relating to MIS, the major structural components of MIS, and information subsystems of the MIS. One major topic remains: how an MIS is developed, operated, and improved. This major topic is the subject of Part Six.

Although development, operation, and improvement are technical activities performed largely by information specialists, it is the manager who has responsibility. These activities can be managed—hence the name, "Managing the MIS."

Chapters 16, 17, and 18 describe the evolution of the MIS from early planning stages through operation and maintenance. As this process unfolds, you will be able to see its step-by-step nature. Chapter 16 deals with how the manager plans the MIS project and establishes a control mechanism. Chapter 17 deals with the work of information specialists in analysis, design, and implementation. Chapter 18 describes the operational system and emphasizes controls that assure the planned performance and security of the MIS.

We introduced this evolution of the MIS in Chapter 1 and used the term *MIS life cycle*. Figure 1-13 shows this life cycle as a wheel of four parts—planning, analysis and design, implementation, and operation. After a system remains operational for some time, perhaps 3 or 5 years, it becomes necessary to modify or replace it. Then, the life cycle starts over. This never-ending life cycle has significance for both the manager and the information specialist. It means that involvement with the MIS never ends. Both the manager and the information specialist continue to adapt the MIS to the changing needs of the user and to incorporate new hardware and software capabilities.

The final chapter of the book, Chapter 19, projects this concept of MIS management into the future by recognizing future trends that will improve performance. In Chapter 19 we attempt to plot the course that MIS technology and methodology are likely to take during the next several years. Here, the control that the manager exercises over the MIS is less clear—but nonetheless it is present.

Future hardware and software will develop in response to unmet management information needs. In this manner, the manager determines the characteristics of not only today's MIS but tomorrow's as well.

Chapter 16

Planning and Controlling the MIS Project

Learning Objectives

After studying this chapter, you should:

- Appreciate that the semi-structured nature of the MIS project makes planning both necessary and difficult
- Understand the scope of activities included in an MIS project, and how such a project is started
- Realize that the MIS progresses through two different types of life cycles—one of a relatively short term as a single MIS project is implemented, and one of a much longer term as the sophistication in computer use increases
- Be aware of the options that exist for assigning responsibility for the MIS project
- Recognize that MIS projects can be initiated to accomplish objectives or to solve problems
- Know two ways to develop an MIS plan from the firm's objectives
- Understand how MIS performance standards logically flow from the firm's objectives
- Know the basic steps of planning an MIS project
- Know five dimensions of MIS feasibility
- Understand the logic of preparing a detailed project plan
- Be familiar with the basics of two project control mechanisms
- Have an appreciation for the factors influencing selection of an MIS project for implementation

Introduction

This chapter, and the next two, will introduce you to a number of activities involved in implementing an MIS. You will need a view from the top before you get involved with the details. Figure 16-1 provides an overview of the basic relationship between the manager and the information specialists. You will note that the manager either plans or controls. A plan is established during the first phase of the MIS project that provides the control mechanism for the following phases. The information specialists support the manager during the planning phase and are then responsible for performing the tasks in the remaining three phases.

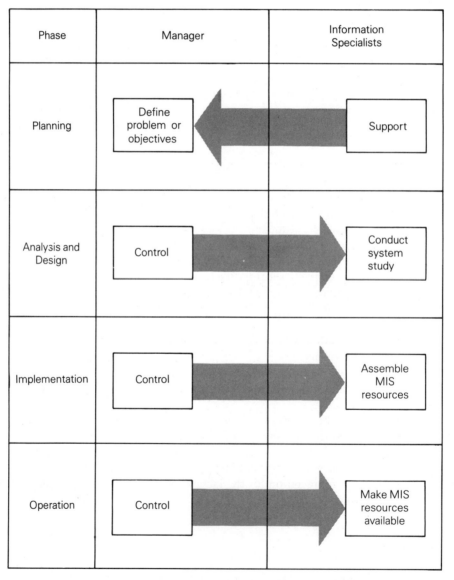

Figure 16-1 The cooperative development process.

MIS Life Cycles

The concept of a life cycle fits anything that originates, matures over time, and sooner or later terminates. We recognized in Chapter 13 that consumer products follow such a life cycle pattern (see Figure 13-11). The life cycle concept also applies to the MIS. In fact, it can be applied in two ways.

First, the life cycle can be viewed as the long-term evolution that a firm's MIS follows beginning with the installation of the first computer. Many large firms installed their first computer 25 years ago, and have continually improved the manner in which the device is used. Perhaps these firms have subsequently used several "generations" of computer technology, and have increased the number of computers in use. Today, the firms implementing their first micro are embarking on this long-term developmental life cycle.

The second view of an MIS life cycle is much shorter, although it may span several years. This view relates the life cycle to a particular MIS project. Perhaps the project is the implementation of the firm's first MIS design, or the project might involve improvement of an already-installed subsystem such as forecasting. Regardless of the project size, there is a specified end product to be achieved.

This second view of the MIS project life cycle is our main topic in this chapter. Before we launch into that discussion, however, let us see where that MIS project might eventually lead—the long-term MIS developmental cycle.

Nolan's Model of MIS Stages

Richard L. Nolan, formerly a Harvard professor and currently a consultant, is credited with defining the stages through which computer use in a firm evolves. His model, pictured in Figure 16-2, has become known as *Nolan's stage model*.

According to Nolan, after a firm implements its first computer, its use progresses through six stages:[1]

1. *Initiation.* The computer is usually installed for the purpose of reducing costs. Frequently the computer is installed in the accounting department since data processing applications dominate. In some cases, a separate computing organization is established.

2. *Contagion.* Word quickly spreads throughout the organization of the advantages accruing from computer processing. New applications are added without any overall plan, and the size of the computer staff grows to meet the new demand.

3. *Control.* Management becomes alarmed at the increasing costs of the computer operation, and institutes controls. Perhaps a high-level committee, called a steering committee, is established to oversee the entire

[1] Richard L. Nolan, "Managing the Crises in Data Processing," *Harvard Business Review* 57 (March–April 1979): 115–126.

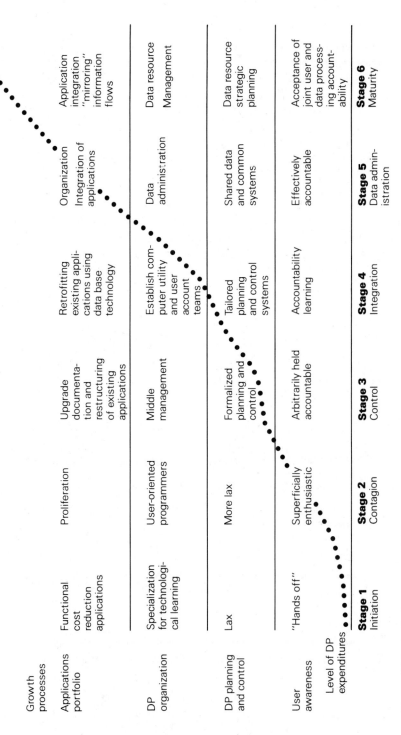

Growth processes	Stage 1 Initiation	Stage 2 Contagion	Stage 3 Control	Stage 4 Integration	Stage 5 Data administration	Stage 6 Maturity
Applications portfolio	Functional cost reduction applications	Proliferation	Upgrade documentation and restructuring of existing applications	Retrofitting existing applications using data base technology	Organization Integration of applications	Application integration "mirroring" information flows
DP organization	Specialization for technological learning	User-oriented programmers	Middle management	Establish computer utility and user account teams	Data administration	Data resource Management
DP planning and control	Lax	More lax	Formalized planning and control	Tailored planning and control systems	Shared data and common systems	Data resource strategic planning
User awareness	"Hands off"	Superficially enthusiastic	Arbitrarily held accountable	Accountability learning	Effectively accountable	Acceptance of joint user and data processing accountability
Level of DP expenditures						

Figure 16-2 Nolan's stage model.

Source: Reprinted by permission of the Harvard Business Review. An exhibit from "Managing the Crises in Data Processing" by Richard L. Nolan (March/April 1979). Copyright © 1979 by the President and Fellows of Harvard College; all rights reserved.

computing operation. This is the point where interest in DSS usually begins. Up until this point, the entire emphasis has been on data processing. Top management not only applies the brakes to the computer spending but also decides to channel some of that investment into decision support.

4. *Integration.* Systems that were implemented separately during the second stage are tied together so that data flows from one area to another. The data processing subsystems are integrated as explained in Chapter 9, and they provide the linkages to the various information subsystems as explained in Chapters 12–15.

5. *Data administration.* Management becomes aware of the importance of the data base to both data processing and DSS. DBMS software is implemented to manage the data resource.

6. *Maturity.* All of the major MIS components are in place. The steering committee exercises overall control, information services is a major functional area of the firm, user areas develop an MIS expertise, terminals and micros are installed throughout the company, and end-user computing becomes a reality.

Much has happened in the computing field since Nolan first presented his model of stages. Advances in hardware, software, and user sophistication require that the stages be updated. The model does, however, recognize that computer use in a firm is dynamic over the long term.

A large number of today's firms, even large ones, have not progressed beyond the control stage. Most large firms, however, have progressed beyond the integration stage and are deeply involved with data administration. Very few firms have reached the maturity stage. For one thing, the membership requirements keep getting more difficult to satisfy. Office automation is an example of maturity that did not exist a few years ago. "Mature" MIS usage is like a carrot on a stick in front of a donkey. A firm can be making real progress, but new technology opens up still more challenges.

We can assume that all computer-user firms, large and small, evolve through some process similar to the one that Nolan described.

With this overview, we now direct our attention to the MIS project life cycle.

The Importance of Planning

Chapter 2 described Henri Fayol's management functions. The first, planning, is the key to satisfactory performance of the others. Managers have learned that time spent in planning pays dividends when other functions are performed.

The efforts of a firm to implement an MIS represent a large-scale activity involving many people and facilities, much money and equipment, and considerable time. The MIS project can require as many resources as the development of a new product, the construction of a new plant, or the entry into a new market. Therefore, the MIS project should receive the same management attention as any expensive, time-consuming venture.

The difficulty of the planning task

This chapter concerns the planning that begins with a decision to consider implementing an MIS and ends before work begins to design and implement the system. It is important that this planning be accomplished before work on the project actually starts. If not, it is likely that the work will be misdirected and have to be redone. Poor planning only delays the benefits of the MIS and adds to the cost of the project.

You would think that planning an MIS today would be reasonably automatic, considering that firms have been doing it over and over for the past twenty years or so. But MIS planning is a semistructured problem. Some structure is provided by previous efforts, but much of the task is undefined as the firm begins a new MIS life cycle. There is usually only a sketchy idea of how the future MIS will perform; thus, the time and resources necessary to implement the system cannot be defined precisely.

The difficulty of the task should not make the manager avoid planning. In fact, the difficulty is the very reason that planning is required. The manager knows that the initial plan is very general and will be changed and made more detailed as the project unfolds. MIS planning is therefore a process of iteration and refinement. Management begins with a general plan that is refined as more is learned about what is necessary to achieve the new MIS.

Initiation of the MIS Project

We use the term *MIS project* very broadly. It can mean a *complete* system, such as one encompassing executive, marketing, manufacturing, and financial subsystems. Such a project would be initiated by a brand new company with no existing MIS or by a firm with an MIS that needs a complete overhaul. Perhaps the need for a complete overhaul is caused by technology, such as the conversion of a manual system to a computer-based system. It could also be caused by structural changes or growth within the firm. As firms increase in size and scope, an MIS that functioned satisfactorily in the past can fall far short of adequacy very rapidly.

We also regard an MIS project as the effort required to implement only one or more of the *subsystems* within the MIS. Perhaps a firm wants to overhaul one area such as its manufacturing information system, or its promotion subsystem, or its method for projecting cash flow. An MIS project can, therefore, be a major effort that involves practically everyone in the company, or it can be a relatively minor change to an otherwise sound MIS.

The need for an MIS project can be recognized by the firm's environment, by the firm's executives, by lower-level managers, by nonmanagers, and by the firm's information services staff.

Individuals and groups in the firm's *environment* will often be the first to recognize a need to improve the MIS. Customers, vendors, the government, the financial community, and stockholders call weaknesses to the attention of persons within the firm—often top managers.

The MIS projects initiated by the *executives* tend to be broad in scope, affecting the entire organization. The executives, expecting the MIS to support the firm as a whole, initiate projects with this objective in mind.

Most requests for MIS projects probably originate with *lower-level managers* in the work areas. These managers are responsible for seeing to it that their systems operate efficiently. They are quick to notice problems or opportunities.

Nonmanagers, such as professional, clerical, and secretarial employees, know the details of the systems better than anyone. When they do not take their system as "given," and recognize the possibility of improvement, they can be a force initiating system change.

In only rare cases will the *information specialists* initiate the project. For one reason, the information services group in most firms is overworked, with a backlog of jobs stretching perhaps two or three years into the future. These specialists are usually not looking for additional jobs. Another reason is because the need for the new system exists outside the information services department. Users, working with an inadequate current system, can see the necessity for a new one better than anyone else.

Firms getting their first computer

Most large firms have been using computers for years. They have all of their data processing applications and many DSS applications converted to the computer. The activity of implementing first computers is currently happening in small firms. They are implementing micros.

In some respects these small firms are at an advantage when compared to larger firms, and in some respects they are at a disadvantage. Small firms are at an advantage in that they can benefit from the years of trial and error by the larger firms. The step-by-step process of implementing an MIS is well defined, and the small firm follows the same steps, generally speaking, as did the large firm. The small size of the firm does not mean that fewer steps must be taken. The same process must be followed, but the difficulty of certain steps might be less. A small insurance company, for example, may have to convert only 10,000 policy files to the computer data base, whereas a large company might have to convert 100,000.

Where the small firm is at a disadvantage is in the area of resources. The large firm can assign greater numbers of skilled persons to the MIS project than a small firm. The large insurance company, as an example, might contract the data base job to an outside computer service bureau. The small firm, on the other hand, might have to involve all of its employees in that activity. One small insurance company divided the policy folders among all of its employees, including the president, and assigned each person the task of coding the contents into a format acceptable to the computer. Each day the president would go to the file room during his lunch hour and do the coding. He was the first to finish all of his folders!

Later in the chapter, we will study the development process of the MIS. As that discussion unfolds, we must keep in mind that smaller firms do not have all of the resources mentioned. The work still has to be done—perhaps more slowly and in a less elegant manner than described.

Responsibility for the MIS Project

Someone within the organization must have overall responsibility for the MIS project. This should *not* be the manager, such as the vice president of information services, who is responsible for the computer.[2] Rather, it should be a high-level manager representing the users of the information system output.

There is nothing wrong with the president of the firm having this responsibility. In fact, that would be an ideal situation. The system is so important to the success of the firm that the president's involvement is justified. The president might not, however, be able to devote as much time to the MIS project as it deserves. In this case, the president delegates primary authority for achieving the MIS to a key top-level executive.

Positions within a firm lending themselves to the type of direction needed are the executive vice president and administrative vice president. Refer back to Figure 12-3 to see where these two executives fit into the organizational structure. The *executive vice president* is usually the senior executive with overall responsibility for assuring that the firm meets its operational and tactical objectives. The executive vice president, therefore, can represent *all* of the interests of the firm relating to both the physical system and the conceptual information system. Since the information system supports the physical system, the executive vice president has the best understanding of the total information needs.

If the firm does not have an executive vice president or if that person is unavailable, the logical second choice is the *administrative vice president*. This person occupies a staff position responsible for providing administrative support to the entire firm. Unfortunately, he or she has no responsibility for, or authority over, the physical system. This person's scope of activity is more limited than the executive vice president's. But the administrative vice president can represent the firm as a whole, in terms of meeting its administrative and information needs.

Throughout our discussion in the remainder of this chapter and the two following, we will use the title executive vice president when referring to the leader of the MIS project. This title is used for simplicity's sake only, knowing that in many firms a person with another title, or a steering committee, provides the leadership.

MIS responsibilities of the executive vice president

The executive vice president is responsible for determining what the MIS will do and then for assuring that it is done. This task involves communicating with other executives and managers in the firm to determine their *general* information needs. The executive vice president, assisted by the vice president of information

---

[2] In this and the following chapters, the title *vice president of information services* will be used to identify the individual with overall responsibility for the firm's MIS. We recognize that not all firms establish this responsibility at the vice presidential level. We also recognize that not all firms have an *information services department*. It may go by another name, or be a part of another department. However, using these terms will simplify our task.

services, meets with the president and the functional vice presidents to determine the major subsystems of the MIS. This information is then augmented with more specific details provided by lower-level managers.

MIS responsibilities of the functional executives

The vice presidents of finance, marketing, and manufacturing all play active roles in the MIS project. First they communicate with the president, executive vice president, and vice president of information services to develop the overall description of the MIS. Then the functional vice presidents work with the vice president of information services to develop the overall description of their functional information systems.

MIS responsibilities of the vice president of information services

During the planning period, the vice president of information services helps the other managers identify their information needs. When the decision is made to implement an MIS, the vice president of information services directs the efforts of the information services staff in design and implementation. Once the MIS is implemented, the vice president of information services is responsible for maintaining the performance of the MIS.

The responsibilities of these executives are summarized in Table 16-1.

The steering committee

Most firms make liberal use of committees. Committees exist on practically every management level. They are used to pool knowledge for a specific project or problem and to improve communication. When the purpose of a committee is to provide ongoing guidance, direction, and control, it is often called a *steering committee*.

The MIS project clearly justifies a steering committee. About half of the computer-using companies have followed this approach. The membership of the steering committee will vary from firm to firm, but it should include executives, information services personnel, and users. As a minimum, the steering committee should include the executive vice president, the functional vice presidents, and the vice president of information services. The executive vice president would be the likely chairperson, and keep the president informed of the committee activities.

The steering committee collectively carries out the responsibilities described in Table 16-1. More specifically, the steering committee performs these functions:[3]

- Define objectives
- Establish priorities
- Review requests for resources
- Resolve conflicts concerning user needs

---

[3] Taken from D. H. Drury, "An Evaluation of Data Processing Steering Committees," *MIS Quarterly* 8 (December 1984): 259.

Table 16-1 Executive Responsibility for the MIS

Executive	Preimplementation period	Implementation period	Postimplementation period
President	Overall responsibility for the MIS		
Executive vice-president	Take primary responsibility for the design and implementation of the MIS		Approve the performance
Vice president of finance	Design the overall MIS Design the executive information system Design the financial information system	Implement the executive and the financial information systems	Make suggestions for improvement
Vice president of marketing	Design the overall MIS Design the executive information system Design the marketing information system	Implement the executive and the marketing information systems	Make suggestions for improvement
Vice president of manufacturing	Design the overall MIS Design the executive information system Design the manufacturing information system	Implement the executive and the manufacturing information systems	Make suggestions for improvement
Vice president of information services	Design the overall MIS Design the executive information system Design the functional information systems	Implement the overall MIS	Oversee the operation and maintenance of the MIS

- Approve capital expenditures
- Establish long-range plans

These functions should be performed with the intent of implementing the concept of information resource management described in Chapter 1.

It is important to recognize the ongoing nature of the steering committee. It is a permanent committee insofar as it is not disbanded when the initial version of the MIS is implemented. Its ongoing nature means that it controls the implementation of small subsystems in addition to overall company-wide systems.

A number of advantages accrue from the steering committee approach:[4]

- Top management involvement
- User representation

---

[4]Drury, p. 260.

- Centralization of authority concerning the company's computer resource
- Insistence on planning and control

The steering committee serves as a vital communication link among the executives, the users, and the information services staff. The committee is a conduit, enabling each group to better understand the needs of the others.

One point should be made clear. Even if a steering committee is formed, the overall responsibility rests with a single individual—the committee chairperson. Shared responsibility seldom works. The committee serves in an advisory capacity to the chairperson.

Putting MIS responsibility in perspective

Responsibility for the design and implementation of the MIS lies in two general areas: (1) managers who will use the MIS, and (2) the information services staff who will create it. This responsibility is distributed among managers on several levels. A top executive (such as the executive vice president) is responsible for the overall effort and is assisted by the other managers who will use the MIS output. The vice president of information services lends support when and where needed.

There has never been any doubt about the necessity of management involvement in a computer project. The scenario presented here, describing active, informed participation at the top level, is a normative model—it describes how the MIS *should* develop. Not all projects are managed in this fashion. But the closer the project management conforms to the description presented here, the greater the chances for success.

Planning the MIS Project

The managers perform each of Fayol's functions as the MIS evolves. During the first phase, however, planning takes precedence. It is also by virtue of this planning that the seeds of control are planted.

Benefits of planning the MIS

Managers engage in planning in order to achieve certain goals. In terms of the MIS project, planning is expected to have the following benefits:

1. *Identify tasks necessary for goal achievement.* The scope of the project is defined. Which activities or subsystems are involved? Which are not? This information provides management with an initial idea of the scale of resources required.

2. *Recognize potential problem areas.* Planning will point out things that might go wrong. It is better to know of potential problems than to wait for them to appear.

3. *Arrange a sequence of tasks.* Many separate tasks will be necessary to implement the MIS. These tasks are arranged in a logical sequence based on information priorities and the need for efficiency. For example, a sales-

forecasting model may be so important to the firm that it is implemented before a less important system. Also, one task usually follows another. A mainframe computer should not be scheduled for delivery until the room has been prepared, for example.

4. ***Provide a basis for control.*** Certain levels of performance and methods of measurement should be specified in advance. The persons in charge of the MIS project should know what needs to be done, who will do it, and when it will be accomplished.

Alternate planning approaches

There are two basic ways to approach an MIS project. One is an *objective orientation*, where the firm uses its objectives as the starting point. The other is a *problem orientation*, where the firm designs an MIS to address specific problems. Recall from Chapter 4 that problem-solving activity also encompasses taking advantage of opportunities. A firm does not merely select between the two approaches. Rather, it follows the route illustrated in Figure 16-3. If a firm does

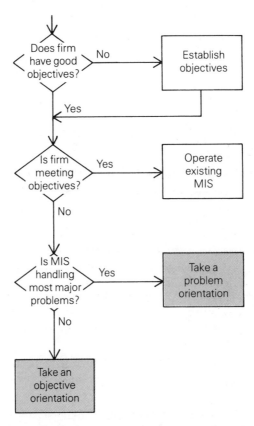

Figure 16-3 Determining the MIS approach.

not have objectives, they must be defined before proceeding with MIS planning. Then the firm must determine whether it is meeting its objectives. There is no need to develop a new MIS if the existing one is doing its job.

If the firm is not meeting its objectives, it must choose between the two planning approaches. The choice depends on how well the MIS is handling most of the major problems encountered. If the MIS is doing a good job, a comprehensive redesign is unnecessary—the existing system need only be modified to correct minor flaws. If, on the other hand, the MIS has serious faults, the firm needs a fresh approach and should follow an objective orientation.

We assume that a new firm, or a firm implementing its first computer-based MIS, will take an objective orientation. Since most computer-using firms have found themselves in this situation during the past several years, a large number of approaches have been devised. The approaches receiving the greatest amount of attention are the total study approach, strategy set transformation, and critical success factors.

The total study approach

The initial approach to defining the MIS plan was to interview each of the firm's managers individually to identify their information needs. The interviewing would proceed from the top management level to the bottom. The assumption was that all of the managers are working toward the objectives of the firm. This assumption led to another—that the MIS could support the firm in meeting its objectives by satisfying the manager's specific information needs.

The total study approach is still being followed. In fact, of the three techniques mentioned, it is probably the most popular. An example is IBM's Business Systems Planning (BSP) methodology. A large number of managers are interviewed, and the findings permit an identification of unmet information needs. A plan is then developed to implement the needed systems. This approach is costly in terms of the resources used to gather the data. A large volume of findings must be analyzed in order to identify and integrate the decision processes.

Strategy set transformation

In 1978 William R. King, a professor at the University of Pittsburgh, coined the term *strategy set transformation* to describe how objectives for the firm can be transformed into objectives and strategies for the MIS operation.[5] Figure 16-4 illustrates this concept.

Overall company strategy is an *organizational information set* consisting of missions, objectives, strategies, environmental constraints, and organizational attributes such as the sophistication of the management resource. Strategic MIS planning converts the information set into an *MIS strategy set* consisting of MIS objectives, constraints, and strategies.

[5] William R. King, "Strategic Planning for Management Information Systems," *MIS Quarterly* 2 (March 1978): 27–37.

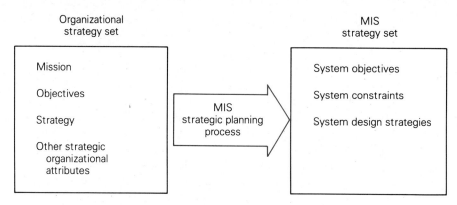

Figure 16-4   The overall MIS strategic planning process.

Source: Reprinted by special permission of the MIS Quarterly, *Volume 2, Number 1, March 1978. Copyright 1978 by the Society for Information Management and the Management Information Systems Research Center.*

The process of developing an MIS strategy set consists of six steps. The first two steps involve the *study* of the firm and its environment. The next step is devoted to the development of *organizational strategy* for the firm itself. The final three steps relate to the development of an *MIS strategy*.

Study phase

1. Define the internal and environmental groups that influence the long-term performance of the firm
2. Identify the goals of each group

Organizational strategy phase

3. Identify and develop the organizational strategy for achieving the desired interface with each group

MIS strategy phase

4. Identify alternate MIS strategies supporting the organizational strategy
5. Evaluate the alternate MIS strategies
6. Select the best MIS strategy

You recognize that the process is an application of the systems approach.

It is the responsibility of the top-management level to accomplish steps 1 and 2. Middle-level managers become involved in step 3. Systems analysts perform steps 4 and 5. Step 6 is the primary responsibility of the vice president of information services.

Critical success factors

One of the first efforts to prescribe the structure of an MIS was by William Zani, a Harvard professor. His 1970 model provided a blueprint for early MIS designers, but at the time its real innovative nature was not apparent. The central element in the model was something that Zani called *key success variables*. He defined these variables as "factors and tasks that determine success and failure."[6]

This idea lay dormant for almost ten years until it was picked up by researchers at MIT who renamed it *critical success factors (CSF)*. The logic underlying the CSF concept is that a firm will meet its overall objectives if it does a few key things (the CSFs) well. For example, a CSF relating to most firms is "human resources"—ensuring that a sufficiently qualified staff is available.

John Rockart, a professor at MIT, is credited with promoting CSF as an MIS design strategy. Rockart believes that the task of the MIS is to keep management informed concerning those items (the critical success factors) that should receive careful and continuous management attention.

Malcolm Munro, a professor at the University of Calgary, and Basil R. Wheeler, a major in the Canadian Armed Forces, incorporated the CSF approach into a series of steps leading to a specification of the contents of the MIS data base:[7]

1. Understand the objectives of the business unit (the firm)
2. Identify CSFs
3. Identify specific performance measures and standards
4. Identify data required to measure performance

This four-step process is illustrated in Figure 16-5. The end product is a data dictionary of all data elements necessary to support the organizational plan.

The current popularity of the CSF approach is due largely to its appeal to top management. It is easier for executives to conceptualize on the few factors that are critical to the firm's success than to describe the decisions that they make. At lower management levels, however, more difficulty may be experienced in conceptualizing the CSFs.[8] Here, a more traditional approach of focusing on decisions, such as that provided by the BSP methodology, might be in order.

Putting MIS planning in perspective

An MIS project is of sufficient complexity and importance to demand a good planning effort. Even a small project will likely involve many people from different areas and span a period of several months. If the existing MIS is handling most major problems, it is necessary to address only those problems that are not

---

[6] William M. Zani, "Blueprint for MIS," *Harvard Business Review* 48 (November–December 1970): 97.

[7] Malcolm C. Munro and Basil R. Wheeler, "Planning, Critical Success Factors, and Management's Information Requirements," *MIS Quarterly* 4 (December 1980): 29.

[8] Andrew C. Boynton and Robert W. Zmud, "An Assessment of Critical Success Factors," *Sloan Management Review* 25 (Summer 1984): 17–27.

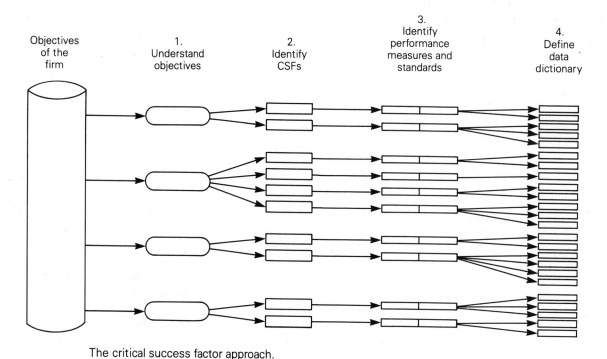

The critical success factor approach.

Figure 16-5   *Source: Malcolm C. Munro, and Basil R. Wheeler, "Planning, Critical Success Factors, and Management's Information Requirements," MIS Quarterly 4 (December 1980): 34. Reprinted with permission.*

being handled well. A complete overhaul is unnecessary. If, on the other hand, a need is seen to revamp the entire MIS, the project objectives should be derived from the objectives of the firm. The total study approach assumes that the objectives will be met by satisfying the individual manager's needs. The strategy set transformation and the CSF approaches make no such assumption and begin with the objectives.

The executives of the firm should continually monitor the effectiveness of the MIS, and when a deficiency is noted, an MIS project should be initiated. The scope of the project will depend on the degree of the deficiency.

MIS Performance Criteria

Although a firm can take an objective or a problem approach in designing their MIS, the end product should be the same. The MIS should support the firm's objectives. A logical relationship therefore exists between the objectives and the expected performance of the MIS.

The firm's objectives determine the objectives that each functional area— and the managers in those functional areas—should attain. The manager's objectives, in turn, determine their information needs. Finally, the manager's information needs determine the *performance criteria* of the MIS—the standards of performance. This hierarchy is illustrated in Figure 16-6.

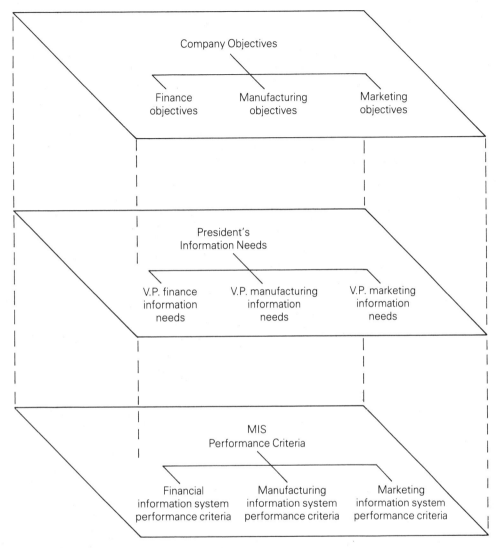

Figure 16-6 Relationship between objectives, information needs, and MIS performance criteria.

For example, a firm might have an objective of realizing a 12 percent return on investment during the coming year. To help achieve this objective, the marketing function might have an objective of $25 million in sales revenue with operating expenses under $1.2 million. In order to meet these marketing objectives, the vice president of marketing might require periodic sales and expense reports. Later in the MIS life cycle, the report requirements will be specifically stated. At this point in the planning phase, however, the criteria are stated in general terms, such as "Provide a monthly expense report that compares actual expenses with budgeted expenses for each operating unit." Similar statements establish the general performance criteria for each subsystem of the MIS.

Planning Steps

The executive vice president and the vice president of information services (assisted by the information services staff) work together in a series of steps to plan the MIS project. The systems analysts support the executive vice president during the initial stages, conduct a feasibility study, prepare a study project proposal for approval, and work jointly with the executive vice president to establish a control mechanism. These steps, illustrated in Figure 16-7, represent the systems approach to planning an MIS. The eight steps provide a finer breakdown of the first step of the systems approach—define the problem—discussed in Chapter 4.

1. *Recognize the problem*. Step 1 is taken with either an objective or a problem orientation. In both cases, the MIS developmental effort is expected to result in some improvement. If problems exist, they must first be recognized.

2. *Define the problem*. Once a manager realizes that a problem exists, he or she must understand it well enough to pursue a solution. No attempt is made, however, to gather all of the information describing the problem. That would require a full-scale systems analysis. The manager is interested only in gaining the understanding necessary to direct an effort aimed at problem solution. At a minimum, the manager should know where the problem exists. Which management level is involved? Perhaps there is more than one level. Which functional area is involved? Again, the problem may exist in more than one area. In addition, the manager should know which system or subsystem is deficient and what the general difficulty is. As the manager, assisted by the systems analyst, isolates the location of the problem, an effort is made to separate symptoms from the real cause. Very often, the manager and systems analyst will pursue a chain of symptoms that eventually leads to the problem cause, as described in Chapter 4.

3. *Set system objectives*. The objectives that the MIS should achieve are specified next. The functional vice presidents play key roles in identifying these objectives, since the MIS should meet the needs of their areas. Lower-level managers will also be called upon to participate.

At this early point in the developmental process, the objectives can be stated only in general terms. The manager should try, however, to assure that the objectives have the following characteristics:

- All MIS objectives should help the firm achieve its objectives.
- Lower-level objectives should support higher-level objectives.
- Objectives should be valid—they should steer the organization in the direction that it wants to go.
- Objectives should be realistic, yet demanding enough to stimulate improvement.
- Objectives should produce measurable standards.

4. *Identify system constraints*. The new MIS will operate under many constraints. Some are imposed by the environment, such as the government's demand

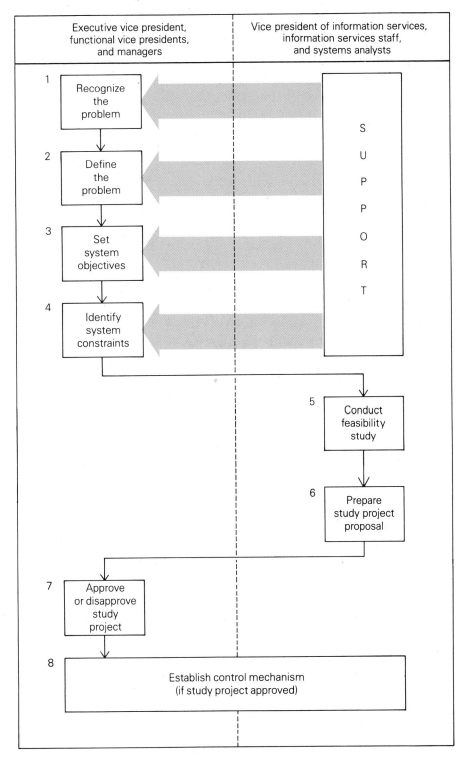

Figure 16-7 Steps in the planning process.

for certain tax reports and the customers' demand for billing information. Other constraints are imposed by the firm's management, such as limits on computer cost or response times.

It is important that these constraints be identified and understood as well as possible before work on the MIS actually begins. In this way, the MIS design will fall within the constraints. Otherwise, the system might have to be completely redesigned to conform to the constraints after they become known. Additional constraints typically arise as more is learned about the new system, forcing a design modification to accommodate them. Attention to constraints during the planning phase is intended to minimize modification later in the project.

5. Conduct a feasibility study. The systems analyst takes the information from the first four steps and uses it as a guideline for conducting a feasibility study. A *feasibility study* is a brief look at the major factors influencing a system that will enable the manager to solve the defined problem or achieve the desired objectives. It is not a full-scale study effort; that study will come later after the project feasibility has been demonstrated.

There are five dimensions of project feasibility:[9]

- *Technical.* Is there hardware and software available to provide the necessary decision support?
- *Economic.* Can the proposed system be justified on an economic basis?
- *Legal.* Will the proposed system operate within legal and ethical boundaries?
- *Operational.* Is the system design such that it can and will receive the support of the people who must make it work?
- *Schedule.* Will it be possible to implement the system within the imposed time constraints?

The systems analyst gathers the information necessary to answer these questions. Upper-level managers are interviewed, records are analyzed, and library research is conducted. The intent is to gather the needed information in the shortest time possible and at the least cost.

6. Prepare a study project proposal. The systems analyst summarizes the findings up to this point in a *study project proposal.* If management decides that the MIS project should be continued, based on the feasibility study, it will be necessary to conduct a full-blown systems study. The *systems study* will provide the *detailed* basis for the design of the new system in terms of what it should do and how it should be done. The systems study will be conducted by the analyst or a team of analysts and will require several weeks or months of effort. The study will therefore involve a considerable expense. The executive vice president must approve this expense and should have some basis or support for the go-ahead decision. The study project proposal serves this purpose.

Figure 16-8 is a sample outline of the study project proposal. Sections 1 through 3 (introduction, problem, objectives and constraints) are developed jointly

---

[9]From John G. Burch, Jr., Felix R. Strater, and Gary Grudnitski, *Information Systems: Theory and Practice*, 3rd ed. (New York: John Wiley & Sons, 1983), pp. 341–342.

1. Introduction—reason for the proposal

2. Problem definition

3. System objectives and constraints

4. Possible alternatives

5. Recommended course of action
    a. Tasks to be accomplished
    b. Resource requirements
    c. Time schedule
    d. Cost recap

6. Anticipated results
    a. Organizational impact
    b. Operational impact
    c. Financial impact

7. General implementation plan

8. Study project objectives
    a. Tasks
    b. Budget

9. Summary

Figure 16-8 The study project proposal.

by the systems analyst and the executive vice president during the first four steps of the planning phase.

Sections 4 through 7 are developed by the systems analyst from the findings of the feasibility study. Section 4 identifies the possible system solutions, and each is briefly described. The analyst determines which alternative appears to be best suited for the particular situation, and that alternative is described in section 5, along with a brief explanation of the resources needed for implementation. *It is the manager's responsibility to decide which, if any, alternative to implement, but the systems analyst can, and should, recommend solutions.* The manager will apply his or her own judgment in deciding whether to accept the analyst's recommendation. Section 6 describes the effects, both positive and negative, on the firm and its operations of implementing the recommended system. Section 7 presents a general implementation plan.

The first seven sections of the proposal relate to the MIS. Section 8 relates to the study project leading to the MIS. In this section, the analyst identifies the tasks involved in conducting the study project and the funds needed.

The study project proposal is a preliminary report. Although the problem is defined in as much detail as possible, more will be learned as the study progresses.

The identified alternatives are stated generally—including the one recommended by the analyst. The purpose of the report is twofold:

1. To provide management with the information necessary to make a decision whether to continue with the project.
2. To provide the participants (managers and information specialists) with the objectives of the system study, assuming that approval is given.

Written copies of the study project proposal are given to executives who will influence the decision, such as all members of the steering committee. The systems analyst, or analysts, may also make a formal oral presentation, complete with visual aids.

7. *Approve or disapprove the study project.* In preparing the proposal, the analyst must be careful not to advocate an unjustified study. The facts should be reported honestly, with attention also given to the reasons why the study should not be conducted and to weaknesses in the proposed general design.

The executive vice president weighs the pros and cons of the proposed project and system design, and takes one of three actions as shown in Figure 16-9. First, the manager asks the question, "Do I have enough information?" If the answer is "no," he or she tells the analyst what additional information is needed. Once

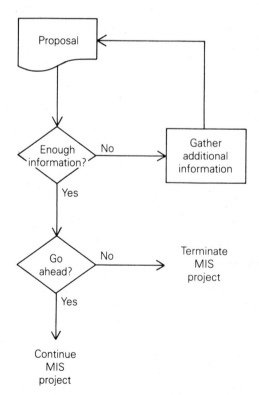

Figure 16-9 The "go/no go" decision.

the executive vice president feels that sufficient information is available, the *go/ no go decision* is made. If the decision is "go," the project proceeds to the study phase. If the decision is "no go," both the executive vice president and the systems analyst turn their attention to other matters.

As the executive vice president considers approving the project, two key questions are asked:

1. Will the proposed system solve identified problems or enable the firm to meet its objectives? These are the performance criteria—the basis for evaluating the performance of the MIS once it is implemented; they also should be the basis for evaluating the proposed MIS.

2. Is the proposed study project the best way to determine the specific design of the proposed MIS? There is no pat answer to this question. The executive vice president must be assured that the analysts have considered all of the feasible approaches to the study. If the executive vice president is to have this assurance, he or she must have an MIS literacy.

8. *Establish a control mechanism.* Before the study begins, the executive vice president must take steps to establish control over the project. Whereas the objective of the MIS is to satisfy the information needs of management, the objective of the MIS *project* is to produce the desired MIS within both cost and time constraints. Project control is the means of assuring that this end is met.

MIS Project Control

The executive vice president and the vice president of information services must work together closely to establish the control mechanism. They need a thorough understanding of the task ahead, which the vice president of information services can provide.

Basic ingredients of control

Two basic ingredients must exist if the executive vice president and the others in charge of the MIS project are to control it—performance standards and a system of progress reporting.

1. *Performance standards.* Standards of acceptable performance are established for three dimensions of the activity: time, cost, and quality. At this stage, the standards can be established only in general terms. This is especially true for the standard of quality.

2. *Progress reporting.* The vice president of information services is responsible for keeping the executive vice president up to date concerning the progress of the MIS project, which is done through scheduled meetings. The meetings usually are held weekly but can be supplemented by special sessions. The meetings take the form of progress reports by the vice president of information services.

Quite often, visual aids are used to illustrate what has been accomplished, what has not been accomplished and why, upcoming activities, and possible trouble spots. At a minimum, the meetings include the executive vice president and the vice president of information services. If a steering committee is formed, that group receives the reports. Other managers from functional areas as well as members of the information services staff are also invited to participate from time to time. The meetings employ management by exception in that the managers devote their attention to critical areas and do not dwell on things going as planned.

Detailed project control

Once the decision has been made to proceed with the systems study, the vice president of information services and the analyst or analyst team that is to conduct the study must plan it in detail. They must specify what needs to be done, who will do it, and when will it be done.

1. **What needs to be done?** The feasibility study produces a list of jobs for the MIS to perform. For example, in the marketing information system the jobs could include:

> *Product Subsystem*
> New-product evaluation model
> Product deletion model
> *Place Subsystem*
> Warehouse location model
> Warehouse layout model
> *Promotion Subsystem*
> Territory assignment model
> Advertising media scheduling model
> *Pricing Subsystem*
> Pricing model

2. **Who will do it?** The vice president of information services next decides who will be responsible for designing each of the subsystem models. The general design specifications identify the types of employees needed. For example, the two warehouse models will probably use linear programming. If a linear programming specialist is not presently on the staff, one will have to be added. The firm must acquire personnel who have the skills necessary to achieve the MIS.

3. **When will it be done?** The vice president of information services must establish a time schedule for the MIS project. Certain things will have to be done at specific times. For example, new computing equipment might have to be scheduled for delivery. The firm will want the equipment delivered when it can be used—not before and not after.

An example of a project schedule

The specification of the project in terms of what, who, and when enables a project schedule to be made. As an example, the following subtasks might be required to develop a model to support the marketing manager in making decisions concerning deletion of products from the line—a product deletion model.

1. Identify the processes that the appropriate marketing managers will use to make product deletion decisions.
2. Identify the information requirements of the managers making the deletion decision.
3. Identify the input data necessary to produce the required information.
4. Prepare documentation of the computer processing to convert input data to information output.
5. Code the program.
6. Test the program.
7. Obtain confirmation from the users that the model satisfies their information needs.
8. Implement the model.

The vice president of information services then determines who will perform each of the subtasks, and how long each should take. Table 16-2 illustrates the detailed schedule.

The time increment in the table is *person days*—the number of days that will be required for one person to accomplish the task. For example, it might be

Table 16-2 Detailed Subtask Planning

	Functional system: Marketing Subsystem: Product Model: Product deletion	
Subtask	**Responsibility**	**Time estimate (person days)**
1. Identify deletion criteria	Systems analyst and product manager	12
2. Identify output information requirements	Systems analyst and product manager	5
3. Identify input data requirements	Systems analyst	4
4. Prepare program documentation	Programmer	5
5. Code program	Programmer	16
6. Test program	Programmer and operations staff	10
7. Approve program performance	Product manager and vice president of marketing	7
8. Implement model	Operations staff	7

estimated that the product deletion model will require approximately 1000 lines of program code. If work standards indicate that a programmer can prepare fifty lines of code per day, the total coding time should be twenty person days. In *some* cases, the number of *calendar days*, the elapsed time from beginning to end, can be reduced by assigning more persons to the project. For example, coding might be accomplished in 10 calendar days by assigning two programmers. In not all cases, however, can calendar time be reduced by assigning more personnel. In the table, the total number of person days is 66, or 3 calendar months (assuming 22 working days per month).

The estimation of time duration is a semistructured problem. At this stage of the project, these estimates can be only broad approximations. They are based on the experience of the vice president of information services and the information services staff.

Monitoring project progress

Once the MIS project has been defined in detailed terms, the executive vice president has a basis for control. The next step is to document the project plan in a manner that will maintain control as work progresses.

There are a number of documentation techniques. The executive vice president and the vice president of information services select the one(s) with which they feel most comfortable. One technique is the *Gantt chart*, a product of the classical management school.

The Gantt chart in Figure 16-10 illustrates how the work on the seven marketing models is phased over time. During the progress report meetings, the

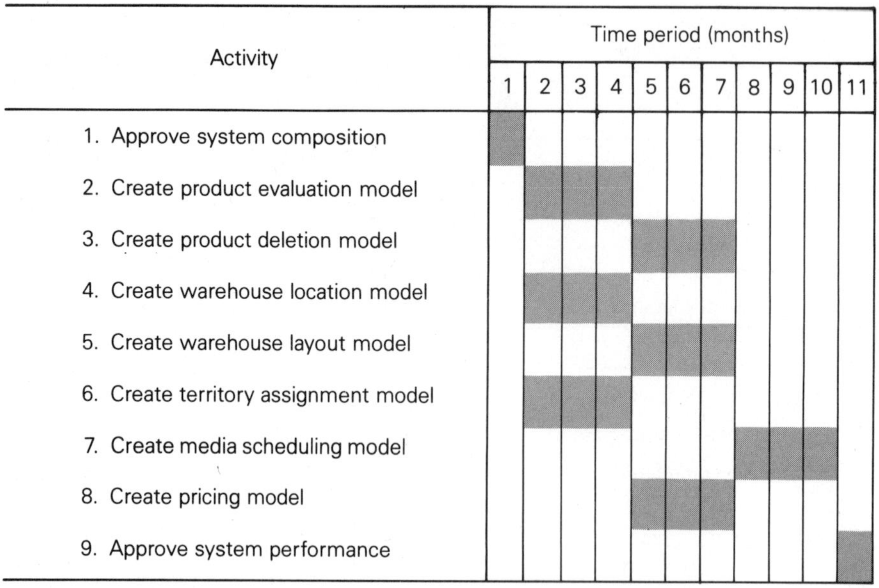

Figure 16-10 Gantt chart of marketing information system activity.

managers can use charts such as this to compare actual performance with the plan.

The main shortcoming of the Gantt chart is that it doesn't show how the activities interrelate. It doesn't explicitly show that work on the seven models (steps 2–8) cannot begin until the system composition is approved (step 1). Also, it doesn't show that the same information specialist may be assigned to more than one model.

These interrelationships can be represented by another documentation technique—*network analysis*. In network analysis, *activities* are represented by interconnected arrows to show how one relates to another. In Figure 16-11 the bars in the Gantt chart have been redrawn as interconnecting arrows. The network diagram shows that activity 9 cannot start until activities 3, 7, and 8 are completed. Activity 3 cannot start until activity 2 is completed, and so on.

The circles are called *nodes*, and they do more than simply connect the arrows. The nodes are numbered, as in Figure 16-12, to provide a better identification of the activities. Each activity has a unique pair of node numbers and is identified by those numbers. For example, when referring to the activity to create a new pricing model, you would speak of "activity 40–70."

Figure 16-12 also shows estimated times just below the arrows. These numbers can represent any time increment—days, weeks, or months. In this example they represent months. By adding up the times for each path through the network, we can identify the critical path. The *critical path* is the one requiring the most time, and it determines overall project time. In the example, the critical path connects nodes 10, 20, 50, 60, 70, and 80. This path requires eleven months. The upper path (nodes 10, 20, 30, 70, and 80) requires eight months, as does the lower path (nodes 10, 20, 40, 70, 80). The upper and lower paths thus allow for extra time, called *slack*. Both the upper and lower paths contain three months of slack. Work in activities 20–30 and 30–70 could be delayed up to a total of three

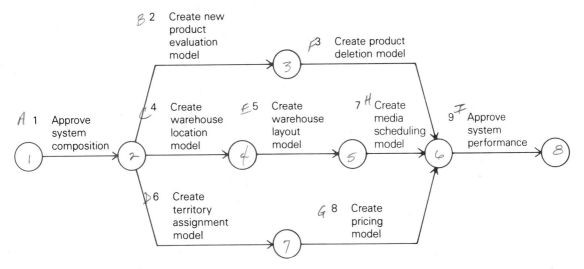

Figure 16-11 Network diagram of marketing information system activity.

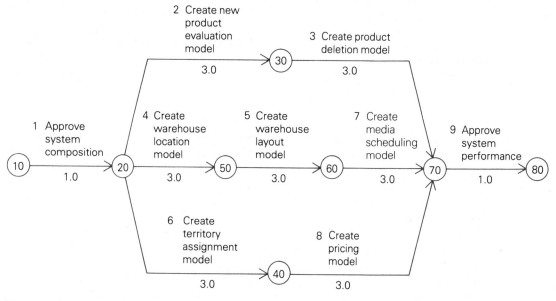

Figure 16-12 Network diagram with node numbers and activity times.

months without affecting project time. The same holds true for activities 20–40 and 40–70. There is no slack along the critical path; that is its distinguishing characteristic.

Figure 16-12 is an example of a *Critical-Path Method (CPM)* network. CPM uses a single time estimate for each activity. The other popular type of network is the *Program Evaluation and Review Technique (PERT)* chart. PERT differs from CPM in using three time estimates—optimistic (T_o), most likely (T_m), and pessimistic (T_p). A formula is used to weigh the most likely estimate more heavily than the pessimistic and optimistic.

$$\text{Activity time} = \frac{T_o + 4T_m + T_p}{6}$$

For example, if T_o = 1.2 weeks, T_m = 4.0 weeks, and T_p = 5.0 weeks, the activity time would be

$$\frac{1.2 + 16.0 + 5.0}{6} = \frac{22.2}{6} = 3.7 \text{ weeks}$$

The real value of the network method is the imposed discipline of requiring that a project be planned in detail before work begins. The networks for small MIS projects can be drawn by hand, and the critical-path calculations made with an electronic calculator. For large projects, a computer-based network package is very helpful. The computer package makes it easy to update the network—a real advantage. Also, the computer can compute the *start date* and the *completion date* for each activity. You specify when the project will begin, and the software computes the dates. For example, if you specify that the product deletion model project will begin on January 10, the network package will compute the dates shown in Figure 16-13. The *early dates* specify the earliest that the activities can be started and completed, assuming no slack in the network. The *late dates* are those for start and completion when the slack is utilized. The slack is the amount of time between the early and late dates, either start or completion.

Project management software

Companies began using network analysis for project control during the first computer generation. Construction firms used CPM or PERT to schedule projects such as building bridges and highways. Those early users had to code their programs using procedural languages, most often FORTRAN. Before long, project management packages came onto the market. These packages, written for mainframes, were offered by both hardware and software vendors.[10]

One of the most popular of the mainframe packages has been EZPERT from Systonetics, Inc. An example of the EZPERT output appears in Figure 16-14. This is a Gantt chart. You can also obtain a network diagram. Both are produced by a plotter.

As you would expect, this has been an area for micro software activity as well. There are more than 25 such packages for the IBM PC alone. Most of the packages can handle only a limited number of activities, such as 200 or 250. One of the more popular packages, the Harvard Project Manager by Harvard Software Inc., fits into this category. A few other packages can handle several thousand activities and therefore offer no real constraints in this regard—at least for projects of realistic size.

The micro packages are interactive, facilitating the what-if game. The mainframe packages are basically batch oriented. The micro packages print the same

NODE NUMBERS	ACTIVITY	TIME	EARLY START	LATE START	EARLY COMPLETION	LATE COMPLETION	SLACK
10-20	APPROVE COMPOSITION	1.0	1/10	1/10	2/10	2/10	0
20-30	NEW PRODUCT MODEL	3.0	2/10	5/10	5/10	8/10	3
20-40	TERRITORY ASSIGNMENT MODEL	3.0	2/10	5/10	5/10	8/10	3
20-50	WAREHOUSE LOCATION MODEL	3.0	2/10	2/10	5/10	5/10	0
30-70	PRODUCT DELETION MODEL	3.0	5/10	8/10	8/10	11/10	3
40-70	PRICING MODEL	3.0	5/10	8/10	8/10	11/10	3
50-60	WAREHOUSE LAYOUT MODEL	3.0	5/10	5/10	8/10	8/10	0
60-70	MEDIA SCHEDULING MODEL	3.0	8/10	8/10	11/10	11/10	0
70-80	APPROVE SYSTEM	1.0	11/10	11/10	12/10	12/10	0

Figure 16-13 Project calendar printed by a network software package.

---

[10] For a review of these mainframe project management packages, see Perry Petersen, "Project Control Systems," *Datamation* 25 (June 1979): 147ff.

SYSTONETICS INCORPORATED
801 EAST CHAPMAN AVENUE, SUITE 201
FULLERTON, CALIFORNIA 92631

NETWORK CHRI | SUBNET CAG
SAMPLE PLOTS FOR BANK SYSTEM
SYSTONETICS DEVELOPMENT GROUP
RUN DATE 30JUN82 | DATA DATE 28JUN82
WEEKLY BARCHART, CRITICAL PATH HIGHLIGHT
DRAWN BY EZPERT, PATENT 3684871, SYSTONETICS INC.

PLANNED BY DATE

APPROVED BY DATE

LOCATION
PAGE 1 OF 1 SHEET 1 OF 1
SYMBOLS
START OR FINISH △
ACTUAL START OR FINISH ▲
LATE FINISH ▽
DURATION (NON CRITICAL)
DURATION (CRITICAL)
TOTAL FLOAT
PROGRESS

PRED NAME	SUCC NAME	ACTIVITY DESCRIPTION	TIME EST.	TOTAL FLOAT	EARLY START	EARLY FINISH	LATE FINISH
5	10	RECEIVE INVITATION TO STUDY	7	0	28JUN82	04JUL82	04JUL82
10	15	DEVELOP SCOPE OF STUDY	14	0	05JUL82	18JUL82	18JUL82
15	20	DEVELOP DETAILED PLAN	7	0	19JUL82	25JUL82	25JUL82
15	25	ORGANIZE STUDY TEAM	7	7	19JUL82	25JUL82	01AUG82
20	25	PREPARE NETWORK DIAGRAM	7	0	26JUL82	01AUG82	01AUG82
25	30	ASSIGN TASK RESPONSIBILITY	4	0	02AUG82	05AUG82	05AUG82
30	35	STUDY FIRM'S ENVIRONMENT	21	0	06AUG82	26AUG82	26AUG82
30	40	STUDY POLICIES AND PRACTICES	7	7	06AUG82	12AUG82	19AUG82
30	45	STUDY ORGANIZATION STRUCTURE	7	17	06AUG82	12AUG82	29AUG82
30	65	STUDY COMPANY HISTORY	7	21	06AUG82	12AUG82	02SEP82
40	50	IDENTIFY INPUTS	7	14	13AUG82	19AUG82	02SEP82
40	55	IDENTIFY OUTPUTS	7	14	13AUG82	19AUG82	02SEP82
40	60	IDENTIFY PROCESSES	14	7	13AUG82	26AUG82	02SEP82
40	65	IDENTIFY RESOURCES	4	17	13AUG82	16AUG82	02SEP82
45	65	PREPARE ORGANIZATION CHART	4	17	13AUG82	16AUG82	02SEP82
50	65	DUMMY	0	14	20AUG82	20AUG82	03SEP82
55	65	DUMMY	0	14	20AUG82	20AUG82	03SEP82
35	65	PREPARE MODEL OF FIRM'S ENVIRONMENT	7	0	27AUG82	02SEP82	02SEP82
60	65	DUMMY	0	7	27AUG82	27AUG82	03SEP82
65	70	PREPARE MODEL OF FIRM AS A SYSTEM	7	0	03SEP82	09SEP82	09SEP82
70	75	GATHER COST DATA	7	17	10SEP82	16SEP82	03OCT82
70	80	STUDY AND DOCUMENT DEMAND DEPOSIT SYSTEM	25	3	10SEP82	04OCT82	07OCT82
70	85	STUDY AND DOCUMENT LOAN SYSTEM	18	10	10SEP82	27SEP82	07OCT82
70	90	STUDY AND DOCUMENT TRUST SYSTEM	21	7	10SEP82	30SEP82	07OCT82
70	95	STUDY AND DOCUMENT TIME DEPOSIT SYSTEM	28	0	10SEP82	07OCT82	07OCT82
75	95	PREPARE COST DETERMINATION SHEET	4	17	17SEP82	20SEP82	07OCT82
85	95	DUMMY	0	10	28SEP82	28SEP82	08OCT82
90	95	DUMMY	0	7	01OCT82	01OCT82	08OCT82
80	95	DUMMY	0	3	05OCT82	05OCT82	08OCT82
95	100	ANALYZE FINDINGS	14	0	08OCT82	21OCT82	21OCT82
100	105	PREPARE MANAGEMENT REPORT	14	0	22OCT82	04NOV82	04NOV82
105	110	RECEIVE APPROVAL TO CONTINUE	7	0	05NOV82	11NOV82	11NOV82

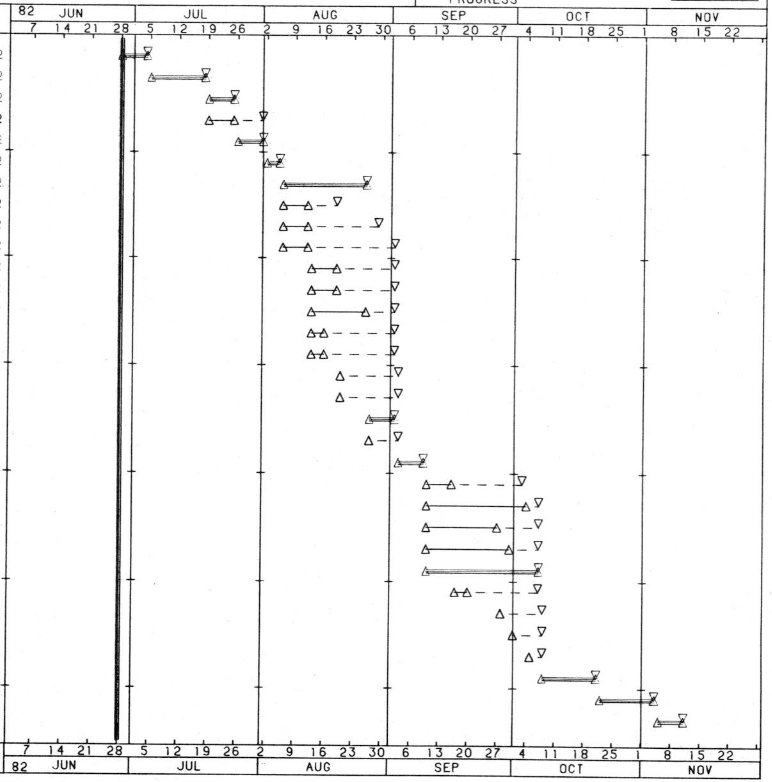

Figure 16-14 A plotted graph of network data.

outputs as those for the mainframes—Gantt charts and network diagrams. The graphics can be produced on a matrix printer with a graphics capability—either across the width of the paper or lengthwise (for long charts).

Computerized network analysis is an excellent control mechanism for complex projects. The availability of micro-based packages means that even the smallest firms can use this approach.

MIS Project Selection

Before we conclude the discussion of the planning phase, some comments relative to MIS project selection are in order.

Factors affecting priorities

Most information services departments have more work than they can handle. Management therefore must decide whether to embark on an MIS project and, if so, its sequence among other projects. Project priority can be affected by several factors.

- *Risk.* Early computer users first installed the applications that they knew best—payroll and inventory. These projects offered the least risk of failure. The failure might be reflected in a cost overrun, a missed implementation schedule, or a system that does not perform as intended. This practice of favoring low-risk projects has been continued, even involving DSS applications. It is called *cherry picking.*

Management does not always pick the project with least risk. In some instances, a risky project will be initiated because the possible benefits are so great. MIS projects that will provide the firm with an advantage over its competitors are of this type.[11]

- *Logical sequence.* It might be necessary to install one system before another. For example, if the order entry system uses information from the accounts receivable file in making a credit check, it might be advantageous to first install the accounts receivable system.
- *Competence of information services.* Any limits on the technical abilities of the information services staff should be regarded as constraints. A project should not be attempted if it requires skills that the staff does not possess. This factor is more likely to affect DSS projects than data processing where the skills are more basic.

---

[11] A good discussion of project risk can be found in F. Warren McFarland, "Portfolio Approach to Information Systems," *Harvard Business Review* 59 (September–October 1981): 142–150.

- *Financial benefits*. Some MIS projects are initiated in an effort to produce measurable financial benefits— reduced costs or increased profits. These benefits are estimated during the feasibility study.

- *Intangible benefits*. Most MIS projects do not lend themselves to quantification of the benefits. The underlying objective of most projects is "better information," and that is difficult to measure in dollars and cents. Several approaches have been advocated for estimating the value of information— incremental analysis, expected value, value analysis, cost-benefit analysis, and weighted scoring.[12] Peter Keen explains the difficulty of the task even when these approaches are used.

   "In managerial tasks there is rarely a clear link between decisions and outcomes, and a DSS can be expected to *contribute* to better financial performance, but not directly cause it. In general, managers describe a successful DSS as 'indispensable' without trying to place an economic value on it."[13]

The fact of the matter is that decisions relating to MIS projects are made with less than perfect information. The decisions are semistructured, and managers subjectively weigh the factors that cannot be quantified. In this respect, justification of the MIS is no different from most challenges that managers face.

Summary

As firms become more experienced in computer use, they progress through various stages. Nolan's model identifies the stages as initiation, contagion, control, integration, data administration, and maturity.

Responsibility for planning an MIS project should be placed in the hands of an executive. The project is important enough to justify such high-level attention. The responsible person should be someone who can represent *all* of the MIS users. The ideal person to have this responsibility is a top executive with total-firm interests and involvement, such as the executive vice president.

The stimulus for initiating an MIS project can originate anywhere—even outside the firm. More likely than not, however, the stimulus will come from a user rather than an information specialist.

Small firms can follow the same steps that have been proven by large firms to lead to successful systems. Small firms, however, usually cannot match the specialized resources applied by the large firms.

---

[12] For details on these approaches, see Robert D. Smith, "Measuring the Intangible Benefits of Computer-Based Information Systems," *Journal of Systems Management* 34 (September 1983): 22–27; Robert T. Keim and Ralph Janaro, "Cost/Benefit Analysis of MIS," *Journal of Systems Management* 33 (September 1982): 20–25; and Peter G. W. Keen, "Value Analysis: Justifying Decision Support Systems," *MIS Quarterly* 5 (March 1981): 1–15.

[13] Keen, p. 9.

Managers plan for four reasons—to identify necessary tasks, to recognize potential problems, to arrange tasks in sequence, and to provide a basis for control.

MIS projects can have either an objective or a problem orientation. A major project usually evolves from the firm's objectives. A minor project can be undertaken to solve one or more specific problems.

The total study approach to identifying MIS objectives assumes that the firm's objectives will be met if the managers receive the information that they need. Strategy set transformation is a top-down evolution of MIS strategy based on an understanding of both internal and environmental influences on the firm. Critical success factors are those few indicators of successful performance by the firm that management should monitor continually. An MIS can be designed to provide measures of CSF performance.

The performance of the MIS will be evaluated once it becomes operational. It is well to identify the performance criteria before the design process begins. The performance criteria are derived naturally from the firm's objectives and the manager's information needs.

Planning an MIS project requires that the executive vice president, the vice president of information services, and the systems analyst or analysts follow eight steps. The first four steps determine the objectives of the MIS and identify its constraints. These steps are the responsibility of the executive vice president, but assistance is provided by the vice president of information services and the systems analysts. The information specialists then conduct a feasibility study and prepare a study project proposal. If the proposal is approved, a control mechanism for the project is established jointly by the two vice presidents.

The vice president of information services and the systems analysts divide each task into subtasks, assign responsibility, and estimate the time requirements. These details provide the basis for project control. Graphical techniques, such as Gantt charts and network diagrams, provide a useful means of tracking the progress of MIS development.

Management usually has to select from multiple MIS projects. Once a project is selected for implementation, it must be given a priority relative to the other projects. Factors influencing the priority are the degree of risk, logical sequence, competence of information services, financial benefits, and intangible benefits. In the final analysis, much of the MIS project selection decision is based to a large degree on intangibles.

Key Terms

Nolan's stage model	problem orientation
MIS project	total study approach
executive vice president	strategy set transformation
administrative vice president	organizational information set
steering committee	MIS strategy set
objective orientation	critical success factors (CSF)

performance criteria

feasibility study

study project proposal

systems study

go/no go decision

person day

calendar day

Gantt chart

network analysis

activity

node

critical path

slack

CPM (critical path method)

PERT (program evaluation and
  review technique)

start date

completion date

cherry picking

Key Concepts

How the concept of a life cycle can be applied to (1) the long-term evolution of an MIS through stages of growth, and (2) the sequence of events incorporated into an MIS project

The use of the term "MIS project" to describe systems efforts of all sizes

The way that planning evolves from the general to the detailed as more is learned about the project

How the initiation of a project can originate both from within and outside the firm

The importance of MIS project leadership representing user interests, and including top-management participation

How the control mechanism evolves from planning

How the firm's objectives influence objectives for the entire MIS

activity, and also for large-scale MIS projects

The problem-solving orientation of smaller MIS projects

The chain reaction leading from objectives to information needs to MIS performance criteria

How MIS project planning corresponds to problem definition in the systems approach

The go/no go option that the manager has for proceeding into the next phase of the life cycle

The development of a detailed plan by answering the questions What?, Who?, and When? in that order

The multiple factors that can influence MIS project selection

The commitment to invest heavily in MIS based largely on intangible benefits

Questions

1. What are the six stages in Nolan's model? At what point does management become interested in DSS?

2. What is meant by the term "MIS project"?

3. From where can the stimulus to initiate an MIS project originate?

4. What advantage does a small firm today have over a large firm years ago in implementing an MIS? What disadvantage does the small firm have?

5. Must a small firm generally take the same implementation steps as a large one?

6. Why is the executive vice president a good person to manage the MIS project?

7. What functions does a steering committee perform?

8. What are the advantages of using a steering committee?

9. What are the benefits of planning?

10. Distinguish between an objective and a problem orientation.

11. Describe the process for deriving the data dictionary from CSFs.

12. Which management level might have difficulty in conceptualizing CSFs? If so, which planning approach would you use?

13. What does the term *performance criteria* mean? Describe how the criteria are derived.

14. Distinguish between a "feasibility study" and a "systems study."

15. What are five dimensions of feasibility? Which one would apply to an IRS regulation that employee earnings be reported quarterly?

16. Why is a study project proposal prepared?

17. What two questions does the executive vice president ask as the study project proposal is evaluated?

18. Would a weekly status report from the vice president of information services to the executive vice president be an example of a control mechanism? Explain.

19. What are the two basic ingredients of project control?

20. How does CPM differ from PERT?

Problems

---

1. Using the activity times in the diagram, (1) determine total project time, and (2) identify the critical path. Time is expressed in days.

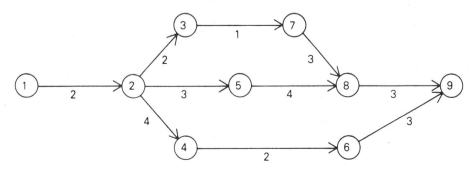

2. Using the following pessimistic (T_p), most likely (T_m), and optimistic (T_o) times, compute total project time for the diagram in problem 1. What is the critical path?

Activity	T_p	T_m	T_o
1-2	3	2	1
2-3	3	2	2
2-4	5	3	2
2-5	4	3	2
3-7	2	1	1
4-6	4	2	1
5-8	7	3	1
6-9	5	3	2
7-8	4	3	3
8-9	4	3	2

3. Draw a critical path diagram of an Indianapolis 500 pit stop. After the car stops, one crew member gives the driver a drink and then cleans the windshield. After the car is raised off the ground, one crew member fills the gas tank, and four members each remove a wheel and replace the removed wheel with a new one. When the wheels have been replaced and the gas tank filled, the car is lowered to the ground. The car then resumes the race.

CASE PROBLEM: Berry Geophysical Exploration

Berry Geophysical Exploration of Midland, Texas, installed their first computer in the late 1960s to do computations on seismic data. Over the years their level of computer use expanded, and today a VAX 11-780 super mini is installed to do both scientific computing and data processing. About a year ago, John Berry, the president, decided to emphasize MIS applications and asked Myrtle Renfro, the vice president of finance, to "get the ball rolling." Berry selected Renfro because she knew computers—her undergraduate degree was in computer science. In addition, Myrtle had earned a reputation of always putting the company first. She had earned the respect and friendship of the other executives at Berry by always being willing to cooperate on issues affecting multiple departments.

Even though Renfro was technically qualified, she didn't solicit the MIS assignment. Her reaction to Berry's offer was "Shouldn't that go to Bert? He's the executive vice president. He would seem to be the likely person." Only when Berry assured her that he had given the matter much thought, and was certain of his choice, did Renfro accept.

Berry asked Renfro to "look into MIS," and the two could get back together in a couple of weeks. When they finally met in Berry's office, John got right to the point: "Who is going to be on your steering committee?"

John seemed startled when Renfro replied that she "decided that would not be necessary." She went on to explain that she wanted to meet informally with John and Buzz Dockery, the director of computing, and then bring in other managers and employees as needed.

John didn't object, and the talk turned to the computer and how it could be used to better support the Berry management team. Renfro spent a good hour detailing the shortcomings of the existing system.

At one point Berry interrupted, "This really sounds depressing. You make it sound like we don't really have an MIS."

"That's right," Renfro replied. "What we really have is a data processing system."

"Well, just how do you plan to go about giving us an MIS?" Berry asked.

Myrtle replied, "I thought that I would make a list of all the problems. Actually, I've already started. Then, we could prioritize them to identify what we should do first. I think we've got enough work to keep us busy for the next five years."

For about a month, the three (Berry, Renfro, and Dockery) met each week in Berry's office. The sessions were productive, and a clearer picture of the MIS began to take shape. But it became more and more difficult for Berry to attend the meetings. His schedule was so busy that he missed more than he attended. Finally, he told Renfro: "Myrtle, you're just going to have to go on without me. You can just keep me posted from time to time concerning what progress you're making. If you ever need my input, you know where to find me."

Assignment

1. Make a list of the errors made in planning the Berry MIS.
2. For each error, write a brief explanation of how it should have been done.

CASE PROBLEM: Saito Electric Corp.

Saito Electric is one of Japan's largest manufacturers of electric and electronic consumer products, including sound recorders, kitchen appliances, and power tools. You are the manager of systems analysis, reporting to Mr. Kiyoshi Hoshina, vice president of computer services. In your weekly planning meeting with Mr. Hoshina and the other computer managers, you learn that top management wishes to establish some performance criteria for the computer division. Mr. Hoshina has given you the task of establishing the standards for the firm's manufacturing information system.

When you get back to your office, you look at your copy of the Saito long-range plan and review the firm's objectives. You find them to be stated in very general terms—"to offer a balanced package of consumer products . . . to maintain a position of leadership . . . to identify new consumer needs . . . to strengthen and maintain community and employee relationships . . . ."

You know that the company objectives are the place to start, but you feel that they are too broad to be of specific help on your assignment. You decide that the next source of information is Mr. Mitsu Saito, vice president of manufacturing. You make an appointment and, after a brief discussion of the weather, ask Mr. Saito about the objectives of the manufacturing division. He opens a desk drawer, retrieves a small notebook, and begins to read: "To make efficient use of manufacturing resources. To maintain production quality at the established level. To manufacture the right quantity at the right time for the firm to meet its sales forecast. To provide safe working conditions for all employees."

As Mr. Saito puts down the notebook, you are still not convinced that you have gotten the specifics that you need. You ask Mr. Saito, "Could you describe how the computer group might help you meet your objectives?"

Mr. Saito replies, "For us to meet our objective of efficient resource use, we must first know what resources we will need. We get this from our material requirements and capacity requirements planning models. Our production scheduling model permits us to have the right quantity at the right time. We achieve our quality objective primarily by selecting vendors who provide high-quality raw materials. We pursue our objective of worker safety by receiving statistics on accidents so that they might be anticipated and prevented."

Now you're getting somewhere. But you still need more specifics before you can begin to put together performance criteria. You ask Mr. Saito exactly what he expects from his MRP, capacity requirements, and scheduling systems: "Is it enough that we simply have those models available?"

"Of course not," Mr. Saito replies. "The models must be accurate. They must be able to handle our volume and variety of production. They must be designed in such a manner that we can use them as frequently as we like, from terminals in our offices, without running up unreasonable computer charges."

"Fine," you say as you jot down some notes. "But what about vendor selection? How should the MIS support you in that area?"

"First," Mr. Saito explains, "we must have in our data base up-to-date financial information on each vendor. Second, we must have an up-to-date price list for each of our vendors. And third, we must be able to query the data base and retrieve summary reports showing the quality records of each vendor's shipment."

"Excellent," you respond, confident you are on the right track. "One more point—what about the safety statistics?"

Mr. Saito adjusts his tie as he talks. "Right now we're getting monthly reports on accidents—where they happen, when, the cause, and the resulting cost in lost production hours so that each department can be ranked by its safety record. We could implement a reward system as a means of making our supervisors more sensitive to the safety issue. I would like to be able to get a weekly status report comparing the safety records of each department."

Before you can thank Mr. Saito for his time, he gets up from his chair and leads you out of his office, explaining, "You must excuse me. I must meet a group of Americans who want to tour our plant. They are very interested in learning as much as possible about our methods and most likely will want to take some pictures. Please come back again when you have developed your performance criteria. I will tell you if you are on the right track. *Sayonara*."

Questions

1. Was it a waste of your time to start by reading the company's objectives?

2. Is Mr. Saito using the MIS to meet manufacturing objectives? Explain your answer.

3. State the general performance criteria for the MRP, capacity requirements, and scheduling systems. Hint: Review Figure 16-6. Mr. Saito has summarized his information needs. Review each of his comments about the three systems. Prepare a general performance criteria statement for each, such as "The MRP model must accurately project material needs."

4. State the criteria for the vendor information portion of the manufacturing intelligence subsystem in the same manner.

5. State the criteria for the safety-reporting system.

Selected Bibliography

Planning and Controlling the MIS Project

Anderson, Robert E., and Raymond K. Cornbill, "When Strategic Information Planning and Management Misses the Mark," *Information Strategy* 1 (Winter 1985): 23–27.

Boynton, Andrew C., and Robert W. Zmud, "An Assessment of Critical Success Factors," *Sloan Management Review* 25 (Summer 1984): 17–27.

Bryan, Shawn, "A Plan for All Reasons," *PC Products* 2 (January 1985): 41ff.

Buss, Martin D. J., "How to Rank Computer Projects," *Harvard Business Review* 61 (January-February 1983): 118–125.

Doll, William, and Mesbah V. Ahmed, "Tradeoffs in Selecting an Executive Steering Committee," *Journal of Systems Management* 35 (January 1984): 6–11.

Drury, D. H., "An Empirical Assessment of the Stages of DP Growth," *MIS Quarterly* 7 (June 1983): 59–70.

Drury, D. H., "An Evaluation of Data Processing Steering Committees," *MIS Quarterly*, 8 (December 1984): 257–265.

Gibson, Cyrus F., and Richard L. Nolan, "Managing the Four Stages of EDP Growth," *Harvard Business Review* 52 (January-February 1974): 76–88.

Howitt, Doran, "Project Management Programs Gain," *InfoWorld* 7 (April 1, 1985): 32–35.

Johnson, James R., "Enterprise Analysis," *Datamation* 30 (December 15, 1984): 97ff.

Keim, Robert T., and Ralph Janaro, "Cost/Benefit Analysis of MIS," *Journal of Systems Management* 33 (September 1982): 20–25.

Keen, Peter G. W., "Value Analysis: Justifying Decision Support Systems," *MIS Quarterly* 5 (March 1981): 1–15.

King, John Leslie, and Kenneth L. Kraemer, "Evolution and Organizational Information Systems: An Assessment of Nolan's Stage Model," *Communications of the ACM* 27 (May 1984): 466–475.

King, William R., "Strategic Planning for Management Information Systems," *MIS Quarterly* 2 (March 1978): 27–37.

Krakow, Ira H., "Three Project Managers: Schedules for Success," *Business Computer Systems* 4 (March 1985): 103ff.

Lustman, Francois, "Project Management in a Small Organization," *Journal of Systems Management* 34 (December 1983): 15–21.

McFarlan, F. Warren, "Portfolio Approach to Information Systems," *Harvard Business Review* 59 (September-October 1981): 142–150.

McFarlan, F. Warren, James L. McKenney, and Philip Pyburn, "The Information Archipelago—Plotting a Course," *Harvard Business Review* 61 (January-February 1983): 145–156.

Melone, N. Paule, and T. J. Wharton, "Strategies for MIS Project Selection," *Journal of Systems Management* 35 (February 1984): 26–33.

Munro, Malcolm C., and Basil R. Wheeler, "Planning, Critical Success Factors, and Management's Information Requirements," *MIS Quarterly* 4 (December 1980): 27–38.

Nocentini, Stefano, "The Planning Ritual," *Datamation* 31 (April 15, 1985): 122ff.

Nolan, Richard L., "Managing the Crises in Data Processing," *Harvard Business Review* 57 (March-April 1979): 115–126.

Nolan, Richard L. "Managing Information Systems by Committee," *Harvard Business Review* 60 (July-August 1982): 72–79.

Robinson, David G., "Synchronizing Systems With Business Values," *Datamation* 30 (June 15, 1984): 152ff.

Rockart, John F., "Chief Executives Define Their Own Data Needs," *Harvard Business Review* 57 (March-April 1979): 81–93.

Rockart, John F., and Adam D. Crescenzi, "Engaging Top Management in Information Technology," *Sloan Management Review* 25 (Summer 1984): 3–16.

Smith, Robert D., "Measuring the Intangible Benefits of Computer-Based Information Systems," *Journal of Systems Management* 34 (September 1983): 22–27.

Wysong, Earl M., Jr., "Using the Internal Auditor for System Design Projects," *Journal of Systems Management* 34 (July 1983): 28–32.

Zani, William M., "Blueprint for MIS," *Harvard Business Review* 48 (November-December 1970): 95–100.

Chapter 17

Implementing the MIS

Learning Objectives

After studying this chapter, you should:

- Know more about information specialists, and how they are organized to develop and maintain information systems
- Understand the importance of communication in the design of an MIS, and ways to minimize communication breakdown
- Understand how the system study evolves in steps, taken jointly by managers and information specialists
- Understand how the systems analyst identifies the manager's information needs
- See how specific MIS performance criteria are derived from the general statements developed during the planning phase
- Understand how a computer configuration is determined
- Know what is included in system and program documentation, and how it is organized
- Appreciate the need for system documentation
- Understand why implementation can be planned in greater detail after the analysis and design phase has been completed
- Recognize how the "make-or-buy" software decision influences the sequence of implementation steps
- Know one way to introduce more structure into the make-or-buy decision
- Understand the process of requesting and evaluating vendor hardware and software proposals
- Recognize the role of the DBA in developing the data base
- Recognize three approaches for cutting over to the new system
- Have an understanding of prototyping—what it is, its strengths and weaknesses, and the effect that it might have on the traditional system life cycle concept

Introduction

The previous chapter described the role of the firm's management in planning and controlling the MIS project. In this chapter, the emphasis shifts to the work performed by the information services staff.

Although this chapter focuses on the information services staff, it is important to understand that their work is aimed at creating an MIS to meet the managers' needs. It is the responsibility of the managers, through the executive vice president or steering committee, to exercise control over the work. In addition to playing a role in the planning and control of the MIS project, managers play an active part in the analysis and design of the MIS. Managers must communicate their exact information needs to the information services staff.

The purpose of this chapter is to help you understand the work of the information services staff. Subsequent chapters will again take up the manager's perspective.

The Information Services Staff

Throughout the text we have included descriptions of the information services staff—its organization and responsibilities. In Chapter 1 we described the "communication chain" that links the user to the computer by means of the information specialists—systems analysts, programmers, and operators. (See Figure 1-15.) In Chapter 7 we described the duties of the DBA, and in Chapter 8 we included a description of the network manager. In the previous chapter we described the role of the vice president of information services and systems analysts in planning and controlling the MIS project.

The MIS project includes the work that creates an MIS to meet the objectives identified by the firm's management. It is the responsibility of the vice president of information services to see that this work is carried out in the prescribed manner and that the schedule is followed. As the work is performed over a period of months, the vice president of information services reports the progress to the executive vice president or the steering committee. As problems arise, actions are taken to get the project back on course.

Refer back to Figure 5-26 for an organizational chart showing all of the information specialists. In the sections below, we briefly describe the operator, programmer, and systems analyst.

The operator

A microcomputer requires only a single *operator*, while a mini or mainframe can require three or four. The operators communicate instructions to the computer through the console, mount and dismount tape reels and disk packs, and put the correct paper forms in the printer.

The operators are part of the computer operations department. In addition to those working directly with the computer, other members of the operations department operate key-driven data entry machines, maintain controls over computer input and output, schedule jobs on the computer, and maintain library files of tapes and disk packs.

The programmer

The *programmer* has the important responsibility of translating the systems analyst's description of system processes into a form that the computer can understand. This translation is accomplished with the *program*—the list of instructions that specifies the computer processes and their sequence. If the computer is to do what is expected, the program must be accurate. Before a program is put into operational use, the programmer subjects it to many tests to assure that it contains no errors, or "bugs."

Larger firms usually have more than one programmer. In some cases, each programmer specializes in writing certain types of programs. For instance, a programmer might specialize in writing programs for marketing or accounting. Smaller firms may have only a single programmer, or none at all. Perhaps one or more employees have programming as a part-time responsibility.

The systems analyst

It is the responsibility of the *systems analyst* to define the computer solution to a problem. The systems analyst must gain an understanding of the problem from the manager. In some cases, the manager knows precisely what is needed. In other cases, the analyst serves as a catalyst by informing the manager of the kinds of information available.

The systems analyst uses a variety of information-gathering methods in an effort to understand the manager's problem. These methods include interview, observation, data search, and survey. The information that is gathered provides the analyst with a sufficient understanding of the manager's needs to develop a computer approach to the solution. Once the approach is defined, it is communicated to the programmer. This communication is accomplished both verbally and in writing. Much of the written communication incorporates diagrams and tables.

The programmer analyst

The jobs of systems analyst and programmer are not separated in all firms. One person often performs both jobs, particularly in small firms. When the jobs are combined, the position is called *programmer analyst*.

In many large organizations one person does both jobs. These are organizations where the computer applications are not too complex for one person to handle the analysis, design, and programming duties. In other industries the applications are so complex that they require one person to do the analysis and design work and someone else to do the programming.

Organization of the information services staff

The organization chart in Figure 5-26 is only one approach. It divides analysts and programmers into two groups. One group is responsible for *systems development*—the creation of new systems. The other group is responsible for *systems maintenance*—the updating of systems already in use.

Another approach is to organize analysts and programmers into teams based on the problems to be solved. As an example, an "inventory system team" might implement a new inventory system, or a "marketing information system team" might have that system as their responsibility.

Whatever the organizational arrangement, the information services staff must interact with managers on different levels and in different functional areas.

The communication problem

The design of an MIS requires two broad types of knowledge: management and information systems. The manager furnishes the management knowledge, and the systems analyst furnishes the information systems knowledge. Representatives from these two areas must communicate, and this is not always easy. Both areas have their separate jargon, educational and career development paths, and professional interests. At some point, however, these two bodies of knowledge and experience must come together. That point is the personal interaction between the manager and the systems analyst. This is potentially the weakest link in the communication chain. If it breaks, no further communication is possible.

Solving the communication problem

Both the analyst and the manager can take steps to assure that the communication link between them does not break. They can both learn as much about each other's job as possible. This effort provides a shared knowledge that can form the basis for a strong communication tie. Much of this shared knowledge can be gained in college and university programs in management and computer science. The remainder is gained through experience by jointly solving business problems.

Another approach to solving the communication problem is to eliminate the need for information specialists. If the manager can communicate directly with the computer, there is no need to use information specialists as intermediaries. This approach, called *end-user computing*, is becoming increasingly popular. The manager prepares the programs (the written communication) and then executes them on the computer or terminal by performing the necessary operating tasks (the physical communication). The computer responds with the information in written or displayed form.

Career opportunities in information services

End-user computing will no doubt have an effect on career opportunities in information services. Users will gradually become more self-sufficient in building their own DSS models, querying the data base, and even designing their own reports.

The users will not be doing all of their own work, however. They will continue to rely on information services to design and (primarily) maintain data processing systems and to develop more complex DSS models.

There will still be opportunities for persons entering the computer field who are intelligent, energetic, and innovative—particularly in the area of decision support.

The Analysis and Design Phase

The preceding chapter described the planning phase of the MIS life cycle and explained how the executive vice president and the vice president of information services worked together. A study project proposal was prepared and approved, and a control mechanism was established. As the analysis and design phase proceeds, the executive vice president retains overall control, but the work of the information services staff is the responsibility of the vice president of information services. Figure 17-1 illustrates how these two executives continue to work together.

The bulk of the work in this phase is performed by the systems analyst(s). A systems study is conducted in steps 3 and 4 to define the needs. This is the *systems analysis* activity. Then a system is designed in steps 5 through 8 to meet the defined needs. This is the *systems design* activity. When the design work is completed, the analysts, under the direction of the vice president of information services, prepare a second proposal. This proposal recommends the continuation of the project through implementation.

It is unlikely that a firm would get this far and then decide to drop the project completely, but it is possible. Very little is known in the beginning about the MIS and what it will do for the firm. As more is learned, management might decide that the results do not justify the cost. The process of implementing an MIS is a series of two key go/no go decisions. One decision determines whether the firm will go through the analysis and design phase. The other decision determines whether the firm will go through the implementation phase. The information services staff must provide the justification for proceeding from one phase to another.

The following sections correspond to the numbered steps in Figure 17-1.

Announce the study project

It is important to recognize the behavioral impact that a new MIS can have on the firm's employees. This impact is characteristic of small systems and small projects as well as large. Nothing is more feared than the unknown, and it is easy for rumors to get started that the MIS will put people out of work.

In the case of large firms, a computer has probably been in use for several years as a data processing system. In this case, the employees have come to accept the computer. Management then only has to explain the new use of the computer as an information system and to ask for the employees' support.

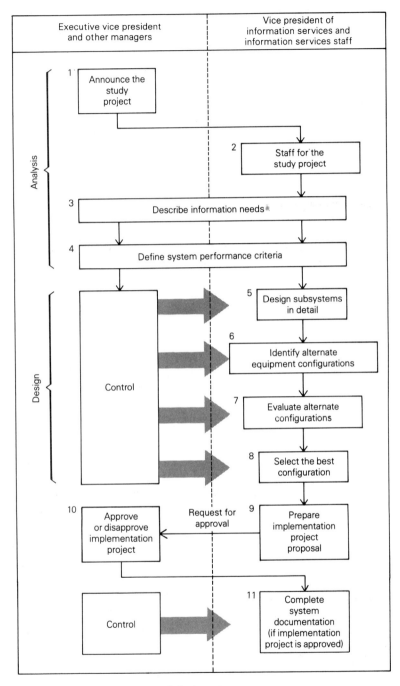

Figure 17-1 The analysis and design phase.

If a firm has no computer history, the situation is different. Here management must overcome the employees' fears by explaining what the computer is intended to do. A company meeting can be called, with the president presiding. The presentation is not technical; it simply summarizes what the MIS will be expected to do and what will be required for implementation. This announcement can be supplemented by an article in the company newspaper and by departmental meetings. The tone of the communications should not be "Here is what we have decided to do." Rather, each employee should be encouraged to participate and to make suggestions. The MIS cannot attain its highest level of performance without support and input from the rank and file of employees.

Staff for the study project

Before the system study can begin, all of the needed resources (primarily systems analysts) must be acquired and made ready. Training might be necessary, and project teams must be formed.

Perhaps all of the needed personnel resources are not presently working for the company. Analysts might be needed who have specialized skills. For example, there might be a need for analysts who are experienced with a particular industry (airlines) or with a particular subsystem (accounting) or with a particular technique (decision modeling).

Since only the analysts participate in the analysis and design phase, the programming and operations staff are not involved at this time. Additional programming and operations resources are not acquired until they are needed. The firm must allow sufficient lead time, however, for orientation or training of programmers and operators before their work actually begins.

Describe information needs

The analysts must now gather information describing the information needs of the managers. This is done primarily by *personal interview*. Personal interviews represent an effective way for the analyst to gather information describing the manager's information needs. During the interview the analyst can react to the manager's answers and direct the line of questioning along the desired path. The analyst guides the discussion with the intent of defining information needs.

The general approach that the firm is taking—objectives or problems—influences the discussion as well. When a firm follows an objective orientation as described in Chapter 16, the analyst can start with the objectives and then successively convert the findings into responsibilities, decisions, and information needs. This is the point where each manager can state his or her critical success factors. In the event that a manager is unable to conceptualize these factors, the interview is refocused on information needed to accomplish objectives.

When a firm follows a problem orientation, the analyst focuses initially on problems, then on the decisions necessary to solve the problems, and finally on the information needed for decision making.

Figure 17-2 illustrates the chain reaction in the interview process for both

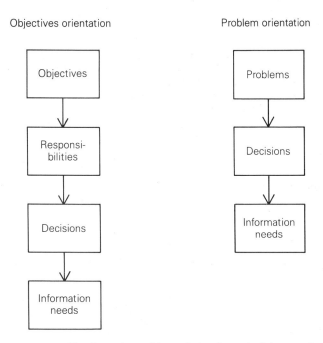

Figure 17-2 The interview ultimately leads to decisions and information needs.

an objective and a problem orientation. As the analyst focuses on the decisions, he or she might pursue the following line of questioning.[1]

1. What decisions do you regularly make?
2. What information do you need to make these decisions?
3. What information do you get?
4. What information would you like?
5. What specialized studies do you request?
6. What magazines and trade reports would you like to have routed to you on a regular basis?
7. What specific topics would you like to be informed of?
8. What do you think would be the four most helpful improvements that could be made in the present information system?

Traditionally, systems analysts have relied largely on interviews to define the manager's information needs. This approach has been criticized as too superficial. Henry Mintzberg, for one, has recommended that systems analysts rely more on *observation*—"living with" the manager for several days or weeks in order to really understand the manager's needs.

It is not suggested that observation replace interviewing. Observation should be used in conjunction with interviewing. The analyst might observe the manager

[1] Adapted from Philip Kotler, *Marketing Management: Analysis, Planning and Control*, 3d ed. (Englewood Cliffs, N.J.: Prentice-Hall, 1976), p. 423.

for some time and then ask specific questions in an effort to better understand the observed behavior.

Another source of information is *data search*, where the analyst reviews historical records in order to understand the details of the firm's operations. Finally, the analyst can conduct a *survey* using a questionnaire to gather information from a large number of managers by mail and telephone as well as by personal interview. The survey is becoming increasingly important as firms implement distributed systems, making it more difficult for the analyst to personally interview all of the participants. Analysis ends when the analyst believes that he or she understands the information needs of the managers.

Supporting roles. Throughout our discussion we refer to the systems analyst. We may be referring to more than one—an analyst team. We should also recognize that other information specialists might be involved. If the firm has a DBA, that person will be a part of the analysis and design team. The DBA will gather information from the managers concerning their data needs. This information gathering will involve the same methods used by the systems analyst and will be coordinated with the work of the analyst. If the firm has a network manager, that person will also be involved. The network manager will gather information needed to design datacom networks.

We do not mention the DBA and network manager in our description, but they play key roles in the analysis and design phase as well as the remainder of the system life cycle.

Define system performance criteria

For the first time in the project, the specific needs of the managers are known. Up to this point, the needs have been defined in general terms, and some have been assumed. It is now possible to specify in exact terms what the MIS should accomplish. These are the performance criteria that were stated in general terms during the planning phase.

For example, a marketing manager might want a certain level of performance from a distribution system such as the one studied in Chapter 9. The manager can insist that customer orders be filled in no more than two days, that no more than 10 percent of the ordered items be back ordered, that invoices be mailed the same day that items are shipped, and so on. If acceptable to both users and information specialists, these specifications become the performance criteria for the distribution system. How well the system does its job will be determined by comparing the actual performance with these criteria. Efforts are made to establish similar criteria for each MIS subsystem. These criteria should be specific and quantitative, where practical, so that performance can be measured exactly.

Design subsystems in detail

When the analyst understands what the new system must accomplish, he or she must next describe the processes that the computer is to follow. Attention is paid to basic computer capabilities rather than to particular pieces of equipment. For example, the analyst recognizes that an online master file is necessary but does not specify that the file be DASD, magnetic tape, or whatever.

Each subsystem of the system is described in terms of its inputs, processes, secondary storage, and outputs, perhaps by using *general* flowcharting symbols as in Figure 17-3. These general symbols are *hardware-independent* (that is, they do not specify any particular type of hardware). Other documentation tools may be used in lieu of flowcharting.[2]

As an example of the design process, assume that one of the subsystems is the order entry system discussed in Chapter 9. Using information gathered up to this point, the analyst prepares the general system flowchart shown in Figure 17-4. If, for any reason, you are unfamiliar with order entry, you should read the discussion of that system in Chapter 9.

Once the systems analyst has an understanding of the general system structure, using system flowcharts, data flow context diagrams, HIPO hierarchy and overview diagrams, or Warnier-Orr diagrams, the analysis becomes more detailed. Documentation is prepared on successively more detailed levels until the analyst feels that he or she has included all of the important features of the system.

In this manner, the analyst "thinks through" the design. It is a *detailed* design in that the analyst identifies the input data, secondary storage data, basic processing and logic, and output data.

Identify alternate equipment configurations

It is now time to think about the information processor technology. All of the systems have been documented in the above manner. If it appears that a computer should serve as the information processor, then a configuration must be selected

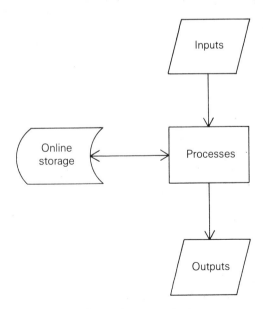

Figure 17-3 General system design.

---

[2] Mel Colter compares various documentation tools in "A Comparative Examination of Systems Analysis Techniques," *MIS Quarterly* 8 (March 1984): 51–66.

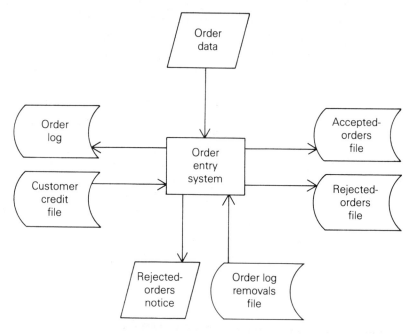

Figure 17-4 General system flowchart of the order entry system.

that allows the programs to function efficiently. The needs of the systems will determine the configuration.

The selection of a configuration is a sequential process, starting with the identification of various equipment combinations that can execute each program. For example, the order entry system can accept order data from CRT or hardcopy terminal input or from OCR documents. The order log, customer credit file, rejected orders file, accepted orders file, and order log removals file can be on magnetic tape or DASD. The rejected orders notice can be produced by a printer, a CRT terminal, or a hardcopy terminal. In addition, data can be processed in batches or online. These alternatives are summarized in Table 17-1. In all there are 576 different configurations (3 × 2 × 2 × 2 × 2 × 2 × 3 × 2).

This doesn't mean that the analyst carefully considers all 576 possible combinations. Some alternatives need not even be considered. For example, OCR input can be dismissed if this is the only place in the overall system design where OCR could be used and the volume of activity does not provide adequate justification. By eliminating obviously unacceptable options, the analyst can reduce the feasible system alternatives to a reasonable number, say from three to six, for detailed study. Table 17-2 identifies three alternatives for evaluation.

Evaluate alternate configurations

The analyst, working closely with the manager, evaluates the three order entry alternatives. The one is selected that best enables the subsystem to meet its objectives, given the constraints.

Table 17-1 System Alternatives

System Elements	Alternatives
Input	CRT terminal Hardcopy terminal OCR
Order log	Magnetic tape DASD
Customer credit file	Magnetic tape DASD
Rejected orders file	Magnetic tape DASD
Accepted orders file	Magnetic tape DASD
Order log removals file	Magnetic tape DASD
Rejected orders notice	Printer CRT terminal Hardcopy terminal
Processing	Batch Online

Table 17-2 Alternatives Selected for Detailed Study

Alternative	Input	Order log	Customer credit file	Accepted and rejected orders files	Order log removals file	Rejected orders notice
1	CRT	Magnetic tape	DASD	Magnetic tape	Magnetic tape	Printer
2	Hardcopy terminal	DASD	DASD	Magnetic tape	Magnetic tape	Printer
3	Hardcopy terminal	DASD	DASD	DASD	Magnetic tape	Hardcopy terminal

Each subsystem is evaluated in the same manner, with the analysts and the manager identifying the best configuration. Then they must consider all of the subsystems together to identify the single configuration that offers the best support to the subsystems as a group. Table 17-3 compares several data processing subsystems.

Table 17-3 Comparison of subsystem configurations

Subsystem	Input devices			Secondary storage		Output devices				
	Hardcopy terminal	CRT terminal	OCR	Magnetic tape	DASD	Printer	Hardcopy terminal	CRT terminal	Plotter	COM
Order entry	X				X	X	X			
Inventory	X		X		X	X	X			X
Billing					X	X				
Accounts receivable			X		X	X		X		
Purchasing	X				X		X			
Receiving		X			X			X		
Accounts payable	X			X		X				
General ledger	X	X		X	X	X	X	X	X	

Select the best configuration

We can use the data processing subsystems in Table 17-3 as an example of how a configuration is selected.

The analysts evaluate all of the subsystem configurations and adjust the device mix so that all subsystems conform to a single configuration. For example, OCR input might be replaced with CRT terminal input for the inventory and accounts receivable subsystems. In the same manner, plotter and COM output might be replaced as output options with printer and magnetic tape respectively. After the analysts have adjusted the configurations, they present their recommendation to the executive vice president for final approval.

In the event that the selected configuration does not provide the support that the manager identified initially, the performance criteria should be modified accordingly. The system will be evaluated using the performance criteria, so the performance criteria should be achievable with the selected configuration. In this manner, the executive vice president selects an equipment configuration, such as the one in Figure 17-5, that best fits the needs of the entire organization.

Prepare the implementation project proposal

Before additional funds are allocated to cover the implementation phase, management requires as much information as possible to justify proceeding. Now that the system has been designed, it is possible to provide this information.

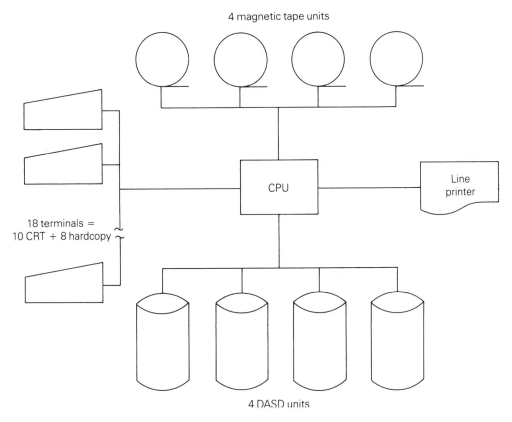

4 magnetic tape units

18 terminals =
10 CRT + 8 hardcopy

CPU

Line printer

4 DASD units

Figure 17-5 The selected equipment configuration.

The information services staff prepares an *implementation project proposal* outlining the work to be done, the expected benefits, and the costs. The format of this proposal is similar to the one prepared for the study project. Figure 17-6 presents a sample outline.

Section 1 briefly reviews the progress to date in completing the analysis and design phase. Sections 2, 3, and 5 represent updated versions of corresponding sections in the study project proposal. Because more is known about these sections now, the information can be more specific than was possible previously.

Unlike the study project proposal, the implementation project proposal does not describe possible alternatives for the firm to follow. The selected design and computer equipment configuration are presented in section 4 along with the performance criteria. The anticipated results of that design are described in section 5.

The study project proposal contained a general implementation plan, which is now presented in detail in section 6. Since the revised plan is such an improvement over the old one because of its more current nature, new documentation of the implementation phase is also prepared—new bar charts, network diagrams, and so on.

1. Introduction—reason for the proposal

2. Problem definition

3. System objectives and constraints

4. System design
   a. Summary description
   b. Performance criteria
   c. Equipment configuration

5. Anticipated results
   a. Organizational impact
   b. Operational impact
   c. Financial impact

6. Detailed implementation plan
   a. Objectives
   b. Tasks to be accomplished
   c. Resource requirements
   d. Time schedule
   e. Cost recap

7. Summary

Figure 17-6 The implementation project proposal.

Approve or disapprove the implementation project

The vice president of information services reports the progress of the information services staff throughout the systems study. These reports are made periodically to the executive vice president or steering committee. This is a healthy situation when proposal review time rolls around. The executive vice president or the steering committee reviews a proposal that they have helped to prepare, not one prepared entirely by the information services staff.

Complete the system documentation

The approval to proceed with implementation indicates a successful analysis and design effort. The analysts have studied the existing system and designed a new system that is satisfactory to the firm's management.

The final step of the analysis and design phase is to complete the documentation of the new system. Such documentation often includes:

1. System documentation
   a. System description (narrative)
   b. Some type of high-level documentation in a graphical form such as system flowcharts, and HIPO hierarchy and overview diagrams

2. Program documentation (for each program or program module within the system)
   a. Program description (narrative)
   b. Some type of detailed process documentation such as program flowcharts, structured English, or Warnier-Orr diagrams.
   c. Some type of detailed data documentation such as data element dictionary descriptions
   d. Output record layouts (such as printer spacing charts and display screen formats)

All of the materials for a system constitute the *system documentation package*. All of the materials for a program constitute the *program documentation package*. The systems analyst provides the initial contents of these packages and the programmer adds the remaining material. The packages are filed in the information services department for the duration of the system life cycle.

The need for documentation

You should recognize that system and program documentation requirements vary widely from one installation to another. Everyone agrees that documentation is desirable because it performs two basic functions. First, it facilitates *communication* among the participants in the system design (primarily among users, analysts, and programmers). Second, it facilitates system *maintenance* at a later date.[3] Proponents of complete documentation believe that the time spent in documenting pays dividends elsewhere during the system life cycle. Computer users should remain open-minded to the different documentation techniques, recognizing that each is best suited to particular situations. The descriptions of each tool in Appendices A through F include an indication of when each should be used and how each affects the manager.

The subject of documentation is very important to users of packaged software. If a user purchases a poorly documented software package, it may be impossible to tell what the package will or will not do. Also, when something goes wrong and a programmer must be brought in to fix the problem, the programmer wastes precious time finding the cause of the trouble.

There is no doubt that much of the documentation of business installations over the years has been busy work. But it would be a big mistake to do away with documentation altogether. Computerized business systems are used by many people over a long period of time. For this reason alone, documentation is a must.

Putting the analysis and design phase in perspective

Although the executive vice president or steering committee has overall responsibility, the analysis and design phase belongs to the systems analyst. The analyst

---

[3] For a discussion of the importance of documentation to maintenance, see Tor Guimaraes, "A Study of Application Program Development Techniques," *Communications of the ACM* 28 (May 1985): 494–499.

is the key to satisfactorily performing this, perhaps the most difficult, phase of the life cycle. The analysis and design phase involves the creation of a set of system specifications from an often vague problem definition. Both the systems analyst's communications skills and technical knowledge come into play at this time. First, the analyst must establish cordial working relations with managers and other employees in the area of the firm being studied. Next, the analyst must be able to creatively identify the possible solutions and evaluate each from a technological standpoint.

In performing this activity, the systems analyst uses the systems approach as the overall guide. Within this framework, the analyst employs her or his various skills. The documentation techniques described in the appendices are the tools of the analyst's trade. The analyst is skilled in the use of these tools, in much the same way that a cabinetmaker is skilled in the use of the various woodworking tools.

The work of the systems analyst does not end with the completion of the analysis and design phase. During the implementation phase, the analyst will work closely with the programmer in developing the needed computer code. The analyst will also be involved in in-house training programs—teaching managers and employees on all levels their roles in the new system. But the end of the analysis and design phase brings the curtain down on the analyst's primary responsibility. The success of the remainder of the life cycle as well as the success of the implemented system depends largely on the analysis and design work performed by the systems analyst.

The Implementation Phase

The implementation phase includes all of the tasks necessary to convert the MIS design into a working system. The analysis and design phase describes the new system and how it will work. The description exists only on paper; it is a model of the planned MIS. What is necessary now is the conversion of that model into the real thing. The MIS will be a physical system consisting of machines, personnel, and materials. *Implementation* is the acquisition and integration of the physical MIS resources to form a working system.

Many separate tasks make up the implementation effort. These tasks involve practically everyone in the firm, whereas the planning and the analysis and design phases involved primarily the managers, systems analysts, data base administrator, and network manager. The implementation phase involves these same people as well as employees throughout the organization and the remainder of the information services staff.

The tasks involved in implementation include:

1. Plan the implementation
2. Announce the implementation project
3. Organize the MIS staff
4. Select the computer
5. Prepare and/or purchase the software library

6. Prepare the data base
7. Educate participants and users
8. Prepare physical facilities
9. Cut over to the new system

The sequence in which these tasks are performed depends on the organization. If a firm intends to develop its own software, the computer selection is made prior to preparing the software library, the data base, and the physical facilities. This sequence is shown in Figure 17-7. If, on the other hand, a firm intends to

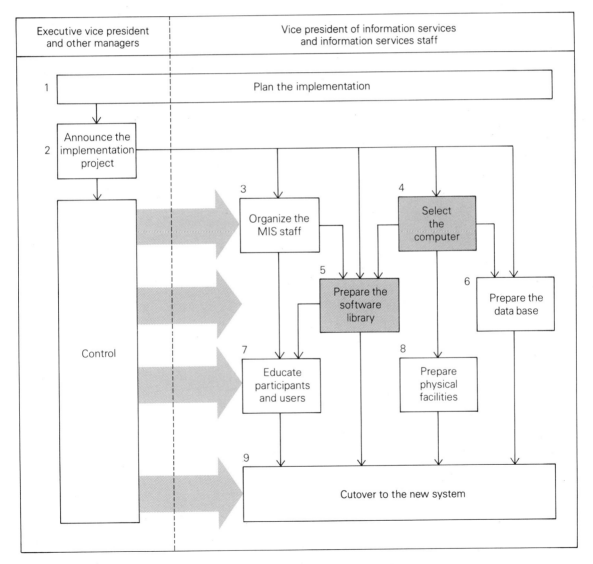

Figure 17-7 The implementation phase—the firm prepares its own software.

obtain its software from a vendor, the software decision should precede and influence the computer selection. This sequence is shown in Figure 17-8.

You will notice in Figures 17-7 and 17-8 that several tasks are going on at the same time. In the earlier life cycle phases the manager and the analyst took steps sequentially. In this phase other resources (such as programmers and operators) are involved, and several can be working at the same time.

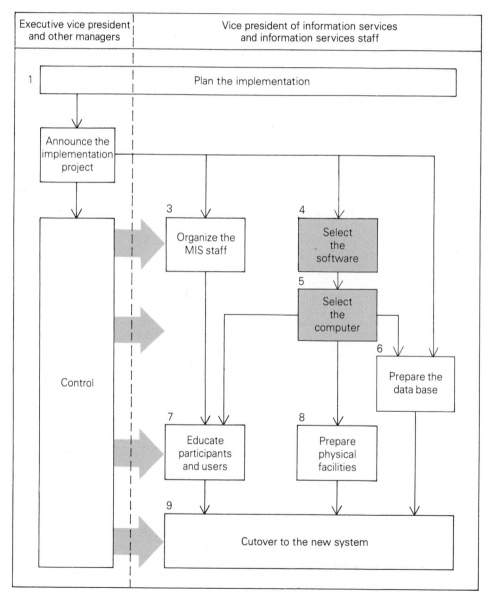

Figure 17-8 The implementation phase—the firm purchases its software.

Each of the nine steps of the implementation phase is discussed in the sections below.

Plan the implementation

You recall that a control mechanism was established at the end of the planning phase in the form of a Gantt chart or network diagram. As more was learned about the project during the analysis and design phase, the control mechanism was updated and made more detailed. Now, only one phase remains before cutover, and the managers and information specialists have a very specific knowledge of the MIS design—knowledge that can be used to develop a detailed implementation plan. This plan specifies precisely what will be needed for software selection and/or programming, as well as data base preparation.

Software selection. The system design identifies the particular software packages needed. All firms will acquire system software, and many firms will acquire application software. The software vendors must be identified, and then time estimates must be made for vendor responses to requests for bids. Sufficient time must be allowed for the bidding process before subsequent activity, such as computer selection, can be scheduled to begin.

Programming. Each of the programs has been designed and documented. The program documentation can be used to estimate the time required for the coding and testing.

In addition to a better knowledge of the required programs, the firm also has a better understanding of the resources that will do the work—the programmers. The programming staff has been assembled, and their numbers and capabilities are known. Specific programmers can be assigned to specific programs, and can participate in the scheduling process.

Data base preparation. The system design includes an identification of all the required data files as well as their contents. Some of these files might currently exist in computer-readable form, such as magnetic tape or disk. Perhaps they will remain as is, or they may be converted to another form, such as from tape to disk. Also, there is a good chance that completely new files will have to be created. The system design permits a detailed plan of all of the file-building activity.

Putting the plan into action. The control mechanism is updated to reflect the details of the implementation plan. Periodic meetings of all participants continue, and increase in frequency as the cutover approaches. From this point on, management attention focuses entirely on control. The final plan has been made; it is time to put it into action.

Announce the implementation project

Just as the analysis and design phase was announced to the employees, so top management must communicate the plans for the implementation phase. Since most employees will be expected to play a role in the implementation, an appeal must be made for their cooperation. Management should explain the roles that the employees will play and the benefits that they will receive.

The announcement can be made in phases. The president can address the entire employee force or can make a statement for the company's publication, explaining the plan in general terms. Then the executive vice president and the vice president of information services can meet with key managers to discuss how each area will be involved. These managers will then meet with their staffs to acquaint them with the upcoming events. The final step includes meetings with each section and department to discuss in specific terms how the implementation will be handled. These meetings are not intended to educate the employees about their role in the operating MIS. Instead, the objective is to inform the employees of their role in implementation.

Organize the MIS staff

The systems analysis group has been in place for quite some time and has completed the bulk of its work in designing the new MIS. Specialists in data communications and data base administration, when needed, also participated in that design work. As the design evolved, recruiting and training efforts were launched to bring the programming staff up to the needed level in terms of quantity and skill.

During this period the staff will be organized into functional groups or teams. The implementation plan specifies what staff members are needed and when their work will begin.

Select the software and the computer

The decision of whether to make or buy application software is made by large firms as well as small. As an example, a large insurance company can consider purchasing packaged software costing hundreds of thousands of dollars even though they have an in-house programming capability. This *make-or-buy decision*, never an easy one, has been further complicated by the increasing variety and improving quality of the packages.

The decision can be made more structured by identifying the factors that have an influence. These factors can be listed on a make-or-buy decision form such as the one pictured in Figure 17-9. In this example, factors 1 though 6 concern the firm and its software needs, whereas factors 7 through 11 concern the software vendors and their products.

A firm will be prompted to "make" its own application software when:

- It already has a large programming staff
- There is little or no backlog of new applications
- The firm processes its data in "nonstandard" ways
- DSS, rather than data processing, is emphasized
- The firm has a strong desire not to rely on outsiders for help
- There is no pressure to implement systems quickly

Instructions: Mark the scale to represent the situation in the firm.

MAKE   BUY

					Numeric Rating	Weight	Points

1. The firm's programming resources are:

large   small
1   2   3   4✔   5

| 4 | .30 | 1.2 |

2. The firm's backlog of application programming projects is:

small   large
1   2   3✔   4   5

| 3 | .10 | .3 |

3. Most of the firm's application programs are:

unique   common
1   2   3   4✔   5

| 4 | .05 | .2 |

4. The application programs have an orientation toward:

information   data
1✔   2   3   4   5

| 1 | .10 | .1 |

5. The firm's desire to be self-sufficient is:

strong   weak
1   2   3   4   ✔5

| 5 | .05 | .25 |

6. The time available for program development is:

extensive   minimal
1   2   3   4✔   5

| 4 | .02 | .08 |

7. The availability of prewritten application software is:

limited   great
1   2   3   4   ✔5

| 5 | .20 | 1.0 |

8. The quality of the available application software is:

poor   good
1   2   3   4   ✔5

| 5 | .02 | .1 |

9. The cost of the available application software is:

high   low
1   2✔   3   4   5

| 2 | .10 | .2 |

10. The reputation of software vendors is:

poor   good
1   2   3   4   ✔5

| 5 | .05 | .25 |

11. Local availability of software support personnel is:

poor   good
1   2   3   4   ✔5

| 5 | .01 | .05 |

Interpretation of total points:
1.00 to 1.99   Strong "make" orientation
2.00 to 2.99   Moderate "make" orientation
3.00 to 3.99   Moderate "buy" orientation
4.00 to 5.00   Strong "buy" orientation

Total Points | 3.73 |

Figure 17-9   Self-administered make-or-buy questionnaire.

- The application software on the market is limited in quantity and/or the quality is poor
- The packaged software is expensive
- The vendors of the needed software do not have good reputations
- There is little or no local assistance available to maintain purchased software

When a form such as the one in the figure is used, it is designed by the managers working jointly with the information specialists. The form is completed by persons responsible for the make-or-buy decision, such as the executive vice president or steering committee.

Each factor is weighted to reflect its relative importance, and points are computed by multiplying the weight times the checked rating. The factor points can be added to produce a total score. In Figure 17-9, the firm has a moderate "buy" orientation, which means that it will probably obtain most or all of its application software from vendors.

The make-or-buy decision applies only to software. All firms obtain their hardware from outside sources. Over the years, a well-defined process has evolved for requesting bids from vendors and then evaluating their proposals. In the sections below, we define the process as it applies to hardware. Be aware that exactly the same process can be followed for purchased software.

Requests for proposals. The system design should be made available to the vendors offering all or any of the types of computing equipment in the configuration selected at the end of the systems study. Many vendors supply only certain units, such as plotters, terminals, or OCR readers. Some of these units may be superior to similar devices supplied by vendors like IBM, Honeywell, and Control Data Corporation who offer complete configurations. The best configuration might integrate hardware from more than one vendor.

Each vendor selected to compete for the order should be provided with a document called a *request for proposal (RFP)*. This document is a summary of the relevant parts of the system study and the implementation project proposals. It is prepared by information services personnel. Figure 17-10 presents an outline of an RFP.

The letter of transmittal explains to the vendor what is expected, including the type of proposal and deadline. Descriptions of the system objectives and constraints, design, performance criteria, and equipment configuration are taken directly from the implementation project proposal. The selected portions of the program documentation packages enable vendors to understand what the equipment is intended to do. The estimated transaction volume and the estimated file sizes enable vendors to estimate how much time will be required to process the data. The installation schedule, included as the final section of the RFP, enables vendors to schedule equipment deliveries to arrive at the appropriate time.

Vendors, therefore, propose equipment configurations to meet specific processing requirements. By specifying the system design for the vendors, the firm assures that all vendors will be proposing equipment to do the same job. If the vendors are left to propose configurations of their own choosing, the firm has no clear basis for comparison.

1. Letter of transmittal

2. System objectives and constraints

3. System design
   a. Summary description
   b. Performance criteria
   c. Equipment configuration
   d. Program documentation packages
      (selected portions)
   e. Estimated transaction volume
   f. Estimated file sizes

4. Installation schedule

Figure 17-10 The request for proposal.

Vendor proposals. If vendors choose to compete for the order, they prepare a *proposal* describing how their equipment meets the performance criteria. In most cases, the vendors prepare written proposals. Some proposals may be nothing more than a letter, while others may be lengthy volumes. An outline of a vendor proposal is shown in Figure 17-11. Section 1 acknowledges that the proposal is submitted in response to the RFP. Section 2 summarizes the vendor's recommendations relating to the type of equipment proposed and the major benefits expected. This section condenses the relevant points of the proposal into a succinct management summary. Section 3 lists the advantages of selecting this vendor's equipment over that of another. Sections 4 and 5 identify the proposed computer system components along with their performance specifications (speeds, accuracy ratings, and so on) and their price. Section 6 addresses the performance criteria,

1. Letter of transmittal

2. Summary of recommendations

3. Advantages

4. Equipment configuration

5. Equipment specifications
   a. Performance data
   b. Prices

6. Satisfaction of performance criteria

7. Delivery schedule

Figure 17-11 The vendor equipment proposal.

program by program. When included, this is the lengthiest section of the proposal. Finally, in section 7, the vendor quotes a delivery schedule, which should meet the installation dates in the implementation plan.

Very often the vendor will also make a formal oral presentation to the key executives or the steering committee. This presentation gives the firm's executives an opportunity to ask questions about specific points in the proposal.

Selection of vendors. When all vendors propose the same types of hardware or software, the selection decision boils down to which one best meets the performance criteria at the lowest cost. How does the firm know that the proposed systems can meet the performance criteria? One approach is to establish *benchmark problems* for the vendors to solve, using the proposed hardware and software. These benchmark problems can be a few of the more important programs or the entire system.

The use of benchmark tests lends a certain degree of structure to the vendor selection problem, but it remains essentially semistructured. The final decision is not based strictly on quantitative proposal data. Consideration must be given also to the vendor's record of meeting previous commitments. A survey of some of the vendor's customers can indicate the consistency with which promises are fulfilled.[4]

When all of the vendor data has been received and analyzed, the executive vice president or the steering committee select the vendor or vendors. The president approves the selection, and the firm places the order(s).

An organization of any size can follow the above approach. The amount of leverage that an organization can exercise over the vendors, however, is a function of the organization's size. If the organization is a branch of the federal government, for example, and the size of the potential order is large, the vendors can be expected to go to any lengths to get the business. Large organizations can make the benchmark tasks very demanding, whereas small organizations cannot realistically consider them as evaluation tools. Small organizations can, however, go through a well-planned sequence of steps in evaluating feasible hardware and software alternatives.

Prepare the software library

When a firm decides to create its own application software, it follows a process like the one pictured in Figure 17-12.

1. The programmer must first understand the problem. He or she reviews the contents of the program documentation package and then prepares documentation on a more detailed level using techniques such as flowcharting or structured English.

---

[4]For a discussion of how to measure the subjective factors influencing vendor choice, see Vishist Vaid-Raizada, "Incorporation of Intangibles in Computer Selection Decisions," *Journal of Systems Management* 34 (November 1983): 30–36.

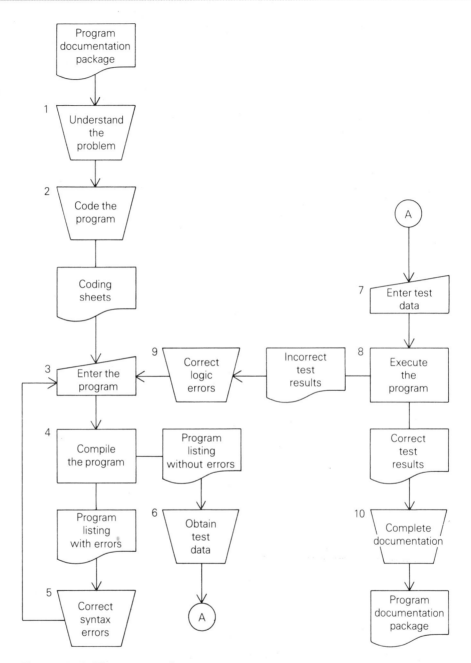

Figure 17-12 The programming process.

2. The program is coded in a procedural language.

3. The program is keyed into the computer.

4. The language compiler translates the *source program* (coded by the programmer) into an *object program* (in machine language).

5. The output from the compilation is called the *source program listing*. *Error messages* identify *syntax errors* that occur when the rules of the programming language are violated.

6. After achieving a *clean compile*—a compilation with no syntax errors— the programmer uses data to test the program logic. Sometimes test data will be fabricated; other times the firm uses live data.

7. The test data is entered.

8. The program is executed.

9. If test results are incorrect, the programmer corrects the *logic errors*— statements that satisfy the syntax but produce the wrong results. The corrected program is recompiled, and steps 3, 4, 5, and 8 are repeated.

10. When test results are correct, the programmer completes the documentation in the program documentation package. The programmer adds the source program listing, the test data listing, and the test data results.

Today, most business programs are written following *structured programming* conventions. The idea behind structured programming is that a program will be subdivided into modules that are arranged in a hierarchy as pictured in Figure 17-13. See Figure A-4 and its description in Appendix A for further details on the transfer of program logic between the modules. The hierarchy of program modules is similar to the structure of both the HIPO (see Appendix E) and Warnier-Orr (see Appendix F) analysis and design techniques. When the systems analyst documents the new system design using HIPO or Warnier-Orr, it is a relatively straightforward process for the programmer to prepare the structured program.

An advantage of structured programming, especially for large projects, is that it enables the programming tasks to be subdivided among several programmers, thus reducing the calendar time. Separate modules can be assigned to particular programmers, and then all of the modules can be combined. The term *programmer team concept* is used to describe the cooperative effort of multiple programmers.

The programmer team concept works best when a top-down, modular approach is followed not only in programming, but in the entire development process. The term *structured development* means that a modular, hierarchical approach is followed in planning, analysis and design, programming, testing, and implementation.[5]

Prepare the data base

Earlier discussions have explained the data base in terms of what it is, how it is organized, and how it is used. The discussion here centers on how the data base is prepared.

---

[5] Kathleen Mendes provides an excellent description of structured systems analysis at Exxon in "Structured Systems Analysis: A Technique to Define Business Requirements," *Sloan Management Review* 21 (Summer 1980): 51–63.

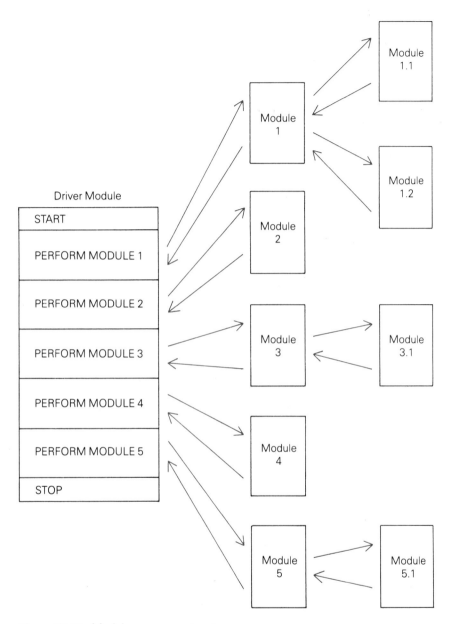

Figure 17-13 Modular program structure.

Preparation can be easy or difficult, depending on the circumstances. The task becomes difficult when (1) the firm is converting from a system of manual files to computer media, (2) the files are large, (3) the files contain very old data, and/or (4) some of the data has not been maintained in the past. The degree to which any of these conditions exist determines the difficulty of the task.

During the 1960s, most large firms converted their data bases to computerized systems. Many of these firms have subsequently converted their data bases to a form compatible with a DBMS. Quite a few large firms are currently involved in this activity. Small firms installing their first computer are faced not only with the task of cleaning up their data files, but also putting the files in a form acceptable to a DBMS such as dBASE III or Rbase 5000. For these small firms, preparing the data base can be just as difficult as preparing the software library.

Responsibility for data base preparation.   We have seen that the data base administrator (DBA) is responsible for all phases of data base activity. This includes the preparation of the data base, which is often the most important and difficult part of the DBA's assignment.

The DBA should be on the scene during the analysis and design phase, working closely with the systems analyst. The DBA interfaces with the users in much the same manner as does the systems analyst, gaining an understanding of data needs.

Once the data base schema has been defined, and a decision has been made concerning which computer to use, the DBA can guide the selection of the DBMS. As in the case of the systems analyst, the DBA acts in an advisory capacity. The executive vice president or the steering committee decides which, if any, DBMS to use. Once the decision has been made, the DBA becomes involved in the preparation of the data base and in the training of users.

Educate participants and users

The MIS will affect many people. Some will make the system work and others will use its output. All must be educated concerning (1) their role in the system, and (2) how the system will benefit them. The education program is aimed not only at members of the firm, but at elements in its environment. The education can be provided by the systems analysts, instructors in the personnel department, or outsiders (such as consultants).

The only groups not needing education concerning the expected benefits of the MIS are the members of the information services staff and top-level management. Both groups have already received this information by virtue of their involvement with the system development.

Employees on the operational level, such as clerical personnel, factory workers, and salespersons, must learn how to do specific tasks. These tasks include filling out forms, operating terminals, and using output. This education is very detailed and specific. All of these people must understand exactly how the system will work.

Managers receive less detailed instruction. Departmental managers must understand the role of their departments, including the flow of data and information to and from other departments. All managers must also understand how to interpret and use the information output. In many cases, the managers will need hands-on training in the use of a terminal.

Education for internal employees is best handled face to face, giving an opportunity for two-way communication. Education for members of the environment, although important, is usually not so intense. Vendors and customers generally need more information on the new MIS than do other members of the environment. Both parties must understand that they are participants in an interfirm information network. The benefits accruing to all network members should be stressed. This message is often communicated in person by representatives of the firm's purchasing and sales departments. Direct mail can support these personal contacts.

If the firm's workers are members of organized labor unions, local union officials should be included in the education effort. The sessions with labor representatives are much like those directed at lower- and middle-level managers: they stress general procedures and benefits. The sessions can be conducted by members of the firm's industrial relations department, assisted by the information services staff.

There is no need for specific education programs for other members of the environment. Any special information needs can be handled as they arise.

Outside education programs. Many hardware and software vendors conduct education programs for their customers. Some courses are free, whereas others require a fee. These courses are aimed at both managers and information specialists. IBM offers a full range of courses and is noted for its customer executive program. One-week sessions at IBM plants give top-level executives firsthand knowledge of how computers produce management information.

Control Data Corporation (CDC) is another computer manufacturer with a strong customer education program. CDC is noted for its courses tailored to information specialists. Some of the courses, however, are helpful for managers.

Many of the educational alternatives come not from hardware and software vendors, but from organizations specializing in education. Some of the organizations have very broad programs, encompassing management as well as computing. Examples are universities and the American Management Association. Other organizations have very specialized interests, perhaps offering courses in a single area such as data communications or office automation.

Table 17-4 provides a flavor of the variety of courses intended to improve the computer and MIS literacy of both users and information specialists. The prices include only the tuition. When travel and lodging are required, the total cost of a two- or three-day course can easily exceed $1,000.

Courses such as these offer excellent opportunities for both managers and information specialists to prepare themselves for their roles in the MIS. The people needing education and the types of education needed should be identified early in the MIS life cycle, and the courses scheduled at the appropriate time—usually just before the learned material is applied.

Prepare physical facilities

The work required to prepare the physical facilities to house the computer depends on the amount and type of hardware needed. If only a few additional units are to be installed (disk drives, terminals, and so on), they can be housed in existing

Table 17-4   Computer-related courses offered by outside firms

Course	Outside firm	Number of days	Cost
Communications networking	The American Institute for Professional Education	3	$695
Methods of forecasting and decision-making for executives	Wharton, University of Pennsylvania	2	$895
Office automation and integration	Data-Tech Institute	3	$595
Computer packages and applications for marketing research	The Burke Institute	2	$650
Factory of the future	Technology Transfer Society	3	$495
Structured testing	The American Institute for Professional Education	3	$695
Networking IBM personal computers	Center for Advanced Professional Education	3	$695
Simulation modeling for decision making	The Institute for Professional Education	3	$895
The IBM PC	Center for Advanced Professional Education	3	$745

areas. Microcomputers and small minicomputers also pose no real physical installation problems; these small systems can simply be plugged into the nearest wall outlet. If, on the other hand, a new mainframe or super mini is needed, a complete construction project may be necessary.

Such a project begins with the specification of the equipment environment (power, temperature, space, and humidity) by representatives of the equipment vendor. These same representatives also recommend the best arrangement of the equipment units for operating efficiency. Once the layout of the computer area has been developed, attention is given to surrounding areas (offices, peripheral equipment rooms, and libraries). The layout of these areas is often done by architects and interior designers. Finally, the design is implemented by a general contracting firm.

Constructing computer facilities is similar to constructing facilities to house any piece of expensive equipment. Representatives of architectural and contractor firms, along with those of the computer manufacturer, can supply expert consultation. All of these activities are incorporated into the overall implementation plan and are controlled in the same manner as work performed by the firm's own employees. It is common practice for the manager of computer operations to have primary responsibility for representing the firm to the various outside groups. The operations manager will often direct that a separate CPM or PERT diagram be drawn specifically for the facilities construction project.

Cutover to the new system

When the above implementation work has been completed, it is time to start using the new system. The process of halting use of the old system and starting use of the new one is called *cutover*. As with a human patient undergoing some type of transplant, the total system must be kept alive while replacing the old part with a new one. The larger the firm and the more complex its operations, the more difficult the cutover becomes.

Basic approaches to cutover. There are three basic approaches to cutover: immediate, phased, and parallel. These approaches are illustrated in Figure 17-14. The approach selected will depend on the characteristics of the firm.

1. *Immediate.* The simplest approach is to convert from the old system to the new one on a given day. This approach should be selected when possible since it is the least expensive and time consuming. However, it is feasible only for small firms or small systems. As the scale of the operation increases, the timing problems of an immediate cutover become too great. It is almost impossible to convert all of the old procedures and files at one time.
2. *Phased.* If the entire system cannot be converted at once, it can be divided

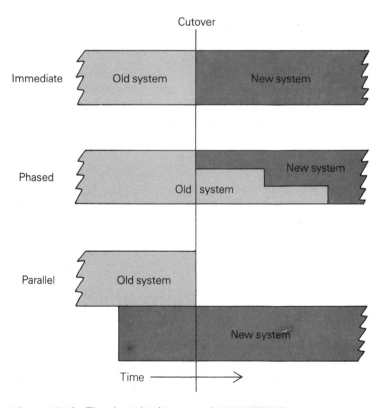

Figure 17-14 The three basic approaches to cutover.

into subsystems and converted a subsystem at a time. This process prolongs the conversion period and introduces problems when one subsystem must be linked to another. The problems can be worked out, however, and this approach is very common. A phased cutover can be followed within a single geographic location or among several locations. For example, at the firm's main plant the order entry subsystem can be implemented first, followed by the finished-goods inventory subsystem, and so on. Or if the firm has suboffices located across the country, each can convert to the new system in succession.

3. *Parallel.* A parallel cutover requires that the old system be maintained until the new one is fully checked out. This approach offers the greatest security against failure, but it is the most expensive and presents problems in coordination. A big advantage is the ability to fully debug the new system, using live data, before the old system is scrapped. The expense comes from maintaining two systems at once. The coordination problems can be minimized by hiring temporary help or contracting with computer service bureaus to perform much of the duplicated work during the conversion period.

Maximizing the opportunity for success.   Effective planning is the best assurance of a successful cutover. In addition, two special techniques can be used to identify trouble spots before full-scale cutover is attempted. *Simulation* is especially effective for checking out online systems, where a mathematical model can simulate the operation of the new system. The model uses transaction volumes during peak as well as average periods to assure that the equipment configuration is adequate. Such models are often available from computer equipment manufacturers and computer consulting firms.

Another special cutover technique is used for both online and batch systems. It is the pilot test. A *pilot test* is a use of the entire system, but restricted to only a portion of the overall operation. For example, if an airline is installing a computerized reservation system, initial use can be limited to travel agents and airline offices in a single city. When successful, the pilot test becomes the first phase of a phased cutover. Both the pilot test and simulation can be used as a preliminary to any of the three basic approaches.

Once the cutover has been successfully completed, the operations phase begins. That phase of the MIS life cycle is the subject of the next chapter. Before we conclude the discussion of the development phases, however, attention should be given to a development technique that is becoming more and more popular—prototyping.

Prototyping

For as long as information specialists have been working with users in designing information systems, there has been difficulty in delivering systems that meet the users' needs. It doesn't seem to matter how well the project is planned and controlled, the problem still persists. In some cases the user says, when presented

with the new system, "That's not what I wanted." In other cases, the user gradually ceases to use the new system.

The problem of satisfying the user's needs has two basic causes: First, the
user often cannot describe what is needed. This is not ignorance on the user's
part. In some cases the problem lacks structure and is difficult to define. Decision
support systems for strategic-planning managers are a good example. In other
cases it takes so long to implement the system that needs change, and the delivered
system misses the mark.

A possible solution

During the 1980s, attention has been directed toward a new way to implement
information and decision systems that might solve the user satisfaction problem.
This new approach is called prototyping. _Prototyping_ consists of quickly producing a system that contains some or all of the essential features required to satisfy
the user's needs. The rough product that is delivered is called a *prototype*. It is
similar in concept to a physical model used by an automobile maker. The prototype is intended to address questions that can only be answered by having a
sample end-product to view and perhaps use. The user responds to the prototype
by providing additional, more specific descriptions. The prototype is refined, and
the process is repeated until an acceptable system is achieved. This activity is
illustrated in Figure 17-15. You can see the iterative process.

The emphasis is on speed. The information specialists try to put something
in the user's hands very quickly—perhaps overnight. Time is not spent trying to
completely define the problem. Also time is not spent in planning, devising control
mechanisms, and documenting.

Since the emphasis is on development speed, you might think that the term
"quick and dirty" applies. It really doesn't. Proponents of the quick and dirty
school try to produce a *final* solution very quickly. Perhaps a program is written
with little regard to built-in controls or to efficiency in terms of operating speed.
The prototype, on the other hand, is not intended to be the final solution. The
prototype is a method of learning what should go into the solution.

As you can see in the lower portion of Figure 17-15, the user can elect to use
an acceptable prototype as the working system, or the prototype can be replaced
with a more permanent working system.

Types of prototypes

Prototyping is new and much remains to be learned, but there is evidence that
different types of prototypes exist. James Johnson, director of systems development at Hallmark Cards, identifies four types:[6]

1. Mock-up—something that just "looks like" the intended system, such as
   reports or screen displays produced from dummy data.

---

[6] James R. Johnson, "A Prototypical Success Story," *Datamation* 29 (November 1983): 251.

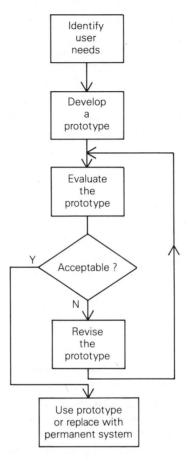

Figure 17-15 The iterative prototyping process.

2. Simulation—an interactive program that consists of only the dialog with the user, but no real processing occurring within the system.

3. Working model—a system incorporating part or all of the necessary processing, but one that is not intended to be the final product. The working model may become the final product, but that is not the intent.

4. Research and development—a system that is refined over time with the intent of eventually becoming the final product.

The first three types are intended only as tools during the analysis phase. The fourth type is intended to be used during analysis, design, and implementation.

Prototyping and the life cycle concept

You can see that prototyping is a different view of system implementation. The traditional life cycle approach is based on the idea that the solution will be right the first time. Prototyping assumes that the solution will not be right, but that the prototype will help in better understanding what the solution ought to be.

Does this new view mean that firms will no longer use the life cycle approach? It is too early to answer this question, but indications are that the type of project is the key. If the problem to be solved is well defined, then the life cycle approach can be followed. An example is a data processing project such as the development of a new payroll system. If the problem is not well defined, then prototyping can be used.

It seems appropriate to regard prototyping as existing *within* the broader life cycle framework. We know that the MIS consists of a large number of data processing, office automation, and decision support subsystems. Prototyping can be used to implement certain of these subsystems, but, overall, the MIS evolves through the cycle. This view is pictured in Figure 17-16.

Advantages of prototyping

The main advantage of prototyping is *user enthusiasm.* Users do not have to wait months to finally get their system. They get fast service and feel more a part of the design effort.

Prototyping offers a greater *opportunity for success* than the life cycle. The prototype contributes to improved problem definition, and there is less chance that the delivered system will be unacceptable.

Because prototyping minimizes the opportunity that an entire project might have to be redone, prototyping should be *less expensive* in the long run.

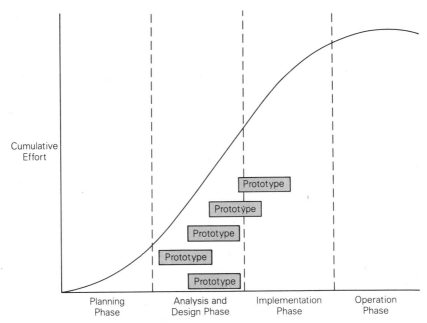

Figure 17-16 Prototyping within the traditional life cycle.

From the standpoint of the systems analyst, the real value of prototyping is the fact that it provides for *good communication* with the user. The user and the analyst have a common reference point. Definition and design effort can be focused on the specifics of the prototype.

Weaknesses of prototyping

The emphasis on speed can produce a project that is characterized by *inadequate controls.* Caution is often thrown to the winds in an effort to provide a speedy product. Costs can get out of hand, and documentation can be poor or even nonexistent. This weakness is not a factor in the life cycle approach where emphasis is on controls.

Firms using the prototype approach have also found that it is sometimes *difficult to maintain user enthusiasm* after the first working prototype is produced. The users perhaps are tricked by the output mock-ups or the simulated dialog into thinking that their problem has already been solved.

Both of these weaknesses can be overcome by proper project management. A policy of establishing and enforcing budget limits and documentation standards can be followed. Also, user education can aim at providing a realistic understanding of how the prototyping activity will proceed.

A third weakness, however, is one that cannot be solved during the short term. Prototyping requires a *sophisticated information services staff.* The sophistication is reflected in a staff capable of using the array of prototyping tools that are available. These tools enable the fast response to user needs.

Prototyping tools

We have previously recognized several of the tools used in prototyping. In general, these are the fourth-generation languages discussed in Chapter 11 (see Figure 11-27). The information specialists can use *graph generators* and *report writers* to produce sample information output. DBMS *query languages* can quickly produce information output from the data base. *Modeling languages* and *very high level languages* can perform some or all of the processing without the necessity of coding lengthy programs.

All of these tools are especially well suited for prototyping decision support systems. *Application generators* offer ways to prototype data processing systems. An example of an application generator is MANTIS from Cincom. Figure 17-17a shows the opening menu listing the various activities that MANTIS supports such as screen design and file building. Figure 17-17b illustrates part of the screen design process, and Figure 17-17c shows how the specifications are entered for each data element to be displayed. Once the screens and files have been designed, the processing can be specified with very powerful and succinct code, as illustrated in Figure 17-18.

```
                              MANTIS
                          MENU SELECTION
RUN A PROGRAM BY NAME ................. 1    RUN VARIOUS APPLICATIONS .............. 9
DISPLAY A PROMPTER ....................... 2    SIGN ON AS ANOTHER USER .............10
DESIGN A PROGRAM ......................... 3    DIRECTORY OF PROGRAMS ................11
DESIGN A SCREEN ............................ 4    DIRECTORY OF SCREENS .................12
DESIGN A FILE ................................. 5    DIRECTORY OF FILES .......................13
DESIGN A PROMPTER ........................ 6    DIRECTORY OF PROMPTERS ............14
DESIGN A LOGICAL VIEW .................. 7    DIRECTORY OF LOGICAL VIEWS .........15
DESIGN AN INTERFACE ..................... 8    DIRECTORY OF INTERFACES ...........16
                    TERMINATE ......................................... PA2
```

(a) The MANTIS opening menu

After the user signs on, MANTIS displays a menu. Each user's menu can be specially tailored to a particular application. This tailoring makes the system easy to use and contributes to security. The user selects the function to be executed—such as DESIGN A FILE.

```
                                            * * * * * * * * *
                                            * NEXT ....... PF1 *
                                            * UPDATE ... PF2 *
                                            * INSERT .... PF3 *
                                            * EXIT ......... PA2 *
                          EMPLOYEE RELATIONS  * * * * * * * *
                          MASTER RECORD FUNCTIONS

EMPLOYEE NUMBER ...................... # # # # # #
LAST NAME ................................ # # # # # # # # # # # # # # # # # # # # # # # # # # # # # #
FIRST NAMES ............................. # # # # # # # # # # # # # # # # # # # # # # # # # # # # # #
SPOUSE'S NAME ........................... # # # # # # # # # # #
HIRE DATE ................................. # # / # # / # #
CURRENT SALARY ......................... $ # # # , # # # . # #
SEX ......................................... # (M OR F)
                              COMMENTS
# # # # # # # # # # # # # # # # # # # # # # # # # # # # # # # # # # # # # # # # # # # # # # # # # # # # # # #
# # # # # # # # # # # # # # # # # # # # # # # # # # # # # # # # # # # # # # # # # # # # # # # # # # # # # # #
# # # # # # # # # # # # # # # # # # # # # # # # # # # # # # # # # # # # # # # # # # # # # # # # # # # # # # #
```

(b) Screen design

Screen design is usually the first step in implementing an application. The user keys in all headings and data fields. The # sign indicates data fields.

```
                                            * * * * * * * * *
                                            * NEXT ....... PF1 *
                                            * UPDATE ... PF2 *
                                            * INSERT .... PF3 *
                                            * EXIT ......... PA2 *
                          EMPLOYEE RELATIONS  * * * * * * * *
                          MASTER RECORD FUNCTIONS

EMPLOYEE NUMBER ...................... # # # # # #
LAST NAME ................................ # # # # # # # # # # # # # # # # # # # # # # # # # # # # # #
FIRST NAMES ............................. # # # # # # # # # # # # # # # # # # # # # # # # # # # # # #
SP
HI   * * * * * * * * * * * * * * * * * * * * * * * * * *
CU   *  FIELD NAME:       EMPLOYEE NUMBER          *
SE   *  INTENSITY:        NORMAL / BRIGHT / HIDDEN *
     *  PROTECTED?        NO / YES                 *
     *  NUMERIC?          NO / YES                 *
     *  PEN DETECTABLE?   NO / YES                 *
# #  *  ALWAYS SENT BACK? NO / YES                 *  # # # # #
# #  * * * * * * * * * * * * * * * * * * * * * * * * * *  # # # # #
# #                                                      # # # # #
```

(c) Specification of data elements

Field attributes can now be assigned. MANTIS automatically highlights the field being defined.

Figure 17-17 Designing screens with an application generator.

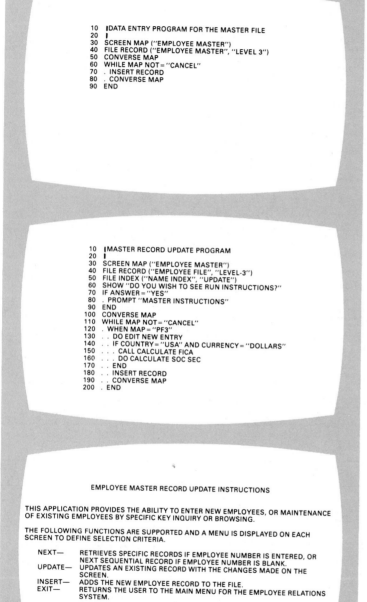

A program to enter data from a terminal and store the data in a file can be written in just a few minutes. The user identifies the format ("map") of the screen and the file to be updated. The CONVERSE command writes and reads data on the screen. The INSERT command writes the record in the file.

The initial program can be made more complex by adding instructions. In this example, a PROMPTER (see screen example below) is inserted to help the user enter data. Some calculations are also added.

This is an example of a PROMPTER. A user can easily design a PROMPTER and can call it into use from the terminal. Or the program can automatically call the PROMPTER.

Figure 17-18 Coding programs with an application generator.

The future of prototyping

Thus far, the results from prototyping are good. Newer tools are being developed, and it should become a widespread implementation approach. As we have seen, prototyping offers some real advantages over the traditional life cycle approach.

Prototyping also represents a possible way to reduce the backlog of user systems awaiting implementation. As such, prototyping is only one of three strategies being followed. The other two are packaged application software and end-user computing. Of the three, prototyping is unique in that it involves the information specialists; it is a way to better use that scarce resource. Packaged software and end-user computing are efforts intended to shift the systems design and implementation away from the information specialists. As larger firms cope with the backlog problem, they will be forced into prototyping as a way to use their information specialists in the most productive manner.[7]

Summary

During the analysis and design phase, most of the work is performed by the systems analyst. This person is assisted by the DBA and network manager when appropriate. During the implementation phase, other information specialists become involved. Programmers and operators are required to produce application software. The information specialists can be organized in various ways, but two popular approaches recognize a division between system development and maintenance, and between application areas.

The communication problem that faces the manager and information specialist can be overcome by both parties becoming familiar with the other's work. Another approach is to implement end-user computing. End-user computing will have an effect on the numbers of information specialists needed to implement small-scale DSSs, but probably not for data processing systems and large-scale DSSs.

The analysis and design phase consists of eleven steps taken for the purpose of defining the new MIS in specific terms. The systems analyst concentrates on the manager's information needs and uses four information-gathering methods— personal interview, observation, data search, and survey. Historically, the interview has been the most effective method, but observation is being recommended as a way to really understand the manager's information needs. Also, the survey is becoming increasingly valuable as the needs of geographically dispersed users must be considered.

After the manager's information needs have been defined in detail, it is possible to establish specific performance criteria for the new MIS. Then the subsystems are designed, with the documentation evolving from the general to the specific. The specific designs permit the selection of a few equipment configurations to be evaluated in detail. The analyst works with the manager in an iterative

---

[7]An example of how prototyping is used at Superior Oil is provided by T. R. Young in "Superior Prototypes," *Datamation* 30 (May 15, 1984): 152 ff.

manner to gradually refine the configurations so that one best suits the entire MIS.

The analyst prepares a proposal explaining how the selected configuration can be implemented. Approval of the proposal by the manager means that only one step of the analysis and design phase remains—completion of the documentation that will be given to the programmer. Each system is described with a system documentation package, and each program in each system is described with a program documentation package. The documentation facilitates communication and maintenance.

The implementation phase begins with detailed planning. This planning draws on the detailed system design to address software selection, programming, and data base preparation. The implementation project is announced, and the MIS staff is organized. If a firm purchases packaged software, the software selection is made prior to the hardware selection. If a firm prepares its own custom software, the hardware selection is made first. RFPs are sent to selected hardware and, perhaps, software vendors. Vendor proposals are evaluated, and selections are made.

Today, most firms follow a structured programming approach. Structured programming can fit within an overall approach of structured development, involving planning, analysis and design, testing, and implementation as well as programming.

The DBA plays the primary role in implementing the data base. This activity consists of selecting a DBMS and then preparing the data so that it is compatible with the DBMS. During this same period, persons inside and outside the company are educated concerning their roles in the MIS. Any work necessary to construct physical facilities is also performed. Cutover can be immediate, phased, or parallel. Firms maximize the opportunity for success by first simulating online systems and by conducting pilot tests of both online and batch systems.

Prototyping is a new implementation approach intended to quickly produce systems that meet managers' information needs. It is an iterative process, redesigning the system using manager feedback. Prototyping is made possible by the variety of fourth-generation languages that are available. Prototyping can be used instead of the life cycle when user needs are not clearly understood. When those needs are understood, however, the life cycle approach is best because of the higher level of control that it provides.

Once cutover has been completed, the firm can begin to enjoy the benefits of the new system. In the next chapter we address the need for operational controls and describe some techniques that are being used.

Key Terms

operator	programmer analyst
programmer, program	systems development
systems analyst	systems maintenance

systems analysis

systems design

personal interview

observation

data search

survey

hardware independent

implementation project proposal

system documentation package

program documentation package

implementation

make-or-buy decision

request for proposal (RFP)

proposal

benchmark problem

source program, object program

source program listing

error message

syntax error

clean compile

logic error

structured programming

programmer team concept

structured development

cutover

immediate, phased, and parallel cutover

pilot test

prototyping

prototype

Key Concepts

Division of responsibilities between the systems analyst and the programmer

Difficulty in establishing a communications link between the manager and the systems analyst

Potential impact of end-user computing on the computer profession

How the analysis and design phase and the implementation phase represent the systems approach to developing an MIS

How the information services staff is assembled during the development process, as the need for specialized skills arises

The various ways that the systems analyst can learn of the manager's information needs

The manner in which the new MIS

design evolves from the general to the specific, and how an overall equipment configuration is selected

The overlapping of several tasks during the implementation phase

The opportunity for detailed and accurate implementation planning

The need for communication to employees concerning their role in the implementation and the operation of the MIS

How the firm's make-or-buy decision influences the sequence in which hardware and software are obtained

How the make-or-buy decision can be made more structured

The solicitation and evaluation of hardware and software vendor proposals

The varying amounts of proposal-related effort that a vendor will expend, depending on the size of the potential order

Structured development and structured programming

Factors influencing the difficulty of the data base preparation task

The comprehensive nature of the educational program—encompassing all levels within the firm plus key environmental elements

Different approaches to cutover, influenced by firm size and resources

How prototyping contributes to an improved understanding of the manager's information needs

The relationship of prototyping to the traditional life cycle concept

---

Questions

1. Under what conditions would an individual perform both as a systems analyst and as a programmer?

2. Name two ways that information specialists can be organized.

3. What is the "communication problem"? How can it be overcome?

4. What steps are involved in systems analysis? In systems design?

5. List four ways that the systems analyst gathers information from managers. Which one does the analyst rely on the most? Which one should be used more often in order to better understand the manager?

6. What are three ways to gather information by survey?

7. What is a "hardware independent" system design tool? Give an example.

8. If a system has 3 input alternatives, 2 processing alternatives, 4 output alternatives, and 2 secondary storage alternatives, how many possible configurations are there?

9. How many configurations does the analyst evaluate in detail?

10. What is included in a program documentation package?

11. What are the two main reasons for documentation?

12. Name three implementation activities that cannot be planned in detail until after the system design is completed.

13. What is the purpose of announcing the implementation?

14. Does the "make-or-buy" decision relate to hardware or to software or to both? Explain.

15. What is an RFP? Who prepares it? Who receives it?

16. Which media do vendors use in presenting their proposals?

17. What is a benchmark problem? Can any firm use it?

18. List three conditions that make data base preparation difficult.

19. Name three approaches to cutover. Under what conditions is each used?

20. Is prototyping an example of a "quick and dirty" approach? Explain.

Problems

NOTE: Refer to the appropriate appendix when working problems 1–4.

1. Document the following process using a system flowchart.
   a. A sales clerk fills out a sales receipt form containing data supplied by the customer (account number) and data from the merchandise tag (item number, price).
   b. The sales receipts are accumulated in batches and sent to the data entry department.
   c. Data from the sales receipts is recorded on floppy disks using a key-to-disk unit.
   d. Data from the floppy disks is read into the computer and added to a monthly sales file on DASD. During the same process, a daily sales report is printed. The sales report is sent to marketing management.

2. Repeat problem 1, using a data flow context diagram and a top-level DFD.

3. Repeat problem 1, using a HIPO hierarchy diagram and an overview diagram.

4. Repeat problem 1, using a Warnier-Orr diagram.

5. Prepare a system flowchart of the system used by Oil Field Equipment Co. to process and fill a customer order. Refer to the case at the end of Chapter 3.

6. Repeat problem 5, using a top-level DFD and second-level DFDs when necessary.

7. Repeat problem 5, using a HIPO overview diagram and detail diagrams where necessary.

8. Repeat problem 5, using a Warnier-Orr diagram.

9. If you worked more than one of problems 5-8, which systems tool do you think did the best job of documenting the procedure? Explain your answer in a short paper.

10. Your instructor will provide you with a list of courses offered by a local computer store. Which courses would a firm use if they were planning on purchasing all of their software? Which courses could the firm's management attend? Are any of the courses of interest to large firms? If so, identify the courses and explain the interest.

11. A firm has decided to implement the eight subsystems of the distribution system described in Chapter 9. They wish to follow a phased cutover approach. Assume that an adequate information services staff exists to cutover more than one subsystem at a time. Draw a top-level DFD showing the sequence of the cutover. Explain the DFD in a short narrative.

CASE PROBLEM: Metroscope Realty

Master of ceremonies: First I'd like to thank the nice folks at the Granada Inn for such a delicious meal. Now it's our pleasure to welcome as our speaker Mr. Arnold Whitmarsh, owner of Metroscope Realty, who will address this monthly meeting of the Fort Wayne Microcomputer Club. Mr. Whitmarsh.

Mr. Whitmarsh: Thank you, Mr. President. It's my pleasure to be here this evening to tell you about our new MIS—that stands for *management information system*. Last summer when my wife and I were vacationing in Iowa, I noticed that one of those computer stores was having a sale. We checked it out and they made me an offer I couldn't refuse. Got a brand new microcomputer for 35 percent off. Brought it back to the office and learned my first lesson about software— you need it. I called the store in Iowa and they sent me five real estate programs for only $29.95 each. Well, I tried to get those programs to work, but I just couldn't do it. I was talking with my brother-in-law, and he said I needed a programmer. So I ran an ad and hired Ray Fletcher, whom you all know. Ray got the programs to run in nothing flat. We started using them and found we didn't even need our desk calculator any more. We're doing calculations now that we never dreamed of before—rental property income analysis, mortgage analysis, depreciation calculations, and much more. (*Applause*) One day Ray came to me and said, "Mr. Whitmarsh, we ought to think about installing a management information system." I said, "What's a management information system?" Ray proceeded to tell me how my agents and I could get a lot of valuable information from the computer. It sounded good, and I gave Ray the green light. "Put as much as you can on the computer," I told Ray. Since then, Ray has been working night and day getting our MIS ready. I thought you might want to ask Ray some questions, since he's the expert, so I brought him along. Take a bow, Ray. (*Applause*) Now, does anybody have any questions?

Club member: Ray, what programs are you writing?

Fletcher: Mostly accounting systems—general ledger, billing, receivables, commission accounting, and inventory.

Club member: Did you consider canned programs?

Fletcher: Not really. Mr. Whitmarsh hired me as a programmer and I felt obligated to give him his money's worth. Besides, I know what we need, and our programs will be tailored to us, not somebody else.

Club member: Have you had a good experience working with the people who will use the system?

Fletcher: I haven't bothered them yet. They're all busy selling, and I don't want to waste their time. I've been in the real estate business off and on for over ten years, and I know what's needed. I plan on getting everything put together in a nice package and then having a training seminar to show everyone how to use it.

Club member: What language are you using, and what kind of documentation are you preparing?

Fletcher: BASIC. And the program listings are pretty much it as far as documentation goes. I include a data dictionary at the beginning of each program, defining all of the variables. Documentation isn't a real problem. I have a good understanding of what's going on and can make changes to the programs very easily if the need arises.

Master of ceremonies: Pardon me, folks. I'm going to have to cut this short. The cleanup crew has to come in and get the room ready for the American Legion dance tonight. See you all next month.

Questions

1. What was the major error Mr. Whitmarsh made in hardware selection?

2. Have any errors been made in the software area? Explain.

3. Is Ray Fletcher doing a good job of developing the MIS? Support your answer.

4. Assume that you are a club member giving Mr. Whitmarsh a ride home after the meeting. He says, "I'd be interested in any suggestions that might help us improve our MIS." Briefly, what would you say?

CASE PROBLEM: New Canaan Business Forms

It seems like only yesterday that you, Jill Marquez, graduated from college with a degree in MIS. The past two years have flown by—moving to New Canaan, Connecticut, and starting your own computer consulting firm; getting the big inventory system contract that paid the bills while you made new contacts; and hiring your first employee, a part-time typist.

All of these thoughts cross your mind as you drive to your 9 A.M. appointment with Betty Kornegay, the president of New Canaan Business Forms. You met Betty at the DPMA (Data Processing Management Association) meeting last week, and chatted with her afterwards about her plans to get a computer. A few days later she called and asked you to come by and talk further. It looks like a good opportunity. New Canaan Business Forms is a growing company, just now reaching the size where it needs to computerize its data processing and begin thinking about an MIS.

Betty: Hi, Jill. Come on in. I'm glad you have time for us to finish our talk. As I mentioned, we've decided to get a computer and have made quite a bit of progress. We hired two systems analysts about eight months ago, and they have just finished their systems study. I'm pleased with the work they're doing. They've established a good rapport with our managers and put together very professional-looking documentation. I'd like you to take a look at it and let me know what you think.

Jill: I'd be happy to. Is that the reason you asked me to drop by?

Betty: No, it isn't. We need to decide whether to do our own programming or buy software packages. We need your help. I'd like to retain you as a consultant to give us guidance as we consider the make-or-buy decision. What about it?

Jill: I'm flattered. I've been involved in these decisions before and know how challenging they can be. I'm sure I can help. But to help me understand your situation better, I'd like to ask you some questions. First, you didn't mention hiring any programmers.

Betty: We haven't gotten that far. We've delayed hiring until we've made the make-or-buy decision.

Jill: That's good. Could you give me some idea of the size of your programming task? Do you have a lot of application programming to do?

Betty: Not too much initially. We plan to implement only the basic accounting systems at first. Our systems are pretty standard—"plain vanilla," I'd say. The analysts tell me we handle things in a typical fashion.

Jill: There's nothing wrong with that. Now tell me, what are your plans for management information?

Betty: At present we're going to hold off. We'd like to get the basic information outputs from the accounting systems and then build on that. We're in no big hurry. I'm a firm believer in taking it slow and easy.

Jill: Do you mind relying on outsiders for your programming?

Betty: Not at all. We rely on outsiders for practically everything else—customers, materials, finances. I can't see that computer programs are any different.

Jill: From what you say, I don't believe you'll have any trouble finding the software you need—not initially, anyway. Later, when you get more involved in management information needs, it might be a different story. I know of several software vendors in the area who have good products and excellent service organizations. I wouldn't hesitate to recommend any of them. And from what I know, their prices are very reasonable. They are not cheap by any means, but they are quite a bit less than what you would have to pay in Boston, for example.

Betty: It's good to know that. I feel that either way we go, we can end up with a quality computer installation. Do you have any other questions?

Jill: I would just like to get a better feel for the relative importance that you place on the factors that will influence your decision. As I name a factor, try to tell me how important it will be in your decision. Do you understand?

Betty: I think so. If I don't understand, I'll stop you. Go ahead.

Jill: The formation of your own programming staff.

Betty: Oh, that's very important—the key consideration, I would suppose. It represents a big expense.

Jill: What about your desire not to be self-sufficient? Do you feel strongly about that?

Betty: Oh no, we really don't have a strong desire. I expect that if we had to be self-sufficient, we would. But that really isn't an important consideration.

Jill: Does the availability of high-quality software and local support personnel from reputable vendors have an influence?

Betty: It certainly does. That would be a major reason for deciding to "buy."

Jill: What about the cost?

Betty: That's not important. We'll pay whatever it takes.

Jill: Am I correct in assuming that since you do not have a big backlog of jobs for the computer, and that your work is "plain vanilla," as you say, those factors have no real bearing on your decision?

Betty: That is correct. I can't see that they are relevant.

Jill: Also, the pressure to do something quickly will have no influence. Right?

Betty: Right. Any more questions?

Jill: No, I think you've answered all of them.

Questions

1. Use the eleven-item scale in Figure 17-9 to determine a make-or-buy score for Betty's firm. Your instructor will give you a blank form. Use the case material as a basis for your entries.

2. What decision do you recommend? Write a short letter to Betty, briefly explaining your recommendation.

Selected Bibliography

Implementing the MIS

Alavi, Maryam, "An Assessment of the Prototyping Approach to Information Systems Development," *Communications of the ACM* 27 (June 1984): 556–563.

Andrews, William C., "Prototyping Information Systems," *Journal of Systems Management* 34 (September 1983): 16–18.

Awad, Elias M., *Systems Analysis and Design*, 2nd ed. (Homewood, IL: Richard D. Irwin, 1985).

Berry, Elizabeth, "A Practical Approach for Standardizing User Documents," *Journal of Systems Management* 35 (July 1984): 8–11.

Bohl, Marilyn, *Tools for Structured Design* (Chicago: Science Research Associates, 1978).

Colter, Mel A., "A Comparative Examination of Systems Analysis Techniques," *MIS Quarterly* 8 (March 1984): 51–66.

Connell, John, and Linda Brice, "Rapid Prototyping," *Datamation* 30 (August 15, 1984): 93ff.

Couger, J. Daniel, Mel A. Colter, and Robert W. Knapp, *Advanced System Development/Feasibility Techniques* (New York: John Wiley & Sons, 1982).

DeMaagd, Gerald R., "Limitations of Structured Analysis," *Journal of Systems Management* 33 (September 1982): 26–27.

Egyhazy, Csaba J., "Technical Software Development Tools," *Journal of Systems Management* 36 (January 1985): 8–13.

Green, Jesse, "Productivity in the Fourth Generation: Six Case Studies," *Journal of Management Information Systems* 1 (Winter 1984–85): 49–63.

Gremillion, Lee L., and Philip Pyburn, "Breaking the Systems Development Bottleneck," *Harvard Business Review* 61 (March-April 1983): 130–137.

Guimaraes, Tor, "A Study of Application Program Development Techniques," *Communications of the ACM* 28 (May 1985): 494–499.

Johnson, James R., "A Prototypical Success Story," *Datamation* 29 (November 1983): 251ff.

Konsynski, Benn R., "Advances in Information System Design," *Journal of Management Information Systems* 1 (Winter 1984–85): 5-32.

Kull, David, "Designs on Development," *Computer Decisions* 17 (April 9, 1985): 86ff.

Langle, Gernot B., Robert L. Leitheiser, and Justus D. Naumann, "A Survey of Applications Systems Prototyping in Industry," *Information & Management* 7 (October 1984): 273–284.

Mendes, Kathleen S., "Structured Systems Analysis: A Technique to Define Business Requirements," *Sloan Management Review* 21 (Summer 1980): 51–63.

Meyers, Edith, "Getting a Grip on Tools," *Datamation* 31 (March 15, 1985): 30ff.

Naumann, Justus D., and A. Milton Jenkins, "Prototyping: The New Paradigm for Systems Development," *MIS Quarterly* 6 (September 1982): 29–44.

Raymond, Louis, "Decision-aid for Small Business Computer Selection," *Journal of Systems Management* 34 (September 1983): 19–21.

Semprevivo, Philip C., *Systems Analysis: Definition, Process, and Design*, 2nd ed. (Chicago: Science Research Associates, 1982).

Vaid-Raizada, Vishist K., "Incorporation of Intangibles in Computer Selection Decisions," *Journal of Systems Management* 34 (November 1983): 30–36.

Wood, Lamont, and Don Leavitt, "Breaking the Applications Logjam," *Computer Decisions* 17 (March 26, 1985): 82ff.

Chapter 18

Controlling the Operational MIS

Learning Objectives

After studying this chapter, you should:

- Understand the role played by control in achieving and maintaining computer security
- Have a better understanding of how the manager can control the MIS development process
- Know how both hardware and software controls can be incorporated into system design
- Know how system operation can be controlled
- Be familiar with two ways to evaluate MIS performance other than economic value
- Understand the reasons for maintaining a system, and the factors that can make that maintenance difficult
- Be familiar with the duties performed by computer operations personnel
- Appreciate the necessity of disaster planning, and understand the types of plans and programs that are possible
- Understand what is implied by the title "corporate information officer"

Introduction

Now that the MIS has been implemented, it can be used on a daily basis to provide the benefits that justified its development. The first three phases of the MIS life cycle (planning, analysis and design, and implementation) probably took several months to a year or more to complete. The firm hopes that this fourth and final phase, operation, lasts several years before it becomes necessary to start the life cycle over again.

We are going to address the operation of the MIS in this chapter. We are also going to recognize the importance of control to the operating MIS. But as we have shown, management does not wait until the operation phase to establish control. Control begins with the planning phase and continues throughout the life cycle.

The Importance of Control

One of the purposes of the MIS is to support managers as they control their areas of operations. But even though the MIS facilitates control, the MIS itself must be controlled. Managers exercise control over the work of the information services staff during the design and implementation of the MIS. Once the MIS becomes operational, its performance must be carefully controlled. We have all read stories of computer crime—how someone embezzled thousands of dollars from a bank by gaining access to the computer data base.[1] We have also heard stories of how computer enthusiasts, called *hackers*, gain access to a company's computer system and destroy or alter data.[2] These intentional acts pose threats to the organization and its information resource, as do unintentional acts such as accidentally caused fires or natural disasters. Management exercises control to prevent those catastrophes that can be prevented and lessen the impact of those where prevention is impossible. In this chapter we focus on the subject of control—where it should be established and how. This is an appropriate topic to conclude our analysis of current MIS technology and methodology. Only by developing a well-controlled MIS can managers have confidence in its output.

The Relationship of Control to Security[3]

The manager exercises control over the system to ensure that it performs as intended. The manager therefore functions as the control element of the system. If system performance is to be maintained, then the system must be kept secure from disruptive influences.

Security may be defined as the protection of both physical and conceptual resources from natural and human hazards. The security of conceptual resources—data and information—is our area of interest. Although a breach of data and information security can take many forms, all fall into the six categories in Table 18-1. The loss can be accidental or intentional, and it can result in modification, destruction, or unauthorized disclosure.

---

[1] See, for example, James Miskiewicz, "DP Security: A Delicate Balance," *Computer Decisions* 17 (April 23, 1985): 104ff, and Martin D. J. Buss and Lynn M. Salerno, "Common Sense and Computer Security," *Harvard Business Review* 62 (March–April 1984): 112–121.

[2] See Gene Troy, "Thwarting the Hackers," *Datamation* 30 (July 1, 1984): 116ff.

[3] Based on *Data Security Controls and Procedures—A Philosophy for DP Installation*, G320-5649 (White Plains, N.Y.: IBM Corporation, 1977).

Table 18-1 Six Ways to Breach Data and Information Security

Accidental	Intentional
1. Modification	4. Modification
2. Destruction	5. Destruction
3. Disclosure	6. Disclosure

Actually, accidental breaches of data and information security are a greater threat than intentional breaches. The intentional acts usually receive the most publicity, but accidents happen more frequently.

System properties facilitating security

If an information system is to keep its contents secure, then it should have three properties: integrity, auditability, and controllability.

A system has *integrity* if it performs as intended. System designers attempt to develop a system that has *functional integrity*, the ability to continue operating even when one or more components have failed. A good example is a distributed processing network that continues to function after one of the processors becomes inoperative.

Auditability means that it is relatively easy for someone to examine, verify, or demonstrate the performance of a system. People who are independent of the system organization, such as internal and external auditors, conduct the audit. For a system to be auditable, it must meet the tests of accountability and visibility. *Accountability* means that responsibility for each event occurring within the system must be traceable to a single individual. *Visibility* means that unacceptable performance is called to the attention of the system managers. A computer program, for example, is auditable when the systems analyst and programmer provide a complete program documentation package and when the program includes the necessary checks for errors.

Controllability permits management to exercise a directing or constraining influence over the behavior, use, and content of the system. One technique for achieving system controllability is to divide the system into subsystems that handle separate transactions. A breach of integrity in one subsystem does not compromise the entire system. For example, one subsystem in a bank is for opening accounts. Another subsystem processes withdrawals. The first subsystem controls the second to prevent unauthorized manipulations of funds, such as someone's opening a fictitious account and transferring funds into it from other accounts.

Managers therefore achieve information system security by developing systems that exhibit the properties of integrity, auditability, and controllability.

The MIS Control Task

Control of the MIS spans all four phases of the life cycle—beginning with planning, and extending through operation. During the life cycle, the controls can be subdivided into those that relate to development, design, and operation. The system *development controls* assure that objectives are identified and that work toward those objectives proceeds according to plan. We have seen examples of how this control is established and maintained during the planning, analysis and design, and implementation phases.

As the MIS is developed, management assures that the design minimizes the chance of error, detects errors when they are made, and corrects the errors for reentry. These are system *design controls*, and they include both hardware and software. *Hardware controls* are incorporated into the equipment by the manufacturers. An example is additional circuitry inside the CPU that detects the loss or gain of electronic bits as bytes of data are transferred from one location to another. *Software controls* are incorporated into system software by the vendors, and in application software by the firm's systems analysts and programmers. An example is an edit program that checks input data for errors.

Once the MIS is implemented, *operation controls* preserve the integrity of the system. One example of an operation control is division of duties among operations personnel in an effort to deter collusion. Another example is locks on computer room doors to prevent unauthorized entry. The operation controls are typically delegated to the manager of computer operations.

Methods of achieving and maintaining control

Management can exercise control in three basic ways, as illustrated in Figure 18-1.

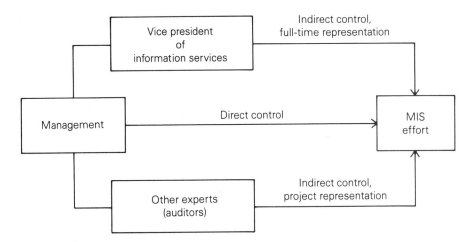

Figure 18-1 Control of the MIS effort.

First, management can take direct control—evaluating progress and performance, and determining what corrective actions are necessary. This approach requires a great deal of computer literacy.

Second, management is represented indirectly in the design effort on a full-time basis by the vice president of information services. This person is an executive who owes allegiance to both the technical staff and the using managers. The vice president of information services is responsible for developing an MIS that meets the managers' needs and then keeping the MIS operational.

Third, management makes use of third parties such as internal or external auditors to evaluate the system and influence its design from a technical standpoint. These specialists represent management on a project basis and provide a degree of computer literacy that the managers cannot be expected to possess.

We will now address the three areas of MIS control—development, design, and operation.

Control of the Development Process

The objective of development control is to ensure that an MIS is implemented that meets the users' needs. The benefits of the control are not realized until the operation phase. Figure 18-2 identifies seven examples of development control and the points in the life cycle where they are applied.

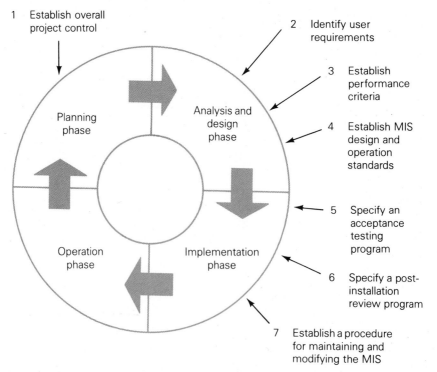

Figure 18-2   Control actions in the MIS life cycle.

Establish overall project control   Top management establishes overall project control during the planning phase by forming a steering committee (if needed), determining the basic specifications of the MIS, and creating a project control mechanism (such as network analysis).

Identify user requirements   Management makes clear the user orientation of the MIS by identifying user information requirements early in the analysis and design phase. These requirements specify problems to be solved or objectives to be attained.

Establish performance criteria   Criteria are established that will be used to evaluate the operational MIS. The criteria are derived directly from the user needs.

Establish MIS design and operation standards   Standards are the guidelines of acceptable performance by members of the information services staff. Three types of outside organizations provide standards that a firm can consider. There are *standards organizations*, such as ISO (International Organization for Standardization) and ANSI (American National Standards Institute, Inc.). The flowchart symbols used in Appendix A are those accepted by ISO and ANSI. In addition, there are *user groups* of different manufacturers' equipment such as SHARE and GUIDE (IBM users). Certain standards are also developed by the *computer manufacturers*, such as the format of file labels and datacom protocols. A firm has a choice of using these externally developed standards, developing its own, or not using standards at all. The last choice is a poor one.

It is a good idea to have a *standards manual* that spells out the conventions that the members of the information services staff are expected to follow. Standards are established for each area of MIS activity (systems analysis, programming operations, data communications, and data base administration). For example, a systems analysis standard would specify the contents of the system documentation package. A data base standard would specify names to be used for data files, records, and elements. Figure 18-3 contains a sample table of contents for a standards manual developed by a large insurance company. It is the responsibility of the information specialists, working under the guidance of the vice president of information services, to develop the manual.

Specify an acceptance testing program   The requirements for approval of each computer program are spelled out in detail. Approval is necessary before the programmer satisfies his or her responsibility for program development and the program is entered into the software library.

Specify a postinstallation review program   Shortly after the cutover, the information services department should conduct an audit to determine how well the MIS is performing. This audit is called the *postinstallation review.* It is not an audit of the system's compliance with accounting practices, but of the system's ability to meet its decision support commitments.

Essentially, the postinstallation review seeks to determine how well the performance criteria are being met. You recall that these criteria were initially stated in the form of general systems objectives during the planning phase, made more

TABLE OF CONTENTS

Figure 18-3 Table of contents from a standards manual.

specific during the analysis and design phase, and modified as necessary during the implementation phase. When the performance criteria evolve in this manner, they usually reflect the features of system performance that management believes to be important.

It is not easy to measure the performance criteria in terms of achieved *economic value*. We have previously recognized the difficulty of placing a monetary value on information. Peter Keen recognizes this difficulty and also points out a problem in measuring MIS performance immediately after cutover. Keen suggests that evaluation consider four *levels of performance*:[4]

Level 1—The MIS leads to *management action*.
Level 2—The MIS leads to *management change* in performing the various management functions such as planning and organizing.
Level 3—The MIS leads to *increased use of decision support tools*.
Level 4—The MIS leads to *organizational change* in terms of its structure and personnel.

According to Keen, levels 1 and 2 can be evaluated shortly after cutover, but levels 3 and 4 require considerably more time. An MIS can therefore be evaluated by using these levels, depending on how long it has been operational.

Another alternative to measuring economic value is to measure *user satisfaction*. The assumption is that satisfaction reflects economic value. It might be appropriate to enlist the services of an unbiased third party to measure user satisfaction shortly after cutover. Perhaps an external EDP auditor or consultant can be retained. However, the information services group and internal auditors can conduct the same type of study.

The best approach is to interview users personally. These personal interviews can be supplemented with mail surveys. Figure 18-4 illustrates a type of questionnaire that can be generated periodically by the computer and mailed to users. Managers can comment on each type of information output they receive. A "yes" response to the final question triggers a personal call from the systems analyst.

It is important to recognize that the postinstallation review is not conducted only one time. It is initially conducted some 30 to 90 days following cutover, after the system has had a chance to settle down. But it is also repeated periodically, such as annually, throughout the life of the system.

Establish a procedure for maintaining and modifying the MIS During the operation phase of the life cycle, the MIS must be maintained and modified. Firms engage in this activity for three reasons. First, it becomes necessary to *correct errors* discovered after the system becomes operational. Second, the MIS must *adapt to changes* in the firm's operations and the managers' information needs. Third, the firm attempts to *make improvements* in system performance.

This maintenance activity is expensive. Estimates of the portion of total software expenditures devoted solely to maintenance range from 40 percent to 75 percent. General Motors estimates that over 70 percent of their software efforts are devoted to maintenance.[5]

The point frequently overlooked is the fact that maintenance is really a "mini" life cycle—involving not only programming but planning and analysis

---

[4] Peter G. W. Keen, "Computer-Based Decision Aids: The Evaluation Problem," *Sloan Management Review* 16 (Spring 1975): 20–22.

[5] Warren Harrison, Kenneth Magel, and Raymond Kluczny, "Research in Software Maintenance," *Journal of Systems Management* 34 (July 1983): 11.

```
TO:        BERNADETTE LONG
           MANAGER, PRODUCT PLANNING

FROM:      ANDREW WENTON
           VICE PRESIDENT OF INFORMATION SYSTEMS

SUBJECT:   PERIODIC EVALUATION OF MIS PERFORMANCE

DATE:      APRIL 21, 1986

LISTED BELOW IS EACH FORM OF INFORMATION OUTPUT PRESENTLY BEING
SUPPLIED BY THE INFORMATION SYSTEMS DIVISION.   PLEASE INDICATE
YOUR EVALUATION OF EACH OUTPUT BY CHECKING THE APPROPRIATE BLANK.
PLEASE RETURN THE COMPLETED QUESTIONNAIRE BY MAY 15.

OUTPUT 1--NEW PRODUCT EVALUATION MODEL

1.   THE ACCURACY OF THIS OUTPUT IS:

     ___  ACCEPTABLE (NO EXPLANATION NEEDED)
     ___  MARGINAL:  EXPLAIN _____
     ___  UNACCEPTABLE:  EXPLAIN _____

2.   THE TIMELINESS IS:

     ___  ACCEPTABLE (NO EXPLANATION NEEDED)
     ___  MARGINAL:  EXPLAIN _____
     ___  UNACCEPTABLE:  EXPLAIN _____

3.   THE COMPLETENESS OF THE INFORMATION IS:

     ___  ACCEPTABLE (NO EXPLANATION NEEDED)
     ___  MARGINAL:  EXPLAIN _____
     ___  UNACCEPTABLE:  EXPLAIN _____

4.   THE PRESENTATION MODE (PRINTED REPORT, CRT DISPLAY) IS:

     ___  ACCEPTABLE (NO EXPLANATION NEEDED)
     ___  MARGINAL:  EXPLAIN _____
     ___  UNACCEPTABLE:  EXPLAIN _____


OUTPUT 2--PRODUCT DELETION MODEL



DO YOU HAVE ANY INFORMATION NEEDS THAT ARE NOT BEING MET?

___ YES;    ___ NO
```

Figure 18-4 MIS evaluation questionnaire.

and design activity. The user must perceive the need for the maintenance and work with the systems analyst to define what is to be done. The analyst and programmer go through the same steps as those taken when the system was originally implemented—although hopefully more quickly.

The difficulty of maintenance is influenced by four factors, relating to the user, the information specialists, the environment in which the information specialists work, and the software itself.[6]

- User sophistication—how well the user can identify the problem and define it in terms of the information system; how well the user can communicate the problem to the information specialist.
- Information specialist abilities—how well the systems analyst can communicate with the user, and the ability of the programmer to modify a program that perhaps he or she did not originally code.
- Information specialist environment—the tools available to the information specialists for communication, analysis, and software and data modification. Examples are automated flowchart generators, application generators, and DBMS.
- Software features—a combination of the complexity of the program and how well it is documented.

When users are not sophisticated, when information specialists have limited abilities, when information specialists have limited tools with which to work, and/or when programs are complex, program maintenance can be very difficult.

These are only a few examples of how management controls the MIS as it evolves through its life cycle phases. In this manner, management ensures that the MIS development project runs smoothly. During this project the systems analysts and programmers build certain control features into the system design. These design controls influence the performance of the MIS once it becomes operational.

Control of System Design

It is possible to design an information system without any built-in controls. The design cost would be less than for a system with controls. While that result might seem appealing, the penalties would outweigh the savings. It would be like buying a car without a spare tire, a fuel gauge, bumpers, and door locks. The cost would be lower, but the reduced safety and security would expose you to hazards that might be more expensive in the long run.

Some subsystems of the MIS demand greater controls than others. Generally, anything involving money needs the tightest controls. A firm cannot afford mistakes in calculating an employee's payroll check or a vendor's payment. On the

---

[6]Based on Harrison, Magel, and Kluczny, pp. 13–14.

other hand, a nonmonetary subsystem such as a report of sales statistics is still useful even if it contains some minor errors.

It is important to recognize that systems controls cost money. A control should not be implemented if its cost exceeds its value. The value is the degree to which a risk is reduced, and this is a difficult estimate to make. For example, what is the value of a control that reduces the risk of producing a bad payroll check? You would have to know how often the error occurs and the amount of money involved.

In spite of the difficulty, the systems analyst must make the user aware of the points in the system where errors can occur and what the consequences might be. This is called *risk analysis*. A good method for communicating this information to the manager is a *control matrix* such as that pictured in Figure 18-5.

Subsystems	Risks		
	Incomplete data	Inaccurate data	Unauthorized transactions
Edit order data	Missing order data • Customer number • Customer order number • Item number • Quantity • Price	Wrong order data • Customer number • Item number • Quantity • Price	
Compute credit check			Exceed credit limits
Log in orders	Missing orders • Never entered • Lost after entry		
Remove filled orders	Inaccurate order log • Filled orders not removed		

Figure 18-5 Control matrix of potential errors in the order entry system.

In this example, the risks have been categorized as incomplete data, inaccurate data, and unauthorized transactions. The system being described is the order entry system. These are all of the risks that could potentially plague the operation of that system. Design controls can be incorporated into the subsystems that specifically address each risk.

Areas of system design controls[7]

The MIS includes many subsidiary systems such as order entry, and most are unique in some way. Each one can be subdivided into its basic system parts, however, and controls can be considered for each part. Figure 18-6 illustrates these basic system parts.

The first part is devoted to *transaction origination*. This procedure involves recording one or more data elements on a source document. The document might be a sales order form or a payroll time card, for example. This origination is external to the computer equipment and precedes any computer processing.

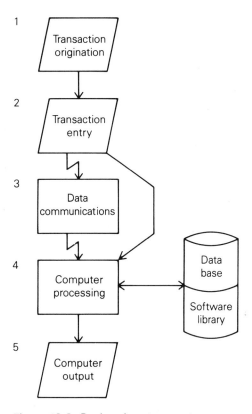

Figure 18-6 Basic subsystem parts.

---

[7]The format for this study of design controls, and much of the content, was obtained from *Systems Auditability and Control: Control Practices* (Altamonte Springs, Fla.: The Institute of Internal Auditors, 1977), pp. 45–86.

After the transaction is originated, it is converted into a computer-readable form, a process called *transaction entry*. This part *does* involve the use of computing equipment. The transaction entry device can be online, such as a micro keyboard or a mainframe terminal, or the device can be offline such as a key-punch, key-to-tape, or key-to-disk unit.

Some systems include a *data communications* part. In other systems, data is entered by transaction entry directly into the computer for processing.

Once the data is entered into computer storage, it is processed by programs in the software library. In many instances, this *computer processing* results in data added to or taken from the data base.

When the processing has been completed, some *computer output* is created. This output can be information for management or data for use by another subsystem.

The following paragraphs address each of these system parts. Some examples of control for each part will be described to provide an idea of the alternatives available. There are many more methods of control than those included here.

Transaction origination   Figure 18-7 provides a further breakdown of the steps involved in originating the transaction. Each of the five parts shown is a candidate for controls. The number and variety of controls built into each part depend on the risks to be reduced and the costs of the controls.

Controls start with the *source document origination*—the order form, the payroll card, or the check. These controls deal with procedures for (1) designing

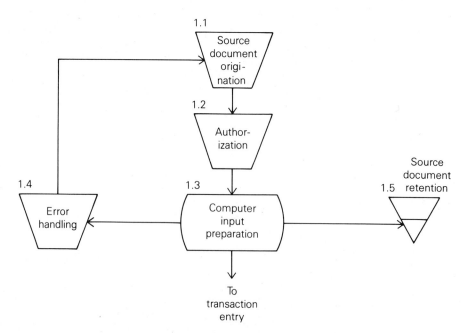

Figure 18-7 Transaction origination control areas.

source documents for use, (2) assuring the security of documents before use, and (3) handling the documents.

Authorization controls describe how data entries are to be made to the documents and by whom. Such control is accomplished by requiring signatures on source documents, involving several persons in the preparation of each document, devising written procedures, and establishing limits on the approval of certain transactions, such as customer credits.

Computer input preparation controls establish a means of identifying input records found to be in error and assuring that all input data is processed. Examples of controls of this type are transaction logs, which serve as a record of transactions to be processed, and the practice of batching source documents.

Error-handling controls provide a systematic way to correct errors and resubmit records for input. This control area is not concerned with detecting errors, but with correcting them once they have been detected. Each subsystem part has an error-handling area.

Finally, controls of *source document retention* specify how documents will be stored after use and under what conditions they will be made available to potential users.

Transaction entry   Transaction entry converts the data from a source document to computer-readable format. The controls attempt to maintain the accuracy of data to be transmitted over a communication network or entered directly into a computer. Figure 18-8 shows how this subsystem part is divided into four control areas.

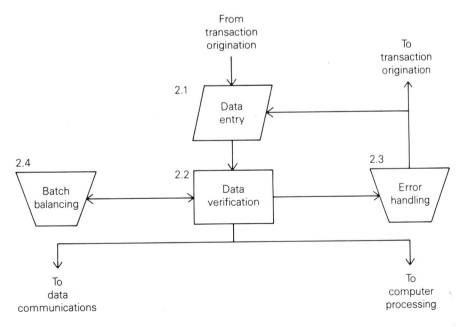

Figure 18-8 Transaction entry control areas.

Controls over *data entry* can apply to either offline or online processes. The controls exist in the form of written procedures and the input equipment itself. The equipment should be located close to the point of transaction origination to reduce delays in entry. Also, an effort should be made to capture the input on a computer-readable medium such as a cassette tape or diskette.

After the data is recorded, it is checked for accuracy. There are two basic approaches to *data verification*—key and sight. In *key verification*, the data is keyed into the system twice, preferably by different operators. The software compares the two inputs and issues a signal when they are not exactly the same. In *sight verification*, the operator views the data on the screen before entering the data into the system. Key verification is the more expensive since the work must be done twice. Because of the expense, key verification is performed only on data that must be free from error, such as financial data.

Control totals such as document count and dollar amounts are accumulated for each batch in a *batch-balancing* process. These totals are compared with similar totals prepared during computer output. An equal comparison indicates that all transactions have been processed.

Data communications   In subsystems where data is transmitted over a communications network, there are three areas where controls are possible: message sending, the communications channel, and message receipt. See Figure 18-9. Error handling is not a separate area but is accomplished by the communications equipment.

Of all the system parts, the one receiving the most attention because of its vulnerability to risk is data communications. This is potentially the weak link in the system because the communications signals go outside the firm's facilities. Unauthorized persons can enter the system through the datacom network and commit two types of intrusion. *Passive intruders* do not make changes to the system but become knowledgeable of its contents. This is a major threat to an MIS since the data base contains information of a highly confidential nature such as strategic plans. *Active intruders* make changes to either programs or data. In this way, computer criminals embezzle money from financial systems. This type of intrusion can also degrade an MIS by changing data as well as the DSS programs that process that data.

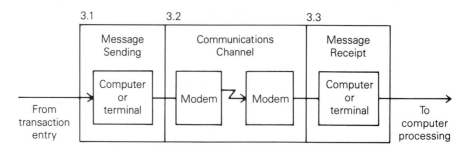

Figure 18-9   Data communications control areas.

Control can be established over the *message sending* portion of the datacom network by using codes to identify both users and terminals and by restricting users to entering only certain approved transactions. In addition, a message log can be maintained of all transactions for periodic audit or follow-up.

Much of the control over message sending can be provided by a DBMS. Some DBMSs provide several levels of security, with user password checking being the most basic level. Additional levels can be provided by user directories, field directories, and data encryption. We discussed these topics in Chapter 7. Recall that we also recognized in that chapter that microcomputer DBMSs are usually weak in terms of their control features.

Most of the controls of the *communication channel* involve hardware rather than software. If the firm has a choice, it is always better to use a private circuit rather than a dial-up one. The private circuit offers greater security from hackers who randomly dial numbers, listening for the distinctive high-pitched carrier tone provided by the modem. These hackers frequently use a micro to automatically dial the numbers.

Not every firm, however, can afford the cost of a private circuit. In that case, the firm can encrypt the data as it is transmitted over the dial-up circuit. *Encryption*, which we discussed earlier in Chapter 8, also provides an added degree of security for private circuits. The logic behind relying on encryption for security is that even if an intruder gains access to the channel, by wiretapping for example, the data obtained would be meaningless.

Encryption is considered by some persons to be the most effective hardware device aimed at achieving security. It doesn't protect the user from all risks, however. Encryption offers no protection against either accidental or intentional destruction of the data. The main problem in using encryption is controlling the key to the encryption algorithm. To date, no effective way has been devised to prevent the key from falling into unauthorized hands.

Controls of *message receipt* include the automatic detection of errors by the receiving units, and requests for resubmission. Errors can be detected when *check bits* or *check characters* are transmitted along with the data, and the bits or characters are inappropriate for the data received. In that case, the datacom equipment either corrects the error automatically or executes a retransmission. Special *header labels* (at the beginning) and *trailer labels* (at the end) can also be added to blocks of records, making it possible to account for all records.

For firms using dial-up lines, telephone numbers of the modems can be changed frequently and kept confidential. All calls can be intercepted by a special hardware unit called a *port protection device*. The port protection device contains a microprocessor that can check the user's password. Some of the devices have a *callback ability*—the user hangs up, and the device calls back after the security check has been completed. Some of the devices also deviate from the modem tone by using a recorded human voice, or simply silence.

The combination of hardware and software controls designed for communication-based systems enables a very high level of security to be achieved. There are indications, however, that management should look elsewhere for the point where the security of the system is most likely to be breached. In a survey conducted by the American Bar Association, it was learned that persons working *within* the information services area are the biggest risks. Programmers, followed by operators, were most often identified as the culprits.[8]

Computer processing   Up to this point, all of the system design controls have been placed on entering data into the computer. With that now accomplished, controls can be built into the programs and the data base. These control areas are shown in Figure 18-10.

Data-handling controls properly identify input transactions and assure the accuracy of data manipulation and computation. Assume that three types of input transactions—identified by codes 1, 2, and 3—can be processed. Through programming, the computer can determine if a transaction is a code 1 or 2. If not, it is a mistake to assume the code is a 3. Perhaps an error was made in keying in a 1 code, and an A was entered instead. It is neither a 1 nor a 2, and it most certainly isn't a 3. Figure 18-11 shows examples of good and bad program logic to test the transaction code.

Another example of a control of data manipulation and computation would be the testing of the result of an arithmetic operation for reasonableness. The monthly commission for a sales representative can be checked for a maximum limit, say $5000. Any exceptions can be flagged for follow-up to verify accuracy.

The *error-handling* control area is concerned with reporting errors and with reentering correct data. When a transaction is found to contain an error, processing of that transaction is suspended. The transaction record is entered into an error suspense file and held until it is corrected. An error report is printed by the computer, identifying the error. Errors in money data fields are corrected with proper debit and credit entries rather than deletion and replacement. If deletion and replacement were allowed, any figure could be entered as a replacement

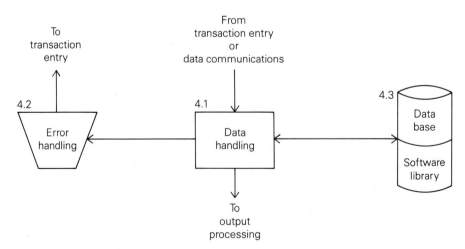

Figure 18-10   Computer processing control areas.

---

[8]Miskiewicz, p. 108.

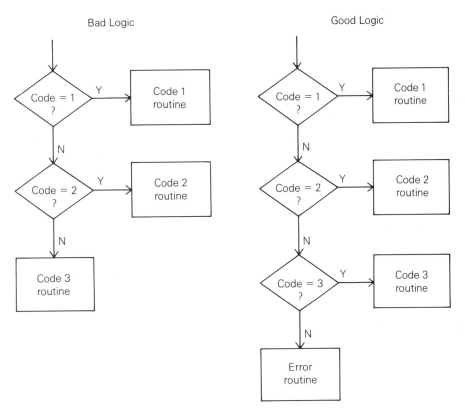

Figure 18-11 Good and bad approaches to code testing.

amount and an error could be difficult to detect. The error suspense file can be used periodically to prepare statistical reports on types of errors, frequency, and source.

Processing controls can also be established on changes to both the *data base* and the *software library*. Passwords and user and field directories protect the data base, as we have seen. This is another point in the system where header and trailer labels can be used. Header labels can assure that the proper file is being used and that a file is retained for the required length of time. Trailer labels can contain control totals for data in the file. Other types of controls can be used to protect the software library. A log of all changes to programs can be maintained in secondary storage, identifying the date and time of the transaction, the terminal, security codes, and password.

Computer output This subsystem part is responsible for delivering the finished product to the customer. See Figure 18-12.

The *computer operations balancing* area verifies that all batches and transactions received from user departments are processed. This procedure is accomplished by balancing computer output totals to totals established at input. Additional controls can be established on money amounts. Computer reports can also

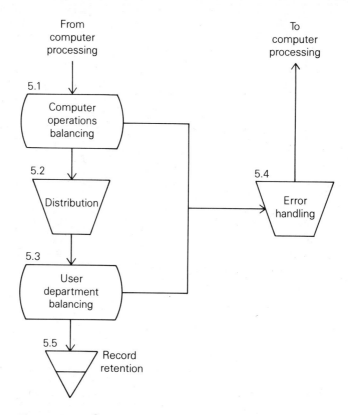

Figure 18-12   Computer output control areas.

be prepared on changes to programs and on transaction volume by terminal to detect unauthorized use.

Controls on report *distribution* attempt to assure that only the appropriate persons receive the output. A cover sheet identifying the recipient is attached to each report, and a log is maintained showing when each output is distributed. Only the correct number of copies is prepared. The recipient can be asked to acknowledge receipt by returning a special form.

User department balancing involves balancing computer output to control totals established when input data was originally prepared. The user department has a responsibility to establish and maintain controls that guarantee system integrity. The responsibility does not rest entirely with information services.

Error handling consists of an error log maintained by a special control group. Errors are corrected, following written procedures, and the corrected transactions are reentered. Upon acceptance by the system, the transactions are removed from the error log. The error log is periodically scanned to identify transactions where correction is overdue.

The final area of *record retention* is the responsibility of the user department. The objective is to maintain proper security over computer output and to control waste disposal. Paper shredders used for out-of-date reports and aborted computer runs represent a control of this type.

It is the systems analyst's responsibility to assure that the system design includes the proper level of controls. The analyst can take the hardware controls as given and can then build in the software controls where needed.

Control of System Operation

The two control areas discussed above, development and design, deal with actions taken prior to cutover to the MIS. After cutover, a third control phase becomes necessary. This is the control over the actual operation of the MIS.

System operation controls are intended to achieve efficiency and security. Computer operations are a complex system composed of the computer, peripheral equipment, personnel, facilities, and supplies that must work together in a coordinated fashion. In addition, the operations are meant to be safe from disruption or abuse by unauthorized persons both inside and outside the firm.

Controls that contribute to the desired efficiency and security can be classified into six areas:

1. Organizational structure
2. Input/output scheduling and control
3. Library control
4. Equipment maintenance
5. Environmental control and facilities security
6. Disaster planning

Organizational structure

The information services staff is organized along lines of specialization. Analysts, programmers, and operations personnel are usually kept separate and develop the skills required of their work area only. This structure contributes to the efficiency of the overall operation, and also to security. It is much more difficult to violate the system when the cooperation of several individuals is required. Controls are built into the system by each category of personnel. One type of employee (say a programmer) might be able to bypass his or her controls, but not the others.

In addition to the separation of operations from analysis and programming, it is desirable to separate the different areas within operations. The main areas are input/output scheduling and control, data entry, media library, production control, and equipment operations. In a department organized as in Figure 18-13, it is difficult for both user departments and operations personnel to violate the system.

The different units within operations play special roles in the flow of computer jobs through the department. These roles are illustrated in Figure 18-14. Data entry personnel convert input data into a computer-readable form. Computer operators perform the necessary computer setups to run the jobs. Operators of peripheral equipment such as decollators and forms bursters (machines that separate the carbons from multiple copy forms and pull apart the separate pages)

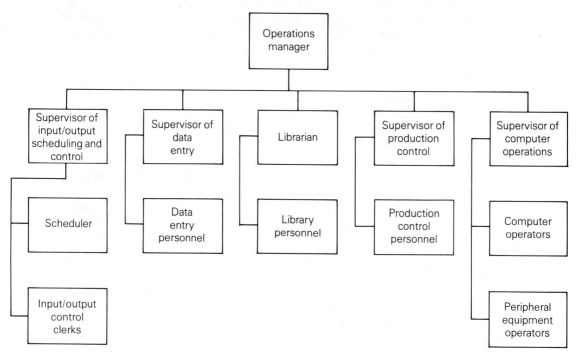

Figure 18-13 Organization of the operations department.

make the computer output available for distribution. Library personnel make data files available for processing. Input and output control personnel establish controls at points of data entry and exit. Production control personnel assure that jobs are run as scheduled. The scheduler establishes the production schedule for all operations activities.

Computer operations can be viewed as a manufacturing operation. Work flows through the plant, and one measure of efficiency is the speed of the flow. *Response time* is measured from the time the user releases the source data (point 1 in Figure 18-14) until he or she receives the output (point 6). *Turnaround time* runs from the time the operations department receives the data (point 2) until the output is transmitted to the user (point 5). Turnaround time measures the efficiency of all of the operations units. *Throughput time* is the time from input into the CPU (point 3) until output from the CPU (point 4). Throughput time measures the efficiency of only the computer processing within operations.

Input/output scheduling and control

In a factory it is necessary to input raw materials, schedule the flow of materials through the production area, and distribute the finished output to the customers. In the computer operations "factory," these tasks are the responsibility of the input/output scheduling and control section.

Often an important responsibility of this section is to serve as a link between the computer and its users. This relationship exists in a batch environment, where

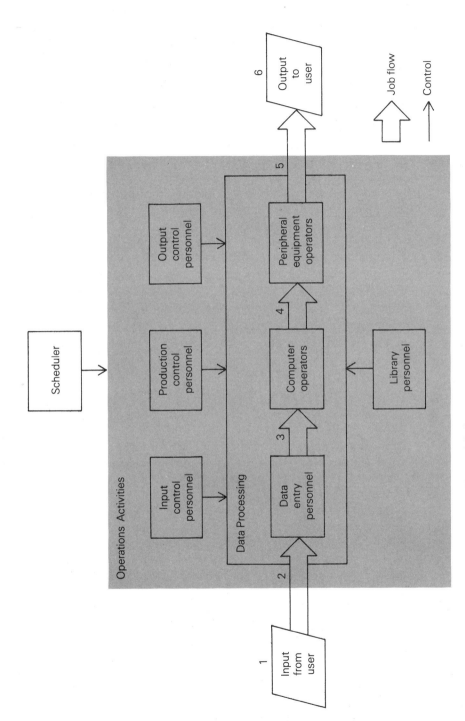

Figure 18-14 Operations organization facilitates job flow.

users submit data in source document form for data entry, batch processing, and the delivery of hardcopy output. The relationship also exists when online users submit jobs to be batch processed. But when input, processing, and output are all online, the input/output control section is effectively bypassed. These relationships are diagrammed in Figure 18-15. The controls applied by the input/output control section are based primarily on the batch balancing activities performed during transaction entry (step 2.4 in Figure 18-8) and computer output (step 5.1 in Figure 18-12).

The supervisor of the input/output control section is also often responsible for job scheduling. The scheduler prepares the daily schedule from one day to one week in advance, based on historical data describing computer use, the recurring jobs and their characteristics, special jobs to be run, and situations unique to that day—operator absences, jobs to be rerun, changed priorities, and so on. Scheduling computer work is very similar to scheduling production work in a factory, and many of the same techniques apply.

The schedule is given each day to the production control section responsible for coordinating the schedule with computer operations. Separating scheduling from production control makes it difficult to run unauthorized programs or make unauthorized changes to the data base. In an online environment, however, that possibility exists. In that situation, security must be achieved by incorporating a mix of the network controls discussed earlier.

Library control

A computer media library is similar to a book library, in that there is a librarian, a collection of media, an area where the media are stored, and a procedure for making the media available to users.

The computer media include reels of magnetic tape and disk packs (see Figure 18-16). These media are stored in racks, some with locks for confidential material. The racks should be housed in a room that is secure from unauthorized access. The same temperature and humidity controls should apply to the library as to the computer room. Only library personnel should be allowed in the library, with computer media being released only to computer operators.

Duplicate copies of files and programs should be maintained, although not in the library. Another location is desirable as a hedge against a disaster in the computer area. Additionally, it is common practice to maintain two *file generations* so that reconstruction can be performed if necessary.

Files organized sequentially are updated on a cycle basis, such as daily or monthly. The file created on Wednesday contains data from the Tuesday file plus Tuesday transaction data. Likewise, the Tuesday file was prepared from the Monday file plus Monday data. The Monday, Tuesday, and Wednesday files represent three generations of data. (This concept is illustrated in Figure 18-17.) The data on the Monday file is not erased until the Wednesday file is created. If anything happens to the Wednesday file, it can be reconstructed by again processing the Tuesday transactions against the Tuesday file. These sequential files can be recorded on magnetic tape or DASD.

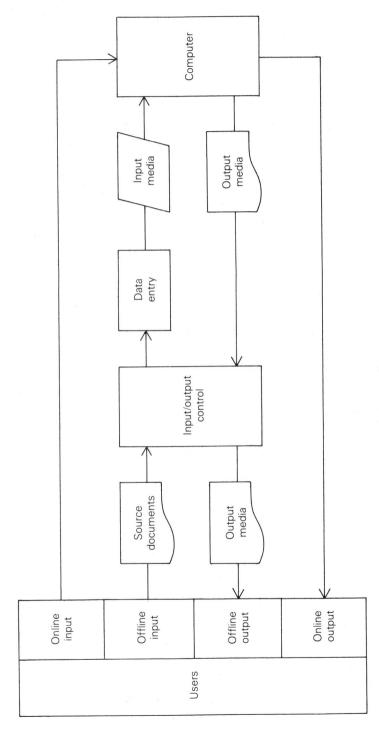

Figure 18-15 Input/output control interfaces with batch users—input or output.

Figure 18-16 A tape library.

A different procedure must be followed for files recorded on a DASD and organized for direct access. File backup can be provided by "dumping" the DASD files periodically onto magnetic tape. The transaction data also is saved so that the DASD file can be reconstructed if necessary.

Equipment maintenance

Maintenance is a greater concern for mainframe and minicomputer users than for micro users. The micro user simply waits for something to break and then takes the unit to the nearest computer store for repair. The greater complexity of

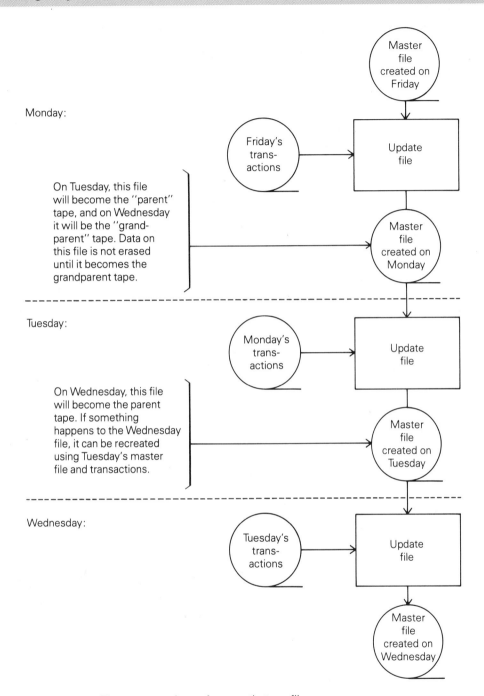

Monday:

On Tuesday, this file will become the "parent" tape, and on Wednesday it will be the "grand-parent" tape. Data on this file is not erased until it becomes the grandparent tape.

Tuesday:

On Wednesday, this file will become the parent tape. If something happens to the Wednesday file, it can be recreated using Tuesday's master file and transactions.

Wednesday:

Master file created on Friday

Friday's trans-actions

Update file

Master file created on Monday

Monday's trans-actions

Update file

Master file created on Tuesday

Tuesday's trans-actions

Update file

Master file created on Wednesday

Figure 18-17 Three generations of magnetic tape files.

larger computers makes them more susceptible to failure and more difficult to fix. The following discussion assumes a mainframe or minicomputer.

It is the computer manufacturer's responsibility to keep the equipment in running order. This service is included in the monthly lease charges or is contracted separately for purchased equipment.

The computer repair persons, called *customer engineers (CEs)* or *field engineers (FEs)*, perform both unscheduled and scheduled maintenance. *Unscheduled maintenance* is performed when the computer develops unexpected problems, as when an electronic component suddenly goes bad. *Scheduled maintenance*, called *preventive maintenance (PM)*, is designed to prevent problems. It is like changing the oil in your car every 4000 miles.

On larger systems it is common practice to provide the FEs with a specific time each day to perform PM, such as from 8:00–9:00 A.M. It is also common for the FEs to have their own area just off of the computer room to house their test equipment, supplies, repair manuals, and so on. FEs can be assigned full-time to the site depending on the quantity of equipment installed.

The manager of computer operations monitors the performance of the computer to ensure that downtime is not excessive. *Downtime* is that period of time when the computer is inoperative for any reason. The manager monitors the performance by observing activities in the operations area, talking with operations personnel and FEs, and receiving reports of system performance. The reports show downtime by time of day, by computer unit, and so on.

Time for PM, adequate FE facilities, and a good monitoring system are controls that contribute to smooth equipment operation.

Environmental control and facilities security

Computers must be given special care to protect the investment and ensure against damage or malfunction. The large models require special environmental conditions—the computer room must be clean, and the temperature and humidity must remain within tolerance limits. Backup electrical power is often available so that operation will continue even when normal electrical service is interrupted.

In the early years of computer use, many firms regarded their systems as showpieces. Computers were frequently located in sidewalk-level rooms with large viewing windows. Passersby could note the progressive nature of the firm. Social unrest during the late sixties changed all of that. Some computer centers were bombed or sabotaged. Computer crime added emphasis to the need for greater security. Now, the trend is to isolate computer areas, making them inaccessible to all but authorized persons. Those persons must use magnetic-stripe cards or door-lock combinations to enter.

The trend toward distributed processing and microcomputers has had an effect on facilities security. Instead of having only one computer installation to protect, the firm now has many. Security at the distributed sites is normally not as strict as it is at the central location. This condition is especially true of micros. Micros are often left unattended, with diskettes containing programs and data within easy reach. This is an especially serious problem when the micros are networked to the host.

A few firms have taken security precautions with their micros, however. As an example, Security Pacific National Bank of Glendale, California, devotes a separate chapter of their security manual to micros, and gives a copy to each new micro owner. There is also a large variety of software and furniture aimed at securing micros. Morgan Computing Company sells a software package called Copy Protector that disables the use of copy and diskcopy commands. Micro-Clear, Inc. markets a package called dSECUR that provides multiple-level security for dBASE II files. Several lockable cabinets are available to house the micro. An example is Data-MATE, a welded-steel hood sitting atop a welded-steel base, which is bolted to the floor.

Disaster planning

The firm that establishes the above controls on system operation can expect a high level of performance. But unforeseen disasters may occur. For example, a fire in another part of the building can destroy remote equipment, such as terminals; a program tape can be erased by mistake; vendor supplies and services can be terminated because of a strike. Management should anticipate and plan for these possible disasters, called *contingencies*, so that the firm can recover and resume operation.

Rather than devise a single, all-encompassing plan, a more manageable approach is to define multiple plans. The most common plans include:

- Emergency plan
- Backup plan
- Vital-records plan
- Recovery plan

An *emergency plan* is not intended to prevent a catastrophe, but rather, to minimize the effects. Top priority is the safety of the firm's employees. Effective strategies provide for alarm, evacuation, and protecting machines with covers or fire-quenching systems.

A *backup plan* details how the firm can continue to function from the time it suffers a loss of capability until it can resume normal operations. Users identify information processing jobs that will be necessary during the recovery period. These jobs, in turn, identify the minimum equipment configuration required. Arrangements can be made for the use of a backup system. When very little system degradation can be tolerated, even for a short time, backup equipment is located on the premises. An airline, for example, has a backup CPU for its reservation system. Some firms even duplicate their entire computing center. Mobil and Shell have done this.

Most firms cannot afford the expense of backup or duplicate systems. A more practical approach is to make arrangements with another firm that uses the same type of equipment. If firm A's computer goes down, it can use firm B's. Firm B enjoys the same privilege.

In 1978, Sungard Recovery Services of Wayne, Pennsylvania, initiated a new alternative for disaster victims. It established a computing facility that is made available on a subscription basis. The arrangement is like an insurance policy—the firm pays from $3,000 to $13,000 a month for the privilege of using the facility when necessary. Sungard has since opened a second site in Chicago so that more than a single customer can be supported at a time.

Installations such as the ones offered by Sungard are named *hot sites*. Most feature IBM mainframes, but some make available NCR, DEC, Burroughs, and Honeywell equipment. Datacom facilities are often included as well. Approximately 20 firms are now in the hot site business.

Another approach is for a firm to construct computer facilities at a second location, and then acquire replacement hardware in the event of a disaster. These facilities are called *cold sites*, or *empty shells*. A firm taking this approach assumes that it can obtain the needed equipment from its vendor. When a disaster strikes only one or a few of a vendor's customers, this high-level support is possible. Security Pacific National Bank received such service when a power system malfunctioned and destroyed four mainframes. They were able to get a backup from IBM within ten hours. However, if several users in the same area are wiped out by the same disaster, such as an earthquake, such fast service might not be possible.

Another plan that works in conjunction with the backup plan is a *vital-records plan*. This plan identifies critical data files and specifies where duplicate copies are stored. The storage location should be some distance from the computer installation.

In addition to the backup and vital-records plans, a *recovery plan* is intended to normalize the firm's computing facility after a disaster. The recovery plan complements the other plans by specifying how the MIS resources can be reassembled. The plan identifies sources of replacement equipment, communication facilities, and supplies.

Firms can also establish *programs* that are followed on a daily basis. Programs deal with topics such as *data classification*. This program determines the relative importance of data elements and specifies those employees who can have access. It is also important to identify the person, known as the *owner*, who is responsible for each data element. Each element should have an owner who monitors data accuracy and ensures that the correct degree of security is maintained. The owner is identified in the data element dictionary.

Another example of a security program deals with *document classification*. Here, each document used within the firm is given a classification. The military has used this practice for years, popularizing the term "top secret." Some firms in private industry take similar precautions.

Plans and programs such as these have only recently been considered necessary. Few firms have achieved the level of disaster planning described here. The plans are costly and are difficult to justify economically. Very often, disaster has to strike before top management sees the necessity of such precautions. The vice president of information services should make the CEO aware of both the risks and how a set of well-thought-out plans and programs can speed recovery. There are several examples that can be cited. A Thanksgiving Day fire at Norwest Bank of Minneapolis destroyed much of their computer operation. A disaster plan had been in effect for only six months prior to the fire, and operations were resumed in leased warehouse space within two days. The computer center at Mazda Motors of America in Compton, California, was wiped out when a rain-soaked roof collapsed. A computer leasing firm was used to set up a new system at a new site in five days. The Washington Post missed an edition when its main CPU went down. A backup system was put into service and the presses were rolling again in six hours.

The vice president of information services can also enlist the support of internal and external auditors as well as vendors of disaster recovery services in making top management aware of the necessity for a comprehensive plan.

Putting MIS Control in Perspective

When learning about all of the ways in which the operational integrity and the security of an MIS can be violated, it is easy to get the idea that a computer-based system is controlled less than a manual one. Nothing could be farther from the truth. Even with all of its risks, the computer system is far superior to a manual system in terms of accuracy, consistency in following procedures, and protection against misuse. The reason for this superiority lies not so much in the electronic equipment as in the fact that more attention has been directed at computer-based systems than manual ones. The first computer-based systems were not secure by today's standards. Over the years, the technology and methodology have evolved that provide the manager with a set of effective control tools.

Why is the manager concerned about controlling the MIS? For one thing, if the MIS is inoperative for any length of time, there probably will be no physical system of the firm to manage. Employees on all levels depend on the MIS for day-to-day support. Recall the important role that the MIS plays in the manufacturing area, for example.

In addition, losing the MIS effectively isolates many managers from the physical system. This is especially critical on the lower levels, since those managers depend heavily on the MIS to signal problems needing their attention. Although upper-level managers also rely on the MIS, their longer planning horizon minimizes the disruption caused by short periods of computer downtime.

More serious than the temporary disruption of MIS output is the effect that data base tampering can have on decision making. Recall that data can be modified, destroyed, or disclosed. The worst act would be *modification* that goes undetected. In this case, the MIS would produce erroneous information that could cause the wrong decisions to be made. The results can also be bad when modification is detected; management's confidence in the entire MIS can be seriously damaged. If data base contents are *destroyed*, then a recovery procedure becomes necessary to recreate the files from backup copies. The disruption to decision making in this case would be minimal. The third possibility, *disclosure*, could cause the firm to lose its competitive position in the marketplace. A competitor could engage in a form of electronic espionage to tap into the firm's data base. Conceivably, the competitor could have available as much information on the firm's operations as the firm's own managers. These same concerns for the data base also exist for the software library.

Primarily as a result of attention focused on computer crime during recent years, management is more aware of the need to control the operating MIS than ever before. Many firms are increasing computer security with the intent of minimizing their exposure to the many risks. As safeguards are installed to protect the firm's financial assets, another valuable resource will also be protected—information. In the long run, protecting information might be more important to the performance of the firm than protecting the firm's financial assets.

The Corporate Information Officer

Throughout the book, we have used the term vice president of information services to identify the person responsible for all of the firm's computing resources. Another title, *corporate information officer*, or *CIO*, is beginning to be used.

This is not just a new name tag; the title carries with it a stature within the organization that has seldom been enjoyed by the top computer manager. The term CIO means that the computer manager is an executive—on the same level as the vice presidents of marketing, manufacturing, and finance. This does not mean stature only in terms of the organization chart, but in terms of influence on the firm's overall operations as well. Acceptance at this level means that the CIO participates in long-range strategic planning for the entire organization. The scope of the CIO's activities therefore exceeds the boundaries of the information services department.

Too many top computer managers have neither solicited nor achieved such executive status even though they might have the title of vice president. In a survey of some 300 information services executives by The Conference Board, 50 percent were found to have the title of vice president. However, only 25 percent of the vice presidents report directly to their firm's CEO.[9]

The expanded scope of the CIO's activities demands that she or he possess general management skills. This is where computer executives in the past have often come up short. Emphasis has been placed on technical skills instead. Ideally, the CIO will have the same managerial skills as other executives, plus enough technical skill to interact with personnel in the information services area.

Critical success factors for CIOs

We saw in Chapter 16 how certain critical success factors (CSFs) can be identified for the firm as a whole. The person who pioneered the CSF approach at that level has also applied it to the CIO. John Rockart has identified four CSFs that seem to apply to most, but not all, CIOs.[10] The CSFs are:

- Service—an ability to meet the needs of the MIS users, and make the users aware of the service being provided.

[9] John Rymer, "Executives to Unlock Technology's Promise," *Computer Decisions* 15 (September 15, 1983): 143.

[10] John F. Rockart, "The Changing Role of the Information Systems Executive: A Critical Success Factors Perspective," *Sloan Management Review* 24 (Fall 1982): 3–13.

- Communication—the two-way communication between the CIO and key users.
- Information services personnel—the quality of persons working in the information services area. Persons must be attracted to the area and retained who can maintain data processing systems and develop new DSS and OA systems.
- Repositioning information services—changing the position of information services in the organization, and how that position is perceived. This CSF has four dimensions— technical, organizational, psychological, and managerial. *Technical repositioning* involves supplying users with more powerful problem-solving tools. *Organizational repositioning* involves integrating the MIS throughout the firm. *Psychological repositioning* means changing the users' perceptions of the computer group from data processing to decision support. *Managerial repositioning* means relocating many information specialists throughout the firm in user areas.

If the top computer manager aspires to be a CIO, he or she should identify the CSFs that apply and establish strategies for implementing each one.

The idea of a CIO is just starting to catch on. It seems to be most popular in banking, insurance, and airlines industries, where the information resource is seen as indispensable. The idea yet has to make an impact on manufacturing organizations where physical resources are so important.

Although we have not used the term CIO, our descriptions of the vice president of information services have assumed such top-level performance and influence.

Summary

The MIS assists the manager in performing the control function. But the MIS must also be controlled. The objective of the control is to assure that the MIS is implemented as intended, the system operates as intended, and the operation is secure from misuse or disruption. Data and information security can be breached either intentionally or accidentally, resulting in modification, destruction, or disclosure.

A system should possess three properties: integrity, auditability, and controllability. A system has integrity if it performs according to its specifications. A system has auditability if it exhibits accountability and visibility. Accountability means that responsibility is established for each transaction, and visibility means that exceptions from standard performance are called to the attention of the system's managers. Controllability permits the manager to maintain a directing influence on the system.

The MIS control task is focused on three areas: development, design, and operation. The manager can achieve control in these areas directly, through the vice president of information services, or through other experts such as auditors.

Control of the development process spans the three life cycle phases leading to cutover. Managers initially achieve control by establishing a project plan based on a mechanism such as network analysis. The analyst next identifies the managers' information needs and the managers establish the performance criteria of the new system so that, from the outset, the MIS is dedicated to user support. The information services department performs its tasks according to standards, such as flowcharting symbols and system documentation contents. The work of the programmer must adhere to an acceptance test that stipulates exactly how the program must perform. Before cutover, managers specify how a postinstallation review will be conducted, and they establish a procedure for maintaining and modifying the MIS. The operational MIS can be evaluated based on the level of changes that are produced, user satisfaction, and economic value. System maintenance is necessitated in order to correct errors in system performance, adapt the system to changes, and make improvements. Maintenance is difficult in the case of lack of user sophistication, unskilled information specialists, an environment of inadequate maintenance tools, and complex software. These development controls are applied to anticipate problems before they arise and to assure implementation and continued operation of an effective MIS.

System design is controlled by incorporating both hardware and software controls into the five basic parts of a system—transaction origination, transaction entry, data communications, computer processing, and computer output. Hardware controls are provided by the manufacturers of the computing and data communications equipment. Examples are port protection and encryption devices. Software controls are incorporated into the system design by vendors and systems analysts. Examples are passwords, batch control totals, and data editing. Input data is verified either by rekeying a second time or by visually inspecting the screen display. The data communications part of the system is potentially the weak link, providing opportunities for both passive and active intruders.

The control of systems operations is based on the organizational structure of the operations department, the activities of units within the department (such as input/output scheduling and the media library), equipment maintenance, environmental control, facilities security, and disaster planning. Most of these controls are the responsibility of the manager of operations. The efficiency of operations can be measured by response time, turnaround time, and throughput time. The effectiveness of the input/output scheduling and control group is being lessened by the trend to online systems. Data base backup is achieved by maintaining generations of files and by locating duplicate copies elsewhere. Backup plans can consist of backup computers, duplicate computer centers, hot site agreements, empty shells, and agreements with other users of the same equipment.

Managers are interested in MIS control because a breach of security can cripple a firm's operations, cut off the managers from the physical system, produce manipulated information that leads to wrong decisions, and make confidential information available to competitors.

The corporate information officer is more of a new view of the role of the top computer manager than a position on the organization chart. Factors critical to the success of the CIO include an ability to provide service, to communicate, to build and retain a professional staff, and to reposition the information services group both physically and psychologically.

This chapter concludes our discussion of how the MIS is managed throughout its life cycle. In the next, and final, chapter we address how the manager can influence future MIS trends.

Key Terms

hacker	response time
security	turnaround time
integrity	throughput time
functional integrity	file generations
auditability	customer engineer (CE), field engineer (FE)
accountability	unscheduled maintenance
visibility	scheduled maintenance
controllability	preventive maintenance (PM)
development control	downtime
design control	contingency
hardware control	emergency plan
software control	backup plan
operation control	hot site
standards manual	cold site, empty shell
postinstallation review	vital records plan
risk analysis	recovery plan
control matrix	data classification program
key verification	data owner
sight verification	document classification program
passive, active intruders	corporate information officer (CIO)
encryption	technical, organizational, psychological, managerial repositioning
header, trailer labels	
port protection device	
call-back ability	

Key Concepts

The relationship of control to security

Auditability of a system

The time dimension of control: system development through operation

How the manager relies on others to achieve control

Areas of system design controls

How both user and information services balance computer input and output

The attention focused on data communications as a weak security link in spite of a higher level of system violations by information services personnel

The manner in which organizational structure facilitates control

The different measures provided by response, turnaround, and throughput times

Generations of sequential files

Subdivision of disaster planning into specialized plans and programs

The importance of MIS control to the manager

Questions

1. Does the MIS help the manager control, or does the manager control the MIS? Explain.

2. What are the six different ways that data security can be breached?

3. How can a distributed data processing network provide functional integrity?

4. What is auditability? How do documentation tools contribute to auditability?

5. What are the three types of controls that can be applied to the MIS?

6. How can a manager control the MIS when he or she is not an information specialist?

7. Who establishes design and operation standards?

8. When is a postinstallation review conducted? Name three ways to evaluate system performance.

9. What are the three major reasons why systems must be maintained?

10. What are the four conditions influencing maintenance difficulty?

11. What are the five areas of system design controls? Identify the one(s) not directly involved with computing equipment.

12. What are the ways that the accuracy of input data can be verified?

13. What distinguishes a passive from an active intruder?

14. At what point, or points, in the system can encryption be used as a design control?

15. What is the effect on system control when one person in a small organization performs all of the operations duties?

16. Which is most important to the user—turnaround, response, or throughput time? Which is most important to the vice president of information services? Which is most important to a computer salesperson? Explain your answers.

17. Which type of file offers the best backup protection— sequential or direct? Explain.

18. How can the operations manager minimize downtime?

19. Distinguish between an emergency plan, a backup plan, and a recovery plan.

20. If a person is vice president of information services, does that mean that she or he is a CIO? Explain.

Problems

1. Draw a control matrix for the inventory subsystem described in Chapter 9. Use Figure 18-5 as a guide.
2. Draw a control matrix for the accounts receivable subsystem described in Chapter 9.
3. Use the program flowcharting technique to design the logic necessary to determine whether the inventory balance on hand has dropped below the reorder point. Use Figure 18-11 as a guide. Also draw a program flowchart showing the logic required to determine if a customer's purchase amount is less than $100, from $100 to $500, and over $500. Include error routines in these two flowcharts as required.

CASE PROBLEM: Ace Toys

Jim Pelzer has been selling for Ace Toys for the past eighteen years. Ace is a toy wholesaler located in Toledo with a nationwide sales and distribution operation. Warehouses in Los Angeles, Chicago, New Orleans, Boston, and also Toledo stock a wide assortment of toys. Sales offices are also located in those same cities, and Jim works out of the Boston office.

Jim likes selling because it puts him in contact with people. Being basically friendly, he has established warm relations not only with the customers in his territory but with his competitors as well. He is extremely close to Bert Wilson, who sells for Destructo Toys. Jim and Bert have been friends for years and play golf practically every weekend.

One Saturday, after finishing a round of golf and also a round of drinks at the clubhouse, Jim says to Bert, "I've never told you about our new computer system. We just put it in last month. You talk about powerful—I can get practically any information I want just by keying a few codes into the terminal that we have down at the office."

Jim told Bert all the details of the system's operation, and Bert seemed genuinely interested. Destructo uses a completely manual system—just like the one that Ace had before cutting over to the computer. Jim could see Bert's interest and asked, "Why don't we drop by the office on the way home, and I'll give you a demo?" Bert replied, "Sure, why not?" and the two drove to the Ace sales office.

They parked their cars in the alley behind the building and entered through the back door. Jim explained, "You can almost always get in this way. The cleanup crew leaves it open." They walked down the hall to a small room housing the terminal. "This used to be the supply room. We walled off part of it for the computer."

Jim sat down in a chair in front of the terminal, and Bert kneeled down on the floor next to him. "See. All I have to do is turn it on, pick up this phone, and dial the computer at the home office. It's an easy number to remember—the Toledo area code and A-C-E-T-O-Y-S. Neat, huh?" Bert only winced as the high-pitched tone of the home office mainframe came through the telephone earpiece that Jim had placed against Bert's ear.

"That buzz means we're connected to the computer," Jim explained. "Now all I have to do is put the phone in this little holder here, push this key, and I can start asking for information." The screen displays a list. "All I have to do is key in a code. See, they're all here on the screen. They call this a menu. I can ask for an inventory status report by typing a '1'. I can get a report of my year-to-date sales versus quota by typing a '2'. I can get a lot of other reports by typing these other numbers. Some just relate to my sales, but some are for the whole company."

"Let's assume that I want to know how many Raggedy Ann dolls we have in stock. I type a '1' for the stock status report. See, the menu goes away, and the computer asks me what the item number is. I know that one by heart, but if I can't remember, I just type 'HELP' and it displays our item number list. Everything works that way. If I can't answer the computer's questions, I just type 'HELP.' "

The screen displays all of the information concerning Raggedy Ann dolls—quantity on hand, price, cost, sales to date, quantity backordered, and so on. Jim presses a key and the menu reappears.

"Isn't this amazing, Bert? This thing is so user friendly. I don't know a thing about computers but it's a breeze. We've even installed an electronic mail system. If I want to check my mailbox, I just key in a '49' and it lists my messages. Here's one that came in yesterday. It's a summary of our corporate marketing strategy for next year." Jim keys in the number alongside the message labeled "Marketing Plan," and the screen fills with a narrative. Jim steps through the narrative quickly by using a key on the keyboard. "Hey, you're not supposed to see that. That's hot stuff, right?" Jim turns off the terminal and hangs up the phone and asks, "Well, what do you think? Can I sell you one of these little numbers?"

Bert gets up slowly saying, "You guys need some chairs in here for your guests. And maybe a little popcorn. No, I'm only joking. I'm really impressed. I wish we had something like that. I can see how it can make your work so much easier. You're going to be tougher to compete against than ever. Well, listen, I had better go. It's almost time to pick up the kids at the Y."

Questions

1. Comment on Ace's new system from a security standpoint. Point out the strengths and weaknesses.
2. What could be the potential damage if a passive intruder gains access to the Ace system?

3. What could be the potential damage if an active intruder gains access? What might the active intruder do?

4. Assume that you have been hired by Ace's CEO to recommend ways to improve data and information security. Write a memo listing your recommendations. The CEO's name is Cynthia Mears.

Selected Bibliography

Controlling the Operational MIS

Allen, Brandt, "An Unmanaged Computer System Can Stop You Dead,"
   Harvard Business Review 60 (November-December 1982): 77–87.

Buss, Martin D. J., and Lynn M. Salerno, "Common Sense and Computer
   Security," *Harvard Business Review* 62 (March-April 1984): 112–121.

Chasen, Irving, "Contingency Planning for Automated Systems," *Office
   Administration and Automation* 45 (June 1984): 57ff.

Colby, Wendelin, "Burnt or Burned?," *Infosystems* 32 (February 1985): 40.

Data Security Controls and Procedures—A Philosophy for DP Installations,
   G320–5649 (White Plains, NY: IBM).

Guynes, Steve, Michael G. Laney, and Robert Zant, "Computer Security
   Practice," *Journal of Systems Management* 34 (June 1983): 22–26.

Harrison, Warren, Kenneth Magel, and Raymond Kluczny, "Research in
   Software Maintenance," *Journal of Systems Management* 34 (July 1983):
   10–14.

Holley, Charles L., and Frederick Millar, "Auditing the On-Line, Real-Time
   Computer," *Journal of Systems Management* 34 (January 1983): 14–19.

Ives, Blake, Margrethe H. Olson, and Jack J. Baroudi, "The Measurement of
   User Information Satisfaction," *Communications of the ACM* 26 (October
   1983): 785–793.

Janulaitis, M. Victor, "Creating a Disaster Recovery Plan," *Infosystems* 32
   (February 1985): 42–43.

Johnson, Jan, "Securing the Network," *Datamation* 30 (May 1984): 52ff.

Keen, Peter G. W., "Computer-Based Decision Aids: The Evaluation Problem,"
   Sloan Management Review 16 (Spring 1975): 17–29.

Kliem, Ralph L., "Disaster Prevention and Recovery for Microcomputers,"
   Journal of Systems Management 35 (March 1984): 28–29.

Leeson, Marjorie, *Computer Operations: Procedures and Management*, 2nd ed.
   (Chicago: Science Research Associates, 1982).

Lewin, Robert E., "Securing and Managing Dial-In Networks,"
   Telecommunications 18 (October 1984): 52ff.

Lockman, Abe, and Naftaly Minsky, "Designing Financial Information Systems for Auditability," *Journal of Management Information Systems* 1 (Summer 1984): 50–62.

Miles, Mary, "Before Disaster Strikes . . . ," *Computer Decisions* 15 (September 1983): 136ff.

Murray, William H., "Security Considerations for Personal Computers," *IBM Systems Journal* 23 (Number 3, 1984): 297–304.

Prutch, Shirley F., "In Praise of Operations Managers," *Datamation* 30 (June 15, 1984): 139ff.

Rockart, John F., "The Changing Role of the Information Systems Executive: A Critical Success Factors Perspective," *Sloan Management Review* 24 (Fall 1982): 3–13.

Rymer, John, "Executives to Unlock Technology's Promise," *Computer Decisions* 15 (September 15, 1983): 134ff.

Seaman, John, "Halting Network Intruders," *Computer Decisions* 17 (January 29, 1985): 82ff.

Summers, Rita C. "An Overview of Computer Security," *IBM Systems Journal* 23 (Number 4, 1984): 309–325.

The Considerations of Physical Security in a Computer Environment, G520–2700 (White Plains, NY: IBM).

Troy, Gene, "Thwarting the Hackers," *Datamation* 30 (July 1, 1984): 116ff.

Walden, Jeffrey, "Cracking Down on Micro Crime," *Business Computer Systems* 3 (October 1984): 40ff.

Wood, Charles Cresson, "Countering Unauthorized Systems Accesses," *Journal of Systems Management* 35 (April 1984): 26–28.

Wood, Michael B., *Introducing Computer Security* (Manchester, England: NCC Publications, 1982), pp. 97–103.

Chapter 19

The Future of the MIS

Learning Objectives

After studying this chapter, you should:

- Understand why users are achieving self-sufficiency in developing their own computer-based systems
- Recognize how the trend to end-user computing is changing the work of information specialists
- Be able to pinpoint areas in the computing industry that offer the career opportunities of interest to you
- Understand current hardware trends
- Understand current software trends
- Recognize the necessity for user-friendly documentation tools
- Become aware of the changing composition of the MIS, and the potential addition of a fourth subsystem—expert systems

Introduction

The computer industry is in the midst of change—the most dramatic change in its short history. The computer has spread from corporate headquarters to branch offices, small businesses, and even homes. People of all ages are exposed daily to ads on TV and in print touting the powers of the computer. No area of our society has failed to grasp the significance of computers in our daily activities and in our hopes for the future.

Nobody is certain where computers will lead us. Undoubtedly there will be new problems. But there will also be new opportunities. Many people have ideas about what may evolve. In this final chapter, we will examine some of the ideas that relate to the MIS.

As you embark on your business career, you will be caught up in the MIS evolution. You don't simply have to go along for the ride, though. With your preparation, you can influence the direction that the evolution will take. There are many opportunities to improve the way that computers are used as data processing, office automation, and decision support systems. The imaginative and resourceful newcomers to the business scene—people like you—will shape the MIS of the future.

The Changing Role of the Information User

The business environment is becoming increasingly computer literate. People are learning about computers at an earlier age and are receiving better training. Computer courses are common in high schools and are becoming more popular at the junior high and elementary levels.

Many high-school graduates will go on to college and take more computer-related courses before pursuing a career. Others will take jobs in industry and government and will become either users or producers of management information. More and more people on all levels will be computer literate and open-minded to new applications. The result will be twofold. First, there will be a greater demand for computer use within firms. Second, users will be able to put some of their own jobs on the computer, without relying completely on information services personnel.

The communication problem

The most serious problem to plague computer users has been communicating with the information professionals. This problem is being solved by making the communication less necessary. If the user can do his or her own work, there is little or no need to communicate. The user can identify and define the problem, identify alternate solutions, evaluate the solutions and select the best, implement the system, and use and improve the system. All of this activity can occur within the user's area without involving the information services staff. In many cases, users will have their own mini or micro.

User-friendly software

To realize this utopian use of the computer, the computer must become easier to use. It is one thing to expect clerical employees or first-line supervisors to put their data and information processing jobs on the computer. The same level of performance at upper-management levels, where problems are less structured and time constraints more pronounced, is difficult to achieve.

Continued improvements in software will be necessary. Languages will become more user friendly. The trend toward widespread use of fourth-generation languages will continue. The newer languages will use English-like sentence structure rather than *alien syntax* of computer-oriented languages. Early versions of such *natural language software* were Ideal from Applied Data Research, Cincom's Mantis, and Software AG's Natural. More advanced packages are Intellect from Artificial Intelligence Corp. and Ramis II from Mathematica. With packages such as these, a manager can build a very powerful computer program more quickly and easily and with a lower level of computer literacy than has been required in the past.

It is unlikely that a manager will want to create a program to process data. Data processing systems will continue to be developed by information specialists. However, managers can be expected to create programs that prepare special, and even periodic, reports. It is estimated that 80 percent of all program maintenance is caused by users wanting to change the output.[1] Special software packages, called *output generators*, will enable users to produce the required changes themselves. Information Expert, from Management Sciences America, is such a report writer that enables users to easily pull information from a data base.

Managers can also be expected to develop their own software to simulate the effects of decision strategies. Managers are acquiring a greater quantitative sophistication in their college courses and are less afraid of statistical packages (such as SAS) and of management science tools (such as linear programming). Modeling software, however, needs to be easier to use. The popularity of general-purpose models (such as Lotus 1-2-3 and IFPS) is evidence of how positively management will respond to a package that is easy to use.

We can expect electronic spreadsheets to increase in use and sophistication. The next generation of spreadsheets will enable the manipulation of data in more than the two dimensions of rows and columns. A three-dimension spreadsheet can display its contents in the form of a cube and can permit the analysis of data such as sales over time (1 dimension) by product class (1 dimension) by customer (1 dimension). More than three dimensions will also be possible.

The Changing Role of the Information Supplier

What effect will this trend toward user independence have on the traditional roles of systems analyst, programmer, and data base administrator? These people are currently in short supply, and the shortage is expected to increase.

It has been common for some users to wait as long as five years to get an application on the computer. These are jobs that the firm and the information services department regard as low priorities. Even if a job should not go on the computer at all, the user equates the long waiting period with poor service. Lack of support by the central computing facility has encouraged the use of small, distributed systems—often without an overall master plan.

This is perhaps the most serious aspect of the proliferation of micros throughout the firm. Individuals are getting their own hardware and software. Very often these new micro owners are misled by the advertising that tells how user friendly the units are. Unable to do their own work, these people turn to the information services department for help. In some cases a planned, organized approach is taken to provide the support needed. The information center is such an approach.

---

[1] David Kull, "Software—What's Ahead," *Computer Decisions* 14 (November 1984): 108.

In other cases, systems analysts or programmers provide individual attention. The goal of this assistance is, or should be, to make these new users self-sufficient.

The requirement to provide assistance to new micro owners is a short-term one and can eventually be satisfied. The only cost is the drain on the already scarce information services personnel resource. A more serious problem is presented by new micro owners who do *not* need assistance or do not *think* that they do. These users can set up systems to meet their own needs, disregarding the overall MIS plan for the firm. This approach is full of potential inefficiencies. Multiple users may be purchasing identical software or, worse still, coding practically identical programs. Security is often totally absent, with both hardware and software accessible to anyone walking in the door. Duplicate data bases are created with no regard to a master plan. Little or no documentation is prepared for both the software library and the data base. All of these inefficiencies seriously undermine the efforts of the firm to have an organized MIS.

The combination of the inability to meet users' needs and the ease with which computing hardware and software can be acquired has considerably lessened the control that the information specialists have over the firm's computing resource. The information specialists must adapt to the trend, assuming more of a user orientation in terms of both attitude and needed skills. Information specialists must function more as consultants and less as technicians. User education should occupy more of the information specialists' attention. In its most severe form, the trend to user self-sufficiency will result in the decentralization of the information services staff. Systems analysts and programmers will be permanently assigned to user areas rather than working out of a central department.

Increasing computer popularity, while representing a new opportunity for users, represents a problem for understaffed information services units.

A Possible Solution

Micro proliferation has come about as the result of several factors—inadequate information services personnel resource, the ever-growing responsibility to maintain installed systems, low-price and easy-to-acquire micro hardware and software, and increasing computer literacy on the part of users. Since there are several causes of the problem, there are several solutions. The main solution is for the firm to implement a program of information resource management (IRM) that includes strategies for addressing the microcomputer boom. In many cases these strategies include an information center designed to provide individual user support. As a minimum, the firm needs to establish a policy concerning hardware and software acquisition specifying the degree to which such acquisition is permitted, standard brands, and methods for achieving coordinated acquisition and use.

The IRM program should also address the problem of personnel resource shortage within the information services department. The information services department cannot continue to attempt to meet all of the information needs of its users. The department must identify that portion of the firm's information-producing activity that it can handle and gain expertise in performing those services. The remaining jobs are going to have to be performed by the user or by outside service organizations.

The evolution of the roles and responsibilities of both users and information specialists will not occur overnight. Realistically, it will never occur completely. Many information services departments will cling to the old practice of encouraging user dependence. But the trend is clear, and the end result will be users who are both willing and able to implement their own decision support systems.

Future Careers in Computing

What effect is this movement toward end-user computing expected to have on career opportunities for information specialists? Nobody knows for certain, but some projections can be made based upon what has happened in the past.

First, the demand for information specialists will likely persist. This demand is guaranteed because of the need to maintain the mass of installed mainframe applications. We have seen where such activity can account for as much as 75 percent of a firm's information services effort. Projecting this maintenance need into the future reveals that many, if not most, future information specialists will be involved in maintaining existing systems rather than developing new ones. This role will come as a shock to graduates who have completed college curricula geared to new system development rather than maintenance. The real world will not be the one that was described in the classroom.

There is nothing wrong with a career of system maintenance for those who find it rewarding. There are those, however, who thirst for the challenge of new system design. In most cases the maintenance will involve data processing systems, and new systems efforts will involve DSS and OA. Many persons entering the computing profession feel that their education qualifies them to work on systems that incorporate the leading edge of technology and methodology. Exactly how does a newcomer aim in the direction offering the best career potential?

Figure 19-1 is a conceptual graph showing how computer applications have evolved. The vertical dimension is any measure of computer use—number of records processed, number of installed jobs, CPU time, and so on. Area A accounts for most of the current activity, and these systems are data processing applications on mainframes. The shape of Area A (and the other areas as well) is estimated rather than based on actual figures.

Area B represents the slow growth of DSS applications in mainframe shops. Areas C and D apply to small systems—micros and minis. Of the two small system areas, Area C is currently the largest—data processing applications. Area E represents the emerging field of office automation.

Figure 19-1 provides a clue as to computer career opportunities. A large number of information specialists will be needed to maintain mainframe systems, but Areas B, C, D, and E will need personnel as well. Realistically, Areas C, D, and E seem to offer limited opportunities. Most of the data processing applications for micros (Area C) will use packaged software. There will not be a need for on-site systems analysts and programmers. It is true that the software houses

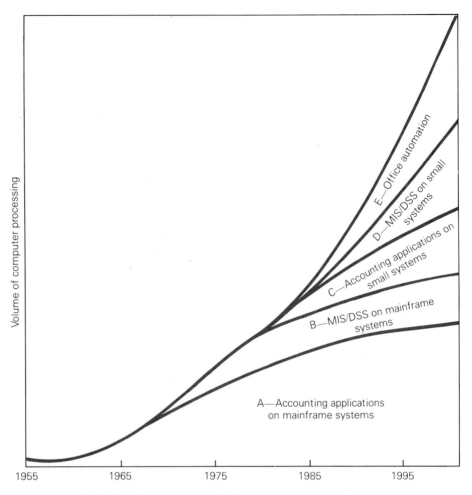

Figure 19-1 Evolution of computer applications in business.

developing these packages will have personnel needs, but the needs will not be as great as if each using firm were acquiring their own staff.

The factors constraining Area C also apply to Area D. Most of the DSS software for micros will be based on packaged software such as DBMSs and electronic spreadsheets. Software houses will be hiring personnel to produce their packages, but the number of job openings will be relatively modest.

Area E is also constrained in that many office automation applications are performed either by hardware or packaged software. The systems are *turn-key* in nature—the user acquires the necessary hardware and software and implements it with little special effort. Some systems analyst time will be required for feasibility study and user training, but the need for programmer participation will be modest.

This rather bleak outlook leaves Area B—MIS/DSS applications on mainframe systems as the only area where a real demand will exist for information services personnel to develop new systems. These new systems will emphasize decision support rather than data processing.

If a college student wants to prepare herself or himself for functioning in Area B, then the necessary knowledge and skills should be acquired. Courses should aim at understanding management responsibilities and needs, and at modern techniques for satisfying those needs—DBMS, statistical packages, modeling languages, graphics, datacom, and even office automation. The person who succeeds in Area B will be the person who can assist managers on all levels in developing and maintaining DSSs that they cannot develop themselves.

The Changing Nature of Computer Systems

Practically all areas of computer technology are changing. During the next few years, we anticipate a continued movement of processor power toward the user. Vendors will develop hardware dedicated to managing the data base, and improvements in storage technologies will increase storage capacities. The methods of entering data into the MIS and receiving information from it will also change. The interest in automating the office may well dwarf the interest in computer use in an MIS or DSS.

Distributed processor power

Computing hardware is moving toward the user. Purely centralized computer installations are giving way to processors located in the manager's area. The most extreme evidence of this distribution is the micro installed to serve the processing needs of a single department or person. Other evidence comes from datacom systems in which much communications processing is off-loaded to front-end processors, remote intelligent controllers, and intelligent terminals, as in Figure 19-2.

In the figure, the user has an intelligent terminal that can perform specialized processes independently of the other systems. A remote intelligent controller can include a local data base, facilitating certain processing independently of the host computer and its centralized corporate data base.

This distribution of processor power will continue as more datacom hardware becomes available. The software, however, is more difficult to provide. The system software, such as operating systems and data communications monitors to support distributed systems, is more complex than packages that support a centralized batch system. The effective use of distributed systems will hinge on improved software (rather than hardware) capabilities.

Data base machines

In addition to the movement of processor power toward the user, there will be a continued movement toward the data base. A micro will be dedicated to interfacing the data base with the CPU, freeing up the CPU for information processing. Figure 19-3 illustrates the offloading of data base responsibility to a *backend*

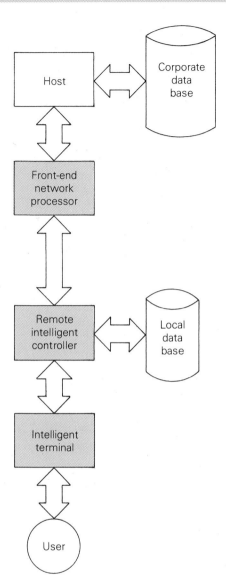

Figure 19-2 Offloading communications processing.

data base processor. Once this offloading is accomplished, computer processing will be performed by three separate processors designed to accomplish three types of processing: data base, information, and datacom network.

A data base processor, called a *data base machine,* performs the functions of a software-based DBMS, only using hardware instead. Interest in data base machines originated in 1977 when ICL announced a system called CAFS (Content Addressable File Store). In 1980 Software AG, vendor of the ADABAS DBMS, began installing hardware systems that incorporated some of the DBMS routines in ROM. Software AG eventually exited the market by switching back to software.

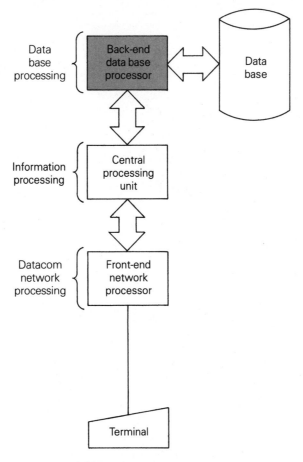

Figure 19-3 Offloading data base processing to a back-end processor.

Today's leader in the data base machine market is Britton Lee, a Los Gatos, California, firm. Britton Lee has sold approximately 450 of their machines designed primarily to support minicomputers such as the DEC VAX. Several models are available that enable from 90 to 400 users to simultaneously access data bases, ranging in size from 320 million to 1 billion bytes. Backup is provided in the form of a cartridge tape drive.

Britton Lee's main competition comes from Teredata, of Los Angeles. Teredata has aimed at the high end of the market—IBM mainframes. Teredata achieves very fast access times by using multiple processors. Their smallest system incorporates six processors, and a new system consisting of 60 parallel processors has been demonstrated. In mid-1985 Teredata had less than a dozen users, but these few users were happy. Citibank handles some 120 to 150 transactions per second. Wells Fargo Bank in San Francisco has dedicated their data base machine to DSS, and management has been impressed with the ease of access.

The trend toward a data base processor is one approach to improving the DBMS. Many firms implementing their first data base will most likely follow this path. The old DBMS firms will probably stick with a software emphasis. Computer users will ultimately be able to select between hardware- and software-oriented DBMSs.

Increasing storage capacity and speed

Since the beginning of the computer era, the search for increased storage capacity and access speed has characterized hardware developments. Both primary and secondary storage have received attention. Semiconductor chips are used for primary storage as well as secondary storage where especially fast access is required. Chips are now available with a capacity of 262,000 bits. Production of a chip with a 1 million bit capacity, called a *megabit chip*, is expected to begin about 1987.

Most efforts to produce an alternate primary storage technology have failed. The most publicized example is *bubble memory*, which was heralded during the early 80s as the primary storage of the future. Today, bubble memory seems to be restricted to only micros. Hicomp Computer Corp. of Redmond, Washington, markets an expansion board for the IBM PC that contains two Intel bubble chips with a 1 million bit capacity each. Other firms are Helix Laboratories and MPC Peripherals Corp., both of San Diego, who make bubble memory boards for the Apple II. All of these products are intended to be used as secondary storage—replacing or augmenting diskette storage.

Bubble memory is *non-volatile*, meaning that it retains the stored data after power has been turned off. Users also appreciate the fewer maintenance problems compared to rotating disks as well as a very low error rate. Bubble memory may succeed in the micro market, after being effectively written off as a mainframe storage medium.

Two developments are under way to improve secondary storage of mainframes. One is *vertical recording* of the data bits using conventional rotating disks. Vertical recording increases storage capacity by standing the bits up vertically, side by side, rather than recording them horizontally, end to end. The other development involves *optical disks*, the type used for recording audio and video material. These same disks can also store data in a much more compact form than both magnetic disks and magnetic tapes.

Optical disks currently suffer two problems. One problem is speed. The optical disks do not offer the fast access of magnetic disks even though individual records are addressable. The other problem is the constraint that data, once recorded, cannot be erased. Current optical disks are *write-once* media. This limitation restricts optical disks to those applications where recorded data need not be changed. An example is archival, or historical, storage. At least 20 firms are working on erasable, or *write-many*, optical disks, but it is likely to be some time before any are placed on the market. One of the leading firms in this area, Storage Technology of Broomfield, Colorado, filed for bankruptcy in 1984.

When write-many optical disks do become available, they will likely replace magnetic tape rather than magnetic disks. Optical disks can store data in one-hundredth of the space required by magnetic tapes and can offer direct access. A firm can use the three storage technologies at the same time—each in a specialized way. Magnetic disks can be used for highly active files where direct access is required. Magnetic tapes can be used for files that can be updated on a less frequent, cycle basis. Optical disks can be used for storage of data that does not have to be changed, but for which direct access is required. The term *tertiary storage* has been used to describe this possible use of optical disks.

Elimination of keyed input media

Offline keyed input, such as keypunch, key-to-tape, and key-to-disk, has practically given way to online input using terminals and to direct input media such as OCR documents. This evolution is illustrated in the conceptual model in Figure 19-4. You will notice that MICR is on the decline, being replaced by electronic funds transfer systems such as automated teller machines. OCR will continue to gain ground in high-volume transactions such as credit card invoices, billing turnaround documents, and department store and supermarket sales. The mini/micro boom will make online keyed entry using terminals the most popular input method of the future. It is still too early to tell whether voice recognition will compete with keyed entry. Most likely, voice recognition will not be popular until the late eighties.

Reduction of printed output

Similar evolutions are under way in output, as shown by the conceptual model in Figure 19-5. Output from computer printers once accounted for practically all

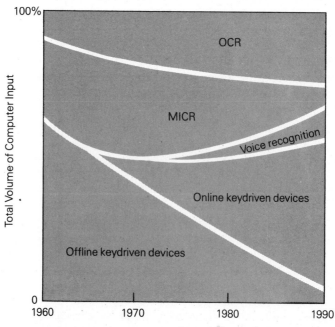

Figure 19-4 Evolution of input devices.

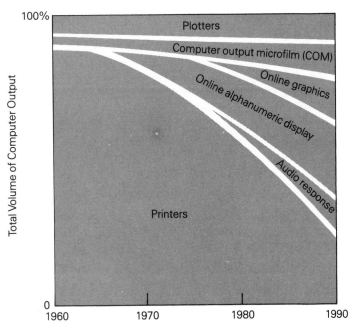

Figure 19-5 Evolution of output devices.

of the information available to the manager. Today these printouts not only are costly to produce and take up unnecessary space, but they lack immediacy and convenience. It is much easier to query the data base from a terminal and receive the information right away. By the end of the 1980s, most printed output will be from serial printers attached to mini/micro systems.

Booming office automation

The microcomputer as a means to automate office clerical routines may attract more widespread attention than similar applications in data and information processing. The micro as a word processor has taken over most of the typing chores in many firms. Other OA applications linking terminals or micros will be the next wave of popularity—electronic calendaring, electronic and voice mail, and computer conferencing. The key to the adoption of these applications will be advances in LAN and digital PBX technology. Optical disks may find a use in storing videotex and microform material.

As firms start to implement office automation systems, their plans should define how these systems integrate into the MIS. If office automation and MIS are regarded separately, neither area will live up to its potential.

The Changing Nature of Software

Both application and system software are moving toward the user in the same manner as hardware. There has always been interest in making the computer easier to use, but only recently have efforts been directed toward the end user. Previously the aim was to ease the programmer's workload.

In Figure 19-6 you can see three clusters of software. The first cluster in the lower left includes Assembler, the first option to machine language, plus the major *high-level languages* that evolved during the first three computer generations— FORTRAN, COBOL, and PL/I. These languages have been used to write most of the programs that are in use today on mainframe systems. These languages are powerful, but not very user friendly. That characteristic is also shared by a more modern language, APL. We recall from Chapter 11 that APL is an example of a *very high-level language* and offers much DSS power but is not easy to use.

The center circle contains two of the more modern high-level languages, BASIC and Pascal, plus an early language designed to facilitate report prepara-

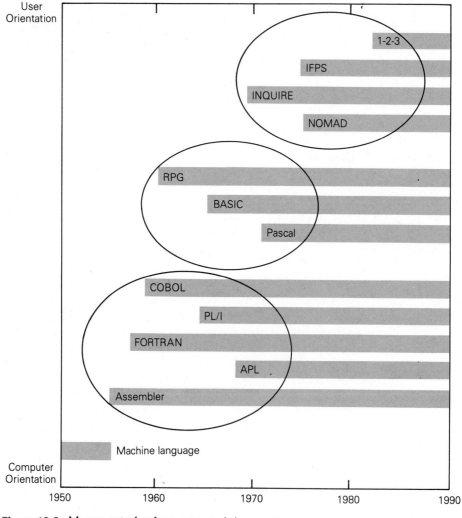

Figure 19-6 Movement of software toward the user.

tion—RPG (Report Program Generator). This software group offers less power than the traditional languages, but more user friendliness. RPG is very easy to use; you only fill out a set of forms. BASIC is more user friendly than FORTRAN, and the structured nature of Pascal moves it closer to the user.

The software examples in the upper-right circle really aren't programming languages as such. INQUIRE and NOMAD are data base query languages, whereas IFPS and Lotus 1-2-3 are decision simulators. Although user friendly, these packages are not as flexible as the less-friendly procedural languages.

You can see that the general trend in Figure 19-6 has been away from the hardware and toward the user. Some exceptions stand out. RPG was ahead of its time in terms of user friendliness, whereas APL and (to a lesser extent) Pascal were not developed with most users in mind. APL is a superior language when the user possesses extraordinary math skills, and Pascal is ideal when the user is proficient in structured programming. Most managers have neither of these skills.

The selection of software in the user-friendly area of the upper right is growing rapidly. The varieties of electronic spreadsheets and query languages are almost too numerous to count. These *are* software systems that users can, and *do*, use. These systems, coupled with user-friendly documentation tools, make the concept of end-user computing one that can be realistically achieved.

User-Friendly Documentation Tools

If the user is to gain self-sufficiency in programming by means of the user languages, he or she should also be proficient in the use of documentation tools. The documentation tools enable the description of an existing or proposed system, revealing all of its basic parts. The person using the tools thus is able to better understand the system and to communicate this understanding to others. We typically think of the tools as being used only by the systems analyst. There is no reason, however, why a user cannot use the tools when developing his or her own systems.

One reason that end-user computing was impractical just a few years ago is that there were no documentation tools that a user could be expected to use. System flowcharts were available for general, top-level documentation, and program flowcharts for detailed, low-level documentation. Figure 19-7 shows that there was no tool to bridge the gap between the general and the detailed documentation. A user might be expected to use systems flowcharts (although few, if any, did), but the jump to program flowcharting was too great. As a result, the user dropped out of design activity early in the life cycle.

Structured documentation tools present a different picture. The figure illustrates three alternatives incorporating the other tools from the Appendix. We can see that Warnier-Orr diagrams offer the greatest flexibility in terms of spanning both general and detailed documentation. A low-level Warnier-Orr diagram can be so specific as to eliminate the need for any other detailed documentation. Both HIPO and data flow diagrams have to be augmented at the lower level with a detailed tool such as structured English.

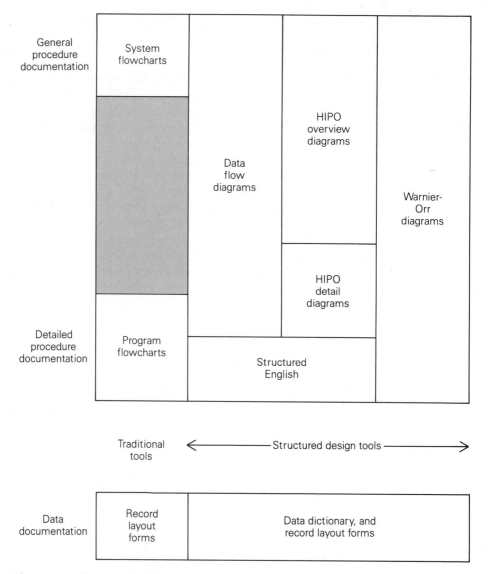

Figure 19-7 Documentation tools.

The lower portion of the figure recognizes the need to document the data. *Record layout forms* such as printer spacing charts are one traditional tool that is also a part of structured documentation. The data dictionary is a structured tool that can be used with any of the structured procedural documentation tools.

Today's user can be expected to use data flow diagrams, HIPO, and Warnier-Orr—at least for the more general documentation. Perhaps the user can draw upper-level data flow diagrams and leave the lower-level diagrams, the structured English, and the data dictionary to the information specialist.

Managers and future managers should learn to use these tools so that they can design their more simple systems and participate to a greater degree in the design of their more complex systems. Colleges and universities should ensure that all business students—future MIS users as well as future information specialists—learn to use the tools. Learning institutions must remain alert to newer and better tools. To do this, the schools must stay in close touch with computer users, quickly recognize the value of new tools and techniques, and pass that information on to the students. Perhaps some new tools will be developed through academic research.

Industry has a giant task in helping the current group of managers to become self-sufficient. Perhaps colleges and universities can help. That would be a proper arrangement. But industry must do much of its own educating.

Control of the MIS

We commented earlier in the chapter how information services is losing its control over the firm's computing resource. This reduction in control is exhibited in two ways. First, the increasingly computer-literate user is assuming greater control of MIS projects. One insurance company, for example, has a policy that the leader of an MIS project team must always be a user. Second, today's decentralized computer networks are more susceptible to breaches in security than the centralized, batch-oriented systems of yesterday.

The big security risk in distributed systems is access to the data base. When the central data base can be replaced by distributed data bases, then the overall security is increased. An unauthorized user, breaking through the security barrier, will have access to only a part of the data base rather than all. This situation assumes replacement of the central data base with distributed data bases. Retention of the central data base in a datacom-oriented system produces the maximum risk. We have seen that the key to data base distribution will be the development of DBMSs that can incorporate distributed as well as centralized data bases.

The Changing Composition of the MIS

We conclude our look into the future by commenting on the trends to expect in data processing, office automation, and decision support, plus a new area that may become a part of the MIS.

Data processing

It is easy to get the idea that computers have been processing data for a quarter of a century and thus have solved all possible data processing problems. That conclusion would be a mistake. Many small firms now implementing their first computers are going through the same evolution that large firms experienced in the first generation. In fact, this *is* the first generation for small-system users. These users are primarily concerned with building a data processing foundation, and are implementing billing systems, payroll systems, and the like.

The data processing problems of small firms will be solved largely by packaged software and eventually by hardware specially built for certain applications. Much improvement is needed here before people with little or no computer literacy can use the application packages effectively.

As difficult as it is to believe, many large firms still struggle with data processing problems. The list even includes Fortune 500 companies. Packaged programs are not the solution here. These firms must determine why they have been unable to implement data processing systems successfully. Once they understand the reasons, they must solve the problems. The shortage of information specialists will hit hardest here. Large numbers of specialists will be needed, and they are not readily available. Perhaps the use of fourth-generation languages such as application development software will prove effective.

Office automation

Initial successes with word processing and electronic mail are encouraging firms to implement other OA applications—computer conferencing, electronic calendaring, and voice mail to name a few.

It is important that firms recognize the potential role of OA in the MIS and consider the various applications. All of the applications, however, do not fit all firms. Three of the applications are geared to firms with geographically dispersed operations—facsimile transmission, and audio- and videoconferencing. A local firm has less from which to choose.

Another limitation of OA is the fact that it communicates primarily internal information. Persons in the environment cannot easily input information into the firm's OA network because of incompatibilities between the different vendors' equipment. The eventual standardization of datacom protocols will solve the problem from a technical standpoint, but firms will have to enlist the cooperation of the external sources.

The next few years should see the development of an executive workstation—combining standard terminal facilities with abilities to retrieve microform images, voice mail, and perhaps participate in videoconferences. Such a workstation has been a long time coming and could encourage executives to become a part of their firm's OA systems.

Decision support systems[2]

The continued success of DSS efforts depends on contributions from both information specialists and users. The specialists must understand how DSS differs from data processing and early MIS concepts. In addition, the specialists should be proficient in the wide variety of technical skills required, and understand their role as catalysts. Users should be willing to invest their valuable time in the design and use of their systems.

---

[2]Based on Ralph Sprague, "DSS Trends," *Computing Newsletter* 14 (March 1981): 2.

Improvement will be realized in *dialog management*—making it easier for managers to interact with the DSS. English-like languages, light pens to enter data and instructions into the CRT, and greater use of the menu display technique will facilitate manager-DSS dialog. Improvements in *data management* will make it easier for a manager to access a small subset of the data base (say forty to a hundred data elements) and to work with that data extensively. As we learn more about how managers use a DSS, the value of making a few key elements available becomes clearer. In *model management*, we can expect to see new modeling languages that permit the user to create a special-purpose model independently of the information services staff, or with only minimal assistance.

A fourth MIS subsystem?

In 1956, four men met at Dartmouth College to discuss ways that computers could simulate human thought processes. The men were Marvin Minsky (now at MIT), John McCarthy (now at Stanford), Nathaniel Rochester of IBM, and Claude Shannon of Bell Laboratories. The meeting gave birth to the term *artificial intelligence*, or *AI*. AI can be defined as "the study of how to make computers do things at which, at the moment, people are better."[3]

During the ensuing years, research into AI continued at a few colleges and universities. Progress was constrained by lack of needed computer power and capacity. Only recently have adequate computer resources become available to the researchers, contributing to the current surge in interest.

AI has grown to encompass research in four separate areas:[4]

- *Natural languages*—systems that translate ordinary human commands into language that computer programs can understand and execute.
- *Robotics*—machines that move and relate to objects as humans do.
- *Visualization systems*—machines that can relate visually to their environments as humans do.
- *Expert systems*—programs that mimic the decision-making logic of human experts.

The AI area of most interest to the MIS is expert systems. During the future, expert systems might become a fourth MIS subsystem, or they might be integrated into the other three subsystems. We will discuss the potential contribution that expert systems might make to the MIS.

Expert Systems

An *expert system* is a computer-based system that can function as an expert in a particular area, in much the same manner as a consultant. The expert system will

---

[3] Elaine Rich, *Artificial Intelligence* (New York: McGraw-Hill, 1983), p. 1.

[4] Elisabeth Horwitt, "Exploring Expert Systems," *Business Computer Systems* 4 (March 1985): 49.

not make the decision for the manager but will help the manager make it—just as a consultant performs the same service.

Expert systems and DSS

This description of expert systems sounds like DSS. Are the two concepts the same, or different? The expert system is actually a step beyond the interpretation of a DSS that is completely controlled by the manager. The DSS concept brings to mind the image of the manager sitting at a terminal playing the what-if game. The DSS responds as it has been programmed to do. The manager solves a problem by knowing how to use the power of the DSS. It is as if the manager and the computer were alone in the room.

An expert system, on the other hand, brings something new to the problem scene—new knowledge in the form of historical data and also processes for approaching a problem solution. The manager identifies the problem, and the expert system executes programmed logic based on the scenario. The expert system might approach the solution in a manner different from the one that the manager would follow. It is as if the manager, the computer, and a consultant were together in the room.

Knowledge engineering

How can the expert system execute logic that the manager might not be able to do? The reason is that someone other than the manager might have furnished the logic that the expert system follows. In designing an expert system, a special type of systems analyst, called a *knowledge engineer*, works with one or more leading experts in the field being studied. For example, if an expert system is being built to suggest ways that the firm can invest its surplus cash, experts might be assembled from stock brokerage houses and investments departments of Fortune 500 companies. The knowledge engineer "picks the brains" of these experts over a period of time to learn how they go about making investment decisions. Thus, when a less experienced manager uses the expert system, he or she has the benefit of the knowledge of persons who are leaders in the field.

The material unique to the problem being solved is called the *knowledge base*. Included in the knowledge base are the *inference rules* that are followed in decision making, plus the *facts* relevant to the decision.

The work of the knowledge engineer is very slow. It might take as long as two years to document the rules and the facts. This problem is confounded by the fact that there are currently only approximately 200 knowledge engineers in the world. This shortage is limiting the number of expert systems projects that can be initiated. The AI researchers are studying ways in which the expert's knowledge can be captured without time-consuming interviewing. Perhaps software can perform the function of the knowledge engineer.

The inference engine

Much of the expert systems activity has been directed at medical diagnosis. At Stanford a program called MYCIN was developed that could diagnose blood and meningitis infections and advise which antibiotics to prescribe. Satisfied with the success of the program, the researchers removed all of the parts that were specific to medicine, and what they had left was a logical *framework* that could be adapted to any type of problem simply by adding special characteristics of the problem. The framework was called an *inference engine*.

The idea of packaging problem-solving logic in such a way that it can be applied to problems of all kinds is significant in that less effort may be needed in designing expert systems. One simply builds upon the framework rather than starting from scratch. To date, however, the success in applying these prepackaged frameworks has been mixed. Best results have been achieved when the inference engine is custom-tailored to a particular problem.

A model of an expert system

The two major parts of an expert system are an inference engine and a knowledge base. Figure 19-8 shows how these parts interact with other parts.

The *workspace* is simply a working area of storage where the problem description and the status of the problem as it is being solved are stored. The *explanation subsystem* explains the reasoning that was followed in problem solution. The expert system is therefore able to tell the user *why* it arrived at its conclusion. This explanation capability is something that an expert system offers that traditional DSS designs do not. The *natural language interface* is the user-friendly software that the user uses to communicate with the expert system. The *knowledge acquisition subsystem* enables the expert system to be "fine tuned" by incorporating additional knowledge as more is learned about the problem-solving process.

Sample applications

Thus far, expert systems have been applied primarily to diagnose particular problem situations and prescribe remedies. Initial success in diagnosing human med-

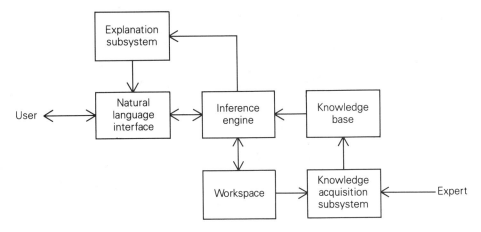

Figure 19-8 Schematic model of an expert system.
Source: Paul Kinnucan, "Computers That Think Like Experts," High Technology 4
(January 1984): 30.

ical problems has prompted AI researchers to apply the same approach to mechanical problems. General Electric has produced an expert system, CATS-1, that can diagnose mechanical problems in diesel locomotives. Once the trouble has been found, a videotape can instruct the repairperson in making the needed repairs. Figure 19-9 is a photograph of an information specialist interfacing with the system using the terminal keyboard. GE's top locomotive repair expert, David I. Smith, is standing. The video monitor used in making the repairs is on the left.

In a similar effort aimed at diagnosing nonhuman ailments, AT&T is using an expert system in Fort Worth to detect problems in its network of underground cables, and to recommend solutions. Each night the program, called Ace (for automated cable expertise), examines crew reports to determine what repairs are needed, and where. It would take a human a week to conduct the same analysis.

Another example of an expert system is XSEL, developed by DEC to assist a salesperson in specifying the configuration of its VAX computer that best satisfies a particular customer need. The program helps the salesperson select from 7,000 parts. DEC believes that XSEL produces specifications that are accurate 95 percent of the time, compared to 75 percent when the salespersons were mak-

Figure 19-9 GE uses an expert system for locomotive repair.
Source: General Electric Research and Development Center.

ing all of the decisions themselves. DEC expects the increase in accuracy to save $10 million a year.

There are several other examples of expert systems. SRI International has an expert system named PROSPECTOR, developed for the U.S. Geological Survey, that is used in mineral exploration. Schlumberger, Ltd., an international petroleum firm, spent an estimated $21 million in creating an expert system named DIPMETER. DIPMETER gives advice when a drilling bit gets stuck deep in the ground. In spite of the huge developmental costs, Schlumberger expects the system to pay for itself since the cost of an inoperative drilling rig can be $100,000 per day.

There are not very many working examples of expert systems considering the time and money that have been invested. To date the systems have been aimed primarily at decisions made on the lower organizational level—telephone cable repairpersons, locomotive repairpersons, and so on. The literature offers *no* examples of how expert systems have been used by business management. It remains to be seen whether such systems can be used in management decision making. This would appear to be an especially justified concern at the upper-management levels. We saw in our study of executive information systems that incorporation of computer-prepared information has been modest. The task of capturing the logic that executives employ in strategic decision making represents a much greater challenge than knowledge engineers have addressed thus far.

Putting expert systems in perspective

The idea of expert systems is not new. We earlier recognized that the AI movement got its start in 1956. Framework systems, containing shells of problem-solving logic, were first developed in the 1970s. The early literature of MIS even includes references to expert systems—although not using that name. Steven Alter's hierarchy of decision support systems included one that "makes decisions." That level of DSS could be considered an expert system. William R. King, writing in a 1973 issue of *Business Horizons*, described "the intelligent MIS—a management helper."[5]

Business systems analysts have always been aware that the computer could possibly capture some of the logic that managers employ. These systems analysts have not been successful in capturing that logic to any real degree. A good example is the logic employed in deciding whether to accept an application for insurance and, if so, what rate to charge. This task, called underwriting, is considerably easier for automobile insurance than for life and health insurance. A computer can be programmed to rate a '58 Chevy owned by a 23-year-old male living in San Francisco. This rating task has been performed by computer for years. But the logical processes of underwriting life and health insurance are still performed by human underwriters in spite of efforts to incorporate that logic into the computer.

The weak point in applying expert systems to management decision making appears to be the knowledge engineer. One wonders what tools this person will

---

[5] William R. King, "The Intelligent MIS—A Management Helper," *Business Horizons* 16 (October 1973): 5–12.

use that have not been employed (and probably developed) by professional systems analysts in designing decision support systems. We have recognized the critical point in DSS design as the communication gap separating the information specialist and the manager. If knowledge engineering comes up with any new tools that shed light on management decision making, then those tools should be adopted as well by information specialists in DSS design.

No doubt progress will be made in adapting expert systems to business applications. Large investments will be made, and the best minds will be focused on the task. Such progress will be a long time coming, however, and accomplishments will be modest if they follow the patterns of computer-based DSS.

This conservative forecast is made in the face of rather widespread enthusiasm for expert systems. Peter Keen, for example, feels that DSS must embrace expert systems if DSS is to survive as a concept.[6] That is certainly the proper attitude to take. Neither managers nor information specialists should ignore the potential that expert systems offer simply because such systems will be difficult to implement. Expert systems represent a challenge for persons developing management information systems of the future. The incorporation of expert systems holds promise of attaining a level of decision support far superior to that envisioned by early MIS and DSS pioneers.

Summary

Computer use is changing rapidly, prodded by the increasing shortage of resources—primarily systems analysts and programmers. The role of the information services department is shifting from doing the work to advising and educating the users so that they can become self-sufficient. This shift in industry roles will be reflected in college and university programs preparing future users and information specialists. The key to the success of this shift will be the continued development of user-friendly software and the ability of educators and information specialists to show users how the software works.

Computer systems are also changing from centralized configurations to distributed networks. In these networks, the orientation of hardware is moving toward the user in the form of terminals, micros, remote intelligent controllers, and front-end processors. Hardware will also orient more toward the data base to perform functions presently handled by DBMS software. Storage capacities will continue to increase, even though the form of that storage (semiconductor chips and magnetic disks) will probably remain the same during the next few years. Input is moving away from source media toward online terminals. Output is moving away from printed reports to displayed reports and query responses. While many changes will occur in the way data is processed, more changes will occur in office automation, where there is tremendous opportunity for improving productivity.

---

[6]Peter G. W. Keen, a speech titled "A Vision for DSS," given at the Fifth International Conference on Decision Support Systems, San Francisco, April 2, 1985.

Software is also moving toward the user. Newer packages such as query languages and DBMS report writers are making it possible for users to specify what information they need without having to worry about the details of how it will be produced.

The software and hardware are only two of the keys to end-user computing. They assume that the user has defined the problem and has formulated a solution strategy that can be transformed into computer logic. In order to do this, the users must master design tools such as data flow diagrams, HIPO, Warnier-Orr diagrams, structured English, and the data dictionary.

Firms implementing datacom-oriented systems become vulnerable to breaches in security by network intruders. One way to minimize the risk is to implement systems that are distributed in terms of both processors and data bases.

During the remainder of the 1980s, we can expect to see office automation playing a more vital role in MIS designs, and small organizations using micros for data processing. Firms that are further along in computer use will expand their decision support systems by concentrating on improvements in the user-DSS dialog, restructuring data bases for easier use, and providing users with modeling languages.

Expert systems, a subset of artificial intelligence, are being promoted as an addition to the MIS that will enrich its decision support capability. A knowledge engineer works with one or more experts to document the thought processes that are used in problem solving. These thought processes comprise the inference engine. The inference rules and facts unique to the particular area are the knowledge base. The other parts of an expert system are the workspace, explanation subsystem, natural language interface, and the knowledge acquisition subsystem.

Although there are a few expert systems achieving good results, the systems generally solve problems typical of lower organizational levels. It has yet to be shown that expert systems will be useful in decision support. The challenge to future MIS and DSS designers will be to harness the potential power that expert systems offer.

A Final Note

The MIS can be defined in one sentence: It is a system that provides information to management. But understanding the resources needed for an MIS and how they interrelate requires considerable analysis. A broad view of the MIS encompasses ideas and techniques from all of the business disciplines—accounting, management, management science, finance, marketing, production, and so on. This is the approach that we have taken. Our task has been to show that the MIS is much more than a computer. We recognized that the computer satisfies only a portion of the manager's information needs, and that other information comes from less formal activities such as personal conversation and reading. But most importantly, the MIS involves people. As we presented the various topics, we described them in relation to the information specialists who create the MIS, and to the managers who use it. You will play one or both of these roles—perhaps soon. We aimed to describe how these roles should be played so that you might contribute to the success of your firm and to your own professional development.

Key Terms

alien syntax	tertiary storage
natural language software	dialog management
output generation	data management
turn-key system	model management
back-end data base processor	artificial intelligence (AI)
data base machine	expert system
megabit chip	knowledge engineer
bubble memory	framework
non-volatile memory	inference engine
vertical bit recording	knowledge base
optical disk	inference rule
write-once medium	explanation subsystem
write-many medium	knowledge acquisition subsystem

Key Concepts

Factors stimulating a movement toward end-user computing

The effect that end-user computing is having on the computing profession

The necessity for changes in academic MIS programs to keep in step with industry's needs

The changing nature of computer use and equipment configuration

The importance of user-friendly documentation tools to end-user computing

The effect of distributed systems on MIS security

The continued importance of data processing system development—primarily in small firms implementing their first computers

The three thrusts of DSS improvements: manager-system dialog, highly usable data subsets, and modeling languages

The inherent appeal of expert systems in spite of modest accomplishments to date

Questions

1. What factors are stimulating the trend toward end-user computing?
2. How must the information services department adapt to the trend to end-user computing?
3. What two key issues should an IRM program address?
4. Where will most of the job opportunities be for persons wanting to work in the area of system maintenance?

5. Where will most of the opportunities be for persons wanting to design new decision support systems? What skills should these persons possess?

6. In what directions is processor power moving?

7. What is a data base machine?

8. Distinguish between a front-end and a back-end processor.

9. What advantages does bubble memory offer? For what class of computers is it being used?

10. Why is current optical disk technology not suited for use as master file storage?

11. In 1990 what will probably be the most common means of entering data into a computer? What about computer output?

12. Give an example of a software system that was ahead of its time in terms of user friendliness. Give an example of a software system that was behind the times.

13. Name three ways to document business systems in detail.

14. Which documentation tool offers the greatest flexibility in spanning the range of both general and detailed design?

15. Which offers the greatest security against intruders—a distributed processing system with a distributed data base or a distributed processing system with a centralized data base? Explain.

16. Comment on the statement, "Firms solved their data processing problems long ago."

17. Will data management of the future focus on larger or smaller files for manager use?

18. What are the four subsets of artificial intelligence? Which have we described in this text? Specify the chapter numbers.

19. Is the concept of an expert system compatible or incompatible with the DSS? Explain.

20. Compare the work of the knowledge engineer and the systems analyst.

CASE PROBLEM: Broadmoor College

Broadmoor is a private liberal arts college in Ohio. The school of business offers an undergraduate major in MIS. The spring semester is drawing to a close, and Amy Klatzkin, head of the MIS department, has called a meeting of the MIS faculty to discuss next year's textbook orders. The faculty includes Irv Forkner who teaches programming, Gwynne Larson, who teaches systems analysis, and Sam Kesters, who teaches the introductory computer course.

Amy: We need to get our textbook orders in for the fall, so I'd like to know if you want to reorder the same texts we used this year. Do you plan to change your courses?

Sam: I've been reading a lot lately about some of the newer software packages such as Ideal, Mantis, and Natural. Should we be introducing our students to them in addition to COBOL, instead of it, or what? I'm talking about the introductory course.

Amy: That's a good point. I'd like to know what the rest of the group thinks.

Irv: I definitely think we should expose our students to them. That's the wave of the future. COBOL is a necessity, but if we limit our students to that, we're shortchanging them.

Gwynne: What do you mean? COBOL is the number one business language. RPG is number two, and nobody ever recommended teaching it. I can't understand all the fuss over fourth-generation software. I think we should wait and see if it is really going to be used. It costs a lot of money to buy a package, implement it on our system, develop our lab assignments, and everything. We could waste a lot of money and time jumping at every new software package that comes along. I think we should stick with COBOL for the time being.

Amy: Sam, what do you think?

Sam: I really don't know. I guess it depends on what we're trying to accomplish. Are we trying to prepare students to be information specialists or users or what?

Amy: Well, we're preparing our MIS majors to be information specialists. But Sam, you've got a lot of future MIS users in your introductory classes. About three-fourths of your students are taking your course because it's required of every business major. And it's the only computer course they ever take.

Gwynne: Do we have the funds to put something like Ideal on our computer?

Amy: I'm sure we do. We've got quite a bit of money left in the budget. But is that the package we want to add?

Irv: I don't see how we can answer that now. We haven't even identified the possibilities. There are many others. Sam mentioned the data base query-type software. There's also the electronic spreadsheets. Perhaps we should consider 1-2-3, or even IFPS.

Sam: Irv, do you think that software packages should be included in your programming courses for our MIS majors?

Irv: I'd rather see them in your introductory course. That's where we have the future MIS users. I can't see that the MIS professional needs that kind of knowledge. I would rather emphasize the mechanics of good program design methods and succinct coding featuring traditional languages such as COBOL, Assembler, or PL/I. Our MIS majors will be expected to develop efficient data processing programs. If we don't give them the basics, nobody else will.

Sam: You're teaching structured design, aren't you?

Irv: Right. That's what I mean by stressing good programming skills.

Sam: Gwynne, are you still teaching structured design in your systems course?

Gwynne: Yes. We've gotten completely away from flowcharting. I'm teaching data flow diagrams and HIPO. The students love it.

Sam: I wish the introductory students had a chance to learn some of those tools. We don't have time to do anything beyond flowcharting. And structured programming is out of the question. We just don't have the time.

Amy: Speaking of time, my next class is in ten minutes. Everybody give me their book orders by Wednesday. Thanks for coming. We need to have more meetings like this.

Questions

1. What should be done, if anything, about the introductory computer course?
2. Should the MIS majors receive exposure to user-friendly software as well as traditional languages? Support your answer.
3. How do you feel about the systems analysis course? Are the proper tools included? Explain.

Selected Bibliography

The Future of the MIS

"Artificial Intelligence: The Next Big Step in Automation," *Office Administration and Automation* 45 (October 1984): 35–37.

"Artificial Intelligence is Here," *Business Week* (July 9, 1984): 54ff.

Foster, Edward, "Artificial Intelligence Faces a Crossroads," *Mini-Micro Systems* 17 (May 1984): 119ff.

Freeman, Raymond C., Jr. "Optical Recording Comes of Age," *Mini-Micro Systems* 18 (April 1985): 65ff.

Fujitani, Larry, "Laser Optical Disk: The Coming Revolution in On-Line Storage," *Communications of the ACM* 27 (June 1984): 546–554.

Hansen, Bill, "Artificial Intelligence—A Short History," *TI Professional Computing* 1 (November 1984): 8ff.

Helgerson, Linda W., "The Optical Disk As an Information Storage Tool," *Office Administration and Automation* 46 (April 1985): 47ff.

Horwitt, Elisabeth, "Exploring Expert Systems," *Business Computer Systems* 4 (March 1985): 48ff.

King, William R., "The Intelligent MIS—A Management Helper," *Business Horizons* 16 (October 1973): 5–12.

Kinnucan, Paul, "Computers That Think Like Experts," *High Technology* 4 (January 1984): 30ff.

Kull, David, "Software—What's Ahead," *Computer Decisions* 16 (November 1984): 94ff.

Martins, Gary R., "The Overselling of Expert Systems," *Datamation* 30 (November 1, 1984): 76ff.

McFarlan, F. Warren, and James L. McKenney, "The Information Archipelago—Governing the New World," *Harvard Business Review* 61 (July–August 1983): 91–99.

Moore, Steve, "The Mass Storage Squeeze," *Datamation* 30 (October 1, 1984): 68ff.

Moran, Tom, "Bubble-Memory Devices Expand Capabilities of IBM PCs," *Mini-Micro Systems* 17 (March 1984): 43ff.

Myers, Edith, "Optical Disks Foreseen," *Datamation* 30 (June 1, 1984): 30–32.

Myers, Edith, "Database Machines Take Off," *Datamation* 31 (May 15, 1985): 52ff.

Perry, Robert L., "Relational DBMS Takes Off," *Computer Decisions* 17 (February 12, 1985): 106ff.

Shurkin, Joel N., "Expert Systems: The Practical Face of Artificial Intelligence," *Technology Review* 86 (November/December 1983): 72–78.

Verity, John W., "Prolog vs. Lisp," *Datamation* 30 (July 15, 1984): 50ff.

Weizer, Norman, and Frederick Withington, "IBM: Mainframes in 1990," *Datamation* 31 (January 1, 1985): 97ff.

Withington, Frederick G., "Winners and Losers in the Fifth Generation," *Datamation* 29 (December 1983): 193ff.

Appendix A

Flowcharting

Flowcharting is the oldest technique used to document computer procedures. Flowcharting was, for all practical purposes, the *only* technique used during the punched card era. Many of the symbols used in flowcharting were used to illustrate processes performed with punched card machines and are not ordinarily used with computer systems. In truth, the flowchart symbols were better suited to the batch systems of the 1960s than the online systems of today.

Flowchart Fundamentals

There are two basic types of flowcharts. One is used by the systems analyst to illustrate how programs and/or noncomputerized processes are linked to form a system. This type of flowchart is the "big picture" of the system and is called a *system flowchart*.

The other type of flowchart is used by the analyst or the programmer to show the steps executed in a single program. These flowcharts are called *program flowcharts*.

Both types of flowcharts are drawn with the template pictured in Figure A-1. These symbols are internationally accepted standard shapes and represent a common language among information specialists around the world.

System Flowcharts

Computer procedures are composed of *data* flowing through a system and *processes* that transform the data. There are therefore two groups of flowchart symbols—those used to illustrate data files and those used to illustrate processes.

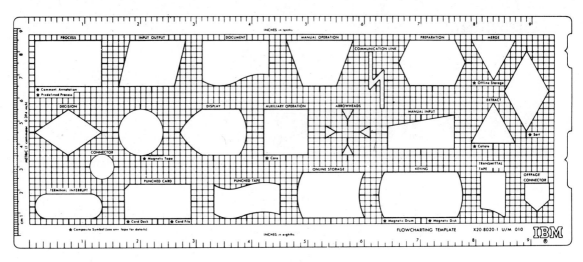

Figure A-1 Flowchart template.

Process symbols

There are three primary ways to process data: manually, with a keydriven device, and with a computer.

Processes performed *manually* are illustrated with this symbol:

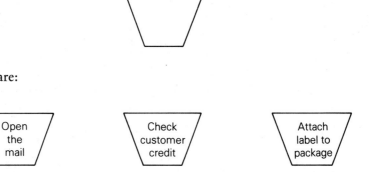

Examples are:

Appropriate lettering is entered in the symbol to provide more information about the exact process involved.

Processes performed by operating an *offline keydriven machine* such as a keypunch, a cash register, or a pocket calculator are represented by:

Examples are:

Keypunch sales cards	Verify sales cards	Accumulate batch totals

Processes performed by operating an *online keydriven machine* such as a terminal are represented by:

Examples are:

Enter order data	Enter decisions	Enter query

Finally, processes performed by the *computer* are illustrated by:

Examples are:

Print payroll checks	Sort sales records	Plant location model

System flowcharts are prepared by arranging the processing symbols in the correct sequence as shown in Figure A-2. For example, a procedure might involve (1) opening the mail, (2) keying the sales order data onto diskettes, (3) sorting the sales records, and (4) printing a sales report.

Symbols are usually arranged in a vertical sequence, with arrows showing the direction of the flow. The steps are often numbered.

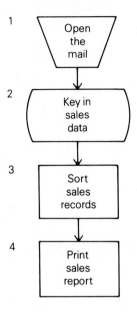

Figure A-2 Process steps.

File symbols

It is also common practice to include symbols representing the files of data or information linking the process steps. These symbols can take the following forms, depending on the file media used.

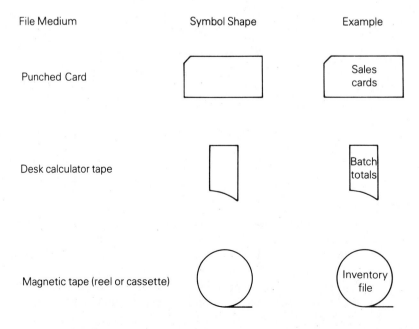

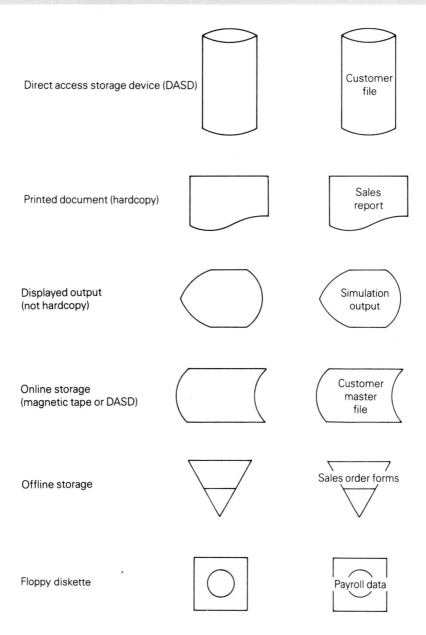

The symbol for the diskette is not a recognized standard. Neither is there a standard symbol for a magnetic tape cassette (we use the tape reel symbol). In addition, there is no symbol for computer output microfilm (COM) and no symbol that can be used for both terminal input and output.

When the file symbols are added to the four process symbols linked in Figure A-2, the system flowchart is complete. See Figure A-3.

The brackets to the right of steps 2 and 3 are *annotation symbols*. They explain the processing of the related step in greater detail.

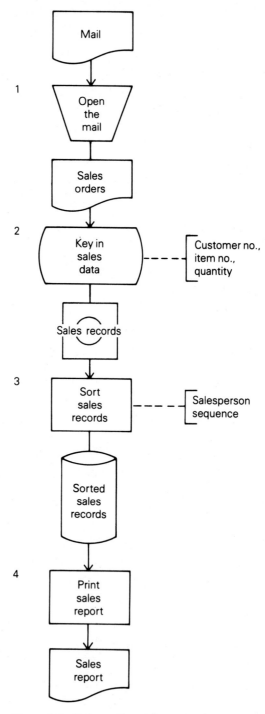

Figure A-3 System flowchart example.

Program Flowcharts

The analyst or the programmer must prepare a program for each of the computer steps in a system. In Figure A-3, for example, a program is prepared for step 4. A prewritten sort program can be used for step 3.

While a large number of different computer instructions can be used in a program, they fall within only five categories. These categories are (1) preparation, (2) input and output, (3) data movement and manipulation, (4) logic, and (5) program terminal points.

The *preparation* symbol is:

Examples are:

The preparation symbol is usually included at the beginning of the program to *initialize* certain data values, to set switches that can be tested with program logic, or to clear primary storage areas.

An *input* or *output* instruction can be illustrated with:

Examples are:

The above are general-purpose input/output symbols; they apply to any type of media.

Data movement and manipulation instructions include the different types of arithmetic processes and also the processes that move data elements from one location to another. The rectangle represents all of these.

Examples are:

Add sales to total	Multiply rate by hours	Compute square root	Move name to output

The *logical decisions* made by the computer usually involve selecting one of two alternatives. The data being examined either agrees with a predefined condition or it doesn't. These decisions are illustrated with a diamond.

Examples of a yes/no decision are:

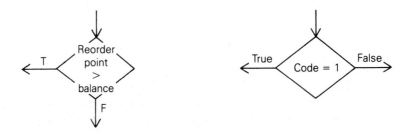

Both of these examples ask a question. The answer is either yes (Y) or no (N). One arrow leads into the diamond, and two exit from it. It makes no difference which points on the diamond are used.

Examples of a true/false decision are:

A statement is made, and the statement either is true or it is false. This technique is especially applicable to IF statements in programming languages.

The diamond is strictly a program flowcharting symbol. It is not used in a system flowchart.

Another symbol limited to use in program flowcharts is the oval.

The oval represents a *terminal point* in a program: the beginning or the end of the program or a major subroutine within it. The beginning and end of the program are illustrated with:

Figure A-4 provides an example of the use of the oval. This flowchart illustrates the *structured programming* technique. The program is subdivided into segments, or modules. Each module begins and ends with an oval. The terminal symbol used to mark the beginning of a module contains the module number (such as 000) and the module name (such as Accumulate sales amounts). The ending symbol either contains the wording "End of program" or "Return."

Program flowchart example

Figure A-4 illustrates a program that reads transaction data and adds the sales amount to a table. The table is a simple list that contains total amounts for each of the firm's 20 salespersons.

Module 000-Accumulate sales amounts is the *driver module*—it "drives" the other modules. Program execution begins with step D1 that directs the "read" module to be performed. (The steps of the driver module are numbered D1 through D6. Steps are normally *not* numbered in this manner; the practice is followed here solely to facilitate your understanding of the flow.)

The control unit of the CPU transfers program control to the read module (800-Read trans record). Step R1 is executed and an input data record is read. Step R2 tests for an end-of-file (EOF) condition. If it is the end of the file (the reading unit cannot read another record), a YES flag is moved to an EOF switch. The *flag* is simply the word "YES," and the *switch* is simply a storage location. If the end of the file has not been reached, the "YES" flag is not moved. When the read module has been executed, control returns to the driver module.

Step D2 is next executed. It causes the "update table" module (110-Update table) to be executed. Step U1 adds the amount of the sale to the appropriate position in the table. Step U2 causes the read module to again be executed. The read module reads a record and tests for the end-of-file condition.

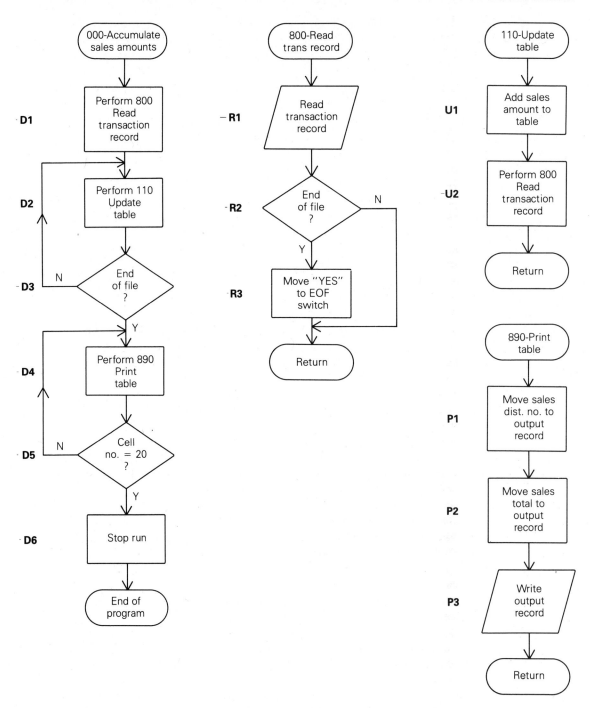

Figure A-4 Program flowchart example.

When the read module has been executed, control returns back to the point in the program that "called" the module. Previously, that point was step D1. Now, it is step U2. The "return" step after step U2 transfers control back to the point that called the update module—step D2.

We are back in the driver module where step D3 tests the EOF switch to see if it contains the YES flag. If not, step D2 is executed and the update module is called (to use the data that was read in the previous execution of the read module). If the end of file has been reached, step D4 causes the print module (890-Print table) to move the first sales district number and its total to an output area in primary storage where the data is printed. Control reverts to the driver module where step D5 tests to see if all 20 table positions have been printed. If not, the print table module is executed again, selecting the next row of data. This printing process continues until all 20 rows have been printed. Then, the "Y" branch is taken from step D5, and the "Stop run" instruction is executed to end the program.

Perhaps you had difficulty in following the transfer of program control back and forth within the program. Keep in mind that our intent here is not to teach structured programming. That is best done in a programming text. We are illustrating program flowcharting, using a structured program as an example. If you understand how the various symbols represent different operations, that is the important thing.

Lengthy Flowcharts

Some problems might require a flowchart too lengthy to fit on a single page. In these cases, some technique must be used to connect the lines on one page with those on another. A special symbol, the *off-page connector*, is used for this purpose.

If the flow goes from the bottom of page 1 to the top of page 2, a pair of off-page connectors makes the connection.

Bottom of Page 1   Top of Page 2

A letter or number is entered in both symbols to show the relationship. This permits the use of more than one set of connectors.

Another connector eliminates long connecting lines on a single page and is called the *on-page connector*.

Figure A-5 illustrates how a long line in the left-hand diagram can be eliminated to produce a less-cluttered structure at the right.

Either letters or numbers are entered in sets of related on-page connector symbols. If letters are used for off-page connectors, numbers can be used for on-page, or vice versa.

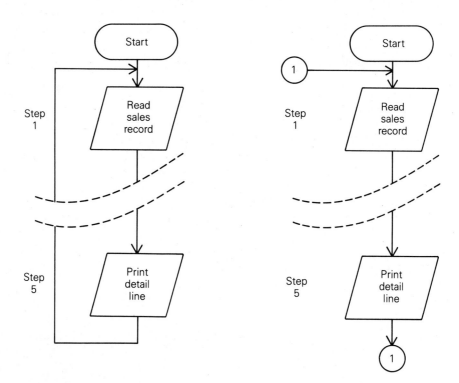

Figure A-5   Use of on-page connectors.

Flowcharts and the Manager

Flowcharts are notoriously user *un*friendly. They provide a good way for information specialists to communicate with each other, but a user can quickly become lost trying to follow the paths of large charts. Perhaps our "simple" program flowchart example convinced you of the difficulty.

System flowcharts are not so bad; usually they are shorter and there is no jumping back and forth. It is possible for a manager and a systems analyst to use a system flowchart as a way to agree on an overall design. But the major weakness of the flowcharting technique is that detail cannot be gradually cranked into the structure. Going from a system flowchart to a program flowchart is like switching off the lights for the user. With flowcharts, the systems analyst loses the user at a very early stage. In other techniques such as data flow diagrams, HIPO, and Warnier-Orr diagrams, the detail can be gradually injected—like gradually dimming the lights with a rheostat. With these other techniques, the user can be involved farther into the project.

System flowcharts are excellent for communicating *hardware-specific designs*— pictures of the different computer units used in certain ways. Since users can follow these flows, system flowcharts will probably continue to be used. Program flowcharts, however, are gradually losing ground. This is not due primarily to their user unfriendliness, but because the programmers prefer the other techniques that are better suited to structured design.

But businesses are slow to change. Flowcharts are likely to be around for some time.

Appendix B

Data Flow Diagrams

In the first few chapters of the book, we recognized how resources flow through the firm. Data and information are conceptual resources, and these flows can be documented using data flow diagrams.

The idea for using data flow diagrams as one of the means to achieve structured design is credited to Larry L. Constantine. His idea began to take shape in 1963 and was described in various journal articles beginning in 1965. In 1979 Constantine teamed with Edward Yourdon to write a textbook incorporating data flow diagrams and other structured techniques.[1]

Fundamentals

Tom DeMarco, author of another early book on structured design, defines a data flow diagram *(DFD)* as:

> a network representation of a system. The system may be automated, manual, or mixed. The Data Flow Diagram portrays the system in terms of its component pieces, with all interfaces among the components indicated.[2]

A DFD shows two aspects of a business procedure—the data flowing through the system and the processes that transform that data.

---

[1] Edward Yourdon and Larry L. Constantine, *Structured Design: Fundamentals of a Discipline of Computer Program and Systems Design* (Englewood Cliffs: Prentice-Hall, 1979).

[2] Tom DeMarco, *Structured Analysis and System Specification* (Englewood Cliffs: Prentice-Hall, 1979), p. 47.

DFD symbols

Only four symbols are used in DFDs—square, arrow, circle, and open-ended rectangle. The square represents something in the environment of the system being documented—an *environmental element*. The element can be an organization such as the firm's customers, or it can be another of the firm's systems. Here, we are talking about the environment of the system—not the environment of the firm. The arrow is used to show data flow. The data may range from a single data element to a complete file. The circle represents a process—some action performed on the data. The open-ended rectangle represents a *data store*, or file. The data store can be a computer storage medium such as magnetic disk or tape, or a noncomputer medium such as a file cabinet.

Much of the appeal of DFDs is due to the few symbols used.

Sample DFD

Figure B-1 is a sample DFD of a payroll system. The firm's employees provide the input data by filling out time sheets (identified by an arrow). The time sheets are printed forms that employees update with their data—name, employee number, department number, total hours worked per day, and total hours for the week. The sheets are prepared weekly.

The arrow labeled "Time sheets" goes into a circle labeled "1.0 Edit time sheets." This is the first process step. In this example, the diagram doesn't identify *who* does the editing; that identification can be accomplished elsewhere. Neither does the DFD identify exactly *how* the editing is done. That also can be accomplished elsewhere—either on more detailed DFDs or other documentation. Our sample DFD shows a general, high-level flow of the data and processes.

There are two arrows coming out of step 1.0. The step transforms one type of input into two types of output. In this case, the editing either approves or rejects the time sheets. Rejected time sheets go back to the employees for correction.

Approved time sheets are input to the second step, where the sheets are accumulated in a file. Maybe a clerk simply files time sheets in a file drawer. Or, if a computer is being used, a data entry person keys the data onto some type of magnetic medium such as a diskette.

The accumulation of data is named a "Time sheet file." The term *file* is so popular in business that it is difficult not to use it. The proper DFD term is *data store*.

The payroll data is retained in the store for a while and then is removed. Perhaps the data is retained for the current month.

You can look at a DFD and get an idea of the rate of the data flow. When two circles are connected by an arrow (such as processes 1.0 and 2.0), the second process is performed as soon as the first is finished. When, on the other hand, a store separates two processes (as in 2.0 and 3.0), you know that there is a break in the action. The data is held in the store until it is time to use it in the next step.

The data that is removed from the store is named "Current period data." This data is processed in step 3.0 to compute earnings (perhaps total hours worked

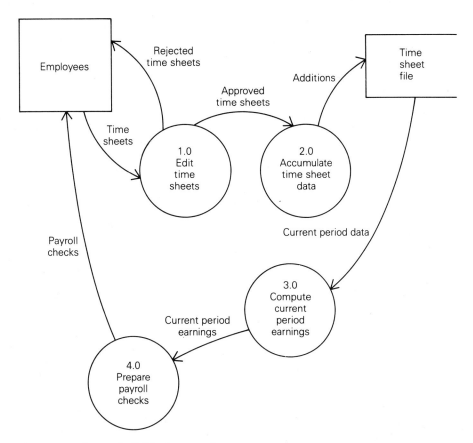

Figure B-1 A sample DFD of a payroll system.

are multiplied times the hourly rate). The computed earnings are used in step 4.0 to prepare the payroll checks, which are distributed to the employees. In this example, the employees both provide input data and receive the output from the system.

Why use DFDs?

There are several major reasons for using DFDs:

1. They are easy to learn. The few symbols and rules can be learned much more quickly than several other documentation techniques such as flowcharting.

2. They communicate information quickly. Because of their graphic nature, they convey data and procedure flow much more quickly than a narrative.

3. They facilitate a structured, top-down approach. This is the design approach that is currently very popular. DFDs can be defined in successively lower levels of detail.

4. They encourage user involvement. Because DFDs are simple to understand, the user can easily follow the documentation prepared by the systems analyst. The user and analyst can therefore work as a team longer into the project than if other, less friendly tools are used.

5. They capture logical design rather than physical. They are therefore not susceptible to obsolescence when technology changes.

6. They are effective for showing both general and detailed flow. Each DFD level can gradually introduce more detail, making it easy for the user to follow the logic as a system is being designed.

Why not use DFDs?

DFDs are better suited for certain situations than others. The systems analyst or user selects the best tool for the situation. Some disadvantages of DFDs are:

1. DFDs don't show enough detail. At some point, it becomes necessary to switch from the graphical style of the DFD to another form, such as a narrative, in order to document details.

2. They are not machine readable. The term *machine readable* means that documentation is very similar to computer code. Machine readable documentation, such as a Warnier-Orr diagram, is very easy to convert to code, such as BASIC. DFDs, on the other hand, are far removed from code. This disadvantage can be minimized by giving careful thought to the names assigned to the processes, as we will see shortly.

Suggested Techniques

There are not a lot of rules governing the use of DFDs. Some general conventions, or practices, have evolved over the past five- to ten-year period as DFDs have increased in popularity. We will incorporate most of the conventions into our description. Since, however, there are no DFD standards (as in flowcharting), there is considerable variation in how DFDs are drawn.

Environmental elements

These elements are represented by squares. Some people shade the square so that it appears to be a box:

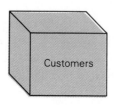

The terms *source* and *sink* are often used to describe these elements. The source provides the input and the sink receives the output. In our payroll example, the employees serve as both the source and the sink.

As you use DFDs in a top-down manner, you will prepare DFDs with successively increased levels of detail. You *never* introduce a new environmental element on a lower level. The top-level diagram includes *all* of the sources and sinks that will be incorporated into the system.

Processes

Processes convert input to output. You will often see DFDs with the processes drawn using rectangles with rounded corners:

```
2.4

Assign
order
number
```

Each symbol, regardless of shape, should contain a *step number* and a *description*. Use numbers like 1.0, 2.0, 3.0, and so on for the top-level diagram. For the next lower level, use 1.1, 1.2, 1.3. Follow with numbers like 1.11, and then 1.11.1. Usually three or four levels are sufficient to document business procedures.

When describing a process, use a *verb* (such as "Edit") followed by an *object* of the action (such as "Time sheet"). This practice is also followed in other structured techniques, so it is a good habit to get into if you will be using multiple tools. The verb/object structure is also compatible with programming, making it easier to convert your DFD into computer code. In this manner, you increase the machine readability of the DFD.

Each process name in a DFD should be unique—no two processes should have the same name. When defining the unique names, use the names of the data flowing into and out of the process as a clue. For example, in step 1.0 of Figure B-1, the input data is time sheets. So, when naming step 1.0, think of "doing what to time sheets?" They are being edited, so a good name is "Edit time sheets."

Data stores

A data store is represented with an open-ended rectangle. The name of the store is entered inside the space.

```
Deduction
file
```

A store is often used more than once in a system. This is especially common when the system is a large one. If you want to indicate that a store is used more than once, you can include some special marking. A popular technique is to include a number of vertical marks. Each set of multiple files would use the same number of marks. For example:

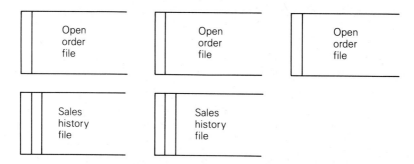

The open order files have one vertical mark inside the rectangle; the sales history files have two. When you see a store with these types of markings, you know that there are other references to the same store in the same DFD. When you see a store without such markings, you know that there are no other references.

Always try to use informative names for the stores. The viewer should be able to read the name and have a good idea of what is contained.

Data flow

Data flow is illustrated with arrows. As with the process and data store names, each arrow name should be unique and should adequately describe the data represented.

Some users do not label arrows coming from a store when the name of the store adequately describes the arrow. For example, we might have this flow:

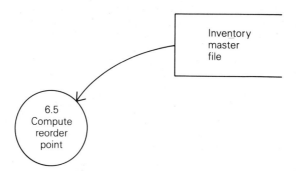

Here, the entire inventory master file is being processed, so there is no reason to name the arrow. You might want to bypass this option and name all arrows just for uniformity. But, be prepared for a lot of arrows on a large diagram. After a while it becomes tedious to continually come up with good, unique names. This option can provide some measure of relief.

An arrow can represent a single data element, a record, or a file. As an example of a single-element data flow, assume that a clerk obtains a rate from a rate book:

An arrow will frequently represent more than one record or document traveling together as a *packet*. For example, we might send a picking ticket, packing list, and shipping label to the warehouse so that ordered merchandise can be gathered and shipped to customers. Here, our task is to come up with a name to describe all three records. We might decide on "shipping documents."

Top-Down Approach

We can use the payroll procedure in Figure B-1 as an example of how a system documentation is successively made more detailed. Actually, when we used the B-1 diagram for our example, we did not use the highest-level diagram. It is possible to describe our payroll system using a single circle, as in Figure B-2. This type of DFD is called a *context diagram*—it puts the system in context in terms of its inputs, outputs, and boundaries. Arrows leading to the circle are the system's

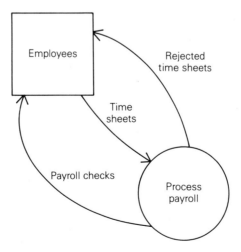

Figure B-2 A context diagram.

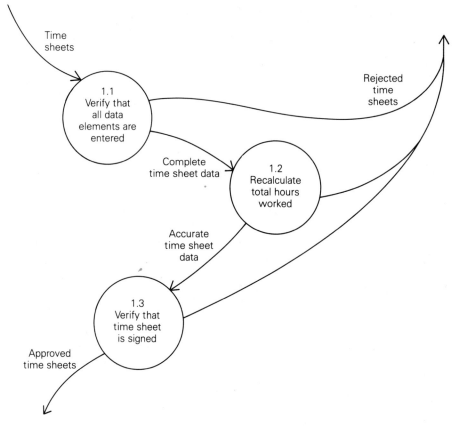

Figure B-3 Second level of system detail for step 1.0—Edit time sheets.

inputs, and arrows leaving the circle are the outputs. Any squares represent the boundaries—interfaces with sources and sinks.

The single process step of the context diagram is not numbered. Notice in the example that you only show the data flows into and out of the system; all other flows are internal to the system, as is the single store.

If we were documenting the payroll system (either the existing system or a proposed one), we would start with the context diagram in Figure B-2. Then we would prepare the *top-level* DFD in Figure B-1.

The next step is to increase the level of detail by subdividing the steps of Figure B-1. Figure B-3 illustrates how step 1.0 in Figure B-1 can be subdivided to provide a second level of detail. We have simply recognized that three basic operations are involved in editing the time sheets. This example shows an anomaly that may be encountered—*converging flows*. All three steps produce rejected outputs that are routed back to the source. (You can also have *diverging flows*—a single flow splitting apart.)

We would subdivide steps 2.0, 3.0, and 4.0 of Figure B-1 in the same manner.

At this point, you may be asking "How do you know when to stop subdi-

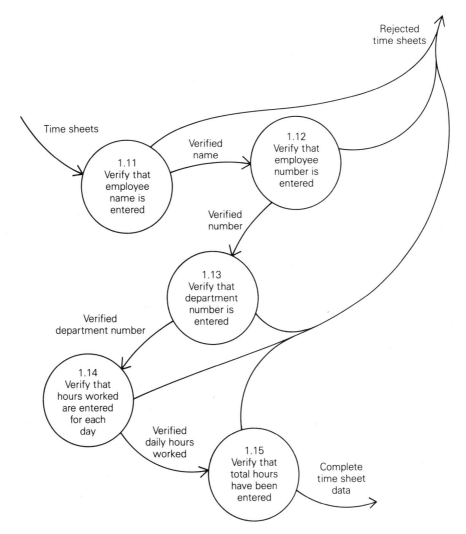

Figure B-4   Third level of system detail for step 1.1—Verify that all data has been entered.

viding?" One answer is ,"When you think that you have revealed enough detail to thoroughly understand the system." Another rule of thumb is to stop when you can prepare a brief narrative describing a process and be able to fit the narrative on a single page. It is common to accompany DFDs with such narratives so as to address the detail adequately.

It is possible that some processes on a DFD should be subdivided, and some should not. Using Figure B-3 as an example, step 1.3 may be detailed enough, but there may be a need to subdivide step 1.1 to indicate exactly what data elements are checked. So, we may subdivide 1.1 but not 1.3. Figure B-4 shows the detail for step 1.1. Steps 1.11 through 1.15 reflect a *third level* of detail.

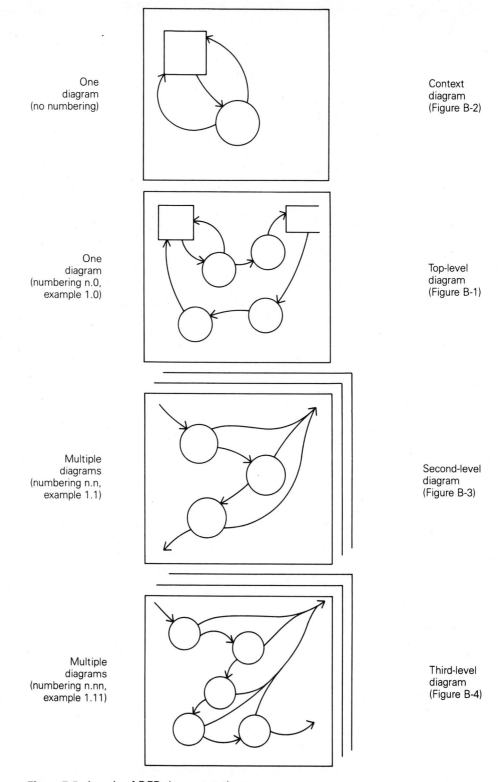

One
diagram
(no numbering)

Context
diagram
(Figure B-2)

One
diagram
(numbering n.0,
example 1.0)

Top-level
diagram
(Figure B-1)

Multiple
diagrams
(numbering n.n,
example 1.1)

Second-level
diagram
(Figure B-3)

Multiple
diagrams
(numbering n.nn,
example 1.11)

Third-level
diagram
(Figure B-4)

Figure B-5 Levels of DFD documentation.

Notice that the data flow names entering and leaving the DFD in Figure B-4 are the same that appear for step 1.1 in Figure B-3. The same names are used from level to level.

The final system documentation would include all of the DFDs on all of the levels as we have begun to do with Figures B-1 through B-4. Figure B-5 illustrates how all of the document levels interrelate.

Accompanying Documentation

It has become a common practice to use DFDs in conjunction with other design and documentation tools at the detailed level. DFDs describe processes in general. These processes need to be described in more detail, perhaps in a simple step-by-step narrative. DFDs also describe data, but only in a general sense. At some point, the records in the files and the data elements in the records must be specified. The DFD provides a natural origin for the *data dictionary* that we introduced in Chapter 7 (The Data Base). The data dictionary, in turn, provides a natural origin for the details of the DFD processes. These details can be provided by several techniques that are quite similar—pseudocode, logically "tight English," structured English, and transform descriptions. *Structured English* is the technique most often associated with DFDs.

Figure B-6 captures the relationships between DFDs, the data dictionary, and structured English. The DFDs are drawn first to specify the overall architecture of the system. Next, each data flow is analyzed in detail and its data elements identified. These elements are described in the data dictionary. With the DFD description of the overall flow, and the data dictionary description of the data

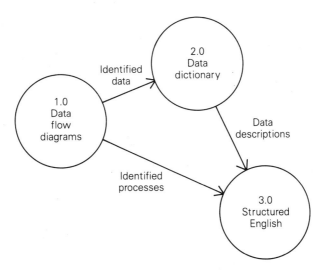

Figure B-6 Logical relationships between design and documentation tools.

contained within that flow, it is fairly easy to document the processes in detail using structured English.

We will describe the data dictionary in Appendix C and structured English in Appendix D.

DFDs and the Manager

The DFD is the most user-friendly of all the design and documentation tools. It is a natural way to illustrate a procedural flow—just sketch out circles representing processes and string them together with arrows. It is quite realistic to assume that a manager can document her or his own system by using DFDs. The DFD offers a manager a way to achieve end-user computing by providing a means of performing the necessary systems analysis and design.

The manager is not so likely to use the other structured tools—the data dictionary and structured English. Information specialists normally create the dictionary, and structured English requires an understanding of program logic—looping and so on.

The manager also benefits when the systems analyst creates the DFDs. The DFDs are so easy to understand, and their detail can be increased in such a gradual way that the manager can be an active member of the design team much longer than when many other tools are used.

Appendix C

Data Dictionary

Note: This appendix presupposes an understanding of data flow diagrams as presented in Appendix B.

In Chapter 7, we explained that the *data dictionary* describes each data element in the data base. Some dictionaries are *computer based*—that is, they are maintained in secondary storage by a special software system. But the data dictionary must be specified in detail on a printed document before it is entered into computer storage. Therefore, a *document-based data dictionary* is a prerequisite to a computer-based one. If the firm does not use a computer-based dictionary, then the document-based dictionary provides the standard description of the firm's data resource. In this appendix, we describe how to develop a document-based data dictionary.

Data Dictionary Forms

The system presented here consists of a set of four dictionary forms:

- Data store dictionary entry
- Data structure dictionary entry
- Data element dictionary entry
- Data flow dictionary entry[1]

The first three forms present the data base contents in the form of a hierarchy. The data store, or file, is the highest grouping. Structures, or records, exist within

---

[1]This set of forms is based largely on the system described by James Senn, *Analysis and Design of Information Systems* (New York: McGraw-Hill, 1984), pp. 125–134.

stores, and elements exist within structures. This is the file/record/element hierarchy that was presented in Chapter 7.

    The data flow form describes each data flow (arrow) on a data flow diagram (DFD). Data flows can consist of single data elements, groups of elements forming a structure, or multiple structures.

    These forms are assembled in a binder to provide (1) the firm's document-based data dictionary, or (2) input to the firm's computer-based data dictionary.

Data store dictionary entry

The *data store dictionary entry* describes each data store in the system. Even though a store might appear several times within a system, only a single data store form is used. Figure C-1 contains a completed sample. The *data store name*

DATA STORE DICTIONARY ENTRY

Use: To describe each data store, or file, on a data flow diagram.

DATA STORE NAME: Payroll transactions

DESCRIPTION   The data used each pay period to prepare employee
payroll checks

DATA STRUCTURES: Employee payroll record
Earnings record
Deduction record

VOLUME: 350–375 per pay period

ACCESS: Restricted to managers and supervisors in
employee's department, plus members of payroll
department

Figure C-1 Sample completed data store dictionary entry.

is entered, along with a brief *description*. The *data structures* comprising the store are listed. Think of the store as a file and the structures as types of records in the file. In the example, the payroll transactions store consists of three types of structures—employee payroll record, earnings record, and deduction record. Perhaps we would have all three for each employee. The structures *occur* a certain number of times depending on the size of the store. For example, in a firm with 1200 employees, the employee payroll record structure would occur 1200 times.

Some indication of the size and activity of the store is entered in the *volume* area. The volume can describe the store in terms of the number of structure occurrences, or it can describe the activity in terms of the percentage of the occurrences involved in processing. For example, the volume can be expressed as "18–20,000 occurrences of each structure," "80 percent of the contents active each week," and so forth. If there are any *access* restrictions, they are entered in the area at the bottom of the form.

Data structure dictionary entry

A *data structure dictionary entry* is completed for each structure listed on the data store and data flow dictionary entries. A sample form appears in Figure C-2. The *structure name* field contains the same name used on the data store and data flow forms. The *description* field describes the use, and the *contents* area lists each data element. At the bottom of the form is a *volume* area, which describes the quantity of the structure (how many times it occurs), and possibly a measure of the rate of flow. For example, the volume could include details such as "1 for each sales transaction," "4,000 per day," or "varies between 10,000 and 12,000, depending on the season."

Data element dictionary entry

The *data element dictionary entry* provides the basis for the data base schema. These forms provide the data element dictionary (DED) described in Chapter 7. A completed data element dictionary entry appears in Figure C-3. The sample is for a customer number. This number appears on order forms, invoices, statements, and many other forms and reports.

A data element form is used for each data element included in all of the structures. But, only a single form is used for each element even though it might appear at several points within the system. The idea is to standardize the description of an element so that the element is used the same way each time.

In addition to the *element name* and *description*, the *type* of data is indicated—numeric, alphabetic, or alphanumeric (combined numeric and alphabetic). The *length* specifies the element size, in number of positions or bytes. If the element has several names, or *aliases*, they are listed. Some indication is provided, when appropriate, of the *range of values* to be recorded for the element, a *typical value*, and any *specific values*. If there are any *other editing details*, they are listed at the bottom. The editing is intended to detect errors.

Much effort goes into a complete description of each data element, but the work is only done once. Thereafter, all users share the same description.

DATA STRUCTURE DICTIONARY ENTRY

Use: To describe a formal data structure, such as a record or document.

STRUCTURE NAME: Picking ticket

DESCRIPTION: The document used by warehouse personnel to select items from the shelves in the process of filling orders

CONTENTS:
Customer number

Customer name and address

Customer order number

Customer order date

Shipping instructions

Item number

Item description

Quantity

Warehouse location

VOLUME: Average 275 per day; peak day = 325; light day = 175

Figure C-2 Sample completed data structure dictionary entry.

DATA ELEMENT DICTIONARY ENTRY

Use: To describe each data element contained within a data structure, data flow, and data store.

ELEMENT NAME: Customer number

DESCRIPTION: The number assigned to each customer to provide a unique identification

TYPE: Numeric

LENGTH: 8 positions

ALIASES: Customer I.D.

Customer account number

VALUE RANGE: 30000001 to 30999999

TYPICAL VALUE: None

LIST OF SPECIFIC VALUES (IF ANY):

None

OTHER EDITING DETAILS: First two digits are always "30." Remaining digits are assigned in sequence. No duplicate numbers. All positions are numeric. Missing numbers are common. Numbers are reassigned when account becomes dormant.

Figure C-3 Sample completed data element dictionary entry.

Data flow dictionary entry

The *data flow dictionary entry* is used to describe each data flow (arrow) in a data flow diagram (DFD). If your DFD contains 43 arrows, then you need 43 data flow dictionary entries.

A sample data flow dictionary entry is included as Figure C-4. The *data flow name* is the same one used on the DFD. The *description* is a brief explanation of the flow, identifying whether it is a single data element, a structure, or group of structures. The description can also explain how the data flow is used. The *from processes* field identifies the process, or processes, producing the data flow, and the *to processes* field identifies the process, or processes, next using the data flow. The *data structures* area lists the structure, or structures, included in the flow.

Complementary nature of the forms

The four data dictionary forms work together as a set. The relationship is illustrated in Figure C-5. The data flow form identifies the structures within the data flow. The data store form identifies the structures within the store. The structure and element forms specify lower levels of the data hierarchy in both the data store and the data flow.

Tailoring the Forms to Your Needs

The set of forms presented here is only one example. There is no standard way to design the forms. If a firm plans to use a computer-based data dictionary system, the input requirements of the DDS will dictate the way that the data is described. Otherwise, the firm is left with the option of describing the data the way that they see fit.

Any approach, however, should include a separate form for each data element, containing standardized characteristics such as name and format. The other descriptions will vary from one firm to the next. The important thing is to take an organized, systematic approach to describing the firm's data resource. The exact manner that is used for the description is secondary in importance.

The Data Dictionary and the Manager

The manager will provide valuable input to the development of the data dictionary by identifying and describing needed data elements. However, the manager will not actually create the dictionary. That task is left to an information specialist—systems analyst or data base administrator.

The manager greatly benefits from the data dictionary in an indirect way. The manager uses the contents of the data base, which are specified by the dictionary. The data dictionary is a step necessary to providing the manager with the data base required for a good MIS.

DATA FLOW DICTIONARY ENTRY

Use: To describe each data flow (arrow) on a data flow diagram.

DATA FLOW NAME: Shipping documents

DESCRIPTION: Paperwork provided to warehouse personnel
enabling them to select merchandise, pack it,
and make it available for shipment to
customers. Consists of three forms--picking tickets,
packing lists, and shipping labels.

FROM PROCESSES: 6.81 Prepare picking tickets

6.82 Prepare packing lists

6.83 Prepare shippping labels

TO PROCESSES: 7.23 Fill order

DATA STRUCTURES: Picking ticket

Packing list

Shipping label

Figure C-4 Sample completed data flow dictionary entry.

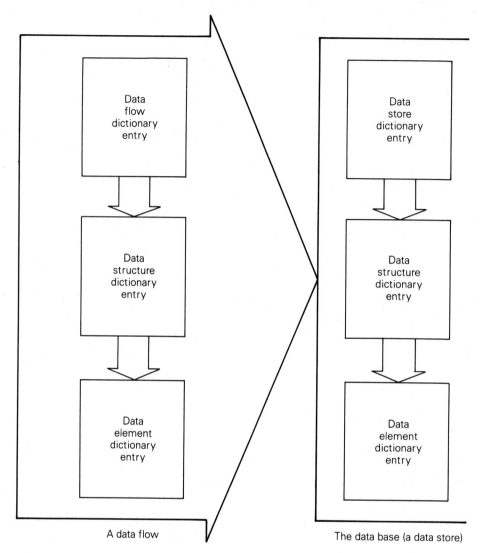

Figure C-5 Interrelationships of the forms.

Appendix D

Structured English

Note: This appendix presupposes an understanding of data flow diagrams as presented in Appendix B.

Structured English is a narrative description of a process, with the sentences and the way the sentences are arranged resembling computer code. There are no specific rules governing how structured English is to be used. The advantage of no specific rules is that a novice can produce structured English with very little training or monitoring. There are some general guidelines, which are presented in this appendix, but much is left to the discretion of the person preparing the narrative.

If the preparer has a strong programming background, then the structured English will closely resemble computer code, such as the BASIC, FORTRAN, and Pascal languages. Such a narrative is said to be *machine readable*, meaning that little is required to convert it to a procedural language. If, on the other hand, the preparer knows little about programming, then the structure will appear less like program coding and more like an ordinary narrative. Also, much depends on the documentation standards of the firm. The standards may specify that the narrative closely resemble a particular language, or that it be more generic in nature.

The objective of structured English

The objective of structured English is to supplement the data flow diagram (DFD) or other documentation technique by providing the detailed description at the lowest level. The various levels of the DFDs describe the overall data flow as the technique is applied in a top-down manner. At some point, the graphical DFD technique becomes less effective than a narrative.

Even though structured English is most often presented in conjunction with DFDs, you should understand that it can be used with other structured techniques as well. Figure 19-7 shows structured English used with HIPO. It could be used with Warnier-Orr diagrams as well.

The origin of "program-like" narratives

Pseudocode is another narrative design and documentation tool similar to structured English. Figure D-1 contains an example of pseudocode.

Structured English, pseudocode, and other similar program-like narratives evolved as a convenient means to design a computer routine before preparing the code. The narrative serves two basic purposes. First, it enables the user (most likely a systems analyst or programmer) to "think through" the logic and arrange the steps in an orderly and succinct manner. Second, the narrative provides a good documentation of the system for persons other than the creator, who later may want to understand what the system does and how it does it.

Pseudocode was the first of the narrative types to receive widespread attention. New people coming into the growing computer field often rebelled against the numerous rules of flowcharting. Flowcharting had been used in business data processing for years and had been effective in documenting procedures that were used over a long period of time. Many of the newcomers were not using the computer for data processing, but for scientific research. Their main intent was to produce a workable program, and they were less concerned about the longevity of the documentation. In many cases, the program would be used only once. Pseudocode became identified as a program-design tool to be used in lieu of flowcharting.

```
Start
Enter order data
Write order log record
Edit order data*
IF order contains errors THEN
      write error list record
(ELSE)
ENDIF
Read customer credit record
DOWHILE this order
      Multiply order quantity times unit price
      giving price extension
      Add price extension to invoice amount
ENDDO
Add invoice amount to accounts receivable
giving new accounts receivable
IF new accounts receivable greater than
credit limit THEN
      Write rejected orders record
      Write rejected orders notice
ELSE
      Write accepted orders record
ENDIF
Exit

*The detail of the editing process is not shown.
```

Figure D-1   A pseudocode example.

During the 1970s, pseudocode became *the* program-design tool for non-business applications. It also enjoyed use in businesses where there was less dedication to flowcharting. Structured English has come into prominence during the 1980s as *one* of the ingredients of structured analysis and design. Other ingredients include data flow diagrams and the data dictionary.

Structured English versus pseudocode

There are four basic differences between structured English and pseudocode:

1. Structured English requires that only the three structures from structured programming be used. These structures are (1) simple sequence, (2) selection, and (3) repetition. They are illustrated in Figure D-2 using the program flowcharting technique. Pseudocode does not require these sequences, but there is no reason not to use them in a pseudocode description.

2. Structured English requires that all data names be defined in the data dictionary. Pseudocode has no such requirement. But again, nothing would prevent a pseudocode user from using only names from the data dictionary, assuming that such a dictionary exists.

3. Structured English is considered to be a part of a package of structured design and documentation tools. Other tools in the package can include data flow diagrams and the data dictionary. Each tool complements the others. Pseudocode, on the other hand, is typically used alone—as *the* documentation tool.

4. Pseudocode has almost invariably been used to document detailed processing steps of a computer program. Structured English can be used in that manner, but it is also used to document noncomputer processes such as filling orders in a warehouse. Structured English is being applied on a broader scale than pseudocode.

Structured English and pseudocode are very similar, and one technique is not necessarily better than the other. The choice depends on the situation. Structured English is preferred when other structured tools are also used. Pseudocode is best when there is no data dictionary or other documentation, and/or when the objective is to execute a one-time program as quickly and easily as possible.

The Process Dictionary Entry

It is possible to write the structured English on ordinary ruled paper. Since the structured English is part of a package, however, a form can be designed that links the narrative to its graphical predecessor—the DFD. Such a form appears in Figure D-3. It is named the *process dictionary entry*.[1]

---

[1] This form design is from James Senn, *Analysis and Design of Information Systems* (New York: McGraw-Hill), pp. 132–133.

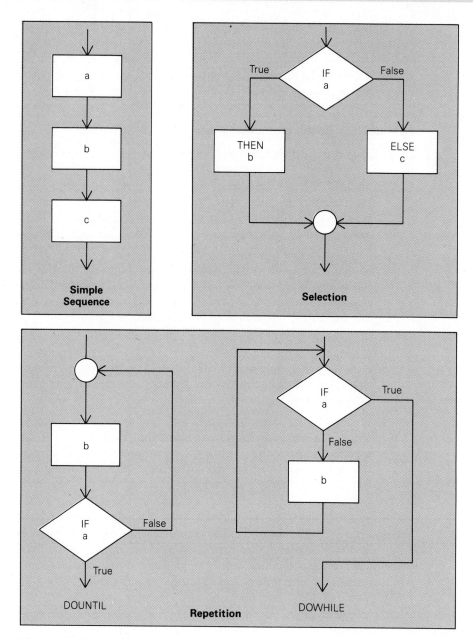

Figure D-2   The three basic program structures.

PROCESS DICTIONARY ENTRY

Use: To describe each process included on a data flow diagram.

PROCESS: 12.25 Compute gross earnings

DESCRIPTION: Gross earnings are computed by multiplying hourly rate times the number of hours. For hours worked over 40, the rate is increased by half ("time-and-a-half")

INPUT: HOURS

RATE

OUTPUT: GROSS-PAY

LOGIC SUMMARY: IF HOURS greater than 40

THEN

multiply RATE by 40

giving REG-PAY

multiply (HOURS - 40)

by (RATE times 1.5)

giving OT-PAY

compute GROSS-PAY =

REG-PAY + OT-PAY

ELSE

compute GROSS-PAY =

RATE times HOURS.

ENDIF

Figure D-3 Sample completed process dictionary entry.

The field labeled *process* contains the number and name from the DFD. There is one process dictionary entry form for each process in the DFD. The *description* briefly explains what the process accomplishes. The DFD does not lend itself to providing this description. The description is best recorded on a separate form such as the process dictionary entry. The *input* fields identify data elements being used in the process, and the *output* fields list the data elements created by the process.

The *logic summary* portion of the form is where the structured English appears. The upper portion of the form is strictly heading information relating the narrative to the DFD. The sample in Figure D-3 computes gross payroll earnings by multiplying the rate times the hours worked. If the hours exceed 40, the rate for the excess is one and one-half times the regular rate.

Notice that data element names in the input, output, and logic summary sections are capitalized. This technique serves to call the viewer's attention to the standardized nature of the names. The names are exactly as in the data dictionary. We should be able to go to the data dictionary and find separate pages devoted to a description of HOURS, RATE, and GROSS-PAY.

You will also notice that the entries in the logic summary section are indented in a certain way. The indenting serves to set apart the THEN and the ELSE portions of the selection structure. The words IF, THEN, ELSE, and ENDIF are also capitalized so that they highlight the selection structure.

The arithmetic steps in the sample are very similar to programming. This particular syntax is almost identical to COBOL. Other styles would be similar to Pascal, BASIC, or another language. The firm most likely will specify which particular style the information specialists should use. End users might have more flexibility.

It should be obvious from the example that an experienced programmer can learn structured English much easier than a novice. The discipline for constructing the narrative can be just as demanding as that of programming.

Other Structure Examples

Figure D-3 illustrates the selection structure. Programmers refer to this as an IF-THEN-ELSE structure, since IF the situation is true THEN you do something, ELSE you do something else.

Simple sequence

In a simple sequence, there are no alternate paths. The entries are performed one after the other until the end of the sequence. An example is the sequence of tasks performed by an order clerk in keying sales order data into a terminal:

```
Enter CUSTOMER-NO
Enter CUST-ORDER-NO
Enter ITEM-NO
Enter QUANTITY
Enter PRICE
```

Repetition

A simple sequence can be repeated a certain number of times depending on a condition. For example, the order clerk would enter ITEM-NO, QUANTITY, and PRICE for each item ordered. This process would be repeated until all ordered items had been entered. This repetition could be expressed as:

```
DOUNTIL no more items
        Enter ITEM-NO
        Enter QUANTITY
        Enter PRICE
ENDDO
```

This is a DO loop—you DO it until there are no more items. The terms DOUNTIL and ENDDO set off the boundaries of the loop. This is the DOUNTIL structure diagrammed in Figure D-2.

The other form of repetition structure is the DOWHILE—you do something as long as a condition exists. As an example, assume that a firm will ship merchandise to a customer as long as the customer's accounts receivable amount does not exceed the credit limit. This repetition could be expressed as:

```
DOWHILE ACC-REC less than LIMIT
     Update inventory record
     Prepare billing record
     Print invoice, picking ticket,
        packing list, and shipping label
     Ship merchandise
ENDDO
```

Structured English and the Manager

If the manager knows programming, then he or she can use structured English to document both computer and noncomputer procedures. Another factor is the manager's attitude about end-user computing. If the manager wants to be self-sufficient, and not rely on the information services staff, then she or he can prepare the structured English narrative.

In most cases, however, the systems analyst will prepare the narrative for high-level descriptions of both noncomputer and computer procedures. The programmer will prepare the narrative for detailed procedures destined for computer coding.

The manager benefits from structured English even if he or she does not actually produce it. There might be times during the system life cycle when the systems analyst will want to review a portion of the detailed logic with the manager. Structured English can serve this purpose. The manager is used to narratives and can understand the structured English format more quickly and easily than many other documentation techniques, such as flowcharting and perhaps HIPO.

Appendix E

HIPO

HIPO (Hierarchy plus Input, Processing, Output) was one of the first structured design and documentation techniques. It was introduced by IBM in the early 1970s. Since it was one of the first efforts to attempt a breakaway from flow-charting, you can see that the break was not clean. There is a lot of flowcharting in HIPO. You could even say that HIPO is simply a way to subdivide flowcharts into levels and modules.

HIPO Basics

HIPO consists of three types of diagrams. One, the *hierarchy diagram* or *structure chart*, shows the subdivision of a system by levels. A hierarchy diagram for the order entry system described in Chapter 9 appears in Figure E-1. The hierarchy diagram illustrates *processes* only—data is not included. You must describe the data elsewhere, with record layout forms or the data dictionary.

The upper box in Figure E-1 represents the system (box 1.0). On the next lower level are the basic processes of the system (boxes 2.0 through 7.0), which are described in greater detail on successively lower levels. The system is usually numbered 1.0. The major processes on the next lower level are numbered 2.0, 3.0, and so on. Lower levels incorporate decimal numbers—2.1, 2.11, 2.11.1, and so forth. The narrative in each box consists of a verb and an object.

A second type of HIPO diagram is the *overview diagram*, which relates inputs and outputs to the processes identified in the hierarchy diagram. Figure E-2 is an overview diagram of the entire order entry system—box 1.0 in Figure E-1. In Figure E-2 the input files and output files are linked to the basic processes by arrows. The files are represented by rectangles in this example. Some analysts prefer to use the flowchart symbols for the various file media. No effort is made to relate specific files to specific processing steps or to show the detail of the processing. That detail is described in lower-level diagrams.

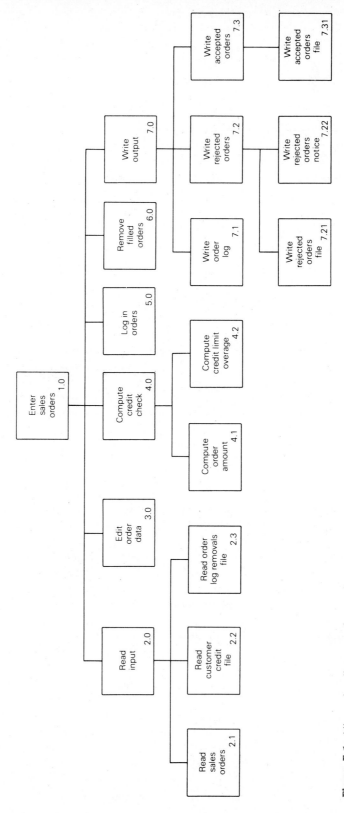

Figure E-1 Hierarchy diagram of an order entry system.

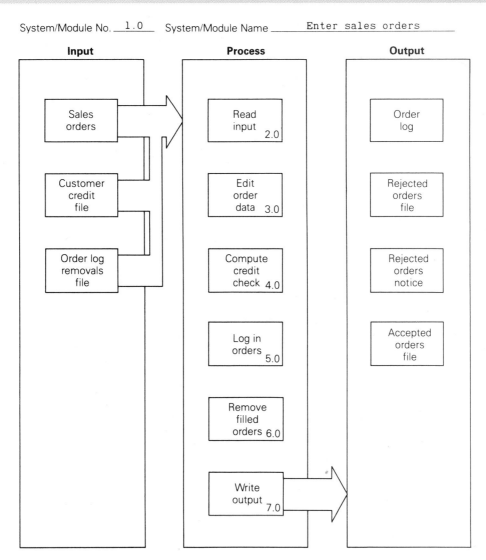

System/Module No. __1.0__ System/Module Name _____ Enter sales orders _____

Figure E-2 An overview diagram.

You normally have several levels of overview diagrams as you gradually increase the detail. The lowest level diagram is the *detail diagram*. Figure E-3 illustrates the detail diagram providing the detail for step 4.0 in Figure E-2. This is one approach to computing a credit check. In the first processing step, unit price is multiplied by quantity for each item ordered. These input data elements are enclosed in boxes to indicate that they are already in primary storage. The output, order amount, is also placed in storage. The second processing step computes the credit limit overage. The accounts receivable amount is added to the order amount, and the updated receivable amount is compared with the credit limit. If the sum exceeds the credit limit, the amount of the overage is recorded

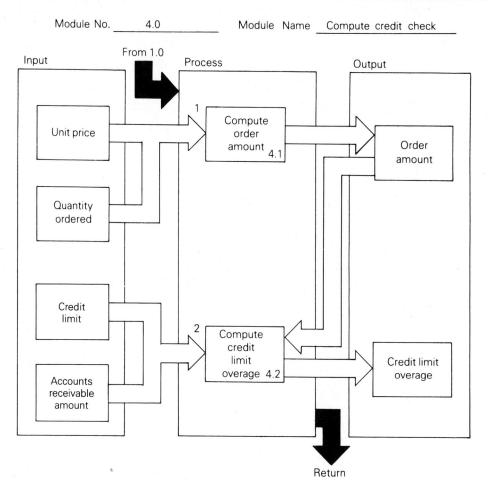

Figure E-3 A detail diagram.

in a storage area. The detail diagram for module 4.0 does not show the detail of the computations in steps 1 and 2. That detail could be shown on a lower-level diagram. In that case, Figure E-3 would become an overview diagram.

The dark arrow labeled "From 1.0" links module 4.0 to the module on the higher level, module 1.0. Also, the dark arrow labeled "return" recognizes that control will be returned to the upper-level module as soon as this series of steps is completed.

An Evaluation of HIPO

It is unlikely that HIPO will ever be a very popular design and documentation tool. In its early years, it had to compete with the well-established flowcharting technique. More recently, it seems to have been passed over by newer structured methods—data flow diagrams and Warnier-Orr diagrams.

HIPO is good for showing top-down system structure. At upper levels, the components can be illustrated with rectangles. As the design becomes more detailed, special flowcharting symbols (for disk stacks and so on) can be used. The overview and detail diagrams illustrate the system in a straightforward input-process-output form. These diagrams are easy for a user to follow.

Since HIPO only describes processes in a general manner, it must be supplemented by other tools that include the data and the detailed processing. A good structured design package would include HIPO, the data dictionary, and structured English. Such a package would retain the graphical appeal of flowcharting, yet incorporate more modern structured techniques.

HIPO and the Manager

HIPO is very user friendly. The manager can easily understand the hierarchy diagram, which looks like an organization chart. The levels of diagrams provide a gradual introduction of detail. It is thus easier for the manager to follow the transition from general to detailed system description. In its early promotion of HIPO, IBM used the term *iterative refinement*, which means that the system structure can be refined (made more detailed) in an iterative manner. Iterative refinement keeps the manager involved in the design process longer than if flowcharts are used. Other structured techniques (data flow diagrams and Warnier-Orr diagrams) also offer iterative refinement.

A manager would likely never draw the HIPO diagrams. They would be drawn by the systems analyst. Therefore, HIPO will not cultivate end-user computing. HIPO will, however, provide a vehicle for the manager and the information specialist to work together in designing systems.

Appendix F

Warnier-Orr Diagrams

The Warnier-Orr technique is based on the work of French mathematician Jean-Dominique Warnier in devising a means of depicting structured program designs. This occurred in the early 1970s. In the late 1970s, Kenneth T. Orr, working for the Topeka, Kansas firm Langston, Kitch, and Associates, refined the Warnier method so that it could fit broader, overall systems designs.

A good starting point in learning the Warnier-Orr method is the organization chart. Figure F-1a shows such a chart, and Figure F-1b shows the Warnier-Orr equivalent.

Warnier-Orr diagrams use brackets to show hierarchy. The upper level is at the left, and the lowest level is at the right. A bracket is used to enclose the basic constructs of the next lower level. In Figure F-1b, a bracket shows that divisions are the basic constructs within the company.

The beauty of Warnier-Orr is that it is equally effective in showing both data and process hierarchy. Figure F-2 illustrates how the structure of a data base can be depicted using Warnier-Orr.

Warnier-Orr, however, usually does not show data structure *explicitly* as in Figure F-2. Rather, the data structure is usually *implied* in a diagram showing the hierarchy of the *processes*. Warnier-Orr diagrams are said to be *data-driven*, in that the data structure influences the processes. This is very logical. The data structure usually preexists. The processing must work within the constraints provided by the data. The data specifications come first (in designing the logical structure of the data base), then the processes follow.

Fundamentals

Warnier-Orr is intended to illustrate a system using only the three basic structures (see Figure D-2 in Appendix D).

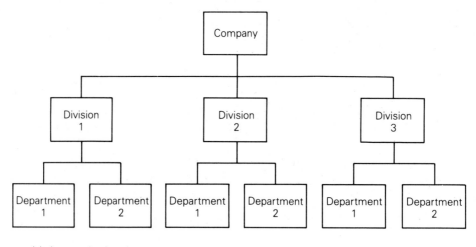

(a) An organization chart

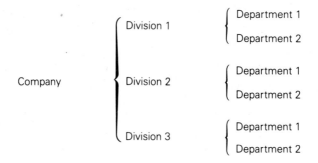

(b) Warnier-Orr structure

Figure F-1 Warnier-Orr diagrams show hierarchical structure.

Simple sequence

The processes included in a simple sequence are enclosed in brackets and are executed from top to bottom:

$$\text{Print detail line} \begin{cases} \text{Move data element 1} \\ \text{Move data element 2} \\ \text{Write the line} \end{cases}$$

Selection

In the selection structure, the different alternatives are separated by a special symbol, a circle containing a plus sign. The symbol is named an *exclusive* and

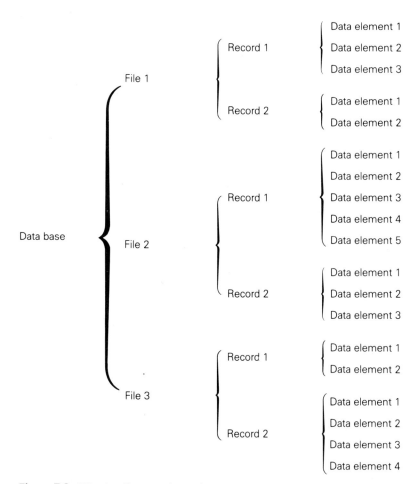

Figure F-2 Warnier-Orr can show data structure.

means that the alternatives are mutually exclusive. That is, you perform one *or* another—you do not perform them in combination. For example, if we only prepare a report at the end of the month, we could illustrate this with:

Sales Report ⎰ Month end   {Prepare report
            ⎱ ⊕
              Not month end {Skip

The word "Skip" means that there is no processing when this condition (Not month end) exists.

The conditions are not restricted to binary choices between two alternatives. You can have multiple alternatives:

Compute sales discount
{
  Order amount < $1,000 — { Compute discount = order amount × .02 }
  ⊕
  Order amount $1,000-$5,000 — { Compute discount = order amount × .05 }
  ⊕
  Order amount > $5,000 — { Compute discount = order amount × .10 }
}

In this example, the firm offers three discounts depending on the amount of the sales order. If the customer orders less than $1,000 in merchandise, the discount is two percent. The discount is five percent when the amount is between $1,000 and $5,000, and the discount is ten percent for orders over $5,000.

Repetition

You show the number of times that a routine is to be executed by including numbers and letters within parentheses. If something is done only one time, you use (1). If something is not always done only one time, you use two numbers, or a number and a letter, within the parentheses. For example, if something is either done once or it is not done at all, you use (0, 1). If something is done a certain number of times (say 20), you show this with (1, 20). If something is done a variable number of times, you show this with (1, n). If something can be done a variable number of times, but it might not be done at all, you use (0, n).

Let us use an order entry example to illustrate repetition. Assume that a data entry operator is keying sales order data into a terminal. Customers can order varying numbers of items, but they always order at least one. This situation is diagrammed as shown in Figure F-3.

The exclusive symbol (⊕) is not used since you always enter both order identification and item data. The three item data elements are entered for as many items as are ordered.

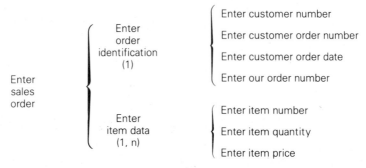

Figure F-3 An example of repetition.

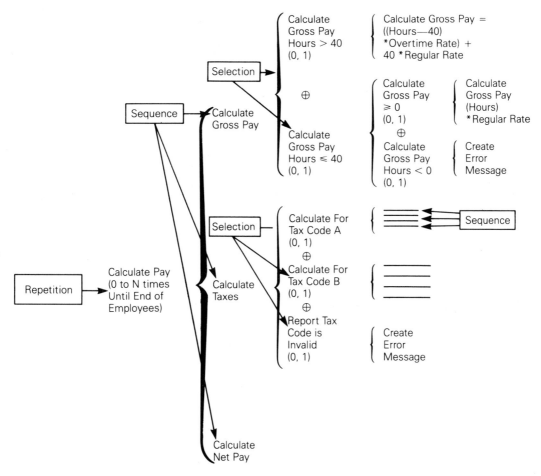

Figure F-4 A payroll system.

Warnier-Orr diagram example

Figure F-4 depicts a payroll system in the form of a Warnier-Orr diagram.[1] This
example identifies the three basic structures. A system or a program usually
consists of a mixture of the structures as shown. Note the error message routines
that are enacted when hours worked are less than zero and when the tax code is
invalid.

An Evaluation of Warnier-Orr

The bottom line is that Warnier-Orr is probably the best, all-around, of the design
and documentation methods. Here are the reasons:

---

[1]Example courtesy of Arthur Andersen & Co.

1. Warnier-Orr is equally adept at showing data and process structures. No other method does this.
2. Warnier-Orr is very user friendly. Its few symbols and rules make it easy to learn and to understand. It is probably much less frightening to a user for showing detailed logic and procedures than structured English.
3. It can illustrate any level of structure—from a top-level system overview to the detailed logic of a program module.
4. Its left-to-right pattern forces a top-down, structured approach.
5. A Warnier-Orr diagram is very machine readable. This does not mean that the diagram can be read by the computer. Instead, it means that very little effort is required to convert the diagram to computer code.

A good tools package would include Warnier-Orr and a data dictionary. The data dictionary offers the explicit description of the data, and Warnier-Orr describes both the procedural flow and its detail.

Warnier-Orr Diagrams and the Manager

When we look at a systems tool through the eyes of the manager, we look for two basic characteristics. First, is the tool structurally sound, yet user friendly enough for the manager to conceivably use it to achieve end-user computing? Second, if the information specialist uses the tool to create the documentation, can the documentation serve as the basis for keeping the user current on the development process? In both situations, Warnier-Orr is excellent. An MIS-literate manager can use Warnier-Orr to conceptualize the solution to a problem and then use a fourth-generation language or prewritten software to convert the solution to a form for computer processing. Tools such as Warnier-Orr make the concept of end-user computing a realistic, achievable one. On the other hand, if the user wishes that the information specialist perform all of the systems work, Warnier-Orr can provide a common basis for communication.

Index